ELIZABETH I

ELIZABETH I

Wallace MacCaffrey

A member of the Hodder Headline Group
LONDON • NEW YORK • SYDNEY • AUCKLAND

First published in Great Britain 1993 by Edward Arnold
First published as a paperback 1994
Fifth impression 1998 by Arnold,
a member of the Hodder Headline Group
338 Euston Road, London NW1 3BH

Co-published in the United States of America by
Oxford University Press Inc.,
198 Madison Avenue, New York, NY 10016

British Library Cataloguing in Publication Data
MacCaffrey, Wallace T
Elizabeth I
I. Title
942.055092

Library of Congress Cataloging-in-Publication Data
MacCaffrey, Wallace T
Elizabeth I/Wallace T MacCaffrey
p. cm.
Includes bibliographical references (p.) and index.
ISBN 0-340-61455-2
1. Elizabeth I, Queen of England, 1533–1603.
2. Great Britain-History-Elizabeth, 1558–1603.
3. Great Britain-Kings and rulers-Biography.
I. Title
DA355.M24   1993
942.05′5′092-dc20   93-3568
[B]   CIP

ISBN 0 340 61455 2

Typeset in 11/13 Linotron Janson by
Rowland Phototypesetting Ltd, Bury St Edmunds, Suffolk
Printed and bound in Great Britain by J W Arrowsmith Ltd, Bristol

Contents

Preface   vii
List of Maps and Tables   xi

PART I. The Lady Elizabeth, 1533–1558

  1. Princess Elizabeth   3
  2. The Second Person   12

PART II. The Apprentice Queen, 1558–1568

  3. Making a Government   33
  4. The Legacies of the Past   43
  5. The Religious Settlement   48
  6. The Pacification of Scotland, 1559–1560   60
  7. The Rise of Dudley   70
  8. Marriage and Succession   82

PART III. Elizabeth and Mary, 1568–1572

  9. The Coming of Mary Stuart   103
 10. The Norfolk Marriage   114
 11. The Northern Rebellion   126
 12. The Ridolfi Plot   135

PART IV. The Struggle for Peace, 1572–1585

13. England and Her Continental Neighbours, 1559–1572 147
14. The Crises of 1572 and Their Aftermath 175
15. England and the States General, 1576–1579 188
16. The Anjou Match 198
17. The Coming of War 218

PART V. The Waging of War, 1585–1603

18. Armada and Counter-Armada 235
19. The Alliance with Henry IV 250
20. The Alliance with the States General 266
21. The Assault on Spain 274
22. Edging towards Peace 283

PART VI. The Practice of Statecraft

23. The 1559 Settlement 297
24. The Rise of the Reformers 303
25. The Puritans in Parliament 310
26. Grindal and Whitgift 316
27. The Queen and Her Catholic Subjects 327
28. Conspiracy and Repression 337
29. The End of Mary Stuart 343
30. The Queen and Her Constituencies 355
31. An Economical Queen 381

PART VII. The End of a Reign, 1590–1603

32. The Earl of Essex 393
33. The Queen and Ireland 417
34. The Queen and Her Successor 434

Epilogue 443
Abbreviations 449
Notes 451
Index 473

Preface

No English monarch — with the exception of Victoria — has left so vivid an impression on the imagination of posterity. The image, however, is not one of photographic simplicity nor even the lively representation of a Holbein or Van Dyke. Elizabeth comes down to us swathed in fold upon fold of myth, the earliest strands woven in her own lifetime and steadily augmented ever since. In due time, like her nineteenth-century successor, she became the symbol of an age, of a whole era of English history. Her very name conjures up a glittering array of achievements — the first fine flowering of a high literary and intellectual culture, the exploits of those daring pioneers of English imperial expansion, Drake or Ralegh, or the Amazonian St George slaying the Spanish dragon. She emerges as the patroness of poets and playwrights, the foundress of the British empire, and the master statesman of her age.

The consequences of this epic myth-making raises for the biographer formidable difficulties, aptly symbolized by the royal portraits. They more resemble the icons of a saint than faithful representations of a living human being. Decked out in her stiff array of richly embroidered robes, set off by a host of glittering jewellery, she seems like some great painted doll — or a baroque Madonna. The icon, by giving Elizabeth a timeless dimension, diminishes for us her historical reality, diverting our attention from the Queen as a practitioner of statecraft, the hard-pressed ruler of a small European state, in a storm-driven age when her own society was at odds with itself and the European polity riven by the bitterest ideological conflicts.

This book focuses on Elizabeth at work in her own royal *métier*, exercising the wide-ranging skills which her exacting calling demanded. The awesome semi-divinity of the office was an asset of immense value, but one which had to be realized to be effective: the sovereign could not, like Shakespeare's Richard II, merely stand passively upon her dignity. Not unlike a modern elected ruler, the Queen had to cultivate all the arts of a politician in order to secure her right to be obeyed, to win the unquestioning confidence of her subjects in her ability to govern them. By the same token, she must by her acts of state justify that confidence. She had to give long-term coherence to day-to-day decisions, to set a course and a destination for her realm — in short, to make policy. It is the unfolding of the tangled history of these actions which is the matter of this book. Like all such histories it records both successes and failures. But those terms must be used carefully, placing the recorded actions within the horizons which bounded contemporary vision and within the particular and personal framework through which the Queen perceived the political landscape in which she lived.

The obligations which I have amassed in the writing of this book stretch back many decades. I owe an initial debt to Professor W. K. Jordan, who first brought me to a serious study of the Tudor age and who directed my first steps as a professional scholar. Among British scholars, Professor J. E. Neale and his successor at London, Professor Joel Hurstfield, were more than generous in the time and attention which they gave and the knowledge they shared with me. In more recent years I have enjoyed and benefited from the counsel of Professor G. R. Elton, particularly in his Cambridge seminars. In the writing of this book I have been well served by the staffs of both Harvard College Library and Cambridge University Library. During the early stages of writing I enjoyed the warm hospitality of the Master and Fellows of Trinity Hall, where I spent a profitable year as a visting Fellow. Lastly, I owe warm thanks to my long-time friend and colleague, Professor Bernard Bailyn, whose reading of the manuscript provided expert and helpful criticism of style and presentation.

W.T.M.
Cambridge
February 1993

List of Maps and Tables

Maps

1. Europe *c.*1560   148
2. The Route of the Spanish Armada, 1588   240
3. Brittany and North-West France, 1589–1594   252
4. The Earl of Essex in Ireland   414

Tables

1. The Habsburg Dynasty   xiv
2. The Succession to the English Crown 1553–1603   xv
3. The Bourbon Dynasty   xvi

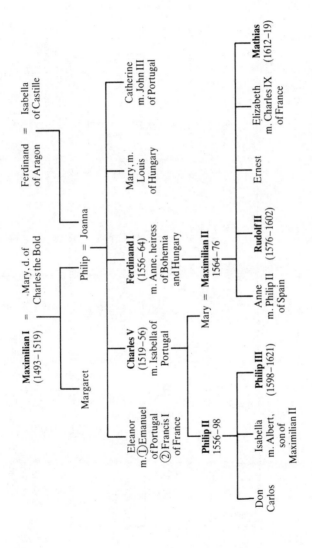

Table 1: The Habsburg Dynasty

Maximilian I = Mary, d. of   Ferdinand = Isabella
(1493–1519)   Charles the Bold   of Aragon   of Castille

Margaret

Philip = Joanna

Eleanor   Charles V   Ferdinand I   Mary, m.   Catherine
m.① Emanuel   (1519–56)   (1556–64)   Louis   m. John III
of Portugal   m. Isabella of   m. Anne, heiress   of Hungary   of Portugal
② Francis I   Portugal   of Bohemia
of France   and Hungary

                      Mary = Maximilian II
                             1564–76

Philip II   Anne   Rudolf II   Ernest   Elizabeth   Mathias
1556–98   m. Philip II   (1576–1602)   m. Charles IX   (1612–19)
                     of Spain   of France

Don   Philip III
Carlos   (1598–1621)

Isabella
m. Albert,
son of
Maximilian II

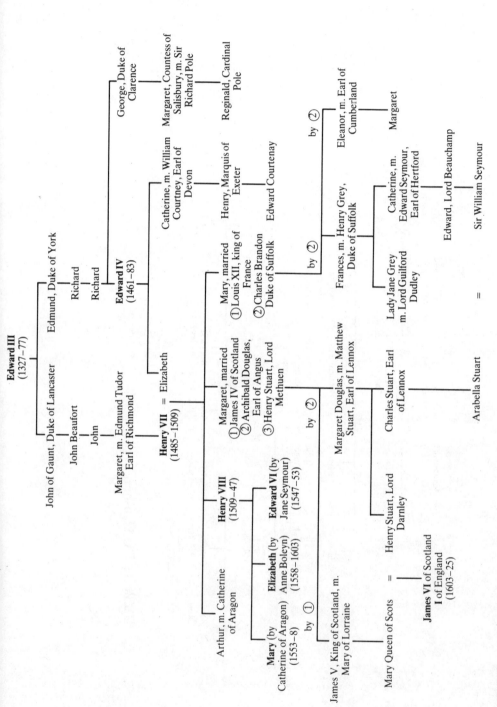

Table 2: The Succession to the English Crown 1553–1603

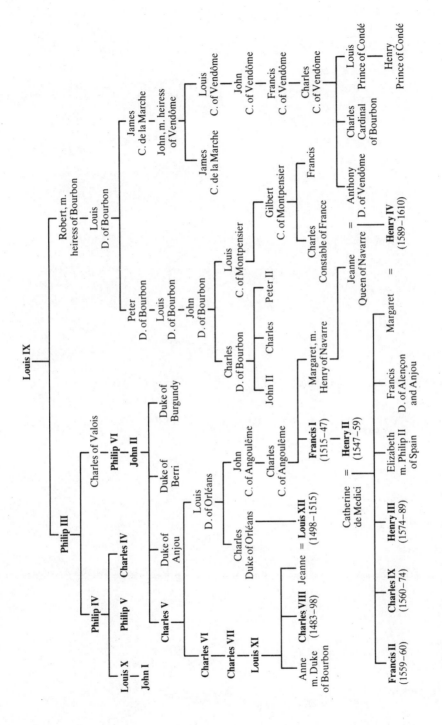

Table 3: The Bourbon Dynasty

Part I

The Lady Elizabeth
1533–1558

1

Princess Elizabeth

*E*arly in September 1533, the Lord Mayor of London and the other civic dignitaries were bidden to attend a great state cere-mony at the royal palace of Greenwich. In the church of the Friars Minors on Wednesday, 10 September, the three-day-old prin-cess Elizabeth, first-born child of Henry VIII's second marriage, was to be christened. There were assembled the entire political elite of the kingdom — the two dukes, Norfolk and Suffolk, nobles with their ladies, bishops and abbots, as well as the royal councillors including the formidable Thomas Cromwell, the King's great minister. The Bishop of London baptized the infant; Archbishop Cranmer stood as her godfather. The rites were performed with appropriate splendour; trumpets blew and the title of the princess was duly proclaimed.[1]

The customary pomp of the baptismal rites masked the fact that the infant was a child of discord. She was heir, at her birth, indeed at her conception, to a long and troubled history; the union of which she was the issue had been six turbulent years in the making. When Henry set out in 1527 to undo his first marriage and clear the way for his second, the road to be travelled had seemed open and relatively free of obstacles. Yet by 1529 that road was permanently blocked. If Henry was to reach his goal he had to find another route. The very act of searching for it led to a transformation of the goal itself. What followed was a course of action which dwarfed the initial enterprise of the annulment. To secure the future of the dynasty, to demonstrate beyond all possibility of cavil that the rending of the old marriage ties and the binding of the new were justified in the eyes of God and man, a vast work of destruction and reconstruction had to take place.

The whole structure of the Christian church in England, both in its governing principles and in its institutional machinery, had to be rethought and reshaped. The authority of the Pope as the successor of St Peter and the Vicar of Christ, the pillar on which the very foundation of Catholic unity rested, would be repudiated. And Henry, in spite of his vociferous denials, would find himself standing on common ground with Lutheran heresy, the tenets of which he had vigorously attacked in the preceding decade. The King and his masterful minister, Cromwell, had done their best to mask the changes by an appeal to the past – the recovery of usurped royal rights, the restoration of a Constantinian supremacy of the lay ruler over the church. But to most contemporaries, reformers or conservatives, these alterations heralded the coming of religious revolution. Anne Boleyn and her supporters were tagged as the standard-bearers of the new order. Her child was at birth enlisted as a partisan in the great wars of truth just then beginning.

The first phase of Elizabeth's life, as princess and heir apparent, was destined to be short. In the first months of her life the necessary statutes were passed to secure her rights in the succession if the longed-for male heir should not arrive. Englishmen were required to swear their loyalty to the new order of things. The King's first wife, Katherine, shorn of her regality, was sent into country exile. Her daughter Mary's household was dismantled; many of its personnel shifted to the new establishment created for Elizabeth. The years of her early infancy were uneventful, passed largely in royal manor houses in the Hertfordshire or Buckinghamshire countryside, varied by occasional visits to court.[2]

Elizabeth was in fact already playing a part on the political stage. Her father was quick to enter her in the royal matrimonial stakes. A marriage between Mary and the French dauphin was already being planned. As early as October 1534 there was talk of a linking match with the French king's third son for Elizabeth. Later on Cromwell hinted to the Imperial ambassador the possibility of the princess marrying the emperor's son, Philip. These manœuvres were, of course, merely the small change of the diplomatic market where Henry sought to protect his position *vis-à-vis* the Habsburgs and to secure international recognition of his second marriage.[3]

Elizabeth's brief role as heiress apparent was about to end. It came with dreadful suddenness in the spring of 1536. As late as January after the death of Katherine of Aragon, Henry carried his infant daughter about the court for the admiration of his courtiers,[4] and she was conducted to mass to the sound of trumpets. But in April the thunderbolt of royal rage struck; Anne was accused and condemned of adultery and in a few short weeks passed from the throne to the block.

The event, terrible as it was, had little immediate effect on the three-year-old girl. Since her father had not only executed but also divorced her mother, Elizabeth was now a bastard and deprived of the title of princess. There was a momentary flurry in her household[5] when her governess, Lady Brian, wrote anxiously to Cromwell asking for direction as to her charge's status and provision for her immediate needs; but by late summer 1536 there was a shared regime for the two daughters of the King, at Hunsdon in Hertfordshire. Sir John Shelton was steward of an establishment costing at least £4,000 a year.[6] Later in 1536 when Mary had submitted to her father's brutal demands and acknowledged her own bastardy, both were at court, the younger, according to a foreign observer, the object of paternal affection.[7]

Their place in the royal family, not only in the narrow social sense but also in the large political perspective, was a matter for conciliar concern. In a memorandum of 1537 the Privy Councillors urged the King to countenance his two daughters, providing them with means and using them as pawns in the diplomatic game by finding husbands who would be useful allies.[8] When in 1537 their brother Edward, son of Henry's third queen, Jane Seymour, appeared on the scene, the two sisters played prominent parts in the christening ceremony. (Elizabeth 'for her tender age' was herself carried by a nobleman.)[9] The King took to heart his Council's advice and in 1538 he was again canvassing for husbands for his daughters. At one stage Elizabeth was ticketed for one of the Habsburg princes; at another for a scion of the French house.[10] None of these overtures came to anything, but they made it clear that the half-sisters' technical illegitimacy was not to disqualify the royal girls for the traditional role of princesses in the diplomacy of Europe. Of even greater importance was the fact that, when Parliament authorized Henry to devise the crown by his will, he placed Mary and Elizabeth, in that order, after Prince Edward. It was now legally possible, however unlikely in fact, that Elizabeth might succeed to the crown.[11]

For Elizabeth the seminal event in her childhood was her father's marriage to his sixth and last wife, Katherine Parr, in July 1543. This pious and cultivated lady set about creating a family setting for her stepchildren; they were all brought together under one roof by December of that year. In Katherine Parr Elizabeth had for the first

time a motherly presence, and the princess responded to the affectionate care of her stepmother. The new Queen renewed the tradition
of Katherine of Aragon's court, notable not only for its blend of piety
and learning but for the insistence that high-born women should share
in the forms of humanistic education which were prescribed for their
brothers.[12] Elizabeth was thus fortunate to be one of that generation
of European princesses who had a rigorous training in the prevailing
humanist curriculum. Her brother was being taught by a staff of Cambridge's best and brightest young scholars, headed by Richard Coxe,
assisted by John Cheke of St John's College. This staff was augmented
a year later by another Cantabrigian, William Grindal, who was
appointed tutor to Elizabeth. The establishment also included a
French master, John Belmaine, and Sir Anthony Cooke, the father of
two famous learned ladies, Mildred Cecil and Anne Bacon. When
Grindal died in 1548 he was succeeded by Roger Ascham, who
remained Elizabeth's tutor until 1550.

Ascham's tribute to his pupil, written after his return to Cambridge,
may owe something of its warmth to her illustrious rank, but it is
clear that she was a responsive pupil. A dozen years later she could
still find time from her royal duties to spend an evening with Ascham
reading the oration of Demosthenes against Aeschines and he could
declare that 'she reads here now at Windsor more Greek than some
prebends of this church read Latin in a whole week'. Her Latin studies
took her into Cicero and Livy, her Greek into Isocrates and Sophocles.
Besides the ancient tongues she commanded French and Italian. Her
competence in these tongues is borne out by the witness of the
Venetian ambassador when he met the princess in 1554, and who
added Spanish to her list of accomplishments.[13]

The practical advantages of this education are obvious; her command of the principal European tongues was invaluable to her in
dealing with the ambassadors of foreign princes. These skills enabled
her to play a direct and commanding role in the exchanges of diplomatic intercourse. How far the more intangible benefits of the humanist curriculum influenced her is harder to judge. Certainly she was not
stimulated to the speculative and argumentative life of the intellect, as
was her equally well-educated Scottish successor, James I. She did not
become a patron of letters or of scholarship. In the Elizabethan court
circle it was her courtiers, rather than the Queen, who were the focus
of its lively literary culture. Though she did not take a lead in patronizing the creators of that culture, she was hospitable to their creations.
It was she who set the cultural tone at court. It was for her pleasure

that the scholars of Oxford and Cambridge performed their Latin plays, and for her delight that gods and goddesses, nymphs and satyrs, entertained her at Kenilworth or Elvetham with pageantry replete with classical allusions and classical imagery. Her learning and her tastes ensured that the English court would be a centre of intellectual sophistication where the high literary culture of the age could flourish.

However, the question remains how far her immersion in the classical authors affected her conduct as a ruler. It might well be argued that Elizabeth's coldly calculating view of politics and her secular view of the function of religion in society owed something to her reading of the classical moralists. There is little evidence that the substance of their argument affected her practice of politics. She was familiar with at least one work of Erasmus, but there is little evidence that his humanist moralism touched her feelings. Machiavelli – had she read him – would have been more congenial to her way of proceeding. Her cool pragmatism owed more to her own harsh experience than to any bookish instruction.

The further question – how far the ancient writers influenced her own personal and inward view of the world – is hardly answerable; so much of the life of Elizabeth Tudor was subsumed in the career of Elizabeth the Queen. One might wonder if Elizabeth's distaste for the religious enthusiasms of her age was influenced by her acquaintance with the secular and civic morality of the Romans. Certainly she was more at home in the rational discourse of Seneca than in the theological polemics of her contemporaries. When she turned her hand to translations in later life, it was Boethius' *Consolations of Philosophy*, Plutarch, and Horace which engaged her attention. But all this is little more than speculation: the inner woman remains locked away from us; perhaps its core was hidden to the Queen herself.

Certainly her teachers succeeded in one vital task. Their tutelage produced a pupil highly literate on paper and tellingly articulate in speech, marked by a distinctively individual style. To a modern reader the royal letters have an 'Asiatic luxuriance' with which James I once reproached a correspondent. One sentence winds sinuously into another until the reader longs for a silken clue to guide him through the maze. The style was no doubt temperamental, but frequently serves to clothe the ambiguities of the writer's intentions. When Elizabeth wished to be direct, she could command a pithy aptness of phrase and imagery and a sardonic irony which struck home, as her speeches to Parliament amply demonstrated.

For Katherine Parr, patronage of humanist studies was part and parcel of a larger goal — the advancement of the 'new learning', of Erasmian piety with its oblique but telling critique of the traditional faith. Her associations with men and women of this bent were conspicuous enough to invite the hostile attentions of Bishop Gardiner, the leader of the religious conservatives in the court. His insinuations of her religious heterodoxy persuaded the King to agree to her arrest on charges of heresy. The dramatic episode in which she foiled the bishop's scheme and regained her husband's confidence is one of the most vivid chapters in John Foxe's martyrology.

How far did the religious influence of Katherine's circle influence her young charge? She certainly inspired the affection and respect of her stepdaughter. In 1545 the latter's New Year gift to her stepmother was a translation of *The Mirror or Glass of the Sinful Soul*, written by another pious princess of Erasmian persuasions, Margaret of Navarre.[14] Elizabeth also compiled a collection of Katherine's prayers and meditations and translated Erasmus's *Dialogue of Faith*. In the covering letter Elizabeth makes a very Protestant-sounding declaration of her belief that faith alone can save.[15] It is unlikely that we should take this as an assertion of deep personal conviction, but it is a clue to the religious atmosphere of her formative years. Certainly she accepted the radical Protestantism of her brother's regime without hesitation, and the ardent Protestant bishop Hooper could write complacently not only of her sound religious belief but also of her capability in defending reformed doctrine against its enemies.[16] Ascham had grounded her in the Greek Testament and in such patristic texts as St Cyprian and modern commentaries such as Melanchthon. She was speaking truthfully when she told Queen Mary at the beginning of her sister's reign that her whole religious education was in the new faith. Future events would test how deep or strong her religious commitments were.

This calm and fruitful era in Elizabeth's life came to an end with the death of her father in January 1547. Edward had already been separated from her, a separation which he regretted.[17] As King he had, of course, his own court. Mary retired to one of her country houses. Elizabeth, however, stayed on with her stepmother, the dowager Queen, a circumstance which would lead to a painful and humiliating episode and to her initiation into the pleasures and pains of adulthood.

Katherine Parr, at thirty-five three times a widow, astonished the court world by accepting a new husband a bare few months after Henry's death. She could hardly have chosen worse. Sir Thomas

Seymour was the younger of the King's two maternal uncles. During the late reign, benefiting by his relationship to the heir, he had held various official posts of some importance. The advancement of his elder brother to the protectorship and the dukedom of Somerset had aroused in him an insensate jealousy. He repeatedly insisted that he should share in the guardianship of the King. With the secret assistance of John Dudley, Earl of Warwick, his brother's rival, Thomas Seymour forced Somerset to admit him to the Privy Council; there followed appointment as Lord Admiral and promotion to the peerage as Lord Seymour of Sudeley. These advancements only whetted his appetite for more. Although irresistibly attractive to women, he was still a bachelor. He had thought of seeking the hand of the Lady Elizabeth but, seeing she was out of his reach, turned to Katherine Parr, whom he had been wooing when he was pre-empted by Henry.[18]

For the next year Elizabeth lived under the same roof as the Lord Admiral and his bride in their house at Chelsea. Life in the Admiral's household had an unbuttoned informality very different from the ordered sobriety of Katherine's royal establishment. Quite soon after the marriage Seymour began the habit of visiting the fourteen-year-old Elizabeth early in the morning before she was out of bed, exchanging pleasantries while slapping her buttocks and back. On one occasion he made as if to kiss her. Sometimes he appeared in nightclothes, bare-legged; at another visit Elizabeth hid behind her bed-curtains while Seymour pretended to seek her. Initially he was accompanied by his wife, but soon he appeared alone. These romps were not confined to the bedroom. One day in the garden, the Admiral ripped Elizabeth's dress to pieces while the Queen Dowager held her fast. However, when Katherine found her husband embracing her ward, there was an end of these dalliances. Around Whitsuntide 1548 Elizabeth went to live at Cheshunt in Hertfordshire although friendly correspondence continued. In September of that year Katherine Parr died in childbed.[19]

Seymour, now free, turned his thoughts again to Elizabeth. Talk began to spread of his ambitions for such a match. The Admiral made overtures; when Elizabeth's London residence, Durham Place, was unavailable, he offered her his house. He proposed a visit to Ashridge (where Elizabeth was living) on his way to the west, a proposal which clearly pleased Elizabeth although she half-heartedly discouraged his coming. At the same time he made use of Elizabeth's two principal servants, her governess, Kate Ashley, and her cofferer, Thomas Parry. They dropped hints about his intentions. Ashley told her that the rumour in London was that 'Your Grace shall have my lord Admiral and that he shall come shortly to woo you'. Parry went so far as to ask his Mistress if she would take Seymour's hand if offered (and the Privy Council approved), to which Elizabeth replied evasively.[20]

Seymour was not only seeking the hand of Elizabeth but also plotting against his brother. In the last months of 1548 he threw himself into a frenzy of feckless intrigue which soon attracted the attention of the Council. In January he was in the Tower; accused of treason, he was attainted and executed.

The investigations surrounding his downfall revealed his relations with the Lady Elizabeth from the time of his marriage. Both Kate Ashley and Thomas Parry were detained and closely examined. It is from their confessions that we know the circumstances related above. Elizabeth herself was submitted to rigorous questioning by Sir Robert Tyrwhitt who, with his wife, was put in charge of her household. She admitted a correspondence with Seymour in regard to a post for her chaplain and acknowledged his offer of a town residence. Ashley had told her of his proposed visit, and intended to warn him against coming lest it arouse suspicion. Writing to the Privy Council, Elizabeth repeated much the same story, insisting that she had always declared she would do nothing without Council approval and denying that her servants had intrigued for a marriage. Tyrwhitt urged her to confess all; the Council, considering her youth, would blame Seymour, but Elizabeth stuck to her story. Baffled, he wrote: 'she will not confess any practice by Mrs Ashley or the cofferer concerning my lord Admiral yet I do see in her face that she is guilty.'[21]

There was nothing more to be got from the stubborn lady. She complained bitterly of the appointment of the Tyrwhitts and would hear nothing against the Admiral. In due time Ashley and Parry were released and allowed to return to Elizabeth's service. The matter was allowed to fade away. It had been for Elizabeth a painfully instructive episode. In its first stages it seems to have been a half-teasing, half-joking romp in which a fourteen-year-old girl, countenanced by her stepmother, enjoyed for the first time the admiration of an attractive male. Later it took a more serious turn when the dowager Queen sent Elizabeth away. When Seymour resumed his attentions after the death of his wife, Elizabeth was obviously flattered and willing to countenance his attentions. Left with no semblance of parental counsel or influence, she responded to the urgings of her servants and indulged herself in a flirtation with a man of whose true character she was ignorant. Before she was compromised the affair was abruptly ended by Seymour's own actions. It was a brutal conclusion to Elizabeth's first (and only) girlhood romance, bringing the painful discovery of misplaced trust as well as a sharp sense of her personal vulnerability. The Council's inquisitorial interest in her behaviour warned her that she was not her own mistress. It was a rough initiation into adulthood.

Elizabeth drew the moral of her experience. Henceforward she was scrupulously careful in her style of life; no shadow of scandal or even the hint of any attachment was allowed to appear. The somewhat surprising assertion of an observer that Elizabeth affected a severe plainness of attire, eschewing jewellery or personal adornment, suggests her determination to present an image of maidenly modesty and decorum.[22]

Through the remaining years of Edward's reign Elizabeth remained in country retirement. She lived either at Hatfield in Hertfordshire or at Ashridge in Buckinghamshire. In March 1550, in performance of Henry's will, Edward formally granted his sister land in half-a-dozen shires, mostly in the Thames Valley or the south Midlands, worth in total about £1,300 a year. The house at Ashridge was part of this grant, along with Durham Place in London. Hatfield was added a few months later. In fact the patent rolls show that these lands were in her possession earlier, possibly from the beginning of the reign. There seems to have been additional income; a surviving household account for 1550–1 gives a net annual income of about £4,800. There were then thirteen gentlemen in attendance and some forty yeomen.[23]

In March 1551 Elizabeth paid a state visit to her brother, accompanied by some 200 lords and gentlemen, and in the following October she was present for the visit of the Queen Dowager of Scotland; but for the most part she remained in country seclusion at Hatfield, where she was residing when her brother died in July 1553. Of Elizabeth's actions during the turbulent days of Jane Grey's short 'reign' we know little. On 29 July, after the conspiracy was crushed but before the new Queen left East Anglia, Elizabeth entered London with a considerable entourage, spent a night at her London residence, and then went to meet Mary. When the Queen entered the capital, Elizabeth rode behind her in the procession. Similarly, in the royal procession from the Tower to Westminster on the eve of the coronation and at that ceremony itself, Elizabeth occupied a prominent position.[24]

2

The Second Person

Elizabeth's very prominence in these state occasions highlighted the new role into which she had now been thrust. Since Edward's death she was no longer merely the old King's daughter or the new King's sister, a minor royalty, slated for whatever matrimonial slot would best serve English interests. She was now the next heir to the throne, the second person in the realm until and if her sister bore a child. This new-found eminence, whatever it might portend for the future, was in the present fraught with the gravest perils. The position of an adult heir was at the least a delicate one, as the fortunes of the French dynasty bore witness in the next decades, when restless younger brothers busily intrigued with the forces of discontent in the country. But Elizabeth's position was one of particular delicacy. First there were the facts of her birth. Mary never forgot the sufferings of her mother — or forgave those whom she held responsible, above all Anne Boleyn. The Queen treated her sister civilly but she found it hard to dissemble her intense dislike.[1]

These antipathies were bad enough in themselves, but they were exacerbated to an almost infinite degree by Mary's judgment on her sister's religious opinions. The ultimate criterion by which the Queen measured all persons was their adherence to the Catholic faith. In her eyes Elizabeth was irredeemably heretical, whatever outward professions she might make. The prospect of her future succession burdened Mary's conscience; in the immediate present she feared her sister would lend herself to conspiracy against the throne. These fears were fed by the urgings of the Imperial ambassador, Simon Renard, who saw Elizabeth as a threat to his master's interests.[2]

There was some justification for the Queen's fears. Her subjects shared her view that Elizabeth was the natural leader of the Protestants and, in a more general sense, of any movement of discontent. She was cast, whether she wished it or not, as the head of what the eighteenth century would have termed the reversionary interest. Hence she was, by the very logic of her position, beleaguered on both sides, by a suspicious court, which saw her very existence as a menace to the regime, and by the unwelcome adherence of conspirators who freely used her name as a stalking horse for their subversive schemes. There was no way she could avoid the perilous role to which history or (as John Foxe, the great myth-maker of English Protestantism would have it) providence had consigned her.

There was another unspoken but surely not unthought of consideration which must have haunted most minds and which made Elizabeth's position all the more significant. Mary was a woman in her thirty-seventh year with a history of poor health. The risks of motherhood would be grave; in any calculation the probabilities that Elizabeth would succeed her sister were high.

The tensions implicit in this role were not slow to surface. Elizabeth had unquestioningly accepted the radically Protestant faith of her brother's reign, legally still in force in Mary's first months as Queen although in the court the old religious practices were already restored. As early as the end of August Elizabeth's absence from mass was noted, and Renard urged this on Mary as reason for not trusting her. The princess, perceiving her sister's increasing coldness, took the initiative. In early September she asked for a private audience where, kneeling and weeping, she protested her ignorance of the old faith and begged for instruction. The Queen agreed readily, and on the feast of Our Lady's Nativity Elizabeth attended mass. Yet within a few days the ever-suspicious Renard noted that she had failed to attend Sunday mass. The Queen, deeply distrustful of her sister's sincerity, bluntly questioned Elizabeth's belief in the Catholic sacrament, to which the latter could only assert that she went to mass voluntarily.[3]

When Elizabeth retired from the court in December, the Councillors Arundel and Paget warned her to be careful of her behaviour. Before her departure she made another assertion of her religious sincerity, and petitioned the Queen not to listen to any evil without giving her a chance to defend herself. *En route* she sent back to court, begging for a supply of chapel furniture to provide for the celebration of mass in her own house.[4]

Elizabeth left behind a court in deep disarray. Mary was determined not only to reverse the Edwardian reformation but to reconcile England with Rome. These goals placed severe strains on the political system. Parliament readily agreed to restore the mass, but balked at the return of a papal power which might threaten their security as purchasers of the monastic lands. However, the root of Mary's problems lay not so much in her religious convictions as in her gender. Her accession to the English throne was to her contemporaries a deeply disturbing anomaly, a flaw in the natural order. When in 1558 John Knox, in a famous pamphlet, assailed female government, his readers understood quite clearly that the regiment (government) of women was indeed a monster, an aberration, a creature which, like a two-headed calf, violated the natural and providential order. Yet for Englishmen there was no alternative; the line of succession stretched in an unbroken female sequence – Mary, Elizabeth, Mary Stuart, Lady Margaret Douglas, the Grey sisters. There was no avoiding a woman ruler, but there was a remedy – to find her a husband. On his shoulders would fall the burdens which only a male could carry. He would, in fact and in right, be a king.

In this solution Mary was at one mind with her male counsellors; she was as willing as they were anxious to find her a husband. For her, more particularly, it was above all important to have an heir who would exclude Elizabeth and secure the future of the Catholic faith in England. The choice of husband was limited: either a prince of the Habsburg house or an Englishman of the blood royal. In the second category there was only one viable candidate, Edward Courtenay, restored by Mary as Earl of Devon, after twelve years in the Tower, where he had lain since his father's execution for alleged plots against the king. A direct descendant of Edward IV, he was highly eligible and widely popular in court circles, in no small part because such a match would preclude a foreign ruler.

The Queen, however, had different views. Powerfully swayed by her Habsburg cousin, the Emperor, she chose his son Philip. It was a choice which was accepted with reluctance by most of the ruling circle of the English aristocracy and utterly rejected by some. Hence the interval between Mary's initial decision in October 1553 and Philip's arrival in the July following proved to be a time of great troubles, fraught with dangers for both sisters. Mary had rebuffed a parliamentary petition that she marry within the realm by announcing her engagement to Philip. Many of the Commons went home in a dangerously disgruntled mood. Among them were those who would look to Elizabeth and Courtenay for an alternative. By marrying, these two could at once provide for the succession and prevent the accession of a foreigner to the English throne.

Even before the marriage was announced, Mary and her advisers were debating what to do with Elizabeth. As early as August Renard, Charles's ambassador, whose overheated imagination saw a plot lurking in every corner, raised the issue. Elizabeth, he argued, clever and sly, possessed indeed of a power of enchantment, would, if she remained at court, be a dangerous plotter. The Queen shared his distrust and considered sending her away, but put off any action.[5] The ambassador and Bishop Gardiner, now Chancellor, a prisoner for his faith in Edward's reign, would have dealt with the problem by sending her to the Tower, but other Privy Councillors, led by Lord Paget, an Edwardian hold-over, resisted such a move. The latter offered a very different solution. Elizabeth was next heir to the crown by authority of Henry's will, which rested on parliamentary statute. It was unlikely that Parliament would repeal that statute. Now that the Queen had chosen a husband, why not marry the rejected suitor, Courtenay, to Elizabeth? Courtenay was of the blood royal and a Catholic in religion, who would keep his wife fast to the old faith. Such a match would reassure the political classes, who looked askance at the Spanish match. The unspoken premiss in his proposal was the likelihood that the Queen would leave no issue.[6]

Mary was unwilling to accept this scheme and her personal preference would have been to appoint her Scottish cousin, Lady Margaret Douglas, descendant of Henry's older sister, as heir presumptive; but Paget declared that Parliament would never accept this. In the end no decision was reached; the matter was passed on to the Emperor, and in December the Habsburgs, father and son, quashed the idea of a Courtenay–Elizabeth match altogether. So things stood at the turn of the new year 1554, as the Spanish plenipotentiaries arrived to settle the terms of the marriage treaty. Elizabeth had been at Ashridge since early December.[7]

Within a few weeks Renard's worst apprehensions were realized. The shadowy plots which he had feared proved to have deadly substance. Late in January revolt broke out in Kent under the leadership of a local gentleman, Sir Thomas Wyatt. Its avowed purpose was to prevent the Spanish marriage. The rebels raised a substantial force, recruited the London militia sent to oppose them, and swept unopposed to the south bank of the Thames, occupying Southwark. There was a moment when panic seized the court, but the Queen's courage rallied her Councillors. London closed its bridge to the rebels, forcing them to a circuitous march to Richmond bridge and back along the north bank to Westminster, where they were easily beaten by the Queen's men. By 7 February it was all over.

There had been a few bad moments, especially when the court and the city seemed to waver, but in fact the government had enjoyed considerable good luck. The conspiracy was widespread; its authors planned coordinated risings in the West, the Midlands, and the Welsh borders, as well as Kent. The first of these had been scotched before it raised its head; the effort of Sir James Croft, a Herefordshire squire on the Welsh borders, was stillborn; only in the Midlands did Lady Jane Grey's father, the Duke of Suffolk, call a handful of men to arms. They were quickly rounded up and the Duke sent to the Tower.

Indeed, the government had many of the strings of the conspiracy in its hands before Kent rose. Gardiner had got hold of his protégé, Courtenay, and squeezed a partial confession out of him. (They had been fellow prisoners in the Tower.) Courtenay admitted that he had been approached by several people proposing that he marry the Lady Elizabeth. He claimed to have rejected them out of hand, declaring he would sooner return to the Tower.[8] The Council had also discovered the outlines of the Devonshire plot and frightened the putative leader in the West, Sir Peter Carew, into flight to France. He and his friends had also hoped for the countenance of Elizabeth and Courtenay.[9]

More was discovered when the conspirators were rounded up. They were a group of country gentry, mostly in middling circumstances. Many of them had held posts under the late regime although, with the exception of Suffolk, none was of major consequence. However, they all had links with important court figures, and they clearly hoped for support from greater men who shared their antipathy to an alien prince. They were held together by a passionate determination to break the Spanish match, which they saw as delivering England into foreign hands. The French ambassador was in their confidence and held out hopes of aid.[10]

Their programme was simple — the use of force to compel Mary to renounce the marriage. Beyond that they were more vague. The Queen's fate remained uncertain, but one item in their agenda was clear: Elizabeth was to marry Courtenay and thus assure a native-born succession to the throne. (Mary, presumably, would remain single.) How far were the two presumptive leaders of the movement parties to it? Were the conspirators merely assuming their cooperation once the movement succeeded? There could be no doubt that Courtenay was well aware of their intentions, but Elizabeth's involvement was much less certain. The Council knew from intercepted correspondence that Wyatt had written to her, urging her to leave Ashridge and move to her house of Donnington in Berkshire which could be fortified. They had also intercepted a package addressed to the French ambassador which enclosed a copy of a letter Elizabeth had just written to the Queen.[11]

These scraps of evidence, their general suspicions, and the urgings of Renard were sufficient to move the Privy Council to summon Elizabeth to court on 29 January (four days after Wyatt called the Kentishmen to arms). If she refused, it would confirm their suspicions of her guilt. The ambassador and Bishop Gardiner wanted to send her directly to the Tower. Elizabeth on receipt of the letter pleaded illness, and asked the Queen's doctors be sent to verify her excuse. On 12 February, after the revolt was extinguished, the Council sent a weighty delegation of courtiers, including Elizabeth's great-uncle, Lord Howard of Effingham, to Ashridge. They found she was indeed unwell, although fit to travel very slowly. It took eleven days for the thirty-three mile journey to London. She entered the city in an open litter, clad in white, the symbol of innocence.[12]

She went, not to the Tower, but to a wing of Whitehall, where she was lodged behind guarded doors and allowed only a tiny staff of attendants. She remained there through the rest of February while the examination of Wyatt proceeded. In the course of the trial more fragments of information emerged. A servant of the princess, Sir William St Lo, was accused of being privy to the plot, but under examination he made no statements incriminating his mistress. The Earl of Bedford's son admitted to having delivered a letter from Wyatt to Elizabeth during the rebellion. An abundance of evidence relating to Courtenay's involvement emerged and he was sent to the Tower, but nothing more turned up regarding Elizabeth. Wyatt admitted to nothing more than having written to Elizabeth advising her to remove further from London, to which she had replied verbally by St Lo with her thanks. On the scaffold he explicitly denied that he had accused either Courtenay or Elizabeth: 'neither they nor any other now yonder in durance was privy to any rising before I began, as I have declared to the Queen's council.'[13]

Elizabeth herself, examined by the Council, explicitly denied any knowledge of Wyatt's or Carew's plans. When Gardiner urged her to put herself in the Queen's hands and ask pardon, she replied that this would be a confession of crime. Let them prove her guilty and then she would seek pardon.[14]

Renard, who never ceased to press for bringing Elizabeth to trial, began to complain of the slackness of the proceedings. He was all the more disturbed by a mysterious voice in a London wall; when bystanders shouted 'God save the Queen', there was no response; when the cry was 'God save the Lady Elizabeth', the answer came, 'so be it'. Matters came to a head with the approaching departure of the court for Windsor. Elizabeth could not safely be left behind. Bishop Gardiner proposed to send her to the Tower. He faced a numerous opposition in the council, including both 'Catholics' and 'Protestants' in its numbers. They argued there was not sufficient evidence such as the law of England required to bring a charge. Gardiner turned their flank by asking which of them would undertake to be her guardian when the court departed.[15]

Faced with the Tower, Elizabeth resorted to a tactic of delay — the oft-quoted scene in which she asked time to write to the Queen, and took so long to compose her letter that the tide had turned and the barge could not run London bridge. It was a measure of her desperation but also of her personal shrewdness, since it allowed her to assert fully and strongly her innocence and to demand she should answer the accusations before the Queen herself. 'I protest before God, whatever malice shall devise, that I never practised, counselled, or consented to anything that might be prejudicial to your person in any way or dangerous to the state by any means. And I therefore beseech Your Majesty to let me answer afore yourself . . . before I be further condemned.' This appeal placed her in the posture of injured innocent, denied a hearing of her case.[16]

On Palm Sunday, 18 March, Elizabeth was taken by barge to the Tower. There are two contemporary accounts of her arrival, both colourful and perhaps embellished in the telling, but agreeing in substance. Refusing to set foot out of the boat, she was roundly told by the Marquess of Winchester that she had no choice. Disembarking, she once again proclaimed her innocence: 'Here landeth as true a subject, being prisoner, as ever landed at these stairs; and before thee, O God, I speak it, having no friends but thee alone.' She came closer at that moment to losing her self-possession than at any other time in her long ordeal. The next two months were the most agonizing of her life. Helpless to do anything but assert her innocence, she could only wait on events. In another examination conducted by Gardiner she was pressed as to whether she had not talked with the conspirator Croft about going to Donnington. At first denying more than mere knowledge that the place existed, she grudgingly admitted that her officers had had talk with him about the matter.[17]

There could be no doubt as to the danger in which she stood. The Habsburgs and their ambassador were convinced that the Prince of Spain would have no safety so long as Elizabeth lived, and Renard was unremitting in his pressure on the Queen. He had an ally of sorts in Gardiner, who shared his views of Elizabeth, but whose effectiveness was hamstrung by his partiality for Courtenay. If he was to save his protégé, he could hardly condemn the Queen's sister.[18]

More important still was the resistance of a major group of Privy Councillors, including the ambassador's usual collaborator, Paget. The latter put it to Renard that if evidence could not be found to condemn Elizabeth, she should be married to a Habsburg ally, the Prince of Piedmont, with the succession (after Mary's issue) vested in them. This, he argued, would reconcile the English to the Spanish match. It was an interesting and highly significant variation of the tune Paget had played the previous autumn, when the bridegroom would have been Courtenay. The English Councillors had a different perspective from that of the Habsburgs. Elizabeth was the last surviving child of Henry; if she vanished, the succession would be thrown open to frightening uncertainties. No doubt the Queen, married, would bear a child and their fears would vanish, but until that event they were too canny to ignore contingencies which had a high degree of probability about them. Moreover, Mary, much as she distrusted her half-sister, was fair-minded enough not to send her to the block without the strongest proofs of her guilt.

Finally the experience of the failed rebellion had been essentially reassuring. However much discomfort they felt about the Spanish match, the substantial leaders of the English aristocracy were not going to risk lives and property to defy it. The English would accept their new king. As the spring wore on and tension eased, many of the minor — and some of the major — figures in the rebellion found mercy at the Queen's hands on the urging of councillors. By the time the court was ready to move to Richmond in May, even the Queen agreed that Elizabeth should leave her prison. Renard would have packed her off to the Catholic north, to Pontefract, with its dismal association with Richard II, but the council thought it wiser to send her into a rural solitude, suitably isolated but not too far from the court, where she could be kept under close surveillance. Woodstock, the old royal hunting lodge in Oxfordshire, was the chosen site.[19]

On 19 May Elizabeth left the Tower, was rowed to Richmond and

then travelled by litter up the Thames Valley to her destination, a
five-day journey. As she passed through the villages *en route*, she was
greeted by the country people with cakes and wafers. At one place
the bells were rung and in another she stopped to see a local festival.[20]

At Woodstock she was lodged in a gate-house, a building in poor
repair, where four rooms had been hastily fitted up for her use. Her
keeper was Sir Henry Bedingfield, a Norfolk squire, an early adherent
of Mary in July 1553, who had been rewarded by appointment as
Privy Councillor and captain of the royal guard. Inexperienced in the
court world, stolid, dull, and literal-minded, he took his responsibilities with great seriousness, nervously anxious to carry out his instructions. He was attended by a garrison recruited from his own servants
and tenants. The instructions from the Queen spelled out his responsibilities.

> The cause of our said sister's late committing to the Tower of London
> whereof although she be not thoroughly cleared yet we have for her better
> quiet and to the end she may be the more honorably used thought meet
> to appoint her to remain at our manor of Woodstock until such time as
> certain matters touching her case which be not yet cleared may be
> thoroughly tried and examined.

She was confined to the house, allowed to walk in the garden in
Bedingfield's company; there were to be no messages and no confer-
ences with any person out of Bedingfield's hearing. Only six servants
waited on her, although her cofferer, Thomas Parry, was allowed to
lodge in the village, since he had to provide for her expenses which
were to be met out of her own estate. Neighbouring gentry were
required to be ready to assist Bedingfield.[21]

From the beginning he found his charge difficult to handle. She
complained of the litter on the way to Windsor and at the castle
insisted on going over the whole building, 'in the which and like
requests I am marvellously perplexed to grant her desire or to say nay'.
This was a lament he would repeat again and again. At Woodstock she
demanded to walk in the park, alleging a Council promise. When
Parry brought her Cicero's *Offices* and a Latin psalm book, Bedingfield
insisted on a Council warrant. Later there was the question of an
English bible for the lady. Then a neighbouring gentleman, who
brought a gift of fish and pheasants, had to be warned off. There was
endless friction about the presence of Parry and the dubious guests
he entertained.[22]

Apart from these continuing skirmishes in which this skilful toreador baited the bull to distraction, Elizabeth sought to make use of Bedingfield in continuing to assert her innocence and keeping her case before the Queen and Council. Within a few weeks of her arrival she accused him 'in the most unpleasant sort that ever I saw her since her coming from the Tower' of preventing her communication with the Council. She bade him write asking for permission to address a letter in her own hand to the Queen. He promised to do this but warned her he could not promise an answer. However, her ploy succeeded: permission did come from the Queen, and Elizabeth wrote a letter, now missing, to which a reply came, addressed to Bedingfield, in late June. He was to communicate the gist of it to his charge at a favourable opportunity.[23]

Elizabeth's letter had denied the validity of the witnesses brought against her. The Queen replied that, since the intercepted letters of the French ambassador revealed 'that divers of the most notable traitors made their chief account upon her, we can hardly be brought to think that they would have presumed so to do except they had more certain knowledge of her favour towards their unnatural conspiracy than is yet by her confessed'. She went on: 'yet cannot these fair words so much abuse us, but we do understand how things have been wrought.' Even if direct proof were lacking, circumstantial evidence was too powerful to ignore. Mary believed 'her meaning and purpose to be otherwise than her letter purposeth; wherefore our pleasure is not to be hereafter any more molested with such her disguise [*sic*] and colourful letters'. The Queen could only hope that the Lord would grant her grace 'to be towards Him as she ought to be'.[24]

Bedingfield was, not unnaturally, hesitant to pass this message to his ward. When he did so, her response was to request him to write at her dictation a letter to the Privy Council, a task which he refused. She bitterly riposted that she was worse off than the prisoners in the Tower or in Newgate, who at least had the right to be heard. Bedingfield still continued his refusal, but conscientiously reported the matter to the Privy Council. Elizabeth's persistence again paid off: it obtained royal consent to the princess's demand. Elizabeth once again appealed to her sister. She asked either that she be allowed to make her case directly to the Queen or that specific charges be brought against her to be answered and tried. To this Mary merely replied that she would consider it.[25]

Elizabeth now took a new tack, demanding she be allowed to send a servant to court to press for an answer to her suit; even wives were permitted this much. Her stern gaoler again refused. By this time

(August) he was so despairing of his charge that he sought the Councillor Bishop Thirlby's help in getting a discharge. His prisoner pushed her cause another step by making a solemn declaration at the mass that she had in all her life 'done nothing nor intended to do, that was perilous to the person of the Queen's Majesty or the commonwealth of this realm'. Calling on God as her witness, she then received the sacred wafer.[26]

These tactics worked; the Council allowed her to write and to send the letter by her own servant, who would be accompanied by one of Bedingfield's. There followed a small comedy. Bedingfield brought Elizabeth two sheets of paper, five pens, and ink (all these had been denied to her by the Council's order). Elizabeth accordingly wrote her letter, but next day she summoned Bedingfield, telling him that she never wrote but by a secretary 'and I am not suffered at this time to have none and therefore you must needs do it'. Reluctantly he obeyed, writing to her dictation. Whereupon she took the copy, added a postscript which she concealed from him, and sealed it.[27]

The royal answer was more encouraging; Mary would not be unmindful of her cause; as good occasion proceeded from deeds, she would be appropriately dealt with. In its wake there was another storm; when the prisoner asked to write to the Privy Council and Bedingfield demurred until he had clearance from his masters, she hurled at him words of 'reproach of this my service about her by the Queen's Highness commandment more than ever I heard her speak before, too long to write'. The next day she polished him off with the withering judgment that, although he might have good meaning, he 'lacked knowledge, experience, and all other accidents in such a service requisite'. He wrote to court, begging for mercy: 'to receive the discharge of this my service . . . were the joyfullest tidings that ever came to me.'[28]

With these letters of October 1554 our knowledge of Elizabeth's sojourn at Woodstock fades; she was to spend the winter there. The order for her release and return to court came in April 1555. Elizabeth had made good use of the year's detention in Oxfordshire. The insistent reiteration of her innocence and the demand for justice, that she be allowed to answer the charges brought against her (with the implication that they were false) had its effect. The hard core of Mary's disbelief in her sister's innocence was at least softened, and the Council was not allowed to forget her grievances.[29]

The Queen and the court had much else to preoccupy them in these twelve months – the arrival of Philip, the marriage at Winchester, and in the autumn the announcement of the Queen's pregnancy. The restoration of the old faith was completed with Cardinal Pole's arrival, bearing the papal absolution. The tremors which had shaken the English political world at the opening of the reign had died down; the regime was firmly in place and hopes for the future ran high. The Queen rejoiced in the assurance that God, who had miraculously preserved the old religion by bringing her to the throne, would provide an heir to assure the future. She could afford to look more gently on a sister whose existence now seemed much less threatening.

With the Queen's confinement imminent, Elizabeth was summoned to Hampton Court where for a fortnight she lived in guarded isolation. She may have been visited by Philip during these weeks, before she met her sister. A delegation of Councillors, headed by Gardiner, visited her. According to Foxe they sought once again to bring her to submit herself to the Queen, an act she proudly rejected as an acknowledgment of guilt. In the Imperial ambassador's account, they tried vainly to persuade her to go to Flanders to the court of the Queen Regent, Philip's sister, a scheme discussed the previous summer by the Council.[30]

Finally Elizabeth was sent for by the Queen. What followed comes on the doubtful authority of Foxe. Kneeling at her sister's feet, Elizabeth prayed for the Queen's welfare, professed her utter devotion, and asked to be believed, declaring that nothing to the contrary could be discovered. Mary, still doubtful, but under pressure from her husband, yielded; a week later Bedingfield and his guards vanished. Elizabeth now, along with the whole nation, awaited her sister's delivery. There was a false report of birth at the end of April; by late August it was painfully evident that there was no child; it had been a false pregnancy. When the royal couple returned to Hampton Court, Elizabeth went to another house three miles off. In October she departed for Hatfield, making a public appearance in London *en route*.[31]

There can be little doubt that the great non-event of this summer profoundly strengthened Elizabeth's position. When Mary met her at Hampton Court in April, she was confident that she would soon be a mother. When Philip left for Flanders at the end of August, he and the whole political world believed — if the Queen did not — that Elizabeth would be the next sovereign of England. That she should be the successor was as important for the Spanish as for the English, since the next in line was the young Mary Stuart, Queen of Scotland and soon to be dauphine of France. Whatever suspicions of Elizabeth as a menace to the present regime lingered on were outweighed by the contingent interest of her future sovereignty.[32]

Elizabeth had survived the two most difficult years of her life. Fate had cast her in two conflicting roles, as contingent heir to her sister's throne and as assumed patroness of Mary's enemies. The tensions which these roles implied were merely latent until the outbreak of rebellion in January 1554. The Kentish rising, although sparked off without her involvement, forced her to the first great political actions of her life. The problems which faced her were ones which would have challenged a veteran politician; yet she had neither counsel nor experience.

The fact that both court and rebels took for granted that Elizabeth would patronize the rising meant that she was left with very little room for manœuvre. All she could do was to reiterate her innocence to a disbelieving Queen. Even before the Kentish revolt began, the Council knew that Carew was planning a rising on behalf of Elizabeth and Courtenay in the West Country. In addition, Gardiner had pried from the latter a confession: the Earl admitted having been approached with the proposal that he marry Elizabeth. Later evidence, gathered after the revolt was crushed, made it clear that Courtenay had been well informed of what was planned.

But what about Elizabeth? How much did she know in advance of the rising? The Council had heard by 27 January (the day the rising began) that she wished to take refuge at Donnington, her house in Berkshire, and to fortify it.[33] This was a distorted version of what was later more accurately known: first that Croft had visited Ashridge, discussed a move to Donnington with Parry; then that Wyatt had sent a letter after the rising began, urging her to remove further from London, to which she had replied verbally through a servant, simply thanking him. Nothing further emerged from the trials of the conspirators.

Piecing together these fragments of evidence, it is possible to reconstruct a possible scenario of Elizabeth's role in these events. We know, of course, that the rebellion failed, but contemporaries, including many of the councillors, thought it had a good chance of succeeding. Elizabeth, too, had to calculate on that possibility. She could do nothing to advance or to halt events. The rebels did not count on her leading the movement; they hoped to overthrow the existing regime by a general rising in the shires which would draw the support of the great court politicians. Only then would Elizabeth and Courtenay be called on to perform their part. Elizabeth warily kept open her options. On the one hand she steadily asserted her loyalty to Mary, but on the other she permitted contact between her principal officer and one of the leading conspirators, Croft. She did indeed receive a letter from Wyatt, and during the crucial days when events hung in the balance she fended off the summons to court, remaining at Ashridge, where she had freedom of movement. By the time the delegation from court arrived, the rebellion had collapsed and she had no alternative but to obey the Queen's summons.

When Elizabeth arrived at Whitehall she was thoroughly frightened, as her desperate effort to avoid the Tower and her failure of nerve when she landed there made apparent. She knew her enemies were seeking her life and the state prisoners who had entered that dread prison had all too rarely emerged alive. Nevertheless, she was not without hope. The princess had left her enemies with very little to take hold of if they proposed to try her for treason. Moreover she had a band of partisans within the Council who would fight for her rights. Her great fear must have been that, either by torture or by holding out the hope of pardon, her opponents would extract from the treason trials some confession which would incriminate her. Renard complained bitterly of the lack of energy in pursuing a prosecution, and as early as the beginning of April the Council was already discussing the possibility of finding a husband for her, but with the coming of Philip, and later the royal pregnancy, she could be consigned to limbo at Woodstock while they waited on events to solve their problem. With the end of the false pregnancy she had to be freed and restored to a place in the political universe.

For the remaining three years of Mary's reign there was something like a tacit truce between the two sisters. Elizabeth, withdrawn to country retirement at Hatfield or Ashridge, remained carefully aloof from all political activity. The court, although still uneasily suspicious, treated her with formal courtesy. On both sides civility and decorum served to mask underlying unease.

The court's ineradicable distrust of the princess was given some colour in these years. Renard, in a memoir of the spring of 1558, bitterly noted that all the plots of the past four years aimed at placing Elizabeth on the throne sooner than the course of nature would permit. Although there were no more open revolts against the Marian regime (with the exception of the mini-insurrection at Scarborough in 1557, crushed at birth), there was abundance of rumour and of half-formed conspiracies. The most serious was the Dudley plot of 1555–6, organized in France, where the government there gave clandestine sponsorship to a cluster of malcontents.[34]

Once again the objective was the replacement of Mary by Elizabeth.

It involved a large network of gentry, mostly men of modest position but many of them well connected. The conspiracy was betrayed from within before it matured. Among those who were involved was Francis Verney, the servant who had carried Elizabeth's letter to court during her Woodstock confinement. During the investigation of the conspiracy Elizabeth's waiting-woman, Kate Ashley, was again a prisoner along with her Italian teacher, Baptiste Castiglione. A guard was thrown around the princess's house, but an elaborate letter of explanation and apology was sent, the guard withdrawn, and her servants soon released. In December 1556 Elizabeth made a state visit to the court, lodging in her London residence, Somerset House. There was another such visit in the spring of 1558.[35]

For the government, the years from 1556 were filled with unwelcome preoccupations. The papally inspired war between France and Spain brought Philip back to England to persuade his reluctant English subjects to add their forces to his. It was an unpopular war and the foot-dragging character of the English effort disgusted the Spanish king. There then followed the sudden French assault on Calais and the conquest of the last Continental enclave of English power. By now both Spain and France were moving wearily towards peace; negotiations were, in Philip's eyes, unnecessarily tangled by the English insistence that he recover Calais for them. The Spanish commitment in the island kingdom, once a promising asset, was increasingly a liability.

In these circumstances Spanish interest in England's internal affairs dwindled. Nevertheless, the sure prospect that Elizabeth would succeed made her marriage a matter of major concern to them. Their favourite candidate for her hand was the Prince of Piedmont. This exiled prince, whose hereditary lands were French-occupied, was a general in the Spanish service. His name came up as early as 1553. In 1554 Paget pushed for the match as a means for reconciling the English to the Spanish marriage. A few years later Renard pressed it on the different grounds that it would link England to the Low Countries, where Piedmont might act as governor. Both saw the Prince as a candidate whose minor dynastic status would make him acceptable to jealous English fears of foreign rule. In 1554 he actually came to England, although he did not meet his proposed bride. Desultory discussion continued over the succeeding years. It was still on the Queen's agenda in the spring of 1558. The Habsburgs never seem to have given it their full attention, and in the end they put it aside, but the greatest stumbling-block was the bride herself. By 1556 her position was far too strong for her to be pressured into a marriage (as she might have been in the aftermath of the Wyatt rebellion). But now it was certain that Elizabeth would not choose a husband to satisfy the needs or plans of the Habsburgs.[36]

When Philip dispatched his special envoy, the Duke of Feria, in the spring of 1558, he was instructed to get in touch with Elizabeth — which he did, but only after Philip had written to his wife to inform her of the plan. Feria saw the princess but since he deferred telling Philip of their conversation until he returned, we cannot know its content.[37] From the late summer on, Mary's health began to deteriorate, and in late October, hearing her life was in danger, Philip sent Feria once again. In early November the Council prevailed on Mary to make a declaration in favour of Elizabeth's succession. Two Councillors were sent to Hatfield to tell the princess of the Queen's decision and to ask that she maintain the old religion and pay Mary's debts.[38]

Feria arrived on 9 November; the Queen's physicians had given up all hope, and in fact the envoy's mission was directed to the rising not to the setting sun. He went very promptly to see Elizabeth in Hertfordshire, to convey his master's assurances of goodwill and his offer of any aid necessary to ensure her peaceful accession. Elizabeth responded with suitable affability. She especially thanked Philip for his aid when she was a prisoner. When Feria, pushing a step further, tried to persuade her that she owed her throne neither to Mary nor to the Council but solely to the King of Spain, he suffered a very tart repulse. Elizabeth expressed her anger at her treatment in the past five years, and went on to declare that she owed her position to the people, who had remained loyal to her. It was they, not the king nor the English nobility, who had placed her where she was.[39]

She knew Philip had wanted to marry her to the Prince of Piedmont, but she was resolved never to marry out of the kingdom. Her sister's fatal mistake, which had lost her the affection of the English people, was to marry a foreign prince. Feria went on to decry the favour she showed to heretics and traitors. He had no doubt there would be a reversal of the whole policy of the dying reign.

When Mary died on the morning of 17 November, Chancellor Heath went before the Parliament then in session to announce that event and to proclaim the accession of her sister. Later in the day solemn proclamations were made at Westminster and in the city. The transfer of power had been altogether peaceful. In large part this was due to the acquiescence of the dying monarch and the cooperation of her ministers, but Elizabeth had also made her own dispositions.

There can be little doubt that there had been contacts with notables in the provinces and quite probably at court although the surviving evidence is very slight.[40] There had also been preparations for active measures if opposition should arise. A letter written nearly forty years later reveals that the writer, a captain at Berwick in 1558, received a letter from Parry in October or November. He was commanded to proceed to Hertfordshire and to bring with him the assurances of support of the other captains in his garrison, with their promise 'to serve for the maintenance of her royal state, title and dignity'. There apparently was a plan and an organization which could have been mobilized if need had arisen.

Elizabeth in the autumn of 1558, at the beginning of her twenty-fifth year, was fully blooded in the great game of politics. Her apprenticeship had been a brutal one; she had to learn her trade without the benefit of a master to instruct her. Faced with danger to her life, she had reacted with courage and a cool self-possession. Except for a moment when she was entering the Tower, she never faltered. That self-possession and cool-headedness enabled her to conceive a strategy of defence and to adhere to it unswervingly. In her tenacity of purpose and action she resembled her sister's stand in Edward's time. Mary, too, had taken a position and held to it unyieldingly. But in Mary's case it was a stand on principle, on her deep-grounded religious beliefs. Elizabeth for her part had no hesitation in shifting her religious practice to the dictates of her sister. The beacon which guided her actions was not one of religious or political principle but, first of all, survival and, beyond that, the pursuit of power. From 1553 the possibility and, from 1556, the certainty of succession directed Elizabeth's footsteps.

In this self-taught course of instruction the princess learned many of the skills of the practical politician, mostly those a darker kind — dissimulation, outright deceit, evasion, the careful concealment of one's own aims. She learned how to suppress her own emotions, to conduct herself, not as an autonomous human being, but as a pawn in a game where every move had to be carefully calculated. Cut off from the normal human associations of family or friendship, she had no one to rely on except her servants, particularly Parry and Ashley. In them she found a sturdy loyalty which she reciprocated, but with the world outside her household, relations were regulated solely by interest, on both sides. In short she had shed many of the attributes of her private persona; she had already, before mounting the throne, acquired a public persona which shaped most of her intercourse with other human beings. She had already entered the awful solitude of a sovereign, to whom all others are necessarily inferiors with whom her relations will always be shaped by the unbridgeable chasm between the anointed of the Lord and the mere subject. The latter could persuade, cajole, flatter, but never engage on terms of equality and rarely with candour.

Elizabeth had undergone a useful apprenticeship in the art of politics, but the skills she had learned were necessarily those derived from her own circumstances of extreme vulnerability. She had developed a strategy of caution, of immobility, playing as few cards as possible, waiting and hoping on events. She was yet to learn the skills required for the exercise of rulership — making decisions, giving commands, and ensuring those commands were obeyed. This was a role for which there was no script and no rehearsals; she had to learn it as the play unfolded itself to an expectant audience.

Elizabeth's experience was very limited. Her life had been led almost exclusively in the seclusion of country houses, with only an occasional and short visit to the court. She had had no dealings with the ambassadors of foreign princes, and only an outsider's acquaintance with the world of the courtiers and the administrators. She had yet to master the management of men — and, as far as possible, of events. Above all, she suffered from the same fatal disadvantage as her sister: she was a woman in a man's seat. Her sister had largely confirmed men's doubts; only the test of time and of events would strengthen or resolve their doubts about her successor.

Part II

The Apprentice Queen

1558–1568

3

Making a Government

When the heralds proclaimed Elizabeth's accession on 17 November 1558 she became, by divine sanction and lawful inheritance, a supreme ruler who by her 'mere will and motion' commanded the obedience of her people. However, these awesome powers, like other gifts of the gods, came with attached special conditions which circumscribed their use. These conditions were of different kinds; some resulted from the action of her immediate predecessors, her father and her siblings — revolution and counter-revolution in religion, the struggle with France over Scotland, the accumulated debt and the empty treasury. These circumstances would force Elizabeth into immediate decisions: often painful, sometimes dangerous, but always unavoidable.

Her conduct of affairs was also circumscribed, more obliquely, by the legacies of a more remote past, the massive complex of institutions built up by the practice of her royal predecessors over nearly half a millennium. Like some ancient manor house, they had been constructed piece by piece, additions being made whenever some new need dictated. These institutions — Council, courts of law, Parliament, plus the tissues of conventions which governed their actual functioning — were at once instruments by which the royal will could be implemented and brakes upon unconstrained use of regal power. Although there had been steady development of political, administrative, and legal institutions across the centuries, the changes which took place had for the most part been slow and gradual in nature, so that they were assimilated almost without being noticed. England had, of course, experienced the violent fluctuations of political life — the bloody rage of faction, contests for the throne itself, the death of princes. If the historical weather had been stormy, however, the historical climate had been essentially stable.[1]

This process of slow-moving accommodation had fortified a deep cultural bias of the medieval European world which viewed with alarm any symptoms of change, evolutionary or revolutionary. Such manifestations of instability or disturbance were seen as malfunctions: repairs were called for to restore the mechanism to good working order. That it might be obsolete and require major modification or even replacement was unthinkable.

Thus Englishmen were totally unprepared for the events of the twenty-five years between Elizabeth's birth and her accession. In those decades Henry VIII, the greatest disturber of the public peace since William the Norman, had performed a major piece of political surgery by amputating the church in England from the main body of Latin Christendom. The severed arteries had been skilfully cauterized by Thomas Cromwell and the separated church tidily integrated into the existing constitutional and legal structure of royal authority. As an afterthought the monarch and his ministers had demolished the whole monastic establishment, destroying an age-old pillar of traditional Christian corporate life.

While English society was still striving to digest these changes, Henry's death placed his nine-year-old son on the throne. The men who governed in his name, riding on the momentum induced by the late King's actions, had gone further still — abolishing the mass and replacing it with a radically different mode of public worship. These enactments placed the English church definitively in the Protestant fold. Then, in a sudden reversal of fortune, the accidents of mortality and inheritance had enabled the King's elder daughter, Mary, to undo the work of both her father and her brother. These dizzying changes had left the nation at large bewildered and disorientated. The alternation between two unrelentingly opposed regimes, one radically Protestant, the other uncompromisingly Catholic, was dividing Englishmen.

All this meant that the new ruler of England faced a society painfully strained by the unprecedented disruption of ancient ways of life, and by the possibility that it might suffer the peculiar horrors of fratricidal strife motivated by profound ideological disagreement. Moreover, these dangers were not peculiar to England; the lines of battle between the two faiths were now drawn across the breadth of western Europe. Not only domestic affairs but also Elizabeth's relations with her fellow monarchs would be shaped by the religious conflict.

This was the heaviest and most troublesome burden which the Queen inherited from her predecessors. There was, however, a second hardly less weighty. The unexpected death of James V of Scotland in 1542, leaving a week-old girl as his successor, opened a window of opportunity which Henry was anxious to exploit by marrying his son Edward to the infant Mary and thus adding another kingdom to his dominions. His clumsy mixture of bullying and sweet-tongued persuasion only succeeded in driving the xenophobic Scots into the arms of their ancient ally, France. The young Queen was sent abroad to be affianced to the French dauphin; French troops supported a French regent in ruling the northern kingdom.

Henry's actions succeeded in turning topsy-turvy England's relations with her ancient foe, France.[2] Although since 1453 England had ceased to occupy French territory (except for Calais), the English kings had retained the same aggressive posture towards her neighbour, using every opportunity to harass her, and had done this with impunity, since France was too preoccupied in Italy to be able to retaliate. Now in a single instant the tables were turned; France, which had long regarded Scotland simply as a convenient stick with which to distract England, saw the northern realm as a jewel to be added to the French diadem. England, for the first time in centuries, faced a Continental foe seated within the island.

Elizabeth's inheritance was thus saddled with heavy liabilities. What about the other side of the ledger? What were her assets — the stock of capital on which she could draw? What institutional and social forces could be utilized to support her in steadying the realm in this painful era of internal and external strain? The throne which Elizabeth inherited was supported by a firm administrative and legal foundation. Of the executive agency, the Council, more is said below. The most imposing institutional structure was to be found in the law courts. The three common-law courts, dating from the thirteenth century, had been augmented more recently by the court of Chancery and by a Tudor creation, the court of Star Chamber. From the subjects' point of view the court system was the *raison d'être* of royal government, the guarantor of their property rights and the scourge of evil-doers. On the crown's side it was seen as the agency which, by easing the frictions generated by personal and local quarrels and by punishing criminals, kept in control the violence endemic in the society. That violence could all too easily escalate into grave public disorder, especially if it were exploited by religious or political faction.

The system of justice was not, however, wholly self-subsistent. The

judges made their twice-yearly visitations in the shires to punish mis-
doers and to adjudicate private disputes, but they were met at the
shire boundaries by a company of the local gentry. It was only through
their cooperation in mobilizing the whole machinery of the assizes
that the judges could accomplish their tasks. These gentry were at
the same time the abiding representatives of royal power in the every-
day life of the local communities. To this end the crown had enlisted
their services as justices of the peace, a role in which they combined
the natural ascendancy of landlordship with royally bestowed powers
of office. The dignity and power with which their commission
endowed them were sufficient to compensate for the onerous – and
unpaid – burdens it imposed. Their routine duties were wide-ranging
and steadily growing in number. In times of emergency they were
even more essential since they were the first line of defence when
local or personal grievance threatened to explode into insurrection.
Such had been their role in 1549, when agrarian discontent was rife
through much of central and southern England and incipient disorders
widely spread. In almost all of the counties affected, the local magistrates rose to the occasion and quelled the disturbances before they
escalated into insurrection. Where they failed, in Devonshire and
Norfolk, armies had to be raised to put down organized revolt.

To guard against such a disaster, it was essential that the crown
and its ministers win the confidence and retain the loyalty of the JPs
and of the class from which they were chosen. These considerations
had become all the more urgent in the wake of zigzagging changes
in religion. There was now the potential for fatal division within the
realm. Whether such a rift could be avoided turned on the response
of the ruling county elites. Only if the new regime could win their
unshaken confidence in its capacity to govern could the spectre of
civil conflict be laid.

In the end that depended on the monarch himself. However awesome the solemnities of the coronation rite or the splendours of court
ceremonial, they were, as Shakespeare's Richard II discovered, inadequate if the sovereign himself did not embody in his (or her) own
person the qualities of rulership. The monarch must be of such a
commanding presence that there could be no doubt of prompt obedience to royal commands by servants and by subjects alike. For three
generations Edward IV, Henry VII, and Henry VIII had measured
up to the demands of the royal office. The last, indeed, had become
a figure larger than life: mixing charm and terror in equal proportion,
restless and wilful, driving his people into costly war or herding them

out of the Roman fold, he had imprinted the majesty of monarchy on the popular imagination. His son had not lived to assume the mantle of sovereignty and his elder daughter had worn it uneasily, anxious to shift its burden to her husband. Whether his younger daughter was equal to the task remained to be seen.

What, of course, loomed menacingly, quite beyond the best skills of kings or queens, were the untamable and unpredictable forces of the natural environment which shaped the lives of a pre-industrial society with an immediacy long forgotten in our age. For Elizabeth and her subjects the vagaries of the weather were not merely incidental to the routines of their daily lives, but essential to their well-being. In an economy overwhelmingly agricultural and of necessity self-supporting, a rainy — or a dry — summer had immediate consequences to every household in the realm. With no reserves in store, the cost of food, the largest item in every family budget, would immediately respond. Each season the farmer waited anxiously for the rain or sun which would make the year one of dearth or of plenty. Less immediately apparent but in the long run even more determinative of the quality of life was the impact of disease on a society quite without medical defences.

The weather patterns of the last half of the century were for the most part normal ones, in which good and poor harvests were distributed evenly enough to avoid the misery of prolonged dearth. The notable exception was the middle years of the 1590s, when crops failed for three seasons running; even here, however, England was spared the horrors of famine.

The other great environmental variable was the incidence of disease — not only by the dreaded bubonic plague but also the whole array of air- or waterborne infections. After a severe visitation in the very first years of the reign the picture brightened, and the 1570s and 1580s were particularly free of disease — as measured by the mortality rates. Here again the 1590s were a grimmer decade, marked by a sequence of disease-ridden years.

The relief from the worst visitations of sickness was to be had at a price. Since the reign of Henry VIII the population of England had been slowly growing. During the 1570s and 1580s the rate of annual increase was higher than at any time before the eighteenth century. When Elizabeth died she was reigning over over a million more subjects than her predecessors.[3] The necessary correlation was an ever-larger number of mouths to be fed, by an agrarian economy which had strictly limited means of increasing its food production. There followed a steady rise in grain prices, spurred by population increase, fluctuating from year to year according to weather conditions, but rising inexorably decade by decade. For a great proportion of the Queen's subjects, her reign was marked by a substantial fall in their standard of living. For a minority, the landowners, the steady rise in grain prices provided an era of unparalleled prosperity and unashamed conspicuous consumption, to which the monuments of the Elizabethan house-builders still bear witness.

The economy was overwhelmingly given over to the tasks of feeding, housing, and clothing the population, and most of this activity was local in character. The one great exception was, of course, the production of woollen cloths for export to the Continent. This industry had grown by leaps and bounds in the half century to 1550, when a market glut and other conditions had brought a check. During Elizabeth's time it would not recover to the peak of these earlier years, but it would continue to be the mainstay of foreign commerce, the money-earner which paid for such imports as wine and Continental manufactures. The revolt of the Netherlands would disrupt the pattern of trade, diverting the shipment of cloth from Antwerp to German or Dutch marts. Bolder and more venturesome exporters would be stimulated to explore new markets, in the Levant, the Baltic, Russia, and, at the very end of the reign, to found the East India Company. In general, the basic patterns of national economic life were but little changed in the Queen's lifetime. Only at its close were there signs that English commerce would break out of its ancient western European limits.[4]

In the first months of her reign, and in the following years, the Queen would have to find her way, step by painful step. She had to choose and then to test the men on whose advice and service she would rely. She had to take painful and often irreversible decisions and learn to live with their consequences. This in turn meant setting goals and devising strategies to realize them. The first decade of the reign would record a long trail of such actions as the Queen struggled to master her new calling. By the opening of the 1570s her apprenticeship was over; she had taken her place among the masters of her elite guild.

The first task — and the first test — of a new monarch was the choice of a council. In form that body had been what each monarch had chosen to make it. Under the first Tudor it had been large and amorphous: Henry VII had consulted whom and when he chose and the collective role of the body was negligible. His son's formidable

secretary, Cromwell, had in the 1530s radically restructured th
tution, separating out a tight inner circle, the Privy Council, ...
members took a special oath, were provided with their own secretariat
and archive, and were intended to act as the sole instrument of royal
power, at once an administrative board and a committee of advisers.[5]
The Privy Council normally included the major departmental heads,
Chancellor, Treasurer, and Admiral (and now the Secretary). To them
were added a contingent of prominent peers, a clutch of household
officers, and a handful of bureaucrats, the equivalent of modern under-
secretaries. In short, the Council consisted of a mix of men of influence
and men of business, with an infusion of the monarch's personal servants. In the past many of the men of business had been clerics, but
this was changing. How effective this body was depended on the
monarch. It could be a finely tuned instrument of power or a hotbed
of faction. Under Mary it had been too often the latter.

Elizabeth moved with dispatch in the choice of her Council. She
first appointed Sir William Cecil as Secretary of State. A veteran of
the Edwardian Council, serving both Somerset and Northumberland
in the same office, he had lost conciliar status under Mary. Politically
agile and religiously adaptable, he had filled minor posts in her service.
Since 1550 Cecil had been a servant of Elizabeth, appointed as her
land surveyor in that year. Such evidence as there is shows him in
frequent contact with Parry, her major-domo, and presumably with
the princess herself. He was certainly a familiar and trusted servant
who commanded his mistress's confidence in the highest degree.[6]

When she arrived in London, Elizabeth turned her attention to
further appointments. She had the practice of her predecessors to
guide her. Tudor policy sought to recruit from a wide pool of men,
rewarding royal servants not only for their loyalty but also for their
proven capacity in the tasks to which they were set. There had
emerged in Henry VIII's late years a new class of professionals, servants of the crown rather than the personal clientage of the ruling
monarch. By his death there existed a core of such men, who had
mastered their skills in the preceding years, jacks of all trades — diplomats, soldiers, administrators.

The absence of an adult monarch after 1547 enabled them to consolidate their position. By 1553 Mary found their services indispens-
able, even though most of them had supported Lady Jane's usurpation.
Reluctantly she appointed them to her Council. That body was an
ill-assorted collection, thirty strong, including those veterans, experienced but only half trusted; a contingent of her household servants,

loyal but unversed in politics; and a clutch of clerics. Its history was marked by internecine feuds and general quarrelsomeness.

Elizabeth had a freer hand in her selection of councillors. Surveying the Marian Council, she chose to dismiss two-thirds of them. The personal retainers of her sister were, of course, dropped; so were the clerics, all firm adherents of the Catholic faith. Ten of Mary's Councillors were retained.

Among the carry-overs were four earls whose prime recommendation was their rank. Two of these, Derby and Shrewsbury, were sleepers, great regional magnates in the north, who (it was taken for granted) would seldom be in attendance at court. The other two, Arundel and Pembroke, were active and experienced politicians, the former the holder of one of the oldest peerages, the latter an *arriviste* who had made a spectacular ascent to property and place under Edward. Elizabeth also retained Lord Howard of Effingham, her great-uncle and reputedly her defender in the Marian court, Lord Admiral Clinton, whose conciliar service began in Edward's time, and Paulet, the aged Marquess of Winchester, administrator *par excellence* and Lord Treasurer since 1550. He continued in that great office. The three surviving commoners were all veteran men of business whose careers dated back to Henry's time — Sir John Mason, a diplomat, Sir William Petre, a former Secretary of State, and another diplomat, Sir Nicholas Wotton — none of them politically prominent.

The new additions to the Council mingled several different types. Sir Thomas Parry, her steward for a decade, was a battle-scarred survivor who had suffered imprisonment in her service; his appointment was brief — he died in 1561. Two other Councillors were blood relations on the Boleyn side, Sir Richard Sackville and Sir Francis Knollys, both former office-holders in the Edwardian regime. The office of Lord Keeper went to Sir Nicholas Bacon, attorney of the court of wards, and brother-in-law of Cecil. Two peers were added, the strongly Protestant second Earl of Bedford, son of a successful Henrician courtier, and Parr, Marquess of Northampton, brother of the late Queen, who had lost his title and very nearly his life for his share in the Grey usurpation. Two newcomers, Sir Edward Rogers, a member of her brother's Privy Chamber and of her Hatfield household, and Sir Ambrose Cave, a connection of Cecil's, filled out the list. In total there were twenty of them, two-thirds as many as in the previous reign. It was a Council in which the men of business, the professionals, formed a substantial majority and had a preponderance of influence. The noble Councillors sat not so much as magnates of the realm as in their capacity as experienced courtiers. It was a body designed for administrative efficiency and for knowledgeable counsel.

In composition this Council was not much different from its predecessors — except for the absence of the clerics — but the complexion of its membership was significant. Ardently Catholic councillors were missing altogether; the bulk of the incumbents were vaguely *politique*, conformists as circumstances dictated. Two, Bedford and Knollys, who had gone abroad in Mary's reign, held markedly Protestant views. The return of Edwardians to office was obvious. Of some interest was the presence in the Council of two participants in the Wyatt rising, Rogers and Parr. Sir Nicholas Throckmorton, whose acquittal for treason in 1554 rocked the Marian court, was ambassador in Paris. The Warden of the Cinque Ports, the Captain of the Guard, and a number of lesser officials of the new regime had been involved in the same conspiracy.

Outside the official ranks of the Council but inside the circle of royal familiars was another group of survivors from the Edwardian past — the Dudley brothers, sons of the late unlamented Duke of Northumberland. The Queen's favour to Lord Robert, the younger brother, attracted wide notice from the first days of the reign when he was appointed Master of the Horse, a lucrative post which required constant attendance on the Queen. His older brother, Ambrose, was appointed Master of the Ordnance. This cosy family party was rounded out by their brother-in-law, Sir Henry Sidney, who, already holding high office in Ireland, became Lord President of the Council in the Marches of Wales.

The Queen now had chosen the men on whose counsel, service, and loyalty she would depend as she set about the governance of the realm. She had paid her respects to the traditional noble elites by including some of their number in her Council; the clerics, on the other hand, were totally excluded. (Archbishop Whitgift, appointed in 1584, was the sole exception in the reign.) The gap left by their absence was filled by men of a new breed, the professional laymen of business. Some were lawyers by training; others had begun their career as clerics but had changed their collars; many were simply courtiers, men who had scrambled up the slippery pole of promotion by service, as soldiers, diplomats, or administrators. But in all these categories the prime qualification was proven talent. These were the men who would form the active element in the business of government.

For her own comfort and ease Elizabeth had surrounded herself with a circle of old and trusted servants, and she had created a kind of family for herself out of her mother's kin. The Queen had two cousins, the children of Mary Boleyn, who had married William Cary. The son, Henry, was now created Baron Hunsdon, and endowed with lands; he was also appointed Captain of the Gentlemen Pensioners and launched on a career which would bring him to the Privy Council. His sister was married to Sir Francis Knollys, Privy Councillor and Vice-Chamberlain of the Household. Sackville, another Councillor and Chancellor of the Exchequer, was first cousin to Anne Boleyn. On his death in 1566 his son, Thomas, was created Baron Buckhurst and in due time joined the Councillors. Their wives became ladies attendant on the Queen.

It was within the Council that the business of state was carried on; but the theatre of politics, in a more general sense, was the court, and more particularly the chamber, the staff of personal servants who filled the more dignified offices of service and were in constant attendance on the sovereign. Out of a total of some fifty, only about a dozen survived from the previous reign. Among the new appointees a high percentage had served the Queen's brother.

Mary's Council had been riven by internal quarrels. Would Elizabeth's be more harmonious? Could they function as a team? Was there among them an incipient Wolsey or Cromwell? Would any one of them establish himself as a special confidant of the sovereign, as a preferred Councillor, moving on an inside track? The Queen had carefully excluded the most prominent and the most ambitious of the Marian councillors, Lord Paget. Among the hold-overs the only one who was likely to push himself forward was Arundel. He fancied himself (among other things) a consort for the Queen, but his ambitions had generally outrun his talents. Among the newcomers, Parry and Cecil were the two who had had close personal connections with Elizabeth before her accession. Parry was a loyal and trusted servant, but inexperienced in the larger world of the court. Cecil knew the ropes, having served as Secretary under Edward, although in a subordinate role to Northumberland. The other new Councillors were unknown quantities.

4

The Legacies of the Past

The Council table was largely filled and the court newly ordered by the new year. Parliament was to meet at the end of January. In the mean time the ceremonial occasion of the coronation loomed, preceded by a state procession from the Tower of London to Westminster, through the city streets. In the Queen's brother's and sister's time the custom had grown up of greeting the new sovereign by an array of decorative arches and pageants presented by the City companies.[1]

This was the first occasion when the Queen encountered a large public; she embraced its opportunities with the enthusiasm of a modern elected politician. She was met with 'cries, tender words, and all other signs which argue a wonderful earnest love of most obedient servants'. To all who wished her well, the Queen, 'by holding up her hands, and merry countenance to such as stood far off, and most tender and gentle language to those that stood nigh to her grace, did declare her self no less thankfully to receive her peoples good will, than they lovingly offered it unto her'. To those who 'bade God save her grace, she said again God save them all, and thanked them with all her heart'.

At intervals along the way there were erected scaffolds with their attendant pageants. At the first, Elizabeth stopped her chariot and bade silence so that she could hear the prepared oration. She listened attentively and 'with rejoicing visage did evidently declare that the words took no less place in her mind, than they were most heartily pronounced by the child'. This scene repeated itself at the successive pageants on the route. She accepted the countless offerings of nosegays from the humblest, and one such sprig of rosemary was seen in her chariot when she arrived at Westminster. This sixteenth-century version of the twentieth-century royal 'walkabout' would be repeated many times in the coming years.

The coronation itself proved to have more than merely ceremonial significance. Normally the consecration of the new monarch fell to the primate, but that office was now vacant by the death of Archbishop Pole. It proved difficult to find a substitute, for by this time the religious views of Elizabeth were deeply suspect in orthodox circles. At the Christmas mass she had retired at the elevation of the host. In the end Bishop Oglethorpe of Carlisle agreed to preside, but the communion service was probably celebrated by the Dean of the Chapel Royal, in English and without the elevation of the host.[2]

With her Council and court assembled, the coronation past, and Parliament about to meet, the Queen now faced a series of momentous decisions which could not be postponed. At the moment when Elizabeth assumed the reins of power, Europe was racked by two great conflicts. The first was the seventy-year-old struggle between the two Continental dynasties, Habsburg and Valois, now about to draw to a close. England, as Spain's ally in the latest bout of war, was a junior party to the peace negotiations now under way. Her representatives' hope was to recover the lost possession of Calais, captured by the French in January 1558; but, since they lacked any bargaining counters, these hopes were slight.

The second great conflict was only just taking shape — the struggle between the new-born churches of the Reformation and the old papal order. In the years after 1540 there had been a steady polarization as each side — at Trent, Augsburg, or Geneva — defined and rigidified its beliefs. That same process contributed heavily to the politicization of the struggle, as the contestants moved down from the high ground of theology, where divine confounded divine, to a more mundane level, where princes strove by diplomacy or arms for the victory of their confession. Once this polarization had set in, no prince could remain aloof from the struggle. By the very fact of membership in the Christian commonwealth he had to define his position. Henry had havered; in the 1540s this was still possible, but by 1558 it had ceased to be so. Under the next two sovereigns England had enlisted first in one and then in the other camp. To which standard would Elizabeth rally?

At a national level the religious problem had at least two dimensions. Henry's initial break with Rome in the 1530s had been more a political and constitutional than a religious act. Using the power of the crown, not to conquer new territories on the Continent, but to crush the parallel authority of the church within his own realm, he predicated a whole new conception of the state, to use a term just coming into use. This bold augmentation of royal power, the assumption of lay control over the moral as well as the ecclesiastical universe, had immense attraction for Henry — and for contemporary European monarchs. It filled his imagination, as the immediate contingencies for which it was devised — the annulment and remarriage — faded away. The exercise of the supreme headship became the King's major goal. He had been timid in dealing with doctrine or worship. Yet unwittingly, in spite of this conservatism, he had opened the sluice-gates through which the doctrine and practice of German reform could enter. The second dimension, the movement for religious reform, although numbering only a small minority of the population, was a visible presence. Towards the reformers the King had been ambivalent, alternating between encouragement and brutal suppression.

It was left to his successors in power, Somerset and Northumberland, to plunge ahead and carry England into the full spate of the Protestant Reformation, repudiating traditional worship and doctrine and instituting a new religious order. Nevertheless, at the end of Edward's reign their work was less than half done; only a devoted minority of Englishmen and women accepted the new faith. The Protestant regime was sustained in power by the authority of the crown. Most of the population continued sluggishly loyal to an instinctive Catholicism, accepting without demur the Marian restoration. Under Mary the old faith, which in Edward's time had failed to rally against the new order, obtained a new sense of self-consciousness and effective clerical leadership. Yet Cardinal Pole and his episcopal colleagues failed to light the blaze of counter-Reformation zeal which was renewing Continental Catholicism. He left behind no corps of organized militants to counter the enthusiasm of the dedicated reformers. Protestantism, tried by the ordeal of persecution, had proved to be a living faith, with ardent supporters among the common people of the south-eastern counties, although few among the upper classes shared any disposition to emulate the example of the peasant martyrs. Yet it was increasingly clear that to root out Protestantism would not be an easy task. All England and half Europe waited expectantly for Elizabeth to reveal her plans for the settlement of religion. There was a general assumption that change would follow, but uncertainty as to its form. That would have to wait upon Parliament.

For the moment it was the first problem, the making of peace, which took precedence even over the religious question. The unwelcome war inherited from the past regime had to be liquidated. A truce had been declared months before, and commissioners were negotiating in the border town of Cateau-Cambrésis. The great antagonists were both exhausted and ready for peace. English claims were an impediment to final settlement. National honour demanded that the Queen insist on the return of Calais, but her representatives came to the table without a single bargaining chip in hand. Their hope was in Philip. As long as his wife was alive he could not decently ignore their pleas, but the Spanish King, anxious for the conclusion of peace, saw the English claims as a nuisance and would give little more than lip service in their support.

Mason, veteran diplomat and Councillor, bluntly told Cecil that it was idle 'to stick upon Calais as though we had the Frenchmen at commandment'. Moreover, the Franco-Scottish royal couple were displaying the arms of England, more than hinting at Mary Stuart's claims in the English succession. In Mason's view the English should settle for whatever they could get.[3] However, at the end of December a letter from the King of France arrived, brought by a private emissary, suggesting a private treaty between the two sovereigns. The Queen made her first essay in personal diplomacy in a sequence of correspondence with Henry II. It was clear to Elizabeth that his hope was to drive a wedge between her and Philip. She checkmated the French king by revealing her correspondence to Philip when it became clear that this correspondence held out no hope of recovering Calais; the correspondence ended, fruitlessly but civilly.

A second line of private negotiation was opened up through a French courtier with English connections and Sir Henry Killegrew, another one of Cecil's brothers-in-law, a diplomatic agent employed by Mary. For a time it seemed possible that a deal might be made, but this too failed. In the end the English decided to bite the bullet, and instructions were sent accordingly. Elizabeth, with the assistance of Cecil (whose corrections appear on the original documents), had handled the negotiations shrewdly. Although she failed to move Henry on Calais (and probably never expected to do so), she saw the window of opportunity opened by the French overtures. Having ascertained that the French were willing to make peace, she avoided the temptation of a separate treaty by taking Philip into her confidence and concluding the peace through official channels in collaboration with the Spanish.[4]

A face-saving formula was patched together which avoided a formal surrender of territory. At the end of eight years France was either to retrocede Calais or pay an indemnity. By 22 March the treaty was in hand.[5] However unsatisfactory the terms of peace, blame for the disaster could be fixed on the defunct regime.

The death of Mary and the coming of peace necessarily ended active alliance with Spain. However, the Spanish had good reason for continuing friendly interest in English matters. The French presence in Scotland and Mary Stuart's lurking claims to the English succession — or the English throne — made them doubly anxious to shore up Elizabeth's government. Their first ploy was to propose marriage between Philip and Elizabeth. The Queen politely but firmly declined the honour. Nevertheless, Philip went out of his way to use Spanish influence at Rome to prevent the excommunication of Elizabeth, which the French were labouring to procure.[6] Thus by Easter 1559 Elizabeth had pulled clear from the morass of the late war and achieved peace with France and Scotland. The loss of Calais was a grievous blow, but the outcome of the peace was not altogether unhappy. Even though the marital link was broken, Spain had a strong interest in safeguarding English interests against possible French aggression. The King of France, on his side, had shown that he had more urgent concerns than opening up a rift with England over the Stuart claim. There was time for the new regime to catch its breath and turn to domestic problems.

5

The Religious Settlement

*L*ong before the conclusion of peace the great question of religion had been opened up, in the session of Elizabeth's first Parliament which began on 25 January. No one, at home or abroad, doubted that Elizabeth's accession would bring another alteration in religion, a repudiation of the Marian settlement and a return to some form of Protestant polity. Mary and her advisers, English and Imperial, anticipated this; so did her opponents, political and religious. The new reign was greeted by the English Protestant community as a divine deliverance; Elizabeth was to be the English Deborah, sent to save God's Englishmen. Thus, to a man, contemporaries assigned her to the Protestant fold, as a matter of course, an historical given. Posterity has made the same unquestioning assumption.

It may be worthwhile to pose what may seem an absurd question. Why in fact did Elizabeth choose the path of reform in 1559? She was not constrained by immediate circumstance. She had herself publicly, even ostentatiously, professed the Roman Catholic faith for five years. The country had accepted the Marian programme, without much enthusiasm but without major resistance. Even Wyatt had not raised the Protestant standard and once the issue of the abbey lands was settled Parliament's obstructions vanished. Protestantism was rooted in English society, but its active adherents were largely among the politically powerless classes. Among the martyrs and, more importantly, among the exiles, the absence of the higher social orders was conspicuous. Men like William Cecil may have privately balked at the Marian changes, but if Mary had lived as long as Elizabeth, he would have died a conforming communicant of the ancient faith. In short, there was not in England in 1558 the kind of activist aristocratic leadership which, linked to popular feeling, ensured the political consequence of the Protestant movements in France, Scotland, or the Low Countries.

The various letters of gratuitous advice with which Elizabeth was showered at the beginning of her reign all assumed she would alter religion, but were unanimous in urging the greatest caution in any move to do so. That ardent Protestant Sir Nicholas Throckmorton would have retained a substantial bloc of Marian councillors, even churchmen, in the new Council. The other would-be counsellors envisaged the high risk of active Catholic resistance. Moreover, to opt for Protestantism at home would automatically place England in a partisan stance on the international stage. What, then, led the Queen to a course replete with uncertainties, beset by real dangers of domestic disturbance and foreign hostility? We cannot, of course, answer this question from the Queen's own mouth. It is in her actions, not in her words, that a record of her motives can be traced. The evidence is circumstantial, but it is plentiful enough to be persuasive.

The simplest explanation of Elizabeth's behaviour is also the best. The Queen was a convinced Protestant. The immediate objection to that proposition is her conformity to Catholic practice throughout Mary's reign. The contrast with her sister, who so obstinately held to the mass in Edward's time, highlights Elizabeth's apparent indifference in religion, and carries the corollary that her motives were straightforwardly political. The explanation lies in discriminating among the varieties of religious experience of her contemporaries. For the earliest English Protestants, a generation older than Elizabeth, the experience of the new faith was necessarily one of conversion, often of a Pauline intensity, involving the trauma of rejection and redemption.

But for those who came even half a generation later, such as Elizabeth, their religious beliefs were already a matter of instruction, not of revelation. Elizabeth's religious education seems to have been a relatively passive process, one of exposition rather than exhortation, in which a ready pupil absorbed the systematic teachings which her tutors instilled without being aroused to any deep personal response. Necessarily, given time and circumstance, much of that instruction was devoted to demonstrating the falsity and corruption of the old faith and the superiority of the new. These teachings, once implanted, remained to her an authoritative statement of Christian doctrine, albeit as much negative as positive in content, a rejection of the old 'superstition', but without a regenerating experience of the new.

How, then, to account for her change of faith under Mary? The answer lies in the particular formation of early English Protestantism. When Henry and his ministers sought to pick the lock of the divorce case, they stumbled on the key to a much larger portal, one which opened to them the dazzling possibilities embodied in the supreme headship. These grasped Henry's imagination as well as those of his Councillors, and took shape in the order set forth in the parliamentary acts which proclaimed his new status. Thus the first pronouncement of the independent *ecclesia anglicana* was political; theology would follow only later. Hence the faith in which Elizabeth was initiated exalted as a first principle the compelling authority of the prince in spiritual causes.

For the subject, the logic of this position necessarily implied obedience to the legitimate prince as his first duty. No one questioned Mary's legitimacy; indeed Protestants had risen to defend it in 1553. Hence she must be obeyed in her lawful commands, issued with parliamentary authority behind them. It took a heroic rejection of the very notion of hierarchical order to pit one's own conscience against the sovereign. The royal authority of Edward had initiated Elizabeth into one set of doctrine and practice; when his sister's royal authority gave another set of instructions, she as a subject must give them the same ready obedience. The position was succinctly put by John Hayward in 1612: 'For the change in religion which then ensued and had also happened not long before was easily foreseen by men of understanding, not only by reason of the consciences of the princes, formed in them by education, but also out of their particular intents and ends.'[1]

Now Elizabeth was no longer a subject but a sovereign and freed from the constraint of obedience which had held her in the past. In her eyes Mary had wrongly abandoned the title of supreme head, indeed, had lacked the power to do so since, as the Henrician statutes made clear, that title was and always had been inherent in the very nature of kingship. To lay it aside was to mutilate the royal office.

Given these convictions, there could be no question that the new Queen would resurrect the act of supremacy and reassert an overarching authority which comprehended English society in both its civil and religious forms — *regnum* and *ecclesia*. It was a corollary of this conception of the royal governance of the church that the sovereign should provide for a uniform mode of public worship which the subject would be required to attend. That compulsion would rest, not on any claim to doctrinal or dogmatic correctness, but simply on the command of the highest civil authority to perform a public duty.

Beyond these large considerations there was a set of highly politic circumstances which impelled Elizabeth to opt for the reformed faith. Although she might be less than enthusiastic at being hailed by Protestant publicists as the English Deborah, the champion of God's oppressed people, she had no doubt as to the value of support from those who saw her accession as a special act of providence. She could count on the unstinting loyalty of the whole spectrum of Protestant sentiment, from the hot Gospellers on the left to the *politiques* like Cecil on the right. They would support her not only as their natural leader, the heir of the Edwardian reform, but also because she was their only hope. She stood alone between them and the dread possibilities of a Catholic restoration under Mary Stuart. She could be certain of an unshakeable loyalty such as her Catholic subjects would not have yielded. As a purely political calculation there could be no question that a Protestant settlement offered advantages too great to be forgone.

In the weeks between the accession in November and the Parliamentary session in late January, the Queen by a series of actions gave clear signals as to the direction in which she intended to move. A prohibition on controversial preaching, nominally neutral, was in fact directed against Catholics and was used to confine at least one recalcitrant bishop.[2] The same proclamation authorized the use of an English litany, according to the practice of the royal chapel.[3] At Christmas the Queen gave an even more conclusive indication of her intentions. She ordered the officiating priest, the Bishop of Carlisle, not to elevate the Host; when he refused, she stalked out after the reading of the Gospel.[4] At the coronation, mass was probably said by her Dean of Chapel in English and without the elevation of the Host.[5] The service in her chapel was by now effectively Protestant in spirit if not in form; it was obviously intended to be a model for the nation to follow.

The stage was now set for the forthcoming drama of Elizabeth's first Parliament. On 25 January the Members assembled in Westminster Abbey to hear the customary mass, but in fact it had already been sung. As the royal procession entered, it was met by the monks bearing lighted tapers, only to be contemptuously dismissed by the Queen: 'Away with these torches, we see very well.'[6] There followed a sermon by the returned exile, Richard Coxe, denouncing the monks for their share in the heresy persecutions and exhorting Elizabeth to destroy idolatry in England. When the Commons adjourned to their own house, they heard a speech from Lord Keeper Bacon expounding the need for 'uniting of these people of the Realm into a uniform order of religion'. He urged 'that nothing be advised or done, which any way in continuance of time were likely to breed, or nourish any kind of idolatry, or superstition', but he also warned against any encouragement of 'licentious or loose handling . . . whereby any contempt or irreverent behaviour towards God and Godly things, or any spice of irreligion might creep in'.[7]

That Parliament should have a voice in such questions was a recent innovation, a necessary corollary to Henry's initial assertion of his authority over the church. So great a matter required an act of the greatest solemnity and unquestioned authenticity, embodying the kingdom's will and binding all its members. Moreover, only an act of Parliament could provide the penal sanctions which would enforce obedience. For the same reasons Edward's government had sought parliamentary action in changing the liturgy, while Mary, trapped by the same logic, had to obtain Parliament's approval for undoing her predecessors' work. Hence, whatever changes Elizabeth proposed to make would have first to obtain the consent of Lords and Commons. It was Elizabeth's first encounter with a body whose members would in the years to come display a disposition to interfere in a wide range of matters hitherto outside their ken. Her reign would mark a new and troubled phase in the changing relations between Parliament and crown.

What about the character of this particular House of Commons, the audience to which Bishop Coxe and Lord Keeper Bacon addressed themselves? The assertion, of sixteenth-century origin, that it was packed is most certainly untrue. Even if packing had been feasible, it would have been pointless. It was not numbers but personal weight which swayed a Tudor Parliament. What was necessary was a nucleus of influential officials and courtiers to take the lead, under royal direction; the House would follow. This meant that seats must be found for Privy Councillors, officials, and courtiers. That was easily done by the use of patronage in boroughs where there was a court interest, and by the collaboration of helpful Councillor-patrons such as Bedford or Pembroke.[8]

In composition this House of about 400 Members was little different from any other Tudor Parliament, with a substantial representation of men who had sat in the past three reigns, 105 of them in Mary's last Parliament. There was the usual mix of country gentry, lawyers, officials, and a sprinkling of townsmen from the larger boroughs. Of the religious sympathies of the members little can be said. A dozen had been abroad in the late reign, but of these only four were clearly exiles for religion's sake.[9] Counting Members whose later activities numbered them among the Protestant critics of the 1559 settlement, there may have been a radical reformist group of some twenty to twenty-five in the House, of whom less than half a dozen were men of influence.[10] There was also a similar group of known religious conservatives, although none of them had been a prominent member of the late government. None of the Commons members of Mary's Council was present – whether by official pressure, their own choice, or rejection by electors to whom they were now useless as lobbyists, we cannot know.

On past performance the Commons were likely to prove biddable on the religious question. They had fallen in line behind Thomas Cromwell in the 1530s and the Edwardian Councillors in the next reign. However, in Mary's time it had taken several Parliaments to complete her programme of restoration. The House had divided, but with a small minority, on the repeal of the Act of Uniformity. On abolition of the supremacy they balked, but not on religious grounds. Approval was delayed until proprietary rights in the former monastic lands had been guaranteed by Rome.[11]

Yet in the thirty years since 1529 the lower house had taken on a new vitality simply by dint of its frequent meetings – twelve Parliaments and twenty-nine sessions in these three decades. It had also been unprecedentedly active in legislation, quite apart from the ecclesiastical statutes. It was likely to be obstructive of royal demands when property rights were touched – such as uses and wills under Henry VIII, monastic lands under Mary – and even then usually under outside stimulus. This had been the case in the Marian House when a Councillor, Paget, had deliberately stirred up opposition to government acts.[12] He was perhaps the first court politician to realize how the lower house could be used as a weapon in factional fights within the Council. He would not be the last.

The upper house was another matter. As a general principle the Lords, intimates of the court, were susceptible to royal influence and likely to be docile, but two groups demurred to that proposition in the 1559 house. First were the bishops. In Henry's time the episcopal bench, with Fisher's notable exception, had been kept in line by crown influence. In 1549 there had been division in their ranks; several of their number who refused to accept the new order were deposed, but the majority conformed. Under Mary there had been a wholesale purge of the Protestant prelates, who were replaced by reliably orthodox Catholics. Now in 1559 the lines of division were clearly defined;

Protestant and Catholic stood in sharp black and white distinction. Yet the government, remembering past experience, may have held to a slim hope that they could divide the episcopal bench. Secondly, they could not be altogether confident of the lay lords. When it came to a question of their faith, these great men had a self-confidence in asserting their independence which was lacking among their humbler colleagues in the Commons.

Though the upper house numbered seventy-seven in all, an average of only forty were in regular attendance.[13] The government had some good luck. The peers spiritual should have numbered twenty-eight; but the break in the Roman link imposed by the war had made it impossible for Pole to fill up eight sees vacant by death. Then, in the short interval before Parliament met, four more prelates went to their graves. Age and illness lopped off two more; a third was denied the customary writ of summons to attend. Thus barely half of the peers spiritual were present. Among the lay peers it was possible to do something to increase the number of crown supporters; five were added at the coronation (two reinstatements and three new creations). Numbers attending were also reduced by the demands of official duties away from Westminster. Yet none of these comings and goings amounted to a concerted effort to rig the House.

Up to the beginning of parliamentary business the evidence for the Queen's intentions and for her actions is reasonably adequate; but from the first day of business a fog of ignorance obscures the history of this Parliament whose actions were so determinative not only for Elizabeth's reign but for the whole future course of English history. The journals of the two Houses provide a bare outline of events, but it is a record which confuses as often as it illuminates. The historian is left with puzzles for which the key is lacking.

The outline of events is clear enough. On 9 February the crown's ministers brought in a Commons bill to restore the royal supremacy,[14] which was debated from the 13th to the 16th and then committed. On the 16th a bill for common prayer and ministration of the sacraments (presumably to replace the mass) was read while on the 21st the two were replaced by a bill combining the provisions of each, in short, a complete programme for restoring the religious order of Edward's time. The legislative history of these three bills is, as Norman Jones writes, 'the ultimate mystery of the parliament of 1559'. J. E. Neale, in a brilliant reconstruction first put forward in 1950,[15] argued that the crown had intended no more than a supremacy act in this session; the two bills for an order of worship were a private Members' initiative which either proposed a return to the book of 1552 or, alternatively, were not bills at all but a reading of the 1552 legislation to remind Members of its content. In any case, he goes on to argue, the combined bill which was ultimately passed was pushed through the Commons by radical Protestants who, waylaying the measure, went far beyond the court's intention by reinstating the 1552 *Book of Common Prayer.* Thus the bill which left the Commons was a measure contradictory to the crown's intentions and a serious setback to royal policy.

A more recent study (*Faith by Statute*, London, 1982) has challenged the Neale thesis, arguing a weighty case which restores earlier readings of the evidence. Jones's solution to the enigma of the two bills for worship is a simple one; the first bill was government-sponsored and reinstated the 1552 book, while the entry for the second bill in fact records nothing more than a second reading. Hence the omnibus bill, which combined both uniformity and supremacy, fulfilled the crown's intentions of wiping out the whole Marian settlement and returning to the status quo of 1553. In this reading of the evidence, the crown is seen as enjoying plain sailing in pushing its planned programme through the lower house.

By either reading, the measure which then went up to the Lords ordered a return to the 1552 liturgy. What happened there is more fully reported. The bishops took the lead in opposing the bill in its entirety.[16] They won the support of enough lay peers to eliminate the proposals for altering worship. However, on the question of supremacy a majority of lay lords was willing to pass it, albeit in a truncated form. They abolished the papal authority, but left it to the Queen's choice whether she would assume the title of supreme head. In this form it was opposed by all the bishops and by two lay lords.[17] The Commons reluctantly and angrily accepted the mutilated act. So did the crown; a proclamation was prepared reviving communion in both kinds, as provided in the act.[18]

The government, in its first great piece of legislation, had stumbled and nearly fallen. It had in fact been faced with an unusual situation in the upper house, the existence of a compact, articulate and organized opposition which included the whole episcopate. The crown lacked effective spokesmen in the upper house to counteract so formidable a force. Indeed, two Privy Councillors, Lord Treasurer Winchester and the Earl of Shrewsbury, had been included in the majority against the bill. The results were embarrassing but not catastrophic. Armed with the required oath to uphold the supremacy the crown could clear the bench of the Catholic bishops, fill it with Protestant successors, and push through uniformity in the next session. A bill was rushed through both houses giving the Queen powers to appoint bishops to vacant sees. Elizabeth made ready to go down to Westminster Palace to close the session.[19]

Then on 4 March, at the last moment, she changed her mind, adjourned the Houses over Easter, and summoned them to return. What were the circumstances of this abrupt change of course? All we know is that a decision made by the Queen, and about to be implemented, was revoked. Who urged this course of action, and on what grounds it was implemented, remain hidden. It would be tempting to devise a scenario, based retrospectively on the Queen's behaviour in the next crisis of her reign, the Scottish expedition of 1560, in which a hesitant sovereign, reluctant to take further risks, was coaxed to a bolder course by the persuasions of an activist Secretary Cecil, for a decisive victory over the papist foe.

In any case, a new plan of action was prepared. The bishops were ordered to prepare themselves for a debate, to be held in Westminster Abbey, where they would dispute three specified questions with a select group of Protestant divines.[20] These included the use of the vernacular in worship, the right of each church to appoint its own rites, and the central issue of the sacrificial mass. This encounter would serve as a surrogate for a debate in the Lords, where the crown had no clerical supporters. It had the advantage that the procedures could be quite shamelessly rigged against the bishops. They were made to appear obstructive and uncooperative, and were manœuvred into a refusal to continue the debate at the second meeting. Two of their number, Winchester and Lincoln, were packed off to prison charged with disobedience to common authority.[21] The Council rushed a pamphlet to the press, presenting in the most unfavourable light the recalcitrance of the bishops and suggesting that their disobedience amounted to disloyalty to the English crown.[22]

A new supremacy bill was now drafted; the title of supreme head was altered to supreme governor, a concession to the masculine unease about a female as head of the church that obtained in the ranks of both religious parties.[23] It was a shift of title, not a diminution of power. The bill also repealed the Marian heresy laws, and revived the Henrician machinery for consecrating bishops.

The bill for uniformity copies in very large part its Edwardian ancestor. The liturgy was, with one important exception, that of 1552. To the words of administration of the latter book which were highly memorialist – 'take and eat this' – were added those of 1549 – 'the body of Our Lord Jesus Christ ... preserve thy body and soul into everlasting life'. Theologians have wrestled ever since with the implication of this conjunction. To contemporaries, the addition had overtones which echoed the old faith while giving voice to the various views which divided Protestants on this great issue. In one other respect the bill diverged from the practice of 1552: it provided that the ornaments of the church and the dress of the clergy should be those of 1549.

The bills were passed unaltered in the lower house; in the upper the supremacy measure was amended in ways which would protect conservatives against persecution under the new regime but which left unaltered its main provisions. Only one lay peer voted against this measure.[24] The Commons accepted this version and its passage was relatively easy. The uniformity bill was, of course, fiercely resisted by the bishops, but this time they lost most of their lay support. Still it was a close-run thing, twenty-one for and eighteen against. Half of the dissidents were lay peers.[25] The enforced absence of the two imprisoned bishops proved telling, but it is clear that the lay peers had been disciplined into conformity by the determined line taken by the crown.

Although our knowledge is painfully restricted, there is enough to suggest the strategy of the crown. The religious legislation of 1552 was adopted wholesale (with the exception of the ornaments rubric and the words of administration). It was very much a scissors-and-paste operation, with clause after clause inserted without amendment. The crown chose to ignore the fact that in 1552 Protestant opinion on central theological and liturgical problems had been in flux. At that time, radicals like Hooper and Knox saw the reform as still in its early stages and the formulation of the second Edwardian act provisional; there was much necessary change yet to come. And, indeed, the gravamen of the bishops' opposition to the uniformity bill lay in the charge that their opponents were themselves in wide disagreement. To which of the many churches in Germany did the English Protestants belong, Bishop Baynes mockingly asked.[26] To open debate on these sensitive issues would expose all the vulnerabilities of the Protestant position. The reformed divines themselves were painfully aware of the charge, which they attempted to refute in a declaration drawn up in April, outlining their doctrinal views and asserting their unity.[27]

These considerations throw considerable light on the change of heart after the passage of the first supremacy act before Easter. Why the sudden switch in plans, in a matter of hours? It is possible (although this is an entirely speculative idea) that it was the Queen whose courage failed for a moment. The future would be replete with instances of her hesitation at such moments of decision. A corollary speculation would be that it was a boldly determined Secretary Cecil who persuaded her to try again. Be that as it may, one of the most powerful arguments for pressing on was the risk of widening the theological controversy, giving the Catholics a chance to press their case and revealing Protestant disagreements. Moreover, it would have been all the more difficult to advance the reformed cause when the Queen's supremacy was so grudgingly and conditionally defined. Whoever made the decision grasped the strategic necessity for a continuing offensive; to fall back on the defensive would have been to acknowledge a major setback in the first great initiative of the reign.

The resulting achievement was well worth the risk taken. The royal supremacy was now finally in place, a well-constructed edifice built on firm foundations. With her powers fully defined, the Queen had, in the supremacy oath and in the ecclesiastical commissions, ample weapons for imposing her will on any opposition. She may have regretted that virtually none of the episcopate was prepared to provide continuity to the new order, but the simple test of tendering the oath made it easy to remove recalcitrant clergy without raising any question of doctrine: it could be presented as a matter of civic loyalty.

What was not so apparent to Protestants in these euphoric days of deliverance from the late regime was that the Queen had also acquired effective weapons against those Protestant radicals who might wish for further change in the religious order. She had been warned in the letters of advice[28] against those who 'would have religion altered but would have it go too far'. These men, finding either the ceremonies still retained unacceptable or their particular doctrine not embraced, would 'call the alteration a cloaked Papistry or a mingle mangle'. With the powers provided by the statutes fleshed out by the royal injunctions of the next summer, the Queen was in full control of the national church, whose officers from archbishops to curates were her servants, the performance of their duties prescribed by her order. How far this religion established by law would fulfil the spiritual aspirations of those of her subjects who were deeply touched by the great religious questions of the age remained to be seen.

In polemics with their Catholic adversaries, Protestant divines would reiterate the conservative and historical argument that the reform was a return to earlier and purer practice, defiled by papal usurpation, but for the ordinary worshipper the new liturgy was nothing short of a revolutionary change in immemorial social practice and habit. Whether the new ways would take root and be integrated into the larger social fabric remained to be seen. The Queen was certain that this could be accomplished only by the rigorous, sustained, and universal imposition of the new order by her civil and ecclesiastical officers.

6

The Pacification of Scotland,
1559–1560

Hardly were the religious acts on the statute-books before the Queen had to turn from the domestic to the foreign scene. The peace of Cateau-Cambrésis comprehended Scotland as well as France but as far as the northern kingdom was concerned it was a paper peace. The roots of the most recent phase of endemic Anglo-Scottish conflict were to be found, like most of the Queen's other inherited liabilities, in the actions of her father. Henry's scheme for marrying the boy prince Edward to Mary, the infant Queen of Scots, had a statesmanlike ring to it, but his elephantine clumsiness in the 'rough wooing', his effort to persuade the Scots to accept such a match, only served to drive them into the arms of their ancient ally, France. Mary, bundled off to France, was affianced to the dauphin while her French mother ruled Scotland as regent. Mary's prospective claims to the English succession through her Tudor grandmother, Henry VIII's elder sister, were now backed by the power of the French crown.

The Scottish tinder-box was set alight when a group of nobles and gentry, resentful of alien domination, took up arms with the aim of expelling the French but also of advancing the reformed faith. The Lords of the Congregation, as they styled themselves, represented that potent combination of aristocratic discontent, resentment of foreign rule, and religious radicalism which was a feature of Reformation politics in more than one place.

Once in arms against the French regent of Scotland, the league of Protestant nobles and gentry came seeking English aid. Their request offered the Queen Hobson's choice; if she acceded to their proposals she would be pitted not only against the government of Scotland but also against its protector, the King of France, but to refuse was to leave the French camped at her back door. Elizabeth faced the first great international confrontation of her reign. Although focused in the British island, it formed a piece in the jigsaw of European politics. It embodied *in parvo* most of the great issues which divided the larger world across the Channel.

Elizabeth came into her inheritance at a moment of profound change in the relations of the European powers, which bore awkward and dangerous implications for England and Scotland, for it threw into flux the main assumptions on which their policy had rested for some generations. Since the final expulsion of the English from France in 1453, they had lived in relative isolation from the great affairs of their Continental neighbours. Those had been governed since the 1490s by the ambition of the house of France to gain control of Italy. The French had been resisted initially by the Spanish rulers of Naples and Sicily. When Charles V, already ruler of the Low Countries and Austria, succeeded to his Spanish and Italian inheritances, the struggle was enlarged to become Europe-wide, fought not only in the peninsula but also in the Pyrenees and on the Picard and Lorraine frontiers.

This was a state of affairs beneficial to English interests. The two Continental giants were engrossed in their own rivalry; the cockpit in which they fought was beyond the orbit of English influence or interest. Moreover, the existence of two more or less equal Continental powers meant that there was little risk that one or the other might achieve a hegemonic position in European affairs. Under Henry VIII, England was content to play a peripheral role; the King offered his services as a makeweight to one or the other of the contenders, usually the Habsburgs. His rhetoric echoed the ambition of the Hundred Years War, but his interventions were short-lived adventures aimed at ephemeral goals, largely the gratification of his personal vanity, at the most the acquisition of a town or two. None of them risked any vital English interest, and at all times Henry was free to withdraw or to change sides without serious danger of retribution.

All this had altered in a very short space of time. The precipitating event was the death of James V of Scotland in the wake of a crushing Scottish defeat. When Henry sought, by wedding his own heir to the infant Scots queen, to unite both British kingdoms under the Tudor dynasty, the predictable Scottish reaction was a plea for French aid, with unanticipated results. Henry II, the ambitious new French King, was already turning his gaze away from the Italian scene and north-wards. Scotland, which to his predecessors had been a mere counter-irritant against England, now became an object of French expansionist design: a match between Mary Stuart, now in France, and the dauphin was projected, while a permanent French garrison was established in Scotland under the French Queen Regent.

Suddenly England, so long the aggressor, found itself in a quite unaccustomed posture of defence, against a foe within the island. At the same time with the accession of a woman ruler, Mary, the English throne itself became a sought-after prize, coveted and acquired by the Habsburgs. For a few years both British kingdoms were little more than satellites in the planetary systems of the two great Continental houses. Mary's death freed England from her bondage but left her vulnerable to a France whose appetite was sharpened by the fall of Calais, and whose horizons were expanded by the prospective claims of Mary Stuart to the English throne.

At the same time the Continental scene was fast changing as the curtain was rung down on the long duel between the Valois and the Habsburgs. The Treaty of Cateau-Cambrésis established a rough balance between the two adversaries. France retired across the Alps, abandoning her claims in Italy, but in the north-east the extension of her territories by the acquisition of the three bishoprics of Metz, Toul, and Verdun foreshadowed a future zone of contention. Philip was engaged in regrouping his share of the divided Habsburg inheritance around a Spanish nucleus, an enterprise which would soon engender resistance in the Netherlands. More immediately he had to turn his attention to the advancing Turkish power in the Mediterranean. As for the French, barely had the treaty been signed when Henry II died of a wound received in a joust and Mary's husband, Francis II, became king. Almost at the same moment, France felt the first tremors of coming religious conflict.

Looming in the background was a grave threat to the peace of western Europe — the confrontation between the two great religious camps. The determinations of the divines at Trent and Geneva made the gulfs between the confessions unbridgeable and stimulated bitter hatred and unappeasable fear on both sides. The rise of popular reform movements within the Low Countries and France threatened civil disorder and equated religious difference with rebellion. When the persecuted reform movements in turn looked to outside help from their fellow religionists, civil strife was likely to escalate into inter-national war.

The Scottish situation contained in miniature most of the elements outlined above when the Lords of the Congregation looked to their English co-religionists for help against their alien rulers. Appeals from Scottish factions for English intervention were nothing new, but in this case, for the first time, the appeal rested on something more than short-term expediency. The English Queen and the Scottish rebels found common ground in two long-term causes — the exclusion of Continental intruders from their island and the advancement of the reformed faith.

The Queen's response to the Scots lords' plea would transform the English political stage. The previous act of the Elizabethan political drama, the meeting of the 1559 Parliament, played out behind the curtains of our ignorance, the actors' voices muted, is largely hidden from posterity. The second act would be played in full view, where it is possible for us to see who played which role and with what success. The events in the north would test the capacities of the new leadership and, more important still, reveal much about the actress at centre stage, the Queen herself.

It was William Cecil who from the first made the running. In August 1559, in the wake of Francis II's accession to the French throne, the Secretary prepared an ambitious state paper which laid out with the boldest strokes a whole new Scottish policy.[1] Declaring that 'the best worldly felicity that Scotland can have is either to continue in a perpetual peace with England or to be made one monarchy with it', he drew out his proposals. England should back the Scottish rebels in securing the expulsion of the French and the establishment of a Scottish government to rule as long as their Queen remained in France. At the same time the Scottish Estates should overturn the papal church and replace it with a reformed polity. Finally, if Mary and Francis refused these terms they should be replaced as sovereigns by the next heir. All this would open the way to a new and enduring unity of action and purpose between the island kingdoms. It was an opportunity which must not be missed. 'Anywise kindle the fire, for if quenched the opportunity will not come in our lives.'[2] Here was a recipe not only for eliminating the French menace but also for establishing a firm and lasting base for the 'perpetual peace' of which Cecil wrote. The ancient hostility between the British kingdoms, which had poisoned their relations since the thirteenth century, would be broken down and replaced by a common interest in the maintenance of a reformed religious polity. The 'auld alliance' with France would be replaced by an Anglo-Scottish comity.

Cecil had a hard task in front of him. The risks of a war with France when England was still exhausted from the last struggle were all too visible to his fellow councillors. More particularly, he had to deal with the Queen's idiosyncratic response to the Scottish crisis. Her angle of view was 180 degrees removed from the Secretary's. First, she objected strenuously to giving aid to rebels. That 'it is against God's law to aid any subjects against their natural princes or their ministers' was a maxim of universal application for her. Secondly, she had no sympathy for the religious view of a company whose chief religious counsellor was the odious John Knox, author of a recent pamphlet against female rule. The Scots had to be coached by Cecil so that their submission to the Queen explicitly repudiated any disloyalty to their sovereigns. All mention of religious revolution had to be excised from the ensuing negotiations.

It took another kind of argument to prod the Queen from words to action. In the same paper[3] Cecil painted in lurid colours the actions of the French court, the doubts cast on the Queen's title at Cateau-Cambrésis, the attempts to persuade Rome to denounce her, the display of the arms of England on the plate and hangings of Francis and Mary. These were actions which touched Elizabeth's most sensitive nerves.

Yet it was not only the Queen who hesitated. In October the Secretary wrote worriedly of 'many more letterers [hinderers] than you would think, some not liking the progress of religion, others less convinced of the French menace' or simply hopeful of something turning up. The doubters in the Council were largely the Marian veterans. Their arguments against action were largely those of English poverty, the superiority of French resources, and the lack of allies.[4] These were arguments that weighed with the Queen and caused her to hang back. At one point Cecil became so desperate he threatened resignation.[5] In the end he dragged his unwilling colleagues into a recommendation to the Queen that she send an army and a fleet northward.

Cecil's Scottish plans became entangled with another issue – that of the Queen's marriage. As relations with France worsened, many hankered after Habsburg support, preferring shelter under the Habsburg umbrella to open confrontation with France. This could be bolstered by Elizabeth's marriage to the Austrian Archduke Charles; an imperial envoy, bearing overtures for a match, had arrived in May, only to be fobbed off with an ambiguous reply, but hope revived in the autumn.[6] At the same time Elizabeth's conspicuous display of favour to Lord Robert Dudley excited even more enthusiasm for the Austrian candidate in many circles. Hence a wide-ranging coalition of divergent interests opposed a war in Scotland.

All this was bad enough; much worse was the stubborn resistance of the Queen. At first absolutely negative, she allowed herself to be nudged, step by dragging step, into piecemeal commitments which ultimately coalesced into full intervention on land and sea. Opponents of the move continued to pressure the monarch, urging a compromise settlement with the Scottish Queen Mother.[7] Then the English army, which had entered Scotland, failed pitifully in an assault on the French stronghold of Leith. (The scaling ladders were too short.) 'I have had such a torment herein with the Queen's Majesty as an ague hath not in five fits so much abated' was the Secretary's sad lament. Elizabeth was finally persuaded to send reinforcements, but Cecil still observed: 'The Queen's Majesty never liketh this matter of Scotland; you know what hangeth thereupon; weak-hearted men and flatterers will follow that way.'[8]

Matters came to a head when Cecil was commanded to go to Edinburgh to negotiate with the Scots and French. He was far from happy in the mission. 'My friends in council think it necessary for the matter and convenient for me; my friends abroad think I am herein betrayed to be sent from the Queen's Majesty.' Elizabeth was in the unhappiest of moods, resentful of events out of her control and impatient for peace. In Cecil's absence it might be all too easy to undo all that he had so arduously accomplished. Cecil's ally, Nicholas Throckmorton, the ambassador at Paris, summed up their worries: 'Who [in Cecil's absence] will speedily resolve the doubtful delays? Who shall make dispatch of anything?'[9]

In fact, Cecil's mission to Edinburgh proved to be a spectacular success. Much was owed to fortune; the Queen Mother, the pillar of the French establishment in Scotland, died almost on his arrival. This clinched French uncertainties about the whole venture. Winter storms had turned back one relief fleet; an English blockade choked off others. Then, in the spring of 1560, there came the first flare of hostilities between French Catholics and Protestants, which ushered in the epoch of civil war. The French government cut their losses and, in the Treaty of Edinburgh, agreed to withdraw all but a token force. To crown Cecil's triumph the Scots Estates now met and by a single act swept away the old religious establishment, proclaiming Scotland a Protestant society. A new government was set up under the aegis of Lord James Stuart, Mary's bastard brother, stalwart

Protestant and of necessity a reliable ally of England. Francis and Mary, however, balked at ratifying the treaty.

The Scottish experience was, of course, a major success for the new regime. The English had eliminated the threat which had hung menacingly in the north for more than a decade — and had done it without a full-scale war with France. However, these credits were counterbalanced by a heavy entry on the debit side of the account. There was now a new colouring to the Queen's inherited title of Defender of the Faith. However unwillingly, she had assumed the role of protectress of a foreign Protestant community. In the Scottish case this was bound to be a continuing obligation. Her assumption of this role had also raised expectations in other quarters. Continental reformed communities came to see her as general patroness of a Protestant *internationale*, to whom they would look for aid in times of trouble. Indeed, the French Protestants had already made their first overtures, seeking her assistance against their Catholic opponents.

While the Queen emphatically rejected such a role, it might not be easy to avoid it. French interest in Scotland, thwarted for the time being, was by no means extinct, and it would be tempting for the English to counter French intrusion into the island by patronizing religious dissidence in that kingdom. Implicit in this dilemma was a larger question. What kind of relations were possible between Protestant and Catholic states? Seemingly they stood on the opposite shores of an impassable moral gulf, each condemning the other as utterly irredeemable, cut off from the body of Christendom. Surely there could be nothing between them but implacable enmity and, as many on both sides urged, a duty to exterminate a deadly menace to the eternal salvation of humankind. In practice, as in other wars of truth, ways were found to establish an uneasy truce, a precarious coexistence. Ambassadors were exchanged and common civility maintained. Nevertheless, there was deep unease on both sides and growing distrust. Every move was watched and, however apparently harmless, interpreted in the most ominous way.

It was in this poisoned atmosphere that Elizabeth had to conduct her relations with her neighbours. She had to face the unpleasant fact that both the Continental states were ruled by orthodoxly Catholic monarchs with whom it would be difficult to maintain long-term relations of trust. She knew, too, that domestic and international politics now intersected in new and frightening ways, in which to the standard armoury, stocked with martial and diplomatic weaponry, there would be added the lethal dagger of subversion from within.

These events had also deeply affected domestic politics. The urgencies of the crisis had been a kind of litmus test which revealed the colours of the individual members of the Council. It revealed Cecil's capacities of leadership as the dynamo who could draw his colleagues to join him in shaping policy recommendations to the Queen. More important still, he could coax, prod, and cajole her into accepting them.

Elizabeth too had been tested by these events. Faced with the need for action, she had shown herself timid and hesitant and had to be chivvied into a series of piecemeal actions. At each stage she halted protestingly, desperately anxious to avoid decisions which could not be reversed. At the very end, when Cecil was already in Edinburgh, she nearly tripped him up. French Protestant agents had made advances for English aid; she wanted to play this off in the negotiations and forbade Cecil to conclude the peace unless Calais were returned and an indemnity paid. Fortunately these instructions were to be valid only if peace were not already signed,[10] an event which had taken place before their arrival.

Moreover, it was plain that the Queen's whole vision of politics differed from that of her minister. Cecil's straightforwardly Machiavellian analysis, which cavalierly trampled on the rights of the Scottish sovereigns and boldly sponsored religious revolution in that kingdom, only served to arouse her deepest antipathies. She was deaf to his arguments for the long-term benefits of such policy. Her frame of reference was so different from his that she seemed, through her royal spectacles, to see quite another landscape. Its principal features were rebels in arms against their lawful prince and religious dissidents with dangerously subversive ideas. It was only with difficulty that she could be brought to agree that her own safety demanded cooperation with the Scottish nobles. Her naïve expectation that the French could be frightened into ceding Calais had nearly wrecked the treaty when the essential goal of expelling the French from Britain was in her grasp. She was very much a novice in her royal profession.

Cecil's colleagues on the Council had showed their colours as they aligned themselves in support of or opposition to his leadership. The veteran diplomats and officials such as Mason, Wootton, Winchester, and Petre were, not surprisingly, the most reluctant to act, preferring to cling to the traditional formula of a Burgundian alliance. On the other hand, the hold-over peers Pembroke, Clinton, and Howard, solidly backed the Secretary, as did all the newcomers save Bacon. Cecil had staked out a position which had implications beyond the immediate crisis. They were spelled out when Spain offered to act as a mediator, even proposing the dispatch of troops to replace the French garrisons in Scotland. The conservatives, acting on the ancient maxim that England should never fight France without an ally, would have embraced this offer of Habsburg protection, but Cecil steadily resisted it.[11] He was determined that England should act on her own. At least within the island of Britain she should be beholden to no one but herself. The dangerous link which had bound Scotland to France should be severed; Anglo-Scottish relations should be a matter solely for the two parties, and should rest on common interest.

On his return from Scotland Cecil, appropriately proud of his achievements, was dismayed by the coolness of his reception. His proposal that subsidies be provided to support the pro-English party in Scotland was emphatically rejected by the Queen. He was soon complaining of the royal indifference to the men who had served her so well in Scotland but who were now left without reward or recognition.[12] By late summer he was even talking of resignation, although this note of despair blended his disappointments over the Scottish venture with his apprehensions about another matter, the prospect of a marriage between the Queen and Robert Dudley.[13]

Elizabeth's refusal to implement continuing support for the struggling pro-English regime in Scotland was partly based on her scepticism about spending her scanty funds on recipients so notoriously fickle as the Scottish nobility. There was also something deeper. In the past few months the Queen had been hustled by her advisers, above all by Cecil, into a series of unwelcome actions. She had been forced to make decisions which wrested control of events out of her hands, leaving it to soldiers out of reach in the Scottish Lowlands or her admirals in the Firth of Forth. Secondly, she had been manœuvred into cooperation with men who were unlawfully in arms against their liege lady, a violation of the natural order. Finally, even more important, she had lost the initiative to her Secretary. It was he who was driving the coach; she had become a protesting but helpless passenger on a perilous journey. They had arrived safely, but she was determined to show that it was she who held the reins. At least some of the coolness towards her councillors which Elizabeth displayed in the late summer of 1560 was a demonstration of her independence. She could not allow herself to be dependent on the guidance of any one servant or group of servants, no matter how good their advice or loyal their intentions. It was doubly important that, as a woman ruler, she should make plain her mastery of men and events.

However, in the autumn of 1560 it was quite another aspect of royal independence which riveted men's attention. The death of his wife had left Robert Dudley a widower, and the court held its breath waiting for the announcement that the Queen would choose him as her husband.

7

The Rise of Dudley

*E*ver since the day of Elizabeth's accession one great topic of speculation had absorbed the attention of her subjects, high and low, as well as the ambassadors in London and their masters at home. When and whom would Elizabeth marry? That she *would* marry was taken for granted: it was unthinkable that she should hold the reins of power by herself. John Knox's blunt assault on female rule might be unpalatable in style and unlucky in its timing, but there was little in its substantive argument with which most Englishmen would have disagreed. Moreover, the matter had an urgency to it even greater than in Mary's case. Elizabeth was the last survivor of Henry's children; who would succeed, if she died childless, was frighteningly uncertain.

By the terms of Henry's will, resting on statute, the heir after Elizabeth was Lady Catherine Grey, sister of the ill-fated Lady Jane, the descendant of Henry's younger sister, Mary, Duchess of Suffolk. Unmarried as yet, she was kept in decent obscurity by Elizabeth. But the Grey claim was shadowed by that of Mary Stuart, Queen of France and Scotland. By the normal rules of inheritance she, as a grand-daughter of Henry's elder sister, Margaret, had superior claims, but that the Queen consort of France should mount the English throne must have seemed unthinkable to most Englishmen. An alternative Stuart candidate was the Lady Margaret Douglas, Countess of Lennox, daughter of Queen Margaret's second marriage. Resident in England and the mother of two sons, she had been prominent in the late court and at one point Mary's candidate as her successor. Beyond her lay a scattering of Yorkist heirs, descendants of Edward IV's brother, Clarence, of whom the most conspicuous was the strongly

Protestant Earl of Huntingdon. If Elizabeth died without issue, the rival claims of these various candidates made civil and/or international war all too probable.

Elizabeth's first Parliament had not hesitated to bring forward the question. A petition urging her to take a husband had been drawn up in the Commons on the first day of the session and presented by the Speaker accompanied by a delegation of thirty members.[1] The Queen duly replied that she preferred to remain single, 'of which trade of life I am so thoroughly acquainted that I trust God . . . would not now of His goodness suffer me to go alone'. However, she condescendingly accepted their petition although warning them sternly against any attempt to limit her choice. She assured them that, should God incline her heart otherwise, she would do nothing with which they could be discontented. Probably most of them refused to take her declaration of single blessedness at face value.

At the time of her accession the King of Sweden had already made a bid on behalf of his brother, but Sweden was too far from the orbit of English interests to be considered.[2] Philip had put himself forward as a suitor in the first weeks of the reign, hoping to retain England within the circle of Habsburg power; the Queen had politely declined the offer.[3] Rumour assigned various names as possible husbands, some English, some foreign. The most plausible was that of the Archduke Charles of Austria, younger son of the Emperor Ferdinand. Of suitably royal birth, he offered the advantages of a Habsburg connection without the risk of foreign intervention in English affairs by the distant power at Vienna. In June 1559 the Emperor had gone so far as to send an envoy, whose offer of his son's hand had been refused but without totally closing the door.

All such proposals soon began to appear irrelevant when it became apparent that the Queen, throwing aside all politic considerations, was casting her eyes on one of her own subjects. Lord Robert Dudley, one of the younger sons of the late Duke of Northumberland, had been involved in his father's plot and condemned but then pardoned and restored in blood. When and how he met Elizabeth we do not know, but at her accession she appointed him to the major household post of Master of the Horse, worth £1,500 per annum and requiring constant attendance on the royal person. His personal attractions for the Queen were more than obvious, but he was married, his wife, Amy Robsart, the daughter of a Norfolk squire. Gossip about the two had circulated widely and not only in court circles. In Essex a woman had retailed the story that the Queen was pregnant by Lord Robert.[4]

The Spanish ambassador had reported that Dudley might divorce his wife.[5] The Duke of Norfolk took the lead among the nobles in decrying such a *mésalliance*, but as long as Dudley's wife was alive it did not seem a proximate possibility.

Dudley was not, of course, of the Council, and so had no direct role in state affairs. However, he plainly enjoyed the private role of the favourite, with the associated public advantages of patronage and influence. A royal familiar who was also a powerful political figure was common enough in Renaissance royal courts, but there had been no such personage in England since the fateful reigns of Edward II and Richard II. Henry VIII had showered ducal honours and wealth on his crony (and brother-in-law), Suffolk, but that nobleman had never figured largely at the centre of power. What Dudley's attractions for the Queen were is not particularly obvious. His portraits suggest a conventionally handsome masculine presence. He clearly lacked the intellectual sophistication and the lively literary culture of such humanist-courtiers as Ralegh or Essex, in a later generation. The attraction seems to have been largely physical although, as events would show, his attractiveness for the Queen would not wane with time, or even with his marriage to the widowed Countess of Essex.

Dudley's privileged position was reflected by the buzz of suitors who hovered around him, including earls, bishops, and ambassadors. Protestant noblemen like Bedford solicited his help for ecclesiastical patronage; the Roman Catholic Councillors of the late Queen looked to him for protection. Correspondents abroad provided news; at Berwick Sir James Croft kept him abreast of Border affairs.[6] Dudley had dabbled in the Queen's matrimonial prospects, offering his support, through his sister, Lady Sidney, to the Austrian candidate, either because he thought the Archduke likely to succeed or, more likely, because he thought that the ensuing negotiations would delay any royal decision.[7] His own prospects were obviously held in check by the existence of his wife.

Everything altered in the summer of 1560; his wife's health failed, and on 8 September she suffered a fatal accident. As we have seen, there was already a sour mood in the court in the wake of the Scottish affair. Cecil confided to the Spanish ambassador that he would retire from office, since the Queen's intimacy with Dudley threatened ruin to the realm. He urged the ambassador to warn the Queen of her misconduct, wished Dudley in the next world and intimated that the favourite might kill his wife. The next day she was in fact dead.[8]

From September 1560 to January 1561 there was a prolonged agony of uncertainty in the English court. Throckmorton, the out-spoken ambassador in Paris, wrote to Cecil that if the match ensued, 'God and religion will be out of estimation; the Queen discredited, condemned, and neglected, and the country ruined and made prey.'[9] Rumours of all kinds floated in the court — of intrigues on behalf of Lady Lennox or the Earl of Huntingdon, of a nobles' revolt, even that the pair were secretly married.[10] Speculation on the favourite's chances fluctuated from week to week; Cecil told the Spanish ambassador the Queen would not marry Dudley; the courtier Killigrew declared: 'Lord Robert shall run away with the hare and have the Queen.' Norfolk, the premier peer, and the clutch of older nobility for whom he spoke were furious at the prospect.

By the end of the year nothing had happened. Then, in January 1561, on the death of the Queen's old servant, Parry, Cecil was promoted to the Mastership of the Wards. The grant of this lucrative office with the vast patronage attached to it was a substantial mark of favour, a clear vote of confidence by the Queen, and a cause for congratulation among the anti-Dudley party that such an outspoken opponent of the match had been given promotion.

The favourite now took steps to advance his own cause. Using his sister, Lady Mary Sidney, as intermediary, Lord Robert proposed to the Spanish ambassador, de Quadra, that if Philip II would back the marriage, the favourite would undertake to restore Catholicism in England through the General Council then meeting. The ambassador, not surprisingly sceptical, approached the Queen herself. Initially evasive, she finally shyly admitted a preference for Dudley, although she had not decided to marry him or anyone else. What would Philip think if she married one of her servants? The next day Lord Robert again urged de Quadra to press the Queen; a little more push might settle the matter. The ambassador wrote home for guidance.[11]

How are we to read this puzzling little history? Did Elizabeth really mean to trade the national church for Dudley's hand? Hardly likely, but there may be at least a speculative explanation of the episode. That Elizabeth was much attracted to Dudley is clear enough. His wife was dead and marriage a possiblity though not a likelihood. Elizabeth, however strong her feelings for Dudley, had not lost her political senses. She knew that if the match were to come off, it must have the solid backing of a substantial interest in council, court, and country. The outspoken criticism of some and the sullen silence of others told her that no such approval would be forthcoming. Dudley, in his anxiety, desperately sought some outside support which would enable him to circumvent some of the objections to the match. The criticism of the conservatives would be undercut if the Habsburgs gave their blessing and cast an air of respectability over the whole affair. Promises about religion could be made but not kept; it would be easy to find opportunities for evasion. The Queen, half-tempted, may have tentatively canvassed Philip's approval for the match.

In any case the Queen soon thought better of it; she brought an end to the intrigue with de Quadra by handing over the exchange with the ambassador to Cecil. Dudley perceived this as a check and, according to court rumour, attempted to storm the gate, demanding either marriage or licence to go abroad. To which the Queen allegedly replied 'that marry him she will not but will not only license him to go over according to his political desire but will make him able to withstand the malice of his enemy'. If true, it was an accurate prophecy of Dudley's future.[12]

In fact, Dudley's matrimonial venture had become entangled with another issue which now drew the attention of Cecil. The Council of Trent was about to reconvene, and the Pope was hopeful of inducing English representation. To that end a nuncio had been dispatched and was making application for a passport from Brussels. de Quadra had hoped to use the leverage of the Dudley match to win royal consent to a visit from the nuncio.

Cecil and his allies were worried that the Queen might give a hearing to the nuncio. Throckmorton roundly asserted that were she Numa Pompilius or Sertorius she might not change her faith. Cecil's pointed comment was that de Quadra had 'entered into such a practice with a pretence to further the great matter here (meaning principally the church and perchance, accidentally, the other also) that he had taken faster hold to plant his purpose than was [my] ease shortly to root up'. Root it up he did, and that very briskly. Seizing a chaplain of the Marian Councillor, Waldegrave, he found compromising letters which enabled him to arrest and imprison the latter, along with two other Marian Councillors, Wharton and Hastings. Enough was uncovered to give the impression of serious Catholic conspiracy. Cecil quite cynically wrote that 'he thought it necessary to dull the Papists' expectations by discovering of certain mass-mongers and punishing them. I take God to record I mean no evil to them, but only for the rebating of the Papists' humours which by the Queen's levity grow too rank. I find it hath done much good.'[13]

This diversionary tactic was highly successful. The Council minuted the Queen against allowing the nuncio's entry, citing the disturbance which the very rumour of his coming had aroused. It is a measure of Cecil's deep-rooted fear of a Catholic renaissance. The Queen might have been willing to engage in a diplomatic flirtation with the nuncio; she wanted to blur the division from Rome as much as possible, both for domestic and for foreign purposes. Cecil, however, backed by the Council, had his way, once again reasserting his leadership in policy-making.

In the mean time although the flirtation with Dudley lingered on, tension in the court gradually relaxed. In the summer of 1561 Lord Robert was singled out for royal attention and Bishop de Quadra was teased with the suggestion that he preside at their nuptials. Dudley once more pressed for a letter of support from Philip, while Elizabeth told the ambassador she would never marry sight unseen and that if she married an Englishman it would be Dudley. It seems reasonably certain that by now the Queen had resolved against marrying Dudley, although she had no intention of dropping him from favour. For the present it was convenient to keep the possibility of a match alive since it fended off pressure for a foreign marriage.[14]

These months from the autumn of 1560 through to the following spring were among the most tempestuous of the Queen's life. She brought herself to the brink of marriage with the one man whom she would have wed. It was a pleasing, a very tempting, prospect, but in the end she drew back. She had not forgotten the lessons she learned in her sister's time. Three years on the throne had confirmed those convictions. Unlike her sister she found the exercise of power exhilarating, and she was loath to yield it to anyone. But for a woman it was a necessary consequence of marriage that a husband would expect to share, even to monopolize power. Moreover, marriage with an Englishman would destroy the inviolability of her position. The independence of her crown and the mystique of sovereignty would be compromised fatally, since the envious hatred of his fellows for her husband would drag the crown down into the morass of factional strife.

For Dudley her decision was disappointing, but he soon discovered, as did others, that if he was not to be a husband, he was to continue as favourite. Insensibly the relationship between the Queen and Lord Robert transformed itself into a less passionate but no less deep-rooted bond, something less than love but as close to friendship as was possible in the inequality which separated subject and sovereign. The court world might breathe with relief as the prospect of a Dudley marriage faded, but it would soon need to take note of a new political fact. The

Queen proposed to patronize the favourite's metamorphosis into a politician.

This transformation was accomplished in 1562. The preliminaries were a flow of bounty which provided the requisite material base for a major political career. First was a large grant of land from Dudley's father's attainted estate. This was followed by a series of patents giving him the coveted right to export 80,000 undressed white cloths over several years. (The annual quota of the Merchant Adventurers, the London exporting cartel, was 30,000.) These licences were, of course, profitably sold to the London exporters. The fountain of favour was to overflow yet again, with an annual grant of £1,000 charged on the customs, to be paid to Dudley until he had lands of equal value. In 1563 he received Kenilworth castle with the Welsh border lordships of Denbigh and Mortimer.[15]

His elder brother, Ambrose, shared in the bounty; restored as Earl of Warwick in December 1561, he was given a large part of his father's land, including Warwick Castle and estates in the same area. Ambrose's earldom restored the family to noble rank. These grants not only enriched the Dudley brothers but ensured that they were no longer mere courtiers, creatures of the royal whim, but men of substance whose position rested on the possession of land, houses, and tenants.

Robert Dudley now had the material base on which to build his political fortunes. What he needed next was the opportunity to exploit his position by launching a political initiative of his own. It arose, not in England, but across the Channel.[16]

In 1562 Elizabeth embarked on her second foreign venture, this time across the Channel. The Protestant movement in France had begun as early as the 1540s. In spite of vigorous measures of repression by the government, it had won increasing adherents; by the end of the 1550s it had become an organized body, with branches throughout much of the country. Moreover, it had won the support of two great princely families, the Bourbons, titular kings of Navarre, and the house of Chatillon. After the death of Henry II the dominance of the ardently Catholic house of Guise in the court of the boy kings, Francis II and Charles IX, had linked the Protestant cause with the rivalries of the great noble houses, no longer effectively checked by a strong monarch. By 1562 these tensions had ripened into civil war.

The Protestant leaders, hard pressed by their opponents, now looked outside the kingdom for help from their fellow religionists in England, invoking the sacred cause of a universal reformed religion. At the same time they lured Elizabeth with hopes of secular advantage. In their first approach, in the summer of 1560, they had talked largely of restoring the glories of Lancastrian times. Now they offered much more solid bait, the retrocession of Calais once they were victorious. In the mean time the English were to hold Newhaven (as the English called LeHavre) as a bridgehead for their assistance and as a gage for Calais.

The Queen's willingness to engage herself in this enterprise not only marked a new boldness in foreign policy but also reflected an important change in domestic politics — the rise of Robert Dudley to political eminence. Lord Robert's opportunity to take a lead part on the political stage came with the feelers put out by the French Protestants. The *de facto* ruler of France, the Queen Mother, Catherine de Medici, herself Catholic, had wavered between repression and compromise. An unstable balance of forces which had preserved a fragile peace collapsed with the King of Navarre's transfer of loyalty from the Protestant house of Chatillon to the Catholic Guises. The Prince of Condé, the Huguenot commander, in desperation looked across the Channel to his co-religionists for help.

There was in the English court a powerful pro-Huguenot lobby. Its most active and vocal member was Sir Nicholas Throckmorton, the ambassador in Paris. He had hinted to the Queen the possibility of recovering Calais by alliance with the Protestants; to Cecil he wrote more frankly, 'Our friends, the Protestants, must be handled and dandled', so that if Spain intervened they 'for their defence or their desire for revenge or affection to the queen, may be moved to give her possession of Calais, Dieppe, or Newhaven'.[17]

As the French overture developed, it was Dudley who took the lead in negotiation and in action. Cecil, so far as the record goes, remained curiously mute; he had tentatively backed a scheme to support German mercenaries in aid of the French Protestants, but otherwise he appeared on the scene merely as the executor of orders, facilitating finance and supply. His sole recorded comment during the weeks leading up to the agreement was a non-committal 'I think the prince shall have help of the Queen of England. I think the Queen shall have Newhaven.'[18] Dudley, who had been in touch with the Chatillons on his own in the preceding winter, entered into a new alliance with

Throckmorton.[19] Sir Nicholas had hitherto been an ally of Cecil and a harsh opponent of the Dudley marriage; now he changed his colours and threw himself with his accustomed zeal into promoting his new patron's cause.[20] Lord Robert negotiated directly with Condé through his brother-in-law, Sidney, while others of his dependants played a conspicuous role in events.[21]

In July 1562, collaboration with the Huguenots was formally proposed to the Council (of which Dudley was not a member). Queen and Councillors accepted without demur. In August agreement was reached by which the English would subsidize Condé to the tune of 140,000 crowns (£40,000).[22] In return they would receive Newhaven, to be held until Calais was returned. English troops would land at Dieppe and advance to Rouen to join their French allies.

In many respects this enterprise seemed to parallel the Scottish intervention two years earlier, but there was a difference.[23] Collaboration with Scottish factions was a long-established habit of English diplomacy, but intervention in French domestic politics was a rarity; the last instance had been Henry VIII's patronage of the Duke of Bourbon in 1524. Secondly, the English were to have a material reward for this intervention, the return of Calais. A traditional goal, the recovery of the ancient possession of the crown, mingled uncomfortably with the novelty of confessional solidarity with the godly brethren. This time the Queen seemed to have shed the scruples she had displayed in the Scottish enterprise and gave her ready consent. The prospect of restoring national honour by recovering what Mary had lost no doubt influenced her; conceivably she was emboldened by the previous success.

Dudley's interest in the expedition became even clearer with the surprise appointment of his brother, Warwick, to command the English forces. The latter's sole military experience was a spell as gentleman volunteer with the Anglo-Spanish army in 1557. He chose to surround himself with adherents of the Protestant radical left, clerics of Genevan persuasion and soldiers of similar outlook.[24] The Dudleys, now collaborators with the French Protestants abroad, were cultivating the Protestant left at home.[25]

Lord Robert was finding his feet as an independent political entrepreneur. He was deliberately choosing to be patron of two overlapping but distinct clientages. One was the band of enthusiasts, the most eminent of whom was Throckmorton, who wanted to cast the Queen as international Protestant champion. Convinced of the hostile intentions of the Catholic princes, they argued that for England the best defence was to support Continental co-religionists wherever they were. The second group consisted of those clerics, and their lay backers, who were pressing for further reform within the English church, along the line of the Continental models.

In October the English forces crossed to Dieppe and Newhaven, followed by their commander. Rouen was in Protestant hands, besieged by the Catholics and desperately in need of English help. At this juncture Elizabeth's normal timidity reasserted itself. She ordered Warwick to keep his forces largely at Newhaven; only a few participated in the defence of the Norman capital. Rouen fell to the Catholics in November. Dieppe followed and the English found themselves isolated in Newhaven. Over the next few months the French parties gradually edged towards an accommodation. When this was accomplished in the spring of 1563, the English were left without a *raison d'être* for their continued occupation of the French port. The rebel promise to deliver Calais had lost all force, and indeed, the contending French parties now united to expel the intruder.

There had been a change in diplomatic personnel during the autumn. Throckmorton, anxious to pursue his career where it could be pushed, at court, had been replaced at Paris by Sir Thomas Smith, a scholar turned civil servant, an Edwardian veteran, and an ally of Cecil's. Throckmorton, caught up in the war *en route* home, sought refuge in the Protestant camp; lingering too long, he was captured by the Catholics, and only reached home in January.[26]

The French venture, unlike its Scottish predecessor, had turned sour. The hope of recovering Calais had gone glimmering. The only question remaining for the Queen was whether to hang on at Newhaven in the hope that another twist in the French struggle would yield possession of Calais – or to cut her losses and bring her army home. Throckmorton pushed for the former option; Smith, at Paris, sought a mediating formula. Behind these two one can dimly perceive the push and pull of their patrons, Cecil and Dudley.[27] The Queen, whose ambiguous attitude towards the enterprise had already manifested itself in her refusal to support the Protestants in Rouen, began to backtrack, refusing money for fortifications at Newhaven. The French resolved the question for the English. They steadily advanced the siege, aided by an outbreak of plague in the garrison. There was nothing for it but surrender, in June 1563.[28] All that the English had to show for the whole futile enterprise was a visitation of the plague, brought home in the soldiers' baggage, which spread throughout the country thereafter. A peace was patched up with the French in the Treaty of Troyes (April 1564). A symbolic payment by France liquidated the issue of Calais and initiated a period of peaceful relations between the two kingdoms.

The English no doubt had hoped to duplicate their previous success in the north. The analogy was badly drawn. In Scotland the English had looked to long-term advantage but expected no material gain from their allies. In France there was duplicity on both sides; Elizabeth cared only minimally for the welfare of the French brethren but eagerly clutched at the chance to recover the lost dominion. The French offered the bait with every hope of not having to pay the price, and Frenchmen of both parties found common cause in expelling the alien.

An examination of Elizabeth's course of action in 1562 as against that of 1559–60 provides a telling comparison. Then she had turned a cold shoulder to Cecil's bold and innovative vision of a new Anglo-Scottish relationship. Now, in 1562, she had moved boldly, even rashly, to a commitment in which she was willing to sacrifice principle by collaborating with rebels in a nostalgic exercise in backward-looking strategy. Cooperation with Scotland offered the solution of an ancient problem; the recovery of Calais a burdensome liability and the running sore of continued Anglo-French hostility. Then, having sent her forces to France, she got cold feet and neutered their effectiveness. The result was a humiliating retreat, although French weakness ensured there would be no further consequences. The Queen had burned her fingers badly. Events had strengthened her doubt both about collaboration with rebels and about the risks of military campaigns which developed their own momentum, beyond effective royal control. Elizabeth had drawn the moral of the lesson to herself. It would prove very difficult indeed to lure her into another such venture.

However, the failure at Newhaven had no adverse effect on that venture's sponsor. Dudley continued to prosper. In October 1562 the Queen gave him a seat at the Council board and, at the very moment of his brother's capitulation, made him a princely gift of land, including Kenilworth Castle and the Lordships of Mortimer and Denbigh.[29] However, there are clear signs that it was Cecil who had the Queen's ear when the question of hanging on at Newhaven arose. And, at the same time that she admitted Dudley to the Council, she promoted his old foe, the Duke of Norfolk, to the same honour.

It is possible to discern here the emergence of a distinctive royal strategy of politics. In the first years of the reign the dynamic energy of the Secretary had taken the initiative from the Queen and driven her along roads she was unwilling to travel. It was not that she did not value the intelligence and skill of Cecil; she had no intention of depriving herself of his service. She could, however, check him by forcing him to share her confidence with a rival Councillor. There would thus be another focus of influence within the Council and another voice of counsel to the Queen. Cecil, no longer able to mobil- ize a united council, would have to fight for a hearing. Hence her lavish endowment of Dudley and his promotion from favourite to Councillor. Although this might seem to give him an advantage, he too had to accept the same limits as Cecil. She made it plain that even though she was staking him to power and place by her bounty, there was to be a level field of play. The privileges which Lord Robert enjoyed as her favourite were not to extend to Dudley the Councillor. Here he must take his place among his equals, fight his own fight, and expect to win or lose on the merits of his case.

For the Queen, the advantages of this system were to give her greater freedom, more elbow-room. Faced with the need for making decisions, she could make her choice from among the differing coun- sels offered her. She would listen, but the decision would be hers. It was a very different system from that which her father had pursued up to 1540, when a single minister monopolized the royal confidence. Elizabeth's system created an uncomfortably tense set of relationships within her inner circle of counsel. They were bound to engender friction, and might foment the kind of internecine quarrels which rent the Council under Queen Mary. Nevertheless, at a moment when the most difficult kinds of choice were about to be thrust on the Queen, her Council would be kept open to diverse opinions and contending policies. At a time of passionate difference on the great questions of state, no party would feel frustrated and excluded, as had happened at moments in Henry's reign and would be classically the case under Charles I. All this was still in embryo in the 1560s, before the most vexing issues had emerged. For the moment it was sufficient that neither of the two dominant men in her Council, each striving to have her ear, had a monopoly of her confidence. It would be clear to the world that her councillors were her servants, not her tutors. It was a long step forward in Elizabeth's mastery of her royal calling.

8

Marriage and Succession

The return of the English forces from Newhaven and the ensuing peace with France ended Elizabeth's experiment in foreign
adventure. French affairs would engage her attention later in
the decade, but, as we shall see, she would keep the Huguenots at
arm's length. Relations with Spain would pass through a troubled
period but would not reach an acute stage until 1568. France and
Spain had their own preoccupations in which England did not figure
largely. It was domestic issues which absorbed the interests and the
actions of Council, court, and the larger political community. Above
all it was the great linked questions of marriage and succession; in
one form or another they would form the stuff of domestic politics
for nearly a decade. In foreign relations events could force the Queen's
hand, and Councillors might cajole or chivvy her into action, but on
the marriage it was she who made the running. Councillors and
courtiers could do no more than follow the course she set, expostulat-
ing as they went.

On the matrimonial question the Queen, by her long flirtation with
Dudley, had early on seized the high ground. This assertion of her
own preferences silenced any discussion of alternatives. As we have
seen, the prospect of such a match dampened the spirits of most of
her Council, but if she persisted, there was, as in her sister's time,
nothing left but sullen acquiescence. The Queen made the most of
her tactical advantage and probably kept the Dudley wooing alive well
after the time when she had in her own mind rejected it.

On the succession question she had less advantage. So long as she
remained unmarried, there was no assurance of a known successor.
The full implications of this dilemma came home with a vengeance

in 1562 when the Queen nearly died of smallpox.[1] According to the uncertain but plausible witness of de Quadra the court, faced with the question of a successor, split three ways, among the adherents of the Lady Catherine Grey, those of the Earl of Huntingdon, and a third party who would have delayed until the lawyers could give an opinion. It was thought that they would have opted for the Stuart claim. (There was a strong Catholic element among the legal profession.) The Lady Catherine Grey had badly damaged her relations with the Queen by having clandestinely married Seymour, Earl of Hertford, and compounded the fault by producing a child. The Queen in her fury had forced an ecclesiastical annulment of the marriage and packed Catherine off to confinement in country exile. Huntingdon was a young nobleman of strongly Protestant bent but not at this stage a major public figure.[2]

The most interesting alternative was represented by an abortive bill proposed for the 1563 Parliament, backed by Cecil. This would have vested interim sovereignty in the existing Privy Council until Parliament chose a successor. It is a measure of the determination of the Secretary and his associates to keep the English crown in the hands of a Protestant ruler, even if it meant overriding the indefeasible line of hereditary descent and throwing the choice of successor into the hands of the ruling elite, resorting to election by Parliament.[3]

Even before the Queen's illness the pieces in the succession puzzle had shifted. In December 1560, death had ended Francis II's brief reign, and Mary, now a cipher in French affairs, had no choice but to make a reluctant return to her native kingdom. Widowhood totally altered her position *vis-à-vis* the English succession. With the albatross of her French throne removed, she was a highly plausible candidate. The question of her possible remarriage, which interested the English as much as the Scots, was a very lively one. One candidate for her hand had already surfaced: the Countess of Lennox began to push the claims of her son, Henry, Lord Darnley. She was the daughter of Queen Margaret Tudor by her second marriage, so the young man stood in the line of the English succession. Although junior to Mary's claim, he was English-born, according to some legists a necessary qualification for an heir. Lady Lennox's dabbling in intrigue at Westminster and at Edinburgh landed her and her husband in the Tower, although after a few months they were released and restored to entrée at court, where the young lord entertained the Queen with his skill at the lute. His name was now on the list of possible husbands for the Queen of Scots.[4]

What followed between 1563 and 1565 was a duel, fought at arm's length, between the two queens. It was they who called the tune and their respective ministers could only follow as best they could. Mary's return to the native land opened direct communication between the cousins for the first time. The initial contacts were not happy. When Mary asked permission to pass through England on her return, she was faced with a demand to ratify the 1560 Treaty of Edinburgh, to which she had so far refused her signature. She declined; licence was refused, and she returned home across a sea haunted by English cruisers.[5]

In Scotland Mary showed herself a political realist by accepting the official Protestantism of her kingdom while retaining her own right to the mass and by working hand in glove with the regime set up in 1560. Her collaborators were her half-brother, now Earl of Moray, and the secretary, Maitland of Lethington. For the time being, Scottish politics seemed stable and reasonably predictable. Mary, however, remembering her former glories as Queen of France, was little content with her fate. She was soon casting about for another husband. There were some tentative overtures to her brother-in-law, Charles IX of France, and to the Infante Don Carlos, the Spanish heir. Catherine de Medici choked off the first, and Philip was interested in the second only as a counter to a renewed Franco-Scottish alliance.

Mary had to turn her attention to lesser princes, such as the Austrian Archduke Charles. If she was not to enjoy another throne, she must turn her eyes towards the English succession. Hence she wanted a husband who could assist her in obtaining recognition of her rights. In the pursuit of this goal she had the services of a devoted and able servant in Secretary Maitland, once her enemy, now her loyal agent. He shared with Cecil the vision of a united Britain, but since it would be under the sway of his mistress's sceptre, he was now arrayed against the English Secretary.[6]

Elizabeth and her ministers followed with deep anxiety the manœuvres of Maitland on his mistress's behalf, and when he returned from a mission in France intimated to him that they would not countenance any match with a Habsburg, Spanish, or Austrian.[7] An English emissary, Thomas Randolph, went north to reiterate this message; it was made more emphatic still in a second mission, late in 1563. Randolph was to tell the Scottish Queen that no son of France, Spain, or Austria would be acceptable to his Queen; she would prefer her cousin to marry an English nobleman. Mary had already acknowledged her readiness to follow Elizabeth's advice in her marriage and now wanted

to hear specific English proposals. In London the name of the preferred candidate was an open secret – Robert Dudley, who in order
to make him a more acceptable bridegroom was now promoted to
the peerage, as Earl of Leicester. But Elizabeth was determined his
name should be put in play by the intended bride, not by the match-
maker. Randolph, charged with this mission, did his best but in
vain. Mary insisted, 'Let me know plainly what your mistress's name
is that I may the better devise with myself and confer with other
and so to give a more resolute answer than by these general words
spoken by you I can.'[8] At last the English Queen had to divulge
her choice.

For the historian it is hard to regard Elizabeth's proposal as anything but preposterous. It seems on its face an insult to her cousin.
If the Scottish Queen were to be compelled to accept an islander as
her husband, she might at least expect a nobleman of unblemished
descent and honourable career. She was offered instead the hand-me-
down favourite of her rival, a mere creature of the court, of dubious
antecedents. No promises were made about the succession although
to sweeten the pill Elizabeth intimated she would not marry. A final
bizarre touch was a suggestion that the three of them might share a
common household, Elizabeth paying the expenses.

The Scots, as Randolph informed London, regarded the proposal
with unbelief. 'Knowing both their affections and judging them [Eliza-
beth and Leicester] inseparable', the Scots could only suppose 'that
no such thing is meant on my sovereign's part and that all these offers
bear a great show and face of good will than any good meaning'.[9] In
that judgment they were probably right, in the sense that Elizabeth
did not really expect Mary to accept the offer. Why then make it? It
was not intended as an insult, so what did Elizabeth hope for? The
simplest explanation is that it would serve to drag out even longer the
futile negotiations between the cousins. The official policy was to
prevent the Scottish Queen marrying outside Britain. Elizabeth may
privately have hoped that Mary would not remarry at all.

The offer of Dudley's hand was also designed to fault Mary in the
cut and thrust of the queens' duel. When Elizabeth insisted on a
British marriage for her cousin, Mary acquiesced, thus pushing Elizabeth to name names. The most obvious candidate would have been
a noble of ancient lineage and high birth – Norfolk or Arundel were
names which would spring to mind. But Elizabeth had no intention
of allowing a match which would give Mary a political base in England.
Hence the offer of Dudley's hand, an offer which Mary would

85

certainly refuse, but by her refusal place herself in the wrong. At the least it was a move that produced stalemate.

There is another possiblity, so speculative as to be offered very tentatively. Given the insensitivity engendered by a more than royal egotism, Elizabeth may just possibly have conceived the scheme would work. For someone whose personal relationships were all those of absolute superiority and unconditional submission, there was a certain crazy logic in the proposal. Since Elizabeth had no intention of marrying, Mary was being offered the prize she sought — at a price. She must tie herself to the apron-strings of her cousin to assure her docility during Elizabeth's lifetime. The lenses through which Elizabeth viewed the world were worn only by princes, and in that exotic landscape the prospective match may have seemed entirely plausible. Surely for Mary the prize would be worth the cost.

Mary, however, did not propose to allow the stalemate to endure. In seizing the initiative she probably had the assistance of her would-be suitor, Leicester. He was no more enthusiastic about the proposed nuptials than was his intended bride. Leicester apparently wrote to the Earl of Bedford, who was conducting negotiations, asking him not to press the suit.[10] Discussion did indeed end when Mary insisted on, and Elizabeth refused, a formal recognition of the former's rights in the succession. Leicester took a further step; he promoted the cause of another suitor.[11]

The exiled Earl of Lennox, long *persona non grata* in Scotland, had been allowed by Mary to return, at Elizabeth's request. The latter's reasons are not clear. It certainly did not suit her purposes that Lennox should participate in Scottish politics during the marriage negotiations. On his return he enjoyed the favour of Mary, who sponsored his restoration in land and rank in October 1564.[12] Mary had an ulterior purpose in her favours to the earl. Her next step was to send an envoy, Sir James Melville, to ask permission for Lord Darnley to join his father in Scotland. Melville's English ally in this effort was Sir Nicholas Throckmorton, now unemployed but acting as unofficial counsellor to Mary and to Leicester. With the latter's assistance, Melville persuaded the Queen to grant Darnley licence to travel. It was one of her major misjudgments.

Darnley arrived in Edinburgh in February 1565. Events moved swiftly thereafter as Mary pressed ahead with her plans. In April she quarrelled with Moray and broke the working arrangement on which Scottish politics had rested since her return from France. Maitland appeared in London with the message that, since Elizabeth would not guarantee the succession, Mary refused the Leicester match. However, in accordance with the English wish that she should not marry outside Britain, she proposed to take Darnley as her husband.[13]

The consternation at the English court led to hasty backtracking. Elizabeth now agreed to examine fully Mary's claims to the succession, and to publish the results, if only the Scottish Queen would take an English noble as husband; the Duke of Norfolk and the Earl of Arundel were mentioned. Elizabeth set her face firmly against the Darnley match; she would give neither approval nor goodwill. Throckmorton, sent north with this message, did his best, but to no avail. When Moray refused to support a Darnley marriage, he was driven from court; Maitland was coldly regarded. The political fabric on which stable relations between the two kingdoms had depended was now in shreds. The royal wooing, in which the lady was even more ardent than the gentleman, was a brief one. In July 1565, less than six months after his arrival in Edinburgh, Darnley was married to the Queen.

Mary had taken the reins away from Elizabeth and driven events according to her own will, throwing the English queen on the defensive. Elizabeth, deeply disturbed by the new development, turned to her Council for advice. The responses of individual Councillors varied in detail but coincided in their assessment of the dangers which the marriage presented. All their fears of a large-scale, well-organized network of international Catholic conspiracy now surfaced. The marriage was simply a new chapter in an old story which harked back to the use of the English style and arms by Mary and Francis in 1559. Temporarily frustrated 'by God and the queen', Mary had now found a way to reactivate the old conspiracy. It aimed at more than the announced claim to the succession. Her goal was nothing less than possession of the throne. The Councillors' unease was heightened by the never-sleeping fear of domestic Catholic conspiracy.[14]

Apart from the flurry at the time of the proposed nuncio's visit, there had been a half-witted plot by Cardinal Pole's nephews, who shared his Yorkist descent, to secure help from the Guises in proclaiming Mary Stuart Queen. They soon ended in the Tower, but the episode poured oil on the fires of suspicion.[15] So did the raids on the Spanish embassy chapel which flushed out English communicants at the ambassador's mass. More weighty evidence came from a survey of 1564, conducted by the bishops, to test the religious sympathies of JPs. It revealed that not more than half of the 850 in the survey could be counted as committed supporters of the religion established by law, while 150 were written down as adherents of the papal faith.[16] It was easy for the Councillors to tot up the dangers to the regime, less easy to suggest any remedies. More rigorous enforcement of the recusancy laws, pressure on the Marian bishops, and, significantly, a relaxation of Catherine Grey's confinement were all they could muster. The episode revealed all too clearly the underlying insecurity which haunted the English leadership.

As for the immediate situation in Scotland, the Councillors agreed in recommending precautionary measures. Bedford was sent to the borders as Lieutenant-General.[17] Some would have gone further and opened hostilities if necessary. However, when the matter was put to the question by the flight of Moray and his associates to the border town of Dumfries, there was disagreement within conciliar ranks about what to do. The Queen momentarily authorized clandestine aid to the Earl, but then hastily retreated. Mary advanced with her forces; Moray and his company took refuge in Carlisle.[18]

Cecil produced one of his papers in his favourite pro-and-contra form. He saw a strong argument for action in the dangers arising from a prospective Franco-Scottish league and endemic Border disorder. On the other side, however, were arguments which certainly chimed with Elizabeth's deepest instincts — the question of dealing with other princes' rebels and the cost of doing so. Cecil's recommendation was to treat with Mary; Elizabeth was in full agreement.[19] She had at first taken a very high line, sending an envoy to Scotland with orders to express her strong displeasure; the Scottish Queen had retaliated in kind. But now Elizabeth lowered her tone, offering to recognize the marriage if the exiled nobles were pardoned and the reformed faith guaranteed. Nothing came of this overture. By midwinter it was known that Mary was with child. Then events took an unexpected and ugly turn. Darnley had soon revealed himself as an immature weakling and lost his hold on his wife's affections. Conscious of his humiliating position, he was easily lured into a plot against Mary's Italian secretary, David Rizzio. A personal favourite of the Queen, Rizzio aroused Darnley's jealousy and the resentment of the Scottish nobles. The aggrieved husband joined eagerly in a scheme to murder the Italian. The deed was committed in the royal apartments in Holyrood House, in the pregnant Queen's presence. It was to prove only the first act of the bloody melodrama which would follow. For the moment, relations between the two courts were in suspense.

Mary had turned the tables on Elizabeth by her marriage; she had met English requirements by marrying a British nobleman of impeccable antecedents. The birth of a son crowned her success. Elizabeth's cry, 'The Queen of Scots has a fair son and I am but of barren stock'[20] was a personal response, but it was echoed with different overtones by her Councillors, above all by Cecil and all those others for whom the prospect of a Catholic successor was anathema. Mary, respectably married, the mother of a son, the tolerant ruler of a Protestant kingdom, had irreproachable credentials as a claimant to the succession. It would be increasingly hard to deny that claim. There was only one remedy for this — Elizabeth's own marriage — and towards that end they turned their energies.

At the beginning of the reign, in the first week of the 1559 Parliament, the Commons had petitioned the Queen to marry. When the next Parliament sat in 1563 the topic faithfully reappeared on the house's agenda. At the time of this meeting there was in circulation a pamphlet, written by John Hales, an exchequer official, promoting the Grey claim to the succession and assailing that of the Stuarts, both of Mary and of the Lennoxes.[21] The author was packed off to the Tower, while a number of eminent court figures fell under marked royal displeasure. Lord Keeper Bacon was forbidden the court for some time, and even Cecil was not beyond suspicion. The appearance of the pamphlet may have led to the prorogation of a prospective 1564 session.[22] The fright suffered when Elizabeth had smallpox in 1562 was a powerful impetus to another parliamentary effort.

These events formed the background to a massive and carefully engineered effort to use Parliament as a vehicle for pressuring the Queen into settling the succession. During the session, informally, and possibly in the House, men exchanged views about the various possible candidates, Mary, Margaret Lennox, Catherine Grey, the Earl of Huntingdon, and the Lady Margaret Strange, another descendant of Henry's younger sister. At least one Privy Councillor, Ralph Sadler, wrote, and possibly delivered, a speech against a Stuart succession which echoed the fears and antipathies of a xenophobic people with fresh memories of an alien ruler.[23] 'Our common people and the stones in the street would rebel against it.' Already on the first day of business a burgess had made a motion for the succession.[24] Two days of debate, during which there were arguments by 'divers wise personages', ended with the appointment of a prestigious committee, including Privy Councillors and the Speaker, to draw up a petition. When it was ready, the House sought and received the furtherance of the Lords and, at an audience in the gallery at Whitehall, the Speaker read the document to the Queen.

Referring to the 'great terror and dreadful warning' of the Queen's late illness, the petition proceeded on the assumption that Parliament was called purposely to resolve the succession problem. After a hair-raising recital of the woes which would follow an uncertain succession and a remembrance that the realm 'from the Conquest to this present day was never left, as now it is, without a certain heir, living and known', they urged her to a statutory settlement of the problem. They also pressed her to marry, but this plea was subordinated to that for the succession.

In her reponse the Queen displayed her formidable oratorical and diplomatic skills. Prolix, laden with conceits, oblique in its reference to the issues at stake, her reply nevertheless made certain things clear. Fears for her death, sharpened by her late illness, were roundly rebuked. 'There needs no boding of my bane — I know as well as I did before that I am mortal. I know also that I must discharge myself of that great burden God hath laid on me.'[25] The matter was too weighty for an immediate reply; she would defer it to another time. Then, rounding on her audience, she reminded them that 'by me you were delivered whilst you were hanging on the bough ready to fall into the mud, yea, to be drowned in the dung', and recalled the obedience which they owed her. She did not dislike the matter and sum of the petition, although she rebuked those 'restless heads in whose brains the hammers beat with vain judgment'. She reiterated, 'I mean upon further advice further to answer'. She acknowledged the worth of their concern but warned them against treading too far on delicate ground.

The Lords in the mean time had composed their own petition, read to the Queen by Lord Keeper Bacon.[26] Phrased in much the same terms as the Commons petition, it asked specifically for an answer such that 'good effect and conclusion may grow before the end of the session of this Parliament'. When no answer was forthcoming, the Lords jogged her memory by considering a bill for dealing with the case should she die without provision for succession being made. This was the bill mentioned earlier to give power to the Privy Council to rule during an interregnum and to Parliament to choose the successor.[27]

At the closing session, Bacon read the speech in which Elizabeth responded to the petitions from the Houses.[28] It was a very carefully constructed composition, as the much-annotated draft shows. In a tone more benign than her answer to the Commons, she gently rebuked them for considering a successor when they yet had hope of her own issue. She denied any determination not to marry: 'For though I can think it best for a private woman yet do I strive with myself to think it not meet for a prince. And if I can bend my liking to your need, I will not resist such a mind.'

As for the succession issue, she took refuge in a cloud of delphic rhetoric. The closest she came to any concrete answer was the promise to consult on the matter, 'as cause of conference with the learned shall show me matter worthy utterance for your behoofs so shall I more gladly procure your good after my days than with my prayers whilst I live be mean to linger my living thread'. There was a vague reference to the proposed Dudley match with Mary.

In fact, by 1565 any hopes she had that this would solve the problem had faded. When the offer of Leicester's hand to the Scottish Queen tacitly ended his availability for Elizabeth's hand, the politicians saw an opening for reviving the cause of other candidates. Even before the end of 1563 Cecil had set about renewing the Austrian suit – that of the Archduke Charles.[29]

Leicester had lost his hopes of the Queen's hand, but he had no desire to be displaced from her favour by a husband. To check the Austrian, he backed another horse but one which was a sure loser. When feelers were put out to the French court in spring 1565 for a match with the young King Charles IX, Leicester became a warm sponsor of the proposal, Throckmorton acting as intermediary with the French ambassador. It is possible that the Earl had persuaded Elizabeth to this initiative as early as December 1564. Since the King was fifteen and Elizabeth thirty-two, the match was improbable. Moreover, it was implacably opposed by Cecil, who had no intention of seeing another reigning monarch as an English consort. The negotiations gave a summer's employment to the diplomats, but neither side was seriously interested in the marriage itself. For Elizabeth it was an opportunity to take the heat off the agitations of the late Parliament; for the French it was a counter-mine to a Habsburg match. At the end of the summer, when the farce had been played out, the French shifted their backing to Leicester.[30]

The jostling between Leicester and Cecil over the rival suitors for the Queen's hand was symptomatic of a malady which was beginning to afflict the English court. The Queen's deliberate juxtaposition of Cecil and Leicester had sown the seeds of faction. Dormant for a while, they now sprang into unhealthy growth. Cecil had always looked askance at the favourite. He had all the contempt of a man who had ascended each rung of promotion by virtue of meritorious service for the adventurer who at one leap had bounded to the top solely because his manly form pleased the Queen's eye. Leicester returned the compliment, aware of the secretary's disapproving eyes and rightly seeing him as an obstacle in whatever the favourite attempted.

Leicester had tried to poison the mind of Guzmán de Silva, the new Spanish ambassador, against the Secretary, and his agent, Throckmorton, had spoken to the French ambassador of Cecil's enmity to his patron.[31] The Earl was anxious to obtain a Council seat for Sir Nicholas; he almost attained it in 1564, only to see it fall through because of Cecil's opposition. Of a later effort to promote Throckmorton, Cecil wrote with bland malice to Sir Thomas Smith in Paris, 'Great means is made for Nicholas Throckmorton to be of the privy council; and so I wish you both.'[32]

To this first crack in the mosaic of court politics there was added a second. The meritocrats loathed the favourite as a dilettante; the aristocrats with equal fervour, as an *arriviste* adventurer. Norfolk, the greatest of the nobles, resented the favourite's usurpation of the place in the royal confidence to which he felt entitled by his rank and birth. Cecil's views were summed up in a memorandum of April 1566.[33] Entitled *De Matrimonio Reginae Angliae cum extero Principe*, it was divided into two columns, 'reasons to move the queen to accept Charles' and 'reasons against the Earl of Leicester'. On the latter his views were emphatic – a man whose study would be to enrich his friends, he lacked riches, estimation, and power. The circumstances of his wife's death defamed him and would taint the Queen. Norfolk was more succinct. Leicester was a man 'who could produce no more than two ancestors, namely his father and grandfather and these both of them enemies and traitors to their country'.[34]

Norfolk's position was appreciably strengthened by the return to court of Thomas Radcliffe, Earl of Sussex, from his long stint as the governor of Ireland. A peer of ancient descent, his mother was a Howard. 'My lord of Norfolk loveth my lord of Sussex earnestly and so all that stock of the Howards seem to join in friendship together,' wrote Cecil.[35] He was soon at odds with Leicester, who attacked his conduct in Ireland; their quarrel soon rose to such heights that supporters of each went armed at court and badges were displayed; Sussex declared his life in danger.[36] Norfolk had more personal grievances against the favourite. During a tennis match the latter had borrowed the Queen's napkin to wipe his brow. The Duke's jealous fury against the favourite was rebuked by the Queen.

Thus in 1565 Norfolk and Sussex entered into alliance with Cecil in their campaign for an Austrian marriage. They also sought the help of the Spanish ambassador. The two noblemen soon became collaborators with the Imperial representative in forwarding the marriage. When the agent dispatched to Vienna that year sent a courier home, it was Norfolk who had first knowledge of the letter he bore. He consulted with Sussex and Cecil how to communicate it to the Queen. Cecil remained in the background but his memorandum, quoted above, was witness to his whole-hearted approval. Charles had the requisite rank and dignity without the conflicting interests of a ruling prince, while the connection would promote good relations with Spain. The Austrian wooing went very slowly; it was not until 1566 that another agent was sent to Vienna, after Norfolk had bullied Leicester into agreeing to back the cause. Bacon, Winchester, and others joined in; Cecil was their benevolent patron. The envoy returned with a doubtful answer since the Habsburgs stood firm on the religious issue, but hope persisted for the renewal of the approach.[37]

The Queen had throughout acquiesced in these negotiations, although without showing any visible sign of enthusiasm; observers remained sceptical about her intentions. She told Guzmán de Silva, a diplomat with whom she had friendly relations of mutual respect:

> If I could appoint such a successor to the crown as would please me and the country, I would not marry, as it is a thing for which I have no inclination. My subjects, however, press me so that I cannot help myself or take the other course which is a very difficult one. There is strong idea in the world that a woman cannot live unless she is married or at all events if she refrains from marriage she does so for some bad reason.

It was a fair comment on sixteenth-century mores.

Yet it did not meet the case. Cecil put it with his usual clarity in a memorandum of this date.[38] 'To require both marriage and stablishing of succession is the uttermost that can be desired. . . . To require marriage is most natural, most easy most plausible to the Queen's Majesty.' To require the succession would be more difficult because of 'the difficulty to discuss the right' and because of the royal unwillingness to deal with it. 'Corollary: the mean betwixt these is to determine effectually to marry, and if it succeed not, then proceed to discussion of the right of the successor.' This was all very reasonable, but in fact Elizabeth was determined neither to marry nor to declare the succession. She would continue for the present to go through the motions of wooing Charles. So things stood when in September 1566, two months after the birth of the infant prince of Scotland, Parliament met again. It remained to be seen whether it could bend the Queen to its will.

Public discussion of the succession problem had continued since the 1563 session of Parliament. The Hales pamphlet was answered by a partisan of Mary's, a Catholic justice of Queen's Bench, Anthony Browne. There followed at least four more treatises, two on either side of the issue.[39] With the birth to Mary of James a Scottish author in Paris produced a poem saluting the 'prince of Scotland, England, France and Ireland'. Pamphlets were followed by broadsheets scattered in the court itself protesting against Elizabeth's failure to provide for the succession. A Puritan divine, the recently deprived Dean of Christchurch, prepared a long petition to the same effect.[40]

The Commons from the start showed signs of restiveness, one of which was their narrow division on the vote for the royally nominated Speaker. However, the first assault on the sovereign came in the Council, where Norfolk, acting as spokesman for his fellows, reminded the Queen of her promise in 1563 to answer the petitions on succession and marriage. Elizabeth angrily retorted that she had no desire to be buried alive or to see a repetition of the visits to Hatfield in her sister's time.[41]

Having failed in this attempt, the agitators shifted their venue to the Commons. A motion on the succession was moved by a Member, Molyneux. Cecil and other Councillors strove to divert the move by asserting that the Queen intended to marry, but in vain. The subsidy bill was held up, and Elizabeth told the Spanish ambassador she was being blackmailed by the House, who were offering £250,000 as a bribe for her consent to their demands.[42] After a vain effort by the Commons to reach the Queen, they turned to the Lords for assistance. The upper house responded by sending a delegation to the Queen. They spoke plainly: her refusal to deal with the succession had led the Commons to a resolve to hold up the subsidy and other legislation until they were satisfied. The Lords asked her to give them an answer or else let them go home. Her answer was short and tart. They were asking her to dig her own grave. Let them do as they pleased; 'as for me I shall do no otherwise than pleases me. Your bills can have no force without my assent and authority.'[43]

The action now shifted back to Parliament, where the Lords agreed to join their voice to the Commons in a petition. When the upper house seemed to be moving too slowly, the Commons dragged their feet, dawdling over legislation, and pushing the Lords into a joint committee meeting. Before they could finish the task of preparing their petition, the Queen acted. She had already turned on her Councillors. Norfolk was called a traitor and conspirator; Pembroke and Northampton felt the rough side of her tongue; even Leicester was not spared. He and Pembroke were forbidden the court for their furtherance of the succession question.[44]

Pre-empting the petitioners, she now summoned a delegation – thirty from each House – to hear her response.[45] It was, as usual, carefully prepared – a mixture of royal anger, well laced with sharp-toothed sarcasm. A grave matter which required the most sober consideration had been brought forward by 'these unbridled persons whose mouth was never snaffled by the rider', who 'did rashly ride it into the Commons House, a public place', wildly asserting 'that unless provision were made for the succession, they must needs perish'. They had then seduced the Lords, who 'of simplicity did assent unto it'. She then derided two (unnamed) bishops who with their long speeches 'sought to persuade you also with solemn matters, as though you, my lords, had not known that when my breath did fail me, I had been dead unto you and that when dying without issue what a danger it were to the whole state'. Coming at last to the questions at hand, she dealt first with marriage. Reproaching them for having doubted her word, sent through her Councillors, that she would marry even though 'of mine own disposition I was not inclined thereto', she reiterated that promise (though not without conditions): 'I will marry as soon as I can conveniently, if God take him not away with whom I mind to marry, or myself, or some other great let happen.'

On succession Elizabeth went on the offensive, accusing them of a fatal misapprehension of the problem. They saw only their interests; they failed to grasp hers. She recalled her own experience in Mary's lifetime: 'I am sure not one of them was ever a second person, as I have been, and tasted of the practices against my sister.' She went on, 'I stood in danger of my life; my sister was so incensed against me: I did differ from her in religion and I was sought for divers ways. And so shall never be my successor.'

She then turned to ridicule, striking at the weakest point in their argument. Who should be the successor? 'They would have twelve or fourteen limited in succession, the more the better.' And these nominees would be so upright, so pious, 'that they would not seek where they are second to be first and where the third to be second and so forth'. She concluded: 'your petition is to deal in the limitation of the succession. At this present it is not convenient without some peril unto you and certain danger unto me.' If a time came when 'it may be done with less peril unto you she would deal therein'. She charged the Lord Chief Justice and Cecil to repeat her answer in their respective Houses.

Cecil did his duty, but not without a careful damping down of the heat and flames of the original speech. Yet even in this watered-down form the gist of the message was clear. The House heard him in silence, but their determination to keep the issue alive was not quenched. Within a couple of days Lambard, the Kentish antiquarian, stood up and resolutely 'began a learned oration for iteration of the suit to the Queen's Majesty for limitation of succession', and debate followed. The royal riposte was prompt, an order, delivered by Vice-Chamberlain Knollys, that they proceed no further in their suit. Thereupon the promoters of the cause changed tactics. Paul Went-worth raised a constitutional question, 'whether Her Highness com-mandment be a breach of the liberty of free speech of the house or not'. And even if it were not, 'what offence is it for any of the house to err in declaring his opinion to be otherwise?' To this the Queen's short answer was to repeat her command and add that any person not yet satisfied should come before the Privy Council to show his reasons.

The House was not to be muzzled so easily. It now set to work upon yet another petition; a committee of thirty was appointed to draw it up. Thereupon Cecil intervened and the resulting document, though carefully tuned to the royal ear, stuck to the main point.[46] On their knees, in the presence of Almighty God, 'whose viceregent we know you to be', with all humility they insist that they 'have no wise intended or prosecuted anything in our late conference but the renewing of a former suit made in the last session', which would tend to the honour and tranquillity of the realm. Then, moving to the free-speech issue, they spoke of the right confirmed in every Parlia-ment 'of a leeful sufferance and dutiful liberty to treat and devise of matter honourable to Your Majesty and profitable for the realm'. The petition was never presented to the sovereign. Elizabeth, faced with another confrontation, changed course. She penned a message which exists in three different forms;[47] it is uncertain which was given to the House. The chilliest in tone simply says that any discussion of the liberties of the House would only produce 'more inconvenience than were meet'. In the more conciliatory version the Queen declares that, since she now understands by good information that the House took no action on the renewed motion, her commands were unnecessary and so are revoked.

Elizabeth followed up this discreet truce with an initiative guaranteed to win the applause of the House — and of the tax-payer. She remitted the third payment of the subsidy now before the House, thus reducing the subjects' burden by one-third. Yet even now the persistent agitators in the Commons sought to pin down the Queen by another manœuvre. They proposed to flesh out the preamble to the subsidy act in which the Queen would be thanked for her promise to declare the succession at convenient time. The royal response to this was predictable. 'Shall my princely consent be turned to strengthen my words that be not of themselves substantives? I say no more at this time; but if these fellows were well answered, and paid in lawful coin, there would be fewer counterfeiters among them.'[48] The act was duly amended to a bare mention of the royal promises.

The Queen had weathered an unprecedented storm. The pamphlet warfare, the debates in Parliament, and the sustained parliamentary effort to force her hand gave to the storm an air of novelty, of approaching modernity, and it is tempting to view these events in the light of later parliamentary history. They might be read as a prologue to the assertion of a new and more assertive role, particularly of the lower house. To do so would be to ignore the special, indeed unique, circumstances in which these events transpired. As with much else in Elizabethan history, the root of the matter lay in the ruler's gender. Royal marriage was usually a public matter in which considerations of state overrode personal preferences. The choice of a royal wife might well reflect relations with neighbouring princes, but it rarely affected domestic politics. (Anne Boleyn's marriage was the obvious exception.) But the selection of a royal husband was a matter of the greatest moment to the whole realm, since it was in effect the choice of a new ruler. How seriously subjects regarded it was abundantly evident in the events of Mary Tudor's first months. The Commons had not hesitated to petition her not to marry outside the realm, and Elizabeth was convinced that her sister's failure to take account of this had done permanent damage to her regime.

Hence the boldness and persistence of Councillors and Parliamentarians alike is not surprising. They were reacting in traditional ways, by petition and counsel, to a novel problem. They felt justified in stubborn persistence because what was at stake was not only the fate of the dynasty but the essential interests of the whole society. It was not an attempt to claim new powers but an effort to utilize old procedures to resolve an unprecedented problem. They had used them tentatively in 1563; by 1566 the question had taken on a new urgency, in the light of Mary Stuart's marriage and the birth of James.

The Queen's response, at least on the succession question, was equally interesting. Although she fell back on a certain amount of royal bluster and made use of a merciless ridicule of opponents who could not answer in kind, she did in fact engage in a kind of dialogue, at least in an effort to persuade her subjects that her position was not merely self-indulgent but a defensible response to a grim dilemma. To this effort she marshalled her whole armoury of rhetorical skills, not least her biting wit, but her speeches are reasoned efforts to persuade her audience, not merely to bully it.

She admitted the grave risks of an unsettled succession, but she set against them the even greater dangers of a present settlement. Her death was a future contingency, a succession statute a present action with immediate consequences. She drew on her own experience in Mary's time when she had been the 'second person' to her childless sister and, worse still, of opposite religious persuasion. The analogue to the present situation did not need spelling out. To appoint a Catholic successor was to betray the present order and to excite the hostility of a powerful party in the realm. To attempt to fix on any other heir would lead to wrangling disagreements. Indeed, to air the whole matter was to open Pandora's box. To leave things as they were, uncomfortable as it might be, was the least dangerous option open to them.

As to marriage she was less frank and less honest. To the straightforward argument that the succession knot could be cut through in one swift stroke if she would but marry, she gave evasive answers, half-promises, carefully circumscribed with multiple conditions. She was determined not to marry, and was honest enough to make clear her personal preference for the single life, but she could not flatly refuse to wed under any circumstances. It would be difficult to defend such a decision on any public grounds; hence the evasiveness of her public statements and the desultory negotiations with Vienna.

In the duel between the Queen and the Houses in these successive Parliaments, Elizabeth showed herself the mistress of the oratorical art, both in her vivid and forceful language and in her marshalling of argument. Her ornate, indeed luxuriant, prose leaves the modern reader puzzling out the syntax in order to find his way through the verbal maze, but the ambiguities served to cloak her devious skill in evading the marriage issue. However, when she wanted to hammer home an argument, she easily found the telling phrase or the apt figure of speech. Her mordant wit mocked her petitioners — 'as though you, my lords, had not known that when my breath failed me, I had been dead'. With earthy imagery she reminded them that she delivered them when they 'were hanging on the bough ready to fall into the mud, yea, to be drowned in the dung'. When she sought to dissuade them from legislating on the succession, her central argument that it would only divide them was driven home with sardonic irony. Were the candidates for the succession such paragons of virtue that each would meekly defer to the next?

The Austrian negotiations had prospered for a time in 1566 but then stalled. At last at Easter 1567 the Queen consented to send a major mission to Vienna, carrying the Garter for the Emperor and a tardy reply to the Imperial response of the previous year. The Earl of Sussex headed the embassy.[49] Although he set out in the late spring, it was a long journey and the proceedings of the Imperial court ponderously slow. It was not until October that dispatches from Vienna arrived home.

On the vexed religious question the Queen instructed Sussex to say, somewhat disingenuously, that England subscribed to the Augsburg confession of Lutheran Germany, which was legally established in the Empire. The Habsburgs were ready to make some concessions. They insisted that the Archduke be allowed his private mass, which no Englishman would be allowed to attend. He would accompany the Queen at public religious services. If these conditions were privately agreed, the Archduke would come to England without further ado. If he were rejected, his dignity would be saved by alleging religion as the stumbling-block.[50]

Given this straightforward answer, the Queen had to cut bait or fish. The Council members were consulted; the result was what might be expected. Leicester and his allies, Pembroke and Northampton, plus the ultra-Protestant Knollys opposed the match on religious grounds. Cecil, Howard, Clinton, and Rogers supported it; Norfolk, ill at home, sent his enthusiastic approval, scoffing at his opponents' pious objections and declaring that once the Archduke was married he could be converted. The nays were saying what Elizabeth wanted to hear, and Sussex was instructed to refuse the demand for separate worship.[51]

The refusal of the Austrian match closed a door which had never been more than slightly ajar. What Elizabeth had consistently said when pressed on the subject was true: she preferred not to marry.

When and precisely why she made this decision we can never know. It had perhaps grown with the years. When she came to the throne she was much attracted to Robert Dudley. When he became free to marry in the summer of 1560 she was sorely tempted; but she did nothing, and what was initially indecision imperceptibly hardened into resolution: Dudley was not to be her husband. By 1564 she was willing to offer him to Mary Stuart. With the exercise of power had come the appetite. If she married, she put it in jeopardy; before the honeymoon was over, there would spring up ugly faction in which the crown could not be neutral. In the end she opted for as much of both worlds as she could obtain. The monopoly of royal power remained intact; Dudley was still her companion, consoled for the loss of her hand by her grants of wealth and status and by the political career which she opened up for him.

There were no such consolations for Cecil and the other councillors. They had to accept the likelihood that their mistress would live out her reign a virgin queen. For the present the succession must remain unsettled. However, a set of startling events would soon scatter the pieces on the chessboard of politics and open the way for a novel solution of the succession problem.

Part III

Elizabeth and Mary
1568–1572

9

The Coming of Mary Stuart

*E*ven as the last hopes of the Habsburg match faded, a succession of melodramas at Edinburgh turned the Scottish political world upside down and left the English in gasping confusion. Mary had weathered the first of these, the murder of Rizzio, with courage and skill. She was able to regain control over her weakling husband and establish at least the semblance of order. When the Earl of Bedford went north for the christening of James, Elizabeth's godson, he carried with him a conciliatory proposal which showed the continuing strength of Mary's position. If Mary would renounce all present claim to the English throne, Elizabeth would undertake, not to recognize her succession rights, but to protect her against any rival claims. Elizabeth's severe treatment of the pamphleteer Hales was cited as an earnest of the proposal.[1] Mary, triumphant in her motherhood, refused the proffered palm-branch. She was putting out feelers to Philip of Spain as a possible patron and dabbling in twopenny conspiracies with various Englishmen.[2]

Hardly three months after the christening ceremony at Edinburgh, the European world was startled by the news of Henry Darnley's murder in February 1567. Mary's regard for him had turned to contemptuous hatred, and he was obviously an embarrassment. It was she who lured him back from Glasgow and arranged for him to stay in the isolated house outside Edinburgh's walls where he was killed. Responsibility for the murder itself was universally ascribed to the Earl of Bothwell, but unpleasant imputations also hung around the Queen's reputation. Bothwell was acquitted after a make-believe trial. Worse was to follow: in July Mary and Bothwell were married. For the Scottish Queen it was an act of personal and political self-destruction. Her new husband was the rogue male among the Scottish nobility, distrusted and feared by his peers. The Scots lords, divided in much else, were united in opposition to the Earl and his wife. Armies gathered and marched to a confrontation which proved bloodless. Bothwell's forces disintegrated, and he fled the country. The captive Queen was carried into her own capital, jeered by the mob, and within a few days the lords had enforced her abdication, proclaimed the infant James King, and locked up his mother in the island prison of Lochleven. Moray, who had departed in disgust a few months earlier, was summoned home from Italy (urged on by Secretary Cecil) to become Regent for his nephew.

Cecil and his associates had every reason to rejoice at the shipwreck of Mary's fortunes. They had pressed Elizabeth to marriage not only for the obvious need to beget an heir but also to avoid the consequence of a Catholic successor. To many of them the event was providential. The Councillor Mildmay piously wrote, 'She hath accorded to the resignation of her estate in marvellous tragedy if a man repeat it from the beginning, showing the issue of such as live not in the fear of God.' Another observer put it more baldly when he said that Scots lords had the wolf by the ears and hoped she would never exercise power again.[3]

Elizabeth's reactions to these events were of a very different kind. Far from rejoicing in the misfortunes of her cousin, she was in a fuming rage at the conduct of the Scottish nobles, who had not only raised arms against their lawful sovereign but had now deposed and imprisoned her. Although she wrote to rebuke Mary for the folly of the marriage, she promised to intervene in her behalf, and Throckmorton was sent northward with all speed. The instructions he carried minced no words. The nobles were roundly condemned for an intolerable act of violence against their monarch. Elizabeth acknowledged Mary's faults, urged a divorce, and accepted the prospect of a conciliar tutelage for her cousin, but the cardinal condition was Mary's liberation and restoration to her throne. There were politic considerations in this move; such a scheme would make both Queen and nobles dependent upon English favour, but above all it would preserve Mary's regality.[4]

The Scots were in no mood to listen to such conditions. Throckmorton warned Cecil: 'for when all is done, it is they that must stand her [Elizabeth] in more stead than the queen her cousin.' He was denied an interview with Mary, and on 29 July James VI was formally crowned at Stirling. The Queen's anger was fanned even more fiercely by these events, and she ordered cooperation with the Hamilton faction, now arming against the Regent in Mary's support. This was in direct contradiction to Cecil's urgings, who was anxious to boost Moray's authority. Throckmorton commented on the Hamiltons: 'their behaviour so inordinate, the most of them unable, their living so vicious, their fidelity so tickle, their party so weak, I count it lost whatever is bestowed on them.' The Regent, in fact, soon brought them to heel, and through the winter of 1567–8 a sullen peace prevailed in the northern kingdom. Elizabeth's wrath cooled only when her ministers pointed out that the Scots lords, if pressed too hard, might kill their captive, a deed for which an unkind world would hold Elizabeth responsible.[5]

The pause in Scottish affairs was brief. The captive Queen charmed one of her warders into assisting her escape. In May 1568 she was free again, at the head of an army provided by the Hamiltons. Elizabeth promptly wrote to congratulate her on her freedom, offered to act as mediator with the lords, with the threat that, if they failed to submit themselves, Mary could count on English arms to support her.[6] Events quickly made the offer irrelevant. A bare two weeks after her escape Mary, her army defeated by the Regent, crossed the Solway firth in a fisherman's boat and, with a tiny entourage, landed in Cumberland.

The speed with which all this happened caught the English government unprepared for such an unwelcome turn in events. There was need for immediate action. Mary had landed at Cockermouth, a lordship of the Percy Earl of Northumberland. That lord, an outspoken Catholic, at odds with the court and highly suspect there, had had some earlier correspondence with Mary. As soon as he heard of her arrival he hastened to the scene, hoping to take her under his wing. He was forestalled by Richard Lowther, a Cumberland squire, deputy to the Warden of the West Marches. Lowther stoutly held off the Earl until the arrival of the Privy Councillor Sir Francis Knollys, dispatched to wait on the Scottish Queen. After a record-breaking journey, he arrived in Cumberland on 25 May, some ten days after Mary's arrival.[7]

The Scots Queen played her cards well. Appealing to Elizabeth's past promises of support, she presented herself as the victim of rebellion, seeking Elizabeth's aid in recovering her rights. She asked to come to the court to make her case and to quiet any doubts that might linger as to past events. That request — after a moment of hesitation — was denied. We cannot know how Elizabeth felt about a face-to-face meeting with her rival; earlier in the decade she had assented to a such a meeting, but then found reasons to cancel it. Dealing with her cousin by correspondence and through emissaries kept the relationship on a coldly official level, where matters could be handled with a certain impersonality and the emotions of a personal encounter avoided. Secondly, Mary's isolation in a northern castle kept her away from the English court and from direct contact with the English notables. Her appearance there would have established that 'second person' whom Elizabeth so dreaded. Cecil gloomily — and percipiently — prophesied that Mary would prove a dangerous centre of infection in the realm.[8]

But what was to be done with the unbidden guest? All the alternatives — to assist her to recover her throne, to allow her to go abroad, or to keep her in England — were equally unpalatable. For the moment she was lodged at Carlisle, half-guest, half-prisoner, under the wardenship of Knollys. The latter, cousin by marriage to the Queen on the Boleyn side, a practised courtier and an outspoken Protestant, could be counted on to keep a firm but courteous surveillance over Mary and limit, although not cut off, her contacts with the countryside. Longer-run policy required thought and discussion. Scotland was now divided between two rival allegiances. Moray headed a 'Jacobite' and Protestant party which naturally looked to England for support. The Marians, a diverse collection of factions, included in their ranks the Scottish Catholics and, looking for foreign aid, had already turned to the Duke of Alva, the Spanish viceroy in the Low Countries.[9]

Elizabeth's view of the matter still reflected her concern for the re-establishment of legitimacy in Scotland, which meant some kind of Marian restoration. Yet even she could see that Moray's regime was a political fact, too potent to be ignored. Reluctantly she agreed to hear a statement of his case, but only if he appeared in the guise of a defendant. Such a manœuvre preserved the fiction of Mary's royal status. It also put Elizabeth in the powerful position of an umpire in Scottish causes. She continued, however, to waver and there were moments when she inclined to a restoration, conditioned only by a promise to eschew French or Spanish links.[10]

To Cecil the latter course would be utter folly; but all choices were grim. Restored, Mary would end the English alliance and plunge Scotland into perpetual disorder; freed, she would go to France to stir up renewed French interest in her claim to the English throne; a prisoner in England, she would intrigue with her friends here for the crown. The other Councillors took a slightly less pessimistic posture, but they were firm in their advice. 'Her Majesty can neither aid her, permit her to come to her presence, or restore her, or suffer her to depart before trial.'[11]

Mary naturally objected to answering Moray's charges, and talked boldly of returning to Scotland or going to France. At Carlisle, barely across the border, it would be all too easy for her to act. The government would have liked to bring her south to some such safe Midlands house as Fotheringay or Tutbury, but she resisted this and they compromised on Bolton Castle in Wensleydale, a property of Lord Scrope, Warden of the West Marches.

Both she and Moray were now pressured to accept the English proposal for a formal hearing before a team of English commissioners. The Regent agreed and, though Mary would make one more plea to Elizabeth for permission to leave for France or Scotland, she finally yielded. France was sinking into another round of civil war; the Regent had gained control of the West Borders, cutting Mary off from the Hamilton fortress of Dumbarton. She would have to make the best of it.

Expectations as to the forthcoming hearing varied widely. The Marian partisan Lord Herries wrote confidently that if the Scottish lords were not found justifiable Mary would be restored unconditionally or, at the worst, with some conciliar tutelage. These reports found such currency in Scotland that Elizabeth had to write to the Regent that, if Mary were found guilty, 'it should behove us to consider otherwise of her course than to satisfy her desire in restitution of her to the government of that kingdom'.[12] Cecil's expectation of the exercise was bluntly put: 'It is not meant if the Queen of Scotland shall be proved guilty of the murder to restore her to Scotland, how so ever her friends may bray to the contrary: nor shall yet there be any haste made of her delivery until the matters of France and Flanders be seen.' He must have taken some pleasure in the Queen's choice of her three commissioners, Norfolk, Sussex, and Sadler. The two noblemen were leaders of the anti-Leicester lobby and Sadler a professional diplomat with long experience in Scottish affairs. This was important because, as we shall see, Leicester and his lieutenant Throckmorton had increasingly acquired the reputation of Marian sympathizers.

When the sittings opened at York in October, it became clear that the Queen's intentions were still different from those of her Councillors. Elizabeth's instructions were less concerned with the hearing itself than with the negotiation of a tripartite treaty among

James's adherents, Mary's, and the English, which would restore Mary but leave her and Moray dependent on the authority of an English umpire.

Moray's representatives, ideologically united under a strong leader, were prepared to take the offensive. Mary's, poorly led and divided in counsel, were on the defensive. The Hamiltons were more concerned to advance their own claims to the Scottish succession than to support Mary. The Regent had two options: some kind of compromise with Mary which cut out the Hamiltons, or a bolder scheme which would banish the Queen from the Scottish scene altogether and completely discredit her followers. To accomplish this latter purpose he had up his sleeve the famous casket letters, on which he counted to establish beyond doubt Mary's guilt in her husband's murder. However, he was still uncertain what Elizabeth would do if he took this all-out line of action. He was afraid she would back away from the implications of the evidence and countenance some kind of restoration.

Moray decided to put the matter to the test. Did the Queen's commissioners have the power to pass judgment on Mary's guilt, and if she were found guilty, what would they do? Elizabeth responded by summoning representatives of Mary, the Regent, and the Hamiltons to court. She still seemed to hope for a settlement on the lines of her instructions to her commissioners: 'You shall have good regard that none of them gather any doubt of the success of her cause, but imagine this conference principally meant how her restitution may be devised with surety of the prince her son and the nobility adhering to him.' Sussex, who had seen some of the evidence, was now convinced of Mary's guilt but foresaw that a trial would only end in stalemate. Mary would stand on her royalty, denying the charges 'on the word of a prince'. He urged a composition by which Mary would be forced, by the threat of a public trial, to surrender her power; if that failed to break Mary's will, the English should simply shift their support to the Regent.[13]

At some point Elizabeth began to listen to this advice. By mid-October the Council had convinced her that, if Mary were found guilty, she should either be delivered to the Regent or detained in England. The signal had been given to Moray to produce the damning evidence of the casket letters.[14] In this advice all the weightier Councillors joined forces — Pembroke, Leicester, Clinton, Howard, Sadler, and, of course, Cecil.

The stage now shifted from York to London; the English commission was strengthened by the addition of Bacon, Clinton, Leicester, Arundel, and Cecil. Moray's agents announced their intention of bringing a formal accusation, and laid the supporting evidence before the English commissioners. When Mary's agents demanded she be allowed to answer the charges in person, Elizabeth disingenuously alleged that the Scottish Queen's presence would give a credibility to the charges which she, Elizabeth, did not find in them. The fiction that the Regent was the defendant was still maintained.

The audience before whom the proceedings unfolded was now enlarged to include the whole Privy Council and six earls. Polled, they approved their sovereign's refusal to see Mary so long as the latter laboured under such imputations. Proceedings were then suspended until Mary answered the charges, either through her agents or in person, to noblemen sent by Elizabeth. This, of course, she would not do. When she asked for copies of the charges, they were refused unless she agreed to abide by Elizabeth's judgment.[15] With proceedings brought to a halt, it was now time to put into practice a version of Sussex's scheme. Mary, they hoped, was now sufficiently cowed to agree to a compromise. She would reaffirm her abdication; Moray would be recognized as Regent, and James brought to England for his education (a tacit recognition of his rights to the succession). Mary, of course, refused.[16]

The hearings now ceased altogether. In February 1569 Mary herself was removed to Tutbury Castle in Staffordshire, under the guardianship of the incorruptible Earl of Shrewsbury. Tutbury lay in the centre of his estates, in an area where he could count on the loyalty of the countryside and where Mary's friends would find it hard to engineer an escape.

Mary's enemies had outmanœuvred her. When she first appeared in England, a fugitive queen, seeking sisterly succour, Elizabeth's queenly instincts had stirred sympathetically. She had sought some way to restore her cousin's rights without destroying Moray. The Council determined that, since fate or providence had delivered Mary into their hands, she must never be allowed to squirm free. However uncomfortable it might be to have her resident in England, it was preferable to leaving her free to make mischief in Scotland or on the Continent. By encouraging Moray to bring forward the casket letters, they had so damaged Mary's reputation that Elizabeth was persuaded to abandon all notion of a restoration.

By pressing Mary to answer the charges, they laid a trap from which she had no escape. If she defended herself she was tacitly admitting that there was at least something to be answered and would, of course, forfeit her sovereign status. But refusal to respond left the charges unanswered, the imputation of guilt still clinging to her. Mary's enemies, English and Scottish, had boxed her into a corner from which, for the moment, escape was impossible.

For Elizabeth, the stalemate which left Mary neither condemned nor acquitted freed her from the embarrassments of a formal judgment. Had the Scottish Queen been found either innocent or guilty, the English Queen would have been forced to act. Yet the prospect was still uncomfortable. Elizabeth could not risk freeing Mary, yet the grounds for holding her in captivity were tenuous. Moreover, Mary, resident in England, was a potential disturber of the peace. All too soon, restless English courtiers would be fluttering, moth-like, around her fatal attractions. For the moment matters had to be allowed to drift.

November 1568 marked the tenth anniversary of the regime. The Queen could look about her with some complacency. There was peace at home and abroad; her first great initiative, the religious settlement of 1559, was taking root. The populace at large and the great majority of the clergy had accepted the reformed religious order without demur. Although there had been ripples of discontent among the more radical Protestant clergy, the angry controversies and the agitating uncertainties of the earlier decades had subsided. The residual Catholicism of the countryside appeared dormant, slowly decaying towards final extinction as the older generation died off. The Queen's goal of a quiescent uniformity of religious practice seemed realizable. The French intrusion into Britain had been repelled, and a substantial pro-English interest now existed in Scotland. The looming rivalry of the Queen of Scots had been severely weakened by Mary Stuart's own acts of folly. A trade war with the Spanish Netherlands had been brought to a successful conclusion. Only the failure at Newhaven blotted the record, and that had left no permanent damage.

More important still was the development of effective political cooperation between the Queen and her Councillors, based on trust on both sides. There now existed a working relationship, stable but flexible, within which ruler and ministers worked together in the common tasks of governance. This achievement stood in stark contrast to the failures of the preceding reign. Mary's regime, after the triumphant vindication of her claims in 1553, had failed to come to terms with the ruling elite. Her uncounselled choice of a husband had offended virtually the whole political community, and though they had rallied to her in the Wyatt rebellion, she had failed to establish her leadership. Internecine squabbles, which she could not control, rocked the council as contending politicians sought to win the queen's ear. With the coming of Philip his strong hand imposed some order, but at the cost of effective English independence. The consequences of this were brought home in the unwelcome and unsuccessful war which ended the reign. The one consistent theme of Marian rule, the restoration of the Catholic faith, was marked by lacklustre leadership which focused on the elimination of heresy rather than the renewal of a lively Catholic polity.

With this dismal experience behind them, English politicians might have feared its repetition under another woman ruler. Elizabeth, a critical observer of her sister's shortcomings as a ruler, had from the first asserted her unquestioned authority over her ministers and made it clear that no decision, large or small, would be made without royal scrutiny. Philip's envoy, Feria, had borne witness to her masterfulness in the first days of her reign. In what precisely did that mastery consist? There are plenty of instances of her high temper and biting tongue, and of the cringing submission of Councillors and courtiers. They hint at but do not explain that inner quality of personality, that mysterious power which was felt by all who encountered it. At the distance of 400 years we can accept their witness, although the vitality of the living presence eludes us.

However potent her personality, her quality as a ruler would depend on the test of time and events. The initial evidence was not reassuring. The first test of her ability not only to assert her will but to convert it into effective action came first with the Scottish crisis and then again in the Newhaven adventure. In the first she had to be shepherded into decisions by Secretary Cecil. In the second she seems, at least at first, to have listened to the persuasions of Robert Dudley, but then to have backed away uncertainly.

Councillors' doubts about her capacities were deepened by the Dudley wooing. Yet it was in the wake of that episode that the outlines of a *modus vivendi* between sovereign and ministers began to emerge. Her care to conciliate Cecil even while promoting Dudley was an early sign of Elizabeth's understanding that her rule depended on broad-based support. Secondly, it was evident that she could distinguish between her private life and her official responsibilities.

Gradually a viable pattern of cooperation emerged. It was not an easy one to live with, since the Councillors had to balance the respect, indeed the awe, in which they held her with their frequent disapproval of her particular decisions. What lubricated machinery which might otherwise have seized up was the knowledge that, however imperious her behaviour, Elizabeth was amenable to persuasion. She could be induced to second thoughts, to a softening of her attitude, and to a reorientation of policy, as the successive phases of her relations with Mary Stuart showed.

The rules of the game became clearer as the players settled into their respective places on the team. The stability which came as fears of the unexpected and the unpredictable receded was setting in. The Councillors came to realize that, once Elizabeth gave her confidence, she would not withdraw it, however roughly she might treat her servants when they displeased her. They might even experience exclusion from the court, but once the storm died down, they resumed their accustomed place. This had a reassuring effect, strengthening the growing sense of corporate identity, common purpose, and coherent continuity.

There were, nevertheless, within the Councillors' ranks plenty of frictions which gave cause for concern. Cecil and Dudley eyed each other warily, mutually distrustful. Norfolk and Sussex glared at the favourite. A player might be tempted to break the rules if that would bring about the downfall of his rival. The Queen had contained for the time being the surging demand for a settled succession, but it was about to break out again in a new and more perilous form. A dangerously volatile newcomer had appeared on the English political scene — Mary Stuart. Her presence would strain the vulnerable political structure to the utmost.

As fate would have it, Mary's presence in the kingdom coincided with other, unrelated events which demanded the full attention of Queen and Council. In the same weeks when the commissioners in London were wrestling with the rival Scottish factions, the government's attention was diverted by the unexpected arrival of Spanish ships, laden with bullion to pay the garrisons in the Low Countries, seeking refuge from the Huguenot privateers who pursued them. This triggered off an unexpected confrontation between England and Spain. The hot-headed reaction of an inexperienced ambassador threatened the peace and poisoned relations between the two courts. After a few weeks of intense strain, the situation eased sufficiently to ensure that there would be no open conflict (see Chapter 13). Even as the tension between the two countries relaxed, the attention of the English court was wrenched back to the domestic scene as they became aware of the audible rustle of intrigue around the skirts of their Scottish 'guest'.

10

The Norfolk Marriage

M ary's arrival in England had set in motion a flurry of activity in several different quarters. The circle in which it raised most new hopes was that of the English Catholics. Scattered, leaderless, and disheartened since the beginning of the reign, they now began to stir. In Mary they saw the possibility of a Catholic successor; but first she must be found a Catholic husband. The Earl of Northumberland, newly reconciled to Rome, had sought to reach her as soon as she landed. When he went to court in December 1568 to attend the hearings on Mary, he took the opportunity of making a nocturnal call on the Spanish ambassador, to whom he suggested a match between the widowed Philip and Mary. While she was still at Bolton, one of the local Catholic gentry contrived to see her and to devise various schemes for her escape. In the spring of 1569, when she was lodged at Wingfield, Shrewsbury's Derbyshire residence, another venturesome English partisan, Leonard Dacre, a cadet of the Border house, clambered on to the roof for whispered exchanges with the prisoner, whose escape he was certain he could organize. All this came to nothing, but these same conspirators were drawn into a much larger scheme with far grander patrons.[1]

None of this was a matter of surprise to that temperamental pessimist William Cecil. 'The fame of her murdering her husband will by time vanish away or will be so by defence handled as it shall be no great block in her way to achieve to her purpose.'[2] Sympathy for her plight and the attraction of her personal charm, which even Knollys admitted, were factors in her favour. More weighty was the bleak realization since the rejection of the Archduke that Elizabeth would not marry. Many of the men who had stirred themselves in 1566 to secure the succession now saw the possibility of a new solution to the problem.

The agitation of 1566 had produced a unanimity among politicians who were normally enemies. Norfolk and Leicester had been linked in the Queen's tongue-lashing when they presented their petition for settling the succession. Leicester, indeed, was moving in a wholly new direction. For some time past he had been making gestures of friend-ship to Mary. His confidant, Throckmorton, had become a partisan of Mary as early as 1565 when he sent her a letter of advice, urging her to woo the English Protestant interest.[3] The Scottish ambassador, Melville, in England in 1566, had found Leicester very cordial to his mistress. In this little political speculation Leicester was doing nothing more than taking an unsentimental but realist view of his possible future. It seemed more and more probable that Mary, nine years younger than Elizabeth, would be the next ruler of England. A sensible man would accordingly take out an insurance policy. This was, of course, a line of thought shared by others. With Mary's arrival in England, concrete action became possible. First Mary's position in her new situation must be regularized. What better way than to find an English husband of suitable rank for her? Her religion was still a bar, but optimists thought she might be converted; others pointed out that Protestantism had thrived under her rule in Scotland. Hints of some such argument had circulated for some time; even that arch-Protestant Knollys thought an English marriage the solution for the Marian problem.

These floating possibilities were transformed into political reality by a new alliance formed by a recasting of the players in the political drama. Most surprising of all was the new-coined *entente* between Leicester and Norfolk, now collaborating as match-makers for the Queen of Scots. The sole duke in England, of unblemished descent, the richest subject in the realm, and conveniently widowed (for the third time), he was the obvious candidate for Mary's hand.[4] Although conforming to the Church of England — and, indeed, employing John Foxe as a tutor for his children — he had Catholic links. His last wife had been a Catholic lady of the Border house of Dacre, and her co-religionists put great hopes in the duke. The seed of ambition may have been sown by the subtle Maitland in an autumn afternoon's hawking at Cawood outside York, during the hearings of Mary's case. If so, it sprouted rapidly. Northumberland knew of a scheme for marrying the Duke to the Scottish Queen when he visited the Spanish ambassador in December 1568. Mary may have been made aware of the possibility by the Lady Scrope, wife to Mary's keeper at Bolton and sister to Norfolk. She regarded him as her friend when the proceedings opened at York.

Rumours of these match-making plans had reached Elizabeth; accused, Norfolk fell over himself with blustering denials. Repudiating Mary as a 'mere murderess and adulteress', he boasted that he was as good a prince 'at home in his bowling alley at Norwich' as Mary in her own kingdom. However, these denials were only a blind. In January the Duke was approached by Moray. The Regent, alarmed at reports of a plot, hatched in the Northumberland circle, to assassinate him on the way home, turned to the Duke for help. In their discussion the Duke forthrightly declared his intention of marrying Mary Stuart. They bargained; Moray promised to support the marriage and to return Mary to her crown with honour, provided Elizabeth consented. In return Norfolk used his influence with the northern earls and secured for the Regent a safe conduct home.[5]

When Moray sent an agent south in March 1569 he found plans well advanced and Mary cognizant of the details. By now the conspirators included Throckmorton, Pembroke, Arundel, his son-in-law, Lord Lumley, and, most important, Leicester, a confidant of the duke's by midwinter. This was, of course, a 180-degree turn for the earl, long at daggers drawn with Norfolk.

There was another, new figure in their ranks – Roberto Ridolfi. Ridolfi was a Florentine banker, domiciled in London, whose banking interests gave him access to court circles. He was a pensioner (and presumably an intelligencer) of both the French and the Spanish. He had also become an accredited agent of the Pope in England. In summer 1568 he wrote to Rome a letter, not now extant, with a plan for restoring Catholicism in England. He now joined the conspirators.[6]

Those privy to the plot were a numerous and very diverse crew. The English Catholics' views were straightforward – the restoration of their church through a Catholic succession. A few of them, quite probably, would have preferred not to wait for the death of Elizabeth before placing her cousin on the throne. However, for the time being the management of Mary's affairs was in the hands of the courtiers, who had, of course, quite different plans. Mary, anglicized and, as they hoped, converted to the established church, would return to Scotland with an English consort to await the day when she would fill both thrones. Moray, in Scotland, was a reluctant adherent, uncertain of Elizabeth's continuing support and hedging his bets. It was an unwieldy and incongruous coalition among men who, for religious and personal reasons, were usually natural enemies.

Their leader was, of course, Norfolk, who threw himself into the enterprise with enthusiasm; but the broker who brought them all together and who acted as manager for the enterprise was Throckmorton, without office since his return from Paris, confidant of both Leicester and Mary. The whole scheme was finalized in a meeting of the principals which resolved that, given the changes in France, Scotland, and Spain, the 'tickle' state of the Scottish Regent, and their own Queen's desire to restore Mary, if she could be sure of her — 'for all these causes and other the said earls and Sir Nicholas were of opinion good provision might be made by the Queen's Majesty and her council as by this marriage Her Highness and the realm might take commodity'. Norfolk, protesting his reluctance, agreed to sacrifice himself for the public good.[7]

Leicester and Pembroke, as marriage brokers, now wrote to Mary with a formal proposal for the match, adding to it a political proviso for confirming the establishment of Protestantism in Scotland and a league between the two kingdoms. The political contract was sealed when Leslie, Bishop-elect of Ross, Mary's new agent, undertook on her behalf the fulfilment of the stated conditions. The Duke's wooing was furthered by personal correspondence and the sending of a ring along with other offerings of his affection.[8]

In the mean time Norfolk and his allies persuaded Elizabeth to approve renewed talks on a reconciliation between Mary and her subjects, with provision for protecting James's rights and Moray's position. They urged that frayed relations with Spain over the seized treasure and with France over support for the Huguenots (now again in arms) made some settlement in Scotland a necessity.[9] From the conspirators' point of view this was meant to be the prelude to the consummation of the plot. Moray would move for Mary's restoration, with the support of the interested Councillors (and the French ambassador). They would then persuade Elizabeth that this would best be done if Mary were safely married to the Duke. It was to be a revival of the Queen's own scheme of 1564, with Norfolk substituted for Leicester. (Norfolk had been mentioned as a possibility then.) But who was to bell the cat, who was to persuade Elizabeth to be a consenting party to such a scheme? Maitland, it seems, was chosen for this delicate operation.

It was in Scotland that the tangled threads of the conspiracy first began to unravel. Moray was quite reasonably apprehensive as to how

Elizabeth would take to the marriage plans. Pressured by Norfolk and his allies to take the initiative for a Marian restoration, he stalled, demanding, contrary to their plans, that marriage precede restoration. Then, gaining confidence as his own position in Scotland strengthened, the Regent summoned a convention of the estates in early August, which politely but firmly refused to hear of the Queen's return. Further emboldened, Moray arrested and imprisoned Maitland on charges connected with the Darnley murder. All this struck a grievous blow to the project, since it cancelled out the very *raison d'être* for marrying Mary. All was now at sixes and sevens.[10]

Through the summer Norfolk busily canvassed support for his enterprise among the English nobles. One agent went north with letters for Sussex, now Lord President at York, for Derby, the great mogul of Lancashire, and for the two Catholic Earls of Northumberland and Westmorland, who had already dabbled in the fringes of the conspiracy. He won varying responses, none of them wholehearted. Northumberland, who would have preferred a Spanish match, went along at Mary's command; Westmorland did not disapprove but warned Norfolk he might be in trouble with the Queen. Derby flatly rejected the scheme, told the Duke to leave well enough alone, and doubted the reliability of his allies when it came to a pinch. Sussex refused judgment and also warned Norfolk against his allies. To his own deputy president, Gargrave, Sussex expressed his fears for the Queen's safety.[11]

By now the foreign ambassadors, French and Spanish, were being drawn into the network, presumably by Ridolfi. The newly arrived Spaniard, de Spes, when he consulted his home government, received no answer from the slow-grinding mills at Madrid until November, and then only a cautious interest. It was left to Alva at Brussels to decide, and he was more than cool towards the whole project. The Frenchman, Fénélon, got speedy instructions to back the match, largely because he persuaded the Queen Mother that the Spanish opposed it.[12] Talk of the marriage was now becoming general: the governor of Berwick reported it was common gossip throughout the north; Cecil certainly knew of it by mid-July and probably much earlier. Time now pressed; the conspirators would have to face the Queen or she would find it out for herself.

There was, however, a second dimension to the plot, linked to it but also tied to quite another set of issues. The conspirators aimed not only at bringing off the match but also at toppling Secretary Cecil. He could, of course, be counted on to offer rock-like opposition to the marriage scheme, and his removal, or at least his neutralization, was a prerequisite for the success of the whole scheme. This was not all; his opponents, above all Leicester, had other aims. They bitterly resented his predominating influence with the Queen, especially in foreign-policy matters. It seemed an auspicious moment to launch an attack on him. The seizure of the Spanish treasure in December 1568 had led to an embargo and the seizure of English shipping in both Flemish and Spanish ports. This risky venture, the first of its kind which Cecil had urged on the Queen since 1560, made her deeply uneasy. At the same time his support of the Huguenots in the current round of civil war threatened a simultaneous crisis with France. On the latter issue there may have already been an attack on the Secretary in 1568.[13] In any case he was more vulnerable than at any time since the beginning of the reign.

Cecil's opponents had support among the London merchants, dismayed by the trade embargo, and, of course, the enthusiastic backing of the Spanish ambassador, de Spes, who hated Cecil with a passion which clouded his judgment. The spokesmen of the anti-Cecil party in the Privy Council were Norfolk and Arundel, but they found substantial support even from Councillors usually his friends. Our knowledge of the events surrounding this episode comes largely from the suspect sources of ambassadorial reports or the correspondence of Ridolfi. Fénélon's are the more reliable; de Spes was too much involved personally to give an impartial account. There can be no doubt Cecil was in trouble, as his correspondence with Sussex in May shows. The Lord President deplored the fact that the Secretary and Norfolk should 'stand in worse terms of amity than heretofore' and Cecil, lamenting the injustice of the Duke's charges, resignedly looked forward to a change; 'I may percase use less diligence in service and gain more quietness.'[14]

The story which emerges from the ambassadorial correspondence is roughly this. During the winter Norfolk and Arundel, using Ridolfi as an intermediary, sent a message in cipher to de Spes, expressing their disapproval of present policy towards Spain and — more astonishingly — talked of a possible Catholic restoration which they would extract from the Queen.[15] The ambassador needed little encouragement; he had already proposed to his French colleague a joint embargo to force Elizabeth to restore Catholicism. (This received a very cool response from Fénélon although his government afterward took up the idea.)[16] The French envoy did, however, think there would be 'some alteration in the affairs of this realm'.

Ridolfi, writing at the time, painted a highly coloured picture of events to come. Norfolk and Arundel, backed by Derby, Shrewsbury, Pembroke, Northumberland, and Lumley, would bring about a restoration of Catholicism; the first step would be the overthrow of Cecil. Leicester would join them in this enterprise, although he was not privy to their religious goals. The French would be invited to cooperate; Ridolfi would travel to Rome for a papal brief.[17]

A more plausible account comes from Fénélon's pen.[18] According to his letter at an Ash Wednesday meeting (25 February), Leicester took the lead in attacking Cecil for conduct endangering the state. When the Queen retorted sharply, Norfolk raised his voice; turning to his neighbour, Northampton, he said, 'See, my lord, how when the Earl of Leicester follows the secretary he is favoured and well regarded by the queen but when he wants to make reasonable remonstrances against the policy of Cecil, he is frowned on and she wants to send him to the Tower. No, no, he will not go there alone.' Northampton agreed vigorously, applauding Norfolk's attack. They then pushed forward a demand that Cecil give an accounting of his policy for the past eight years. When the Secretary pointed out that Leicester would be involved in such an investigation, the latter declared he had only followed Cecil's lead. It is probably no coincidence that Cecil's great state paper, reviewing the past decade and exploring the future, dates from just this time. The debate over further aid to the Huguenots, on the table at this juncture, gave the plotters another stick with which to beat the Secretary. They warned of the risk of war with both Continental powers. The Queen pooh-poohed this but expressed her anxiety for peace.[19]

In April Ridolfi, pushing for a Franco-Spanish embargo, was urging Pius V to lend the weight of his authority to the proposal. Norfolk and his fellows on the Council considered a bloc abstention from business, which would bring the Queen to yield to them. In May they seem to have made some headway in forcing Cecil to give a greater share in business to other Councillors (possibly referred to in Cecil's letter to Sussex). They had, as we have seen, persuaded the Queen to renew negotiations for a Marian restoration, which was, of course, part of the marriage plot. But in June the balance shifted decisively, and Cecil could write exultantly that God had favoured him, saving him from 'some clouds or mist in the midst whereof I trust my honest actions are proved to have been lightsome and clear ... I find the Queen's Majesty my gracious good lady without change of any part of her old good meaning to me.' Relations with Spain were easing;

the tension with France was at least no worse. The assault was dispersed and Cecil stood unharmed.[20]

Cecil had been able to disarm one of his opponents. He was in a position to do a considerable favour for Norfolk. The Duke was involved in litigation arising from the inheritance of his late wife, whose first husband had been Lord Dacre. Norfolk was laying claim to the Dacre lands in behalf of his stepdaughters. Cecil, as Master of the Wards, had the power to favour the ducal claims, and the judgment given on 12 July was indeed in Norfolk's favour.[21]

What is to be made of these fragments of unclear and uncertain evidence? Cecil's own letters reveal that the Queen's confidence in him was under strain. The very considerable risks of war with Spain in the wake of the seizure of the treasure, added to the concomitant crisis with France, were just the kind of situation which irritated and agitated the Queen. Since both were of Cecil's making, it is probable that his opponents were able to play on Elizabeth's irritability. Cecil may have made a tactical retreat by conceding a larger share in deliberations to other Councillors; but as soon as it became clear that the Spanish would not retaliate by force, royal nervousness diminished. The conspirators did persuade the Queen into reopening the question of Mary's restoration. Beyond this they made no headway with Elizabeth. The Queen was quite prepared to check Cecil's plans when they pushed her into unwelcome difficulties, but she had no intention of being manœuvred into his dismissal by a clique of clamorous courtiers.

In the mean time the marriage conspiracy was foundering under its own weight. Maitland could not perform his part; Leicester agreed to take over as interlocutor with the Queen, but then procrastinated from day to day, always with a new excuse for not acting. Mary was demanding of the Duke what he would do if Elizabeth refused the scheme. Norfolk, increasingly desperate, flitted from one one confidant to another, begging advice — Leicester, Throckmorton, even Cecil.

He waited too long. The Queen through her ladies caught wind of the plan; Leicester took to his sick-bed and then tearfully spilled the whole story to his mistress. The court was on a summer progress through Surrey and Hampshire, and it was to Titchfield House in the latter county that Elizabeth summoned the Duke to explain himself. There in the gallery she heard his stammering confession, and he felt the whole force of her royal wrath. She commanded him to give over the matter altogether. According to one account, he attempted to make a case for the wisdom of the match and asked that the Privy

Council consider it. The Queen contemptuously replied that the Privy Council had nothing to do with it. The chill of royal disapproval soon pervaded the court. Norfolk's allies, Pembroke and Arundel, were in the country, and the courtiers present hastened to ostracize the unlucky duke. Leicester, duly penitent, found royal forgiveness without difficulty. He speedily withdrew his countenance from his former ally.

Abashed, Norfolk set off for London without leave, stopping to see Pembroke *en route*. Arundel wrote warning that the conspirators were in danger, while Ridolfi, Lumley, and the Bishop of Ross urged seizure of the Tower. Ross visited the Duke secretly in London, bearing Mary's reproaches and demanding to know what Norfolk would now do. The latter stoutly replied that he would return to his country house and consult Pembroke, Arundel, and other friends. But, the Bishop countered, what if the Queen orders him brought to court by force? 'There would be no nobleman in England accept that charge at her command, for he knew their whole minds, especially those of the North, who would assist him and if he might once have that open quarrel against the queen, that she did did first pursue him . . . he would have friends enough to assist him.'[22] His actions soon belied his boastful words.

When the Queen now summoned Norfolk to the court at Windsor, the Duke, struck down with migraine, lingered at Howard House. Then, fearing that the Tower loomed, he fled to his country house, Kenninghall in Norfolk. A Queen's messenger followed him with a peremptory summons to court; the Duke took to his bed and begged a delay.[23]

The court was now fully alarmed. Orders had already gone out to Lords Hereford and Huntingdon to assist Shrewsbury in strengthening the security of Mary's confinement, while the forces in the Tower were augmented and the ports closed. The potentialities were grave. The Howards enjoyed in East Anglia a dominating regional pre-eminence, dating back to the late Middle Ages. There was no countervailing magnate presence of sufficient weight in the area, and the local gentry of Norfolk and Suffolk were long accustomed to look to the dukes as their natural overlords.[24] The nightmare which hovered in the background of Tudor consciousness, of a rising triggered by a great regional magnate in support of a national grievance — the syndrome of the fifteenth-century disorders — seemed about to become real.

The Queen wrote to Lord Wentworth, the leading East Anglian

peer after the Duke, ordering him to consult with the sheriff on necessary measures of security. At the same time a circular was sent to the lord-lieutenants of the shires for distribution to the JPs. In a very conciliatory vein, it asserted that Norfolk had gone to Kenning-hall in fear of the Queen's displeasure, but added that he had written he would remain a faithful subject, 'and so we heartily wish and trust he will, considering there is no other cause.' To counter malicious rumours the circular goes on to say: 'Her Majesty hath not meant any wise towards the said Duke of Norfolk any manner of thing to him offensive.' She wanted only to explain her prohibition on his match in the presence of the whole Privy Council. The duke is 'a just and true servant.' The nervous and apologetic tone of the document is a sure indication of the court's very real fears about the Duke's intentions.[25]

The Duke, at Kenninghall, attempted to justify himself, expressing his fears of imprisonment without a fair hearing, reiterating his intention to do nothing without royal approval, and reaffirming his loyalty. The Lieutenant of the Gentlemen Pensioners now arrived with a second summons; the two versions which he bore reflected the court's uncertainty about the Duke's behaviour. One was threatening in tone, the other conciliatory; the lieutenant was presumably to choose the one appropriate to the situation at Kenninghall.[26] The Duke had had consultations with his East Anglian gentry clients; they were firm in urging him to obey the summons. Yielding to their advice, Norfolk set out for Windsor, only to be intercepted at St Albans by an order to place himself under house arrest at Burnham in Buckinghamshire. His train of forty attendants was dismissed without incident, and a week later the Duke was lodged in the Tower. On the road from Norfolk he had written to the northern earls advising them not to rise; at Royston a message from Throckmorton warned him not to try to shift blame to his confederates; if he did, he would forfeit their support.

The other conspirators were civilly invited to court, where the three peers, Pembroke, Arundel, and Lumley, were kept in house arrest. Ridolfi and the Bishop of Ross were detained in the custody of Francis Walsingham; Throckmorton was confined. Leicester got off scot-free; as Cecil discreetly put it, 'considering he hath revealed all that he saith he knoweth of himself, Her Majesty spareth the more her displeasure towards him'.[27] None of them suffered severely: Pembroke was readmitted to council and office (he died in March 1570); Arundel was detained longer and sent into genteel exile at

Nonsuch; Throckmorton was restricted to his farm at Carshalton.[28] As for the Duke, the official line was that his actions were ill-judged rather than criminal, the result of poor advice. In any case, on what was known it would have been difficult to mount a successful prosecution. For the time being he lingered in the Tower.[29]

In retrospect it is tempting to write off the whole enterprise as grossly misconceived and curiously amateurish. Yet these were no inexperienced politicians but practised courtiers from the inner circle of power, who presumably anticipated success. It requires more analysis. First one needs to look more closely at the participants in the plot. Three at least were discontented men. Norfolk was conscious that his importance in the royal counsels came nowhere near matching his princely rank. He resented the upstarts who surrounded the Queen and enjoyed her confidence. Arundel, similarly, was a peer of ancient lineage who felt himself consistently undervalued. Throckmorton was a politician of large ambitions whose prospects seemed bright at the opening of the reign. Brash and outspoken, he pushed his views a little too noisily on the Queen. His early alliance with Cecil faded when the Secretary's influence was used to exclude him from the Privy Council. After his return from France he looked to the patronage of Leicester, or even to a link with Mary, to advance his blocked ambitions. All three saw the marriage scheme as an avenue to greater influence.

Leicester's case was different. Partly he was moved by the opportunity which the marriage scheme offered to dislodge his hated rival for the Queen's ear, Cecil. Secondly, he was making a political calculation as to his future. His position rested solely on the Queen's favour; he did not yet have the kind of independent power base in the country which would sustain his fellow nobles under a changed ruler.[30] Hence it seemed political common sense to throw out a line to the Marian camp, to the probable heiress to the English throne. A subsidiary consideration may have been the calculation that once a successor was in place there would be no more talk of a marriage for Elizabeth, no rival for her affections.

The logic of the scheme the cabal proposed was fundamentally sound. If there were an official demand from Scotland for the restoration of Mary, Elizabeth could hardly refuse it, but then the question of a husband who could keep her in hand became urgent. The Duke of Norfolk, mentioned as a possibility earlier on, was the inevitable candidate. But the scheme depended on formal Scottish pressure, and it was here that the structure was flawed. A key role was assigned to

Moray, a conspirator not by choice but by force of constraint. It is hardly surprising that he sought the first opportunity to escape. Nor was the analogy on which the conception relied a sound one — Elizabeth's plan for marrying Mary and Dudley in 1564. One bridegroom would be substituted for another. This, of course, overlooked the fact that in the earlier year Mary held the best cards in her hand and Elizabeth was desperate to find a husband who would bend the Scottish Queen to her will. Now the Queen's object was to prevent another marriage, with all its attendant implications for the succession.

The conspirators began to lose their nerve in the summer of 1569. The Scottish phase of the plot had gone awry altogether; Cecil was firmly established in royal favour. The prospects that the Queen would consent to the match were ever fainter. Increasingly they behaved like a pack of schoolboys, indulging in a forbidden prank and terrified of being found out. After all their busy comings and goings, their solemn conclaves, and their formal exchange of agreements, none of them dared approach the sovereign. It took but a puff of the royal breath to send their house of cards tumbling.

The Queen's lenient treatment of the major offenders reflected her cool contempt for their actions. Leicester came to heel quickly, whimperingly repentant. Arundel, Pembroke, and Throckmorton were sent off to cool their heels in rural retirement. Norfolk was a more difficult problem. He had been the principal offender, offering his hand to Mary and setting up as a prospective royal consort. His wealth and rank had made him momentarily a threat to the public safety, and even in prison he remained a source of worry. His fall had been peculiarly humiliating to one of his great rank, dressed down by the Queen and sent to prison not as a dangerous traitor but as a political fool. His personal honour was touched by his abandonment of his betrothed bride. Weak, vain, easily led, he was something of a loose cannon. Cecil shrewdly urged that he be found another wife before he was tempted again.

11

The Northern Rebellion

The courtiers' plot was now firmly in hand, but there was a second core of discontent much more dangerous to the crown than the scheming of a few discontented court politicians. Norfolk on his way to captivity had sent an urgent warning to the two northern earls, Northumberland and Westmorland, that if they should rise his head was forfeit. The message was a clear indication of the seriousness of the earls' disaffection as well as the extent of Norfolk's association with their doings.

Northumberland had from the beginning been a reluctant recruit to the Norfolk marriage plot. His goals diverged widely from those of the courtiers. Never happy with the changes of 1559, he blurted out in his blunt way the hope that Cecil 'with his singular judgment' would be 'blessed with godly inspiration to discern cheese from chalk ... and to bring Her Majesty to the truth.' In 1567 he was formally reconciled to the Catholic fold by the returned exile priest, Copley.[1] When Mary arrived in England he had sought to reach her, and through his associates had kept in touch with her thereafter. As we have seen, he also visited de Spes, putting out a line to Spain. Besides his religious convictions, Northumberland had other reasons for discontent. The Percys' hereditary pre-eminence on the Borders, shattered under Henry, restored by Mary, had now been set aside by Elizabeth. Northumberland had been deprived of the wardenship of the marches and excluded from the council of the north. In addition, he had been denied what he felt were valuable mineral rights. He was encouraged in his disaffection by another aggrieved northern aristocrat, Leonard Dacre, brother to the late Lord Dacre and, in his own eyes, rightful successor to the title. The Neville Earl of Westmorland shared many of these bitternesses with his brother-in-law Northumberland.

Their objectives were nothing less than the restoration of the old religion. Mary, liberated and proclaimed the Catholic heiress, would be free to find a suitable Catholic husband, presumably abroad. They did not hesitate to seek foreign assistance towards their goals. Leonard Dacre had apparently told the Spanish ambassador, in June, that if Philip sent a force to England, the Catholics would raise 15,000 men. For the present, however, they were constrained by the advice of Mary herself to go along with the Norfolk match. From their point of view Moray's defection and the Queen's flat refusal to sanction the match were good news. The Duke would now be driven to arms and the ball would bounce back into their court. With his influence on their side they could hope for a general uprising to support foreign aid.[2]

They were all the more furious at what they saw as Norfolk's cowardly collapse. He had, indeed, left them in an exceedingly uncomfortable position, where it was dangerous to advance or retreat. As Northumberland's messenger put it to de Spes, the choice was 'to yield my head to the block or be forced to flee and forsake the realm for I know the Queen's Majesty is so highly displeased at me and others here that I know we shall not be able to bear it nor answer it'. The other alternative was to attempt a rising, but Northumberland's doubts about this move were reflected in his plea for 20,000 crowns to finance insurrection – or an assured refuge in Flanders. De Spes could do no more than send a messenger to Alva and urge the earls to keep quiet, advice in which Mary and her adviser, Ross, concurred.[3]

Before this advice reached them the earls had taken up arms. With the Duke hardly in the Tower, rumours had swept the North Riding and the bishopric of Durham of an impending rising. Sussex immediately summoned the earls to York (9 October); on their appearance they swore to oppose any such movement. The Lord President optimistically put a good face on it and urged the court that no further action ensue, 'until winter when the nights are longer, the days worse and the waters bigger to stop their passage if there be any stir.'[4]

The Council in London was less optimistic; it sent down orders for a 'general state' of each shire, an assessment of its political and religious loyalty, while all JPs (and ex-JPs) were ordered to take the supremacy oath. Finally, the Queen herself commanded Sussex to order the two earls to come to London. When Sussex passed on this order Northumberland pleaded business, while Westmorland more honestly declared: 'I durst not come where my enemies are without bringing a force to protect me as might be misliked.' Sussex's final effort foundered when the jittery Northumberland was scared off by a false report of impending arrest by force. On 14 November the earls rode into Durham and raised their standard of revolt.[5]

What had brought the earls to this desperate resolution? Neither of them wanted to take to arms, and they had twisted and squirmed in an effort to avoid doing so. In part the answer lay in their own panic fears that they were so compromised that their heads were already forfeit. Partly it was the persuasions of the imperious Lady Westmorland, who scornfully told them that their inaction would shame them forever and leave them nothing but to crawl into their holes. Similar persuasion came from their adherents among the neighbouring gentry. Behind Lady Westmorland's words loomed the whole inheritance of the Percys and Nevilles. Hereditary overlords of the border counties for generations, they were prisoners of their own past. Their ancestors, endowed by the crown with wide powers to keep order and to defend these troubled borderlands, had enjoyed virtually palatine autonomy, but since the end of the last century the crown had consistently eroded that authority by substituting its own officials. Hence the rising was in some measure a last pathetic assertion of a fading greatness.

Northumberland and Westmorland found themselves political dinosaurs, trapped in a change of climate. Their northern compeers, Shrewsbury in the West Riding and Derby in Lancashire and Cheshire, had made shift to adapt to the new order. Both were Privy Councillors, and the Queen was so assured of Shrewsbury's loyalty that she entrusted him with the custody of Mary Stuart. The two border earls stumbled on blindly, committing political suicide by dabbling in plots with the Queen of Scots and the Spanish ambassador until, trapped by their own feckless miscalculation, they were left with no alternatives but foredoomed rebellion.

The rebels had commenced operations by seizing Durham, entering the cathedral, where they pulled down the communion table, threw the Book of Common Prayer on the ground, and commanded the celebration of mass. This presumably signalled that religion was the motif of their actions. In fact, they were quite unsure of their strategy. In debating their course before raising their standard, they had divided bitterly. Northumberland's supporters urged religion as their cause, while Westmorland declared such quarrels were accounted rebellion in other countries, and 'he would not blot his long stainless house'. The fact that Elizabeth was still uncondemned by Rome troubled those who urged the sanctity of a legitimate prince. They were torn between habits of obedience to their anointed sovereign and their lingering loyalties to the old religion. Consequently they spoke with more than one voice in their manifestos. At Ripon they displayed the banner of the Five Wounds of Christ, evoking the tradition of 1536, while mass was celebrated in the collegiate church. In this version of their proclamation, evil counsellors threatened the 'true and Catholic religion towards God'. Yet in another proclamation, sent to Lords Derby and Monteagle, they barely mentioned religion, only mumbling about the consent of 'sundry the principal favourers of God's Word'. The thrust of the document lay in the question of succession, and appeal was made for the support of the 'high and mighty prince the Duke of Norfolk' and 'divers others of the ancient nobility of this realm' in laying it to rest.[6]

The course of the rebellion reflected the confusion, the ambiguities, and the half-heartedness of the opening days. The occupation of Durham occurred on 14 November. The possibility of a dash southward to free Mary was closed off by the promptness of the government in placing her in safe keeping. The Lord President marshalled his local forces while the militia of the Midlands moved northwards. Berwick, Carlisle, and Newcastle held firm for the government; the northern nobles to a man not only refused support to the rebels but mobilized for the crown. By the end of the year, without having fired a shot, Northumberland and Westmorland were fugitives in Scotland, the former soon a captive in Mary's old prison at Lochleven.

Consequently the process of suppressing the rebellion was less a campaign than a mere military demonstration, accompanied by extensive looting of the helpless countrymen. Hunsdon, the governor of Berwick, had come north immediately to assist Sussex in the initial mobilization before going on to his command. In the west Lord Scrope, Warden of the West Marches, and the Bishop of Carlisle rallied Cumberland to the crown's service. A relief army moved up from the Trent Valley, commanded by the Privy Councillors Clinton and Warwick. The only obstacle they encountered was the snow-blocked roads.

There was an after-shock in the new year. Leonard Dacre was in London when the rising broke out; by the time he reached the borders, the earls had fled, but his own involvement in their schemes was now plain to the government. Desperate, he obtained some help from across the border and raised his own tenants. In February Lord Hunsdon, the Queen's cousin, won the rare honour of a note of royal thanks when he encountered and destroyed Dacre's forces in the only engagement of the campaign. Dacre followed his allies into exile.[7]

Primary responsibility for dealing with the outbreak lay with the Earl of Sussex, Lord President of the North. Sussex's public career had begun in Ireland; after his return in 1565 he had attached himself closely to the Howard interest, had become an outspoken opponent of the Dudley marriage, and had been sent on the ill-starred mission to Vienna to woo the Archduke. Norfolk had sought his support for the marriage scheme, but Sussex had refused to give an opinion and had warned the Duke not to trust his fellow conspirators. However, strong suspicions of the Earl's loyalty hung around his head when the rising exploded. The Queen was critical of his failure to secure Northumberland before the revolt began and wrote to rebuke him. His bastard brother Egremont Radcliffe joined the rebel ranks. There were plenty of detractors at court to taint his reputation. However, his prompt handling of mobilization, the ill success of the rebels, and the warm recommendation of the trusted veteran Sadler won the royal trust, although even in February 1570 it was necessary to defend the Earl's innocence in the previous summer's intrigues.

Sussex's steady and efficient loyalty was a valuable asset to the government, not only in the obvious sense of his services in the north, but because the support of such an eminent 'conservative' served to bring back into the fold that segment of opinion which had been disaffected by the failure to deal with the succession and half-inclined to look to a Stuart solution. He was duly rewarded by a place in the Privy Council and the lord chamberlainship in the next year.[8]

In retrospect the rising was a non-event, but at its outbreak the government's worries were real enough. The crown and its ministers had two fears. One was a repetition of 1536, a mass rising throughout a region where disaffection to the established church was widespread. The second, linked to it, was a national rising of the substantial body of Catholic sympathizers to whom the Earls had somewhat hesitantly appealed. Neither happened; the coalition of separate grievances, knitted together by court intrigue, which had made the rising of 1536 so formidable was entirely lacking in 1569. The Earls could command the support only of their own tenants and dependants; the countryside, perhaps a little sluggishly, rallied to the crown's representative.

Nor did the second danger materialize. The logistics of a hastily organized rising in a remote corner of the country were hardly favourable to its spread. Only two southern Catholic peers acted; Lords Montague and Southampton took ship for Flanders. (Adverse winds brought them home again.) Only at Kenninghall in Norfolk was there a pathetic demonstration by the local peasantry in support of ancient custom and the liberties of God's church.[9]

Yet however feeble the Catholic response within England had proved, these events had served to jar into decisive action the highest authority in the Catholic world. The Papacy, which for a decade had withheld its thunders against the heretic English regime, responded to the pleas of the rebel earls by a declaration of war. The bull *Regnum in Excelsis*, issued in March 1570 (and received in England in May), formally deposed the Queen and dissolved the bonds of obedience of her Catholic subjects. For the moment Rome was a paper tiger, but it would now exert all its efforts to stir up the Catholic princes to act against the heretic Queen.

Nevertheless, with the final suppression of the revolt Elizabeth had good cause for self-congratulation. As Cecil complacently observed, 'The Queen's Majesty hath had a notable trial of her whole realm and subjects in this time when she hath had service readily of all sorts without respect to religion.'[10] A decade earlier, at the beginning of her reign, Elizabeth had enacted a series of sweeping changes in the national religion. She and her ministers were well aware that, although there had been no overt resistance to the new order, many of her subjects, great and small, were at the least no more than lukewarm about it, and many hankered after a restoration of ancient practice. What could not be calculated was the intensity of this feeling and the likelihood of its taking the form of overt opposition. The events of 1569–70 had provided a satisfying demonstration of the political weakness of the Catholics and the loyalty on which the regime could count.

The Queen and her ministers had cause for their satisfaction, yet they had also been favoured by fortune. The rising had taken place in an outlying region, away from the centres of population and under a very locally based leadership. They were also lucky in a sense which was still veiled from their view. The insurrection occurred before the dynamic impulse of the Catholic reform took root in the English Catholic community. Catholicism was still dormant, looking nostalgically backward, without a sense of direction. A decade later the risks might have been far greater; for the time being the government could breathe a sigh of relief. As in other matters, it had been singularly fortunate in the timing of events.

The dawn of the new year 1570 saw the English political skies rapidly clearing as calm weather set in again, but north of the border the barometer, more or less steady since Mary's flight, was falling fast. On 20 January the Regent Moray was assassinated by one of the Hamiltons at Linlithgow. Even as Mary's English fortunes plummeted, her party in Scotland took new hope. The event threw all English calculations into disarray now that the column around which they had built their Scottish policy had fallen. The Marians set up an alternative government in their Queen's name, while their opponents squabbled among themselves. A new Regent was not chosen until July. The problem was compounded for the English by the presence of the fugitive earls and the fear that they could find means in the chaos of the border to mount a new attack.

Elizabeth's policy towards the Scottish conundrum was shaped by her rigid disapproval of illegitimate regimes. She steadfastly declined to recognize the legitimacy of James's government, and now refused to lend English backing to any of the factions among his supporters, jockeying for the regency. This, of course, did not prevent her ordering Sussex to move into Scotland to clear out the nest of border lairds who sheltered English fugitives. However, when the Earl went beyond his remit, taking advantage of his advance to oust the Marian lords from Linlithgow and pursuing them into the Clyde valley, the Queen recalled him.[11]

Her reasons for caution lay not only in her own conservative disposition but also in the re-emergence of French intervention in Scottish affairs. French interest was twofold. The English had been fishing in the troubled water of French civil strife, and this was a chance to give tit for tat by diverting English attention elsewhere. Secondly, they were anxious to keep Mary out of Spanish hands, knowing as they did of her supporters' bid for Philip's support. They forthrightly demanded English withdrawal from southern Scotland, and Elizabeth, anxious to avoid a 'kind of war', ordered Sussex to pull back. Charles IX cancelled plans for the dispatch of forces from Brittany.[12]

Behind these actions lay hours of anxious debate in the Council. As early as March 1570 a group of Mary's friends, led by Leicester, were pressing for her restoration, for a settlement with Spain, and for the release of Pembroke and Arundel. When French pressure was added to their persuasion, the Queen reluctantly agreed to treat with Mary about a restoration.[13] Leicester's motives in this episode reveal a turning-point in his career. He was moving away from the merely careerist direction of his previous actions to a newfound public role. His support for Mary rested on a larger base than concern for her immediate fate. In his reading of the political runes he foresaw Spain as the looming menace to English security. Now that Philip had overcome the Morisco rebellion at home and Alva had recovered control over the Low Countries, Leicester was deeply suspicious of the Spanish ruler's future intentions. Fear of Spain dictated friendship with the French government and that, in turn, the restoration of Mary.[14]

Cecil read the signs differently. The immediate menace to English security lay in the Catholic-dominated court of France; England must support her natural allies, the hard-pressed Huguenots, taking a chance on stopping French intervention in Scotland by force if necessary. Mary was to be kept in strict confinement; some even hinted that her life ought not to be spared.[15] All this dissension among her advisers was very trying to the Queen; she complained bitterly about the divided counsel they offered her.[16] In the end, events seemed to turn against Cecil. The Huguenots made peace; the Morisco revolt was crushed; the papal bull was launched against Elizabeth; and the Spanish massed a fleet in Flemish harbours, allegedly to escort home the new Queen of Spain, but many Englishmen suspected a descent on Scotland. The Secretary resignedly capitulated: 'God send Her Majesty a good issue of this Scottish matter whereunto the entry is easy but the passage within doubtful and I see the end will be monstrous.'[17]

Elizabeth saw no alternative; as she admitted to Sussex, it was difficult to see how Mary could reasonably and honourably be kept under continued restraint.[18] Mary, by acceding to harsh preconditions for a treaty, had further cut the ground out from under the objectors. Elizabeth's retreat, however, was a merely tactical one, since she appointed Cecil and his close ally, Mildmay, to deal with the Scottish Queen, and the demands they carried with them would reduce a restored Mary to a mere cipher in her own kingdom.[19] James would be brought to England; Mary's enemies would occupy all the important offices, and Scottish foreign policy would be tied to English. For all this Mary was to have an implied right of succession after Elizabeth's lifetime. By sending such commissioners with such powers, Elizabeth was doing all she could to impede the success of negotiations. The English agents and James's representatives between them kept the bargaining at Chatsworth dragging on, month after month, into the spring of 1571.[20] By March Cecil was already putting together a scheme for Mary's permanent detention, and in May Elizabeth found a way to adjourn proceedings until the Scottish Parliament met.

In Scotland the infant King's party had on the whole prospered. In the summer his paternal grandfather, Lennox, was chosen Regent and

Dumbarton, the Hamilton stronghold, was taken. On the other hand, Edinburgh, castle and city, had fallen into the hands of Grange of Kirkcaldy, the castle's commander, who refused to acknowledge either side.[21] Playing for time by dragging out the treaty with Mary had paid off. By early 1572 the kaleidoscope of French politics had brought the Huguenot party into a working alliance with the French Queen Mother. Their suggestion of a match between her younger son and the English Queen was taken up by her. This new amity put paid to Mary's hopes of French assistance. The Scottish pot ceased to boil and could be set on the back burner for the time being.[22]

12

The Ridolfi Plot

The opening of the marriage negotiations with the French court and the improved position of the King's party in Scotland relieved Elizabeth of the pressure to continue treating with Mary. For the Scottish Queen this turn of events was crushing. Ever since her arrival in England she had pinned her hopes on her English friends and played her cards accordingly. The collapse of the Norfolk marriage scheme and the crushing of the northern rebellion had been discouraging setbacks, but the death of Moray had renewed her prospects in Scotland and she had counted on the joint efforts of her Scottish adherents, her friends in the English Council, and the French court to win her freedom. Now all these hopes had vanished; the Scottish Marians were in retreat while an Anglo-French *entente* seemed to be in the making.

These disconcerting circumstances led her to recalculate her diminishing assets and to the making of a fateful decision. She must adopt a new strategy. Since she could not count on either English or Scottish support to achieve her goals, she must look abroad — not to faction-ridden, war-torn France, but to Spain. This meant playing a different hand. Her strongest card in this game was her Catholic faith. In order to woo an English clientele, she had made gestures which suggested she might be brought to a change of religion. Now, to arouse Spanish interest, she must become resolutely Catholic and present herself not only as the rightful heir but also as the Catholic heir whose accession would bring back the old religion. Moreover, she must abandon the semi-public manœuvres of the last couple of years for clandestine conspiracy with the Spanish court and the prospective use of foreign invasion to forward her cause. It was, of course, a measure of her declining fortunes that she should have to turn to such desperate, and dangerous, courses.

There was to be a new drama with a new plot and a different set of actors; but one performer from the previous production was called on to play the lead in this new one. For Norfolk Mary's enchantments had not lost their potency; even before he went to the Tower he had written to her, and the correspondence continued through 1569 and 1570. At Christmas and again at midsummer the Duke sent rings to her. There was consultation on her negotiations with Elizabeth and the Scots, and she advised him on his submission to the English Queen in summer 1570. In the mean time Norfolk's friends in the Council (including Leicester) pressed hard for his release, and in August 1570 he was allowed to move from the Tower to Howard House, although still under restraint. Then the correspondence lagged; still expressing his devotion, he showed himself lukewarm in doing anything on her behalf which might incur risk to himself.[1]

In January 1571 another actor returned to the stage, the Florentine banker Ridolfi. Released after a brief detention, he had been busy printing copies of the bull which Pius V had belatedly issued in support of the earls and in distributing papal alms to the English exiles in Scotland.[2] He was now to play the role of tempter; the apple which he offered was nothing less than a letter from the papal nuncio in Paris promising papal funds to pay for a Spanish army of invasion if Mary's English friends would rise to join the invaders. After some hesitation, Mary made the fateful decision to cast in her lot with these new patrons.

Her first step was to write to Norfolk. Her letter contained a realistic survey of her chances. France was interested in her only as a pawn in dealings with England and in blocking a Spanish match (Don John of Austria, for instance). Philip would support her, but only as the standard-bearer of Catholicism. She might marry Don John, but she preferred Norfolk, who, she believed, could restore the Roman Catholic faith in his country. This tickled the Duke's vanity; more truthfully she should have said that she needed an English husband if she was to enlist English support for her scheme.[3]

The Bishop of Ross pressed Norfolk to see Ridolfi, and after two clandestine meetings the Duke agreed to head a rising if Alva came with 10,000 troops (including 4,000 horse). When Ridolfi demanded a letter of credence to carry with him, Norfolk would go only so far as to give a witnessed verbal agreement. In the documents which reached the Pope, Norfolk declared himself a faithful Catholic anxious to restore his faith, and agreed to prepare either Harwich or Portsmouth for Alva's reception.[4]

The logic of Mary's decision is fairly obvious, but what had led Norfolk to such perilous courses? Pretty clearly he had never abandoned the dream of a royal marriage and future royal status for himself. Nevertheless, he was slow to take any steps to realize it. Ridolfi had just the sharp tool in hand with which to prod the Duke into agreement. The Florentine reproachfully pointed out that the Duke's failure of nerve had betrayed the northern earls and left Mary stranded. If he failed to respond to her appeal, Mary would have to look to Don John or some other prince. This touched Norfolk in his most sensitive point, for he was a man acutely conscious of his princely status, aware that it was not matched by political consequence, and bitterly humiliated by the events of 1569. His honour was at stake. He gave his sullen assent to the terms Mary demanded. Ridolfi set off for the Continent in the late spring of 1571. Alva's response was simply to send him on to Rome and Madrid; the Pope recommended him to Philip (with the reminder that nothing could be done that year), while the Spanish King agreed only to further consideration of his proposal, while warning Mary's adherents not to act without his support lest they suffer the same fate as the northern earls. Later in the year, after de Spes communicated the failure of the scheme, Philip set aside 200,000 crowns for possible use in an English enterprise.[5]

Ridolfi vanished from the English scene forever, returning to his native city where he died full of years in 1612. His comet-like flight across the English horizon would lead the Duke to the scaffold and fatally damage Mary's prospects in the English succession. The conspiracy he had woven consisted of the merest gossamer, spun by his fecund imagination, and floating far above the cold earth of political reality. That he should have taken in anyone is a matter for astonishment but also a clue to the levels of unreality in which Mary and her adherents now lived.

The government, of course, initially knew nothing of these plottings. They did know of various schemes devised by private parties, including some of the Stanley family (but not the Earl of Derby), the Spanish ambassador, and several Catholic peers; but none of these was really serious.[6] The first inkling they had of the Ridolfi scheme came by chance when a passenger at Dover attempted to pass certain packages which aroused the officer's suspicion. They contained ciphered letters addressed to the Bishop of Ross; even then, they nearly passed when Lord Warden Cobham's brother persuaded him they would ruin the Duke of Norfolk, and induced the Warden to substitute fake letters. However, the messenger was imprisoned, and by tapping his correspondence the government discovered there was something afoot involving Ridolfi and proposing a Spanish invasion. They placed Ross under detention (in the Bishop of Ely's household) but found out nothing more. All this was deeply worrying, and additional proof that the Queen of Scots' very presence poisoned the body politic. Elizabeth's advisers even attempted vainly to halt the Queen's summer progress. Ironically, it was while she was staying in one of Norfolk's own houses that they finally stumbled on the silken clue which led them to the heart of the mystery.

Even then it was a byway which led to discovery. Fénélon had asked Norfolk to expedite funds for the Marian party in Scotland; this was done through the ducal servants on the northern estates of his Dacre inheritance. It was the discovery of this correpondence which led the Council to examine the Duke's secretary. Secretly arrested and taken to the Tower, he broke down and by his revelations opened to their eyes the whole scope of Ridolfi's conspiracy, as well as the dealings of Mary and Norfolk since 1568.

Norfolk was soon back in the Tower (September 1571). The crown then moved to build its case against him. The widest publicity was given to the evidence available. A meeting of peers heard an account of it in the Star Chamber, a gathering of Londoners in the Guildhall, while pamphlets were printed and circulated to the country at large. The trial took place in January 1572, under the deeply respected Earl of Shrewsbury as Lord Steward, assisted by twenty-six lords, virtually half the peerage and including almost all the earls. The crown was anxious to avoid any imputation of a rigged trial.

The main charge of treason was that of conspiring to overthrow the Queen and alter the constitution of church and state; this rested on the evidence both of the Ridolfi plot and of the earlier scheme for marrying Mary. The crown argued that Mary laid claim to the throne in her own right, that Norfolk knew this, and that he intended to pursue it by force. 'All these matters considered, the seeking of this marriage in this form must needs be high treason within compass of the statute of 25 Edward III.'[7] The government took the opportunity to lay out the details of all Mary's doings in the fullest possible way, those with Norfolk and those with the Spanish ambassador. The trial was intended not only to end the Duke's life but to destroy Mary's reputation.

Yet thanks to Elizabeth the Duke in fact survived for some months after his condemnation by his peers, in spite of the virtually unanimous clamour of the royal advisers for his execution. Cecil (Baron Burghley since February 1571) summed it up by his argument that mercy would only endanger the Queen by giving hope to her adversaries: 'What more hope can be given to the evil than to see impunity which some impute to fearfulness of the queen, some to lack of power in her hands by God's ordinance; yea, some to the Scottish queen's prayers and fasting.' Nevertheless Elizabeth, faced for the first time in her reign by the shedding of noble blood, and that of one of her servants, drew back. There was in her a deep aversion to placing her signature to a document which doomed a member of her circle to death. For weeks she wavered, signing and then revoking. It took the meeting of Parliament to push her to act. There the clamour was not only for Norfolk's life but for that of the Queen of Scots. The Queen could ease her conscience by shifting the burden to other shoulders. On 2 June the Duke finally went to the scaffold.[8]

That event closed the book on a chronicle which had opened four years earlier, when Mary crossed the Solway Firth in May 1568. The fears that Cecil had expressed at her arrival were borne out by events. This wild foreign fowl set loose among the domestic English flock had set them all quacking and fluttering, creating chaos all about her. Now her wings were clipped and she was shut away where she could do less harm.

In these years Elizabeth's attitude toward her cousin gradually hardened. Initially her royalist prejudices made her sympathetic to Mary's plight and outraged by the insolence of the Scots lords. Under the pressure of events that sympathy began to wane. Although Elizabeth stubbornly refused to recognize James as King of Scotland, she did in fact do business with his government. Faced by the probable consequences of a restoration, she shifted ground. Brute political fact edged aside even her deepest feelings about royal inviolability. Mary's role in the events of 1569 forfeited what remained of Elizabeth's sympathy. It was all too clear that Mary was her enemy, and a very dangerous one. When circumstances forced negotiations for a restoration in 1571, the English Queen took good care to cripple the proceedings. Henceforward Elizabeth's attitude towards Mary was one of determined but coolly measured hostility. Everything was done to ensure that the Scots Queen should be politically neutered and that her public reputation should be blackened. But in her personal capacity she was still royal, to be treated with the respect owed to her rank, a royal bird in a gilded cage, free to twitter as much as she pleased but never to fly free.

However, if Elizabeth was resolved to neuter her cousin politically, she was equally determined to protect her life. This became clear when, in the Parliaments of 1571 and 1572, Mary's enemies mounted a campaign calling for her head. The government had been keen to give as much publicity as possible to the misdoings of Mary. How effective these efforts had been was revealed when the Parliament of 1571 met. Indeed, their success proved an embarrassment as the tide of anti-Marian sentiment threatened to rise beyond the bounds the Queen wished to set. The royal ministers had in the wake of the papal bull of deposition prepared a bill to strengthen the treason law. Based on Henry's act of 1534 (partially repealed under Edward) it provided penalties for speaking or writing of the Queen as a heretic or usurper. Upon its first reading, that stout Protestant and general 'man of business' Thomas Norton offered another bill, to be tacked onto the first. It was aimed at any persons (or their children) who had or would make a claim to the throne in Elizabeth's lifetime or 'say she hath not lawful right or shall refuse to acknowledge her to be undoubted queen'. In addition, it would make treasonable the aiding or maintaining of such a person, or the assertion that the Queen in Parliament could not determine the succession. Norton's intent was clear – the total exclusion of Mary and James, mother and son, from laying claim to any right in the English succession.[9]

There followed vigorous debate, in which the main issue was the retrospective character of the intended legislation; but government efforts to keep the two bills separate failed, and a merged bill went up to the Lords. The next stage of its legislative history is obscure; pretty certainly the Queen intervened. She objected that 'others might unaware be trapped' (she meant James) and so 'we misliked it very much; being not of the mind to offer extremity or injury to any person'.[10] What resulted after further consultation between the Houses was a bill which eliminated the retrospective provisions but disabled any would-be successor who in the future claimed a right to the throne, usurped the royal title, or refused, on demand, to recognize Elizabeth as lawful sovereign. To this the Queen gave her approval.

Only a few months after the dissolution of 1571 the horrid facts of the Ridolfi plot were uncovered. In January Norfolk was tried and condemned. But what of the royal accomplice? Was existing law sufficient to deal with the acts of a foreign sovereign? There was undoubtedly widespread pressure on the Queen to summon a Parliament. Ambassador Smith, writing from Paris, threw up his hands: 'God preserve Her Majesty long to reign over us by some unlooked for miracle, for I cannot see by natural reason that Her Highness goeth about to provide for it.' To make things worse, Elizabeth fell dangerously ill. She finally consented to the summons of a new Parliament, although not until the Treaty of Blois with France was safely signed.[11]

On 8 May Lord Keeper Bacon apologized for a session at this unseasonable time of the year (as the plague season began), but asserted that the causes for its summons were weighty and brooked no delay. New treason laws must be devised to protect the Queen's life in the light of the recently revealed 'great treasons and notable conspiracies'.[12] The Speaker, Robert Bell, broached the matter more openly. Some believed, he said, that there was a person in the land whom no law could touch. He denied this was so; if it were, it defied common reason. 'Sure it were much like as one should maintain that the killer of a phip [sparrow] should be punished and a murderer go scot-free.' The law was adequate, yet it might be best to take the matter to Parliament, where the whole matter could be fully considered and further remedy devised. In conclusion, Bell reiterated what was to be a common but heart-felt theme, the benefit of Elizabeth's rule. She had freed them from foreign rule, unsound doctrine, and persecution of the faithful. Greater yet, 'God hath inclined your heart to be a defence of His afflicted church throughout all Europe'.

The court then laid the grounds for legislation. Thomas Wilbraham, Attorney of the Court of Wards, in a long report to the Commons, laid out all the Queen of Scots' hostile acts since the beginning of the reign. Her use of the royal English style in 1559, her refusal to ratify the Treaty of Edinburgh were retailed along with more recent matter – the Norfolk marriage plot, her connections with the northern rising, and finally, in great and explicit detail, her dealings with Ridolfi, including the scheme to bring a foreign invader into the island.[13] In the debates which raged in the House in the next few days Members did not hesitate to call for Mary's head and to urge the execution of the condemned Duke of Norfolk. Norton declared Mary's execution to be a matter 'of necessity; it lawfully may be done ... a general impunity to commit treason was never permitted to any.' One Member who attempted a defence of Mary was ordered to appear at the bar of the House to answer charges.[14]

The main business of the session continued when Wilbraham reported for the joint committee of the two Houses two alternative bills to deal with the matter. Based on the judges' opinion that the facts against Mary showed treason in the highest degree, one bill would simply attaint her, with the usual penalties. It would disable her from claiming the crown and would make it treason to allow her title. The other limited itself to pronouncing her incapable of succession. The Queen preferred the second; the first would involve hearing and examination of the culprit by a committee of the Houses, and would risk Members' lives in the plague season. This was met with a storm of protest from the floor. The risks to the Queen were too great for delay; the snake must be crushed before it lashed out again. The House resolved as a whole 'to make choice of proceeding against the Scottish queen in the highest degree of treason and then to touch her in life as well as in title and dignity'. The upper house gave its support.[15] A petition followed, replete with biblical citations provided by the bishops, but sharpened by the blunt lay argument that there was no safety for the Queen while Mary lived. It availed nothing with the Queen.[16]

A bill, backed by Councillors, was then introduced into the Lords, approved there, and sent to the lower house. After more debate it was passed. Inordinately long, it contained a flat denial of Mary's right in the English succession and condemned any action by her to obtain it. She could be tried under the procedure for peers' wives. An attempt to lay a claim after the death of Elizabeth would condemn her followers as enemies of the realm.[17] The bill then waited on the Queen's pleasure. It was expressed at the close of the session. To the dismay of her councillors, the royal response was 'la royne s'avisera', the traditional formula of a royal veto. The Queen diluted her refusal to sign by asserting a mere suspension of judgment. She liked the substance of the bill, but found flaws in it not to her liking. Parliament was adjourned to November, when it was 'to repair hither again for the further accomplishment of her pleasure'.[18] The Councillors could only wring their hands at the royal unwillingness to strike down a foe so dangerous to herself and to her realm. Parliament did not meet in November, nor again until 1576. Nevertheless, their fears were not, for the time being, realized. Not until the late 1570s did circumstances once again make Mary an active threat to Elizabeth's security. It would be well into the next decade before the fate of Mary Stuart would once more monopolize another parliamentary session.

In spite of the revelations of the Ridolfi plot, of Mary's involvement in schemes for invasion, Elizabeth remained resolute in her determination to limit reprisals against the Queen of Scots to constrained seclusion in an English country house. She was allowed the usual amenities of such a life and when problems of health rose was permitted to visit the baths of Buxton. She was accorded the dignities of her royal rank; her claims to the English accession were never quite wiped out and her son's reversionary rights were protected.

It is clear that during both the 1571 and 1572 Parliaments Elizabeth was under the heaviest pressure from within the Council and court to kill her cousin. There was no difficulty in stirring up an excited Parliament to demand Mary's execution. The Queen, cool-headed and dispassionate, gave them their head, allowed them an invigorating canter, and then pulled in the reins. She saw to it that maximum damage was done to Mary's political reputation, that she was plentifully tarred as an intriguer who plotted the invasion of the realm by alien armies. Yet black as her deeds might be, she was in the Queen's eyes a fellow sovereign and a kinswoman, who stood above the common course of justice and whose actions were not to be submitted to the judgment of subjects. Nor were the inalienable rights of her royal son to be jeopardized by the sins of the mother. Elizabeth was determined at all costs to defend the rights of her own order.

What the turbulent years from 1568 to 1572 brought home to Englishmen and to their Queen was that their domestic politics, like those of France, had been 'internationalized' in an age of fifth columns. In 1562 Elizabeth had exploited the vulnerability of her neighbour, and her fishing expeditions in the troubled waters of French politics had continued, albeit with reluctant royal consent. Now, although they had escaped the disaster of civil war, the English found themselves uncomfortably vulnerable to the attention of their neighbours. Up until the arrival of Mary in Cumberland, England had seemed relatively immune to outside meddling in her domestic affairs. Now the Stuart Queen's presence provided a person and a cause around which English Catholic discontent could organize, while the papal bull of deposition had given the highest sanction to their efforts to overturn the existing regime. However, as they were well aware, they were too weak to hope for success without foreign aid. Both the northern earls and Mary Stuart had turned almost instinctively to the Catholic King as their saviour. He himself had responded tardily, but not dismissively, although Alva remained more than cool to the English overtures and Philip's ambassador had intrigued damagingly. Nevertheless, the door had been opened; Philip's attention had been secured. When circumstances were favourable, Mary and her supporters could hope for renewed Spanish interest. The English crown had won the first round, but was served notice that it must be on the alert for a second encounter.

Part IV

The Struggle for Peace
1572–1585

13

England and Her Continental Neighbours, 1559–1572

France 1568–1570

Mary Stuart landed in Scotland in May 1568, precipitating a prolonged domestic crisis; in the autumn the French civil war, in which the English were soon entangled, broke out. In November 1568 the fugitive Spanish treasure ships arrived, and England was flung into a confrontation with Spain which was still festering when the rising of the Dutch rebels at Brill in April 1572 opened up a new source of friction. While Elizabeth struggled to deal with her unwelcome Scottish guest, she had also to cope with two major crises in her relations with France and Spain.

Events abroad from 1568 to 1572 inaugurated a new and prolonged phase in Elizabeth's reign in which her attention was drawn away from the insular problems of the last decade towards her troubled relations with her Continental neighbours. That turbulence resulted largely from convulsions within the Continental monarchies rather than from English actions. In the end, the Queen's decade-long struggle to preserve peace by diplomatic means faltered and then failed. By 1585 the last hope of a peaceful outcome had gone; the grim fact of war had to be accepted, however reluctantly.

The Treaty of Cateau-Cambrésis (1559), which brought general peace to western Europe after decades of intermittent war, concided with definitive turning-points in the affairs of both the French and the Habsburg monarchies. When the ambitious and aggressive Henry II died from an accident in 1560, he left the French throne to a brood

Map 1: Europe c.1560

Kingdom of Sweden

Territories of the Spanish Habsburgs

Territories of the Austrian Habsburgs

Miles
100   200   300

0   100 200 300 400
Kilometres

Dom.
of the
Teutonic
Order

Muscovite Dominions
(Russia)

Baltic Sea

Duchy of
Prussia

Grand Principality

Kingdom
of Poland

of Lithuania

Khanate of the
Crimea

Archduchy
of Austria

P. of
Moldavia

P. of
Transylvania

K. of
Hungary

P. of
Wallachia

Black   Sea

Republic

K. of
Naples

Ottoman Empire

Constantinople

Aegean Sea

Sea

Crete

Cyprus

Syria

of under-age sons. The first, Francis II, died within less than two years; he was succeeded by the ten-year-old Charles IX; effective rule fell to the Queen Mother, Catherine de Medici. The weaknesses of a regency were compounded by the resurgent ambitions of the great noble houses. The greater French nobility still enjoyed a degree of power which their English counterparts had lost at the end of the Wars of the Roses. Kept in hand by the late King and his predecessors, they now jostled one another in their competition to dominate the court of the boy King. Worse still, their resurgence coincided with the rise of a thrusting and rapidly growing Protestant movement. Popular in origin, it soon recruited from the higher social ranks, and the struggle between the old and new faiths became intertwined with the rivalries of the Catholic house of Guise and the Protestant Chatillons, while the royal cadet house of Bourbon (nominal kings of Navarre) and the Montmorency clan weighed in first on one and then on the other side. By the early 1560s these clashes of interest, religious and political, had exploded into open conflict.

Catherine de Medici, desperately manœuvring to maintain the peace, was able to do no more than engineer temporary short-lived truces. The infection of civil war was now endemic in the body politic, and bouts of raging fever would recur with dreadful regularity for some three decades. As we have seen, the Protestants, the weaker party, looked abroad for assistance from their co-religionists, above all the Queen of England. However reluctant Elizabeth was to become the patroness of international Protestantism, she could not ignore the fact that a Catholic triumph in France would bring to power the house of Guise. Not only were they ardent Catholics but they were the natural patrons of Mary Stuart, whose mother, the late Regent, was a daughter of their house. They could be expected to show an all too lively interest in intervening in Scottish – and English – affairs.

For the house of Habsburg, 1559 was no less a turning-point. When the Emperor Charles V retired from his many thrones in the mid-1550s, he split the family inheritance; the Imperial title with the central European dominions had passed to his brother, Ferdinand. The rest – Spain, the Low Countries, Naples, and Milan – had been bestowed on his son, Philip. In Charles's time the Habsburg 'empire' had been a multicultural collection of lands held together solely by his personal lordship. Chameleon-like, he had been German, Flemish, Spanish, or Italian in turn as his peripatetic court moved from one territory to another. Philip's vision of his role was entirely different from his father's neutrally cosmopolitan outlook. The son identified himself as a Spaniard; in 1559 he left the Low Countries for Spain, and would never leave the peninsula again. From the Escorial, his great palace-monastery outside Madrid, he set about transforming his Netherlandish and Italian possessions into provinces of a Spanish empire, as subordinate to Madrid as the colonies in America. In the Low Countries, where the tradition of local autonomy of each province was strong, this policy met a sturdy resistance led by the great nobles, pre-eminent among whom was the Prince of Orange.

Here, as in France, the appearance of noble dissidence coincided with an assertion of mass-based and militant Protestantism, particularly strong in the great cities of the provinces. And here, as across the border, divergent parties of discontent joined hands. But in the Netherlands, as in Scotland, there was added the resentment against alien rule. In the mid-1560s noble protest was accompanied by iconoclastic riots in the Flemish towns, and in 1568 by civil conflict. The successful suppression of this rising drove multitudes of refugees across the North Sea to England. As in the French case, there was the same expectation that the Protestant Queen of England would support her co-religionists. And, as we have seen, English Catholics — and Mary Stuart — looked to the ardently Catholic King of Spain as their protector. Hence the Spanish threat was seen as more actively dangerous than the French. From the late 1560s English leaders came to fear Philip's intentions towards their nation. Some saw him as the standard-bearer of an international Catholic crusade; even the less excitable Cecil regarded him as an enemy held in check only by constraining circumstance. For the Queen to dabble in Low Countries affairs was to risk war with the strongest power in Europe; to remain neutral was to give too many hostages to fortune. Philip, triumphant in the Netherlands, might then turn his energies to the re-establishment of a Catholic regime in England. In every direction to which the Queen turned her gaze there were menaces too grim to be ignored.

The years following the Treaty of Troyes (April 1565) were quiet ones in Anglo-French relations, varied only by the summertime flirtation between the Queen and Charles IX (see Chapter 8 above), a thoroughly dishonest proceeding on both sides which, however, served to delay the Austrian wooing, to the benefit both of the French and of Leicester. In France the peace of Orleans, concluded between the religious factions, continued to hold until the autumn of 1567, when there was a brief outbreak of fighting which raged until the following March. In this episode English intervention seems to have been negligible; only a stray letter of thanks from Admiral Coligny to Cecil[1] hints at English aid to the Protestants. The renewed peace proved to be illusory. By early September 1568 the Protestants were once again in arms.

This bout of civil war — it would last a full two years — reopened for the Queen the painful problem of how to deal with cries for help from Continental Protestants whose confessional credentials were impeccable but who were tainted in her eyes by the sin of rebellion against their anointed sovereign. The moral dilemma, however much it touched the royal sensibilities, left her Councillors indifferent. For them the issue was a pragmatic one: how to exploit their neighbours' disorders to the fullest advantage without provoking retaliation from the French government. Cecil put it succinctly when he propounded his maxim that the forces of discontent in France should 'be comforted not to desert from their natural defence' since 'they may with less charge annoy the principal enemies than to attend to make an army to issue out of the realm and so consequently the hazard of them is less dangerous to the realm than to send force of the English'.[2] This reflection was Cecil's judgment on the Newhaven venture, engineered by Leicester.

During the first months of renewed strife the Huguenots, while using the English ports to dispose of their prize booty, were allowed to 'borrow' from the royal armoury, and finally a loan of £20,000, secured on pledged jewels, was granted them.[3] However, when the imbroglio with Spain over the treasure ships plunged England into a quarrel with that power, the French government took a strong line and in an ultimatum of February 1569 asked whether it was to be peace or war; the English Council hastily reassured them that it was peace.[4]

In fact the Council was deeply divided; the Queen had to listen to radically diverse counsels. On the one hand Cecil urged continued aid to the Huguenots (all the more urgent after their recent defeat at Jarnac). It was imperative to avert a Catholic take-over at the French court when England already faced the hostility of the other Catholic power. Cecil's opponents, led by Norfolk and Leicester, sought to frighten the Queen with the spectre of simultaneous hostility with both France and Spain, and urged a reconciliation with Philip which would reanimate the ancient Burgundian alliance with the Habsburgs. Simultaneously they proposed to ease tension with Paris by abandoning the Protestants. Along with a changed foreign policy, they aimed at dislodging Cecil from the royal confidence.

Cecil's enemies seem to have scored a momentary gain in diminishing his role in Council, but he soon turned the tables; by early summer he was enjoying full royal favour. The French crisis became less urgent as the Protestants proved unexpectedly resilient, while English attention was distracted by the domestic events of summer and autumn 1569. However, the issue of aid to the Huguenots flared anew in 1570. There was heated argument in Council, and on one occasion the Queen's anger flashed in a rebuke to Cecil: 'Whatever it may be, Mr. Secretary, I want to get clear of this affair and understand what the king [of France] sends me and not to involve myself any longer with you and your brothers in Christ.'⁵ On another occasion she gave vent to her anger at the divided counsel she was offered. In the end the veering compass of French politics provided a resolution to the situation. With a religious truce, the Queen Mother was now balancing the Huguenots and the Catholic Guise parties. In this atmosphere there was, as we shall see below, opportunity for an entirely new relationship between England and her ancient foe.

All this turbulence at home and abroad tested the Queen's mastery of men and events. She dealt with the squabble within the Council with firmness but not without a wobble in her confidence in Cecil. In foreign policy her touch was less certain. When France took to the offensive in spring 1569, she backed nervously away, and again in 1570 her distaste for dealings with the French rebels surfaced. She was willing to dabble on the fringes of the pond, by allowing free trade, volunteers, and even a well-secured loan, but she was determined not to be identified as the religious champion of foreign Protestantism.

The Low Countries, 1559–1570

In the first decade of Elizabeth's reign, relations with her ancient enemy France, always troubled, threatened open conflict no fewer than three times, yet early in the next decade the two nations would draw together in alliance. Relations with the ancient ally, the Habsburgs, less openly ruffled, slowly deteriorated until there was an open break in trade and diplomatic relations. By 1569 Cecil would count the King of Spain as among Elizabeth's ill-wishers.

In part the growing frictions between the princes arose from maladjustments in the diplomatic machinery, in part from the personal shortcomings of individual diplomats. Philip's departure from the Low Countries in 1559 disoriented the traditional arrangements of English diplomacy. Hitherto the main point of contact between the English and Habsburg courts had been Brussels, but now that city had shrunk into a mere provincial capital; essential decisions were made in Madrid. Elizabeth accordingly shifted her embassy from the easily accessible Belgian city to the remote Spanish royal seat. Given the difficulties of communication, either by land or by sea, the successive English ambassadors in Spain found themselves cut off, isolated, and ill-informed. More awkward still was the fact that the main business between the two crowns arose from the commercial relations between England and her Flemish market. There was no longer anyone of diplomatic status at Brussels to represent English interests, while the government there had to refer every matter of moment back to Madrid. Philip's ambassador in London regarded himself as representing Spain, and knew little and cared less about Flemish problems.

This was awkward enough; the situation was not made better by the personality of the first Spanish ambassador accredited to Queen Elizabeth, Bishop de Quadra. This cleric, uncomfortable in the alien religious culture of Protestant England, won neither the respect nor the trust of Elizabeth and her ministers, who treated him with a mixture of levity and contempt. He, on his side, hostile to the religious regime, reported the actions of the English government in the most unfavourable light. His relations with the court sank to a new low when his secretary sold out to the English, providing them with a full budget of his indiscretions.[6] His opportune death in August 1563 may well have forestalled his recall.[7] In his behalf it should be said that, like his English counterpart at Madrid, he was neglected by his home government, badly informed, and underpaid. His plight reflected Philip's minimal interest in English affairs in these years.

De Quadra's successor, Guzmán de Silva, another cleric, was cut from a different cloth. Urbane, flexible, soon at home in the Elizabethan court, he hit it off with the Queen, who favoured his company and made him something of a confidant. His presence eased English relations in the wake of the trade war of 1563–4 and soothed English suspicions when later they were aroused by Alva's policy. He won not only the Queen's but Cecil's commendations.[8] Yet de Silva after a few years' service in London wrote home begging for a transfer from the infected atmosphere of this heretic court. His psychological discomfort was a disturbing sign of the ideological gulf which separated the two kingdoms.

Elizabeth's first two ambassadors to Madrid, veteran professionals, served her competently in what little business they had to conduct.

Their successor, John Man, Dean of Gloucester, was a poor choice; a Protestant cleric was unlikely to be *persona grata* at the Escorial. He proved quite unequal to the task, offended the Spanish court by his indiscretions, and had to be recalled after he was sent into country exile outside Madrid. He departed in 1568; there would not be another resident English representative in Madrid during the Queen's lifetime.

The malaise engendered by the inadequacies of diplomatic personnel offer only a partial explanation of the slowly deteriorating relations between Elizabeth and her former brother-in-law. In sharp contrast to Anglo-French relations in the 1560s, there were no obvious frictions between London and Madrid. The former were bedevilled by a host of painful episodes — the lost dominion of Calais, the French incursion into Scotland, the Newhaven venture, and in the background the traditional English vision of France as the prime enemy. All these matters produced a state of high tension, demanding the constant attention of the Queen. With the withdrawal of Philip from the Low Countries to Madrid, where for nearly a decade he was enmeshed in Mediterranean affairs, Spain drifted into the outer orbit of the English diplomatic universe. One detects to some extent a certain conscious distancing of England from the 'Burgundian' tie after the uncomfortable intimacy of the previous reign. When Brussels offered to intervene in the Scottish crisis of 1560, the government there was politely but firmly warned off.

The most important bond between England and Flanders was, of course, the commercial one, and it was here that friction first arose, in the trade war of 1563–4. The great entrepôt of Antwerp was the focal point of English overseas trade, where the whole cloth export of London was sold and the great bulk of the nation's imports, other than wine, procured. Across England the cloth trade employed thousands of workers; in the City, the Merchant Adventurers provided the principal pool of credit to which the government increasingly looked for financial support.

A series of English enactments, beginning at the end of Mary's reign, had irritated the Antwerp business community. A new rate-book, issued in May 1558, had much increased customs duties. The Act of Frauds, regulating customs procedures, and the Acts of Employment, which required foreign merchants to spend their profits in the purchase of an equivalent amount of English goods, had been enforced more rigorously, while a worrying incidence of piracy in English waters added to the whole array of grievances. From the perspective of the new English government, these were urgently necessary measures to increase its all too scanty revenues. There was also an increasing disposition to use state power to protect the English merchant against his foreign competitors.[9]

A special Flemish envoy, d'Assonleville, sent over with a full statement of grievances, was courteously listened to by the Queen, but no redress was forthcoming. He, on his return, urged strong measures of retaliation against the English, emphasizing the dependence of their whole economy on the Flemish trade. Vigorous action would soon bring them to heel. In December 1563 two decrees, one authorized by Philip, the other launched independently by the Regent at Brussels, embargoed English trade with the Low Countries.

The motives which entered into the embargo decrees were not wholly mercantile. Antwerp, proudly autonomous, was the centre of a growing heretical movement, and Cardinal Granvelle, the Regent's chief minister, hoped to humble the city politically as well as to coerce the English merchants, since Antwerp would suffer no less than London by the suspension of trade between the two. The Cardinal had also the larger hope that discontent in England would be great enough to provoke a popular rising against that heretical regime.[10] The English hesitated between sending an agent with conciliatory proposals and a plan for a general conference on trade or flinging down a challenge; they opted for the latter. A new treaty with the German port of Emden enabled them to shift the whole cloth trade to this new destination. It was a counter-offensive to the Flemish attempt to constrain the English economy and, indirectly, to destabilize the regime. It was also a tentative declaration of economic independence, breaking a network of bonds which had linked the economies of England and Flanders for generations. There can be little doubt that the guiding hand in these moves was that of Secretary Cecil.

The Emden experiment enjoyed some success; and while trading conditions were not so favourable as at Antwerp, the rupture of the old order encouraged initiative in other areas. However, these measures failed to revive employment to a satisfactory level. The government at Brussels was under similar pressure from the unemployed artisans of Antwerp; both governments were pushed to the bargaining table, where they came to an agreement to reopen trade in January 1565.

This confrontation produced fewer problems than the simultaneous frictions with France. There were no complicating ideological considerations; it was a straightforward wrestling match of a kind which had recurred in Anglo-Flemish affairs. The Queen had no hesitation in lending her weight to Cecil's aggressive response to the Flemish challenge. She was willing to follow a line of policy which widened the distance between England and her traditional ally. It was a step in a direction which both she and Cecil favoured, the gradual loosening of ties which limited the English crown's freedom of action. The conclusion of the Emden agreement reassured the Queen that the risks of such a challenge to Brussels were minimal. There was an underlying confidence that in relations with the Low Countries England held the stronger suit. The royal overlord in Madrid had his plate too full with the problems of the Mediterranean world to give his full attention to his Netherlands domains.

That attitude was soon to change. In 1566 a series of dramatic domestic events at Antwerp, in which the English had no direct role, went far to alter Elizabeth's assessments of Philip's intentions towards her and her kingdom. A radical religious reform movement in the Low Countries which had been clandestinely gathering strength exploded into iconoclastic riots of such violence as to frighten the Regent into toleration of public Protestant worship. The toleration was short-lived and the disturbances were suppressed without great difficulty, but the episode shocked Philip II into a drastic decision – to extinguish all trace of heresy in his Low Country dominions. To accomplish this task he sent the Duke of Alva, equipped with a Spanish army, to supersede the Queen-Regent as governor. The Duke's vigorous and unrelenting campaign of suppression was initially successful, but at the cost of losing thousands of skilled artisans, many of whom sought refuge in the Protestant fastness of England.

The English government, during the rising of 1566, behaved with exemplary correctness, as did the English merchants in Antwerp.[11] The Queen declared her express disapproval of the rebels and her satisfaction in their suppression. She told the ambassador that it was not religion which occasioned the uprising. Nevertheless, he believed overtures had been made to her by the rebels, and the very ease with which England granted refuge to the exiles gave rise to distrust.

The coming of Alva's army was, in fact, viewed with dismay and alarm at the English court. There had been rejoicing when Spanish forces left the Low Countries in 1561, and there was now corresponding concern at their return. The Queen questioned the ambassador closely. Why was it necessary to send Spanish troops now that Flanders was quiet? His explanations did not satisfy her; she returned to the subject. In November she reported the rumour that an intended voyage to Flanders by Philip was a cover for an invasion of England, nervously adding that, of course, she did not believe it. A few months later she reported hearing from Germany and elsewhere that a Catholic league — the Pope, Spain, and France — had been concluded. While listening to de Silva's denials, she feared Philip was persuaded by his advisers that there would be no quiet in Flanders as long as England remained Protestant.[12] Later Cecil half-jokingly related the rumour that the Spanish, obsessed with an ambition for world dominion, would assault England.[13] Norris, at Paris, was feeding the home authorities with a steady diet of similar kind. The circulation of such rumours is an index of the smouldering fears, igniting so quickly into a blaze of near-panic, which the English leaders harboured towards the Spanish crown.

In 1568 de Silva in his turn became suspicious of English behaviour, specifically about the Flemish exiles in England, who were using the country as a base to arm themselves for a return home. Appeals to the English authorities to halt such activities got little hearing, and although a royal proclamation was finally issued, the ambassador had little confidence in its enforcement.[14] When Louis of Nassau, brother to the exiled Prince of Orange, the leader of resistance to Alva, took up arms against the Low Countries government that summer, de Silva absolved Leicester from correspondence with him but still believed the Earl had been in touch with the Prince of Orange. He reported a collection on behalf of Nassau organized as a clerical subsidy of a twentieth in the pound,[15] as well as a private subscription to which Privy Councillors were contributing. In the same dispatch he angrily wrote that the English councillors were constantly showing their ill will to Spain and their hopes for a Spanish setback.

When his departure was first bruited, de Silva had written that Anglo-Spanish relations were in a healthy and harmonious state;[16] by the time he had left in September 1568 they were in obvious disarray. Distrust of Spanish intentions made the English edgy, while Spanish suspicion of English backing for the rebels grew. It was, however, a wholly unanticipated event which tore apart the weakened fabric of the Burgundian alliance and opened a permanent rift between the two monarchies.

Alva's normal supply line from the homeland followed the overland route from Genoa, across the Alps, and then down the Rhine. In March 1568 the Elector Palatine had stopped supply barges in the river and impounded a large sum of money on its way to Alva's paychest, a deed which excited Elizabeth's stern disapproval.[17] The Palatine justified his action with the excuse that the money was legally property of Genoese bankers, from whom he proposed to borrow it.

This turn of events forced Alva to turn to the alternate sea route across the Bay of Biscay. These were dangerous waters, infested by privateers sporting commissions from the Queen of Navarre or the Prince of Orange and waylaying shipping of any kind.

A flotilla of Spanish ships set out from Santander in November, laden with new-coined money borrowed from the Genoa bankers. Three of them, pursued by French privateers, took refuge in English ports, two in Cornwall, one at Southampton.[18] de Spes, the Spanish ambassador who had replaced de Silva in September, asked the Queen for protection of the ships against the French, which was granted, and at Southampton an attack was warded off by the local authorities. Elizabeth offered either overland transport of the treasure to Dover or a convoy of royal ships. While Alva hesitated, the situation became more perilous and there was pressure to land the treasure for safety's sake.

Just what happened at this juncture is not entirely clear. According to a memoir of Cecil written in January 1569, the Spanish vessels had been protected by Admiral Winter's royal ships waiting to convoy the wine fleet to Bordeaux. When he had to sail, the Spaniards were no longer safe and the treasure was accordingly landed. But the Secretary's explanation was somewhat disingenuous, since he had written a letter (now lost) commanding the vice-admiral in Cornwall and the captain of the Isle of Wight at Southampton to unload the money. Champernoun in Cornwall responded: 'I have of late received from your honour a couple of letters both tending to one end, which was that I should under cover of friendship use all policy to recover such treasure of the King of Spain as is presently within our western ports.' He recounted his execution of the task and promised to take any blame for the seizure, hoping that when the storm died down he would have royal favour. He added that he was of the mind 'that anything taken from that wicked nation is both necessary and profitable to our commonwealth'. Champernoun, a keen partisan, was later to lose his life fighting with the Huguenots. Horsey, the captain at Southampton, had persuaded the Spanish captain to cooperate, but he was 'so prepared as easily I would have had it whether they would or no'.[19]

In the mean time the English government had been informed, probably by the Italian merchant, Benedict Spinola, that the treasure was still legally the property of Genoese bankers. They had certain proof of this after 24 December.[20] When de Spes, hearing of the landing at Southampton, hastened to court, asking for an audience with the

Queen, he was put off for some ten days; it was not until 29 December that she received him. In the interim de Spes became convinced, on what evidence is not clear, that the Queen intended to seize the money for her own use.[21] He accordingly wrote to Alva urging the seizure of all English shipping in Low Countries ports and, as soon as possible, in the Spanish ports.[22] When the ambassador saw Elizabeth on 29 December, Alva had already taken the suggested action, a fact not known in London until 4 January. In this audience the Queen told the ambassador that she understood the treasure belonged to the bankers. According to Cecil's version, she told him she would give him an answer on the disposition of the money within four or five days. In de Spes's account, the Queen declared she would retain it for her own use, giving him proof of its present ownership within three to four days.[23] In any case the damage was done; as soon as the Queen's government heard of Alva's action, they clamped a seizure order on all Spanish and Flemish ships and goods in English ports. de Spes was shortly thereafter confined to his residence.[24]

What are we to make of this tangled sequence of events? Both sides made haste to justify themselves, placing the blame for the rupture on the other. There can be no doubt that direct responsibility for the embargoes rested on the shoulders of de Spes; his fateful dispatch of 21 December determined all that followed. He wrote out of the conviction that the Queen had decided to seize the treasure. That conviction was shaped as much by his predispositions as by factual evidence. Although instructed to assure the Queen of Philip's friendship and to maintain a civil relationship, he had almost immediately plunged into intrigue, receiving the Earl of Northumberland in a nocturnal visit, corresponding with the Queen of Scots, and entertaining a clandestine visit from her agent, the Bishop of Ross.[25] Moreover, before his audience with the Queen, he had already proposed to the French ambassador a joint Franco-Spanish embargo on English trade in order to overthrow Cecil and then to restore Catholicism.[26] He had also prepared an elaborate treatise to be presented to the Queen in which, with much theological argument, he demonstrated the incontrovertible truth of the Roman Catholic faith and called upon the Queen to submit herself to the Council of Trent, promising Spanish aid against any opposition.[27] With such a frame of mind he was quick to jump to preconceived conclusions about English actions.

Yet it is not absolutely clear what English intentions were. It is impossible to believe that the Queen and Cecil would have deliberately ignored the consequence to the English economy of a break with

Spain. The merchants of London were quick to lay their fears before the Privy Council in the last days of December.[28] Nevertheless, there are certain ambiguities to be explained. The Spanish ambassador was put off for nearly ten days when he asked for an audience. During those ten days, rumours of a possible seizure of the funds were circulating, as the anxieties of the merchants show. Nor was Cecil's memoir altogether disingenuous, since it was not a response to Admiral Winter's departure but a command sent by the Secretary which led to the landing of the silver. Champernoun's letter suggests there was intent to deceive the Spanish captains; it also hints that Cecil was at that point acting on his own. Finally, the Queen's answer to de Spes, even if we discount his assertion that she told him she would retain the money, is ambiguous. She merely promised a decision in four or five days. Clearly the English government did consider the possibility of retaining the money, and may have decided to seize it before de Spes had his audience.

Once the crisis had broken, the English took as harsh a line as possible in exploiting its possibilities. When Alva made an overture by sending over an agent, d'Assonleville, he was given a very cold shoulder, and it was made plain that restitution of the money depended on a general settlement of grievances, both commercial and diplomatic. Cecil's own state paper of these weeks laid out his conviction of Philip's ill will to the Queen. A whole litany of grievances was listed, including the expulsion of ambassador Man, alleged discourtesy by Alva to the Queen, and refusal to ratify the old treaties of friendship. The paper argued forcibly that Spanish intentions towards England had been unfriendly since the opening of the reign.[29]

The English advantage in these negotiations was much strengthened once they were able to find a new outlet for the cloth trade. This was accomplished by implementing an already existing treaty with Hamburg. The first cloth fleet to sail to that port departed in May. Although Hamburg was not a wholly satisfactory substitute for Antwerp, it was to remain the main trading base for the cloth trade for the next decade.[30]

With these advantages on her side, the Queen showed no intention of yielding to the persuasions of Alva. The Duke was anxious to arrive at some accommodation with England, but his efforts were undercut by the blundering intrigues of de Spes, whose links with the Queen of Scots and the northern rebels in the autumn of 1569 further soured English feeling towards the Spaniards. An emissary, Chiapin Vitelli, dispatched by Alva just as the revolt broke, was widely seen as a spy, even as the potential commander of an invasion force, and in the end was advised to leave the country.

There was some shifting of attitudes in 1570, when the interned sailors and merchants were freed on both sides,[31] but no settlement ensued. De Spes's involvement in the Ridolfi plot and his subsequent expulsion from the country ruptured diplomatic relations altogether. Only a Spanish merchant in London, de Guaras, remained as an unofficial agent. In the mean time, major shifts in the French political scene opened up new possibilities which turned English attention in a new direction. Relations with the Habsburgs were allowed to drift; it was not until 1574, under much-changed conditions, that a settlement was patched up in the Treaty of Bristol. It conceded the terms the English had demanded at Bruges almost a decade earlier, but by this time the Dutch revolt had ruptured the whole pattern of English trading relations with the Low Countries.

The Queen showed herself much bolder than she had been nearly a decade earlier in the Scottish crisis. She accepted the risks entailed in laying hands on the treasure, and supported the strong line taken with Alva in the aftermath of the embargo. Her only sign of wavering came in the spring of 1569, when there were embroilments with France and Spain simultaneously, but this was a short-lived hesitation. Relations with the Habsburgs did not at this point involve dealings with rebel subjects of another sovereign. Unlike the French, with their Scottish connections, Spain lacked the power to retaliate. Nevertheless, Elizabeth's conduct in this affair suggests a new confidence and a willingness to take risks which would have caused her to falter in the past. In her dealings with Spain and with France, Elizabeth was striking out into bolder and more aggressive actions.

The events of 1568–9 had precipitated a diplomatic revolution. Ever since the religious settlement of 1559, England's relations with her ancient ally had been beset by a lingering uncertainty. The Queen's decision to opt for Protestantism had been viewed with dismay in Spain, and necessarily chilled the atmosphere of mutual confidence. However, it was only after the dispatch of Spanish troops to the Low Countries that the hostility latent in their religious differences began to surface. Every aspect of their intercourse was now seen in a new light. Philip's conduct at Cateau-Cambrésis, his attempted intervention in the Scottish crisis in 1560, the trade embargo of 1563–4, even Alva's tardiness in writing to the Queen on his arrival in the Low Countries, were all interpreted as unfriendly acts. Even the well-regarded de Silva had been unable to quiet English fears, and the feckless intrigues of de Spes went far to confirm them. The longstanding ties with the 'Burgundian' ally were already dissolving in the poisonous miasma of suspicion even before December 1568.

In this darkened landscape each event was distorted into menacing shapes; every action was seen as malign in intent. Philip's intended voyage to Flanders became a mere guise for invasion; the journey of his new Queen from the Netherlands to Spain aroused the same alarm. The lack of English representation at Madrid or Brussels worsened the situation, while de Spes plied his masters with an account of English affairs designed to show the islanders in the worst possible light. Henceforth, every action of the English government would be affected by the fog of distrust and ignorance through which both sides were constantly stumbling.

The Entente with France

The pacification of France which took place with the Peace of St Germain in September 1570 not only lessened the tensions produced by English aid to the Huguenots but opened the way for a possible *entente*. In October one of the Protestant Chatillons, who now, in the new dispensation at the French court, had access to the Queen Mother, suggested the possibility of a match between her second son, the Duke of Anjou, and Queen Elizabeth, a pairing which had been briefly considered in 1565. It would, he argued, draw England away from an Austrian match, and it would provide for the ambitions of this restless and troublesome prince. Catherine listened; Elizabeth expressed her willingness to hear 'of motion and suits for marriage with princes and great estate'.[32] The new ambassador, Francis Walsingham, who arrived in France in the new year, received hints from the French court, and in March Lord Buckhurst, the Queen's distant cousin, was sent over for private conversations with the Queen Mother.[33] There followed formal negotiations for a marriage treaty.

The solemn wooing of a thirty-seven-year-old Queen by a twenty-year-old suitor had a note of the ludicrous about it, which was not lessened by the widely entertained doubt that Elizabeth meant to marry at all. Nevertheless, once the Queen had pronounced her willingness to proceed, the machinery had to be geared up to full power. Through the summer of 1571 diplomats came and went and there were endless exchanges of documents. What were the bare political facts behind the 'suits for marriages with princes and great estates'?

Elizabeth had earlier hinted at the possible renewal of the Habsburg match,[34] and Fénélon thought her motives in pushing the French marriage were primarily to drive a wedge between France and Spain.[35] He was sure she had no real intention to marry. English opinion is reflected in a draft memorandum, corrected by Cecil, in which the pros and cons were set out in stark array. The advantages of alliance with France heavily outweighed the liabilities. There was less to be said for the marriage; in another document the Secretary morbidly considered the possibility that Anjou might shorten Elizabeth's life and make himself King.[36] There was not likely to be much enthusiasm for a consort who might become King of France.

Nevertheless, the negotiation had to be conducted in all seriousness. It had obvious short-term advantages. It cooled French zeal for the cause of Mary Stuart, and eased the nerves of English statesmen who were made anxious by England's lack of allies. The Queen Mother and the King were – or chose to seem – committed to the match; Charles IX would no doubt have liked to see the last of his brother. Anjou was more elusive. Throughout the negotiations the question of religion was the main point at issue. It was convenient for both parties, since each, by taking the high ground of religious principle, could decently veil his – or her – ultimate insincerity in the wooing. When the negotiations ran into the ground in the autumn of 1571, the excuse of religious difference provided a dignified withdrawal for both parties.

Matters had come to a standstill by late autumn,[37] since Anjou stood firm in insistence on his own faith. Walsingham fell ill at this juncture, and at the beginning of January 1572 Sir Thomas Smith returned to his old post at Paris. He was charged with pressing for the match, but Elizabeth was adamant that Anjou must conform to the English church. As a fall-back Smith was to sound out the possibilities of a defensive treaty. It seems probable that the Queen was well aware the marriage proposal was dead and that Smith's real mission was to persuade the French to an alliance.[38] Indeed, it may be that the whole marriage negotiations were meant to be a prelude to real business.

Just after the ambassador's arrival Catherine enquired whether he had a commission for an alliance. Articles for a possible treaty were quickly drawn up; by the end of January Smith was discussing them with French ministers, and in February English Privy Councillors were pursuing the discussion with Fénélon. The changing complexion of French politics during these months helped the process along. The Queen Mother, in her unceasing efforts to reconcile the unreconcilable, had taken into her confidence the Protestant magnate, Admiral Coligny. He had in hand a scheme for French support for the Low Countries malcontents, a direct challenge to Spain which the young King was disposed to favour. Coligny's influence no doubt advanced the signing of the treaty, but it also gave cause for English nervousness. French intervention in the Netherlands might be less attractive than the continuance of Alva's regime.

After several hiccups in the treaty-making process, agreement was reached and the treaty signed on 19 April. A league defensive, it provided that each country would provide 6,000 men and eight ships if its terms were invoked. Scotland was to be settled under a stable government. Smith wrote home that he thought Charles IX 'went as sincerely and *tam bona fide* as any prince can'. Although the treaty was intended as a bulwark against a possible Spanish attack, Burghley took care to reassure Philip of the continuing goodwill of his mistress, and she publicly honoured the intermediary who conveyed these wishes.[39]

The treaty was modest in scope and its execution contingent on conditions which might or might not obtain. There was on each side civility but not much more. Nevertheless it was a change in direction, a turning away from a partnership with the rulers of the Low Countries – whoever they were – which reached back to the Middle Ages. For Elizabeth it was an important change of direction. For a decade she – with the events of the 1550s much in mind – had regarded France as her most troubling neighbour. She had patronized the forces of disruption, openly at Newhaven, more cautiously thereafter. Now she was cultivating an *entente* with that neighbour and, ever so tentatively, compromising her own independence of action. This move signalled the strong sense of insecurity and of isolation which haunted the English rulers as they looked out at the bleak world of the 1570s. Elizabeth trusted none of her neighbours, but the events of 1569 and the following two years had convinced her that Spain was more to be feared than France. Even before the treaty was signed, the new *entente* was to be severely strained by the sea-beggars' (Dutch privateers') seizure of Brill.

A Regime Established

For Elizabeth, 1568 was a year studded with unwelcome surprises. Mary Stuart arrived in Cumberland in May; in the early autumn civil war resumed in France; and in November the arrival of the fugitive treasure ships precipitated a dangerous quarrel with the Spanish. All three events intertwined with one another; all three constrained the Queen into actions which she fiercely resented but from which there was no escape. As Cecil aptly put it in a state paper written in early 1569, the Queen was now 'pacient', i.e. suffering, the victim, the passive recipient of external actions, while the Pope, France, and Spain were the 'workers and authors of her misery'.[40] His unstated but, to him, incontrovertible premise was that the underlying dynamic of European politics was the re-establishment of universal papal power by the Catholic princes. The English settlement of 1559 had necessarily cast England as an enemy of the faith, and the prime Catholic objective henceforward was the overthrow of Elizabeth and her replacement by Mary Stuart. In Cecil's perspective, that England, 'another Eden, demi-paradise, this fortress built by nature for herself against infection and the hand of war', was in grave danger of losing that immunity, surrounded on every side by foes who only waited their chance to strike.

As Cecil saw it, only a series of accidents had preserved England so far – the death of Henry II of France, the quarrels between the Guises and their rivals, the religious strife in the Low Countries, France, and Scotland, internal upsets like the Darnley murder, Spain's wars with the Turks. Now, with the impending defeat of the Huguenots and Alva's successes, the moment was fast approaching when a great coalition of the Catholic powers would throw its weight against England.

From our perspective, with a knowledge of Alva's and Philip's intentions denied to the Elizabethans, it is clear that Cecil's worries were overblown and largely mistaken. With a host of other problems on his plate, conflict with England was a very low priority for the Spanish ruler, however repugnant the English religious polity was to his Catholic sensibilities. What is important is the tone and mood of English perception which Cecil's paper reveals. Given that he was the most moderate and cool-headed of the Queen's advisers, the alarmist character of his views is a measure of the profound fears which permeated English calculations about the danger in which their country stood.

To deal with the immediate problem of the Scottish Queen Cecil had a series of prescriptions which would and, as events proved, could check her intrigues and render her impotent. But the larger, international problems were not so amenable to management. England's poverty in men and money and, above all, her lack of military skills and experience, begotten by the long peace, made war unthinkable.

Cecil wrote vaguely of possible alliances with the Scandinavian kings and the German Protestants, but more practically urged all possible support — short of war — for the forces of discontent within the Catholic monarchies. In the end, however, he believed England must turn to her own resources for solution. To convince his mistress and his colleagues of the necessity of treading these dangerous paths would put him to a severe test.

How far did the Queen share his views? We know her anxious concern for peace. In part it was a feminine revulsion towards blood and violence, in part a realistic estimate of her kingdom's limited resources in relation to her neighbours. Above all, it was a politic perception that the coming of war would wrest from her effective control over men and events. However, she reluctantly acknowledged the paradox that war could be avoided only by playing the dangerous game of diplomatic bluff, a sustained exercise in brinkmanship. Only thus could she win enough respect from her neighbours to warn them off her territory. How far and how well she had learned these lessons would be made apparent by her role in the shaping and in the execution of English foreign relations in these trying years.

By 1572 Elizabeth had served out her years of apprenticeship. Her first step in mastering domestic politics had been her skilful promotion of Robert Dudley from favourite to councillor without forfeiting the confidence of William Cecil or destabilizing the elite political structure. The Secretary never lost his distrust of Dudley or his conviction that the favourite was a self-seeking adventurer, yet he came to understand that the Queen's decisions would not be swayed by personalities but by her assessment of the state's needs. Dudley in his turn showed himself a slow but intelligent learner. In the early 1560s he exercised his patronage indiscriminately, cultivating any interest which might enhance his prestige, Catholic, Protestant, French, Spanish. By the end of the decade he was focusing much more sharply on the patronage of the evangelical party in the English church. That interest in turn led him to the development of a considered view of foreign relations. He saw its survival in England as tied to that of the Continental Reformed communities. While sharing in Cecil's general assessment of England's position, he was groping his way towards a more militant stance in supporting the Reformed cause wherever it existed. His share in the Norfolk marriage plot and the effort to unseat Cecil was his final fling at personal and factional intrigue. It was the last time in which he proposed to push the Queen into a decision by using his personal powers of persuasion. Interestingly enough, his nerve failed him at the clinch.

Yet even as the Queen learned how to assert her mastery over court and Council and her royal elevation above faction or personalities, she became herself an active participant in the continuing conduct of affairs, above all of foreign relations. In their intercourse with the English court, the foreign ambassadors soon found that audiences with the sovereign were no mere exercises in polite formalities or vague generalities, but tough and exacting diplomatic exchanges with a well-informed interlocutor. They found themselves involved in a vigorous cut-and-thrust in which, although the Queen used to the full her royal prerogative of setting the tone and determining the substance of discussion, she heard them out.

In all such business the Queen's closest collaborator was the Secretary. The complaint of Norfolk and his cronies that Cecil monopolized public business and the Queen's confidence was a justifiable one, to which the ubiquitousness of state papers in Cecil's hand bears witness. Every historian who has examined Elizabethan history has had to assess the respective contribution of sovereign and minister to each act of state. There can be no easy weighing of their relative inputs. There was, after a dozen years of experience, a bond of trust and respect on both sides and a remarkable similarity of temperaments. Both shared a certain dispassionate distance from the business of their vocation, a professional objectivity in striking contrast to the violent and often immoderate passions of many of their contemporaries. Yet there were differences. The Queen's royal isolation augmented her temperamental incapacity to enter imaginatively into the passionate convictions of a Philip II or of her own Puritan subjects. Secondly, although her underlying disposition was coolly dispassionate, in her surface reactions she had a short fuse, likely to explode noisily and to lead to hasty and ill-conceived actions. Cecil, calm and considered in his reactions, did not share the idealistic aspirations of a Grindal or a Cartwright, but he did entertain the deepest abhorrence of what was for him the idolatry and superstition of the Catholic faith. His was a conscious moral commitment, albeit negative rather than positive in content; hers was a supremely unselfconscious certainty, resting on the unique assurance of her own regality.

The question of their relative weights in the making of decisions of state cannot be definitively settled, but the advantage clearly lay with the sovereign. Their relationship was one of trust but not of equality, and there was in Cecil's attitude towards his mistress a genuine sense of awe, a tribute to the sacral nature of her office, a recognition that the royal will, although not always wisely exercised, had an inherent power which must be obeyed. The royal judgment might go awry in a particular case, but the subject must yield to a power in which providence had invested the right to give incontrovertible commands. The sovereign might be advised, persuaded, urged to a certain course of action, but in the end her judgment could not be constrained by human agency.

The storms which had racked the political landscape since 1568 were dying away; but another low-pressure area was approaching, not in this case from the Atlantic but from the Continent. The men who would have to bear the brunt of this new storm would include a number of new faces; many of the old would be missing. It was not only a changing of the guard, but the inauguration of a long epoch — some twenty years in duration — in some respects the golden years of the reign, characterized by stability in the governing circle around the Queen and in the larger political world outside the court.

Time and nature were working their changes at the Council board. In 1572 two veterans of Edwardian times died — Winchester, the Lord Treasurer, and Howard of Effingham, Lord Chamberlain. Pembroke had predeceased them in 1570; Arundel, his reputation tainted by his association with Norfolk, remained a nominal Councillor until his death in 1580 but was rarely seen at court. Cecil, now Lord Burghley, succeeded to the Treasurership. Sir Thomas Smith, twice ambassador at Paris, returned to the Secretary's office he had once filled under Protector Somerset.

In the following year a second Secretary was appointed, also recently ambassador at Paris, Sir Francis Walsingham. This dark-visaged man, whom Elizabeth dubbed her Moor, soon assumed a leading role in Council, where he became a kind of *de facto* foreign secretary and the organizer of a highly efficient intelligence network. Single-minded in his political passions, he embodied an intense anti-Catholicism which saw the religious problem in an international perspective. The Catholic world, the Pope, and the Catholic monarchs loomed as the enemies not only of divine truth but also of Elizabeth's England, the secular stronghold of Protestant orthodoxy. Walsingham would never cease to urge the imminence of the threat. In the developing foreign-policy crisis of the next decades he would be the steady advocate of intervention in the Low Countries and in France, and outspoken in his hostility to Spain. It was an outlook little sympathetic to the Queen's coolly secular temperament, and Walsingham would constantly deplore her lukewarmness in the cause, yet he retained her respect and trust.

Howard's post as Lord Chamberlain was filled by the translation of the Earl of Sussex from the northern Presidency, bringing the experience of a long career, first in Ireland and lately in the turbulent north. He would carry weight as a Councillor until his death in 1583, his old enmity with Leicester now muted as the marriage issue faded into the past. He would be the initiator and keenest supporter of the Anjou match. Lesser appointments to the Council included the Earl of Shrewsbury (1571), a permanent absentee, tied to his post as Mary Stuart's warder. Two members of the Dudley family circle joined the Council board – Leicester's older brother, Ambrose, Earl of Warwick (1573) and his brother-in-law, Sir Henry Sidney (1578). The latter, Irish Lord Deputy and Lord President in the Welsh marches, rarely joined his colleagues at court.

In the latter years of the 1570s further changes occurred. Smith died (1577), to be succeeded by the colourless Dr Thomas Wilson, no more than a superior bureaucrat, a political cipher. When Lord Keeper Bacon died in 1579 another lawyer, Sir Thomas Bromley, said to be have been promoted by Leicester and Hatton, succeeded. Two years earlier, Henry Cary, Lord Hunsdon, Elizabeth's Boleyn cousin, Captain of Berwick, had been elevated to the Council, where he would prove a steady attender and a useful workhorse although not a powerful voice.

Far and away the most important appointment, after Walsingham's, was that of Christopher Hatton, who entered the Council in 1577. He had been for some years past an established royal favourite, rival and eventually equal to Leicester in the royal affections. His rise, though widely noted, had not evoked the agitation surrounding Robert Dudley's early career. Hatton was, of course, not a prospective royal husband. Tradition has it that the Queen first noticed him when he danced in a masque at the Inner Temple in 1561. Born in 1540, the son of a minor Northamptonshire squire, he was enrolled in the Inner Temple in 1559. He had no obvious patron, although he may have had some backing from Sir Edward Saunders, Chief Baron, or Parr, Marquis of Northampton, both distant kinsmen.[41]

In any case, in 1564 he entered the corps of Gentlemen Pensioners, the elite royal guard of fifty gentlemen whose duties were more ceremonial than military. Their feats of arms were largely performed in the tilt-yard, and Hatton was to make numerous appearances there in his first years of service. By 1566 he was a court functionary, appointed to such duties as attendance on Bedford at the christening of Prince James. From 1568 he began to collect various offices, wardships, and small grants of land, culminating in the acquisition of the Corfe Castle estate in Dorset in 1572.[42] He was increasingly employed in official business, particularly in Parliament, where he sat, first in 1571 for Higham Ferrers and then, in 1572 and successively thereafter, as knight of the shire for Northampton.[43] In 1572 appointment as Captain of the Yeomen Guard gave him a major household office and close attendance on the Queen. Five years later he was shifted to the Vice-Chamberlainship and entered the Council.

Although Hatton was universally regarded as co-equal with Leicester in the Queen's personal esteem, his relationship with Elizabeth and with the court world was entirely different. His rise to favour was gradual; there was never a question of marital status; and he was not part of any family or factional grouping. He seems to have owed his advancement solely to Elizabeth's own patronage and to his own political sense. Hatton avoided identification with any partisan interest, keeping on civil terms with the established figures. He had a reputation in Catholic circles as a favourer of their cause, even as being a secret co-religionist. He had Catholic family connections and may have been brought up in that faith, but as a courtier conformed unhesitatingly to the established religion and played some role in ecclesiastical politics. Aylmer of London was thought to owe his bishopric to Hatton's backing; Bancroft, successor to both Aylmer and Whitgift, was certainly his protégé.[44]

Hatton made no attempt to found a clientage or espouse a cause as Leicester did. His career was built on the personal regard of the Queen and his role correspondingly shaped as a loyal and reliable executor of her orders — as a trusted man of business. He shone particularly in Parliament, where along with Sir Walter Mildmay he became a prime spokesman for royal policy, put up to press subsidy bills in 1576 and 1581, to quell the Puritans in 1584 and 1586, or to present the case against the Queen of Scots in the same year. His faithful service was rewarded with a surprise advancement to the Lord Chancellorship in the following year.

Since he was never in the running in the marital stakes, his personal relationship with the Queen was quite unlike Leicester's. There, real passion had cooled into companionship. In Hatton's case, although the attraction was real enough, the game was played by other rules. As the Queen's junior (by seven years) he was cast as the perpetual suitor, paying court to an adored but inaccessible mistress, forever sighing for her favouring glance, forever her faithful servant. His letters, signed as her (eye) 'lids' or her 'sheep', when for his health's sake he went to Spa in Flanders, are full of the anguish of the lover separated from his mistress, and of his consuming desire for her presence. The reverse of this coin was, of course, the skilful administrator and supple politician, one of the inner circle of confidants on whom the Queen relied for all the great business of state.

In the last dozen years of his career Hatton was a member of the quartet, along with Burghley, Walsingham, and Leicester, who, under the Queen's tight control, were at the centre of power. These years, from the early 1570s to the beginning of the 1590s, were probably the happiest in the Queen's life, both personally and politically. She was surrounded by a congenial cluster of familiar faces on whom she playfully bestowed nicknames – Burghley her spirit, Walsingham her Moor, Hatton her lids or sheep, and Leicester her eyes. The Queen's resolute loyalty to her ministers, her politic willingness to overlook their indiscretions, and her refusal to allow any one of them to monopolize the royal confidence gave them a sense of security which blunted the mutual rivalries and personal antipathies among them.

Hatton's success encouraged other, younger men to emulate him. During the Queen's middle years a cluster of hopefuls sought to scramble up the slippery pole which led to court advancement. Unlike Leicester, whose cultural achievements were nil, or Hatton, whose literary remains are at best fragmentary, these younger aspirants were all men of literary pretensions, and indeed most of them would win at least a niche in the English literary canon. For the middle-aged Elizabeth the bait which attracted her was not mere physical handsomeness (although that counted). She demanded a lively wit, a ready tongue, and an eloquent pen, the accomplishments of courtiers cast in the mode of Castiglione.

The best-known and most indulged was Edward de Vere, seventeenth Earl of Oxford. Of ancient descent, Burghley's ward and later his son-in-law, hereditary Great Chamberlain, he had easy access to the court, where he became from the beginning of the 1570s a frequent attender. His literary talents were notable but, wayward, restless, and self-indulgent, he wasted his fortune, misused his Cecil wife, and flirted with Catholicism. None of these abated the Queen's regard; in 1579 she granted the now impecunious earl a princely annuity of £1,000. For a moment during the Anjou affair Oxford assumed a political role, as advocate of the match and enemy of the Dudley interest, but when out of pique he betrayed his Catholic associates,

Henry Howard and Charles Arundel, he lost credit and gradually subsided into relative obscurity. He lacked the steadiness necessary for a political career, but the Queen's snobbish regard for noble birth and his literary accomplishments assured him of place and fortune.

Among the other younger men drawn, moth-like, to the royal presence both Philip Sidney and Fulke Greville came well-connected, the former Leicester's nephew and putative heir, the latter the son of an eminent Warwickshire family with close ties to the Sidneys. Sir Edward Dyer was less favoured, heavily reliant on the patronage of Leicester. All of them won some small rewards in grants of land or office and were employed on minor missions for the crown. Sidney's ambitions, of another sort, were tragically realized in the fateful Zutphen campaign. Greville, not much more than half-hearted in the arduous competition for place, was content with modest but profitable sinecures. Dyer, who hoped for more, obtained less.

In 1581 a new star appeared in the court firmament, dim at first but rising meteor-like to a dazzling brilliance. Walter Ralegh, son of a small Devon squire, adventurer in France and Ireland, rose, like Hatton, solely by a personal magnetism which entranced the Queen. Within a few years he received substantial grants of land, the Wardenship of the Stannaries in Cornwall, and in 1587 the Captaincy of the Guard. Yet in the end he did not penetrate the inner sanctum of the Council. Royal indignation at his marriage – in sharp contrast to her tolerance of Leicester's or Essex's matches – excluded him from court for several crucial years. Ralegh too, like Sidney and Essex, hankered after another sort of career than the courtier's; the wilds of Virginia or of Guiana held more attraction for him than the gardens of Hampton Court or Nonsuch.

The comings and goings of these lesser figures were flurries which ruffled the surface waters; but at a deeper level these two decades were an era of political equilibrium, the least troubled of the reign. The great mischief-maker of the previous decades, Leicester, had now changed his spots. There were no more factious plots to dislodge a fellow Councillor. He had been cured of any further temptations to flirt with the Queen of Scots and now stood forth in a more respectable role as patron of the evangelical Protestant interest at home and as champion of the Protestant *internationale* abroad. Yet the underlying personal tensions between Leicester and his colleagues had not vanished. Burghley would distrust him to the end of his life; Sussex's death-bed message was 'beware the gipsy'. Nevertheless, they accepted him as a colleague. Leicester's new-found sobriety and the more consensual atmosphere within the Council owed much, of course, to the gravity of circumstances as Elizabeth was drawn more and more into the vortex of Continental conflicts.

These were also the years in which the Queen took the initiative in seeking to control events. It was her hand which guided the conspiracies with the French princes; above all it was she who conceived and directed the grand strategy of the Anjou match. The ability of the Councillors to deflect or to modify the course of policy decisions was less in these years than in any other period of the reign. She whistled and they danced, however unwillingly.

The Queen's determination to assert her independence of action, drawing the Councillors relentlessly in her wake, had an important side-effect which prevented the hardening of partisan or doctrinare positions. The interventionists would be deeply disappointed by her refusal to give all-out aid to the States General, while her more cautious advisers would look askance at the scope of commitments implied by the programme of the Anjou match. As a result, divisions within the Council remained fluid and reactions pragmatic. Many voices continued to be heard; there was no party of sullen malcontents, embittered by their exclusion from the royal councils, such as the 'Aragonese' party of the mid-1530s.

Stability within the Council had important resonance in the larger political society: here too, fluidity at the conciliar level communicated itself down the political and social scale. Aspirants to promotion in the court world, as well as suitors seeking to enhance their local prestige and influence, knew on the one hand who were the patronage brokers at court but also, on the other, that no one person or party commanded the approaches to the cornucopia of royal bounty. There was more than one route which might serve, and the knowledgeable practitioners spread their bets accordingly.

The credit of one patronage broker or another varied with the vagaries of the royal temper, but there was no need to fear a convulsion within the inner circle of power which might suddenly alter the whole political landscape, as the fall of Wolsey or of Cromwell did in the Queen's father's time. Clashes of personality, as one courtier jostled another in the intense competition of the court world, were common enough, but they did not jar the fundamental stability of the governing circle. Not until the beginning of the last decade of the reign, with the passing of a generation, did that stability begin to crumble.

14

The Crises of 1572 and Their Aftermath

In England the year 1572 witnessed the last acts in the disturbing sequence of events which had begun in May 1568 with Mary Stuart's flight from Scotland and ricocheted on through the marriage plots, the rising of the earls, and the clashes with both France and Spain. Norfolk went to the block in June while an angry Parliament needed no prodding to proclaim Mary a public enemy. She herself disappeared into guarded seclusion.

1572 also marked the close of another and much longer epoch in English political history, dating back to the 1530s and the first moves of Henry VIII against Rome. His acts in that decade had shaken the English polity to its roots and on his death had left it dangerously unsettled. The acts of his two successors had worsened the situation drastically. Their dizzying zigzags first to the left and then to the right had created the potential for the same fatal conflict which was now tearing France apart.

Elizabeth at her accession had chosen a course which she hoped would rally the country behind her and open the way for restored political and social stability. Fortune had favoured her in the weakness of the Catholic party at the time of her accession; adroit management had helped, but for the first decade of the reign it was uncertain how far the new regime had taken root. The eruption of Mary on the scene threatened to reopen the religious rift and to destabilize the political order. The struggle to contain these disturbances had tested the regime to the full; its success was a triumphant demonstration of its robust health. Above all it was a triumph for the Queen. She had now not only mastery of her Council and the court elite but the enthusiastic loyalty of her subjects. Since at least 1570 there had been spontaneous popular celebrations to mark her accession day, 17 November.[1] The official image of the Queen, propagated in Parliament, court, pulpit, and print, of a ruler devoted solely to her people's welfare, a peace-loving protectress, who had ended the ceaseless and fruitless wars of her predecessors and checked restless discontent within the realm, was now being vitalized into a popular and national myth. It would stand her and the kingdom in good stead in the difficult years ahead.

For the next twenty years, when those external pressures were at their greatest, there would be at the centre a structure of leadership robust and flexible enough to contain radical differences as to the conduct of policy without shaking the effective functioning of government at home and abroad. It would be supported by the active loyalty, indeed devotion, of the local aristocracies to a sovereign who was becoming in her own lifetime a larger-than-life myth. The forty years of disturbing uncertainties initiated by Henry's break with Rome, punctuated by violence and intrigue, and troubled by bewildering reversals of the magnetic pole of religious orthodoxy had come to a close. If the domestic skies were clearing, however, the foreign horizon was already darkened by storm-bearing clouds.

The regime had dealt successfully with the domestic threats to its security, but in its relations with its neighbours had achieved little more than a breathing space in a continuing struggle. The conclusion of the Treaty of Blois had brought a France where, for the moment, the Protestants, led by Admiral Coligny, had a major voice at court into a tentative alliance with England. The future of the new-found *entente* as an effective force in European politics depended on the continuance of a potent Protestant voice in the French court, a highly speculative probability. The English had been careful to reassure the Spanish that the treaty was not directed against them. As a practical demonstration of goodwill, some measures were taken to ease the rupture of commercial relations while the two countries edged towards a resumption of normal trade.

These hopeful auspices of a calmer season were quickly blasted by the two great seminal events of 1572 which shook the Spanish and French monarchies — the rising in Holland and Zeeland and the massacre of St Bartholomew. They would shape the destiny of the two Continental monarchies for decades to come. They would have no less effect on the fortunes of the English monarchy. The consequences which flowed from these events would preoccupy the Queen and her ministers down to the last day of her reign.

France, 1572

Even before the signing of the Treaty of Blois, the new-formed amity was put to a severe test. On 1 April the pirate/privateer de la Marck, sailing under the colours of the Prince of Orange, made what was intended to be a raid on the little Zeeland port of Brill. To his surprise it triggered off risings across Holland and Zeeland and escalated quickly into an insurrection which provided the Prince of Orange with the base for action which he had hitherto sought in vain. The English government played a key role in this event: it was a royal proclamation denying de la Marck the use of English ports which drove him to his attack on Brill. There is no evidence that this was what the Queen desired. Her action in issuing the prohibition was dictated by complaints about piracy from Hamburg, at the time the English cloth staple; she could not ignore them.[2]

Although the Queen expressed her horror of the rebellion to Alva, the immediate reaction of the English government to the event was to allow some hundreds of Flemish exiles, armed and supplied, to flock home. The object, as Burghley succinctly put it, was 'to let them of the Low Countries pass home to the liberty of the country; and I think it were done rather by themselves than others [the French] that percase would not suffer them long to enjoy their liberty when it should be recovered.'[3] The same consideration obtained when English volunteers began to arrive in Zeeland in May. They were under direction from the English government; although they had come over to aid the rebels, they were instructed that, if French interest threatened to take over the uprising, the English bands should go to Alva's assistance.[4]

In the end Coligny's scheme for intervention in the Low Countries was defeated by the Queen Mother's opposition and by events. An Orangist invasion under Louis of Nassau, launched from French soil, was crushed immediately. Before the end of the summer the convulsion at the French court ended any possibility of French intervention, although as late as August Burghley was warning the English captain in Flushing that the garrison there should contain no foreigners except Englishmen.[5]

Yet even as the English sought to check French intervention in Zeeland, possibilities of a new tie between the English and French courts were being pursued. After the failure of the Anjou marriage proposals, the French had offered a substitute bridegroom, the prince's younger brother, the Duke of Alençon. This scheme was now under active discussion.[6] Then, suddenly, the flimsy fabric of the Anglo-French *entente* was ripped apart by a bolt of political lightning. Catherine de Medici had now resolved on a devastating reversal of policy, nothing less than the wholesale slaughter of the Huguenots, beginning with the assassination of their leader. Coligny's murder on St Bartholomew's eve, 24 August, was followed by the mass slaughter of thousands of his co-religionists all over France.

The reaction of many Englishmen was predictable. Burghley saw the massacre as an example of divine wrath, as did Leicester.[7] Walsingham, writing from Paris, pointed to the obvious secular consequences. With Coligny gone, the Guises again in the ascendancy, his pithy comment about the French was: 'I think [it] less peril to live with them as enemies than as friends.'[8] Burghley would have recalled Walsingham, leaving only a secretary to represent England. The Queen, more coolly calculating in her reaction and moved by political rather than religious considerations, determined otherwise. She received the French ambassador, Fénélon, in solemn silence, reproached and rebuked his master, but then allowed him to state his case.[9] The French court did its best to compose a credible justification for its acts; the Queen was at least willing to listen, and in the end pretend to believe. In October Elizabeth agreed to be godmother to a new French princess. Relations remained intact, and by Christmas Fénélon was once again *persona grata* in court circles.[10] London was filled with refugees, and when it became apparent that the Huguenot cause survived, supplies began to flow again. French fears of English intentions re-emerged while the English carefully watched for signs of French interest in the pro-Marian garrison which held Edinburgh castle. Nevertheless, thanks to the Queen, the alliance, however tattered and torn by recent events, was still in place.

The years 1573–6 were an era of whirling confusion in French politics. In France, as in the Low Countries and Scotland, confessional divisions criss-crossed the rivalries of the great noble dynasties. In the years after St Bartholomew these dimensions became more and more visible as the *politique* clan of the Montmorency moved towards alliance with the Protestant Bourbon interest, led by the Prince of Condé. Added to these complications were the bitter rivalries within the Valois brotherhood. The King's health was failing, and it was the Duke of Anjou who took the lead in assaulting the remaining

Protestant strongholds while his younger brother, Alençon, flirted with moderates of all stripes. Anjou, to the King's relief, accepted the throne of Poland in 1573; but Alençon proved more troublesome than his older brother, and the last days of Charles IX (who died in May 1574) were troubled by a conspiracy which involved both Alençon and the Protestant prince, Henry of Bourbon, the King of Navarre.

Amidst this turmoil it is hardly surprising that the English were bewildered in their search for the clue which would guide them through these mazes. One objective remained clear, the provision of aid to the surviving enclaves of Protestant power, above all the port of Rochelle. The organization of an unsuccessful Huguenot expedition for the relief of the town was winked at by the English in 1573, and a large-scale attempt on Normandy was launched from Jersey in the following year.[11] A much more difficult question was the conduct of relations with the French court. Protestant power must be preserved, yet at the same time the integrity of the French monarchy must be maintained. A France torn apart by civil war would no longer be a reliable counterweight to the other great Continental power, Spain. For England the best solution would be a France governed by moderates — by *politiques* — who would keep it out of the clutches of the ultra-Catholics with their scheme for a Catholic *internationale* and see that it remained a reliable counterweight to Spain. These were men whose views chimed with Elizabeth's — cool, detached, and resolutely anti-ideological.

In practical terms this meant seeking out those elements in the French court which sought to check the post-Bartholomew drive to extinguish the reformed faith altogether. Apostate Protestants, like Navarre and others who had conformed out of fear, together with Catholics who decried the whole policy of suppression as merely leading to further violence, were the likely recruits for such a policy. Hence it was necessary to keep open whatever lines possible which offered the possibility of a working *entente*. In this difficult operation the Queen took the lead; for the next several years English policy towards France was the work of Elizabeth herself.

It was she who opened up a dialogue by responding to the French proposal for reactivating the Alençon courtship in March 1573.[12] Burghley was anything but enthusiastic about the proposal: 'I do force myself to pursue it with desire.' Both Walsingham and Leicester thought the French were merely playing for time until their own affairs were more settled. However, the Queen insisted the talks be kept alive by demanding an interview with the suitor (which was promised as soon as the Duke finished his duties at the siege of Rochelle). She also sent an envoy offering her services as a mediator. He arrived just as Anjou's acceptance of the Polish throne relieved Rochelle and opened the way for a patched-up peace.[13] It was now the turn of the French to send an emissary to England to sing the Duke's praises and draw up plans for an interview.[14]

A Huguenot attack on Normandy ruffled relations again, and was almost immediately followed by the discovery of the Alençon/Navarre plot, a high-placed conspiracy in the French court in which the English government had at least a finger if not a hand. The two ranking princes of the blood royal, Alençon and Navarre, concocted a plan to join the Huguenots at Sedan, outside French jurisdiction. (Some even wrote of a flight to England.) Captured, they were imprisoned. When the English ambassador, Dale, saw them in their confinement, they begged for a secret token from the Queen or Cecil as a gage of friendship. Burghley went so far as to conceive a scheme for bribing their guards to help them escape. He wrote fearfully of the 'tyrant that shall come from Poland'. An emissary was rushed to Paris to reconcile the King and Alençon, but Charles IX died just after his arrival.[15]

There was nothing to do but wait for the arrival of the new King, Henry III. Elizabeth dispatched a special envoy with a formal offer to renew the alliance of 1572, but got little change out of the new ruler. His return, far from restoring order, led to a broad-based opposition, a coalition between the Montmorency interest and the Protestants which in turn brought on renewed war in early 1575. During the winter of 1574-5 the English court received one of the Montmorency brothers, bearing the manifesto issued by their party.[16] Their aims went beyond the confessional issue, including toleration as part of a far-ranging programme of political reform. This was to be accomplished with the assistance of a German mercenary army under the Elector Palatine. Elizabeth's proposed role would be the provision of money (£30,000). The French envoy drew a comparison with her Scottish intervention of 1560: success in the present scheme would create a French government linked to the English by common bonds of interest.

This time the Queen, taking a bolder line than in previous French ventures, yielded so far as to offer £15,000 (to be repaid by the Elector Palatine). This was done in great secrecy so that it did not interfere with concurrent negotiations with the French court; the alliance of

1572 was solemnly renewed and Henry III given the Garter; discussion of the match with his brother was renewed. (The Duke now assumed his brother's former title of Anjou and so is designated henceforth.) The money for the German mercenaries was held up. The Queen was waiting to see which way the cat would jump, keeping all options open.[17] She had her answer when Anjou escaped from confinement and proclaimed himself as 'governor general for the king and protector of liberty and the public weal'. He had thrown himself into opposition to the court and open to alliance with the Huguenot/Montmorency coalition.[18]

The Duke now turned to England for support, as did Condé, the Protestant leader, and Montmorency, now collaborating with the Duke. The confusion increased when the King of Navarre escaped from surveillance and retired to the Protestant-held lands in the west. Elizabeth initially gave guarded promises of support. However, when in April 1576 she sent off an agent, he was accredited not only to work for reconciliation between the King and the coalition but secretly to keep Anjou firm in his support of Condé and Montmorency. Elizabeth's house of cards collapsed when Catherine put the French humpty-dumpty back together in the Peace of Monsieur. How much hope Elizabeth had invested in the success of this intrigue was revealed by her angrily bitter letter of disgust in which she reproached Navarre for a false peace, ruinous to him and his cause.[19]

In the four years since St Bartholomew Elizabeth had fumbled uncertainly on the fringes of French politics, seeking to hold in balance two contradictory aims — the preservation of the Protestant interest and the maintenance of the *entente* with the French court established in 1572. The Queen had seized on the Alençon/Anjou match as a possible line of action. To encourage the Duke to assume the leadership of the anti-Catholic forces would provide the base for a coalition, endowed by princely patronage with legitimacy, which could hold in check the ultra-Catholics of the French court with their pro-Spanish sympathies. The Duke's confinement balked the scheme for some time, but Elizabeth continued — and extended — her patronage to the coalition led by Condé and Montmorency.

Elizabeth's support for the Condé–Montmorency alliance marked an important step away from previous English policy towards France. More significant still, this was a policy in which the Queen, at her own initiative, assumed a new and bold interventionist style. Hitherto her stake in the French political game had been minimal; now she had raised it to a serious bid for a winning place. In the past, intervention in

France had meant aid to the Protestants, permission to use English ports, and the provision of asylum in times of adversity. In addition the Queen had looked through her fingers when English ports served as a base for Huguenot assaults on the French homeland. Now, by supporting a coalition which was only in part confessional in character, she was able to throw off the mantle of Protestant champion and by her patronage of the two princes, Alençon and Navarre, could hope to become an arbiter, an umpire, in French affairs. This willingness to take so active a part in her neighbours' domestic affairs marks a new phase in Elizabeth's public career. For the first time she was prepared to move from a cautiously defensive posture to an active participation in the European scene which risked, if not her material resources, at least her reputation.

The role of pacifier and mediator suited Elizabeth far better than that of a partisan. It fitted her feminine image as the promoter of peace, the pacifier of conflict. It enhanced her prestige since her influence would now broaden out to encompass a wide coalition of interests. It would serve her own needs by assuring that France would remain an obstacle to a Spanish/papal crusade against Protestant England. Yet the Queen's posture was more than a merely politic tactic. The obverse side of her indifference to the religious passions of her age was her cool conviction that there was no issue on which reasonable rulers could not reach accommodation. Surely all must see the obvious truth that nothing was more fruitless or destructive than war. Here one may perhaps detect not only temperamental inclination but also its reinforcement by her reading of the classical moralists, the product of her humanist education. Unluckily, the French princes did not share such convictions, and her carefully laid scheme came apart in her hands.

That failure is in part explained by the obverse to this coolly calculated conduct. As early as 1572 there had been an obscure and very curious intrigue, involving Alençon (as he then was). Through a mediator named Maisonfleur, a poet and courtier, a scheme was concocted by which the Duke would slip away from France (accompanied, if possible, by Navarre and Condé). On his arrival at the English court he would wed Elizabeth. In its outlines it duplicated the circumstances of the 1576 plot.[20] How seriously we should regard it is difficult to guess; the Queen took it seriously enough to delay Walsingham's departure from his Paris embassy. This scenario, borrowed, one would think, from one of the court romances, casts light on a side of the royal character normally submerged and quite out of keeping with her usual behaviour. She could swerve from time to time from her usual paths into devious courses which were not only risky but quite unrealistic, unlikely to succeed and foreign to her usual pragmatism. Such impulses emerged again in the 1576 intrigue. Now, as then (and again in 1578), they focused on the person of the Duke.

For success, the 1576 scheme required the cooperation of a cluster of different leaders with varying interests, while it was to be led by Anjou. The Queen trusted too much in the cooperation of that slippery Duke and on her ability to lure him into dependence upon her. It is just in this detail that the lucidity of the plan is smudged. Did she really intend marriage with the Duke? Less would surely not tempt him into her net. Her ministers thought her more serious in intention that at any time since the Austrian match. A sure witness to her seriousness of purpose was her fury at the failure of the enterprise. Whatever her intentions about marriage, she had intended something more than a short-term manœuvre to gain a breathing space. She glimpsed herself as the arbitress of the French political scene.

The Habsburgs, 1572–1576

During these years Elizabeth had to grapple with another version of the problem she faced in France. It was now the turn of the Netherlands, where civil war cast in confessional terms had erupted and another reformed community was claiming the help of the ruler whom they saw as the grand protectress of the Protestant *internationale*. The Queen's dilemma was heightened by the existing ill will between the English and Spanish crowns, and by rising English suspicions and distrust of Philip's long-term intentions.

Although the attack on Brill and the subsequent rebellion were in themselves unexpected events, they took place in a society where the political temperature was already dangerously high. When the rising occurred, the Prince of Orange and his brother Louis of Nassau were once again plotting an insurrection in the provinces. They had approached the English authorities and probably entered into correspondence with Leicester. When de la Marck's venture exploded into a major eruption, English volunteers landed before the revolt was more than a few weeks old. The government, as we have seen, was initially concerned to check French interference, but the men who went and their backers at home saw the Spanish as the enemy. England was already host to some thousands of Flemish refugees, exiles for religion's sake, whose cause awakened strong sympathies in evangelical

Protestant circles. Her ports had served as host to countless sea-beggar ships over the past few years. For the evangelical party in the court, aid to the rebels was an almost reflexive action. That party numbered among its most active members both the Earl of Leicester and Secretary Walsingham.

The situation duplicated in obvious ways the English position *vis-à-vis* the French Protestants, but there were important differences. In France there was an ambiguity to the scene lacking in the Habsburg provinces. The goal of the French Protestants was some kind of accommodation which would allow them to practise their faith. Their strength in the country was such that they had a fair chance of bullying the crown into such a settlement. In the Low Countries it was all or nothing: Philip was determined to destroy every last germ of heresy and to crush local autonomy; inherent in the rebels' goal was the declaration of independence from the Spanish King which would follow in a few years. Moreover, the struggle, as it took shape in the months after the raid on Brill, was far more unequal than in France, the might of the Spanish Habsburg empire against the burghers of a few towns in the two provinces of Holland and Zeeland.

Hence it behoved the English to move very cautiously in their support for the rebellion. It might well be snuffed out and England left alone to face an angry Spain. Yet neutrality might be no shield. A victorious Spanish army — as many Englishmen feared — might well be used to carry through the plans of an international Catholic conspiracy. Even if one rejected so melodramatic a scenario, the control of these coasts was a matter close to England's most vital interests. Cecil had written of the danger of French rule in the provinces: 'our sovereignty of the narrow seas will be abridged with danger and dishonour.'[21] A hostile and militant Spanish regime would be no less dangerous and even more threatening. To abandon the rebels to their fate or to lend them aid — either course was attended by grave dangers. To choose the former was to win short-term safety but at the cost of giving too many hostages to fortune. There was no alternative to some kind of assistance to the rebels.

The first phase of rebellion was a short one. In the summer, William of Orange and his brother raised forces for an invasion of the southern Netherlands; defeated there, the prince withdrew to Holland, now his base and the focus of his actions. French intervention faded even before St Bartholomew. The English companies at Flushing were officially recalled in November, but this did not halt the flow of English volunteers into the rebels' service.[22] It was clear by now that the rebels' position was strong enough to ensure that they would not be quickly overcome.

Elizabeth and her Councillors patterned their response to this new challenge on the same cautious model they had followed in the earlier stages of the Huguenot revolt. Their aim was to allow the rebels free access to English ports and English trade and unchecked recruitment of manpower while at the same time cultivating civil, indeed cordial, relations with Brussels and Madrid. With this latter end in view Elizabeth moved to a final settlement of the trade dispute; agreement was reached for the reopening of ports on both sides at the end of April 1573.[23] The Spanish tried to exploit this new atmosphere of harmony by buying powder in England, but they were blandly told that supplies were too low to permit export. A Spanish attempt to buy the services of English sailors (under Martin Frobisher) was quashed by the English authorities.[24] At the same time the Queen evaded Alva's request for a prohibition on English volunteers by insisting that they went over against her express commands. When the fall of Edinburgh castle in 1573 released a supply of unemployed soldiers on the market, she encouraged the Scottish regency to allow them to join the rebel forces.[25] On the other hand, every effort of the Prince of Orange to obtain open support from England was firmly rebuffed. When the rebels interfered with English shipping the Queen retaliated by counter-measures against their shipping. The façade of even-handed neutrality was carefully maintained.[26]

Significantly, Elizabeth, following again her French strategy, proposed herself as mediator between the contestants. She tried to persuade the Spanish King to such a move in 1573; the effort was rebuffed.[27] When the Treaty of Bristol of 1574 concluded a comprehensive settlement of trade issues, the Queen, going a step further, sent a special envoy, Sir Henry Cobham, to Spain, proposing mediation based on a settlement which would have restored the *status quo ante* in the provinces – reinstatement of the ancient liberties, suspension of the Inquisition, and the removal of Spanish troops. Philip would go no further than allowing the Protestants to emigrate.[28] He might reasonably object that the self-proposed mediator was less than neutral. The terms she proposed were as much advantageous to her as to the disputants. Elizabeth, rebuffed for the present, would resume her efforts at mediation when the opportunity offered.

Underneath the cool rationality of these sober diplomatic exchanges ran a quivering, almost hysterical stratum of fear. In 1574 the Spanish government began assembling a fleet in its northern ports to provide naval reinforcements for the Brussels government. In April it asked permission for Spanish ships to put into English ports in case of emergencies. The Queen unwillingly consented, but the whole country buzzed with apprehension. The royal ships were mobilized and Bedford sent to arm the West Country. Requesens, the Spanish governor at Brussels, on his side heard rumours of a joint Anglo-Dutch–Huguenot fleet in the making. Philip went so far as to send a special messenger with a reassuring letter. In the end the Spanish, their resources overstrained, abandoned the plan. The reactions of parties on both sides showed how deep and how irrational were their fears of each other.[29]

During these years the fortunes of the rebels rose and fell; in 1573 they lost Harlem, but saved Alkmaar; the next year saw the epic defence of Leiden, yet slowly their position was weakening. In 1575 the Spanish siege of Ziericksee bade fair to cut the vital link between mainland Holland and the island province of Zeeland. Only the financial exigencies of the Spanish treasury, which left Requesens's troops unpaid and ultimately mutinous, saved the day for the rebels. With both sides hard pressed to continue the struggle Elizabeth took another initiative late in 1575, again urging mediation and a compromise settlement in which each party made concessions. She was frank in telling Requesens's representative in London that she feared a Spanish regime on the repressive model of Alva, and urged the withdrawal of Spanish troops as a reassurance both to the provinces and to their neighbours. In addition, local home rule should be restored. The rebels on their side were told they must return to Habsburg rule and content themselves with freedom of conscience, equivalent (according to Elizabeth) to the Catholics' status in England. Neither side showed any sign of budging. Within the next few months unanticipated events would shuffle the jigsaw into a whole new pattern.[30]

The Queen's policy from 1572 to 1576 had had two aspects. On the one hand it was a holding operation, waiting upon the outcome of events the English could not influence. Would Orange or Alva be the victor? Until the unexpected breakdown of Spanish power in 1576 that question remained unanswered. The other and constructive side of Elizabeth's actions was her determined efforts to mediate between the two parties. As in France, there were short-term advantages to fishing in the troubled waters of a neighbour's pond, but in the long run English interests were best served by a stable Netherlands regime, capable of withstanding French pressure in the area but left free to run its own internal affairs.

This was the scheme of settlement which Elizabeth repeatedly urged on the combatants. As an intelligent and dispassionate solution to the struggle it was admirable, but the Queen's tone-deafness to the more strident notes on the political scale flawed it fatally. In part her difficulty arose from her own insularity. Acute and clear-sighted in her diagnosis of England's position, she could not make the imaginative leap required to grasp the case of the Spanish or the Dutch. Linked to this insensitivity was her own temperamental coldness to the passionate politico-religious convictions of her contemporaries. To her coldly secular intelligence, the sheer waste of lives and money in continued war set against the advantage of compromise seemed compellingly convincing and to require no discussion. She simply could not comprehend the unshakeable determination of the Catholic King to preserve his faith at whatever costs and the rock-like resistance of the Netherlands Calvinists to every such effort.

15

England and the States General, 1576–1579

U p to the events of 1576–7 Elizabeth had trodden a narrowly
defined path within which her freedom of action was strictly
limited. The indirect aid which she could offer the rebels
could not determine the outcome of the struggle; there was nothing
English assistance could do to prevent the fall of Harlem or deliver
Leiden from its besiegers. As long as the probability of a Spanish
victory was high, the English government could not risk any action
which would expose them to Philip's wrath. Then, suddenly, a startling sequence of events, following in rapid succession, turned the
political landscape of the Low Countries topsy-turvy. Until 1576
revolt was limited to a patchy scattering of towns in the two provinces
of Holland and Zeeland; the other fifteen provinces remained at least
passively loyal. Now the death of Requesens, the paralysis of government at Brussels, the disintegration of the unpaid Spanish armies, and
the ensuing mutiny jolted the local states into action. Their leaders,
gathered in a confederal States General, were shocked into reviving
the demands for the ancient liberties which had been the watchword
of the aristocratic opposition in the mid-1560s crisis. In these demands
they found common ground with the Prince of Orange. In the
urgencies of the moment, disagreements about religion could be
placed in cold storage.

For the English these sudden changes provided hopeful opportunities but also created large new risks. The demand of the States General
for the expulsion of alien soldiers and the restoration of local self-
government chimed perfectly with the proposals reiterated by Elizabeth in her peace proposals; but whether they could extract these

terms from the Spanish King was a question clouded with uncertainty. Very early on, the shaky interim regime turned to England for financial and, more hesitantly, for military assistance. Elizabeth was faced with the unpleasant fact that to realize the kind of regime which she ideally envisaged, and which now seemed within reach, would require English intervention of a much more open and far-reaching character than heretofore. A great prize might be won, but the costs — and the dangers — were high. How much was the Queen willing to risk in this gamble?

The decision was made all the more difficult by the appearance of a new cast of characters on the political stage, most of them newcomers and unknown to the English. Philip with his accustomed deliberation pondered for months over Requesens's successor, finally settling on his half-brother, Don John of Austria, the victor of Lepanto. A portionless prince, ambitious for a throne of his own, he was bribed to take on the difficult task in the Netherlands with the promise that, once he had re-established his brother's power there, he could make a bid for the hand of Mary Stuart and the English throne. His immediate problems, however, were with the leaders of the Netherlands aristocracy, particularly the Catholic house of Croye, headed by the Duke of Aerschot and, of course, the Prince of Orange, now fully master of the two rebel provinces and legitimized by the recognition of the States General.

There were also several other foreign intruders on the scene. The States General anxiously sought to counter Don John's appointment by placing their own candidate in the governor-generalship. The Prince of Orange proposed the Duke of Anjou. The Catholic nobles checkmated this candidacy by bringing forward a rival in yet another cadet prince, Archduke Matthias of Austria, brother to the Emperor Rudolf. Finally, another German princeling crowded onto the well-filled stage: Duke Casimir, a cadet of the Palatine house, and prospective commander of a mercenary army to be hired by the States. With all these participants the English now had to make contact in a bewildering maze of negotiations, where the making of choices was infinitely more difficult than in the simpler era before 1576 and the consequences of their choices more far-reaching.

Lastly, a difference of quite another character arose from the changes in perspective among the Queen's advisers, changes which reflected profound differences, arising not out of personal faction but out of divergent opinions as to strategy and, beyond that, about the long-term goals of English national aspirations. While there was common agreement as to the immediate threat to the Protestant polity of England from its ideological enemies, a menace which was more and more seen to be embodied in the King of Spain, there was increasing disagreement as to the proper response to these dangers.

One group, led by the Earl of Leicester, with strong support in Council, in the court, and in a growing body of popular sentiment, urged all-out support, military as well as financial, for the rebellious provinces. In part their argument rested on the need for the confessional solidarity of the Reformed religion, a rallying to the cause of Continental Protestantism, but it also contained a substantial political ingredient. The newly opened window of opportunity in the Netherlands offered the possibility of a definitive settlement of English relations with the Low Countries on a long-term basis. A regime freed from Spanish domination could be fostered which, linked by trade and religion, would look to England as the guarantor of its wellbeing. Some of the advocates of this view went well beyond the merely defensive goals of such a policy; they would have responded positively to Orange's offer to the Queen of the lordship of the two provinces. As protectress and regent of the Low Countries, she would preside over a grand enterprise in English national expansion.

Opposed to these expansionists were those who, led by the Lord Treasurer, shared his wholly defensive view of what could and should be done. In the best of all possible worlds, Burghley would probably have preferred an isolation which relied on England's own naval and military strength to create a hedgehog defence, so bristling as to frighten off all marauders. Such a policy had seemed feasible at the end of the 1560s, but now it would be prohibitively expensive and would throw away the opportunity to distract the French and Spanish governments by encouraging their rebels. Hence Burghley fell back on a minimalist policy which would measure every act of assistance to Continental allies by its precise value to England's security. So far as possible this would rule out active English military involvement. England's interests in Continental affairs should be limited solely to promoting an international power structure in which states of equal strength would automatically check any attempt at another's hegemonial expansiveness. The result would be a guarantee of English immunity from the unwelcome attentions of either France or Spain. Such a strategy was not necessarily bounded by strict confessional considerations. For the Queen, these changes meant not only that the task of assessing her interests and determining her actions was more difficult but that, in making her choices, she would have to listen to dissonant voices among her Councillors, urging divergent paths by which to proceed.

The avalanche of events which during 1576 swept away Spanish power in the Netherlands began with the death of Requesens in March. At the same time the resources of the Spanish treasury, even though fed by the stream of American silver, had become overstrained. Money was lacking for the army's pay and arrears of wages mounted. Just as the capture of Ziericksee seemed to put victory within the Spanish grasp, the soldiers' patience snapped and they mutinied. The mutinies spread through the provinces and in July the acting government, the Council of State, proclaimed the soldiers traitors. The native-born councillors then turned on their Spanish colleagues, arrested them, and on their own authority summoned a meeting of the States General, which convened on 25 September. Events moved rapidly thenceforward. Negotiations were opened with the Prince of Orange; spurred by the mutineers' sack of Antwerp, they culminated on 8 November in the agreement known as the Pacification of Ghent, in which all seventeen provinces joined in a demand for the expulsion of Spanish forces. The edicts against the Protestants were suspended; the religious issue was to be settled by the States General. The Prince of Orange was acknowledged as *Stadhouder* (regent) of Holland and Zeeland. Don John, newly arrived in the Low Countries, had no choice but a sullen acquiescence in the terms of the pacification.

The new authorities in the Low Countries were quick to get in touch with the Queen's government. An envoy from the States General arrived in November, followed by one from Don John in December.[1] The States sought Elizabeth's intervention with Philip for acceptance of their terms; she readily agreed, and dispatched Sir John Smith to Madrid, while a protégé of Leicester's, Edward Horsey, attended on Don John, urging him to accept the proffered terms and offering English aid against any French intrusion.

A more definitive step was taken just before Christmas. Another States agent, Sweveghem, a familiar figure in London from earlier negotiations, came cap in hand, asking for the loan of £100,000. The Queen agreed without demur, while her agent in Brussels intimated that military aid might be available – provided the States continued loyal to their King.[2] Such a need seemed to recede when, in February, Don John accepted the States' terms in the peace of Marche-en-Famine. This was, as events soon proved, no more than a truce, since it left unsettled the question of religion and the status of the two Orangist provinces. Orange was again urging on the Queen a separate alliance with Holland and Zeeland, a proposal to which she responded with vague talk of a general Protestant league, comprehending the German princes.[3]

In July 1577 Don John's seizure of the fortress of Namur ended the fragile peace and foretold the Spanish decision to mount a campaign of reconquest. English reactions were swift; in early August the Queen[4] announced her determination to continue support of the States General (even though they had defaulted on repayment of their loan). She readied some 500–600 men for dispatch overseas, and wrote to the Scottish Regent that he should send on the bands recently dismissed there.

Leicester during these months was in close contact with the Prince of Orange,[5] acting as godfather for the prince's new child, and was regarded in the Low Countries as a man devoted to the Dutch cause. When the States General readied a new embassy to London headed by the Marquis de Havré, he was instructed to ask for money and an army.[6] The Marquis was received by the Queen on 27 September. He made his plea in familiar terms, stressing the ill faith of Don John and his disregard for their ancient liberties. This time, however, there was a new and important consideration, the massing of French troops under the Duke of Guise on the frontiers. The Marquis asked for 5,000 foot and 1,000 horse under the conduct of a leading English lord. Without hesitation the Queen, acting with startling decisiveness, acceded to both requests, pledging her credit and that of the City for the loan and promising soldiers in case of need (on condition of their continued loyalty to Philip).[7] The soldiers would be led by Leicester. In the euphoria of the moment the Earl happily busied himself with his plans for mobilization.[8] Yet within a month he was writing worriedly of a chill in English ardour. Division within the States General ranks, as evidenced by the coming of Archduke Matthias, put up by the Catholic lords to checkmate Orange, aroused doubts as to the stability of the regime. Leicester, aware of its fragility, had hinted at a radical solution, nothing less than the offer to the Queen of the sovereignty of Holland and Zeeland.[9]

Bad news followed quickly when the States General, swayed by anti-Orangists who feared English influence,[10] declined the offer of men, although still anxious to have the money, a move 'misliked by honest and well affected gentlemen here', as Walsingham wrote. A miscalculation by Orange's rival, Aerschot, made him a prisoner at Ghent and gave the Prince the opportunity to reverse the decision on the English troops. The Queen gave orders to ready soldiers for service overseas, but doubt was already seeping in.[11] The uncertain role of the Archduke, the continuing divisions within the States General, the slowness of business, and the slackness of their military arrangements aroused more hesitation in the royal mind.[12] Don John's agent reported that the Queen had rejected an offer by the States General to hand over Dutch ports to the English as 'cautionary' towns as gages for the loans, a move which would openly affront Philip. Leicester had sought to persuade her; Burghley had succeeded in dissuading her, according to the envoy.[13]

Burghley's own cogitations at this time weighed the reasons for suspecting Spanish hostility and the possible advantages of acting now. A paper of December recapitulated the danger of an attack by Don John once he conquered the Low Countries, but concluded that the Queen was disposed not to act because aid to the States General would be an encouragement to rebels; it would incite the Catholic powers to attack England (which they would not otherwise do) and finally it would mean the sacrifice of English lives for foreigners.[14]

However, in early January 1578 Elizabeth signed a treaty with the States, affirming her offer of money and men; but at the same time she sent off a mediating mission to Don John, seeking an armistice and suggesting terms which would preserve the Catholic faith in the provinces.[15] Another memorandum of Burghley's asserted the necessity for the provinces returning to the ancient order, neither subdued by Spain nor dominated by France — the *status quo ante* of the Emperor Charles's time.[16] The re-establishment of Spanish government would open the way for plots and conspiracies against the English, backed by Don John. The States (and the Archduke Matthias, who had arrived in Brussels on 18 January) were urgent in their clamour for immediate aid, and Orange made arrangments for the debarkation of English forces.[17] The urgency of the situation became even more apparent when Don John crushed the States army at Gembloux on 29 January.

The Queen, however, was already shifting ground. The quarrel within the States leadership between the Catholic nobles and Orange, and the rumours that some provinces were turning to French aid or even to Don John, were reasons for deferring action.[18] A new possibility now emerged. The States had been planning to hire mercenary forces from Germany or Switzerland.[19] Their prospective commander, Duke Casimir, brother to the Elector Palatine, now took the lead in sending an agent to visit both the Queen and Orange.[20] Elizabeth seized the opportunity for substituting a mercenary army for English forces.[21] In mid-February she announced to the States envoy in

London that she would spend part of the loan to pay for Casimir's forces, and in March she formally proposed that the Duke bring a force of 6,000 foot and 5,000 reiters (cavalry) for which she would put down £20,000 immediately with an additional £20,000 to follow. She justified this radical swerve in policy on the ground that the entry of English troops into the Low Countries would trigger a reciprocal French intervention, for France would see this move as leading to English domination.[22]

For Leicester, the Queen's retreat from open support for the States was a bitter disappointment. 'I have neither face nor countenance to write to the prince, his expectation being so greatly deceived.' God had 'found us unworthy of a longer continuance of his former blessing'.[23] His hopes that his sovereign would hoist her standard as the protectress of the reformed religion in the Low Countries, in a move which would replace Spanish predominance in the provinces by English, were hopelessly crushed. Elizabeth, having for a brief moment come forward and boldly confronted the King of Spain, found the bracing air far too chill for her comfort and hastily retreated into her shell.

Since the collapse of Spanish power in 1576, Leicester and his allies had been able to move their mistress into open support of the rebel States; she had doled out £20,000 in December 1576 and, more important, had bullied Don John with threats of intervention if he did not yield to the States demands. Relations with the rebels had remained reasonably warm in spite of their failure to repay the first instalment of the debt on the due date, and the Queen had remained faithful to her reiterated promise to aid the provinces if Don John broke the peace. The high-water mark of the Earl's success had been the treaty of early January 1578 with its promises of money and men. In both cases a determining factor in the Queen's decision to act had been the fear of French intervention. Now, with the abandonment of the expeditionary force the brief interlude of royal support was over.

In the years since 1572, circumstances had enabled her to steer a course which avoided any irreversible commitments. Now, faced with the demand for just such a decision, she brought herself to the starting-point but then balked at running the course. Nevertheless, the promised subsidy for Casimir's mercenaries still stood. However indirectly, Elizabeth was pledged to continue giving material support to the States General. She returned to her favourite role of mediator; but she could hardly claim to be wholly impartial, for she now backed a set of conditions which would compel Philip to pull down the pillars on which his whole policy towards the Netherlands had rested since 1559. That policy was integral to his whole conception of a Spanish imperial polity. Elizabeth, from being merely a mediator, had now become a protagonist in the struggle over the future of the Low Countries. If she had her way, she would thwart the whole thrust of Philip's programme. Philip's awareness of Elizabeth's expanding role in the Low Countries led him to reopen the Spanish embassy in London, closed since de Spes's expulsion in 1571. The States General reluctantly accepted the new terms in March, but it would be some three months before Casimir could arrive. The Queen returned to the old gambit of mediation, using the formula of a return to the pre-1559 order with the significant additional demand that Don John be replaced. Another envoy trotted off to the latter's headquarters to begin another weary round of futile negotiation.[24]

At this point the States General, disillusioned by their English patroness's tergiversations, turned in desperation to the French alternative, the self-promoting Duke of Anjou, more than ever eager to press his services now that there was peace at home. The French Duke was an enigma to the English. Would he come on the scene with his brother's support or simply on his own? Was his offer to the States General made in good faith? Or was he blackmailing both them and Don John? The latter was Orange's view; in his estimation this left the Dutch with no alternative but to accept his services.[25]

The Queen's response was a counter-blackmail of her own. The States General were to be told that, unless they ended the negotiations with Anjou, the Queen would cut off the first £10,000 payment for Casimir's troops. She was now sufficiently alarmed at events in the Low Countries to send off a high-powered embassy, headed by Secretary Walsingham and the Warden of the Cinque Ports, Lord Cobham, to deal directly with the Low Countries principals. Their instructions were double-edged; if the States were willing to accept French intervention, the envoys were to push an alliance of Don John and Casimir to prevent it; alternatively, should the States resist the French, they were to pair them with Casimir in resistance. In the latter case, if their combined forces were inadequate, the ambassadors could offer English aid.

Walsingham and Cobham were to spend an unhappy summer and autumn in wearying and altogether fruitless diplomacy. The Queen clung with a blind obstinacy to the hope of peace. The newly appointed second Secretary, Wilson, warned the ambassadors, 'Do you endeavour for a peace and you shall have thanks on your return.

Otherwise if you tell us of war and the necessity thereof, I tell you plainly we cannot abide to hear of it.' The Queen raged at the States for proposing unacceptable terms to Don John and refused to release funds for Casimir's troops, insisting that she first be repaid for the first instalment already advanced. The ambassadors wrung their hands in despair. Could the Queen not see that she was driving the States into Anjou's hands? 'God of His mercy give us all hereabout of His grace ... for never was there more need nor never stood this crown in like peril.'[26]

Negotiations between the States and Anjou dragged on into August; not until then was there a tentative agreement. Anjou, playing both sides of the street, had pulled out of storage the rusty marriage proposals, and at the same time the Queen had veered around to a new-found hopefulness in the Duke's intentions. Then, abruptly, the royal weathervane reversed direction; doubting Anjou altogether, she offered the States 10,000–12,000 men and £100,000. Burghley warned the ambassadors that 'though this be for the moment earnestly meant I can assure nothing'. At this point fear of French aggression swayed all. It was in any case too late; the States signed up with Anjou a few days later.[27]

This spasm of distrust died down quickly; the order for assisting the States was rescinded on 29 August. The Queen was now looking with increasing favour on the Duke. 'She believes Anjou will do her bidding; convinced of her ability to direct all these causes without such charges as we lay down for her and so resteth assured Monsieur will do nothing without her liking.' Leicester warned Walsingham to be careful how he spoke or wrote of the Duke. The Earl thought the Queen not enthusiastic about the match but persuaded by those who favoured it. Walsingham brought himself to write that the Duke was wise and well-spoken, less deformed than formerly, and matured by experience. Had he not been heir to a foreign throne, the match was not to be misliked. In another and franker letter the Secretary wrote that if the Duke were as well furnished with good parts as Don John, the match would be worthwhile. 'I find Venus is presently ascendant in your climate. But when I consider the retrograde aspects that the present course in hand is subject to I can hope after no great good.'[28]

Walsingham's pessimism, reasonable enough in light of the summer's experience, was not borne out by the evils of the autumn. Don John fell victim to the fevers raging in his depleted forces and died in September. The promised cooperation of Anjou and the States came to nothing, and at the end of the year the Duke disgustedly returned to France. Casimir's forces, unpaid, were little more than an embarrassment and the disillusioned commander set off for England where, under Leicester's sponsorship, he was accorded almost royal honours but came away without any material benefits.[29] Don John's death proved only a brief check on Spanish plans; his place was immediately assumed by his lieutenant, Alexander Farnese, Prince of Parma. Parma moved quickly to take advantage of the weaknesses of the States. He disposed of Casimir's soldiers by the shrewd device of paying off their arrears and sending them home. During the summer Protestant discontent had erupted in the Flemish cities as the reformers demanded the right of public worship. This set Catholic nerves on edge and opened the way for negotiations between Parma and the Malcontents, the Catholic and anti-Orangist party in the southern provinces. Orange and his party were already drawing away from the Brussels regime by establishing a closer union among the northern, predominantly Protestant, provinces, in the Union of Utrecht.

16

The Anjou Match

The French peace of 1576 had coincided with the moment in that summer when the Dutch rebels' cause was most desperate, and Anjou had first entered the Low Countries when Orange offered him the sovereignty of Holland and Zeeland; the Queen Mother quashed that scheme.[1] In 1577 the Duke was engaged, as the Catholic League's leader, in renewed confrontation with the Protestants, but once again Catherine lowered the temperature and procured a truce in the Peace of Bergerac in September. At odds with his brother and in prison for a time, Anjou turned his attention to the Low Countries and to the English Queen. At first, as we have seen, hostile to his intended entrance into the Provinces, she softened towards him and by summer 1578 moved hesitantly towards support of his venture. Walsingham and Cobham were told that 'in some sort Her Majesty would be content that the duke [Anjou] should deal in the Low Countries'.[2] In June 1578 marriage negotiations with the Queen were officially reopened.

The Queen was more than ever disillusioned by the States conduct. Casimir's army had been effectively thrown away.[3] Walsingham, dejectedly surveying the scene, reported the Queen's withdrawal from all participation in their affairs, even as a mediator. More and more she put her trust in Anjou, whose wooing prospered as the future of the Low Countries declined. The Queen, Walsingham declared, seeing Philip's refusal to budge, thought her only safety lay in the French match.[4] Anjou's intervention would give the impression, whether or not true, of his brother's backing and open up a rift between France and Spain. In fact, Elizabeth anticipated that Henry III would be in no position to act and his brother must look to the Queen for help, a situation which would make him her dependant.

Her Councillors thought that it would take more than a flirtation to tame the Duke into doing the Queen's bidding. Sussex wrote that it was useless to 'dally with him in talk of marriage whereby to stay other actions, he will give fair words and proceed in deed to his best advantage'.[5] Only the bonds of matrimony would make him her obedient servant. The Queen herself seems to have arrived at the same conclusion. During the summer of 1578 the negotiations moved at a stately pace through the customary ritual. Anjou's agent was cordially received at court while Elizabeth again urged a face-to-face encounter. If they suited, the details of the marriage treaty could follow quickly. The French were polite but unresponsive, and Anjou with his usual inconstancy intrigued with the Flemish Catholic Malcontents. Only after his total failure in the Low Countries did he turn seriously to thoughts of wedded bliss.

In January 1579, with the arrival of Anjou's Master of the Wardrobe, Jean Simier, at the English court, matters took a more serious turn. Eagerly taken to the bosom of the court, he was dubbed her 'ape' by the Queen and overwhelmed by royal attentions. It was Elizabeth herself who now breathed life into the negotiations by becoming the wooer. For the first time in the history of her courtships it was royal ardour which sparked the process; the lady gave every appearance of wanting to marry the gentleman. To convince Simier that the Queen was sincere in the wooing, every resource was mustered for his entertainment. Music, dance, food, wine, masques, and jousts were all laid on for his benefit. Elizabeth plied him with small gifts for Monsieur — handkerchiefs, gloves, or, more significant, miniatures of herself. She chattered constantly about marriage, and became so lively in the exercise that Simier declared she looked fifteen years younger.

Leicester was mobilized by the Queen to add credibility to the wooing. He had — so he said — purchased his array for the nuptial celebrations, clothes, horses, and all that was necessary. Huntingdon, Bedford, along with the Earls of Shrewsbury, Rutland, Pembroke, and Arundel, were dragooned into a commitment to the match. Let the Duke but come and he would have no task but that of making love.[6] The Queen added her blandishments, hinting at a wedding before Easter and urging the Duke to come as soon as possible. At the end of March formal negotiations on the actual clauses of a treaty were commenced. Such practical questions as his income, his possible coronation, and his public role had to be ironed out.[7] This time, unlike all past courtships, it was the Queen who was pressing the Councillors to action. The usual tactics of delay, above all the question of religion, were not allowed to slow the process; in late June the Queen demanded completion of the arrangements in time for the Duke's arrival in August.[8]

The royal allurements prevailed; the Duke agreed to come and on 17 August arrived at the English court, travelling incognito. However, his ten-day stay was anything but a secret in court circles; the Spanish ambassador was able to relay a fair amount of detail to his master.[9] Nicknamed her frog by the Queen, the Duke passed with flying colours the test of acceptability and thus matters were brought to a head. The courtship was over; the suitor had duly presented himself, been inspected, and found acceptable. It was now the Queen's move; she must give a plain yes or no. She turned to her Council for their advice; in October they reluctantly faced up to a decision which they had evaded for nearly six months.

The case for the marriage had been laid out by Burghley in one of his pro- and- contra papers when the suit became serious in the spring of 1579.[10] The match was to be the keystone of an imposing structure which, when completed, would accommodate all the parties to present disputes. It would cement an alliance with France resting on the influence of the royal husband in his brother's court. With Elizabeth and Francis as guarantors for their good behaviour, the Huguenots could be accorded toleration and civil war ended. Catholic conspiracy in England, backed by France and in favour of Mary Stuart, would cease. Above all, the triple alliance of the two sovereigns and the new Duke/King would be strong enough to compel Philip to grant reasonable terms to his Low Countries subjects. The States would have the reassurance of an English guarantee, while any possibility of French aggression in the area would be held in check.

The far-reaching consequences of the marriage were triumphantly summed up in one of the position papers:

> The Queen's Majesty by this marriage shall be a peace maker over all Christendom; shall by her greatness keep a hand over France, the Low Countries, Spain and Scotland, and all her own dominions . . . [and] shall have more fame than ever king was in Europe a thousand years past, shall live happily upon the earth and shall be blessed in the sight of God.[11]

The Queen now turned to the Council for advice. It was by no means the first time the Councillors had discussed the matter; there had been a week's worth of day-long sessions on the subject in the spring. And, indeed, it was a Councillor who had first floated the scheme of an Anjou match. The Earl of Sussex had always kept his eye on the French role in the Low Countries. In 1577 he warned that their presence there was as great a menace as that of Spain. A year later, in the troubled summer of of 1578, he drew up a letter to the Queen in which the whole strategy of the match was put before her. A conversation with Bussy d'Amboise, the Duke's agent, convinced Sussex that the Duke truly sought the marriage and looked to the Queen for his future advancement to greatness. If she refused, he would turn to friendship with Spain. (He was rumoured to be seeking the hand of an Infanta.) Henry III and the Queen Mother would back him simply to keep him employed and out of the country. Sussex then outlined the advantages of a match in much the same terms as Burghley's memorandum, while matching the Treasurer's rhetoric with the promise that 'your fame shall exceed all other princes that were ever in Europe'.[12] The contingency of Anjou's accession to the French throne was dismissed as remote; the suggestion that he would attempt to seize power in England 'not to be thought of by a Christian prince'. Writing to Walsingham a short time later, Sussex reaffirmed his conviction that Anjou could be tamed to obey the Queen only by the marital tie, and that marriage alone would forestall the nightmare of either French or Spanish domination in the Low Countries.[13] As we have seen, the seed he sowed in the Queen's mind began to grow during the ensuing months.

By the time conciliar debate began in the spring of 1579 Burghley had crystallized his thoughts. They were expressed both in the Council and in a speech to the Queen in the presence of a group of senior Councillors.[14] His support of the match was firm. Many of the premises of this argument echoed his paper of a decade earlier, at the time of the Spanish treasure crisis, but the conclusions he drew were different. Now, as then, he laid great stress on the Queen's isolation in the face of grave external threats. Both France and Spain were menaces to her security. A Guisean France, backing the claims of their Stuart kin and seeking a Catholic restoration in England, could raise rebellion in the country while sending forces to Scotland and Ireland. Spain, goaded by Elizabeth's intervention in the Low Countries, could strangle England by embargoing her trade while buying off Anjou with a Spanish marriage. What could England do to counter these threats? Defensive forces could be raised, an army employed, but only at ruinous cost. Allies might be sought, but they were pitifully weak, compared to Spanish or French might – Condé,

Navarre, Casimir, possibly the King of Denmark. Merely to make such an argument displayed its futility.

The confidence which Burghley had felt in 1569 had evaporated. Then he believed a policy of armed isolation would serve; now it was clear there was only one remedy — marriage and an heir. Only then could the virgin queen insure herself and her realm against her foes. Objections as to the risks of child-bearing or attempts by Anjou to seize power were lightly brushed aside. The prospect of a future in which England and France were jointly ruled by an offspring of the match was welcomed. England under a viceroy would be guaranteed against French or Spanish aggression. It was a very different tone from that of the confident Secretary Cecil of a decade earlier.

In this round of discussion there seem to have been few counter-argument by the opponents of the match. Walsingham had made plain his distaste for the proposal ever since it emerged, although there is no record of his speaking out at this time. But before the conciliar debate was renewed in October, discussion of the question had moved from the seclusion of the palace to a much wider audience. As early as March sermons were being preached against the match, and the angry Queen threatened the preachers with whipping; in the summer it became the focus of faction within the court. The Dudley–Sidney–Pembroke circle mobilized in protest. Leicester's enemies on their side launched a dangerous rocket against the Earl when they revealed to the Queen his clandestine marriage with the widowed Countess of Essex. Lampoons appeared on the Lord Mayor's doorstep and anti-Anjou ballads circulated. Philip Sidney's challenge to the Earl of Oxford reflected the larger issue.

But the most formidable attack on the match came with the publication of John Stubbs's 'A gaping gulf wherein England is like to be swallowed by another French marriage if the Lord forbid not the bans by letting Her Majesty see the sin and punishment thereof'. The author was a respectable lawyer, kin to the noble (and Protestant) house of Willoughby de Eresby as well as being brother-in-law to the Puritan divine Cartwright. His book was a carefully conceived and cogently argued attack on the marriage. The Queen, beside herself with fury, issued a proclamation banning it and set her clergy to work confiscating all copies and muting any pulpit reverberations among their congregations.[15]

Arrested, along with his printer and bookseller, Stubbs was tried under a statute of Philip and Mary which some lawyers thought had expired with that reign. One protesting lawyer went to the Tower and one of the justices of Common Pleas resigned after a sharp reprimand.[16] Stubbs and the bookseller, Page, were brutally punished. Each lost his right hand, chopped off by a cleaver. Camden, an eyewitness, reported the silence of the crowd, 'either out of horror at this new and unwonted kind of punishment or out of commiseration towards the man, as being of an honest and unblemished repute; or else out of hatred of the marriage, which most men presaged would be the overthrow of religion.' Stubbs was held in prison until 1581; in later life he was patronized by Burghley.

His was not the only voice raised in protest. The rising star among the younger generation of courtiers, Sir Philip Sidney, already celebrated as an author and a patron of letters, took pen to write a letter to the Queen, respectfully urging her to abandon the match. An even more famous poet was enlisted in the cause. Spenser's *Shepheardes Calender* (printed in 1579 but circulating in manuscript earlier) echoes the Protestants' fears in two of the eclogues; Mother Hubbard's Tale has a complex allegory involving Anjou, Burghley, and the Queen herself. At quite another level were the ballads criticizing the match. The church weighed in with a treatise by Richard Cox, Bishop of Ely and former tutor to the Queen. The marriage faced a formidable barrage of anguished opposition.

It was by no means spontaneous. Behind it stood the Earl of Leicester and his entourage.[17] He had already assailed Simier's role in promoting the match when the latter came over in the spring of 1579. The Frenchman had struck back by inducing two courtier allies of his, the crypto-Catholics, Henry Howard and Charles Arundel, to reveal to the Queen Leicester's marriage.[18] Simier claimed the Earl had tried to have him assassinated. Leicester had obvious reasons for opposition: any royal husband would dislodge him from his privileged position with the Queen. But he also spoke as the patron of a powerful interest. Committed Protestants, inside the court and out, were profoundly shocked by the prospect of a consort from a ruling house tainted with the deed of St Bartholomew. Untouched by the political rationale behind the scheme, they saw it as straightforward betrayal of the cause of religion. The Queen had promised in her proclamation against Stubbs that the matter would come before Parliament; their voices would certainly be raised there.

When the Council finally came to debate the question, so much of the argument paralleled what Stubbs had said as to arouse royal suspicion of collusion.[19] Sounding a sequence of notes which touched many chords among his readers, Stubbs had singled out three circumstances of 'this strange wrought marriage by France and England' which should 'affect every Christian heart, in respect of the detriment to the Church of Christ, every English heart, in respect of the detriment to England, and every honest and affectionate heart of an Her Majesty's loving true servant, in regard of the great danger thereby coming to her royal person'.[20]

On the first issue, that of religion, he drew a series of vivid parallels with Old Testament history by which he condemned the match as outright treason to the reformed religion. Such a marriage would be as shameful as that of a Hebrew with a Canaanite, for as holy Israel was to pagan Canaan so was England to France, the former 'a region purged from idolatry, a kingdom of light, confessing Christ and the living God', the latter 'a den of idolatry, a kingdom of darkness, confessing Belial and serving Baal'. He reminded Elizabeth that it was she 'by whose hands the Lord hath quite expelled idolatry' from England. Sidney echoed this argument, reminding her of her role as champion of the faith and warning her that the match 'giveth occasion to all the truly religious to abhor such a master, and so consequently to diminish much of their hopeful love they have long held in you'.[21]

The second note sounded by Stubbs was that of a strident nationalism. Alien rule was abhorrent to nature; God's law proclaimed, 'Choose a ruler from among thine own brethren'. He went on: 'if the want of an English heart doth disable any from ruling the ship of our realm, shall a French heart be kindlike enough to rule our queen?' Again he reminded her that 'the first and chief benefit done to this kingdom' by Elizabeth was that she had redeemed it from a foreign king.[22]

Thirdly, the pamphleteer insisted on dwelling on some frightening contingencies. Suppose the Queen — forty-seven years old — died in childbirth. Who would succeed? Again, what if Anjou succeeded his brother as King of France? What would England's position be? Or, assuming there was a child, what would become of England if he inherited both thrones? For Stubbs the answer was obvious; England would shrink into a mere satellite, such as Naples or Sicily were to Spain.

Stubbs belittled the alleged advantages of the alliance. That Anjou had the backing of a substantial party in France was mere fiction; his following was negligible. Nor did Stubbs believe in the reality of a French alliance. Who could trust the ancient enemy? Why should they now be more reliable than in the past? As for the argument that

Philip would come to terms: 'Now the Spanish genet will soon clasp this cake bread snaffle asunder.' Last but not least, the pamphleteer lost no opportunity to mock the presumed virtues of the French prince, hammering home again and again his fickleness and inconstancy to every cause he had touched. In sum, no good could ever come by bringing in 'this odd fellow, by birth a Frenchman, by profession a Papist, an atheist by conversation, an instrument in France of uncleanness, a fly worker in England for Rome and France in this present affair, a sorcerer by common voice and fame'.[23] The emperor's nakedness was all too visible.

On 2 October[24] the Council was summoned to advise the Queen on the marriage. Each Councillor had to give his separate opinion. Walsingham and Leicester were not present: they were labouring under royal displeasure due to their views of the marriage. Burghley summarized the pros and cons, reiterating his former arguments but adding the warning that Mary Stuart's followers would not scruple to kill Elizabeth in order to win the throne for their mistress. If the marriage were rejected the Queen would have to find allies, build her strength at home and at sea, pension James VI, and give all possible aid to the Huguenots and the Dutch. All this would require unprecedented sums of money.

In the end he plumped for the marriage but little more than halfheartedly. Of bad choices the least bad must be chosen. Not to marry at all would be bring more dangers than opting for the match. The risks of the latter alternative were contingent, those of the former certain. Among the other Councillors the most outspoken was Sir Walter Mildmay.[25] He rejected the match on every ground. The Queen was too old to marry; religion would be fatally endangered by Anjou's presence. Henry III was not likely to live long and the resulting linkage of the two realms would be disastrous, doubly so if there were an heir to both.

Others had less to say. Sadler and the Lord Chancellor agreed with Mildmay. Hatton (a Privy Councillor since 1577) announced that, though he had formerly favoured it, he now had changed his mind. Hunsdon and Wilson supported the match, as did the Admiral and Sussex. In the end no resolution was made and the Queen was to be pressed to show her own mind.[26] When this was communicated to Elizabeth, she burst into tears; she condemned herself for having committed the cause to them 'for that she thought to have rather had an universal request made to her to proceed in this marriage than to have made doubt of it'. Those who feared for religion were rebuked, marvelling that anyone would think her unmindful of God's cause.

A week later, and again at a meeting at the end of October, the Council gave a formal and sullen assent to the marriage.[27] Since they all desired an heir, since the Queen made it clear that Anjou was her only possible choice, and since she looked to them for approval, they made suit to her to marry. At the later meeting, they simply offered to favour the marriage with all their power — if the Queen liked it. The ball had been neatly tossed back into the royal lap. While not openly opposing the match, they made clear the lukewarmness of their sentiments. Elizabeth, too acutely shrewd to press an unpopular marriage against a tide of popular disapproval, knew she must retreat.

The surrender was decently cloaked. A committee of senior councillors was ordered to draw up a contract of marriage which was signed by Simier and taken by him to Paris in December. It had a telling proviso, suspending its operation for two months, while the Queen sought to persuade her people, but by the end of the year the Queen was admitting defeat, dejectedly writing to Anjou that public opinion was too adverse to allow her to yield to her desires.[28] This was no diplomatic fiction; the Queen had promised the marriage would be submitted for parliamentary discussion and for the necessary legislation. Her Councillors had made it clear that the project would have rough going in such an assembly. Elizabeth had been balked by a burst of popular feeling, carefully orchestrated from within her own court and Council. The Queen was not going to be called upon to make her sacrifice at the nuptial altar. The Councillors had sufficient braking power to drag the courtship to a dead halt. However, theirs was a purely negative power. They could not offer an alternative plan to deal with the problems which the Queen had sought to resolve. While English policy remained in suspense for nearly a twelve-month, events elsewhere did not stand still.

In the Low Countries, Parma methodically laid his plans for his campaign of reconquest. In 1579, having consolidated a base in the Catholic southern provinces, he had been able to recover most of the lands east of the Zuider Zee. Orange, once again, turned towards Anjou as the only hope; negotiations moved very slowly, but by autumn 1580 a preliminary agreement was reached, with final acceptance by the Duke in spring 1581. For Philip 1580 had been a busy but propitious year. The throne of Portugal fell vacant, and the Spanish King had little difficulty in asserting his claim and in adding the smaller Iberian kingdom and its possessions to his empire. His new acquisition substantially increased his naval strength.

The English leadership had now to face the unwelcome prospect of Anjou's acceptance as governor by the States General, although that prospect was lessened temporarily by another round of civil disorder in France as both sides squared off once again. Two strategies were considered by the English: substantial aid in men and money to Orange if he staved off the appointment of Anjou, or, a quite different line, subsidizing Casimir to enter France in support of the Huguenots. Renewed peace sank the latter scheme. Elizabeth refused to buy the former, pressed, of course, by the interventionists, Leicester and Walsingham.[29]

Then, when peace returned to France, that court made overtures to the English for a possible alliance. First moved in September, they had led by Christmas 1580 to a resurrection of the 1572 treaty as the basis for a general league.[30] Both parties had new occasions for concern. France had taken alarm at the Spanish acquisition of Portugal; England had felt the first prick of danger in her soft underbelly, Ireland, where a papally backed expedition had landed in 1579, followed by a second in 1580. The first sailed from Lisbon, the second from Spain. An Anglo-French alliance, defensive and offensive, designed for collaboration against Spain in the Low Countries and Portugal, was now in the air. For the English an additional urgency rose in Scotland, where the pro-English regent Morton had been overthrown by the influence of James's newly arrived French cousin, D'Aubigny, thought to be a creature of the Guises. The spectre of a Scotland unsettled by Continental conspiracy, reviving the Queen of Scots' cause, rose to haunt the English.[31]

A French mission arrived in April 1581, officially charged with a renewal of the marriage treaty; the English were anxious to shift discussion to a straightforward alliance, but the French showed no interest.[32] With increasing urgency the English now pushed, through Sir Henry Cobham, their ambassador at Paris, for a joint sponsorship of Anjou in the Low Countries and of the Portuguese pretender, Don Antonio. The French held to marriage as a precondition for a treaty.[33]

These futile negotiations finally pushed the Queen into a crucial new adaptation of her policy. No less a person then Secretary Walsingham was sent off to Paris to persuade Henry III to a far-reaching alliance, offensive and defensive, which was undisguisedly anti-Spanish.[34] Walsingham had several tasks in hand; first he was to induce Anjou to give up his matrimonial hopes. This would clear the way for an alliance, disentangled from the marital link. The Duke agreed, and Walsingham went to deal with the King and the Queen Mother. With them he was to argue that a bond of mutual interest, 'grounded upon necessity and where both parties profit by the confederacy', would be a better basis for cooperation than a marriage 'ingrateful' to Elizabeth's people and necessarily involving an unpopular war with Spain. It was the last consideration which weighed most heavily with Elizabeth. An open rift with Spain must be avoided at all costs. Her alliance with France would be public, but aid to Anjou must be clandestine. Even if – as reserve instructions allowed – she consented to marry, the subsidy for Anjou must remain hidden from all the world.

It is not surprising that these proposals were sceptically received at the French court, in spite of Walsingham's desperate pleas of English sincerity. They seemed nothing more than a cunning plan by which England would hold France's cloak while the latter duelled with Spain. The French tested Elizabeth's intentions, first offering to bear the whole cost of a Flemish expedition – upon the conclusion of the nuptial celebrations. Then they changed to an alternate version – no marriage, but sharing of costs. The Queen skittishly shifted her ground, consistent only in her unwillingness to commit herself. Walsingham bitterly complained that the Queen was destroying her own credibility. It was said

> that when Her Majesty is pressed to marry then she seemeth to affect a league and when a league is yielded unto then she liketh better of marriage. And when thereupon she is moved to assent to marriage then she hath recourse to the league, when the motion of the league or any request is made for money then she returneth to marriage.[35]

The clue lay in the last sentence; as soon as the question of any English contribution, in men, money, or ships arose, the English representatives were ordered to plead absence of instructions. These antics simply confirmed French suspicions of English bad faith; they themselves began sounding out Madrid, and amidst mutual distrust the negotiations faded out.

Circumstances, however, forced action on both parties. Anjou, pressed by Parma, was becoming desperate. He sent an agent to England begging for 100,000 ducats. The Queen, after some procrastination, yielded to a loan of £30,0000, while Henry III made a contribution for his brother's needs. That much of the failed treaty was of necessity agreed to.[36] The Queen's unaccustomed liberality signalled a turn in policy. Anjou was now welcomed as a visitor at the

English court. Arriving on 2 November he stayed on into the year, publicly and lavishly entertained. Just after the annual accession celebrations there ensued a bit of melodrama in what proved to be the final episode in Anjou's long-playing courtship of the Queen. Camden coyly tells us that 'the force of modest love in the midst of amorous discourse carried [the Queen] so far that she drew off a ring from her finger and put it upon the Duke of Anjou's upon certain conditions betwixt them two'. The Spanish ambassador added that she told the assembled courtiers, 'He shall be my husband.'[37]

The court was thrown into utter confusion. 'The courtiers' minds were diversely affected; some leaped for joy; some were seized with admiration; and others were dejected with sorrow.' According to Camden, Leicester, Hatton, and Walsingham assailed the marriage as ruinous to religion and to the realm. The Queen's gentlewomen 'lamented and bewailed and did so terrify and vex [the Queen's] mind that she spent the night in doubts and cares without sleep'. In any case, on the following day the Queen withdrew her consent, leaving Anjou to curse the lightness of women and the inconstancy of islanders.[38]

However, this episode did not abate the hospitality offered the Duke; he lingered on into the new year. Concurrently there was an exchange of offers and counter-offers with the French court which failed to produce agreement.[39] Nevertheless, the English now came to terms with Anjou. He was given a loan in two instalments of £60,000 and, flush with cash, set off for Zeeland where he landed on 10 February 1582, accompanied by the acting Lord Admiral, Howard, Leicester, and the Queen's cousin, Lord Hunsdon. They stayed on as witness to his inauguration as Duke of Brabant. The States had now formally thrown off their allegiance to Philip and were thus vesting the Duke with sovereignty. The English were at last giving their blessing to an act of rebellion and implicitly recognizing a new sovereign in the Low Countries.[40]

The events of the ensuing year were anti-climactic. Through 1582 Anjou failed to take any action against Parma while the latter besieged and took the key fortress of Oudenarde. His excuse for delay was the expected arrival of French reinforcements. In fact when they came, they provided the Duke with the resources for a predictable – and predicted – act of treachery when he attempted to seize Antwerp. Soundly beaten in the attempt, he retreated, tail between his legs, to Dunkirk, and then in June 1583 went home for good. The Queen clung to the belief that it was the States and not he who was at fault;

but when in September 1584 he asked her for money even she turned on him in contemptuous dismissal.[41]

The long melodrama in which the lead parts were taken by the Queen of England and the Duke of Anjou had finally played itself out after a full decade's run. It had begun in the obscure scheme for bringing him to England in 1572; it had reached its climax when she chose him to play the key role in the grand design of 1579. Throughout he had exercised an attraction over the Queen which is hard to account for. His record was there for all to read from the earliest days of his public career — restless ambition, feckless scheming, habitual, almost compulsive, treachery, neither respected nor trusted, a commander of proved incompetence. Nor did his personal attractions make up for his moral delinquencies. Bandy-legged, pock-marked, he was appropriately nicknamed her 'frog' by Elizabeth. Yet she chose him as her principal instrument for the accomplishment of the most important initiative of her political career. All this is the more puzzling because in the choice of her own servants she consistently displayed shrewd and accurate judgment.

The answer lies in part in the illusions created by Elizabeth's isolation. Her world was a small and an insular community. The political elite — the Council, the court, the dozen to fifteen ranking nobles, and a significant segment of the county aristocracies — formed a compact society in which the Queen moved familiarly. She was godmother to their children; their wives were her ladies-in-waiting; she visited them in their homes. In such a world she could charm or awe or bully at will, assured of her power to command obedience and with the passing years more and more self-confident in her own judgment. That self-confidence betrayed her in her dealings with foreign princes. With Anjou, as later with Henry IV or James VI, she had no doubt that she would bend their wills to hers, as she had with her English servants. Whatever flaws there were in Anjou's past record could be written off to bad advice or adverse circumstance. Now, his ambitions gratified by a consort's crown, with assured resources of men and money, he would, under the sage direction of his wife, fulfil the role assigned him.

There may also have been a trace of royal snobbery in Elizabeth's attraction to Anjou. He was the first prince of the blood of the oldest Continental dynasty, the most eligible bachelor in Christendom, unmatched in birth and descent. For a ruler of such high notions of her own regality, Anjou was the only suitor who could match them. However, having said all this, one remains baffled by her illusion that the Duke could match the talents of Parma as leader of the States armies and governor of their provinces. His record was plain to read; only wilful blindness could fail to see it.

The fatal attractiveness of the unlovely duke casts a light on the larger problem which confronts our understanding of these crucial years between 1577 and 1583, when it was very much the Queen's move on the chess-board of English politics. Ever since the Newhaven expedition, certainly since the late 1560s, the Queen had kept a firm hand on the tiller. Nevertheless, she had made her decisions in tandem with her Councillors, above all with Burghley. Her policy had been cautious, constrained by the narrow limits of diplomatic space in which she had to manœuvre, leaving England to play a back-stage role.

The real test of her statecraft came when the collapse of Spanish power opened up wide ground for manœuvre and broad possibilities of action. Opportunities of the grandest scope beckoned, glittering prizes to be won if she were willing to take the risks they entailed. Leicester and his allies lured her with the prospect of a Continental presence unknown since Lancastrian times, as patroness — or sovereign — of the Burgundian provinces and protectress of the reformed religion in north-western Europe. They fortified their argument by insisting that such a strategy of offence was the only way to secure her own security.

Elizabeth hesitated for a moment; with the offer of money and men she seemed ready to throw her weight behind the new order in the Low Countries. As we know, she soon reversed direction, utterly rejecting such a course, to the keen disappointment of Leicester and his hawkish allies. Initially she had no clear-cut alternative to suggest. The subsidization of Casimir proved a barren scheme, and for the next months Elizabeth squirmed and struggled to escape from the toils of Low Countries politics. She desperately hoped that the contending parties could be brought together in some kind of peace. As this hope faded, she turned to the solution which Sussex and possibly Burghley had been offering her — marriage with Anjou.

Once convinced, she took matters into her own hands. The Duke under her command would be the instrument for bringing peace to the Low Countries and stability to western Europe. Balked of marriage, she continued to patronize him in increasingly futile endeavours until even she had to admit his utter worthlessness for the purposes in hand. With his ignominious retreat and subsequent death, her policy lay in ruins. By 1583 England had earned the hostility of Spain, lost the confidence of France, and stood by helpless while Parma inexorably added town after town to his dominions as he marched towards the Rhine mouths.

How are we to assess the Queen's role in this unhappy sequence of events? With her own hand she set the course of English policy in these years. The destination and the route were of her choosing and the crew, whatever their forebodings, had to obey her. The direction in which English policy was to move was definitively set by her in 1578 when she eschewed the potential prizes of intervention and chose a strategy of indirection. It was a case of Hobson's choice. Intervention ran the immediate risk of involvement in the partisan divisions of the Low Countries as the unstable regime of the States General began to split apart from internal pressures. In the longer run the possibility of collision with Spain loomed. Every fibre in the Queen's body shrank from this possibility. She chose the alternative which required least immediate commitment and left more freedom of manœuvre, but abandoned hope of repeating something like the Scottish triumph of 1560.

As a conceptual scheme for the solution of the problems it proposed to deal with, the grand design of 1579 was both logical in structure and sound in analysis. It was built on an assessment of the non-negotiable interests of each party. That assessment, resolutely *politique* in charac-ter, de-emphasized ideological considerations and fastened on what Elizabeth assumed to be rational calculations of minimal needs. Each party – Philip, Henry III, Anjou, the States – was to obtain some advantage, but at the cost of compromising maximum demands. Above all, the strategy offered the promise of domestic peace in France and the Low Countries and an end to the menace of international war. Unhappily, it was seriously flawed by the Queen's mistaken conviction that the two sides could be brought to the bargaining table. She consistently failed to understand both Philip's ineradicable determi-nation to exterminate heresy and to reassert his power in its fullest and the conviction of the Prince of Orange and his colleagues that theirs was an all-or-nothing fight for survival. Nor did she accu-rately assess the suspicions with which the French would greet her advances.

Finally, she underestimated the strength of domestic opposition to the marriage. In the very first stage of proceedings the Queen encountered a stumbling-block too ponderous to be removed. Her tone-deafness to religious questions prevented her from understand-ing how the zeal of the committed reformers and the propaganda of her own government had created a deep-rooted Protestant ideology, characterized by an almost reflexive anti-Popery. Mobilized by Leicester and Walsingham, these men stirred up a hornet's nest of angry protest. Nor were they likely to be limited to purely verbal opposition: as her Councillors warned the Queen, Parliament would have to be persuaded to accept the match, and the protestors' voices would certainly be heard there. Elizabeth could have imitated her sister and insisted on going ahead, but she knew — and had, indeed, argued — that Mary's decision had done lasting damage to her whole reign.

The demonstration against the Anjou match highlights a long-term shift in the underlying stratum of English political life which was taking place in these years. The very process by which Parliament had enacted religious reform, repealed it, and re-enacted it implicitly set new limitations on the crown's freedom of action. What the popular reaction of 1579 revealed was the existence of a massive body of public opinion which could be offended at great risk to the monarchy. The anti-Popery so deeply entrenched in a powerful segment of the ruling elites constituted a permanent low-grade infection in the body politic which could be raised to a fever pitch of fear and suspicion by the prospect of a Catholic consort. The Anjou match provoked the first manifestation of a phenomenon which would recur with ever increasing intensity for more than a century. Elizabeth had drawn a moral from her experience which her Stuart successors ignored to their cost.

The abandonment of the marriage and the subsequent attempts to negotiate an alliance with France also had far-reaching resonances. The instructions which Walsingham bore and the consultations of the Queen and Council which preceded them throw light on a moment of signal transformation in the long history of English foreign policy. The catalytic event was Philip's conquest of Portugal. While it posed no immediate problems for the English, its longer-term implications served to crystallize a maxim of state policy which would have a long life ahead of it.

That maxim had been spelled out already in a document of 1577–78.[42] The writer asserts that 'the old policy observed by the Kings of England, France and Spain . . . is whensoever two of these princes seeth that one of them groweth to be a conqueror, the third will give aid to the weaker to restrain the mightier from growing overgreat.' In Walsingham's instructions the doctrine was applied to concrete circumstance, the quantum jump in Spanish power produced by the acquisition of Portugal, which made it imperative to impress on the French sovereigns 'how necessary it is for the Crown of France as well as for ours, yea, for all Christendom, that the King of Spain's greatness should be impeached.' Again Henry III was warned by Elizabeth how foolish they would both be 'to leave the King of Spain to increase to such greatness as hereafter neither the force of France nor England nor any that be confederate with them shall be able to withstand anything that the King of Spain shall attempt.'[43]

The argument, as it was now put to the French, moved away from the particular problem of the Low Countries to an altogether higher level of general considerations. The English perspective now embraced the whole west European scene and their case rested on a naked appeal to *raison d'état*, based on a balance-of-power argument. It bears witness to the ways in which the making of English policy had shifted since the days of Elizabeth's father. In a world in which the protection of a national security under continuing threat dominated their thought, the English leadership cast aside the purely dynastic aims which had governed the policy of a Wolsey. He had aimed largely at securing some tactical advantage in the constant jockeying for advantage among the European monarchs. He had rarely sought more than some augmentation to the personal fame and glory of his master, a town gained here or there, a marriage arranged, a 'summit meeting,' in which Henry could spread his peacock feathers to the full.

Elizabeth and her Councillors, above all Burghley, were forced to think in national rather than dynastic terms; although they were not aware of it, this moment was a landmark in the metamorphosis of the English monarchy from a dynastic enterprise to the first stages of an early modern nation state. Circumstances — the ruler's sex, the ideological gulf, the acute external threats, heightened by Spain's new acquisition — broke the mould of traditional thinking about the objectives of royal policy. Sovereign and Councillors were no longer involved in a glorified version of the joust but in a struggle to preserve not only the sovereign's person but also the polity which she symbolized. They were struggling to perserve what they saw as a set of larger interests, the existence of which was symbolized in the new terminology which was now in common use among the Queen's servants. They wrote, unconsciously but with increasing frequency, of 'the Queen and the state'. Beyond the person of the prince lay the larger entity which the crown embodied, a structure of power which blended political, economic, and religious elements into a whole and which comprehended the interests of the whole people within its bounds.

For the moment it was the religious element which was given play. It was now a world in which 'princes contend not so much for rule as they do for religion; not who shall rule this country or that but what God we shall profess.'[44] Yet it was not only the fate of Protestant England which was at stake. The international Catholic conspiracy was headed by a super-power whose resources were so great as to threaten an irresistible hegemony over all western Europe. Hence the struggle was not only against a religious foe but also against a would-be universal monarchy which threatened the independence of every other state, Protestant or Catholic. In seeking assistance against this threat, therefore, considerations of ideological purity must be subordinated to the needs of survival. For Protestant England, struggling for survival, alliance with a Catholic France was licit. By the same argument France should embrace the proffered overture, since it was the survival of all the sovereign princes of Europe which was at stake. Protestant and Catholic princes alike could survive only by making common cause against the Spanish giant.

Yet however cogent and penetrating the *Realpolitik* force of the English case, it failed to cut any ice with those world-weary sceptics, Henry III and Catherine de Medici. That failure has to be laid at the door of Elizabeth herself. She had won high marks as an expert practitioner of the diplomatic arts, but she failed to grasp the underlying principles on which the game was played. Her skills in deception and delay, in hints and half-promises, in simulated anger and feigned cordiality, had served short-term advantage most admirably when the objective was to play for time or to walk a tightrope of equivocation between two adversaries. But now, when the cards were down and she was urging the French rulers to open confrontation with Spain, she was not prepared to commit the resources of money and men which would give teeth to the alliance. She lacked the nerve and the courage to put to the test the master-plan which she had devised. It was a failure of nerve and of judgment.

The English government no longer had any means by which it could influence events in the provinces – this at a moment when the States were suffering one calamity after another. In 1582 Orange was wounded in an unsuccessful attempt on his life from which he recovered only slowly; two years later, in July 1584, there was a second and successful one. The States were left without a leader at a moment when Parma was enjoying unbroken success in his systematic reconquest. His strategy of isolating, blockading, and starving one city after another into surrender seemed unstoppable. At the time of the

Prince's death only Antwerp, Brussels, and Mechlin of the inland cities still held out, the latter two blockaded and the third invested by a besieging army.

The States leadership now resumed their search for an external protector to fill the post vacated by Anjou's retirement. A futile effort to secure his return preceded his death by only a few months. That event, in June 1584, rippled out with devastating effect first on French, then on Dutch, and finally on English affairs. Most immediately, it polarized French politics in an ominous new way. The heir to Henry III was now the Protestant King Henry of Navarre. The Catholic party in desperation turned to Philip of Spain for protection and, if necessary, assistance. The Treaty of Joinville (31 December 1584) guaranteed them a substantial subsidy and promised resolute support. For the English it raised the horrid spectre of a French government dependent on a Spanish patron.

And, of course, it vitally affected Dutch hopes and plans. Even before the death of the Prince of Orange, the Dutch had offered Henry III his late brother's office, with the right to send troops into Flanders and Brabant. At the same time they threw out another line to London, appealing to Leicester to back their request, first for 1,500 recruits but then shifting the ground, for a royal army of 6,000 foot and 3,000 horse plus military supplies. They made no secret of their offer to the French King, not very subtly suggesting they would prefer Elizabeth's protection.[45] The Queen, while refusing the Dutch offers, kept a close eye on events, dispatching a new agent, William Davison, to the Low Countries.[46] Negotiations between the States and France came to a head at the beginning of 1585 with an offer of sovereignty to Henry III. In March he gave them a firm refusal. The Catholic leaders, the Guises, were about to take up arms, and the French were frank in admitting to the States envoys that their King's estate was 'so tickle and unsound' that he could afford them no help.[47]

All this was bad news for the English. Any prospect that they could secure French cooperation in checking Philip in the Low Countries was fast disappearing. On the European scale this meant that the premise of the balance-of-power strategy, enunciated in 1581, no longer held. The crucial three-cornered juxtaposition which was supposed to insure against single-power hegemony no longer existed. Events now hastened to a showdown which could no longer be evaded. Brussels had fallen; Mechlin soon followed; Antwerp, closely invested, could not hold out indefinitely. Negotiations for an English alliance had been under way for months, but the Queen hesitated and delayed;

it was not until late August that the Treaty of Nonsuch sealed an alliance between England and the States; it came too late to save Antwerp, which surrendered even as the first royal forces landed on Walcheren.[48]

For the Queen the coming of war was a hard blow. The whole episode of the Anjou match was the most important event in her political career. In 1577 she had turned away from military intervention and devised the grand project which, by her marriage, would cure the deadly disease in the Netherlands and the French bodies politic which threatened to infect the English. Her subjects had prevented the Anjou marriage; the French had rejected the proffered alliance; and Anjou had betrayed the cause he was hired to serve. The King of Spain had watched these efforts of the Queen with growing distrust, a distrust mounting into a conviction that Elizabeth was a deadly enemy who must be destroyed if he were to recover his Netherlands dominions. The Queen's grand strategy to preserve the peace had led to a war in which England stood almost alone, her only ally the beleaguered remnant of the rebellious Provinces who were desperately resisting Parma's seemingly irresistible progress.

17
The Coming of War

The decision to assist the States with armed force was precipitated by events in the Low Countries and France in 1584 and 1585, but it came at the end of an unhappy deterioration of Anglo-Spanish relations dating back to 1578. In that year Don Bernardino de Mendoza had arrived to reopen the Spanish embassy in London, closed since de Spes's enforced departure in 1571. Philip's renewed interest in England was, of course, connected with the collapse of his authority in the Low Countries and English intervention in that arena. Paradoxically, most of the business that Mendoza would transact in London would have little directly to do with Low Countries events. There was no reciprocal return of an English ambassador to Madrid. The occasional messengers dispatched by the Queen with particular communications were coldly received, indeed, rebuffed. What intelligence England had from Spain came through Walsingham's spy network. Diplomatic relations were conducted solely through Mendoza in London.

Although the Queen might be flattered by the rank and dignity of the new envoy, she would soon find him a very unsatisfactory representive of his master in this sensitive post. In spite of the long absence of formal Spanish representation at London, relations between the courts had been amicable, particularly since the settlement of the trade embargoes in 1574, and Mendoza's instructions were conciliatory in tone. The ambassador was to maintain civil relations and do all he could to dissuade the Queen from intervention in the Provinces, although he was given little leverage to accomplish this other than the general argument that English self-interest lay with the avoidance of frictions which might lead to war. During the

Anjou match negotiations he could do little to avert the marriage except orchestrate an obbligato of warnings about French duplicity.

Mendoza was ill-suited for the implementation of such a low-key strategy. In temperament and character he embodied the English sterotype of the proud Spaniard. He made no attempt to disguise his assurance of Spanish superiority, his contempt for the English, and his abhorrence of their heretical religion. His arrival coincided with the resurgence of English Catholic piety, and the arrival of the missionary priests, which so alarmed the English authorities. This in turn was paralleled by the appearance of Catholic lay conspiracy aimed at replacing Queen Elizabeth by Queen Mary. These developments produced a burgeoning anti-Popery of a ferociously intolerant kind. At the same time Mendoza's task was made more difficult still by the emergence of two new areas of Anglo-Spanish friction – the New World and Ireland.

The death of King Sebastian of Portugal in the year of Mendoza's arrival and the prospect that his aged successor would soon be replaced by Philip had stimulated Elizabeth's overtures for a French alliance; and once the Spanish King was installed at Lisbon, active support for the native pretender, the exiled Don Antonio, was canvassed in the English and French courts. Antonio actually arrived in England in 1581, although Elizabeth backed away from participation in the French-sponsored Azores expedition of 1583. However, collaboration with the pretender and intervention in the Atlantic islands remained a live option. His flag was a convenient cover for the growing fleet of privateers preying on Iberian colonial commerce. Interest in the Portuguese islands formed part of larger designs on the Spanish New World. Hawkins's voyages in the 1560s had been an effort, half-commercial, half-piratical, to break into the protected market of the Spanish colonial empire. After he was crushed by the Spaniards at San Juan de Ulloa on the Mexican coast in 1569, English voyages in American waters became unashamedly piratical in character. Drake won his spurs in such enterprises, while the prospective returns lured court patrons, including Leicester, into backing individual enterprises.[1]

The Queen entered this scene as a tacit patroness when she became a silent partner in Drake's famous voyage of 1577–80. She had been reluctant to authorize an earlier scheme, pushed by a Devonian syndicate in 1574, but in 1577 she gave her assent to Drake's enterprise. No royal ships or money were involved, but a clutch of grandees were among its backers, Walsingham, Hatton, Leicester, Lord Admiral

Lincoln, but not Burghley. In return for her assent the Queen was assured of a share in whatever profits the voyage yielded. The departure was, of course, kept as secret as possible, but on Drake's return, triumphant and laden with booty in 1580, Elizabeth gave him full public recognition, culminating in his knighting in April 1581.[2] At the ceremony the Queen taunted Philip by declaring that he had demanded Drake's head; she had brought a gilded sword with which to strike it off. By now relations with Spain, amicable enough when Sir Francis sailed from Plymouth, had soured to a point where Elizabeth had no hesitation about a public challenge to Philip. In the interval England and Spain had come into hostile contact in a new theatre, Ireland.

When Mendoza brought forward his recriminations about Drake's depredations, Elizabeth skilfully evaded him by pushing her own grievance against his master. In 1579 and again in 1580 Philip had allowed two papally backed expeditions, manned in part by Spanish volunteers, to sail for Ireland. The first left from Lisbon, but the second departed from a Spanish port. The 1579 expedition had triggered off the Desmond rebellion which ravished the province of Munster for the next several years. The Queen insisted that she be given an explanation of these enterprises before she would grant Mendoza an official audience.[3] She kept the humiliated envoy dangling for nine months while she flirted with Don Antonio. Two stormy interviews followed: after the first Mendoza demanded his passports; after the second he was told he would in the future see only Privy Councillors.[4]

Mendoza had provoked the royal irritation by his hectoring manner and implied threats even before he was denied access to the Queen. When he sought recall to Spain his master tacitly rebuked him, urging him 'not to snap the thread of negotiation as you will do if you leave and will plunge me into obligations which at present are best avoided.' The ambassador replied that it took 'more prudence than I possess to deal with people so evil-minded, cautious, and fickle'. At the bottom of Mendoza's mind there lurked the conviction that the English regime must sooner or later be destroyed. That conviction pervaded all the reports he forwarded home and were bound to add to the Spanish king's growing hostility, already provoked by English patronage of the rebels. In the last interview Mendoza had with Elizabeth in October 1581 he recited the whole roll of Spanish complaints — the Portuguese pretender, Drake, the Low Countries — only to be angrily told by the Queen that since he came he had done nothing but make complaints. This provoked the high-tempered ambassador into the retort that perhaps cannon would make her hear better. This ended his usefulness at the Elizabethan court; he lingered on, shunned by courtiers and Councillors, for another two years.[5]

If Mendoza ceased to deal with the court in his official capacity, he did not hesitate to dabble unofficially in intrigue against it. He was instructed by Philip carefully to abstain from involvement in any plots against the Queen, although he was to give a friendly reception to any English Catholic who approached him. In fact, like his predecessors, he found it impossible to separate his role as ambassador from that of protector of the English Catholics. Initially he stuck to his brief and repelled the overture of the Marian party in Scotland.[6] However, when in 1580 Mary Stuart, despairing of help elsewhere, took matters into her hands by offering to place herself, her son, and her kingdom in Philip's hands the ambassador was gradually drawn into a web of conspiracy which would end in his ignominious expulsion two years later.

From 1581 he became a confidant of the Scottish queen and pressed her case with his master. This led him into cooperation with English and Scottish Catholics, using Jesuits as go-betweens. He allowed himself to be entangled in a complicated intrigue by which the French Duke of Guise, with Spanish blessing, would bring a force to England to rescue his Stuart cousin. Mendoza was opposed to any scheme which was not dominated by Spanish influence, but the Queen of Scots was not in his control. His dealings with Mary ultimately involved him in a plot, the Throckmorton conspiracy, in which Guise, Mary Stuart, and a cluster of English lay Catholics had a hand. Mendoza's voice was one of moderation, but he did not control the strings. Quite early on Walsingham's agents tapped into the conspiracy, and when the plotters were unmasked the ambassador's role was widely publicized by the government. Mendoza himself was sent packing in January 1584. He left behind him among Englishmen an almost hysterical distrust of his countrymen, and took with him a conviction that only force would bring the English to their senses.

In the months after the death of William of Orange in July 1584, England moved hesitantly but inexorably towards war. When the Dutch sought aid from both England and France, the Queen's responses had been contradictory. While she was fearful of French intervention in the Low Countries, she hoped for some form of collaboration by which she could keep them in rein, but French responses to any suggestion of collaboration were unhopeful.

In October 1584 she turned to her council for advice on the most difficult question they had faced in her reign. First, if the French refused cooperation 'shall Her Majesty take in hand to defend and protect them [the Low Countries], to recover their liberties and freedom from the tyranny and persecution of the Roman Inquisition?' Secondly, 'if Her Majesty shall not take them into her defence, then what shall she do to provide for her own surety against the King of Spain's malice and forces, which he shall offer against this realm when he hath subdued Holland and Zeeland?'[7] The second question posited that Philip saw England not only as an obstacle to his reconquest of the Low Countries but as an enemy in its own right, whose destruction was the next item on his agenda once he had crushed the rebellious provinces.

The argument for intervention rested on familiar grounds, the long-standing 'ill mind' of Philip towards England, going back to 1558 and based on 'his mortal enmity against all persons not of the Romish religion'. Once victorious in the Low Countries, with abundance of men and ships at his disposal, he would turn his resources against the Queen. War was inevitable; better to forestall it by acting now while Dutch resistance was still alive, for once triumphant in the Low Countries, Spain would be 'so formidable to all the rest of Christendom as that Her Majesty shall no wise be able with her own power nor with the aid of any other neither by sea nor land to withstand his attempts'. The opponents of action urged that the leaderless States were likely to fall apart, that the cost would be too great even to be estimated, and that intervention would bring war with a power that now had Portugal and the riches of the East Indies at its disposal. Most of the Low Countries had returned to obedience; the French king was neutralized by his own domestic problems; the Emperor was Spain's ally; even the King of Scotland might join the enemy; the Queen stood alone. Spain hardly needed to resort to force; a commercial embargo without military action would bring the kingdom to its knees.

The advice papers went on to say that if the Queen should decide to aid the States, she must have two ports in her control, an English noble commander for the States army, English oversight of taxes and finance; and the assured dependence of the King of Scotland. The King of Navarre should be encouraged to attack his lost lands across the Pyrenees and even to venture into the Indies. Casimir should be hired (with Dutch money) to invade Friesland and Guelderland.

If the Queen should decide to leave the Low Countries to their fates, she must strengthen her navy, hire mercenaries to guard the Scottish borders and the sea coast, and take measures against the

English Catholics. Such a bristling hedgehog would 'become impregnable on every side, be secure at home and a terror to her enemies'. The States were dismissed as rebels against their lawful prince, who had forfeited the liberties which they enjoyed only by their ruler's grace. If Elizabeth aided them, she would meet with the same ingratitude as the French Protestants displayed in 1563.[8]

The bulk of the Council backed the interventionist position, but the Queen still hoped for French cooperation. At one point — to Walsingham's dismay — she even considered French domination of the Low Countries preferable to Spanish restoration.[9] In January 1585, when the States delegation arrived at Paris, Davison, her emissary at The Hague, was allowed to hold out hopes of English aid. In March, when it became certain that French help would not materialize, Leicester wrote with cheerful assurance that 'the Lord will appoint them a better defence'. Elizabeth had given Davison authority to tell the States that 'rather than that they should perish', she would take them into her protection — on her terms.[10] In April the Queen authorized Davison to proceed to negotiations, but in the same letter in which Walsingham retailed this information, he added in a despondent postscript that 'those whose judgment Her Majesty most trusts [are] so coldly affected to the cause that I have no great hope of the matter'.[11] The reference was, of course, to Burghley.

Antwerp, totally surrounded, was not under close siege; but in spite of its urgencies, the matter moved slowly, partly because of the Queen's hesitations, partly because of Dutch delays. Leicester and Walsingham suspected Burghley of dragging his feet,[12] although the Treasurer stoutly denied it. The commissioners arrived in June; bargaining was keen on both sides. Then in July the Queen was pushed to decision. Her first action, the dispatch of Drake's fleet to the West Indies, was triggered by Philip's seizure of an English grain fleet. Spain was always a grain importer; at this moment the prospect of a deficient harvest made the situation urgent, and the King invited the dispatch of English grain, offering safe conducts to the ships. When they arrived, he seized them and arrested their crews. One ship escaped to bring the news home. The English had at the same time intercepted a royal Spanish letter which referred to the fleet preparing against England.[13] The Queen responded by embargoing Spanish ships and commissioning Drake to sail for the Spanish coast and the West Indies on a mission of reprisal.

Ostensibly this expedition was launched in retaliation for the grain ship seizure. These had in fact already been released by the time

Drake sailed. His real purpose, carefully planned in advance, was a raid on the principal West Indian ports. Most of the ships were provided by private subscribers, largely Londoners or courtiers, who hoped to turn a pretty penny on the profits of plunder. They were to be disappointed: Drake captured both Santo Domingo and Cartagena, but the adventurers' returns gave them only fifteen shillings on each pound invested. This was to be the first of a series of expeditions in which incompatible goals jarred one another. The political purpose of the expedition was presumably to fire a warning shot across Philip's bows by displaying English power to harm him and his subjects. But for Drake and his investors the object was profit. There was also a vestige of some larger enterprise of Sir Francis in an aborted plan to seize and hold Havana. The net result strategically was substantial damage to Spanish property; but Philip was more convinced than ever that he must destroy Elizabeth's regime before he could reconquer his own Low Countries provinces.[14]

The Queen was now prepared to make solid commitments to the States, yet even in late July she reverted to her earlier insistence that it be clandestine.[15] However, on 2 August she signed a treaty for the relief of Antwerp, and on the 12th at Nonsuch a general treaty of assistance was sealed. When the Dutch commissioners came to say farewell, the Queen cheered them by her words: 'You see, gentlemen, that I have opened the door, that I am embarking once for all with you in a war against the King of Spain. Very well, I am not anxious about the matter. I hope that God will aid us and that we shall strike a good blow in your cause.'[16]

The 4,000 troops who arrived in late August at Flushing were commanded by the veteran Sir John Norris, returning from Ireland to the scene of his earlier exploits. This was a temporary arrangement. The importance of the post of commander and the urgency of the time demanded that the general be someone of noble rank who also carried great political weight. Leicester was the obvious candidate. An earl and the Queen's confidant, he had been the backer of the Dutch cause ever since 1572 and had many connections in the Provinces. Dutch expectations ran so high that one enthusiast proclaimed him a reborn Prince of Orange.[17]

The decision was, of course, the Queen's, and neither she nor Leicester were quite so confident about the choice. When Walsingham wrote that the fall of Antwerp had not altered royal intentions, the Queen commanded him to ask if Leicester were still prepared to accept the command. Leicester dutifully accepted a post which was

God's service as much as the Queen's; but what worried him was Elizabeth's attitude. How firm was her commitment? Her repeated hesitations, her disposition to halt, even to turn back at each step, raised grave doubts as to her resoluteness in the whole enterprise. Would she make the all-out effort which the situation demanded, or would she be only half-hearted in dribbling out inadequate aid?

> Yes, Mr Secretary, I must deal plainly with you . . . I do find all sorts of men . . . so daunted with this conceit as those who would have run to this service at the beginning will slowly go now if they be entreated for they will not believe that Her Majesty will so deal in it as they hope either of good assurance or such counsel as is fit for men that must go hazard their lives.

Drake had just managed to escape from Plymouth before another change of the royal mind halted him.

After her initial bid for his acceptance of the command, the Queen now turned around 180 degrees. Walsingham was sure it would not be given to Leicester; Lord Grey, a former Irish deputy, was spoken of. The Queen feared that Leicester 'would carry with [him] too great a troop', assume too great a state for a subject. Moreover, she could not bring herself to face his absence; she was beset by irrational fears that she would not live to see his return. When she finally brought herself to consent to his going, it was only to reverse the decision within three days and then, a weathercock, swinging around again, to approve his appointment. It was not until 22 October that the formal commission was issued.[18]

Elizabeth's concern that Leicester would display too great state was not merely royal disapproval of a subject's ostentation, but a reflection of the fact that Leicester's appointment had a dual nature — political as well as military. As her general he had a daily allowance of £6, but the Earl had borrowed £25,000 from the City (secured by a royal guarantee for which he mortgaged his estates to the crown). This was to provide for the personal household of seventy-five which accompanied him, and to pay for the footmen and horse recruited by him. There went with him a retinue of some twenty knights and gentlemen, as well as his stepson, the Earl of Essex, and Lord North.[19] All this stately show was in part intended to manifest the dignity and power of his royal mistress; but it also anticipated the role he expected to play in the Low Countries, and which the Dutch assumed he would play. By the terms of the treaty the English general would command all the forces of the States, while two Englishmen would sit on their small executive board, the council of state. Elizabeth clearly expected the English to have a preponderant role in all decision-making, yet at the same time she was adamant in rejecting the States' offer of sovereignty. There was to be no slightest suggestion that she coveted another prince's lands. Her general would be a curious hybrid, something more than an ambassador, a good deal less than a viceroy.

The Dutch saw matters rather differently. They had ousted Philip as their sovereign ruler, in his various Low Countries capacities, by their declaration of 1581. Anjou had been solemnly sworn in as Count of Flanders and Duke of Brabant, and as Governor-General of all the provinces. When he retired there had been plans to install William of Orange, as *Stadhouder* (regent) in the two counties of Holland and Zeeland. It was now expected that Leicester would assume supreme powers even though the Queen had rejected them for herself.[20]

Leicester, on his arrival in the Low Countries, made a progress which rivalled in its splendour those of his mistress through her English counties. This was followed in early January 1586 by the offer of the governor-generalship of the provinces, as it had been held in Charles V's time. The Earl had no hesitation in accepting without consulting his sovereign. He quite disingenuously claimed that the States General's invitation was a surprise. In fact the matter had been discussed before he left, and the Earl had insisted he must have the same powers as 'any other governor or captain general hath had heretofore'.[21]

Elizabeth's reaction was one of unbounded fury. She ordered the Earl to lay down the office, admitting that he had acted in contempt of her authority and dishonoured her in the eyes of the European princes. The Queen, by no mean reconciled to war with Spain, was determined to avoid any provocation which might close the door to negotiation.[22] It took all the soothing skills of Burghley and Hatton to calm the waters, and eventually the Queen agreed to Leicester's retaining the title. Yet a month later she reversed herself, and it took another round of ministerial diplomacy to end the matter. The whole episode was an unedifying start to Leicester's expedition and a warning of the differences between the Queen and her commander.[23]

Leicester was not acting alone. When Parliament met in February 1587 there was a bold move by a group of Privy Councillors, including Hatton, Mildmay, and Knollys along with a number of weighty Commons members. The minutes of a parliamentary committee reveal a proposal to offer the Queen a special tax, over and above the subsidy, to be levied on wealthier subjects for an indefinite term — if she would accept the sovereignty of Holland and Zeeland. The Queen promptly quashed the scheme, but it is indicative of the determination of the activist party to turn the intervention in the Low Countries into something more than support of the Dutch; it was to be an essay in English imperialism.[24]

Leicester in the mean time was struggling with logistical problems which were exacerbated by Elizabeth's half-hearted backing for the war. Given the lack of any permanent English military establishment, Leicester had to make do with a structure built from scratch. Its basic administrative principles derived from a time when each commander was a military contractor, paid wholesale for his services and responsible for paying and equipping his men as his employees. Sums of money were sent over to the treasurer at war in Holland, who in turn disbursed these moneys to the captains of the companies. Theoretically this was done only when a muster was taken; in practice the money was handed out in 'prests', loans to each captain for which accounting would eventually be made. The system was riddled with opportunities for private gain. But problems were compounded by the Queen's reluctance to expend her resources in a war which she had so reluctantly entered. Thanks to the Queen's fits of 'sparing humour', the money came to the Low Countries in irregular dollops. Usually, by the time it arrived it served only to liquidate the loans incurred while the treasurer at war awaited its coming.

The manpower situation was as desperate as the fiscal. Rates of desertion and sickness were high, but the Queen was loath to levy replacements; and when they did come, fresh from plough and shop, ill-equipped and untrained, they were the despair of the commanders. In short order an acrimonious correspondence sprang up between Leicester and the home authorities, each blaming the other, while the Queen stormed at the Earl for his incompetency and wastefulness. It is not easy to allocate blame, given the built-in defects of the machinery, but it would be hard to give Leicester high marks as an administrator. Yet one cannot but sympathize with a commander who was left without adequate funds or troops through the Queen's unwillingness to release them for his needs. Under these circumstances it was unlikely Leicester would accomplish much militarily. In fact, he did clear the way for reopening trade up the Rhine, but was then deflected to the rescue of two beleaguered towns, Grave and Venlo, both of which were lost to the enemy. To offset these setbacks, Leicester was able to recover Doesburg from the enemy and to isolate Zutphen. In the 1586 campaign the Earl had at least held further Spanish advances in check; the Spanish for the first time had only minor successes to record at the end of the campaign year.

While Leicester went about his summer's business, his position and that of the Anglo-Dutch alliance was being undercut by the activities of his sovereign. She was repeating her performance of the pre-war years. Just as she had backed away from committing her arms to the French in the early 1580s, so now, even though she had signed the Treaty of Nonsuch, she had not fully accepted the finality of that decision. Ever hopeful of staving off war by some compromise, she now pinned her hopes on a settlement negotiated with the Duke of Parma. A private initiative by a merchant had opened a tortuous path which ultimately provided access to Parma. Rumours of some sort of peace feelers were circulating as early as the end of 1585, and in May 1586 actual contact was opened with the Duke. The initiator on the English side was Sir James Croft, Comptroller of the Household, who had served as an informant to Mendoza and had always taken a pro-Spanish line. Flemish merchants acted as intermediaries. In July the Queen wrote directly to Parma, asserting her aims to be simply her own safety and her neighbours' freedom.[25]

A series of exchanges ensued. Rumours of their existence spread widely and the States protested vigorously in March 1587, but the Queen stuck to a set of proposals which more or less reiterated the line she had always followed — a return to the *status quo ante* of the Emperor Charles's time.[26] Negotiations moved at a very halting pace; it was not until September 1587 that Burghley drafted instructions for a mission to meet with Parma's representatives; it was February 1588 before the commissioners crossed the seas, and another month before they met the Duke's representatives at Bourbourg near Ostend. The Spanish yielded little or nothing in negotiation, while the English, on royal command, abandoned one condition after another. The farce came to an end in late July with the arrival of the Armada. The brute fact was that the Queen had allowed her desperate hopes for peace to blind her to the realities of the situation. The Spanish had been delighted to keep her in play while they completed their naval preparations. For Elizabeth it was both a humiliation and a betrayal.

This whole episode had angered the States General and badly eroded Dutch confidence in English intentions. It added to a whole bundle of accumulated grievances that troubled relations between the allies and made life miserable for the increasingly unhappy Leicester. Already in the spring of 1586 his letters home were full of laments that the Queen had no confidence in him and was indeed using him to mount a diversion to help bring Parma to terms. He believed himself abandoned by his allies: 'I see all men have friends but myself.'[27] In September the Council was debating his recall, and 'such as do not love him' were reputed to be in a majority. The Earl was summoned home, reaching England in late November.[28]

There were many causes for criticism of the Earl's record in Holland. Leicester, the amateur, had tangled with Norris, the professional, and although there was a temporary reconciliation on the Earl's departure it was short-lived; Norris would eventually be hauled before the Privy Council at Leicester's instigation. Nor had the latter been happy in his relations with the Dutch leadership. He showed little judgment of persons or grasp of problems, and was soon embroiled in factional politics of which he had little understanding. Then his reputation and that of the English were badly battered by an event of January 1587. Deventer was occupied by an English garrison in Dutch pay under Sir William Stanley, a protégé of the Earl. Unpaid for six months, he preyed upon the citizens, who in turn complained to the States General. Money was sent, but too late; Stanley defected to the Spanish with his troops.

This event, along with general discontent about the Earl's government, led to an important, indeed, definitive shift of direction by the Dutch leadership. Abandoning the traditional premise that the Provinces required a single governor, the representative of an outside protecting power, they moved to the formation of a truly sovereign state. Led by Oldenbarnvelt, the Advocate of Holland, in alliance with the Dutch general Hohenlohe and Count Maurice, son of the late prince and head of the Orange interest, they asserted that sovereign power lay with the States General. This was a direct challenge to Leicester, who responded by supporting their enemies among the Dutch politicians.

Thus things stood at Leicester's departure for England at the end of 1586. The Earl, cordially received by the Queen, nevertheless found himself obliged to give an account of his rule. Sulking, he withdrew to Bath. The Council was bombarded with complaints from Norris, the English commander, and Wilkes, the English member of the council of state. Over the winter things drifted, but in the spring of 1587 Leicester's presence was needed in the Low Countries as Parma began his approaches to the strategic port of Sluys. The Queen delayed, sending Lord Buckhurst on an investigative mission to Holland. In the end, against much advice, she ordered the Earl's return.

He asked for a loan of £10,000 but got only £6,000, secured by a mortgage on his sweet wines farm and his farm of alienation of fines.[29] This time the Queen backed him against the States General, demanding for him the executive powers she had denied him at his first arrival. Dutch eagerness to grant them had now soured, and his return reopened hostilities with them.

Leicester soon lost control of the States forces in Holland and Zeeland; the pro-English faction controlled only the garrisons of the inland provinces, Overyssel and East Friesland. The Earl fiercely attacked his colleagues Norris and Wilkes; the former was summoned before the Privy Council, the latter dispatched to the Fleet prison. Amidst this unseemly wrangling, Sluys fell to Parma. The States General were filled with angry suspicion about the dealings with Parma on which the Queen was placing her hopes. The temperature of Anglo-Dutch relations had sunk nearly to freezing point. Leicester, tired, defeated, and sick, begged for relief, and in December 1587 left Holland for good. In spite of his lack of success overseas, the Earl's personal credit with the Queen was little diminished, and in what would prove to be the last year of his life he would be called to great responsibilities in the defence of the realm against the Armada.

From the time of Anjou's departure from the Low Countries the Queen had been faced with a series of unpalatable choices as one calamity after another narrowed her range of action and pushed her towards open conflict with Spain. Hitherto her options had always allowed her a margin of manœuvre; her commitments were limited, often no more than tentative. The furthest she had gone was to give financial support to the States, directly or indirectly by her subsidy to Anjou. In all her commitments she had always left a door open through which she could withdraw. Once the French made clear their inability to respond to the Dutch plea, the last door had closed. Antwerp stood poised to fall; leaderless, the two Provinces threw themselves at the Queen's feet. If she refused to act, all the probabilities pointed to final Spanish reconquest. Then, according to the majority of Elizabeth's Councillors, Spain would turn on England. Under these pressures the Queen had to give way; yet hardly had her troops departed for Zeeland than she began groping for some way to squirm out of her commitment to the States. Frantic, she clutched at straws and deceived herself into thinking she could make a deal with Parma. The resulting manœuvres revealed the Queen at her worst as, ostrich-like, she refused to face the consequences of her own past actions and to accept the fact that Philip regarded her as his prime enemy. It would take the betrayal at Bourbourg and the thunder of the Armada's cannon to jar her into accepting the bleak reality of all-out war.

Part V

The Waging of War
1585–1603

18

Armada and Counter-Armada

The year 1588 was foretold by the soothsayers as an 'admirable year'. German chronographers presaged that it would be the climacteric year of the world.[1] Contemporary Englishmen were certain, by its opening months, that Spain was preparing a great invasion fleet of unprecedented size; through the spring reports of its mobilization poured in, including a false report in March that it had actually sailed.[2] Philip had now been persuaded by his advisers that he must strike down England first if he wished to recover the rest of the Low Countries. These arguments were amply justified by the record of the past dozen years, in which the islanders had consistently supported the rebel cause with men, money, and diplomacy, and now by open intervention. Beyond these mere temporal considerations was the crying evil of the heretical English regime, proclaimed by the Popes to be a cancer within the body of Catholic Christendom. The acquisition of the Portuguese galleon fleet, used so successfully in the naval operation against Don Antonio's base in the Azores in 1583, gave Spain the resources for a naval attack.

Elizabeth had now to face the eventuality she had striven so long and so hard to avoid. Indeed, she did not give up hope to the very last; her commissioners were dealing with Parma's when the Armada reached the Channel. For the Queen there was now nothing for it but to shoulder the heavy burdens of full-scale war with her powerful enemy. What were the resources at her disposal?

The century had been one of rapid development in the war-making capacity of the Continental monarchies. Some of them now maintained permanent standing forces of men trained in the use of firearms or the pike, under officers who made a lifetime career of military service. In these developments England had lagged greatly. Her armies were still scratch forces of raw recruits, raised for the occasion, usually for no more than a single campaign season. The only sustained campaign in which English soldiers had fought was the attempt to bully Scotland into submission between 1547 and 1550. There was no permanent administrative structure to provide for supply of food or clothing; contractors were called in to serve these needs. An ordnance office in the Tower provided a rudimentary organization for the procurement and supply of arms. Since then, except for small garrisons on the Scottish border and in Ireland, the crown had maintained no regular soldiery. However, since Edward VI's time provision had been made for a militia. All able-bodied men were liable for service, but the new plan now adopted established a select body in each county, the trained bands, who received annual training. They were officered by the local squirearchy under the overall command of a lord lieutenant; a permanent magazine was maintained in each county. These forces were designed for entirely defensive use.

Weakness in land forces was an acceptable risk so long as an enemy could be halted at sea; and here the English had kept abreast of important changes in naval warfare. Since the beginning of the dynasty the crown had maintained a fleet in being based on permanent dockyards on the Thames and Medway and at Portsmouth. These provided bases for a new type of warship. With them began a whole new epoch of naval warfare. Heavily armed, these sailing vessels, abandoning the ancient practice of boarding, depended on their artillery to destroy their opponents. Under Henry VIII the fleet was built up to a peak of over fifty ships, but under his successors its numbers and efficiency declined. Elizabeth and, more particularly, Burghley undertook its renovation, although on a smaller scale than in Henry's time. There was now an embryonic navy board with a staff of permanent professional officials. This body in the early years of Elizabeth's reign consisted of a group of men who, although competent professionals, used their offices as opportunity for building their own fortunes. A new chapter in the history of the navy began with the appointment in 1577 of John Hawkins as treasurer of the navy. A Plymouth merchant by origin, he had made his name as the buccaneer-trader who attempted to force his way into the Spanish colonial market by providing slaves from west Africa. His last voyage had ended in spectacular disaster at the Mexican port of San Juan de Alloa in 1569. He won his new office by a promise to cut maintenance costs, a sure bait for royal approbation. He was able to persuade Burghley (to whom he reported rather than to the Lord Admiral) to privatize the whole maintenance of the navy, which Hawkins contracted to accomplish for a fixed annual fee.[3] In this happy instance the royal passion for economy could be satisfied along with the strategic needs of naval defence.

Hawkins was more than an efficient naval administrator and entre-preneur. He was also an innovative strategist with large conceptions of the offensive potential of English sea-power. Until now the navy had been conceived largely as a defensive force, operating in home waters against possible invaders. Hawkins, with his oceanic experience, sought to make the royal fleet an instrument of attack. Such a strategy necessitated a change in naval architecture, the shift from the top-heavy caravel with its high castles rising from the deck to the narrower and low-built galleon. Under Hawkins many of the Queen's ships were economically rebuilt to the new model. More seaworthy, more manœuvrable, and capable of venturing beyond the home seas of Britain, these ships could be put to new and bold enterprises. They were prime weapons in Hawkins's grand strategy, which sought to move away from the cautiously defensive posture of the past to a deliberately offensive thrust against the power of the Spanish empire. Hawkins saw the life-line of Spanish power in the annual plate fleet which delivered the Peruvian silver to Cadiz each year. Cut this artery, and Spain would be brought to her knees, at England's mercy. Not only would the Spanish menace be wiped out but the way would be open for Elizabeth to assume an imperial role herself.

In 1585 such a strategy of offence was essayed in Drake's Indies voyage, the first attempt to use English naval power to assail the enemy on his own ground. Drake's successful raid on the West Indian ports displayed the potentialities of England's striking power. A vari-ant mode of attack was adopted in 1587, when Drake raked the Iberian coasts in an effort to cripple preparations for the Armada. What strat-egy should be used now, when invasion loomed close?

Preparations for the coming onslaught began with a commission to Lord Admiral Howard as commander-in-chief of a navy and army preparing for sea against Spain in December 1587.[4] Land preparations began at the same time with mustering instructions for the lord lieu-tenants.[5] At Plymouth the urgency of the situation led to work on the ships being carried on by torchlight.[6] As the ships were readied, Drake pressed on the Council a plan to forestall the Spanish by another attack on their coast,[7] which he retailed in letters to the Queen.[8] She, however, still hopeful of some result from the negotiations with

Parma, held him in check. The Lord Admiral wrote angrily to Secretary Walsingham that the Spanish merely sought to deceive the English, adding his hope they would not have cause to curse the grey beard with a white head. The Secretary knew whom he meant – the Lord Treasurer,[9] the sponsor of the mission to Parma.

In June there was finally movement. The Spanish fleet under its reluctant new chief, the Duke of Medina Sidonia, put out early in the month, only to be forced back by storms. This was not known at Plymouth until late June.[10] By 6 July Howard and his ships were at sea, spread out from Ushant to the Scillies.[11] Believing the Spanish to be seriously damaged by the late storm, the Admiral boldly sailed for the Spanish coast, and was only forty leagues north of Galicia when the winds changed and drove him back to Plymouth.[12] They were watering and revictualling there for another sally when on 19 July they were apprised of the Armada's arrival. The southerly winds which had brought them back home had wafted the Spanish northward to the Channel mouth. The Admiral piously blessed God for turning his fleet back.[13]

Up to this point Elizabeth had retained control of naval operations, holding her sailors in check, like bears tied to the stake while assailed by dogs, in the Admiral's bitter words,[14] while she dispatched her mission to Parma. In June, while yielding to the Admiral's wish to sally out, she nervously urged that he keep to a westerly course lest he miss the Spanish *en route* to a landing in northern England. Her nightmare was a scenario in which the Spanish arrived off an undefended English coast while the English fleet was at sea, seeking the enemy.

Once the Armada had arrived off Cornwall the Queen had to leave decisions to her admirals; until the invaders were dealt with, events were out of her hands. The ensuing ten-day battle tested for the first time the new technology of the armed warship in defensive encounter. The manœuvrability of the English ships stood them in good stead as they pursued the foe up the Channel, peppering his ships with constant gunfire although inflicting only light damage. Medina Sidonia had the unenviable task of shepherding a squadron of troop-laden transports while keeping the English fleet in play, all the while pressing forward to his anticipated rendezvous with Parma at one of the Flemish ports. The climax of the engagement came at Calais, where Medina Sidonia was anchored, frantically seeking contact with Parma, who in his turn was waiting for the Admiral to clear the Channel of English ships so that the Spanish forces waiting on the

Flemish shore could cross. The English launched their famous fire-ships; none of which achieved its intended goal, but the panic they created served to break up the formation of the Spanish fleet, scattering its vessels along the Flemish coast, where duels were fought by individual ships with some losses to the invaders. The crux of the matter lay in the dispersal of Medina Sidonia's fleet and the fact that he was now driven northward beyond any possibility of junction with Parma. There was no option left for him but to return homeward by the circuitous north Atlantic route around Scotland and Ireland and back across Biscay. A bout of appalling weather accomplished what the English had failed to do; not much more than half the fleet limped into Spanish ports in the early autumn.

With the arrival of the Spanish off the south coast, the English put into action their plans for land mobilization. Two major armies assembled, made up of county contingents. One, commanded by Leicester, was assembled in Essex with headquarters at Tilbury, since an attempted landing at the Thames mouth was expected. This numbered on paper 22,000 foot and 1,000 horse. A second army, under Lord Chamberlain Hunsdon, the Queen's cousin, was to protect her person. It numbered some 36,000 all told.[15] If the enemy landed, Leicester would pursue a scorched-earth policy of strategic withdrawal. The brevity of the naval struggle meant that these arrangements were barely in place before the Spanish were fleeing northward and luckily their efficiency was not to be tested.[16] There were very quickly difficulties about provisioning forces of this size; the Essex contingent arrived to find neither beer nor bread. Earlier, the fleet had been long delayed at Plymouth while its provisioners scoured the countryside in search of supplies. Had the army been kept together for a longer period, the problem would have been acute.

Leicester now invited the Queen to visit the camp at Tilbury and show herself to her troops.[17] Elizabeth, at St James's, responded readily, and on 9 August (after the Spanish were well in flight but before fear of their return had subsided) she arrived at the camp. Mounted behind Lord Chamberlain Hunsdon, she rode among her troops, 'sometime with a martial pace, another whiles gently like a woman', holding in her hand the truncheon of a leader. This appearance at the head of her forces gave Elizabeth a chance to assert her royal leadership at a moment when her sex seemed to deny its exercise. Woman she might be but she was no less a king. 'I know I have the body of a weak and feeble woman, but I have the heart and stomach of a king, and of a king of England too, and think foul scorn that

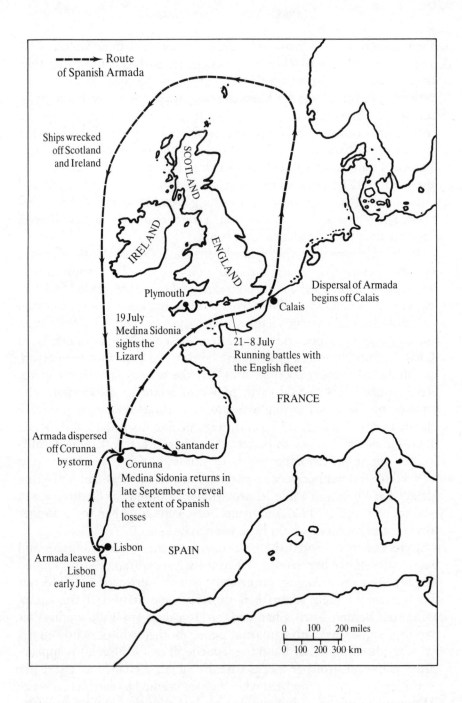

Route
of Spanish Armada

Ships wrecked
off Scotland
and Ireland

SCOTLAND

IRELAND

ENGLAND

Plymouth

19 July
Medina Sidonia
sights the
Lizard

Calais

Dispersal of Armada
begins off Calais

21–8 July
Running battles with
the English fleet

FRANCE

Armada dispersed
off Corunna
by storm

Santander

Corunna
Medina Sidonia returns in
late September to reveal
the extent of Spanish
losses

Lisbon

SPAIN

Armada leaves
Lisbon
early June

| 0 | 100 | 200 miles |

| 0 | 100 | 200 | 300 km |

Map 2: The Route of the Spanish Armada, 1588

Parma or Spain, or any prince of Europe should dare to invade the borders of my realm.'[18]

Later there was official thanksgiving for the victory. On 24 November the Queen rode into the city, in a chariot throne under a canopy supported by four pillars, drawn by two white steeds. She was accompanied by a great company of nobles and courtiers, met by the City corporation at Temple Bar and by the Bishop of London and the Dean of St Paul's at the cathedral door. The bishop of Salisbury, Pierce, preached the sermon; the sovereign dined at the Bishop's palace and then returned by torchlight to St James's.

Commemorative medals were struck. One mocked the Spanish with its play on Caesar's line,[19] *venit, videt, fugit* (he came, he saw, he fled). More remembered was the inscription *flevit Deus et inimici dissiparunt* (God blew upon the waters and dispersed His enemies). In fact, the strategic lessons to be drawn from the event were mixed. The English ships had skilfully out-manœuvred their adversaries and maintained the initiative. However, English fire-power had had little effect on the Spanish galleons; losses by direct English action were small. The flawed strategy of the attempt to coordinate the efforts of Medina Sidonia and Parma, which had never won the latter's wholehearted appproval and which was almost impossible to achieve, had much to do with the Spanish failure to invade England. The destruction of the fleet had been largely the work of wind and waves. Moreover, the losses to the Spanish warships, the great galleons which were the core of its fighting strength, had not been great. Their continued existence, and the knowledge that Philip had the power and the will to launch another Armada, were sobering thoughts which shadowed the aftermath of victory. One battle had been won, but there was a war yet to be fought.

Parma's deceitful tactics in prolonging the Bourburg negotiations, protesting the while that he knew nothing of Spanish preparations, profoundly affected the Queen. She had been defeated at her own game in which she thought herself unbeatable. Her confidence that somehow she could, as in the past, by stringing out negotiations avert the ultimate catastrophe of war had been shattered. It left her with a deep bitterness, and an ineradicable distrust of the Spanish which would surface a decade later when the possibility of peace emerged.

The events of 1588 also hardened the English view that Philip's goal was nothing less than all-out extirpation of the English regime. This, of course, had always been the claim of the ultra-Protestants, but now even the sceptical Burghley came around to accepting this judgment of Philip's intentions. In a speech to the Lords in 1593, he compared this struggle with the wars of the first half-century, drawing a sharp contrast.[20] Then Charles V and the Valois kings made wars in which 'none is intended anything more than to be revenged of supposed injuries by burning and winning of some frontier town by besieging'. After inconclusive fighting, the rulers made a truce and sealed it with a marriage. No one ruler by his acquisitions made himself a danger to the others. Now 'the King of Spain maketh these mighty wars by the means only of the Indies, not proposing to burn a town in France or England, but to conquer all France, all England and all Ireland'. Had Burghley, like posterity, had access to the Spanish archives he might have abated some of the rigour of this judgment. As it was, the English were to fight the war in the conviction that the enemy aimed at universal sway so that it was a life-and-death contest. Moreover — a novel factor which was implicit in Burghley's diagnosis — this was a war with no visible end in sight. English military experience, since the end of the Hundred Years War, had been one of short, seasonal campaigns, with mobilization rarely extending beyond a few months. The only approximation to an extended campaign was to be found in the Scottish enterprise of the late 1540s. Since 1585 England had been committed to an indefinite support of the rebel provinces; now those commitments were likely to be extended in other areas.

For Elizabeth this turn of events was a bitterly painful moment. Her whole policy of the past three decades lay in ruins, and with it her vaunted reputation as the guardian of her kingdom's peace, who had kept her people clear of the fire-storm which was raging among their Continental neighbours. Worse still was the loss of control which she now faced. The disadvantages of her sex were borne in upon her. Hitherto she had been able to keep all the strings in her own hands as she manœuvred to piece together a diplomatic combination which would bring Philip to the bargaining table and secure a bloodless outcome. There had been ample opportunity for the techniques of postponement and evasion at which she was so skilful. After the failure to lure Henry III into alliance in 1581 and the fiasco of Anjou's career in the Low Countries, her freedom to manœuvre had steadily contracted; but even after signing the Treaty of Nonsuch she had not given up hope of escaping the tightening net which was forcing her to the arbitrament of war.

Now her independence was straitened, her freedom to assert her untrammelled will sadly diminished, she was forced to take up the role of a warrior queen who could not evade the grand responsibilities of high strategy, where and by what means to assail the enemy. In the urgencies of a campaign the movement of men or ships would not wait on her wavering hesitations. Events quite beyond her control foreclosed the possibilities of choice or the luxury of delay. Moreover, the very nature of the decisions to be made was conditioned by military and naval expertise which Elizabeth necessarily lacked. She was compelled to submit to the judgment of men whose purposes she more than half distrusted, soldiers and sailors whose martial ambitions for professional renown countered her own instinctive fear of risk-taking and her despair at the wasteful expenditure of her slender means.

It is not surprising that these were years when the Queen's political indisposition to act, her instinctive inclination to procrastinate, became more marked than ever. Armies dispatched to the Low Countries or to France, ships sailing away to the Azores or the West Indies, slipped away from her control. The companies sent to Holland or Brittany dwindled away; the demand for more men, more money, more supplies was unending. Her subjects had to be coaxed into doubling and then tripling their taxes, yet the treasury remained empty. The image of the beneficent goddess whose reign was to be a golden era of peace and prosperity faded as the war dragged wearily on, year by year. Nature itself conspired against her as plague raged and the crops failed. Save for Cadiz, there was no Blenheim or Waterloo to dispel the clouds, only the monotonous succession of sieges in Friesland or Gelderland or the slogging campaigns of attrition in Ulster. The reign would close not in the exultation of victory but in gasping relief which greeted the light at the end of a long tunnel

When the Queen and her ministers took counsel as to their conduct of the war, they faced a bleak prospect. At the moment France, the only power which could hold Spain in check, was in the grasp of the ultra-Catholic Guises. Henry of Navarre was in arms against them, but that fact only served to emphasize the paralysis of France on the international scene. Nothing was to be hoped for from that quarter. As for England's only ally, the rebel Provinces, they were now reduced to little more than Holland and Zeeland, their leadership in disarray, with Parma poised for an assault on their remaining strongholds, making them as much a liability as an asset. England stood virtually alone against what its leaders saw as the threat of universal Spanish monarchy.

At home, there was among the ranks of the Councillors to whom the Queen turned for advice a notable vacancy. In early September 1588, Leicester suddenly died. In the previous year, after his return from the Low Countries, he had for a season fallen into royal disfavour; but at the height of the summer crisis the Queen proposed to appoint him her *alter ego* as lieutenant-general of the realm, until Burghley and Hatton dissuaded her from this course.[21] The Queen's notation, 'his last letter', bears mute witness to the end of a thirty-year relationship, the most significant in Elizabeth's personal life.[22] His disappearance left a gaping hole in the team of confidants on whom she had relied for two decades past. A second member of that team, Walsingham, was to die in April 1590. These changes had a profound effect on decision-making at this crucial moment. Leicester and Walsingham had been the most forthright advocates of maximum aid to the Low Countries rebels and of open opposition to Spanish policy. They had looked with dismay on the Queen's effort to reach an accommodation with Parma. Burghley, the prime promoter of that scheme, and the long-term proponent of a minimalist foreign policy, now enjoyed an unchallenged pre-eminence in the royal confidence, heightened even more when Lord Chancellor Hatton went to his grave in November 1591.

The terms of the debate were necessarily altered now that the question was no longer war or peace but how the war should be fought. What strategies should be followed to win it, and what should be the goals they sought to achieve by victory? Two bodies of opinion were clearly apparent. The hawks among Elizabeth's counsellors pressed for all-out attack on Spanish power on its own territories in Iberia, in the Atlantic islands, and in the Indies. The boldest of them believed that English naval power could be used not merely to defend English shores but to break Spain – even more grandly, to make the Queen the arbitress of Europe and reduce the Spanish ruler – in Ralegh's words – to a mere 'king of figs and oranges as in old times'.

Opposed to this expansive vision stood the resolutely insular perspective of Burghley, who insisted that England must tailor her effort to her meagre resources and her goals to the minimum necessary for the security of the kingdom. For him, the war was to be fought not to open new vistas of expanded power but to recover the security of isolation. As things stood, with the disappearance of the three other pre-eminent Councillors, Burghley, by the early 1590s, had no opponents who could sing their siren songs to the Queen. His was the sole voice that had resonance in the royal ear. The hawks no longer had a spokesman in high places. The young Earl of Essex, his stepfather's prospective heir as patron of the hawkish party, enjoyed the Queen's personal favour but as yet had no place in the Council. Ralegh was another spokesman for the activists, but he too lacked the clout of a high official position and soon, by his marriage, forfeited his place at court. The soldiers, Roger Williams and John Norris, and the sailors, Drake and Hawkins, could speak with professional authority but were outside the inner circle of influence.

At least one contemporary pamphlet survives to voice the proposals of the forward party. It was written by a serving soldier, Captain Anthony Wingfield.[23] He recognized that England already had a military commitment in the Low Countries, and that many would prefer to concentrate on those 'wars in the Low Countries which are in auxiliary manner maintained by Her Majesty'. In their eyes 'it stood more with the safety of our estate to bend all our forces against the Duke of Parma'. This was a dead end. In the Low Countries, studded with fortresses and walled towns, large commitment of men and resources would bring at the best a meagre return. Used against Spain they would bring a bonanza of rich rewards. According to Wingfield, Philip had 'set down in council that to recover the Low Countries he must bring war to England'. The defeat of 1588 would only strengthen his resolve to try again. Hence English strategy should aim at a counter-blow of the same kind, establishing a foothold on the Spanish coast by landing 20,000 men, or at least a full-scale blockade of the Baltic ships which brought grain for the feeding of the Spanish population. This was a strategy which, of course, coincided with Hawkins's pre-war proposals and with the practice of 1585 and 1587. It would be consistently pressed on the Queen not only as the key to a conclusion of the war but as the means for a triumphalist victory which would cripple Spanish power.

The debate over strategy was not only over longer-term goals; it had an immediate locus. The English knew by the winter of 1588–9 that the bulk of the Armada survivors, particularly the war galleons, lay in the northern Spanish ports. They were apprehensive that these ships would soon be available for a renewed assault on England. From our perpective such a fear seems exaggerated; from theirs it seemed all too likely that Philip would take the first opportunity to revenge his defeat. In any case it was important that these galleons, the core of his war fleet, be destroyed. It was certainly the Queen's first concern. The experience of the Armada was seared on her mind; haunted by fears of another invasion attempt, she would always give first priority to preventive action.

How to eliminate the war galleons was a matter fraught with difficulty. Such an enterprise required a costly outlay in ships and money and, undertaken solely under crown auspices, it would impose new and heavy charges on a treasury already burdened by the annual subsidy of £126,000 to the States and one which had just laid out £161,000 in defending the country against the Armada. More worrying still, from the Queen's point of view, was the risk to her most precious asset, her war fleet. Throughout the war she would prove more than anxious about any action which might destroy even one of her ships.

Recent experience offered a helpful precedent which would ease the financial burden and spare the royal fleet. In 1585, and again in 1587, Drake had assembled a naval expedition composed of a small core of royal ships augmented by a squadron of privately owned merchantmen converted for the occasion into armed ships of war. They were provided by a list of adventurers, investors lured by the prospect of lucrative returns from plunder and from prizes. The same scheme of a semi-private venture was now to be employed in 1589. However, if profits were to be realized, something more than the destruction of the Spanish galleons would have to be attempted. The result was an expedition with a threefold purpose; all of the goals were desirable; each was incompatible with the other two.

In October 1588 Drake, England's premier seaman, and John Norris, her most experienced soldier, were commissioned to organize an expedition against the Spanish coast and 'to invade and destroy forces of the invaders'. At the same time a bargain was struck with Don Antonio, the Portuguese pretender, then resident in England. Elizabeth would undertake to restore him to his throne; in return he would bear the costs of the expedition and enter into alliance with the Queen. The instructions issued to Drake and Norris in February incorporated this goal with that of scotching the ships.[24] After completing that task, the commanders would proceed to Lisbon, where they were assured a rising in Antonio's favour would take place. Then yet a third goal was added. Once the Portuguese king was reinstated on his throne, Drake and Norris could sail for the Azores with the intent of seizing one of the islands as a base.

These glittering prospects — the possibility of sacking Lisbon if there were resistance — were offered as bait to the London merchants. They responded eagerly: a fleet was assembled consisting of six

Queen's and twenty adventurers' ships.[25] The scope of the enlarged undertaking now encompassed the strategic goals of the minimalist party, the destruction of the invasion fleet, while those of the hawks would be accomplished, first, by wresting one of Philip's kingdoms from him and thus gaining a foothold in the Iberian peninsula and, finally, by seizing one of the Atlantic islands which lay athwart the plate fleet's home-bound route. The enterprise was as grand in its scope as the Spanish effort of the previous year. It was also cursed by the same incompatibility of strategic aims.

The strategy of a semi-privatization was successful in assembling the necessary shipping; but it was a poor recipe for realizing the primary goal of destroying the remaining Armada ships. Drake had made his career as a privateer (less politely, as a pirate). The private backers of the expedition naturally expected a handsome return on their investment. A give-away as to their intentions is to be found in the actions of the Earl of Essex. Strictly against royal command, he slipped away with Roger Williams, and before the expedition sailed took ship and made directly for the Portuguese coast, where, he took for granted, he would find the expedition.

The royal instructions were explicit; the fleet was to discover where the Spanish warships lay in the northern Spanish ports and there to destroy them. The commanders did in fact make a pass at the port of Corunna on the Galician coast, landing and taking the lower town but failing in an assault on the fortified upper town. No ships were destroyed. They laid their failure to the royal refusal to provide artillery. Now, having given due notice of their presence on Philip's coast, they sailed for a Lisbon fully prepared for their coming. Troops were landed at Cascaes up the coast from the capital; when they arrived at the gates of Lisbon they found them tight closed and well manned. Not a single Portuguese stirred in favour of the pretender; the Spanish had them well in hand. Drake lay off the Tagus mouth but dared not contest the forts lining the entrance to the port. In the end the troops made an ignominious retreat to the coast, already stricken by sickness, and re-embarked. They made another feint at the Spanish coast at Vigo, where they burned the town (but no ships). An attempt to send a part of the fleet off to the Azores was frustrated by the weather. The scattered ships limped home to Plymouth, with some 8,000 to 10,000 dead and nothing but a squadron of Baltic grain ships as booty. (These had to be returned to the owners.)[26]

The Queen's unhappiness with the commanders' proceedings surfaced early in the voyage, when they landed at Corunna but failed to carry out their mission of destruction. The full scope of her disapproval was conveyed in her articles of complaint of autumn 1589.[27] Why had the commanders attacked Corunna, where there were only a few ships, instead of Santander, where there were many? The gist of a somewhat confused defence was that experience at Corunna had proved that only with cannon and more soldiers could they achieve their goal, since they had first to capture the forts which protected the harbours where the ships sheltered. The other northern Spanish ports posed the same problem. The commanders' request, from Corunna, for such reinforcements had been refused by the Queen. They were also assailed for having landed in Portugal without assurance of a native uprising, to which they riposted that only by landing could they test Portuguese opinion. The Queen's angry conclusion was that they had put profit before service, although she shifted her grounds when she spoke of '[be]haviour of vainglory which obfuscates the eyes of judgment'. However, she could hardly exonerate herself from the issuance of instructions, incompatible in aim, or from the refusal to give them artillery support. The latter was probably a typical piece of royal penny-pinching, but it is hard to believe that the commanders did not have their eyes fixed on Lisbon from the start.

The first great offensive effort of the English against their Spanish foe had been a resounding failure. The confusion of incompatible goals as well as the headstrong behaviour of the commanders had contributed heavily to it, but the initial under-funding of the expedition had made their task almost impossible. A contemporary seaman commented that anyone who undertook 'so great an enterprise without a prince's purse shall shall surely be deceived'. To assume 'so great a charge with so little means' was a recipe for ill success.[28]

The failure of the Portuguese voyage confirmed the Queen's scepticism about an offensive strategy. At the same time, the urgent demand for help from the new King of France, whose accession occurred almost as the fleet returned home, diverted her attention and her resources. Drake was relegated to the sidelines for half-a-dozen years. Yet the Queen's hope of diverting some of Philip's treasure into her own coffers kept alive royal participation in maritime ventures. Purely naval expeditions which included royal ships were launched each year from 1589 to 1592 to prey on Spanish and Portuguese shipping. At various times Hawkins, the Earl of Cumberland, and Sir Martin Frobisher were involved, but with only modest success in financial terms. In 1591 a more ambitious undertaking was led by a set of younger leaders, Ralegh and Lord Thomas Howard, with the intention of surprising the plate fleet off the Azores. Plans for a sizeable concentration of ships fell through, and in the end the commander, Howard, with only six warships, faced a Spanish fleet of fifty-five vessels. He prudently retreated, but one of his captains, Sir Richard Grenville in the *Revenge*, lingered behind and engaged the whole Spanish fleet. His epic defence of his ship was to become part of the national naval myth.

1592 proved to be the one year marked by a notable success, when a mixed squadron of privateers and Queen's ships captured the richly laden East Indiaman *Madre di Dios*; the Queen, on an outlay of £3,000, made £80,000. Less spectacular but cumulatively more important were the captures made by the private enterprisers; 236 during the years 1589–91. In 1589 there were 86 ships active. In contrast to the publicly backed expeditions of these years, the privateers did very well. In the three years after the Armada their prizes netted £400,000. The annual average for all the war years down to 1603 may have been somewhere between £100,000 and £200,000.[29] It probably balanced the losses incurred by the suspension of the Iberian trade. While privateering did not inflict dangerous wounds on the enemy, it did force him to divert resources to the protection of his trade a time when the strain on Spanish finances was at its maximum.

19

The Alliance with Henry IV

H ardly had the Lisbon fleet straggled back into port before events on the Continent transformed the international situation. On 1 August Henry III of France was assassinated by a Catholic zealot. By rightful hereditary succession his successor was his Bourbon cousin, Henry of Navarre, but in the eyes of Catholic France that prince's Protestant faith nullified his claim. Already in 1584, French Catholics, organized in the Holy League, had made a treaty with Philip of Spain to support their candidate, the Cardinal of Bourbon. Within a few days of his accession Henry IV was appealing to the Protestant Queen of England for aid in men and money to sustain his beleaguered throne.

His cry for help opened a new chapter in relations between England and France. Hitherto Elizabeth had given cautious backing to the Protestants in arms against their sovereign; now she was to become the ally of a new monarch striving to make good his claim to the French throne. Already before the death of Henry III Elizabeth had begun to play a more active role on the French scene. Since 1585 Navarre had been in arms; in 1587 the Queen had lent him £30,000 to pay for a German mercenary force, only to see it defeated by the Catholic armies. Navarre, however, was still in arms in the south, and his envoy was negotiating for a loan in 1588. At the end of that year Henry III broke free from the Guises with the murder of the Duke and his brother the Cardinal, and joined forces with Navarre.[1] By July 1589 there was talk of an English loan to the Valois king if he would enter a general anti-Catholic league.[2] The dramatic change in French affairs offered the Queen long-term advantages but short-term liabilities. If Henry IV could master his kingdom, the counter-weight of a

France hostile to Spain would re-establish a balance of power sufficient to thwart the hegemonial ambitions of Philip II. More immediately, if Parma were drawn into the French conflict, pressures on the Dutch would be lessened. But for both these blessings a heavy down-payment was immediately required.

Henry, under heavy pressure from his enemies, fell back on Normandy with a force half the size of theirs. There was a great risk he might be trapped with his back to the sea. By 24 August, barely three weeks into his reign, he was begging for reinforcements. The Queen was prompt in her response; by 9 September men were being conscripted from the south-eastern counties.[3] Lord Willoughby, recently recalled from his Low Countries command, was pressed into service with a commission dated 20 September. There was a hitch at this point since on 21–2 September Henry decisively beat the Catholic army at Arques. The Queen now drew back, reluctant to send any of her troops 'unless there be very apparent and urgent necessity to employ them'. With the news of Arques she restrained her soldiers from embarkation. The English ambassador assured Willoughby that Henry was out of danger and that there was no need for the army to embark. Nevertheless, Willoughby, thrusting aside this news, took his men across. The angry Queen ordered him to return his forces unless Henry urgently required them. The King, who had been told Willoughby would not come, naturally found reason why he should stay. The English soldiers were promptly pressed into service, first in an abortive siege of Paris and then in a whirlwind drive through Normandy and Maine which established some semblance of royal authority north of the Loire. The campaign ended in December, when some 3,000 of the original 3,600, exhausted and unpaid, returned home.

Such was the first breathless episode in Anglo-French cooperation. The emergency was so sudden and so seemingly great that there was no time for more than a reflexive response by the Queen. No treaty of alliance was yet written; Willoughby was simply placed at the French King's disposal, to be used as seemed best. When the victory at Arques cancelled the immediate need for help the Queen would have held back her soldiers, but Willoughby and the King between them thwarted her will. Henry had used the English soldiers essentially as unpaid mercenaries: the English exchequer had to bear the costs. It was not a model likely to be followed in the future.

There was now a pause in active cooperation between the allies as Henry's military needs eased. He defeated the League at Ivry in March

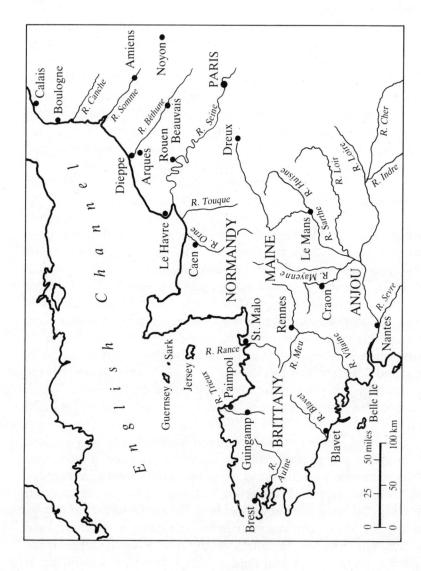

Map 3: Brittany and North-West France, 1589–1594

1590, but his siege of Paris was broken by Parma's intervention. Henry's most urgent problem was money to keep intact his ramshackle assortment of native and foreign mercenary soldiers. Elizabeth had paid over £40,000 in 1589; she now added another £10,000 in the following September, but the necessitous French King was clamouring for yet another advance.[4] What he wanted now was an English contribution to a fund which would pay for a German mercenary army. Elizabeth's wary response was to send a diplomatic agent, Horatio Palavicino, to negotiate the raising of this money from the German princes with a lukewarm half-promise that the Queen would make a contribution.[5] This came to nothing, as Elizabeth probably thought it would. In November 1590 Henry renewed pressure for this scheme, sending the Huguenot grandee, Viscount Turenne, as his envoy. Elizabeth grudgingly offered £10,000 towards a total sum of £60,000. Turenne finally succeeded in raising his force, which was to be ready in early 1591.[6]

Elizabeth had no intention of becoming a mere milch cow for Henry's needs. She was not prepared to commit further resources until she could see her way to an initiative directly beneficial to English as well as to French interests. There were several options available: one was collaboration with the States' forces in an attack on the important port of Dunkirk which would distract Parma's intervention in France; this was actively considered in 1590 but not pursued. Now, with the coming of the German mercenaries, new possibilities presented themselves. There might be, for instance, a three-cornered cooperation against Parma by diverting the mercenaries to Flanders to combine with the Dutch and English in penning up Parma in that province. This appealed strongly to the Queen for financial reasons: it could be carried through with the English forces currently in the Low Countries, thus avoiding additional costs.[7]

These calculations were complicated by a new development. The Spanish sought to assail Henry by encouraging regional magnates to assert their autonomy wherever possible. One such instance was Brittany, where the Duke of Mercœur, a Guisean connection, relying on his wife's inherited claims to the province, set himself up as local satrap under Spanish auspices. In October 1590 a Spanish force arrived at the Breton port of Blavet. This move rang alarm bells in England, for the Breton harbours were well placed to serve the Spanish as an invasion base.

Elizabeth's two senior soldiers were consulted for their advice. Roger Williams was hopeful about the mid-term future; in six months, with the German mercenaries on hand, Parma could be beaten or starved out, but the immediate future was much grimmer, given the weakness of the French royal forces. The Spanish could consolidate themselves in Brittany; there might even be a junction between them and Parma. On balance, Williams favoured action in the Low Countries, which would keep Parma out of France.[8] Sir John Norris in his advice dampened royal interest in the scheme for Anglo-French–Dutch cooperation since, he argued, it could only be rendered effective by additional levies of English soldiers from home. He saw Brittany as the first priority; the presence of the Germans on the eastern borders of France would at the very least inhibit Parma's freedom to invade France. Williams in a second memorandum again pushed for collaboration with the French King's army against Parma.[9]

The Queen finally moved to a decision in the spring of 1591. The prospect of Spanish invasion from bases on the Breton coast, exciting her endemic fear of another assault, persuaded her to give priority to that theatre of war. Taking the initiative, she approached Henry with a proposal to send 3,000 of her troops to Brittany on the condition that he matched her effort. The King was ready with promises for an equal force, supplies for the English, and the hint that Brest could be used as an English base. In April the Queen contracted with him for 3,000 men, costing £3,500 a month, the sum to be repaid by France at the twelve month.[10]

Norris, having pressed for the Breton expedition, now found himself in command of the force sent there. Sceptical of effective action in that province, he would have preferred to hold the troops in Normandy until further arrangements for their reception in Brittany could be made; but he obeyed orders. In May 1591 he and his forces were decanted into Brittany at Paimpol, on the western side of the gulf of St Malo. The situation he faced on his arrival was not a favourable one. Even before the death of Henry III the province had largely fallen under Catholic control. Only pockets of royalist resistance remained, at Rennes on the eastern borders and in the two ports of Brest and St Malo.[11] When Norris arrived, he made contact with the royalist commander, the Prince of Dombes, and they enjoyed an initial success in the capture of Guingamp, a town close to Paimpol; but after that the English found no useful employment. Languishing in inactivity, the force was eroded by sickness and desertion. At the end of summer Dombes moved inland, to Norris's dismay, since this took him away from the strategic coastal areas which he wanted to interdict to the Spanish. In December 1591 the royalists broke up their local army and left the English to live off the country as best they could. By February their numbers were down to 1,700.[12]

Elizabeth's reaction to this discouraging train of events was one of frustrated anger. She could fire off indignant reproaches to the French King, threatening to withdraw her forces, but he knew these were paper threats. If the English went home, the only beneficiaries would be the Spanish and their Leaguer allies; the menace of the Spanish bases in Brittany would be unabated. The unfortunate victims of these circumstances were Norris and his men. The Queen would not withdraw them, but she would not waste any of her resources by sending reinforcements or supplies. In the spring of 1592, when Norris's situation was becoming desperate, Elizabeth summoned the commander home for consultation. In his absence catastrophe struck: an attack by Mercœur so battered the English forces that only 800 survived, of whom 200 were no longer fit for service.[13]

The bitter truth which was forcing itself upon the Queen was that her intentions and those of her French brother were in this quarter wholly divergent. From Henry's perspective Brittany was a mere sideshow. His attention was centred on his northern frontiers, threatened by another invasion by Parma. Elizabeth, on the other hand, obsessed by the threat of invasion, saw Brittany as an area of dangerous sensitivity. Henry's cavalier failure to keep the promises he had made, indeed, his refusal to pay any attention to the Breton scene, left the Queen sputtering with helpless fury. Nor was Brittany the only source of friction between the two monarchs.

. In the spring of 1591 when Norris sailed for Brittany, the English were already involved in the neighbouring province of Normandy. Since 1590 Henry had been urging the dispatch of some 6,000 English troops to cooperate in the siege of Rouen. Taking advantage of the agreement over Brittany, he renewed this proposal. He was not entirely ingenuous in his expressed intentions. His main fear was of another descent by Parma at a time when his own forces were sparse and the Germans had not yet arrived. A reinforcement of 4,000–5,000 English would be invaluable.[14] However, while they waited to see which way the Duke would move, they could be employed in clearing the Leaguers from the lower Seine valley and besieging the Norman capital. The matter was brought to a head by a local crisis at Dieppe, where the royalists were threatened by a League attack. Urgent appeals from the governor there got a surprisingly quick response from Elizabeth: 600 men under Roger Williams went over in April, a month before Norris's departure for Brittany.[15]

Williams, Ottywell Smith, the English agent at Dieppe, and the French officials there now bombarded the Queen with dispatches urging the importance of Rouen and the necessity of taking it from the Leaguers. Williams insisted that Henry's present strategy was useless; he must concentrate on taking the principal towns; otherwise, in a prolonged war he would be worn down by Philip's superior resources. Also – and this struck a chord with the Queen – the King would transfer the tax revenues of Rouen to her as a means for paying off his accumulated debts. For a ruler constantly preoccupied by the shortage of money, this had alluring appeal. Elizabeth was persuaded, and she now offered to second the Breton expedition by another force of similar size in Normandy – if Henry would undertake the siege of Rouen.[16]

The Norman campaign provided a new freedom of action for the Queen. Hitherto, the allocation of her military resources had largely been dictated by circumstance. In the Low Countries her troops had to be thrown in to resist Spanish pressure wherever it was most acute; the initiative lay with the enemy. In 1589 Willoughby's disobedience meant that her soldiers were hustled off to be placed at Henry's disposal, to use as he saw fit. In Brittany it was the enemy – and her feeble allies – who called the tune. Now in Normandy the Queen was taking the initiative in planning a campaign which would work to her advantage and over which she expected to exercise considerable control.

Moreover, it gave Elizabeth the chance to bow the French King to do her bidding. In Henry she had to deal with an ally who was of equal status (albeit dependent on her goodwill) and, moreover, at least in her eyes, a novice in the royal trade. She was determined to assert her seniority in this relationship. Writing to him in the spring of 1592,[17] she told him that he 'must pardon the simplicity of her sex; but from her experience of government she knew what became a king and that Henry would conquer her enemies if he followed her advice'. Elizabeth looked forward to a Norman campaign in which Henry, dependent on his allies, would have to conform his actions to her pleasure and to English advantage. In the bargaining which attended the agreement, she made clear her superior position (and gratified her penny-pinching instincts) by denying the heavy cannon and the pioneers needed for a siege and reducing the number of troops she would supply. It was yet another example of the royal disposition to confuse fiscal and military, with precedence always going to the former.

She was soon to be disillusioned. Henry's eyes were always fixed on his first goal – the capture of Paris. More immediately he had to deal with Parma, if possible to defeat him in the field and thereby shift the whole balance of the struggle. The siege of Rouen was a secondary matter; more important was the presence of English soldiers who could be pressed into use on the battle-field if the Duke advanced. Elizabeth fancied herself a more skilful player in the royal game than her inexperienced ally, new to the duelling grounds. In her overweening self-confidence, she badly underestimated him. In both the agreements – for Brittany and for Normandy – she allowed herself to be overreached by taking at face value his facile promises of performance.

The choice of a commander for the 4,000 soldiers scheduled to go to Dieppe was not easy. The senior professional, Norris, was already engaged in Brittany; Roger Williams commanded the advance guard of 600 already on French soil. His professional credit was high, but other factors had to be considered. The English commander would be dealing directly with the King, and he had to be of a rank commensurate with his responsibility. Noble English commanders were in short supply. Willoughby, the most obvious choice, was in ill health. There was, of course, a self-promoted candidate, the current royal favourite, Robert Devereux, second Earl of Essex. This young man had risen rapidly in royal favour since his introduction under the wing of his stepfather, Leicester, in the late 1580s. He had served as a volunteer in the Low Countries in 1586 and had raced off, in direct disobedience to royal command, to join Norris before Lisbon, where he had had the satisfaction of hurling a lance at the city's closed gates before bowing to the royal will and returning home.

Essex had hoped for the command in the 1589 French expedition and now, in 1591, was unremitting in his demand for the post of general. He won the backing of Henry and the French envoy, Turenne.[18] His insistence and the necessity for appointing a noble commander wore down royal resistance. The Earl was to command the army, but the Queen intended to keep him on a tight leading string. He was accompanied by a clutch of royally appointed counsellors who were to keep him under close supervision, even though 'commonly young noblemen at the first do not embrace advertisements of things to be reformed'.[19] A new ambassador, Sir Henry Unton, assisted by a veteran diplomat, Sir Henry Killigrew, and the Earl's uncle, Sir Thomas Leighton, governor of Jersey, were called to act as his minders. Essex was subordinated to the commands of King Henry but empowered to object to particular orders.

The Queen's expectations that, with a dependent ally and a biddable general, she would control the course of events in Normandy were doomed to disappointment. The King, distracted by Parma's movements, remained at Noyon and summoned the Earl to meet him there, where the two men hit it off very happily. The Queen, furious that the siege was not pursued, now ordered the Earl's return to England, to be followed by that of his forces. Essex, beside himself with frustration, did indeed return; the mediating effort of Burghley and other Councillors had by that time softened Elizabeth's stance sufficiently to allow her commander's return to France, reconciled to his mistress, whose anger was for the time being appeased. The siege at last got under way with the arrival of the King, and the Queen conceded a reinforcement of 1,000 men; but Henry's attention was soon diverted by Parma's movements. His request for yet more men met with emphatic refusal, and Essex was instructed to remain at Rouen if Henry marched on the Duke. The futility of the proceedings became increasingly evident: the Queen would give no more money or men; the English forces were steadily dwindling. The Councillors urged the Earl's return from what was a humiliating situation, and in January 1592 he left France for good.

There was now a flurry of negotiation between the two sovereigns, with plain speaking on both sides. The Queen listed the delinquencies of the French in both theatres of war. Her envoy, Sir Thomas Wilkes, was to tell Henry that 'Her Majesty plainly mindeth except she may receive good satisfaction for these doubts to revoke her forces from thence'.[20] Henry retorted in kind. The Queen, he said, 'made war at this time good cheap against so great an enemy . . . and he wished he had such another fool as Her Majesty had of him to make war against the King of Spain that he might look out the window, as she doth now, and behold the tragedies between him and his enemies now in action'. A memorandum in the English papers draws the moral of these actions: 'if ever the Queen succour the king again, let it be with money [i.e. instead of men]'. The King would get more service from his own people than from the raw English forces.[21]

The Queen in fact conceded something to her ally's demand: 1,600 more men, to join the less than 1,000 effectives remaining under Williams's command. When the siege of Rouen was raised in April, they accompanied the King in his abortive duel with Parma, during which the Duke succeeded in victualling Rouen.[22] The Queen was left to a rueful casting up of her accounts. There was little to show on the credit side. Lives and treasure had been spent in vain; none of the hoped-for results had ensued. The episode threw into relief the basic incompatibilities in the relationship between the allied sovereigns.

They were wholly at odds in their aims. Henry's goal was to destroy the League and obtain the mastery of his kingdom. To accomplish this he had to rely on a polyglot mercenary army, its ranks filled from Germany and Switzerland. For him the English contingent was simply an added ingredient, distinguished by the fact that these men came with pay provided by their sovereign. His strategy was necessarily a fluid one, and he had to be free to use his men wherever they were needed. Elizabeth's view was equally self-centred. She, of course, was anxious that he should master his enemies and secure his throne. However, she was prepared to give aid only when his circumstances were absolutely desperate or when her intervention would serve some English interest. Hence her willingness to commit her soldiers to the Breton and Norman campaigns, theatres where she assumed that she and Henry had common interests. When this proved to be anything but the case, relations between the monarchs subsided into bouts of ill temper and spasms of mutual dissatisfaction.

The year between the raising of the siege of Rouen (April 1592) and Henry's conversion to Catholicism (summer 1593) was one of flux in dealings between Elizabeth and Henry. Parma's campaign of 1592 proved his last; he died at the end of the year, and Spanish participation slackened as their fortunes in the Low Countries waned. The English forces under Williams, although involved in some small actions, hung about uncertainly on the Norman coast. Henry resumed his demands for more English troops. Elizabeth occasionally dribbled out small reinforcements. Williams contemplated the possibility of seizing a Norman port to hold as a gage against the French debt, on the model of the Dutch cautionary towns. Finally, in April 1593, Williams was summoned by Henry to join the royal army in the siege of Dreux.[23] This siege preceded by only a few weeks Henry's change of faith. The Queen's reaction to this decisive event is discussed below. Its immediate consequence was the royal decision to withdraw from Normandy altogether; this was done in the early autumn of 1593.[24] In Brittany, however, Norris's forces still hung on.

After the defeat at Craon in May 1592, the Queen wavered between reinforcing her army in Brittany or withdrawing it altogether.[25] She was pushed into a further commitment by rumours of a peace negotiation between Henry and the League. When these failed the Queen agreed to a new effort in Brittany, and in July a contract was signed for the dispatch of 4,000 English with the promise of an effective French counterpart force.[26] Once again Elizabeth brought herself reluctantly to trust to Henry's promises to support her forces in Brittany; she was to repeat the unhappy experience of the previous campaigns.

It took time to assemble Norris's forces; their ranks were not filled until the new year of 1593. The promised French aid shrank from a paper total of 4,000 to a bare 800 (plus 100 horse) in the field.[27] The Queen and her ministers again hesitated between staying or departing; their only firm decision was to refuse further reinforcements. The choice of whether or not to stay was thrust onto the shoulders of the unhappy Norris. He chose to hang on, begging for help from home. He got none of the latter, but by sheer stubbornness he kept his dwindling bands together. So things stood when rumours of Henry's impending conversion sent a shock through the English Council. Forewarnings of the change flowed in through the spring, so that its actual occurrence in the early summer of 1593 was no surprise. A French emissary was quickly dispatched to London, asking for men and a loan but primarily concerned to retain English support so as to strengthen the King's hand in the delicate negotiations with the League for a truce.

The English put their best face on it. A state paper of Burghley's began, 'the affairs of France being more to be lamented than remedied'. There followed formal disapproval of the change, which aligned the French with Elizabeth's deadly enemy, the Pope. 'And yet though Her Majesty shall do well in this sort to censure the French king yet it shall be considered what shall be meet in policy for Her Majesty to do to help the king against the King of Spain, the Guises, and such as will not submit themselves upon his conversion.'[28]

Elizabeth's real concern was Henry's intentions *vis-à-vis* Spain. Would he continue the war against Philip if he was able to destroy the League at home? To pressure Henry, she ordered the withdrawal of all her forces from France. The Norman contingent, as we have seen, did indeed retire, but she allowed her Councillors to change her mind and authorized Norris to stay. This was the first of a dizzying sequence of royal orders and counter-orders – depart, remain, leave, stay. The royal compass wavered back and forth through the whole autumn of 1593, until news of Spanish reinforcements in Brittany finally determined that Norris was to remain.[29] He clung on through the spring of 1594 until a new factor began to influence English thinking at home and in Brittany. The Spanish were building a fort on the approaches to Brest which would control that vital port. This concentrated English attention and provided a clear-cut objective for action.

By June the Queen became so convinced of the danger at Brest as to order preparations for reinforcements and the dispatch of ships under Frobisher to lie off the coast.[30] Once again, a threat to English security served to move the Queen to act. Norris was simply instructed to focus his efforts on cooperation with the governor of Brest, abandoning any larger commitments in the province. Events now moved with decision and speed. The West Country levies arrived in Brittany by September, and on 1 October Norris commenced the siege; by mid-November the fort was won. There had been last-minute uncertainty: the Queen had flinched when an early assault failed. With difficulty her Councillors dissuaded her from withdrawal, and nerved her to continued support.

1594 had proved the determinative year in Elizabeth's French policy. With Henry's conversion in the preceding year, she had drawn back, uncertain of his further intentions towards Spain as Leaguer resistance weakened. She had pulled out of Normandy altogether and then tortured herself, her Councillors, and her commander through a long agony of indecision. Mercifully, events had forced her hand when the Spanish moved to seize control of the approaches to Brest. This jolted her into a few months of decisive and prompt action – marred by one hesitant pause – which had been duly rewarded by the success of her arms.

That success led in turn to another and final move. The Queen gave orders to Norris to transport himself and 2,000 of his men to Ireland; the balance were to return to their homes. The General protested in vain; at home there was general relief at freedom from the French albatross. Burghley had complained: 'unhappy is the time when Her Majesty is forced to join with such as have no other regard of her state but to ease themselves with throwing their burdens upon her.' Ralegh agreed: 'We are so busy and dandled in these French wars which are endless, as we forget the defence next the heart.'[31] Now, with the League crumbling on every front, Elizabeth could free herself from an entanglement which she had always resented. The turns and twists of that involvement – marked by repeated bouts of

royal exasperation, denunciation of French faithlessness, counter-
manded orders to withdraw — were even more complex than the
account given here. Yet there was an underlying consistency to the
royal behaviour. The Queen never lost sight of her prime interest in
seeing the restoration of a strong, and anti-Spanish, French monarchy.
But, as in other theatres of action, she had limited her aid to the bare
minimum necessary for Henry's survival. His Catholic advisers, who
insinuated to the King that Elizabeth would support him just enough
to keep him from sinking and no more, were not far from the truth.

Brittany was, of course, a special case which touched a very sensitive
royal nerve — the fear of invasion. Here the Queen was tried almost
beyond endurance by French indifference, and more than once she
resolved on withdrawal. It took the combined efforts of her Councillors and the obstinacy of her commander on the scene to hold her on
course. However great the delinquencies of the French, to withdraw
was to yield the game to the Spanish.

The retirement of the English forces from Brittany brought to
a close a chapter of Anglo-French collaboration marked by mutual
dissatisfaction, acrimonious disagreement, and a trail of failed enterprises, redeemed, for the English, by their one military victory. Yet
the end of this little history was for the English a happy one. The
premise on which Elizabeth's foreign policy rested was the abiding
rivalry of the two Continental giants. This guaranteed, first, that
neither of them should establish hegemony in Europe. Secondly, that
same rivalry was an assurance that neither would allow the other to
endanger England's independence. That position was now restored.
Elizabeth could congratulate herself on having supported her French
brother, but she could hardly claim that English support for Henry
IV had weighed significantly in the balance. It was his military prowess
combined with political suppleness which won him his crown.

Henry's success in claiming his throne was a matter for rejoicing
in England, but his very achievement opened up new questions in the
relations between the two realms. What would be his relations with
Spain? Would he be willing to commit his ravaged kingdom, barely
emergent from civil conflict, to the stresses of contest with his great
neighbour? What would be his relations with the States? Would there
be renewed interest in a French push into the Netherlands, renewing
the ambitions of the 1570s? Henry's initial response to these questions
was reassuring. In January 1595 he declared war on Spain, and began
to push for a joint offensive against the common foe. The Queen's
cautious reply emphasized the great contribution she had already made

in Normandy and Brittany. She would continue to make war on Spain where she could be most effective. (Her Councillors were already planning the Drake–Hawkins expedition.)[32]

These indeterminate exchanges were given concrete form when the Spanish successfully invaded Picardy, taking Doullens and Cambrai in late summer 1595 and placing Calais in danger. The Queen offered to send forces to defend that port and Dieppe, but she made conditions; her soldiers must be admitted into Calais. Henry preferred to seek Dutch cooperation. This led to an angry spat between the two rulers. Elizabeth hinted that hostile advisers were sowing suspicion of English intentions as to Calais. A French envoy, rushed over after the fall of Cambrai, made much the same assertion about those among the Queen's Councillors hostile to the French. Elizabeth now bluntly declared she would give Henry assistance only when she saw that French events imperilled English interests. That message, in somewhat more conciliating tones, was confirmed by a new ambassador sent to Paris, Sir Henry Unton.[33]

Elizabeth was now, at the opening of 1596, faced by a new worry. Rumours of peace negotiations between France and Spain were confirmed by Unton's reports. Henry spoke reproachfully to the ambassador of England's refusal to assist him in Picardy; without that aid he would be unable to sustain the struggle and would have to seek peace terms.[34] Unton found his own instructions so contradictory that he was ashamed of his message, and at his wit's end to counter French arguments. Further exchanges were fruitless until a new crisis, the Spanish capture of Calais, shocked the parties into a new initiative. Elizabeth mobilized forces under Essex to relieve the port, but it fell before they could be dispatched. Henry now proposed a full alliance, offensive and defensive, between the two crowns; England to provide 4,000 men for six months of each year, to serve on the north-eastern frontier. France would send 6,000 men to the Queen's service if she needed them. The States were to be a third partner to this alliance.

Elizabeth diverted this diplomatic offensive with considerable finesse. Her preliminary response was a cordial, even enthusiastic, acceptance of the proposed terms. But then she began to make limiting conditions, first for postponing the 'league general' for a year and then for reducing her commitment of soldiers. Exigencies in Ireland were such that she could offer, not 4,000, but only 2,000 men this year, and these to be used only for garrisoning the French channel ports if the Spanish threatened them — and if the King himself were present with an army. As a modest sweetener she offered a loan of

20,000 ecus. Elizabeth congratulated herself on her generosity, 'a better sister than a queen', who put aside the adage that charity begins at home.

Offered this meagre fare, Henry reluctantly accepted it but hinted at his interest in the peace feelers thrown out by the Archduke Albert, Philip's governor-general at Brussels. After more delay two treaties were signed, but in such form as to make them virtually inoperative. Henry's effort to draw England into an active alliance against Spain had failed.[35] Even the pitiful contingent of 2,000 promised for Picardy were held back on the ground of alleged plague in that province. More and more conditions were imposed on any potential assistance. There ensued a total farce. Henry caved in on the English demands for a postponement of the troops' dispatch, only to see Elizabeth swing around and dispatch her men to Dieppe. This reversal was triggered off by her panic fear that a Spanish invasion fleet then approaching the Channel would use Calais as an invasion base. She followed up with a proposal for a joint Anglo-French–Dutch attack on the port, to which Henry wryly responded that he would rather see his enemies take the town than his friends. Elizabeth's enduring fear of another Spanish assault on her coasts had thrown her off course. The invasion fleet was dispersed by storms, but for a moment Elizabeth had abandoned her resolute determination not to involve herself in the French theatre.[36]

The victims of this muddled affair were the luckless 2,000, useless to either English or French purposes. Henry, in fact, had opted out for a season and was sunk in delicious torpor in the company of his mistress. The English contingent rotted in the miseries of the Picard winter. It took a new Spanish offensive, which netted the town of Amiens in March 1597, to rouse Henry to action. Other fronts sprang into life and talk of peace receded into the background. However, nothing would persuade Elizabeth to increase her forces in France; not even Henry's desperate offer of Calais as a cautionary town to be held in gage for the French debt (once the Anglo-Dutch had taken it). After a time, military activity died down; both sides languished in exhausted inaction. The English contingent, unused and unpaid, suffered the usual erosion of disease and desertion. However, the King at last nerved himself to action, and Elizabeth grudgingly dispatched replacements. It was not until September 1597 that Henry recovered Amiens. That accomplished, the English promptly departed from France, for the last time in the war. Henry took advantage of his new strength to advance purposeful peace negotiations, which would soon pose awkward problems for the Queen and her Council. Before following these events, it is necessary to turn to another theatre of war, the Low Countries, and to relations between England and the States.

20

The Alliance with the States General

The wartime partnership between Elizabeth and Henry IV was an unhappy one, frayed by constant friction and, from the English point of view, barren of immediate advantage. The actual experience of collaboration was one of utter frustration. English money was poured out in ample sums and countless English lives were sacrificed in a series of futile enterprises. True, the triumph of the Bourbon king fulfilled one of England's war aims by restoring a powerful counter-check to Spanish ambitions in Europe. Yet it also substituted for the problems of an exigent dependent those of an aggressive rival whose course of action would now be independently determined.

The partnership with the Low Country provinces proved a much happier one. Relations, cool at first, even distrustful, gradually warmed into successful collaboration. The initial auspices were poor. Leicester failed to realize the hope of military recover which his coming aroused. At the same time, working at cross-purposes with his sovereign, he ineptly cobbled together a pro-English party in the provinces, thus leading to a clash with the rising Dutch leadership of Oldenbarnevelt and Count Maurice of Nassau, the second son of the late Prince of Orange.[1]

The Queen for her part regarded the whole enterprise with distaste. The Dutch were, after all, rebels; she would persevere through the 1590s in attempts to re-establish at least the semblance of Habsburg authority in the provinces. Moreover, the States government was an anomaly in the ordered hierarchy of European sovereigns. The Queen was not disposed to give these burghers the status of equals. Beyond these general considerations she was less than half-hearted in her support of Leicester's military effort; she was more concerned to keep her forces intact than to risk them in action. The Queen totally opposed Leicester's meddling in Dutch politics. When he departed, she left the Leicestrian party to wither on the vine; they were soon swept from the scene by the Oldenbarnevelt–Nassau coalition. Worse still, the Queen, frantic for some kind of accommodation with Philip, through Parma, floated a series of proposals which utterly disregarded the States' interest and their announced goals. These efforts climaxed in the Bourbourg negotiations; they left a very bad taste in Dutch mouths.

From 1588 onward Elizabeth's attention was diverted, first by the Armada, then by the Portugal expedition, and finally by intervention in France. At the same time the hawkish party in the English Council reoriented its interests. Previously the zealous advocates of English intervention in the Low Countries, even of extending English sovereignty to those provinces, they now shifted their attention towards Spain and her empire. They began to press for a naval assault on Spain's own territories, relegating the campaign in the Low Countries to a back seat. The English had in any case little respect for Dutch military capabilities. Even when Maurice chalked up a series of successes in 1591, they dismissed his achievement as a fluke, occasioned by the enemy's 'want at that time [of] the common use of his sense in preventing their attempts'.[2]

English indifference to the States' interest had, however, an advantageous side. It gave them a freedom of movement they were quick to seize. Oldenbarnevelt and Maurice had drawn a clear lesson from their unhappy experience with Leicester. Henceforth they must stand on their own feet, abandoning the policy, pursued since 1577, of finding a foreign patron to act as their leader. Under the Treaty of Nonsuch the English had the right to appoint two members to the Council of State, the executive branch of the States regime. When Bodley, the new English agent, arrived in 1589, he perceived that the party headed by Oldenbarnevelt was deliberately eroding the power of that body to make decisions, shifting them to the confederal representative assembly, the States General. (This body consisted of delegates appointed by each of the provincial states.) When Bodley, with Walsingham's backing, protested at a manœuvre which sidelined the Queen's representatives, he was briskly answered by the Dutch leaders 'with indecent and malapert terms wherein they offend in several places'. They advanced the radical proposition that sovereignty rested collectively in the States General, and that the Council of State was a merely delegated executing body, standing to the States General as the Privy Council stood to the Queen. This was a doctrine hard to swallow in a monarchic age unable to conceive a popular sovereignty. English resistance on the issue was worn down by Dutch stubbornness. Reluctantly the English retreated, and imperceptibly the relationship between the two parties shifted from dependence to equality.

English willingness to back down was initially a product of diminished concern by a government distracted by more pressing matters. It took on a more positive note from 1590 on, as the Dutch marched from one military success to another. Oldenbarnevelt and Maurice aimed not only at establishing the sovereignty of the States but also at solidifying their claims by solid achievement. Maurice's systematic annual campaigns from 1591 to 1594 effectually cleared the Spanish from the inland provinces, recovered Sluys, and drove a wedge into Brabant. English statesmen began to conceive a new respect for allies whose military capabilities they had totally discounted only a few years earlier.

The road which led to a viable working relationship between the English and the Dutch was scarred by disagreements but also smoothed by compromise. Bodley's career as English agent at The Hague was inaugurated by a disastrous quarrel over the mutinous English garrison at Gertruydenburg. Neither Willoughby, the English general who succeeded Leicester, nor the Dutch authorities were able to deal with the problem, and in the end the garrison was bought off by the Spanish. Mutual recriminations ensued and Willoughby, sore at his treatment, retired. Over the next year or so the English sought uneasily to arrive at some understanding with the Dutch leadership. Initially they looked with suspicion on Oldenbarnevelt, but soon came to yield him a grudging respect. Various schemes were put forward by the English seeking to maintain the authority of the Council of State and reduce that of the States General.[3] At one stage things grew so acrimonious that each side haughtily declared it could do very well without the other.[4] Some in the English Council, Burghley among them, would have been willing to concede a great deal to the Dutch in return for a reduction in the English subsidy. The Lord Treasurer grumbled unhappily about the infinite charges of a war to which he could see no end, a sentiment which his mistress no doubt shared. The Dutch stubbornly stuck to their position that the States General was a sovereign body and gradually the English gave way.

Improvement came with the appointment of a new commander for the English forces. The energies of the most conspicuous English captains were now committed to the French campaigns. The replacement for Willoughby was neither another nobleman nor a veteran general but a twenty-nine-year old soldier with some three years' solid experience in the field. Sir Francis Vere, a cadet of the ancient noble house of the Earls of Oxford, was appointed Sergeant-Major-General, third in rank after the vacant offices of Lord-General and Lieutenant-General. He quickly won the confidence of Count Maurice, and the two entered into a fruitful collaboration. Parma's distraction in France opened the opportunity to reverse the roles of the adversaries and for the Dutch at last to take the offensive. They did so brilliantly with the surprise capture of Breda in March 1590, in which Vere and his men participated.

The needs of Henry IV now began to impinge on Anglo-Dutch affairs. The Queen wanted to withdraw half her Low Countries forces in order to divert them to Normandy, depleting the field army to do this. This was not the first instance in which Elizabeth snatched away some of her forces for her own use. There had been a similar demand at the time of the Portuguese expedition, to which the Dutch had reluctantly conceded; but this had been a short-term enterprise of a few months, and also fell at a time when they were not on the offensive. To this new demand the Dutch naturally objected, urging that the King of France could best be helped by the campaign in the Low Countries they were about to launch. In the end, bargaining between the two sides brought about a mutually satisfactory solution. The English sent off to France were replaced by new levies from home. The precedent was a fruitful one. By tacit agreement a *quid pro quo* was established. The Dutch commanders became the surrogate trainers of the raw English recruits, whipping them into shape. The English commanders were quick to realize the superiority of these veterans in their own campaigns. The Dutch were willing to continue this arrangement on condition that the English would fulfil the treaty terms by dispatching an equal number of replacements from England. The alliance now took on a vitality which sprang from immediate mutual advantage. What had begun as an *ad hoc* compromise would become an institution which would long out last the war.

The history of this arrangement was by no means untroubled. Elizabeth's drafts on her Low Countries companies came irregularly and unpredictably, governed by the erratic course of French events, while Maurice's campaigns were masterpieces of careful preparation and detailed planning. These disparate strategies necessarily clashed from time to time.

In 1591, while the English launched their two ventures in France, Maurice began the task of expelling the Spanish from the inland provinces of the north. To secure the line of the Yssel, he seized Zutphen, where a daring operation by Vere helped win the day. Maurice then moved on to take Deventer, again with Vere playing a key role, and when Parma was diverted to France there was a third triumph in the capture of Nijmegen, climaxing a season of unprecedented Dutch success. In 1592 the Dutch prepared for another major campaign, designed to complete the task of clearing the Spanish from the inner provinces of Friesland, Groningen, and Drenthe. The Queen, on the other hand, obsessed with the possibilities of success in Normandy, wished to withdraw more troops, and even urged the Dutch to send forces to join Henry. Maurice did in fact send a Dutch contingent to France, but he stubbornly insisted on the priority of his own campaign and firmly rejected additional aid for Henry. In this he had Vere's strong support.

When in May Maurice opened his first operation of the campaign, the siege of Steenwyck, his forces included an English contigent of 1,350 soldiers, a substantial fraction of his army.[5] Then peremptory orders arrived from the Queen commanding immediate withdrawal of Vere's forces from the siege lines for service in France. Vere and Count Maurice, acting together, fended off an immediate response to the royal command by a reference to the States General. There were a few anxious moments, especially when the first assault on the town failed, but by 24 June Steenwyck was in Dutch hands. This crisis was barely surmounted before another royal demand of the same nature followed on its heels. The Dutch had moved to the second phase of the campaign, the siege of Coeverdon. Elizabeth, balked in her first effort, now demanded the immediate withdrawal of 2,000 of her troops for service in Brittany. Another diplomatic fencing match ensued; the States General stood obstinately on the terms of the treaty, that the English should remain in the field until the army returned to winter quarters. These exchanges were cut short by events, the approach of a Spanish relief force. Vere, acting on his own, threw his men into the breach and assisted in the repulse of the attackers. It was a lucky gamble; the fall of Coeverdon followed promptly. After that the States relaxed their stand and allowed the departure of Vere's troops.[6]

The Queen's attitude towards the States did little to forward the process of cooperation. Heedless of Maurice's plans, she had no hesitation in recalling her troops at the very moment Vere's army was poised for the final assault on a key Spanish stronghold. Only Vere's evasive tactics and Dutch persistence had held the Queen in check long enough to allow the completion of their operations. The contrast between English and Dutch efforts in the 1592 fighting season was striking, the former with nothing but a series of disappointments, the latter with a string of victories. The English were still slow to appreciate the scope of the Dutch achievement, writing if off as the conquest of a few towns, but by the close of the year Bodley admitted their gains were beyond any expectations. He also noted the growing self-confidence of the States General and its willingness to stand up to the Queen as her equal, not her dependant.[7]

The following year, 1593, marked a slackening in the military effort in the Low Countries; in France it proved to be the pivotal moment of Henry's conversion. A scheme pushed by Vere for joint action in Brabant came to nothing, and there was little to show for the year's campaign in the Low Countries except the recapture of Gertruyden-burg. However, an important step in cooperative relations was made when Vere, the Queen's commander, was, with her hearty approval, appointed by the States General as commander of the English companies in their pay. This mark of Dutch confidence ensured optimum use of all the English soldiers in the Low Countries. Nevertheless, a fall in Dutch morale towards the end of the year worried the English. Both Vere and Gilpin (the English agent at The Hague in Bodley's absence) were concerned about the reliability of a populace 'given to change and novelties and of the humour that if they once take a head it is hard to stay and much less to revoke them'. It was not the only time when English doubts about the stability of this anomalous regime, lacking the cement of royal and aristocratic rule, surfaced.[8]

By 1594, as Elizabeth was pulling the last of her troops out of Normandy, Maurice made plans for another major push, this time against Groningen, the most important Spanish post remaining in the inland provinces. He needed the service of 3,000 English. After some bargaining, Elizabeth allowed him the use of 1,500 of the soldiers returned from France while allowing him to recruit 1,500 more for service in his own forces. The Queen gratified her ally but also shifted a substantial share of the costs from her shoulders to the States's.[9] At first all went well; the siege of Groningen was mounted in May. Then, in a repetition of the earlier campaigns, the Queen proposed to snatch away the English contingent among the besiegers with a demand for the return of all English-born troops to serve in Brittany, where the crisis at Brest loomed alarmingly. The States General naturally objected, but came forward with a compromise, offering to replace the English garrisons at Ostend and Flushing with their own men while retaining the services of the English in the field army before Groningen. They also offered naval assistance on the Breton coast. The Queen acceded to this bargain. Groningen did in fact fall in July. In September, six Dutch ships sailed for Brest; 1,100 soldiers had already departed from the Low Countries.[10]

With the successes of 1594 came a lull in the Dutch resurgence. The pause which followed gave time for a move towards a readjustment of Anglo-Dutch relations, relations which were increasingly reciprocal. The English could now draw more or less at will on their trained reserve in Dutch service. The States on their side could recruit freely in England when they needed to augment their armies. This arrangement was particularly gratifying to the Queen, since it reduced her financial burden as more and more of the English troops passed from her payroll to that of the States. In addition, the Dutch were now able and willing to join their naval force with hers — a matter of moment when the English decided to mount major naval operations against the enemy. The military successes of the Dutch, their growing wealth, and their expanding self-confidence gave them flexibility in acceding to Elizabeth's demands while meeting their own needs.

With the upturn in Dutch fortunes the Queen displayed a new interest in their affairs, since it opened the way for discussions about repayment of the debt owed her. As always, financial matters had priority with Elizabeth. The Treaty of Nonsuch had provided that the costs of the expeditionary force should be met from the English exchequer but with the understanding that it would be repaid by the allies. The Queen now argued that the Dutch, with their interior provinces liberated, with trade thriving, and with the Spanish governor at Brussels making overtures for negotiations, should begin to pay off the accumulated debt.

Bodley was initially ordered to ask for an immediate lump sum, to be followed by annual instalments in the future. Rebuffed by the States General, who excused themselves by pointing to the burden of their aid to France, the irritated Queen became more specific. Reckoning the accumulated debt at £700,000–800,000, she demanded £100,000 immediately, with annual payments of similar size to follow. She filled the air with her reproaches for Dutch ingratitude, and talked of with-drawing her forces. The States General retorted by listing the burdens which consumed their resources. However, Oldenbarnevelt did circum-spectly hint at the possibility of a £20,000 annual payment during the war years and £100,000 a year after the conclusion of peace. Finally, in November 1595, there was a loosening of the log-jam. England was now preparing for a naval assault on Spain, so the Queen was willing to postpone the repayment issue for the present if the Dutch would give naval assistance.[11] Dutch ships did in fact join the Cadiz expedition, but wrangling over the terms of repayment rumbled on through 1596 without agreement. It became mired in the discussions about a tripartite alliance to include the States with the two sovereigns, which was in fact signed in November. In 1597 the islands voyage again led to the dispatch of a Dutch naval contingent. Such was the state of affairs when the possibility of French negotiations with Spain turned into probability in the early months of 1598.

The relative harmony of Anglo-Dutch relations in these years owed a good deal to the benign neglect of the Queen. Her attention was distracted by her long duel with Henry IV; she paid little attention to the slogging campaigns of Count Maurice in the watery lands east of the Zuider Zee. The Dutch came to her notice only when she wished to draw soldiers from their service. In her high-handed way she laid claim to these companies with total disregard for the campaign plans of Maurice. The supple diplomacy of Oldenbarnevelt, aided by Vere, turned the flank of these raids on Dutch manpower and imper-ceptibly won Elizabeth to a *modus vivendi* advantageous to both sides. By the time the Queen turned her attention to the repayment issue, the Dutch were able to offer a *quid pro quo* which, for the present, held the issue in abeyance. With the coming of peace between Henry IV and Philip II, and the Spanish overtures to England, the basic terms of the alliance necessarily came up for reconsideration.

21

The Assault on Spain

When the French and Spanish plenipotentiaries gathered at Vervins in spring 1598 to negotiate peace between their royal masters, the English Queen, faced with the probable loss of her French ally, needed to take stock of her position after more than a decade of war. She could look back on three major military efforts against the enemy. One, in France, had been fruitless in its immediate purposes (save for the victory at Brest), but events outside English control had achieved their ends, with the re-establishment of a strong French monarchy, hostile to Spain. The second effort, in the Low Countries, where under Dutch leadership English soldiers had played a significant role, had been a history of success. Not only had Spanish advance been halted; it had been rolled back. Substantial territories had been recovered, and a self-subsistent Netherlands state had emerged which, it was increasingly apparent, was invulnerable to Spanish reconquest. There had been a third, almost wholly English effort, on the high seas, in three successive naval expeditions. How had they fared?

After the fiasco of 1589, and with her resources largely engaged in France and the Low Countries, Elizabeth had little appetite for another sea-borne offensive. In 1595, however, she was persuaded to change her mind. In three successive years she authorized major expeditions, each of which was to assail Spanish territories, directly in the homeland or in the West Indian or Atlantic islands. What brought about this radical change of course from a defensive to an offensive strategy? It was primarily intelligence reports of a new armada in the making, said to be larger than the 1588 fleet. The reappearance of an invasion fleet, Elizabeth's deepest fear, was the one stimulus which would prod her into taking the risks and meeting the expenses of an offensive action. These fears now opened the way for the kind of assault on the enemy which the hawkish party had always urged as the only route to victory. The release of her forces from Brittany and the diminished demands of the Dutch campaign gave her more room to manœuvre. Developments in Ireland were another incentive to preventive measures: the Gaelic chieftains had approached Philip for aid, and rumour had it that the new fleet might be sailing to that island.

Each campaign was to adopt a different strategy, but each was aimed directly at the enemy on his own soil. The first of these was designed to carry the war back to the theatre last visited by Drake in 1585 – the Caribbean. His sponsor in the Council was the Earl of Essex, now the spokesman of the hawks, the ardent advocate of full-scale offensive against Spain. What was planned was in its organization another version of earlier efforts, a half-privatized enterprise for which the Queen would provide six ships, to be accompanied by thirteen merchantment funded by London investors. However, the crown was to bear two-thirds of the costs. Command was shared between the two veteran sea-dogs, Drake and Hawkins. Hawkins's choice may have represented Cecil's influence, to provide a moderating influence on the impetuous Sir Francis. A commentator wrote that the latter was 'better able to conduct forces and discretely govern in conducting them to places where service was to be done than to command in the execution there', and added: 'but entering into them as the child of fortune it may be his self will and peremptory command was doubted'.[1]

When the expedition was ready to sail, in summer 1595, a Spanish raid on some Cornish fishing villages frightened the Queen into countermanding their sailing. Her fears were increased when it was reported that a Spanish fleet would sail for Ireland before the winter and, worse still, that an armada more powerful than its predecessors would sail in June or July 1596.[2] Hence, the plan was altered; the admirals were to visit the Spanish ports, raiding shipping as they went, and then sail on to intercept the plate fleet returning from America. The original goal, a campaign in the Indies, was given third priority. Moreover, the admirals had to give a firm commitment to be at home by May 1596, lest the English coast should lie naked to invasion in the following summer.

These new instructions triggered vigorous debate in Council, where the patrons of the voyage raised their voices in loud protest, citing the losses to the investors. The general commanding the soldiers in the fleet urged Essex

> to second this our journey in such sort that we may go forward in our first pretended course without being limited to so short a time ... for who is he so unadvised to undertake the performance of such a voyage wherein there is so great expectations of so great things to be done in so short a time?[3]

The critics of the expedition pointed out the risks of voyages 'into hot countries' and the dangerous absence of Queen's ships from the threatened English coasts. Some proposed converting the whole scheme into an offensive cruise on the Spanish ports. The debate raged, 'checked from above or crossed underhand, not without a great destroyer of humour on both sides for a few days'.[4]

What swayed the Queen's final decision was a chance event; reports came in of a great galleon, disabled at sea, now anchored off Puerto Rico with a cargo of bullion worth 2.5–3 million pesos. The lure of that mass of glittering silver dissolved all the Queen's timidities. The project for crippling the enemy's preparations was shunted aside, and the admirals sent in hot pursuit of the Puerto Rican silver. The expedition was an unmitigated failure. The Spanish, forewarned by Drake's insistence on raiding in the Canaries, were more than ready, and even he shrank from an attack on the fortifications of San Juan. Just at this moment Hawkins, at odds with his fellow admiral, died. Drake now returned to the original intentions of the voyage. He landed on the isthmus of Panama, attempting but failing to reach Panama City. He made one last assault on the Spanish by a landing in Nicaragua, but before his men could get ashore the admiral himself was dead of dysentery. The fleet crawled home, a fifth of the men dead, with a pitiful £5,000 in booty.

Yet even before the fate of the fleet was known, the leaders of the forward party had persuaded the Queen to authorize another enterprise. This also was a repeat performance of a former effort. A fleet and army were to sail for an assault on Spanish home soil. Plans were in the making from November 1595; they took shape in the form of a squadron of seventeen Queen's ships plus twelve merchantmen and a detachment of eighteen Dutch warships. They would carry an army of 6,800 men. To transport this armada there was assembled a fleet of 100–120 ships, bearing 12,000–15,000 participants. The older generation of sea-dogs, Hawkins, Drake, and Frobisher, were dead. Their places were largely taken by younger men, gentlemen players rather than professionals. Two commanders were appointed by the Queen to share control — the Earl of Essex and Lord Admiral Howard. The latter had, of course, seen sea service in 1588, when he had relied heavily on the professionals of his war council. Essex had commanded in the field at Rouen but never at sea. It was very much a court venture. Besides the two Councillors in command it included Ralegh, Captain of the Queen's Guard, and Lord Thomas Howard, the commander of the 1591 expedition to the Azores.

In the midst of the preparations, the Spanish capture of Calais momentarily diverted English attention; Essex was granted a commission to relieve the town, but it fell before action could be taken. The French, through a weighty embassy, lobbied against the naval undertaking, and the Queen wavered. At one stage she proposed to remove the two Admirals and replace them with inferior officers. A faction on the Council wanted to eliminate the soldiery, turning the expedition into a solely naval enterprise, aimed at the capture of the plate fleet. From the Queen's comments on the return of the fleet, it seems probable she would have preferred this option, but she was persuaded into approving the original plan. On 1 June 1596 the fleet sailed.[5]

Its official goals, spelled out in the Queen's instructions, retailed the fear of another invasion, destined for Ireland, in 1597. The admirals were to destroy ships and supplies. If they found a defenceless town, they might attack it, but without hazarding the lives of their men. A council of advisers was appointed by the Queen with power to check the commanders. As before, there was a hopeful addendum to the instructions — the interception of the American treasure ships or the East Indian carracks.[6]

The Earl of Essex chose to put his own interpretation on the royal instructions. In a letter written after his departure from Plymouth, he outlined his programme. Starting with the premiss that 'it is better to do something in another country than to attend the enemy' at home, he urged the necessity of a swift and short campaign, aimed at the enemy's jugular. What he proposed to do was to seize and hold a Spanish port 'to be made a continual diversion', which would be 'a thorn sticking in his foot'. This was a strategy aimed not merely at containment of the Spanish menace but at delivering 'all Christendom from the fearful usurpation' of Philip II.[7]

Ignoring the tenor of the royal instructions, the fleet moved directly against a target the commanders had selected in advance — the key port of Cadiz, the largest of the cluster of ports lying near the mouth of the Quadalquivir and the entrepôt of the American trade. In spite of an unseemly scramble for first place among the commanders, the English captured the city with ease. Absorbed in the excitements of a sack, they neglected the cargo-laden American fleet anchored in the upper bay, waiting to sail. This gave the Spanish time to destroy the ships after unloading most of the cargo.

The town taken, what should they do with it? Essex had no doubt as to their next move. Cadiz stood on what was virtually an island, linked to the mainland by a narrow strip. The Earl envisaged a permanent foothold for the English, one which, supplied by sea, could be held indefinitely. The Admirals' council agreed to this, and to a scheme for sending Howard and Ralegh, with some of the ships, to the Atlantic islands to lie in wait for the East and West Indian squadrons. Thus placed, Essex wrote, 'we shall cut his [the Spaniard's] sinews and make war upon him with his own money'.[8] The Earl's dream was short lived. The Lord Admiral and the other officers soon had second thoughts, which led them to reverse their earlier decision, alleging the lack of royal instructions and the shortage of supply. Bitterly disappointed and blaming his associates, Essex produced a second-best plan, a division of the fleet, the army to be carried home, the rest of the ships to make for the Azores, there to stalk the Indian galleons. Lord Admiral Howard and Ralegh both opposed this scheme. They did agree to search the northern Spanish ports for shipping but, finding Corunna and Ferrol empty, insisted on a return home.

The Queen had watched these proceedings from afar with a sceptical eye. Hearing of the landing at Faro (*en route* from Cadiz to Corunna) she sourly noted that this promised no profit. She then sent off an order echoing Essex's defeated plan, to send the army home while dispatching the fleet in pursuit of the American fleet, laying heavy emphasis on the importance of the treasure to her exchequer. If this failed to reach them before they returned — as it did — they were to pick up supplies waiting at Plymouth and set off post-haste for the Atlantic islands. It was an order demanding the impossible; the sea-worn and disease-infested ships were in no condition to return to sea.[9]

Further royal response to the expedition awaited them at Plymouth.[10] Far from the congratulations they might have expected for their exploit, they received a witheringly contemptuous assessment of their actions. 'The inconvenience which we suspected would follow this journey ... that it would rather be an action of honour and victory against the enemy and particular spoil and profit to the army than any way profitable to oneself.' So much for the martial glories of her admirals. She reminded them that she had argued against an army which, besides the cost, would only consume victuals and render a further sea action impossible. There were now the bills to pay and nothing to pay them with. 'All of which matters were not overseen [unforeseen] by us, if you can both remember but were, as divers other things, neglected and contradicted both by yourself and soothed by others to our no small discontentation.'

What all this royal wrath suggests is that the Queen's reluctant assent to the enterprise had been given in the hope of another booty-laden capture like the *Madre di Dios*. As it was, she had neither treasure nor any major damage to the Spanish war fleet to show for a major effort. All that remained was a substantial pile of bills to be paid. At one point she contemplated docking the sailors' pay on the grounds they were sufficiently rewarded by their share in the plunder.[11] All this was true, but it did less than justice to her commanders' achievement. There was the intangible blow to Philip's pride which worried him into the hurried dispatch of an ill-timed invasion fleet, only to see it broken up by the autumnal storms of Biscay. There was the destruction of the American supply ships, and the loss of credit which resulted in the Brussels government's bills of exchange being refused in Italy.[12]

Throughout the autumn months, the government was distracted by the approaching invasion fleet. Preparations were made to mobilize defence, but by early December news began to filter in of a Spanish catastrophe. As early as 17 November storms had dispersed their ships, with heavy damage. Nevertheless, the Queen was still very uneasy about Spanish intentions, especially towards Ireland, where endemic disorder was fast swelling into dangerous insurrection. Discussion followed as to what measures to take. Essex predictably called for a large-scale operation against Spain with a dozen royal ships, twenty Dutch, and twelve Londoners, along with 5,000 soldiers. Preparations, however, halted for a time, distracted by a court faction fight as the Cecils and Essex squabbled over the appointment of a new Lord Warden of the Cinque Ports and by the French clamour for another expeditionary force after the fall of Amiens. The Spanish alternative prevailed over the French, but the Queen remained sceptical of another overseas enterprise and for a time, in May 1597, suspended preparations. In June she finally yielded her consent.[13]

The expedition in its final form mustered 6,000 soldiers and employed nineteen of the Queen's precious ships. Essex had overall command, with Ralegh and Lord Thomas Howard as Admirals under him. Vere commanded the soldiers. Their instructions from the Queen again combined an attack on the Spanish ships lying in Ferrol harbour, followed, if successful, by an attempt on the homecoming plate fleet. Essex was given permission to seize the island of Terceira in the Azores, but the Queen hung back on any commitment to a continued occupation. Essex again entertained a much grander view of the potentialities of the expedition. He would destroy Spanish sea power, capture both the treasure and the island, and open the way for a West Indian venture. 'To conclude Her Majesty would be absolute queen of the seas.'[14]

The strategy was clear enough, the tactics needed to achieve it much less so. Ferrol lay at the end of a fjord-like bay with fortifications on the hills at the entrance. An army victory was a necessary prelude to naval success, but just how a landing and succeeding operations were to be managed remained quite uncertain. The issue was not to be tested. As usual there was a delay, occasioned this time by the Queen's sudden fear that the two fleets might pass unseen on the high seas and leave England naked to attack. Essex was allowed to sail on 10 July, only to encounter bad weather which scattered his ships in every direction. Howard alone arrived off Corunna to wait in vain for Ralegh and Essex. They had in fact crawled home to Plymouth. By 31 July the English were in their home ports, nothing accomplished.[15] After an interval of confused debate during which Ralegh and Essex suggested sending the fleet to the West Indies, most of the soldiers, who were eating up their rations and spreading infection, were sent home.[16] Deprived of an adequate army, Essex had not the slightest chance of taking Ferrol. Nevertheless he set off once again for that destination with the intention of assailing the Spanish fleet with fireships. Opinion within military circles and in the Council discounted his chance of achieving anything.

In the event the wind blew the ships so far westward that they never saw Ferrol. Essex, thwarted here, now sailed for the Azores. The plate fleet was in fact on hand, but it eluded the English and retired to safety under the guns of Terceira, leaving the discomfited Earl to return dejectedly home. In the final act of this comedy of errors, the English ships were battered by the same storm which dispersed yet another ill-timed Spanish armada. The Spanish commander had sailed from home just as Essex left the Azores. Some of his ships were seen off Falmouth, but the winds once more thwarted their hopes. By 31 October the English could demobilize their ships.

The party of the offensive had had full innings, three large-scale expeditions, two of which were total failures. Many factors entered into their lack of success, not least the rivalries of the commanders and sheer bad luck. Yet overriding the particular obstacles was the mismatch between the visions of the naval strategists and the means at their disposal. To carry through a sustained English presence at Cadiz or in the Azores would have required resources in money, men, and supplies which were simply not to be had. These deficiencies were incapable of remedy because of the very nature of Elizabethan monarchy. The Queen, far from sharing the expansionist dreams of the hawkish party, was contemptuous of what she regarded as their irresponsible pursuit of the bubble reputation. Essex and his associates were indeed obsessed with the thirst for martial glory, sharing the world view of their Continental counterparts, for whom the chief business of monarchy was the waging of war. It was linked, of course, to their aspirations for a greater role for their country in the world of European politics. The opportunity for achieving military renown was necessarily tied to an aggressive pursuit of power by the English state. Such an attitude predominated in the courts of Spain and France. Along with it went the ruthless determination of the rulers to squeeze the maximum financial support from the general populace. These resources would be poured into the formation of professional standing armies equipped and trained to the highest possible level of competence. Heavy taxation in its turn begot a whole new administrative structure to collect and disburse it. There had to be continuous experimentation and innovation by the masters of the state.

Against all this Elizabeth steadfastly set her face. Perpetually haunted by the spectre of an empty exchequer, fearful of the loss of control which delegation of power to her commanders necessitated, and nervously unwilling to risk the popularity of the regime by excessive taxation, she resolutely declined to consider any alterations or adaptations of existing practice in order to fight the war. Even the one weapon which she did value, her navy, was run on the most economical, not to say parsimonmious, lines. Its size meant that armed merchantmen had to be enlisted for every major naval enterprise. Armies (with the exception of the Low Country forces) were raised from scratch and dissolved at the earliest possible moment. The costs of recruitment and mobilization fell upon the local magistracies and their communities, a process which did not diminish the weight of the burden but diffused its incidence.

Such a conception of government, minimal in scope, irenic in external relations, resting on the unpaid services of a social and political elite and on the assumptions of a static society, was antithetical to the ambitions of martially minded aristocrats and expansionist Councillors. This said, the fact remains that Elizabeth did authorize three major overseas offensives. What led her to these deviations from her normal line of policy? First, probably, was her fear of another Spanish attack on her realm, a threat which events proved to be real. Each of the three expeditions was intended to cripple Spanish preparations, although the first was sidetracked by the lure of the disabled silver galleon. That, of course, points to the second motive which moved the Queen to loose her forces on the enemy. In every case there was the desperate hope of intercepting the plate fleet, or at least of another haul like that of the *Madre di Dios* in 1592. After the return from Cadiz, Elizabeth would have sent her weary sailors off on another treasure chase. Her disappointment at their failure cancelled out any satisfaction she might have felt in her commanders' exploits. At times it seemed that the Queen was more interested in paying for the war than in winning it.

The difference between the horizons which bounded the world of Essex or Ralegh and those of the Queen could hardly have been wider. The spacious skies of the two men's vision looked down on a universe of far-reaching splendours, rich in untold — and undiscovered — wealth, and of empires yet to be conquered. The Queen cast her eyes no further than her own domains, a housewife glumly surveying her empty cupboards and bare rooms, distrustful of her neighbours and apprehensive of thieves at the door. Essex dreamed of conquest, a new English empire; the Queen sought nothing more than survival.

22

Edging towards Peace

*B*y the time the last of the expeditions returned home, the air was rife with rumours — and more than rumour — of an approaching peace between France and Spain. From the time when Henry IV mastered the Holy League and asserted his authority over his unruly kingdom, English and Dutch leaders alike nervously worried about his next move. Having won control at home, would he continue to fight abroad? Down to 1597 he waged a war with Spain which was primarily defensive. We have seen the wary jockeying between Elizabeth and Henry as he attempted to inveigle her into substantial support for an offensive in the Low Countries, and the agility with which she squirmed away from any such commitments. Henry's frequent hints that failing such help he would have to seek peace ceased to be mere feints when in 1597 he wrote to say that the enemy now sought peace. What were Elizabeth's views? Would she join in such negotiation? Or, alternatively, would she participate with the States in a tripartite attack on Calais in spring 1598?[1]

The Queen chose to respond by sending a high-ranking embassy to talk face to face with the French monarch. Heading it was Sir Robert Cecil, since summer 1596 the principal Secretary of State. With his father sinking into his final decline, the son was fast becoming the dominant figure in the Council. Essex still stood high in the royal regard, but he was becoming a fifth wheel. As the prospects of peace waxed so did his hopes of another bid for fame and glory wane. However, in the spring of 1598, gratified by his recent promotion to Earl Marshal, which marked his victory over the Lord Admiral's pretensions to be the victor of Cadiz, the moody Earl was in a stable phase. During Cecil's absence in France — given the grave illness of

Burghley — someone had to stand in for the Secretary as the Queen's right-hand man. For Cecil it was a great risk to leave the field open to his rival, with whom there had recently been bitter hostility. However, a pact was struck between the two; Essex faithfully kept his word and watched carefully over Cecil's interests during the latter's absence. Indeed, his conduct won the praise of Burghley himself.

Cecil travelled to France with two fellow envoys, the experienced Wilkes (who died *en route*) and the Second Secretary, Herbert, plus a staff of eighteen gentlemen. The voluminous instructions with which Cecil was laden bear witness to the conflicting hopes and fears of the Queen at this point.[2] Spanish inactivity on the military front and their abandonment of their Breton ally, Mercœur, indicated the seriousness of Philip's desire for peace. What Cecil needed to find out was how far Henry, now in a position of strength domestically, was prepared to deal with his foe. Secondly, he was to sound out the position of the States, whose delegate, Oldenbarnevelt, was also *en route* to the French court. On the answers he received from these questions the Queen could base her own decision whether to participate in the talks with the Spanish.

The Queen was deeply distrustful of Philip, and her instructions recalled the betrayal in 1588. If discussions with the Spanish did ensue, there would have to be guarantees for the security of the United Provinces. To the Dutch themselves Cecil was to propose a return to the formal *status quo ante*, a recognition of Philip's sovereignty, but reduced to a shadow by the withdrawal of Spanish forces and officials, with toleration for Protestants. The Dutch were to be warned that their refusal to accept these terms would leave the Queen free to pursue her own interests. If the war were to continue, Elizabeth expected the States to carry the whole financial burden in the Low Countries, while the French were to be bluntly told they could expect no military aid except when English interests were directly touched. Further, Cecil was to ask for repayment of their debts by both French and Dutch. This was not a very strong hand to play if France were to be dissuaded from making peace, and suggests the Queen's prior resignation to the inevitability of a Franco-Spanish treaty. If such were English expectations, they were confirmed by what Cecil saw as he and his colleagues journeyed across the devastated French countryside to meet Henry at Nantes. In initial discussions Cecil and Henry sparred with one another, the King decrying English strategy, emphasizing his people's war-weariness, and seeking to pry out English intentions towards the Dutch.

In the mean time the English Council had now in hand a packet of documents revealing that the preliminaries of peace between Henry and Philip were already signed. Final conclusion was being held up solely to obtain a commission from Madrid to open the possibility of English inclusion in the treaty.[3] When Cecil received copies of these documents from home, he roundly confronted Henry, who did not deny the facts, but pressed the Secretary as to whether England would treat now that a commission from Madrid had arrived. Cecil evaded this by saying that his commission was only to discuss continuation of the war. In a final flare-up, when Henry declared he had not treated Cecil as an ordinary ambassador, the Secretary retorted that he served 'an extraordinary prince, a prince that ought to be extraordinarily respected . . . and if without arrogancy I might speak it, I might take myself (considering my place) as no ordinary ambassador'.[4] There was little more to say. The English blamed Henry for refusing to consider the continuation of the war; the King riposted that it was his ally's refusal of support which drove him to sign the peace. The mission returned to England in mid-April; on 2 May the peace was signed at Vervins.

Henry had re-established his authority within the kingdom, and when Spain offered the restitution of Calais and the other captured towns, he could not refuse to accept their terms. His country, ravished by decades of disorder, was exhausted and a breathing space urgently needed. However, so long as negotiations continued, he was anxious to keep alive the appearance of an active alliance with England (and the States) as a makeweight in bargaining. Elizabeth desperately wanted to have her cake and eat it — to see France engaged in active hostilities with Spain but to promise nothing substantial in the way of English aid. Faced with the hard choice proffered by the King of France, she stood by her most fundamental principle. She would offer nothing more than a commitment to act when she thought English interests directly involved. To this Henry could only respond by acting as he did. For Elizabeth there was nothing for it but to swallow the pill and move on to the questions which the new situation now posed. Should she treat with the Spanish herself? What were the intentions of the States?

Cecil had met and talked with Oldenbarnevelt in France; the latter made it clear the Dutch would not accept Elizabeth's proposed terms for a shadowy Habsburg sovereignty. When it was certain that Henry would make peace, Cecil persuaded Oldenbarnevelt and his colleagues to follow him to England instead of returning directly home. The best cards were now in the Queen's hand. If the Dutch had to face the undivided attentions of the Spanish armies, their need of English assistance was more than ever necessary and a harder bargain could be struck with them. Cecil told the Queen he would have 'these two, which are the best ministers the States have, humble petitioners to you in England'.[5]

Oldenbarnevelt expected that Elizabeth would in fact make peace while retaining the cautionary towns, and had to be persuaded that it was worth his while to make the journey to England. The Queen gave him and his colleagues a cold reception, reproaching their stubbornness in refusing to consider a peace, but then, in a series of leading questions, hinted that she might want to continue the war if the treaty terms could be renegotiated. With that hopeful message Oldenbarnevelt set off for home to persuade his sceptical fellow-countrymen to such a course. Vere soon followed with concrete proposals. He was to emphasize England's heavy burdens in Ireland and to play up the inducements for England to treat with Spain. The Queen had before her a clear choice — 'either harken to peace when the offer made on so honourable circumstances or follow war with good probability of success'.[6] What inducements could they offer to persuade England to continue so burdensome a war? All this was, of course, meant to pressure the Dutch into maximum concessions. What Elizabeth wanted was relief from her financial commitments under the Treaty of Nonsuch. The Dutch were to assume all charges for the English troops serving in their armies plus those of the cautionary garrisons. Repayment of the debt was to begin, and the States must pledge themselves to assist England in any attack against Spain in Europe or overseas.

The Dutch remained deeply suspicious of English intentions, and Oldenbarnevelt had to work hard to obtain support in the States General and the provincial states. There was a party among them which would have responded to the feelers being put out from Brussels by the Archduke for a settlement. In the event negotiations with England, once opened, moved briskly. The English were aware of the fragility of Oldenbarnevelt's position. A compromise was reached on the debt; the Queen accepted their figure for its total size; they agreed to hers for the amounts of the annual payments. The total (£800,000 against the English claim of £1,000,000) was to be paid off, half in £30,000 yearly instalments, the balance after peace was made. The treaty was signed on 26 August 1598.[7]

The Queen had thus dealt with one of the two questions left hanging in the air after Vervins was concluded. The English would continue to support the States, but only at arm's length. English soldiers would continue to fill the ranks of the States army, but entirely at Dutch expense. The English were assured of Dutch naval support if they chose to mount another offensive against Spain. It was neither war nor peace; it assured the continuance of Dutch resistance, but left open a door for an English response to the offer held out by the Spanish commissioners at Vervins.

The coming of peace betwen Spain and France disappointed Elizabeth's hopes and posed new and awkward problems for her decision. At the same time it restored her to a freedom of action which she had lost a decade earlier. Since 1585, and especially since 1588, she had been the unwilling warrior queen, waging a war which she had sought so desperately to avoid. It was a task which she loathed and for which she was ill-equipped. Lobbied by the advocates of offensive strategy, driven by events over which she had no control, she had, by her timidity and hesitation, tormented her commanders and by unwise economy undercut their efforts. Now, when diplomats were crowding the soldiers from the stage, she could once again exercise her own *métier* and recover control of men and events. With the peace-making process under way, she could act with a sureness of touch which she had lacked in the war-making years.

Having settled a new agreement with the States, she could now turn her attention to the second question, the possibilities of an accommodation with Spain. The Spanish had conveyed through Henry IV an invitation for discussion of a possible settlement which was to remain open for six months. Elizabeth was appropriately coy. Cecil provided the French intermediaries with a memorandum which asked for repayment of the loan made in 1577 to the States General and insisted that the cautionary towns would be returned to the States.[8] These were merely bargaining terms, neither of which the Spanish would accept. They were meant to show that, if there were talks, the English would drive a hard bargain; but at least it left the door open for further approaches.

Any further exploration of possibilities was delayed by the death of Philip II in August and the consequent return of the Archduke-Governor Albert to Madrid for consultation with the new regime of Philip III. This prince and his wife, the daughter of the late King, had been appointed to the Low Countries as the agents of a new policy. They were given a wider range of autonomy and the possibility was held out — if there were issue — of a separate branch of the dynasty. They hoped to rally the flagging loyalty of the war-weary southern provinces while wooing the pro-peace elements in the north. In the mean time the English Council plunged into anxious debate as to what position they should take up in response to the Spanish overture. These discussions were coloured throughout by a profound scepticism as to Spanish sincerity. The Queen, who had never forgotten Parma's deception in 1588, doubted of 'some like accident to accompany this bare offer in the name of the cardinal' (the Cardinal Andreas, acting governor).[9] The initial response was thus a very cool one. Peace could not be made without Dutch agreement, and for the present the States General declined to treat. Elizabeth thanked the French King, but appointed no commission to act. However, she remained open to any move the other side might make. The ball was tossed into the Spanish side of the court.

If the enemy came forward, what answer should be given? The opponents of a peace, led by Essex, emphasized the treachery at Bourbourg in 1588 and repeated the familiar argument that Catholic rulers were not bound to keep faith with heretics. Spain would simply use the opportunities offered by a peace to regroup and prepare another assault. Their opponents on the Council argued that the main goal of the war, as set out in 1585, was to secure the liberty of the United Provinces. That was now achieved, and the presence of a strong anti-Spanish regime at Paris ensured their future. English interests in the Low Countries, as in France, were now protected; no more English substance should be consumed in furthering enterprises no longer vital to the Queen and her subjects. Spain, weakened by decades of war and faced by a resurgent France, was no longer to be feared. Nevertheless, she was too strong for any further allied military action to succeed.

Burghley, a dying man, was strongly in favour of negotiation. What weighed with him were domestic considerations. It was the 'nature of the common people of England [to be] inclined to sedition if they be pressed with extraordinary payments'. Underlying this was Burghley's conviction that 'there was an inbred disaffection in the vulgar towards the nobility'. The burden of taxation must be eased. After a dramatic scene in which the Treasurer quoted Scripture against Essex – 'Men of blood shall not live out half their days'[10] – the peace party won the Queen's support, at least to the extent that Elizabeth would listen to Spanish proposals and, if they seemed fit to consider, she would carry the discussion to the bargaining table.

What the English specifically called for was, first, by an act of oblivion to wipe the board clear of the past decades, and a renewal of the treaties of friendship of 1520 and 1542. A fresh start could then be made on the substantive issues between the crowns. Philip III would have to renounce his claims to the English succession, made in his father's time, end all dealings with the English Catholics, approve English aid to the States, and allow England to retain the cautionary towns until the Dutch repaid the Queen her outlays in their behalf. Trade was to be free of restrictions, particularly religious constraints, and English traders were to have entrée to the Indies. As far as the States General was concerned, the clock would be turned back to the Emperor Charles's reign, with the addendum of complete toleration in the northern provinces and freedom of conscience in the southern. The terms of the peace would be guaranteed by a tripartite Anglo-Dutch–French commission. All foreign troops were to leave the Spanish provinces while the States could continue to recruit in England. These were maximum terms and might be negotiated, but they reflected Elizabeth's deep suspicions of Spain's designs on her realms. Any firm peace would have to assure the existence of an unassailably strong Dutch state which could no longer, in Alva's intentions, be 'as it were a bridge to come into the realm'.

The Queen was determined to force the Spanish to make the first move, and, indeed, at the close of 1598 the acting governor at Brussels, Cardinal Andreas of Austria, pushed his pawn forward and in the first days of the new year dispatched an Antwerp jurist, Jerome Coomans, on a secret mission to London. His message was a simple one: the Cardinal offered his services as a mediator.[11] If the Queen accepted, Andreas would write to Archduke Albert and Philip III for permission to initiate talks with the English government. The Queen gave a cautiously favourable answer; she would listen to any overture. The next move from Brussels was to propose the appointment of deputies by both sides; again Elizabeth agreed, on condition the Spanish representative had full powers from Madrid. There were various delays after that, and it was not until October 1599 that Coomans resumed his visits.

In the interval, discussions continued in the English Council. Essex continued his opposition until his departure for Ireland in April. Elizabeth once again tried to enlist Dutch participation in the negotiations but, when she was turned down, decided to act on her own. In January 1600 Thomas Edmondes, an experienced diplomatic agent, was sent to Brussels to arrange the details of an actual conference. He was fêted *en route* by the war-weary Belgian towns. It was agreed that the meeting should be held on French soil at Boulogne. (Henry had already agreed.)

The Archduke in turn sent an envoy of rank, the audiencer Verreykens, to London, where he had audience with the Queen; in an expansive vein, she went so far as to declare she had so desired peace with Spain that she would have gone to Philip II in person had not religion deterred her. Philip, she was certain, had been misled by evil advisers. In a meeting with Councillors — Cecil, Lord Admiral Howard, Buckhurst, and Hunsdon — Verreykens offered for discussion a draft alliance, loaded with the maximum Spanish programme. This comprehended a renewal of the old Burgundian treaties, an offensive and defensive alliance. Elizabeth was to agree to a rupture of relations with the States, a trade prohibition, and the return of Flushing and Brill to Spanish hands.[12]

As was to be expected, the Queen rejected the proposal for an alliance, which could entail war against Protestants. She countered with a demand for repayment of the 1577 loans of £100,000 to the States General, a six-month interval to allow for possible Dutch participation in the treaty, and a guarantee, should the States refuse, that no fleet would be launched against them from Spain. Further talks yielded little in substance, but it was clear the Spanish wanted the conference to take place. Cecil, still sceptical, supposed 'that seeing they desire to meet we ought to imagine they have a purpose to accommodate'.[13]

Preparations now reached a final stage. The English commissioners were headed by Sir Henry Neville, currently ambassador at Paris, who was recommended by Cecil as a man without 'private passion or prejudicate disposition either violently to war or blindly to peace'.[14] His fellow-commissioners were the Second Secretary, John Herbert, Robert Beale, the experienced Clerk of the Council in the North, and Thomas Edmondes, earlier employed in the preliminary discussions. It was a group of experts, but lacked either a dignified figurehead or a weighty councillor. Their opposite numbers were of the same ilk — Richardot, president of the Archduke's council, the audiencer Verreykens, and a Spanish councillor, Carrillo. The royal instructions directed the commissioners not only as to the substance of their demands but also as to strategy. First of all, they were to stand on the Queen's dignity in matters of protocol. There was to be no question but that they should at all times take first place in precedence. They were allowed to compromise so far as to allow alternating days of 'preseance', but it was to be crystal-clear that Elizabeth came to the table as an equal, not as a suppliant — as a foe who had withstood all Spanish efforts unbowed. The Queen's representatives were to refrain from any initiatives, thrusting on the Spanish the onus of proposing terms and again highlighting the argument that Elizabeth had been the innocent victim of Spanish provocation. It was for the King of Spain to make amends by taking the lead in repairing the harm done.[15]

Consequently, the English commissioners were instructed to concede virtually nothing to Spanish demands. They were to decline entering an offensive and defensive alliance, limiting themselves to a mere treaty of amity, a restoration of civil relations. Elizabeth would retain the cautionary towns even if Spain offered to pay the debts secured on them. Trade with the United Provinces was to be unrestricted. Elizabeth feigned inability to recall those of her subjects who had 'volunteered' to fight with the Dutch, but she would no longer pay their wages. On the freedom of trade in the Indies, she was willing to concede exclusion from the settled colonies but not from unoccupied lands. When the delegates actually met at Boulogne on 20 May it was a question of protocol, not of substance, which engaged their attention — the prime question of precedency. The Spanish adamantly refused to concede in the slightest degree; an English compromise proposal, alternating days of precedence (i.e. who had the honour of presenting, and thereby initiating, business) was turned down. The most the Spanish would do was to refer back to Brussels, promising a reply within a fortnight.

The English Councillors, Cecil, Lord Keeper Egerton, and Buckhurst, became suspicious. Then the Spanish in informal conversation showed their hand. A treaty would be meaningless without Dutch participation. At this very moment another conference was being held at Bergen-op-Zoom, between deputies of the United Provinces and those of the Spanish lands. Would not the Queen act as mediator to draw the two parties together? There was a short history behind this meeting. When the Archduke took office in 1600 he summoned the States General of the Spanish provinces, who immediately demanded a colloquy with their northern counterparts. Albert reluctantly agreed, but the northerners stubbornly refused to listen until Maurice's failure at Nieuport to break through to the relief of besieged Ostend brought them to the bargaining table. What the Spanish now sought was English pressure on their allies to compound with the southern states.[16] Meetings of the Anglo-Spanish negotiators could then be held on Dutch or Flemish soil, where protocol would allow Elizabeth the 'preseance.' The Queen firmly backed her commissioners' refusal to be drawn into such a position. Cecil's shrewd comment was 'that howsover they may resolve to conclude with England rather with neither yet the main point they most effect is to draw the Low Countries to a tripartite covenant'. He had little hope that 'they who have raised themselves to such a height will ever become servants'.[17]

The Queen came to similar conclusions; Spain wanted peace with the Dutch; their interest in England was solely as a decoy to entice the States to the bargaining table. Whether they were desperate for success or hopeful of agreement, England was of secondary interest. Given a choice 'whether to have the Low Countries without the Queen or Her Majesty's amity without then, they will leave her to take them'.[18]

Finally Verreykens returned from Brussels to report unyielding Spanish determination to have the precedence. English suggestions for negotiations by writing only were refused. The English Councillors gave their agents considerable leeway in schemes to resolve the precedency question, but when the English requested a delay for further consultation home over the Spanish scheme for a move to Holland or Flanders, their adversaries refused to wait and went home. Sketchy proposals for a continuing conference maintained the fiction that it was a 'discontinuance rather than an absolute dissolution'. Contacts did indeed continue; there was a desultory correspondence. In the spring of 1601 the Queen and the Archbuke came close to an agreement for reopening the conference, but it broke down over the Queen's insistence that it be entirely secret. The siege of Ostend and the Spanish expedition at Kinsale checked further contact. It was half-heartedly resumed in 1602. Cecil was by this time in regular correspondence with James VI and at the latter's insistence dissuaded the Queen from pursuing the negotiations.[19]

English behaviour in the prolonged negotiations from 1598 on make it clear that the Queen, backed now by an undivided Council, wanted peace, but on her own terms. She demanded neither territorial gains nor financial compensation. She was willing to yield on free trade in the Spanish colonies, but on the great central issue for which she had taken arms in 1585 was adamant. The goal which then had been the defence of Netherlandish liberties was now the independence of the Dutch state. She was willing to offer the Spanish a figleaf of formal sovereignty to veil the bare fact of defeat, but no more. The Spanish were hopeful either of separating the English from their Dutch allies or, failing that, of using England to draw together the two Low Countries parties, counting on war-weariness in the north to force a peace.

The English for their part nursed hopes of a resumption of Franco-Spanish hostilities. War between France and Spain's protégé, Savoy, in 1600 raised these hopes, but they were dashed when a peace was patched up. English expectation of renewed conflict remained lively. Cecil offered a less hopeful prognosis of Spanish intentions towards England. He believed that Philip III's government intended to make use of the Irish rebellion to bring pressure on the Queen. Events would soon prove him right.[20] England's first priority must be the extinction of the Irish rebellion. Until that was completed, peace with Spain suited neither London nor Madrid.

Part VI

The Practice of Statecraft

23

The 1559 Settlement

T here was no area of English life about which the Queen had more determined ideas and clear-cut plans than the reorganization of the national church. She moved decisively at the opening of the reign to implement those plans. Once in place, the structure she had erected was inviolable. When critics from within the Protestant ranks sought to bring about change, Elizabeth was unyielding in her rock-like resistance to any alteration. She would resist successfully to the end of the reign and leave behind a church stamped in a mould which would endure for generations to come. No other aspect of the Queen's work had such lasting consequences.

Apart from the criticism the Queen met from the reformers' ranks, she was faced with a faithful remnant among her subjects who refused to abandon the old faith. Here her initial hopes that time and mortality would erase the lingering survivals of the Catholic order were disappointed, and she had to abandon the tolerance of the reign's early years for a policy of ruthless persecution. This too failed, and at the close of the reign it was becoming apparent that the English Roman Catholic community could not be destroyed without far more rigorous measures than the English government would or could undertake.

The religious problem which Elizabeth faced at her accession was, like the rest of her untidy inheritance, a product of her three predecessors' actions. It owed its chequered history to the contrasting intentions of her father, her brother, and her sister. Henry had struck out boldly in his initial repudiation of Rome's authority, and his minister Cromwell had done an effective job in the reconstruction of ecclesiastical institutions, but the King had faltered in the task of enunciating a coherent doctrinal position. He wavered between overtures towards the Continental reformers and reaffirmations of traditional doctrine. At the close of his reign English religious life was clouded with confusion, with a national church which was in papal eyes schismatic and in the Protestant view stuck half-way on the road to reformation.

Edward's government had shown no hesitation in repudiating both the doctrine and the practice of Rome and in instituting a new order of worship, but at the end of that short reign new uncertainties began to appear. By then the two dynamic forces of the English Reformation were out of phase. The brittle alliance between two divergent groups — laity determined to subordinate the ecclesiastical order to their control and divines who entertained the vision of a national spiritual revival — was now strained at the seams. There followed a ruler, Mary, who knew quite certainly what she wanted to do and what was necessary to accomplish her ends. They were simply to undo, as far as was possible, all that her two predecessors had undertaken, by restoring the *status quo ante* of 1529, a church once more in full unity with Rome.

Her successor, too, was sure of her goals — another about-face which would turn the clock back to 1552, to the Edwardian religious order. It proved easy to dismantle the Marian regime but far less easy to decide what to put in its place. Mary had had the advantage of a hallowed model; it was simply a matter of putting the pieces into place again, of putting Humpty Dumpty back on the wall. For Elizabeth the tentative, half-finished Edwardian structure offered far less authoritative guidance, since many of its adherents had regarded it as an experimental phase in an unfinished process. Of one thing Elizabeth was certain — that the process of fluctuating change must come to an end. Unlike the Protestant divines returning from exile, she saw what was to be done as the final stage of a cycle of reform, not merely another phase in the continuing process of evangelical renewal in which the further purposes of providence would be made manifest. To accomplish this end the new Queen moved briskly to a wholesale restoration of the Edwardian structure, with a minimum of discussion.

Elizabeth in the formation of her religious policy spoke to the instincts of a profoundly conservative society to which all change was deeply alien. The Queen was anxious to establish as quickly as possible a new stability, a fixed pattern of public worship which would become a part of the rhythm of daily life. In mode it must be uniform, sustained, and unvarying if the new religious ways, by hardening into the cake of custom, were to supplant the immemorial tradition of the mass. Such a policy, responding to the deep-lying conception of an unchanging, indeed timeless, social fabric, ran counter to the transforming vision of the reformers, who sought to replace the inertial religion of custom and habit with one of passionate and active conviction.

The statutes of 1559 which provided the constitutional framework of Elizabeth's new order were straightforwardly political and juridical in character. Making extensive use of scissors and paste, their authors cobbled together an Act of Supremacy which re-established the Henrician legislation of 1534–6 and repudiated Roman authority, repeating the same condemnatory rhetoric which assailed the Pope as a usurper of power not rightfully his rather than the more radical Protestant argument in which he appeared as the corrupter of true religion. Its provisions were largely concerned with severing the juridical and fiscal ties which bound England to Rome.

The Act of Uniformity similarly re-enacted the statute of 1552, re-establishing the second Edwardian prayer book as the only lawful form of worship, with the one small but significant alteration in the words of administration in the sacrament of holy communion, an alteration which threw a crust to the adherents of the old faith but also reflected Protestant uncertainties about the true nature of the sacrament. More important was the fact that the Act was largely shaped by lay hands. The sources are obscure, but they suggest at the most a cursory consultation with such Protestant divines as happened to be available.[1] Clearly, the Queen and her advisers wanted to move with all possible haste and least possible discussion. Division in the reformers' ranks would have been perilous, and the government presumably chose a course of action calculated to provoke minimal disagreement. Debate in the Lords, about which we are better informed, did indeed raise the question as to which version of the reformed faith was being adopted, and the reforming clergy made haste to publish an assertion of their unity.

What was entirely lacking in the legislative settlement was any statement of the church's theological stance, on the model of the confession of Augsburg or those of the Swiss churches. The principles laid down in the royal programme were simple and straightforward. The clergy were bound by law to the celebration of the rites prescribed in the *Book of Common Prayer*, and to no other. The laity were obliged to attend divine service each Sunday. For the clergy, the penalties for non-observance of the statute were loss of office; for the laity, a one-shilling fine for each Sunday absence. This essentially negative formulation neatly sidestepped any doctrinal issues. No profession of faith was required, although the obligation laid on clergy and civil officers to take the oath of supremacy obviously meant the repudiation of papal authority. The possibility of a trial for heresy remained, but the crime was so defined as to make its actual prosecution an exceptional event. This provision may well have been pushed through by the conservatives in self-protection, but it chimed with the royal determination to damp down doctrinal divisions and to disentangle the secular power from the task of governing men's beliefs.

Behind the bare words of the statutes lay a far-reaching and novel conception of the relations of state and church, to which Elizabeth was profoundly committed. Its basic assertion was the overriding responsibility which under God rested with her for the regulation of religion in all external matters. Those external matters were extended to include all forms of public worship and church government. Hence, the lay subject in attending church, or the priest in celebrating the sacraments by the prescribed rite, was merely fulfilling a civic obligation. He was called upon for a passive obedience to the ecclesiastical supremacy as unquestioning as that by which he acknowledged the Queen's civil authority. Encoded in this deceptively simple scheme was a dilemma of conscience which the Queen steadfastly refused to acknowledge. Conformity to statutory commands by participating in public worship might constitute, for a faithful Catholic, assent to heresy or, for a conscientious Protestant, disobedience to God's revealed commands. Neither Catholic nor radical, Bible-oriented Protestant could accept the lay power's right to regulate worship. At sword's point on all other issues, the dissidents at both ends of the spectrum joined in placing God's rights, whether expressed by the Vicar of Christ or in the sacred text, before the prince's.

What was conspicuously absent from the statute-book was a confession of faith, a statement of the English church's theological position. Such a statement had been drawn up in Edward's time, but it would be a decade before it was brought out for parliamentary confirmation, and then much against the Queen's will. Definitions of this kind by their very nature emphasized difference and stimulated controversy. The Queen would delay promulgation as long as she could.

The skeleton of the legislative acts was fleshed out by a set of royal Injunctions.[2] In considerable part they merely copied Edward VI's Injunctions of 1547, but with substantial additions which spelled out Elizabeth's interpretation of their intent. They consisted of very specific instructions as to the performance of divine service, regulated the conduct of the clergy in detail, and laid out the religious duties of the laity. Over and over again they echoed the theme of royal authority in all matters of religious practice; the congregations were to be frequently reminded that no foreign potentate had any such authority. The oath of supremacy was defended against allegations that it offended conscience; it merely asserted that the Queen had sole sovereignty and rule over all persons, ecclesiastical or temporal. The Injunctions explicitly denied that Elizabeth claimed 'authority and power of ministry of divine offices'.

Catholic practices such as pilgrimages or shrines were denounced, but no doctrinal questions were raised, and indeed the Queen bade 'all manner her subjects to forbear all vain and contentious disputations in matter of religion', and to avoid such words of reproach as papist, schismatic, or sacramentary. Throughout, the tone of the Injunctions is one of a sober Erasmian piety, moral rather than theological, emphasizing daily conduct rather than inward experience. Above all it projects the vision of a civic religion. The clergy were to be as much agents of the crown as they were servants of God. The Queen, as sole ruler of all her subjects, was responsible for their obedience to the divine precepts for the conduct of their lives. They were bound to observe the rules she laid down for this purpose, but she gave no instruction as to the content of their beliefs. The hidden premiss was that men might be constrained by the crown in all matters of social behaviour and public worship without any obligations being placed on inward belief. This was a divorce between belief and action that would sit very ill with the consciences of ardent Catholics or rigorous adherents of the new faith. Therein lay the seeds of vexatious problems to come.

However, the inauguration of the new order went forward with ease. Although all but one of the Marian bishops refused the new oath and were accordingly removed from office, they accepted their fate without demur. Some were imprisoned, others placed under lighter restraint; but none showed the slightest signs of initiating resistance. Nor were the putatively Catholic lay nobles any more active. A substantial number of cathedral clergy and a few hundred parish priests refused to accept the new order.[3] Among the laity loyal to the old faith there was confusion and uncertainty as to the lawfulness of church attendance; judgments from Rome in 1562 strictly forbade it, but how far the average worshipper was aware of these is doubtful.[4] Recusant priests, protected by faithful lay patrons, continued to celebrate the mass in private houses, but there was no recruitment of successors. The government could reasonably hope that the lingering loyalty to the old faith, unnourished by priestly care and the sacraments, would gradually fade away. Until very late in the decade of the 1560s this seemed a real possibility.

In 1561 there was a flurry of agitation when the Pope proposed to send a nuncio to England with an invitation to the Council of Trent.[5] For a moment it seemed possible that the Queen might receive such an agent; she seems to have been more amenable to the proposal than her Councillors. The hopes of the Spanish ambassador, Bishop DeQuadra, soared, but in fact the Queen consistently made it clear that she would send representatives only to a 'free' council, i.e. one not subject to papal preconditions. Elizabeth was adamant that she would not give any recognition to papal authority.

The problem of Catholic recusancy remained in abeyance, and the Queen might congratulate herself that the new order was settling down with minimal strain; but with the meeting of Convocation in 1563 there appeared the first signs of restlessness among the most devoted of the Protestant clergy, many of them exiles in the late reign. It was a moment characteristic of all revolutions, when a separation arises between those who feel they have arrived at their intended destination and those who insist that there are roads to choose and miles to go. The Marian exiles had in Germany and Switzerland direct experience of communities far more radically reformed than the England they had left. In Geneva especially they saw a pattern of social order, permeated by what they believed to be the principles of social Christian life laid down in the New Testament. Here was the Gospel not only preached and read but embodied in communal practice. Measured against this model, Elizabeth's church order was but 'halfly reformed'. 1559 was not a terminus but only a temporary stopping place. Now, with the Marian order providentially overthrown, the way lay open for the further fulfilling of Divine purposes with which Englishmen were particularly charged.

24

The Rise of the Reformers

*I*n 1563 an influential group of zealous clergy in the lower (representative) house of Convocation put forward a modest package of proposals which they saw as the natural next step in promoting the work of reformation.[1] What they proposed were, most immediately, changes in liturgical practice and, in the longer term, measures to improve the quality of pastoral care. They also urged stricter measures to compel church attendance by those who still hankered after the old religion. Specifically, they would have eliminated or made optional such surviving Catholic observances as the sign of the cross in baptism or kneeling at communion. They would tighten the screws on recusants by fines for non-reception of communion or failure to attend catechetical instruction. Clergy themselves would have been required to engage in 'further education', with regular instruction by the archdeacons or rural deans. The private lives of the laity would have been brought under tighter clerical supervision, with public penance for sinners. Taken together, all these proposals aimed at a religious regime quite unlike that embodied in the royal establishment. The goal was that of a church filled with evangelical enthusiasm, of a clergy whose task was not the mere passive instruction of their parishioners but the active stirring up of each of them to a sense of his — or her — spiritual condition. The church would be an agent for change, for the spiritual renewal of every individual, and for this task it was necessary to have an educated and militant clergy, themselves exemplars of a robust and active piety, and preachers exhorting their flocks to the same strenuous Christian life.

It was a far cry from the routine round of sober instruction drilled into docile hearers and the decorous celebration of an ordered liturgy envisaged in the Injunctions. What the reformers envisaged implied a religious society pursuing goals separately — although not in conflict — with those of the state, a whole realm of activity outside the purview of the civil authority. Such a conception was anathema to Elizabeth, for whom uniformity of practice and of teaching within the church were a *sine qua non* for harmony within the state. An active preaching clergy would stir up once again all the disagreements and controversies which had troubled her predecessors' times, and in so doing reopen fissures which could endanger the civil order.

The proposals in the lower house of Convocation, promoted by a core of émigrés and other Edwardian reformers, came close to a favourable vote in the lower house, although this would have done nothing more than place the proposals before the bishops in the upper house. Many of the upper house — some fourteen of them returned exiles — probably agreed with the petitioners, but royal pressure halted any movement towards alteration of the 1559 settlement. Discreetly but firmly the Queen checked even the modest measure of change proposed by the reformers. They offended her not only by attempting to tamper with the established order, and thereby renewing disunity within the church, but also by taking into their hands an initiative which trespassed on her ecclesiastical prerogative. Her authority as supreme governor of the church was of a strictly descending order; all power to act was vested solely in her; no inferior jurisdiction possessed any powers of initiative.

The Queen might halt proceedings in Convocation, but the real test of her policy came at the grass-roots level, in the parishes. When Elizabeth went on progress in East Anglia in 1561 it was noted that individual clergy were acting independently, altering the letter of the liturgy by omissions or abridgements. In short, they were taking matters into their hands by putting into practice the alterations proposed in the 1563 Convocation, implicitly challenging the whole conception of uniform religious practice. A paper of Burghley's (possibly of 1564) lists an array of such variants. However, it was not until 1565 that the Queen herself became concerned. Who it was who directed her attention to the matter we do not know, but the royal indignation was made explicit in a letter to Archbishop Parker of Canterbury of January 1565.[2]

It contained a succinct exposition of the Queen's whole position. She referred to the 'the two manners of government [civil and ecclesiastical] without which no manner of people is well governed'. Through the ecclesiastical structure she exercised authority given by Almighty

God for 'the defence of the public peace, concord, and truth of His church', in which all men should live according to their several callings in unity and concord without diversity of opinion or novelties in rites and manner, without maintenance or breeding of any contentions about the same. Nevertheless, there had crept in, 'for lack of regard' by the bishops, 'varieties and novelties not only in opinions but in external ceremonies and rites'. The Archbishop and his episcopal colleagues on the High Commission, the delegated body through which the supreme governorship was administered, were to investigate, ascertain the facts, and then 'proceed by order, injunction or censure' to correct these abuses. Uniformity must be established.

Archbishop Parker and his colleagues acted with speed, and by early March had prepared a set of articles which were presented for the Queen's signature. They largely repeated earlier regulations on preaching, the liturgy, and clerical apparel, but gave them teeth by adding the requirement that future appointees to clerical office should subscribe a declaration promising to observe the contents of these orders. (They did make a significant concession in reducing the vestment requirement for parish clergy solely to the surplice.) The Queen, to Parker's great disappointment, declined to sign. The Archbishop threw up his hands in despair. If the Queen would not sign 'the most part be like to lie in dust for execution of our parties, laws be so much against our private doing'. And again, 'If the ball be tossed to us and then have no authority by the Queen's hand, we will sit still . . . I will no more stir against the stream, fume or chide who will.'[3]

A year passed without action being taken. The Archbishop declared himself defeated, while the dissidents became bolder than ever. Then, in March 1566, the articles were resubmitted for royal signature since, as Parker pointed out, the bishops were forbidden by statute 'to set out any constitutions without licence obtained of the prince'. Again the Queen refused, and the timorous primate was finally driven to issue them under joint episcopal signatures as 'Advertisements', a species of public act not known in practice.[4] At the same time he and Grindal of London brought the issue to a head by summoning the whole body of London clergy to his presence and demanding subscription to the Advertisements, especially the articles regarding the wearing of the surplice and ecclesiastical street garb, under penalty of immediate sequestration and, if they persevered in their delinquency, removal from their livings. Of 98 present, 37 refused subscription. Parker was altogether pessimistic:

I trust Her Majesty hath devised how it may be performed. I utterly despair therein of myself, alway [*sic*] wanting either her toleration or further aid. Mr Secretary, can it be thought that I alone, having sun and moon against me, can compass this difficulty?

A number of the London refusers did in the end conform; other nonconformists were speedily provided with new livings by sympathetic lay patrons.[5]

This initial confrontation between these recalcitrant parsons and the authority of the supreme governor revealed a number of things. First was the sheer scale and tenacity of resistance to the requirements laid down in the Advertisements. Indeed, the London demonstration was only the tip of the iceberg. Grindal, writing to a Swiss correspondent, declared that many of the more learned clergy seemed to be on the point of forsaking their ministry, while their parishioners began to resort to private meetings for worship. Indeed, rumour had included Grindal himself among the supporters of the non-signers, and the Bishop of Durham's resignation was bruited. Grindal admitted that he and others had had a severe struggle with their consciences but, having failed to move the Queen, had reluctantly submitted. The Queen had bent the bishops to her will. Nevertheless, it was apparent that discontent and unease were not limited to a few hotheads or a lunatic fringe, but were shared by sober men of substance, with deep convictions, including a large proportion of the episcopate.[6]

Uneasy, even conscience-ridden, they might be, but the options for action were grim. The Queen had them in a vise. Weighing the alternatives, they could not fail to see that flaring disagreement in the reformed ranks, led by ranking clergy, would benefit no one except the papists. The particular scruples of individuals must yield to the overriding necessities of the reformed faith, threatened as it was from all sides. Inherent in the choice was an acknowledgment of the logic of the Queen's argument. Unity in the ranks was imperative for survival. There was also a corollary. Once they began to exercise the coercive powers of their office they were *ipso facto* executors of the royal policy. Consciously or unconsciously they were defending the existing order; some would soon take up arms in its justification.

The bishops had to submit, but the dissidents had strong support among the nobility and gentry. Their power to act, as patrons of benefices, was untrammelled, and they made full use of it. Sampson, dismissed from the deanery of Christ Church Oxford, was newly beneficed as master of a hospital at Leicester by the Earl of Huntingdon. Leicester was reckoned by Parker as one of his strongest obstructors.

The Queen had henceforth to face the open disobedience of some of her clergy and the foot-dragging reluctance of more, encouraged and patronized by powerful laymen.[7]

Then there was the question of Elizabeth's own reaction to these events. It was she who instituted action by her firm instructions to the bishops. Yet when they responded, she refused to give royal backing to their action. Nor did she press the matter; a year elapsed before the Advertisements, still without royal affirmation, limped onto the stage. How can we explain the disparities between her express orders and her unwillingness to lend her will to their execution? The answer lies in the Queen's vision of her ecclesiastical supremacy. The felicity of her chosen motto, *semper eadem*, was never more apparent than in ecclesiastical matters. The statutes and the Injunctions of 1559 were for her sacred texts, never to be altered in a single syllable, as the bishops discovered in the vestiarian crisis. These rigid convictions would not alter. Consequently, any variation from the prescribed order ignited a blaze of royal anger, as in 1565. But having given peremptory orders for the suppression of the disorder, she lost interest, indeed, became bored and irritated in the details of enforcement. The pattern was to repeat itself — fits of angry royal interference, with imperious commands to act, followed by a lethargic indifference to the problems of execution. As she saw it, once the machinery for ecclesiastical government was in place — High Commission, bishops, and their subordinate officials — her clerical servants could be left to operate it on their own, even as the Privy Council and the judges in her civil government did, without explicit royal backing. The functioning of the Privy Council or of the courts of law did not require her participation; neither should that of the ecclesiastical institutions.

Apart from these conceptions of her office, there was an element of temperament. The Queen had no interest in the theological questions in which her father had so eagerly dabbled, and lacked the intuitive piety of her sister. Discussion of such matters irritated her; the niceties of conscience which troubled a Grindal exasperated her. Clerical refusal to conform to the regulation of their external conduct roused her to a pitch of fury. In an age of acute religious sensibility she remained untouched, unresponsive to such feelings and impatient with what she saw as irrelevant scruples. All this made life very difficult for her ecclesiastical servants. First of all, her rigidity of principle placed them between a rock and a hard place, royal implacability on the one hand and gnawing conscience on the other, compelled, often against their convictions, to enforce measures which could only arouse the most tenacious resistance. Worse still, in the absence of royal backing for their commands, it was they who bore the blame in the minds of the dissidents. All too soon the gravamen of complaint would be directed against the episcopal office itself.

The Queen failed to perceive the fragility of the new ecclesiastical order. In a legal and constitutional sense the Elizabethan bishops were the direct successors of the deposed Marian prelates. The Queen had taken care to observe the legal niceties in their appointments. Yet in fact they were a new and different breed. They themselves were deeply uncertain as to their identity. In the reformed churches of the Continent, the office had been largely abolished or had survived in a supervisory and administrative function without any superior spiritual status or authority. In England the bishops had lost their aura of apostolic authority without receiving any clear new definition. They still had sacerdotal superiority in their power of ordination and wide judicial and visitatory authority over the parish clergy, but many of them felt uncomfortable in these roles and preferred to think of themselves as pastoral leaders, exemplars and guides to their brethren rather than governors. Some would have gone so far as to share their authority with a committee of parish clergy.

In the civil order they were still lords of Parliament, peers of the realm, yet they had ceased to be members of the political elite. Gone were the days when they filled many of the great offices of state. Now they were essentially provincial officials, heavily laden with civil administrative duties, glorified justices of the peace. Nor were relations with their lay neighbours easy. Shorn of much of their wealth by the deliberate policy of Elizabeth in forcing them to yield episcopal manors in exchange for the less substantial income of the tithes of parish churches impropriated for the crown, and encumbered with families for whom they needed to make future provision, they had lost prestige in the eyes of the county elite.

Finally, they were faced with recalcitrant subordinates who contested the very nature of their authority, turning against them the very weapons of scriptural command with which they had belaboured their papal opponents and using the same epithets of abuse. For many of them, especially those who had been exiles, it was not easy to find the answer to these awkward questions. Moreover, their critics were backed by powerful lay patrons. Led by nobles like Leicester or Huntingdon or Councillors like Francis Knollys, many of the critics were the gentry neighbours of the bishops in their sees. These were men of the new faith, who shared in the Protestant conviction of the equality of laymen and clerics and accorded far less respect to the clerical office than their fathers had done.

To all these considerations the Queen remained largely blind. Her insensitivity to the reformers' scruples about such matters as clerical attire or liturgical niceties and her distaste for their evangelical enthusiasm led her to treat them with exasperated contempt. An unbridgeable gulf existed between the monarch and an articulate and determined segment of her subjects. Nor, on the other hand, did she perceive the contradictions in her own ecclesiastical policy. She wanted the bishops to exercise their authority in firm suppression of nonconformity, yet at the same time her policies lowered the prestige and authority of the episcopal office. The persistent downgrading of the bishops' political status and the diminution of their incomes severely hindered their capacity to exercise authority, civil or ecclesiastical. Elizabeth's failure to throw the weight of her royal office behind them was counterproductive for her own policies. At a moment of flux when a new order was struggling to come into being, she left the principal executors of her policy painfully vulnerable, assaulted by their enemies, neglected by their patroness.

25

The Puritans in Parliament

The would-be reformers of the church, to whom the name Puritan now began to be given, thwarted in Convocation, had no hesitation in taking their cause to Parliament, thus defying both the prevailing convention that bills dealings with matters of state, i. e. issues of national import, should originate from the crown and the royal conviction that ecclesiastical jurisdiction was the Queen's alone, not to be shared with Parliament. In 1566 a whole budget of measures was introduced by Puritan members, all but one of which dealt with longstanding grievances, such as pluralism, absenteeism, and simony; but a more significant measure proposed to give parliamentary authority to the Thirty-Nine Articles, accepted by Convocation in 1563 as a confession of faith. Both Cecil and the bishops backed the bill. The Queen angrily accused the latter of being its authors, which they denied. She peremptorily ordered the Lord Keeper to halt the bill. Her objection was not so much to the substance of the bill as to the procedure followed. She bitterly resented any act touching ecclesiastical matters which did not originate from her own order. Bills of this sort were an intolerable intrusion on the ecclesiastical prerogative. Parliament continued to drag its feet on other legislation but failed to move the Queen.[1]

When Parliament met again in 1571 the reformers were given some encouragement by the preliminaries of the session. Bishop Sandys of London preached in the Abbey with a call to purge the church of idolatry and superstition, particularly 'Judaical and heathenish rites', while Lord Keeper Bacon, speaking for the Queen, urged them to consider first 'whether the ecclesiastical laws concerning the discipline of the church be sufficient or not, and if any want shall be found to supply the same'.[2]

Given this lead, the reforming members brought forward bills to give parliamentary sanction to the Thirty-Nine Articles (the Edwardian confession of faith) with a requirement for clerical subscription, as well as another to resuscitate Cranmer's abortive Protestant canon law code. There was a special twist to the bill on the Articles: it would have omitted those on the homilies, the consecration of bishops, and others distasteful to the reformers. This was an attack aimed not only at the 1559 settlement but also on the bench of bishops. It not only forfeited their support but forced the bishops into opposing the reformers.

Then a zealous member named Strickland riled the waters with a bill which would have recast liturgical practice by abolishing such practices as the wearing of vestments or kneeling at communion. This assault on the settlement brought a peremptory response from Elizabeth: the promoter of the offending bill was sent to the Tower. This opened up yet another zone of contention. There was aggrieved complaint about the abridgement of free speech in the house, implicitly calling into question the scope of royal prerogative power. Confrontation was evaded when Strickland was freed, but his bill vanished from sight. There was a continuing struggle over the legislation for the Articles. The radical recission of sensitive articles was quashed, but the bill finally passed by both houses limited clerical subscription to those articles 'which only concern the confession of the true Christian faith and the doctrine of the sacraments'.

Elizabeth grumpily approved the bill, but the bishops took care to enforce subscription to the full Thirty-Nine Articles. These skirmishes were the first rounds in a duel between the Queen and the reforming party in the Commons which would be repeated in almost ritual form in future Parliaments. Regularly the latter would present measures for reform which were bolder and bolder in their assault on the 1559 settlement. With equal regularity the Queen would halt their progress through the houses, not hesitating to confiscate their bills or even to imprison the promoters. The reforming party would fail to win a single foot of ground, but the Queen's manifest opposition to their measures equally failed to discourage them.

As things stood at the close of the 1560s, the Queen found her ecclesiastical policy challenged by a small but shrill band of critics within the establishment who were willing to risk their careers rather than accept the demands laid down in the Injunctions. Her bishops had proved reluctant enforcers of these requirements but eventually bowed to the royal will. At the same time their sympathies were being outpaced by the radicals, who were pushing for changes too strong for the episcopal stomachs. Slowly, painfully, and often against their will, the bishops were being pushed by the Queen into a partisan stance as defenders of the royal polity, which they only half-embraced, against reformers with whom they had lingering sympathies. The Queen might congratulate herself on having forced the bishops to become defenders of the established order, but she had also opened a rift within the fabric of the national church which would be hard to mend. She could drive the dissidents from their pulpits but, given the porous nature of the ecclesiastical structure, they could easily re-enter the scene under the aegis of one of their lay patrons who could, by their influence at court or by control of patronage, confound the efforts of the bishops.

Parliament met again in 1572, primarily to deal with the aftermath of the Ridolfi plot. The reformers siezed the opportunity, and pushed a bill allowing each parson to vary the form of the liturgy to his own taste (with episcopal consent). Their conciliar patron, Knollys, sanitized the bill, but predictably the Queen rejected it, albeit with less acrimony than in 1571. By now there was widespread skirmishing between the establishment and its critics. The High Commission, the supreme ecclesiastical court, was vigorously pursuing the most vocal of the reforming clergy, depriving them of their livings when they refused to subscribe to the whole Thirty-Nine Articles, use of the *Book of Common Prayer* and of the surplice. One such deprived cleric was John Field; he soon hit back.

Even while the 1572 Parliament was still sitting he wrote, along with Thomas Wilcox, a pamphlet which initiated a much more far-reaching attack on the existing ecclesiastical order and a searching critique of its underlying premises — *An Admonition to Parliament*. Published before 30 June, it was reissued later in the summer and followed before the end of the year by a *Second Admonition*. The authors were promptly arrested and sentenced to a year's imprisonment for their attack on the Act of Uniformity, but this episode proved to be only the first battle in a long campaign of paper warfare.[3] Many participants would join the fray over the next few decades.

What Field and Wilcox demanded was nothing less than a revolution in the whole ecclesiastical structure. 'We in England are so far off from being a church rightly reformed, according to the prescript of God's word that as yet we are not come to the outward face of the same.' On three counts – the preaching of the Word, the administration of the sacraments, and ecclesiastical discipline 'which consisteth in admonition and correction of faults severally' – the English church was radically deficient. The standard by which they judged it was absolute: the Scripture. Prescriptions for outward government of the church were laid down in the New Testament, and were not a matter for merely human appointment. Only very radical measures could remedy the faults of the existing order. The *Book of Common Prayer*, 'an unperfect book, culled and picked out of that Popish dung-hill, the mass book of all abominations', was defective in every detail. Furthermore, the hierarchic government of the church by bishops and their subordinates was roundly condemned: 'Instead of an Archbishop or Lord Bishop you must make equality of ministers.' The whole diocesan bureaucracy must be replaced by a congregational order: 'You have to plant in every congregation a lawful and godly seignory.'[4]

This revolutionary manifesto brought to a larger audience an academic dispute which was troubling the University of Cambridge. There Thomas Cartwright, Lady Margaret Professor of Divinity, in lectures given in 1570, had laid out in formal academic mode the basic argument of the *Admonitions*. He expounded the scriptural prescriptions for a church government founded on equality of all clergy, entailing the end of episcopacy and the existing church courts, with all authority shifted to an elected minister and his congregation.[5] Cartwright was by no means an activist; deprived of his Cambridge chair, he retired to Geneva. From there he would conduct a classic exchange of polemics with another Cambridge don, John Whitgift, with historic consequences for the development of Anglican doctrine; but that was for the future. In the early 1570s the English episcopate had to deal with the unrest of militant parsons who refused to obey their commands and some of whom questioned their very existence as an order.

For a year or so after the publication of the *First Admonition* the seeds which it had sown seemed to sprout into rampant growth all over the kingdom. A secret press printed and distributed their polemical pamphlets. An embryonic Presbyterian classis came into being in London and may have been experimented with elsewhere. More informal versions of Puritan organization flourished in the provinces. In Northamptonshire, with episcopal sanction and the approval of the magistrates, a simulacrum of Genevan practice was established, with a regular cycle of preaching and catechizing. In some parishes the authorized service was replaced by psalms and sermons. Individual preachers disseminated the doctrines and practice of the Puritans wherever a sympathetic patron gave them a pulpit. What was abundantly evident was the enthusiastic patronage of a substantial body of nobles and gentry, not only notables like the Dudley brothers, Huntingdon, now Lord President of the North, or Councillors such as Knollys or Mildmay, but a solid phalanx of prosperous gentry, well-endowed with ecclesiastical patronage, scattered widely across the country. These laymen had no hesitation in flouting the explicit will of the Queen.

One of these Northamptonshire gentry, writing to Burghley, boldly stated that people of all degrees so hotly desire God's truth 'that they will not [re]frain themselves to favouring the laws and ordinances set forth by the Queen in God's matters but such as are void of all offence and reformed according to sincerity'. They should not be punished, he argued, but bound into a military elite to support the Queen, and allowed to have their own separate churches in England and Ulster.[6] Faced with these widespread manifestations, backed by the most respectable elements in society, finding indifference if not obstruction in the Council, the bishops were soon cast by their opponents as persecutors of God's people. 'As for the Puritans I understand that throughout the realm, among such as profess themselves as Protestants, how the matter is taken; they highly justified and we judged to be extreme persecutors.'[7]

Sandys, Bishop of London, urged that 'a sharp letter from Her Majesty would cut the courage of these men. Her Majesty's proclamation took none effect . . . not one book brought in.' (He referred to the royal proclamation against the *Admonition*.) The Archbishop and Sandys, in an appearance before the Council, were unable to secure authority to silence the popular Puritan preacher, Dering, then delivering a series of lectures at St Pauls.[8]

The Queen seemingly remained deaf to these pleas until her complacency was shattered by the attempted assassination of Christopher Hatton by a religious fanatic. He actually attacked John Hawkins, whom he mistook for the favourite. (Hatton was popularly regarded as a patron of the conforming party.) The threat to the latter jarred Elizabeth into action. One proclamation enjoining religious conformity, largely disregarded, had been issued. Another, stricter proclamation followed. Special commissions were set up to examine clerical disobedience, and the assize judges were ordered to emphasize these matters. In the reaction which followed, deprivations took place in the Midlands while a clutch of London ministers went to prison. Cartwright and some others fled overseas. The persecution was not long-lived after the furor over the attempted assassination died down and official anxiety relaxed.

Throughout these troubled years the Queen remained coolly aloof to the bishops' difficulties except when an episode such as the attack on Hatton touched her personally. Even then she blamed the bishops for having used their powers of visitation to raise money instead of instilling obedience. Her behaviour paralleled her reactions during the vestiarian episode – flaring anger when her attention was aroused, irritable rebuke to the bishops, followed by neglect and indifference – while Leicester found it easy to protect his protégés against ecclesiastical judgments.[9]

26

Grindal and Whitgift

A Reforming Archbishop

In May 1575 Archbishop Parker died; the latter years of his reign at Canterbury had been marked by a querulous defensiveness, a certain air of persecution, and an increased regard for the dignity of his office. His irritation with the attacks from the firebrands of the left was paralleled by his frustration when his efforts at discipline were thwarted by royal lukewarmness or noble obstruction. Longing for the quiet life, he sought compromise where he could.

He was succeeded, after a six-month interval, by Edmund Grindal, a Marian exile, appointed to London at the accession and translated to York in 1570. The only English bishop with an international reputation, he was universally revered for his deep and active piety. He shared many of the concerns of the reforming party, and had been hesitant to move against the vestiarian nonconformists in London. His goals, like those of the more moderate reformers, were a renewed spiritual life in the church, charged by the energy and skills of a learned and zealous clergy. His conception of his episcopal role was close to the functions of a Continental superintendent. However, for him sympathies for the reformers and their goals were not incompatible with submission to the royal establishment. The wearing of the required vestments or particular features of the liturgy might be repugnant to his feelings, but they were secondary considerations compared to the cure of souls. He had been regarded as 'soft' in his handling of London nonconformity, and the six-month interval before his appointment may have reflected royal hesitation. Nevertheless, Elizabeth gave her consent to his translation.[1]

His promotion to Canterbury was backed enthusiastically by Burghley and applauded by moderate Puritans. Parker, under pressure from the crown, thwarted by the Privy Council, and vilified by the evangelicals, had lost heart and ceased to give direction to the church leadership. Grindal, with a more positive vision of his task, with the confidence of his colleagues and of the leading Councillors, was in a better position to give a lead to a church troubled by deepening disagreements as to its role and purpose. The Queen's conception of a clergy limited to drily routine instructional functions, instilling a code of outward uniformity and obedience, denied them a prophetic voice and sadly diminished their spiritual vocation. It ignored altogether the spiritual aspirations of a devoutly pious laity who were impatient of the merely passive role assigned them in the royal scheme of things. They wanted a clergy equipped to lead a participating religious community, men of ardent and active piety, able above all to preach the Gospel, for them the central act of corporate worship.

In the years since 1559 there had been much experimentation in efforts to achieve such goals. The practices which were devised in these efforts were to lead in the 1570s to another head-on collision, this time between the Queen and the new primate. These experiments had pinpointed the most difficult problem facing the Elizabethan church, the provision of a ministry able to fill the demandingly active role of the Protestant pastor, particularly as a preacher of sermons, a skill in which the great majority of incumbents were totally lacking. Except for the small body of university-educated clergy, most incumbents were capable of little more than the performance of their ritual duties. In the long run the universities might provide the solution, but in the short to medium term other arrangements would have to be devised.

What could be done? The natural unit of local life was the market town and its catchment area. It was easy to organize meetings of the clergy from a town and the neighbouring rural parishes, for what was termed 'exercises'. These grew from an informal conference and social gathering into regular programmes for the continuing education of the clergy of the district in doctrine and in preaching, commonly termed prophesyings. Led by the most learned clerics among them, the less learned were put through their paces by examination and by practice preaching, followed by a formal concluding sermon to which the laity were usually admitted. Some expanded into a more public mode, in which the laity were present to hear not only the principal sermon but also the disputations in which the participants expounded an exegesis of a chosen biblical text. The proceedings ended with a dinner for the clergy at the local inn, where they engaged in censure of the doctrine discussed and of one another's personal conduct. The prophesyings became in many instances public events to which the laity flocked to hear a well-known preacher, and to participate in occasions at once religious and social. By the mid-1570s they were to be found all across the Midlands, in East Anglia, and in Kent, Surrey, Sussex, and Devon.[2]

In effect the prophesyings were subtly subverting the whole hierarchic structure envisaged by the Queen's programme. Although episcopally approved, they shifted the initiative down the scale to informal gatherings of local clergy, acting on their own. They created a venue for public religious life outside the prescribed occasions of the prayer book. Moreover, they were designed to promote the cause of a preaching clergy, to train up men lacking the necessary skills to carry out the prime mission of their calling. These were goals which moderate evangelicals shared with their more radical brethren.

Grindal and many of his fellow bishops saw the prophesyings, properly managed, as useful vehicles for continuing progress in the reformation of the English church. It was not to be: to the supreme governor such local initiatives, with all the variety and individualism which they implied, were utterly alien to her vision of regulated uniformity. The encouragement of preaching could only lead to diversity of opinion and to the rending of the seams in the social fabric. Moreover, though they won wide approval and episcopal authorization, the prophesyings were in some instances a vehicle for radical propagandizing. Not surprisingly, for preachers of an evangelical bent, including some who had refused to conform, their informal structure, outside the bounds of official worship, made them effective platforms for advancing their aims. For the Queen, such instances were sufficient to condemn the whole practice.

With her usual indifference to ecclesiastical routine, Elizabeth took no notice of the prophesyings until 1574. Then, when it emerged in the course of the current prosecution of nonconformists that some of the suspended clergy were using the prophesyings to gain a hearing for their views, her attention was engaged. This led to a royal order to Archbishop Parker, which he passed on to Bishop Parkhurst of Norwich, 'to suppress those vain prophesyings'. The latter, as apprehensive of local reactions as of royal disapprobation, appealed to the Council for help. A letter from Smith, Mildmay, and Knollys, all of them sympathetic to the reformed cause, encouraged the bishop to ignore the order. Parker protested, but Freke of Rochester assured his colleague of Norwich that no other bishop had received such an order. Nevertheless Parkhurst, on reflection, thought better of it, bowed to the royal command, and dissolved the prophesyings in his diocese. However, upon his death in the following February they resumed. The Queen apparently made no effort to follow through on this episode.[3]

The matter surfaced again a year later. The Queen now heard of a prophesying at Welwyn in Hertfordshire, and ordered Bishop Cooper of Lincoln to suppress it, which he did, along with all but one other in the southern half of his vast diocese. How did the Queen come to know such matters? Probably it was in the by-play of local quarrels – one faction seeking to discredit its rivals. Cooper had warned Grindal of 'some that seek to creep in favour, not only by their well-doing, but by the discrediting of other's doings and so to suspect I have greater cause than I may conveniently put into writing'.[4]

The crunch came, however, in 1576. In June Leicester, Walsingham, and Burghley all warned Archbishop Grindal of disorderly preaching in Northamptonshire and Warwickshire. Names were specified, and Grindal promptly ordered the accused to appear in London.[5] The Queen now summoned the Archbishop to court and personally commanded that, if the reports were true, he should dissolve all such exercises and at the same time limit the number of preachers to three or four in each shire. The primate then consulted his colleagues in a questionnaire circulated that summer. The questions were specific as to the benefit of the exercise, their regulation, and whether the laity should be permitted to attend. Out of fifteen respondents only four rejected them; eight responded favourably, and they were from the dioceses where the prophesyings were most commonly to be found. With this in hand the Archbishop proposed a regulating code which would have closely supervised the exercises. This was to no avail; the Queen would have none of it.

Grindal now decided to present the Queen with a reasoned argument on behalf of the prophesyings. Turning to weightier authority, he spent weeks in a meticulous search through the sources, for all relevant precedents. This massive collection comprehended the authorities from the age of Ambrose and Augustine to that of Calvin and Beza. Fortified by the weight of theological opinion, Grindal saw no way in which he could execute the Queen's command. He sat down to write one of the most extraordinary documents addressed to a Tudor monarch by a faithful subject.[6] He began by explaining that he would not offend the Queen, unless it were in the cause of God and His church and by necessity of his office and conscience. It was the duty of churchmen to speak plainly; the Old Testament prophets had not hesitated to rebuke kings. Indeed, King David, so rebuked, had not scrupled to change his mind.

Then he got down to cases. The plain and central message of Scripture was that the Gospel be preached. As Solomon had said, 'When prophecy shall fail the people shall perish'. Biblical citation followed citation to clinch the case. Moreover, present conditions and present expectations required preaching of a much higher standard than was currently available. The reading of the homilies, Elizabeth's favourite prescription, was a poor second-best. It was to remedy this deficiency that the exercises were set up – for the 'edification, exhortation and comfort of the clergy'. They were conducted under strictly disciplined conditions; all controversial matter was barred. The results – and Grindal cited the testimony of ten bishops – were striking, forty preaching clergy where previously there were but three. Given all this, 'I cannot with safe conscience and without the offence of the majesty of God give my assent to the suppressing of the said exercises'. If the Queen wished to remove him, he would bow to her decision without demur.

Then, moving to larger issues, the Archbishop politely but firmly urged Elizabeth to follow the example of the Christian emperors in taking counsel on religious matters from divines, even as she looked to the judges to advise her on legal questions. Citing Ambrose's letter to the Emperors Theodosius and Valentinian, he asked, 'Who can deny that in cases of faith bishops were wont to judge emperors, not emperors of bishops?' He went on: 'You would not use to pronounce too resolutely and peremptorily, *quasi ex auctoritate* as you may do in civil and extern matters.' In God's causes it was His will, not that of any earthly creature, which must prevail. Finally he warned her that, though she had enjoyed great felicity in her reign hitherto, she must persevere to the end if she were to continue in such favourable courses. If she turned from God, He would turn from her. 'Remember, Madam, that you are a mortal creature' – who will have to appear before the judgment seat.

This was plain speaking; he had no hesitation in warning the Queen that she was about to burden her conscience with wrongdoing, and refused for his conscience's sake to obey her. But he carefully avoided any attack on her authority over the church; there was no hint of the presbyterian claim to place kings under ecclesiastical condemnation. He asked only that she listen to the appropriate counsellors. Having given his advice, he was willing to accept dismissal; he acted only to satisfy his own conscience, not to raise an opposition to the royal policy.

Five months of ominous royal silence followed while the Archbishop carried out the normal functions of his office. Then on 7 May 1576 a royal letter was sent to all the bishops and judges on circuit that, contrary to law, ministers were using new rites and forms as well as 'inordinate preaching, readings, and ministering of the sacraments'.[7] There had been unlawful assemblies; people had gone from their own parishes to hear 'disputations and new devised opinions upon points of divinity, far unmeet for vulgar people'. These prophesyings, these exercises, led only to idleness, schismatic divines, and violation of the law. 'It was like that religion, which of his own nature should be uniform would against his nature have proved milliform, yea, in continuance nulliform, especially in rites and ceremonies and sometimes also in matters of doctrine.' There was to be no service except as specified in the *Book of Common Prayer* and the Injunctions, preaching only by licence, and by those conformable to the rules of the church. Where there was no suitable preacher, the homilies were to be used. Offenders must be imprisoned and their names sent to the Council.

As for Grindal, the Queen would have deprived him of his office, but the legal difficulties and the discreet dissuasions of Burghley and Walsingham prevented this. Gradually the royal anger cooled to a more tepid temperature. Grindal was allowed to carry out the routine functions of his office, but was excluded from any active role in the church. Friends made various efforts to reinstate him in favour. His downfall coincided with the larger crisis of foreign policy in the years 1577–81, and fearful Protestants saw his fate as part of a general threat to the reformed polity: 'But if the bishop of Canterbury shall be deprived then up starts the pride and practice of the Papists'.[8] However, efforts to rehabilitate him foundered on Grindal's own refusal to acknowledge any fault in his refusal to carry out the royal command. Resignation, by mutual agreement, was in preparation but still incomplete when he died in summer 1583.

This unhappy history was a personal tragedy for Edmund Grindal; it was also a milestone in the history of the English Reformation. Elizabeth's accession in 1559 had been hailed by the English

Protestant community as a providential deliverance and seen as the dawn of a new era of spiritual revival. When the leaders of the evangelical party among the clergy sought to promote further measures of reform in Convocation and in Parliament, they had found their path resolutely blocked. They found also that, at the Queen's direction, the bishops were constrained to use their authority to enforce a rigid conformity to the 1559 Injunctions rather than to use it for the reform of abuses within the church. This had not deterred them (or many of the bishops) from pressing ahead with *ad hoc* programmes aimed at the fundamental problem of a clergy inadequately equipped to carry through an evangelical revival.

Grindal in his submission to the Queen had defended these exercises both as fulfilling the primary mission of the church and as practical programmes of proven efficacy, operating within the existing institutional framework. The Queen's angry rejection of his argument brought home all too vividly the wide gulf which separated the royal vision of the English religious order from that of the committed leaders of the Protestant clergy. The very notion of a preaching clergy cut directly across the grain of Elizabeth's conceptions. The minister's task was to teach, not to preach, to instruct a docile and passive audience in habits of obedience to a received body of wisdom, not to exhort them to a more strenuous and demanding spiritual life. Now, by suppressing the prophesyings and repudiating Grindal, she had dimmed hopes that reform might be achieved within the existing institutional framework. The more impatient critics of the regime began to look for more and more radical alternatives.

The Queen's decision was, of course, a reaffirmation of the policy she had enunciated in 1559. In her inflexible determination not to alter a single item of that settlement, she may well have missed an opportunity to strengthen the fabric of the ecclesiastical order she had brought into being. The acts of her first Parliament had provided an institutional skeleton which needed to be given life by the devoted service of a reforming clergy inspired by the vision of a renewed spiritual life in the nation. The prophesyings offered one possibility for harnessing the enthusiasm of the evangelicals by adaptation of the established order. The royal rejection meant that that enthusiasm would flow into diverse channels. Individual clergy, with the backing of sympathetic lay patrons, would labour at their task in a patchwork of parishes scattered across the country. Prophesyings would not disappear but would continue, sometimes with and sometimes without episcopal encouragement. Concerned Protestants hopes that the home-grown measures for self-improvement among the clergy — which were the necessary prelude to a revived spiritual life among their flocks — would be accepted, under official auspices, into the practice of the established church were now doomed to disappointment. The more impatient of the reformers, restless enough already, would turn their backs on the establishment, repudiating its credentials. Abandoning the strategy of reform within the existing structure, they would experiment with radical alternative models of government and of liturgy drawn from Continental and Scottish experience.

In the mean time much of the energy of the established hierarchy would be devoted to the enforcement of the royal conception of uniformity. The generation of bishops who had lived through the heroic age of martyrdom and exile were passing from the scene. The established church by its very existence generated institutional loyalty. Threatened by Protestant nonconformity and by Catholic intransigence, its leaders would seek to justify and to defend it as it was.

The Royal Counter-Attack

The unhappy experience of Grindal's primacy at last brought home to the Queen that if her religious policy were to succeed she had to place a strong hand on the ecclesiastical tiller, a primate who shared her views and was prepared to enforce them. Secondly, she would have to give the full weight of royal support to his efforts. The appointment of Grindal's successor at Canterbury reflected this new determination. It opened a new epoch in the history of the Elizabethan church which would bring to a dead halt the Puritan efforts to pressure the Queen into accepting their proposals and signal the royal success in rooting the 1559 regime in the social order.

The new primate was John Whitgift, Bishop of Worcester. Born in 1530, he belonged to the first truly Elizabethan generation, whose career had unfolded under the aegis of the new religious regime. In his prolonged debate with Cartwright, Whitgift had constructed a reasoned defence of the established order which fleshed out the bare bones of statute and injunction with a coherent ecclesiology on new and original lines. Its core argument would be expanded on a grand scale in Hooker's classical rationale, the *Laws of the Ecclesiastical Polity*.

It was not only Whitgift's polemical skills which recommended him to the Queen but also his proved ability as an administrator, first at

Cambridge as Vice-Chancellor and then as Bishop of Worcester. In that see he established his position among the neighbouring gentry, and was employed as vice-president of the council in the marches of Wales. His translation to Canterbury brought to the primacy a prelate of firm convictions, prepared to act on them uncompromisingly. In him the Queen had at last found a fellow spirit, a churchman who shared her own outlook and in whom she could repose her confidence. His conduct in office soon assured her that she would no longer need to intervene when episcopal feebleness sold the pass to the Puritan agitators. Whitgift was prompt in launching a vigorous attack on nonconforming clergy. He sent for the Queen's approval, readily given, three articles to which all clergy were required to subscribe.[9] One, affirming the royal supremacy, was innocuous, but the other two, declaring that the prayer book contained nothing contrary to the will of God and that the Articles of Religion were agreeable to the word of God, touched the nonconformists on the quick. These articles were promulgated at the end of October 1583, only a few months after Whitgift's accession to his new see.

It was easy enough to issue the new edict, but it was a different matter when it came to enforcement. Refusals to sign were widespread even when the refusers, numbering some 300–400, were suspended from office.[10] Behind them stood a solid phalanx of gentry support. The pressure was great enough to force a partial retreat by Whitgift, by which an equivocal promise to use the prayer book was allowed to stand for outright subscription. This concession quietened resistance from all but the most determined of the protesters. Against the latter, now isolated from the more moderate majority, Whitgift devised a new strategy, the *ex officio* oath, a rigorous legal procedure which by its very form forced the accused to incriminate himself.[11] This aroused even more formidable opposition to the Archbishop's efforts. The Queen's chief ministers, led by Burghley, raised their voices in protest against procedures which the latter compared to the Spanish Inquisition.[12] The Archbishop's policy was opposed by powerful elements in the counties and by virtually the whole Privy Council. Hatton alone stood his friend.

The assault on the Archbishop reached a climax in the Parliament of 1584–5. A petition was organized in the Commons, addressed to the Lords, the Councillors Mildmay and Knollys among its promoters. The petition contained a comprehensive programme for abolishing the requirements of the three disputed articles as well as the *ex officio* oath. Going beyond that, they outlined a series of radical changes, including a modified presbyterianism in which ordination of clergy would be performed by the bishop, assisted by lesser clergy.

This news brought a message from the Queen, delivered by Burghley, shunting aside the petition; some of the issues were to be dealt with by Convocation, others by the Queen herself, and 'some were not fit to be reformed as requiring innovation and impugning the Book of Common Prayer'.[13] A more direct royal intervention came in a scene at court when Convocation's subsidy was formally presented. The Queen took the occasion to condole with the bishops on the attacks made on them in the Commons, threatened she would 'uncouncil' Mildmay and Knollys, and delivered her views on preachers: 'there is more learning in one of these [the homilies] than in twenty of some of their sermons.' Elizabeth reiterated these views in a message to the Commons. She declared herself opposed to any innovation in 'the religion or the Church of England [as it] stands established at this day'. Then, to make the point once more: 'For as she found [the state ecclesiastical] as her first coming in so hath maintained it these twenty seven years, she meant to in like state, by God's grace, to continue it and leave it behind her'.[14] It was a ringing affirmation of her support for Whitgift.

There was one final Puritan assault, the most daring of all, carefully prepared and supported by an active lobbying effort. In the Parliament of 1586–7 a bill was brought foward which proposed nothing less than the abolition of the *Book of Common Prayer* and the episcopacy. On its introduction the lower house gave sympathetic hearing to the proposal that it be read; but before that event took place, the Queen had confiscated the bill and aborted the whole scheme. This did not prevent continuing debate, and the redoubtable Peter Wentworth once more raised his voice in behalf of parliamentary free speech. Thereupon he and four colleagues were dispatched to the Tower, there to remain at least until the end of session.[15] The Queen followed up these actions by dispatching three weighty Councillors to lecture the house on the enormity of the proposals. Defending the excellence of the present order, they went on to point out that the bill would have utterly destroyed royal supremacy and brought the whole structure of the national church to the ground, abandoning it to the untrammelled licence of a Presbyterian polity.

The crushing repulse of their supreme effort ended the long parliamentary campaign of the reformers. There was a final hiccup of protest in the 1593 Parliament, but after that, religion ceased to figure in the remaining sessions of the reign.

Under an active and determined Archbishop, who shared the royal views on the ordering of the national church, the full institutional apparatus of the ecclesiastical courts could be brought to bear on the Puritan dissidents, and in the final years of the reign the Puritan movement lost impetus. The older generation of clerical leaders were passing from the scene, as were their lay patrons, Leicester, Knollys, and Warwick. Among the younger generaton of reformers there was now a core of zealots who, abandoning hope of realizing their goals within the official structure, were turning to the solution of separate and independent congregations wholly outside the established church. At the end of the reign this movement was still embryonic but full of vitality.

The religious question, which had bulked so large in the Queen's concerns since the 1560s no longer compelled her attention. The structure she had reared at her accession and which she had so stubbornly defended in Parliament after Parliament stood intact, unaltered. Yet it was a flawed victory. The uniformity which was the keystone of the system was largely but not quite fully achieved. There were ragged edges. Clandestine celebration of the mass continued in manor houses all over the country; a coherent, organized Catholic community existed, and the government had tacitly admitted its inability to destroy it. On the other fringe was the tiny cluster of underground Protestant congregations and, more importantly, within the church a substantial segment of ardent Protestants who, far from comfortable with the Elizabethan order but bowing to necessity, reluctantly conformed.

Elizabeth had shaped the English church in a form which would endure for generations. By the end of her reign the new order had supplanted the old religious forms of the medieval Catholic world in the consciousness of the English people as part of the natural and timeless order of things. Yet two groups, small in number but firm in conviction, had escaped the net; their existence would pose grave and intractable problems for Elizabeth's successors.

27

The Queen and her Catholic Subjects

B y the end of the 1570s, however troubling the dissensions within the reformed church were, they paled in comparison with the threat from without, from a resurgent Catholic militancy which struck at the security of both state and church. The somnolence of English Catholicism throughout the 1560s came to an end first with the northern rebellion and then, a few years later, with the invasion of the missionary priests.

The eruption of rebellion in 1569, alarming in its outbreak, nevertheless boosted governmental confidence, since the feeble response showed the weakness of Catholic activism. The somewhat uncertain sound of the northern earls' trumpet call on behalf of the old faith aroused no echoes outside their own immediate entourage. In the wake of the rising, in June 1570, the Queen issued an explicit statement of her policy towards Catholics, read out by the Lord Keeper in Star Chamber. Denying any intention to inquire into 'men's conscience in matters of religion', it declared that recent action had been levelled solely at those who broke the law by refusing attendance at church.[1] Camden summed up these early years of the reign as a time when 'fair and calm weather shone upon the Papists in England who by a merciful connivance enjoyed their own service of God in their private houses in a manner without any punishment' other than the shilling fine. This coloured the picture too brightly, but it probably represented the government's own image of its conduct towards the Catholics in these years.[2]

In any case, this mild weather was now overcast 'by little and little into clouds and tempests'. The first such cloud was the bull of

February 1570, issued by Pius V in the wake of the northern rebellion, excommunicating and deposing the Queen. Invoking his full panoply of apostolic power as Peter's successor, lodged in the see of Rome as protector of the Catholic faith outside which there was no salvation, the Pope denounced Elizabeth as 'the servant of wickedness', as a usurper, and as a mere pretended queen. As a heretic and favourer of heretics, she was excommunicated and deprived of her pretended title. Her subjects were absolved from all obedience, and those who continued to serve her were comprehended in the same anathema. Yet for all its thunder and lightning it was but a paper declaration of war, since the Pope himself lacked the power to execute his sentence and no Catholic prince was prepared to act as his agent.[3]

There was widespread indignation in England, and the zealot who had pinned the bull to the Bishop of London's palace was hanged for his pains, but the official reaction was restrained. A proclamation of 1570 referred to the circulation of infamous scrolls and bills 'and bulls as it were from Rome' which slandered the nobility and Council and uttered high treason against the Queen. Anyone concealing such works was to be imprisoned.[4] It was not until the Parliament of 1571 that more vigorous measures were adopted. The houses, backed by Burghley and the Council, passed a bill requiring not only church attendance but reception of the Anglican sacrament. The Queen, consistent with her earlier promises, vetoed this measure, which would have faced the faithful Catholic with a stark choice between private conscience and civic duty. An act was passed, however, which condemned anyone formally reconciling a subject to Rome (and those so reconciled) to the penalties of high treason. The importation of religious objects was forbidden under pain of forfeiture of property.[5]

For the first time the English government had been forced to identify the Catholics as enemies to the Queen and her realm. Hitherto it had merely enjoined an act of obedience, conformity to the worship of the established church. Now it specifically forbade profession of another faith, and that faith was singled out by name, as the enemy of the Queen. The papal bull had pushed the Queen into a direct confrontation with the papal church, something which she had carefully avoided up to this point. Henceforth there was an avowed hostility and an expectation of warfare. In fact that hostility was to remain latent for some years to come: not until 1577 was a priest prosecuted under the 1571 act.[6] The deposition decree of 1570 marked the commencement of warfare between the English state and the papacy which within a decade would be fought out with weapons of a highly secular character, marshalled by the Pope's lay lieutenant, the King of Spain. Before that contest got under way, another, quite different set of events would open another front.

The Marian church had been but little touched by the fervour of the Catholic Reformation, and lacked the services of its principal agents, the Jesuits. It was not until a decade after Elizabeth's accession that these impulses reached the English Catholic community. In 1568 William Allen, an exiled priest, had founded on his own a college for his Catholic fellow countrymen at Douay for which he had later obtained papal patronage. The infant institution rapidly developed into a nursery for missionaries, for an English Catholic priesthood to be sent to their native land to rescue the divided and leaderless flock of those loyal to the old faith. Their immediate mission was not that of converting non-believers but of preserving a remnant who were in danger of perishing by neglect. This, however, was a first step: in a more distant future lay, of course, the hope of restoring England to the Roman fold. The first Douay-trained seminarians arrived in England in 1574, four that year, forty in the following three. Their reception was enthusiastic, and within a surprisingly short time they had transformed the scattered pockets of passive and dispirited resistance into an organized and self-confident body with a sense of purpose and effective leadership.[7]

The government was slow to realize the impact of these new arrivals. It was warily watchful of the political activities of the Pope and his lay allies, but it was less aware of the campaign of spiritual subversion which was going forward on its own soil. Parliament had taken note of the flow of recruits departing for Douay in 1571; 'fugitives beyond the seas' would forfeit their property unless they returned. A carrot was held out to encourage them to repentance. They would recover their property if they returned, while a conciliatory provision allowed the maintenance of their families out of the forfeited estates.

It was only slowly and reluctantly that the government faced up to the intense ideological conflict which divided so many of the western European societies in these decades. Up to now Elizabeth and her Council had hoped that in England Catholicism would die of inanition. The disappointment of these hopes as the tide of Catholic activism rose forced Elizabeth to an unwelcome retreat from the policy of leniency hitherto pursued. The action which was now taken placed an intolerable strain on the Queen's doctrine of freedom of conscience.

In 1577 the priest Cuthbert Mayne was tried and executed under the 1571 Act, the first of some 123 priests who would suffer death by 1603. The government was painfully anxious to establish the proposition that these men suffered not for their religious beliefs but as traitors to the crown. The Pope had, of course, given them ammunition by the bull of 1570, deposing the Queen. It seemed logical to argue that his agents, seeking to secure the allegiance of English subjects to his authority, were thereby conspiring to overthrow Elizabeth and her regime. Hence it was altogether just to execute them as traitors.[8] To this the Roman Catholics rejoined by accusing the government of brutal persecution, of the judicial murder of innocent men whose mission was entirely spiritual. This was the defence mounted by Edmund Campion in 1580. He argued truthfully that his instructions forbade him to deal in political matters. Around the death of Campion and his successors the Catholic authorities built a martyrology which celebrated both the innocence and the courage of the priests, while painting a very ugly picture of a hypocritical government which, while claiming to leave men's consciences free, sent them to their death for exercising that freedom.

Stung by these accusations, the English government not only pointed to the bull of Pius V but also to an official explanation of later date which permitted the faithful to continue loyal to Elizabeth until such time as the bull of deposition could be put into effect. This explanation did not carry actual papal authority, but it did serve as a guide to Catholic behaviour.[9] With this in hand, the English government accused the priests not only of treason but of shameless dishonesty. Yet the unease of the government revealed itself in the nature of the legal process against the seminarians. In 1577 Mayne suffered under the law of 1571 against reconciliation to Rome. Campion and his colleagues were tried under the basic treason statute of 1352.[10] In the following year, Parliament strengthened the 1571 Act so as to make explicit the link between spiritual and temporal obedience to Rome. To these statutes was added that of 1585, banishing Catholic priests on pain of death if they did not depart.[11] None of these measures answered straightforwardly the question whether the priests' execution of their spiritual tasks amounted to treason. Basically they were condemned as guilty by association.

On the other hand, such priests found themselves in difficulty when pressed by awkward questions as to their loyalty to the Queen, most specifically whether they would defend her against invasion by a Catholic force. The papally backed attempts on Ireland in 1579 and 1580 and the plots against the Queen's life in the ensuing decade made the distinction between their spiritual and temporal loyalties harder and harder to maintain. The government insisted that, since the 1570 bull declared the Queen to be no queen, any expression of obedience to the Pope was necessarily an act of disloyalty, indeed of forthright treason to Elizabeth. The argument followed that men who heard confessions, absolved the penitent, and celebrated the mass were leading people away from the duty they owed the Queen. This was plainly an act of treason, and could be dealt with only by the full rigour of the law in such cases. The onus for the priests' plight lay with their master's assertion of his power to dissolve the temporal authority in the realm.

The anxiety of the government to absolve itself from the charge of religious persecution led Burghley himself to compose a defensive polemic, *The Execution of Justice in England*, written in 1583.[12] The Lord Treasurer pursued the favourite line of the English reformers since Henry VIII's time. Using essentially historical arguments, he denounced Rome's authority as an usurpation of powers rightfully vested in temporal princes. Moving from the general to the specific, he cited the bull of 1570. The seminary priests were the spies or scouts sent out to explore the scene of intended invasion. They claimed to have come only 'to inform or reform men's consciences from error in some points of religion',[13] but in fact their purpose was to win acceptance of the bull's commands to be ready to take arms in rebellion when the time came. True, they had not come armed, but it was 'their direction and counsels [that] have set up rebellion'.[14] Burghley went on to point out that at their trials they were questioned solely on these activities. 'No point of doctrine or faith' on which the English and the Roman churches differed had been raised.

Burghley's whole argument emphasized that the difference between the adversaries lay in the nature of jurisdiction. A long historical catalogue of papal encroachment on royal or imperial authority was unrolled, backed with appropriate quotations from St Paul to the Romans and the second epistle of St Peter. What he carefully avoided was any discussion of the bounds between secular and spiritual authority, and particularly of the royal power to regulate belief. Tacitly he denied such a power when he boasted that no doctrinal questions were put to the priests. By treating their claim to be executing a strictly spiritual commission as mere pretence, he avoided dealing with the question whether such a mission could be legitimate. By resting his case on the traditional anti-papal argument, inherited from the

331

papal–imperial debates of the Middle Ages, he ignored the fact that Elizabeth's ecclesiastical policy radically shifted the boundaries between lay and spiritual jurisdiction. Unlike her father, the Queen eschewed any claim to meddle in matters of faith or doctrine. Yet, at the same time, she redefined the content of these terms by placing public worship and ecclesiastical government in the province of the prince, not the bishops. What Burghley and his mistress refused to admit was that, for Catholics, liturgy gave voice to the central doctrines of the faith. The royal assertion that she offended no man's conscience necessarily fell on deaf ears. Similarly, the authority of the Pope was to the faithful not a historical accident but a divinely ordained power, which in spiritual matters at least must be obeyed.

Burghley's pamphlet soon evoked a response from the leader of the English Catholic community, William Allen, founder of Douay, now a cardinal, whose *Defence of English Catholics* appeared in 1584.[15] A much longer work than Burghley's, it laid out the Catholic case against the Elizabethan regime. It began with an attack on Burghley's insistence that the priests were condemned for political, not religious, actions. Allen had no great difficulty in making the case that the English government had refashioned the ancient conception of treason to suit its immediate needs and had manipulated legal process to secure convictions. Against Burghley's claim that no priest was questioned on doctrinal matters such as transubstantiation, he retorted that they were pressed to say when and how often they said mass or reconciled penitents to the Catholic church. He then pressed the argument in greater and bolder terms in order to justify their whole mission. He condemned *in toto* the English church as a false and heretical organization. Echoing Thomas More, he denied the power of the crown and Parliament to renounce papal authority or to regulate worship. He made it clear that the priests' mission was one of reconversion from a false religion. From this he deduced the papal right to depose such rulers. It was an exposition of the Roman position in its most sweeping terms, in which the pontiff was portrayed as a universal sovereign, dealing with the rebellion of a refractory province.

However, when he came to the specific case of Elizabeth, Allen became evasive. Playing down the significance of Pius V's bull, he noted that there were no further papal condemnations, and cited the exception by which Catholics could continue to give temporary obedience to Elizabeth. Most frequently he insisted that he was only dealing with principles, not with specific cases. Refusing to make a judgment himself, he left it to his superior — or to God — to pass a final decision on the Queen's case. Papal intervention in Ireland was justified as a response to the appeal of a persecuted flock.

At the end of the work the argument took an unexpected turn. The Cardinal had no doubt that right would be victorious in the end, but in the interim he proposed nothing less than a legalized toleration of the Catholics. He offered Switzerland and Germany, even the Huguenots, as models. Could not the Queen give her suffering Catholic subjects these rights in return for their acknowledgment of her temporal power? He left it unclear whether that allegiance would be withdrawn if she were attacked by a Catholic crusade. It was perhaps the first foreshadowing of a recognition that the most the English Catholics could hope for was survival, as a ghetto within a Protestant state.

Allen, like his protagonist, Burghley, left out one essential block in the edifice he was building. The Lord Treasurer refused to admit that the Queen was in fact making demands on her Catholic subjects' conscience. The Cardinal's evasiveness as to Elizabeth's legitimacy as a ruler pointed up the dilemma of the missionary priests. Their mission was purely a spiritual one, but the Pope was also opening a political front in his assault one the Elizabethan regime. He was conspiring – or seeking to conspire – with the Catholic sovereigns to place Mary Stuart on Elizabeth's throne. It was fair enough to argue that Campion and his colleagues had nothing to do with such designs; but one could hardly blame the English government for assuming that, once their work was done, their flock would obey the papal decree against the Queen. There was no common ground on which they could meet when each proponent denied his opponent's basic premise.

Allen's argument, however impressive as a statement of their case, was little consolation to the English Catholics. The government had determined if possible to destroy the Roman Catholic priesthood while making life an intolerable misery for the laity. The execution of priests would go on to the end of the reign, some 78 priests by 1590 and another 88 by 1603. The laity provided their share of martyrs, some 60 between 1577 and 1603. The government's strategy was based on the supposition that the vitality of the Catholic community lay in its priesthood. If the head were cut off, the body must perish. Those laity who actively assisted the priests had to pay the same penalty, but the majority were to be harried by fines which only the wealthy could meet. This was aimed at the Catholic gentry, whose protection was the mainstay of the priests and whose leadership sustained their co-religionists of lower rank. The assault on the priests was softened somewhat, first by substituting banishment for execution in many cases and secondly by setting up prisons in which they could be held, the most famous being Wisbech in the Isle of Ely.

These modifications bore witness to the government's growing realization that, even with its network of informers and spies, it could do no more than hinder the efforts of the priests. They had done their work too well. They had first of all succeeded in inspiring the English Catholic community with a spiritual fervour which ensured the continued recruitment of young men who would risk their lives for the faith. Ninety-eight of the Douay seminaries would be put to death by 1603, but that was less than a quarter of the 438 who were sent out to England during these years. Secondly, they had transformed the demoralized remnant of the lay adherents of the old faith into a strong, disciplined, well-organized community capable of withstanding persecution and confident of its survival.[16]

Beyond these positive checks on the government's initiatives created by the Catholics there was a negative check, resulting from the lukewarm cooperation of the Protestant gentry. The enforcement of the recusancy laws required the zealous activity of the local magistrates in reporting delinquents and presenting them in the courts. In fact, they fell far short of expectations. The Council through its informants compiled lists of recusants which were then sent to the appropriate county officials. Such a list, of December 1582 contained 1,939 recusants in 22 counties. Yet only 55 appeared as paying fines during the next five years. In four years the fines from eighteen counties and two cities brought in the meagre total of £6,356.[17] This pattern repeated itself over time and across the country. The gentry were displaying a curiously paradoxical response to the Catholic problem. Sitting at Westminster as MPs, they invariably outpaced crown and Council in the ferocity of their proposals to penalize the Catholics. At home, on the other hand, they proved sluggishly indifferent to the Council's efforts to implement the penal statutes. The agents of anti-Christ, participants in a grand conspiracy against the whole Protestant world, would-be assassins of the Queen, creatures of the Spanish or French embassies, were one thing, but neighbours of long standing, gentlemen of ancient descent, who quietly maintained a priest to say a clandestine mass, were another. Unless there was a zealous Protestant magistrate to egg on the prosecution, such individuals were likely to be left unmolested.[18]

What of the Queen's role in the mounting tide of anti-Catholic legislation? From the early days of the reign she had always interfered on the side of leniency. The legislation of 1563 which extended the scope of the supremacy oath may have been stronger than the crown wished. Notably, presumably at the Queen's urging, the lords were exempted from its requirements. The most sweeping provision, which would have made treason a second refusal of the oath by an ecclesiastic, was aimed directly at the Marian bishops. Elizabeth took care to subvert this clause by an order to Archbishop Parker forbidding the oath to be offered.[19]

We have seen her statement of policy of June 1570 in which freedom from 'inquisition or examination of their consciences in causes of religion' was promised.[20] This was just before the appearance of Pius V's bull faced her with an open declaration of war. This was necessarily reflected in the Parliament of 1571. A bill was put forward with conciliar backing and with episcopal blessing which, among other measures, would have compelled reception of the Protestant communion under penalty of fine. This would have forced many a 'church papist' into open revolt. Attendance at morning prayer might be squared with his conscience, but reception of the sacrament would have been mortal sin. This clause was included in a bill which passed both houses, but was vetoed by the Queen. Once again she clung to the principle that no Catholic should be faced with a challenge to his conscience. In 1572 and again in 1576 there were attempts to revive such legislation, but in both cases they were blocked by the Queen.[21]

In 1581 there was general agreement that stringent penalties must be passed against the Catholics. The houses, with conciliar backing, produced two bills; both were withdrawn and replaced by a consolidated bill which became law. While there is no direct evidence, there can be little doubt that it was royal intervention which led to the altered — and milder — terms of the final statute. What were these changes? First, compulsory reception of the communion was once more omitted. Secondly, a whole array of clauses which would have excluded Catholics from the professions were dropped. The fines for recusancy introduced in the bill were reduced to £20 a month against the Commons' proposals for escalating fines, culminating in forfeiture. Lastly, there was a small but significant alteration in words which affected the strengthened penalties for conversion of a subject to Rome. While this was linked to the withdrawal of civil obedience, the insertion of the words 'for that intent' preserved at least a legal distinction between religious conversion *per se* and conversion accompanied by a political act. It was to be of no benefit to those tried under the Act, but it still preserved at least the fiction of the royal determination not to persecute for religion's sake.[22]

By the 1580s the Queen's hopes that the Catholic problem would fade away by the mere passage of time were long gone. She was faced with a determined community defiantly resolved not to conform to the religion established by law. It was a refusal which in official eyes endangered not only religion but the state itself. The Queen had to compromise on principle. As Camden put it,

> Such were now the times that the Queen (who was never of opinion that men's consciences were to be forced) complained many times that she was driven by necessity to take these courses unless she would suffer the ruin of herself and her subjects upon some men's pretence of conscience and the Catholic religion.

Even now, although she believed 'these silly priests' guilty of plotting against their country, she blamed their superiors, who used them as instruments of villainy.[23] Like many of her countrymen, the Queen distinguished between the busy minority of conspirators and their ill-guided but loyal flocks.

The English government was committed to a brutal programme of persecution, principally against the priests but not sparing those laity who actively aided them. The Queen accepted the necessity of such actions, but even as the fires of blind bigotry blazed up among her subjects, the Queen kept aloof from the partisan hatreds of her subjects. She was prepared to punish the deeds of the Catholics but not to condemn their beliefs. Indeed, she reserved her active and personal distaste for the other band of nonconformists, the Puritans. A Catholic, if he would only meet the bare requirements of the law by attendance at church, was an obedient subject. The Puritan's perverse refusal to obey her injunctions as the governor of a reformed church lacked in her eyes even the excuse of conscience.

28

Conspiracy and Repression

F rom 1574 a devoted band of exile priests strove to restore the spiritual health of the English Catholic community by their pastoral ministrations. In these same years, both the spiritual and secular leaders of the Catholic world were feeling their way towards another goal, the overthrow of Elizabeth and her government by internal conspiracy assisted by foreign aid.

Elizabeth's decision of 1559 was of more than mere domestic consequence. As she well knew, in casting her lot with the reformed faith she had chosen sides in a conflict which polarized European politics. The opposed forces were not only combinations of power designed to advance dynastic or national interests; the adversaries saw themselves as fighting under the banners of darkness and light, of truth and falsehood. Elizabeth's choice of a religious polity left the papacy with no alternative but to declare her a heretic, an outcast, and a dangerous enemy of the faith, and to set as its unshakeable goal the suppression of this dangerous infection in the body of the Catholic church. The Pope could achieve this end only through the Catholic monarchs; but while the latter acknowledged the justice of Rome's condemnation, they were replete with excuses for delay. The Most Catholic King of Spain and the Most Christian King of France distrusted each other. Each feared the other's ambition to reduce the British kingdoms to his control. In the preceding decade Scotland had been ruled by a French prince and England by a Spanish. However, for the time being, each of the Continental powers was preoccupied with pressing problems of its own, growing civil and religious tensions in France, the dread Turkish menace in Spain's Mediterranean world.

This happy state of affairs cheered the English government; so long as it obtained, England could hope to remain free of the pressing attentions of France or Spain. However, the government was acutely sensitive to the possibility that shifting circumstance would destroy this fragile security. It never forgot that Rome's hostility was unrelenting, and saw in every changing disposition of political or military resources the sinister hand of the Papacy at work. As often as not they mistook shadow for substance, yet there was indeed ground for their fears. From the mid-1560s onward the Papacy did in fact press with increasing intensity for direct action against Elizabeth. At the same time other parties entering the scene added their persuasions to such a course.

The first such group was formed by the English Catholic exiles. Largely clerical in composition in the first decade of the reign, they were augmented by an increasing lay element after the failure of the 1569 rising. Galvanized by that disaster, the leading clerical exiles began to urge Rome to an overtly aggressive stance. Their increasing influence over the English Catholic community, once the missionaries were on the scene, gave weight to their counsels; they came to play a steadily more important role in the succeeding years. The goal of the Catholic party was, of course, not merely the overthrow of the heretic usurper but her replacement by a worthy and reliable Catholic successor. Here fortune favoured them, since the undoubted next heir was indisputably orthodox. The Queen of Scots reciprocated this interest since, with her eyes fixed forever on the English succession, she came to pin her hopes on Catholic support, English and foreign. This was not always the case; in the 1560s she had shown no interest in dislodging the ruling Protestant elite in Scotland, and after her exile in England she had at least made conciliatory gestures to Protestant opinion in England. Only after 1572 did she put all her eggs in the Catholic basket, as a claimant first to the succession and then to the throne.

Both Mary and the exiles knew that their hopes could not be realized without substantial foreign assistance. Their one certain hope lay in the Catholic king. Only Spain or France could mount the force necessary to the enterprise. The *politique* court of France, struggling with its own internal dissidents, was too lukewarm to offer much hope except at the rare moments when the Catholic Guises were able to sway policy. The genuinely pious Philip offered much better hope. Warily cautious, slow to act, and distracted by the many problems of an empire reaching from Antwerp to Lima, he was nevertheless inexorably hostile to the regime in London, which affronted his deepest religious convictions and, by its independence of action, crossed a policy which deemed an England submissive to Habsburg interests vital to Spanish security. However, his sense of religious duty, strong as it was, was kept in check by the counter-claims of worldly policy. These distractions required at least civil relations with the heretic Queen in London. It was to be a long and difficult wooing before this reluctant actor could be induced to take on his assigned role as the champion of the Catholic claimant against the English Jezebel.

It was among the exile community that the first stirrings of a demand for direct action against the Elizabethan regime rose. They were slow in coming. From 1559 the English exiles congregated at Louvain, not too far from home, and the seat of a lively and hospitable university where some of them won chairs. Mostly deprived ecclesiastics who had refused the supremacy oath, they devoted their energies to a vigorous polemic against the new English church. By 1570 the arrival of a younger generation with fewer ties to the past, along with fugitives from the 1569 rising, gave a new direction to their activities as they shifted from paper warfare to plans for a direct assault aimed at bringing down the hated usurper and her adherents.

In 1573 they chose the accomplished scholar and polemicist, Dr Nicholas Sanders, to go to Rome and then to Madrid as their lobbyist. In Spain he found two new allies. One was the Irishman, James Fitzmaurice, a member of the ruling clan of the Fitzgeralds of Desmond, a fugitive after a futile rebellion raised in the name of the old religion. The other was an expansive self-promoter, the adventurer Thomas Stukely, a man of many careers, lately fled from the English service in Ireland. He won Sanders's support of his campaign to lead a papal expedition to Ireland.[1]

Philip and Pope Gregory XIII were attracted to the idea of a papal expedition with clandestine Spanish backing, but were not persuaded of Stukely's suitability to command it. A more promising candidate for their purposes was Philip's half-brother, Don John of Austria, the victor of Lepanto. Restless, ambitious, and hopeful of a throne of his own, he looked to the possibility of a match with the widowed Mary Stuart. Events forwarded his hopes when Philip appointed him Governor of the Low Countries with the promise that, once he had reconquered the provinces, he could take an army to England to rescue the captive Scottish Queen, marry her, and share her new-won throne. The scheme won general consent. Mary had already contemplated him as a husband,[2] and the exiles looked forward to their imminent return under these happy auspices. But Don John had his task of

Hercules to perform before the prize could be attempted, and in this he failed. His death in 1578 came opportunely, when his career was faltering towards stalemate.[3]

Although this scheme proved abortive, it had brought together for the first time a significant coalition, the Pope, Philip of Spain, the English exiles, and the Queen of Scots. If the Pope were to realize his goal of recovering England for the church, it must be through placing Mary, rightful claimant and orthodox princess, on the throne; the exiles promised the active support of a popular uprising once the armies of the Catholic King landed on English shores. It was some variant of this recipe which would govern all future efforts to restore the old faith in England until the death of Mary Stuart.

The English government was well aware of the Scottish Queen's activities. When the match with Don John was broached Secretary Walsingham soon got wind of it,[4] and by July 1577 was fully informed.[5] Similarly, he was early on informed as to Stukely's enter-prise[6] on which the exiles now pinned their hopes. They again looked to Stukely as a prospective leader for an invasion of Ireland. Pope Gregory, after some persuasion, agreed to back him. A force was recruited in the papal states and set out from Città Vecchia, carrying some thousand men. They were sent to Lisbon, since Philip was anxious to conceal his connection with the voyage. His contribution was a gift of 20,000 crowns. What ensued was a bizarre anticlimax; Stukely was seduced by the Portuguese King into joining the crusade in Morocco, where both perished along with their army.

The desperate Sanders now determined to join forces with the Irish exile, James Fitzmaurice. They assembled a fleet of three ships and sailed from Ferrol in June 1579. Their intention to land in Ireland was already well known in London, although not their exact desti-nation.[7] Once landed, Sanders issued a proclamation calling on the Irish to rise against their unlawful ruler, the 'she-tyrant' Elizabeth. Although Fitzmaurice was killed in a skirmish a few weeks after land-ing, Sanders found allies among the Fitzgeralds and eventually enlisted the reluctant Earl of Desmond to the cause. The rising spread through much of southern Ireland. In 1580 reinforcements, 600 strong, arrived from Spain, paid for by Philip, who now began to show signs of more hearty support. However, the second expedition, trapped on the Dingle peninsula, was wiped out by the English deputy, Grey, and by the end of 1580, using the most ruthless means, he had reduced the wasted country to submission. Sanders perished of illness in the spring of 1581.

For the English government it was a sobering experience. The invasion forces were negligible in size, but their capacity for making mischief was huge, given the disaffected state of much of Ireland. The government had good reason for fearing that a rebellious Ireland, with Spanish aid, might become a British version of the Low Countries. Moreover, the expeditions were the first instance of overt Spanish hostility. They were so cited in Parliament in 1581, and loomed large in all future justifications of English action against Spain.

After Sanders's death, dominance in exile affairs passed to two purposeful and energetic clerics, William Allen, the founder of Douay, now relocated in Rome, and Robert Parsons, SJ, recently returned from the English mission he shared with Edmund Campion. Allen, like Sanders before him, moved from a spiritual to a political role. Parsons became the indefatigable, single-minded promoter of aggressive action to destroy the Elizabethan order. Official support for the missionaries, of course, remained unstinted, but Parsons was too impatient to await the slow erosion of the mission process. He wanted to take much more direct measures to bring the Protestant regime tumbling. The opportunity came in Scotland, where the pro-English regime of Regent Morton had fallen in 1581.

Working through the new royal favourite, James's French cousin, D'Aubigny, papal agents put together a complex conspiracy, combining not only Spanish but also French (Guisean) armies of invasion; D'Aubigny undertook to persuade the young King to the scheme; Mary gave her maternal aproval. This scheme foundered first on the fall of D'Aubigny at the hands of a Scottish nobles' junta and then on the coolness of Philip.[8]

Undiscouraged by this setback, the conspirators now listened to a proposal by Guise to sponsor an attack on Elizabeth's life. The assassin was to be paid 100,000 francs, the sum to be provided by Rome and Madrid. This too fell through when the assassin backed out.[9] The papal nuncio in Paris and the English exile leaders now returned to more traditional measures with a plan for a double invasion, one prong a Spanish army to land in Scotland, the other a French in England, the latter under Guise's command. Mendoza would take responsibility for organizing the English Catholics at home. Allen pressed the plan on Gregory XIII.[10] A central figure in this conspiracy was Francis Throckmorton, who had dabbled in Mary's affairs earlier, acting as her postman. Recruited for the present plot, his role was to organize an English Catholic rising when the invaders arrived.[11]

Once again Walsingham's skilful organization of counter-intelligence, aided by a bit of good luck, paid off. Throckmorton's frequent visits to the French embassy aroused suspicions; he was watched and, at the appropriate moment, seized, along with a bundle . of incriminating documents. The Secretary was soon in possession of full details about the proposed landing of Guise's army in Sussex, Spanish financial aid, and Mary's approval of the whole enterprise.[12] What was now laid before the eyes of the Queen and her Council was a master plan for a wholesale assault on both British kingdoms, orchestrated by the Pope and the English exiles, executed by the Duke of Guise and paid for by Philip of Spain. Its immediate object was the liberation of Mary and toleration for Catholics in England, but Throckmorton admitted that if the Queen resisted, she would be deposed.

The revelations of Throckmorton and the Scottish Jesuit Creighton tore the network of conspiracy into shreds. Guise's interests were already being distracted by events in France, where the death of Anjou opened the prospect of a Protestant succession in the person of Henry of Navarre. Guise, as leader of the Catholic League, would soon conclude a pact with Philip, and his energies would be diverted to these urgent domestic causes. Mendoza was sent packing by the English authorities in January 1584; relations with Spain sank to a new low, and Philip began to listen to those advisers who urged that he must take matters into his own hands and launch a direct and large-scale action against England.

29

The End of Mary Stuart

I n the English court circle the revelation of the conspiracy confirmed the argument laid out by Burghley the previous year in
his *Execution of Justice in England*. Here was proof, with chapter
and verse, of the scope and magnitude of Catholic hostility. While it
did not involve the missionary priests, it left no doubt as to the intentions of their superiors, English and Roman. There was, not surprisingly, a spate of new penal legislation in the 1584–5 Parliament, while
the persecution of the priests and their lay protectors became fiercer
than ever. For the next fifteen years the fortunes of the English Catholic community were a subplot in the grander drama of Anglo-Spanish
war.

For the Councillors of the Queen the gravest threat was to be found
at home, in the castle of Tutbury where Mary had been newly moved
under new and stricter guardianship. The conviction that Elizabeth's
throne and, indeed, her life would not be safe so long as Mary lived
was stronger than ever. In spite of the strictest precautions in controlling Mary's correspondence, it was only a piece of good luck that had
revealed the latest plot. However, any proceedings against Mary faced
the opposition of her most resolute protector, Elizabeth.

The Queen could have few illusions as to the inveterate hostility
of her cousin. Assuming that as a given, she had taken every precaution
to isolate Mary and by adroit publicity to blacken her reputation
among the English people. Yet she had always resisted direct measures
against Mary's person, and had never failed to treat her royal captive
as a fellow queen. Elizabeth was confident that with adequate safe-
guards the genie could be kept in the bottle. Her Councillors shared
no such confidence: the ranks of those who thought that only Mary's

death would secure safety for their Queen grew steadily. For the present, however, they were held in check by the decision of Elizabeth to enter another round of negotiations with her cousin, with a view to some final settlement of Scottish affairs.

At this juncture the attention of the Council was suddenly drawn in another direction. Hard upon the trial of Throckmorton there followed another plot.[1] This time the plotter was a single Englishman, but his object was simply to kill the Queen. William Parry had had a very chequered career. A spendthrift, he had run through two fortunes and had been reduced to making a living as a spy for the government. In this role he had dealt with Mary's agent in Paris and penetrated a scheme for Elizabeth's assassination. For this service he had won royal approbation. In 1584 he had a seat in Commons. Once again penniless, he had now taken to desperate measures by trying to inveigle a fellow-subject into an assassination plot. This he had done, so he averred, in order to betray his confidant and win an appropriate reward. The scheme backfired; his confession of having made the proposal for killing the Queen was taken at face value and he ended on the scaffold. It was a bizarre episode, but it occurred at a moment when it became clear that no holds were barred in the assault on Protestant leadership. The Prince of Orange, seriously wounded a year earlier, had now fallen prey to a successful attempt on his life. Faced by this dreadful evidence, English nerves were strung up to breaking point.

This event led directly to a novel but striking strategy devised by the Councillors on their own initiative, the Bond of Association. Embodied in an oath to be subscribed by subjects everywhere, it created a sworn brotherhood of voluntary defenders of the Queen. By its first clause they were bound to obey the Queen, and to resist to the death all who should attempt anything against her. The second clause was aimed directly at Mary, although she was not anywhere named. It bound the signers never to accept as successor anyone 'by whom and for whom any such detestable act shall be attempted'. In short, if there were an attack on Elizabeth's life, Mary was to be destroyed even though not a party to the act. So ambiguous was the wording that it seemed to include James as well.[2] By the late autumn of 1584 thousands of subjects all over the country had signed and sealed copies of the Bond. The Queen, reassured by this outpouring of loyalty, nevertheless felt uneasy about the violence of the second clause.[3]

When Parliament met in November 1584 there was a move

immediately to embody the Bond in statutory form, led by Mildmay and Hatton as the Council's spokesmen. A series of draft bills failed to bring agreement between the houses and the Queen, since Elizabeth was determined to prevent indiscriminate action and to exempt James VI from the terms of the measure. The bills were set aside for a time, and only later in the session was an act passed which was acceptable to the Queen and to a grudgingly acquiescent Parliament. It provided a commission to determine guilt before action was taken, and carefully excluded an innocent heir from the penalties laid on his parent. The Queen's cool-headedness and her successful effort to check what would have been little more than lynch law reflected again the dispassion with which she regarded her rival. All the terror of the law was readied for use, but it was not to countenance a merely arbitrary act, deprived of at least the form of justice.[4]

Elizabeth might ensure that Mary should not be lynched by her angry subjects, but she could not hide from herself the fact that the Queen of Scots was her deadly enemy, who proposed to utilize any means available not only to win her freedom but to seize Elizabeth's own throne. The Queen was willing to live with this uncomfortable fact; her ministers were not. They had no doubt that Mary had been fully cognizant of the late conspiracy, but there was no evidence sufficient to bring her to legal condemnation. If the Queen were to be persuaded to move against her cousin's life, the legalities of the charge would have to be beyond cavil. Mere plotting with the Guises and Spain would not be enough; there would have to be impeccable proof of Mary's consent to an assassination attempt. Elizabeth, like her father, was acutely sensitive to the charge of arbitrary or unlawful action. Like him, she insisted that all her acts should be fully justified by the full panoply of justice.

In the wake of the Throckmorton revelations, Mary, transferred to the greater security of Tutbury, was placed under the charge of Sir Amyas Poulet. It was a change of regime of more than passing importance. The Earl of Shrewsbury, her warder since the 1570s, was a peer of ancient descent whose presence lent a certain air of dignity and honour to the scene, which in some measure glossed over the grim fact of her captivity. Poulet, a stern Puritan of Walsingham's cast of mind, was straightforwardly her gaoler and she his prisoner. In the general tightening of the restrictions on the Scottish Queen, the Secretary ended the arrangement by which her correspondence passed through the hand of the French ambassador. Even then the letters were opened and read by the Secretary, but now, with a new and untrustworthy ambassador, it was ordered that Mary address her correspondence directly to Walsingham.[5] About the same time Mary was moved, for reasons of health, to Chartley in Staffordshire.

Mary's friends had been seeking some way to open secret correspondence with her, now that the channel of the French embassy was closed. They seemed to have found one in Gilbert Gifford, a former student at the English seminary at Rheims and cousin of Dr William Gifford, an eminent figure among the exile clergy. Gilbert Gifford established contact with Mary's agents in Paris and by them was given a letter of recommendation to their mistress. Landing in England in December 1585, he was promptly caught at Dover and sent to Walsingham, who persuaded him to change coats and become a spy in the English service.[6] Walsingham made use of Gifford's recommendation to Mary; he was to offer himself to her as a postman through whom she could reopen correspondence with the French ambassador and thence to the outside world. The Secretary took great care in the arrangements; the letters were to pass in the barrels of beer which supplied the household at Chartley. A local brewer was suborned to act as an accomplice. When the system was in operation the letter passed from the brewer to Gifford, thence to Walsingham, then back to Gifford, who delivered them to the French ambassador, Chateauneuf. The interception soon yielded dividends. It was plain that Mary was urging invasion, and taking steps to accomplish it.[7]

These hopes began to take concrete form when the first strands were woven in a new plot. Although its initial goals were those of its predecessors — invasion coupled with a Catholic uprising — it differed in character from them. First of all it was a highly amateur, almost freelance, affair. The prime instigator was a priest, John Ballard. Returning from a tour of England in 1585, he went to Paris in 1586 to urge the Marian agent, Charles Paget, and Mendoza (now Spanish ambassador to France) that the time was ripe for action. He was sent to England to contact a Catholic gentleman named Anthony Babington. The latter had acted as an intermediary for some of the Scottish Queen's correspondence in the recent past. Ballard talked largely about Spanish and French forces ready to invade, but Babington remained sceptical that anything could be accomplished so long as Elizabeth lived. Ballard, assisted by another ex-seminarian, John Savage, suggested that that difficulty could be dealt with. Babington was soon committed to a plot which would combine the rescue of Mary, foreign invasion, and the assassination of Elizabeth.

The participants were thus a very mixed assortment, but one conspicuous element was missing. Except for Mendoza, whose role was peripheral, the great actors, papal, Spanish, and French, were absent from the scene. The prime instigators were drawn from the tainted underworld of spies, informers, and intriguers begotten of the underground struggle between the English state and the exile community. Walsingham's secret service, like others of its kind, was honeycombed with adventurers who played both sides of the street. Some, like Ballard or his fellow, Savage, were self-promoted freelances, striking out on their own initiatives; others like Gilbert Gifford were men who, to save their skins, had turned double agents. These were the men who pulled the strings, but open rebellion and the dangerous task of rescuing Mary Stuart were to be undertaken by a crew of Catholic gentry, enthusiastic adherents of their faith, ready to die in its service. As Babington, the principal among these men, put it, they were led to act by 'persuasion of such as abused our zeal in religion and the youthful ability of our bodies and minds, ambitious of honest fame.'[8] Indeed, it took all the skills of the instigators to keep their pawns up to mark. The whole thing might have evaporated in talk, but for their constant prodding. What the manipulators — except Gifford — did not know was that Walsingham's agents were shadowing every move they made from the very inception of the scheme.[9]

Babington recruited a dozen or so like-minded friends to the enterprise; six of them were to be detailed to kill the Queen; another squad would rescue Mary. It was, of course, necessary to inform her and obtain her cooperation in their plans. Encouraged by Paget, Mary's agent in Paris, Babington reopened his correspondence with the Scottish Queen and in a letter of July 1586 outlined their plans and sought her approval. The letter, of course, first passed across Walsingham's desk before it was forwarded to Chartley. The Secretary watched anxiously for the response; he had not long to wait. After some nine days his agent, the counter-intelligence expert, Phelippes, triumphantly reported, 'You have now this queen's answer to Babington which I received yesternight.'[10] Mary's partisans have vehemently insisted that she was the victim of Walsingham's manipulation, that sinister interpolations were added to the key letters or that there was wholesale fabrication of documents. That the whole plot was manufactured by the Secretary and his agents seems more than doubtful; that there were interpolations in the letters is possible although unprovable.[11] In any case, they formed the basis for the formal legal prosecution of Mary which now followed.

Walsingham had kept his tapping of Mary's correspondence a secret not shared even with Burghley or Leicester. The latter had a hint of it in early July; the Queen knew of it later in the month, presumably as soon as Mary's answer to Babington was in hand.[12] She took charge of the ensuing measures against the Queen of Scots. She gave detailed instructions for the surprise detention of Mary, the seizure of her papers, and the arrest of her secretaries. Poulet was rewarded by a royal letter in which fulsome praise of his service mingled with angry references to 'yon wicked murderess' and her treacherous dealings towards one who had been 'the saviour of her life for many a year.'[13] Nevertheless, when the Babington trial came on, the Queen insisted that full evidence of Mary's guilt should not appear in the proceedings; the reason given was that it might spark off an attack on Elizabeth by Mary's supporters.[14] In fact at the trial, both in the indictment and in Babington's confession, Mary was implicated.[15]

In the mean time Mary's secretaries had been examined by a committee of Privy Councillors and confirmed that their mistress had indeed written the fateful letter to Babington. The Queen now allowed preparations to go forward for a formal trial. Her consent was grudging, and at each stage she exasperated her councillors by her delaying tactics. She wavered for days over the choice of venue for the proceedings, finally settling on Fotheringay in Northamptonshire. When the commission for the trial was drawn up, she quibbled over its terms, driving Walsingham to a grumbling wish she 'could be content to refer these things to them that can best judge of them as other princes do.'[16] The commission of Councillors and peers finally opened the proceedings on 12 October and brought them to a close by the 15th. Mary reluctantly agreed to appear before them, but protested at each stage of the trial and ended with a demand to appear before Parliament or the Queen in person. On the Queen's order no judgment was rendered at Fotheringay; the commission was adjourned to meet at Westminster on 25 October.

In the mean time a new Parliament had been called, which met four days later, on the 29th. Again the Queen had balked at summoning it at all, but the Council persisted in order 'to make the burden better borne and the world abroad better satisfied.'[17] Its opening had been delayed pending the conclusion of the trial. When it met, the Queen absented herself from the opening because the matter at hand was so repugnant to her feelings. The Chancellor, Bromley, in his opening speech, made plain that they were called together not for their usual legislative business but to give faithful counsel to the Queen, newly escaped from the late horrid conspiracy. All save one of the conspirators had paid the penalty; she lay under condemnation of the law. How should the Queen act?[18]

In the Commons, Hatton's and Mildmay's speeches fired the opening guns in a denunciation of Mary Stuart in which their 'front-bench' colleagues from the council joined. All rehearsed the long catalogue of Mary's iniquities reaching back to the 1560s. All emphasized the never-ending conspiracies of the Pope and his confederates on her behalf. There was, all agreed, but one remedy; she must 'suffer the due execution of justice according to her deserts'. The two houses resolved jointly to petition the Queen, urging that imminent dangers to her person, to the realm, and to religion rendered imperative the death of the Scottish Queen. An audience was sought and granted, but only after the houses agreed to insert a reference to the Bond of Association in the Speaker's brief. This was a delicate royal hint that there were other ways of dealing with the threat than a public execution of Mary.

The Speaker pleaded the houses' case in lengthy argument, heavily larded with Old Testament precedents. The Queen responded in a characteristically diffuse oration.[19] She revealed that she had written to Mary urging a frank confession to her privately and promising there would be no public hearing, but to no avail. She chilled their blood by telling them she had seen a signed bond in which the signatories swore to kill her or be hanged. There was much pious reflection on her providential escape, philosophic musings on the horrors of the proposed deed, a defence of the choice of a special court of the greatest and noblest, and, finally, an assurance that after due seeking of divine guidance, she would give them her resolution.

The houses were then invited to consider whether there was any way the safety of the sovereign and the realm could be secured without shedding the blood of the Stuart Queen. None was put forward; the common voice again demanded that she die. The Queen granted a second audience in which this advice was offered. Her response this time came in another rambling disquisition in which she protested her unwillingness to shed blood and lamented 'that only my injurer's bane must be my life's liberty.' After some passages of self-congratulation on her strict adherence to justice, she finally delivered her delphic response.

> Therefore, if I should say, I would not do what you request, it might peradventure be more than I thought; and to say I would do it, might perhaps breed peril of that you labour to preserve, being more than your own wisdom and discretions would seem convenient, circumstance of place and time being duly considered.

The voice of counsel, of Parliament and of her ministers, was unmistakable. Yet the labours of the houses seemed to be in vain. Burghley wrote that it would be but 'a Parliament of Words'.[20] The Queen proposed to prorogue the houses until March. Worse still, she declined to sign the proclamation of the judgment against Mary, the necessary legal prelude to execution of the sentence. At last, however, under conciliar pressure, she yielded on 2 December; the houses were adjourned, not prorogued, and only until 15 February 1587. The sentence was duly proclaimed, two days later on 4 December, amidst public jubilation.[21]

Burghley and Walsingham made ready the necessary documents for the final scene, but they lay unused.[22] Now there was another cause for delay. Ambassadors came from France and Scotland to plead for Mary's life. They were duly heard and dismissed. At last the Queen seemed to have emptied her bag of tricks; there could be no more excuses for delaying the decision. But there was still one more at the bottom of the bag, which she now pulled out. Secretary Walsingham, at the Queen's command, wrote to Poulet and Drury, Mary's gaolers, expressing her displeasure that they had not found a way to shorten their prisoner's life. She could not bring herself to shed the blood of one of her own sex and rank, so near in blood. They, on the other hand, as subjects, could do what she, as a woman and kin to the prisoner, could not. The Bond of Association and the judgment of Parliament commanded them to the deed and absolved them from the guilt. To this invitation to do murder, Poulet, for himself and Drury, replied by appealing to yet another and higher sanction. He roundly refused 'to shipwreck his conscience and leave so great a blot to his descendants.'[23]

The Queen was now face to face with the most painful decision of her life. There were politic reasons why she should hesitate. Both the Scottish and French kings were interceding for Mary's life. To alienate either of them was a risky business at a moment when the possibility of Spanish invasion loomed, but it was a reasonable calculation that their protests would not lead to a serious disruption of relations. The reasons which moved Elizabeth lay deep in her own heart. That she abhorred shedding even noble, let alone royal, blood had been apparent in the case of the Duke of Norfolk. Beyond that lay deeper, indeed, paradoxical feelings. Her attitude towards Mary had always had a schizophrenic twist to it. Fear and distrust of a rival who had asserted her claims from the first days of the reign and had never ceased to pursue them were inherent in their relationship. Elizabeth had not hesitated to checkmate Mary's designs or those of her partisans, by intrigue or by violence when necessary. Everything had been done to taint Mary's reputation, as a party to her husband's murder, as a plotter who intrigued with English rebels and foreign powers to murder Elizabeth and bring down the English regime.

Yet through all the turns and twists of Mary's melodrama, Elizabeth had never lost sight of her sacrosanct status as an anointed monarch, one of God's earthly lieutenants, and above all human judgments. When the Scottish queen was dethroned and imprisoned at Lochleven, Elizabeth had become almost hysterical in her reproaches to the Scottish nobles and had been reluctant to acknowledge James's sovereignty. We have seen how, when the Parliament of 1572 would have hounded Mary to death, Elizabeth stayed their hand. Even Throckmorton's revelations failed to move the Queen to action, to the despair of her ministers. Only the evidence which Walsingham's strategem uncovered led her to assent to the trial. Her message to Parliament asking if there were not a way to secure her safety and the realm's without shedding Mary's blood was as much a *cri de cœur* as another device for delay. Elizabeth, however, was now resolved that Mary should die. The revelation that Mary was ready to countenance assassination had finally broken through her scruples — or broken her nerve. At this juncture she had tried to shift the responsibility for the deed on to Poulet's shoulders. It was a sophistical argument that she made in her letter to him and a revealing one, for it showed that her scruples were no longer those of her private conscience. What moved her now was an overriding anxiety to preserve her public fame from the guilt of regicide.

Her behaviour when she was finally trapped in a corner from which there was no escape was of a piece with what had gone before. She had ordered Burghley to draw up a warrant for Mary's death just after the sentence was officially proclaimed on 4 December.[24] He left it with Secretary Davison with instructions to get the royal signature. After the Scottish and French ambassadors had departed, the Queen summoned Davison and signed the warrant. He had, of course, to go to Lord Chancellor Bromley in order to pass the Great Seal, but was told to keep the matter secret, although she jokingly suggested he should let Walsingham, sick in bed, see it: 'The grief thereof would go near to killing him outright.' It was then that she ordered that the letter be written to Poulet and Drury with the proposal for assassination. Davison urged against such a move, knowing they would refuse, but the Queen overruled him.

351

The next morning a royal messenger arrived with an order that Davison was to see Elizabeth first if the warrant had not passed the Great Seal. Davison saw her, only to report that this was already done. Why the haste, she asked, and then once again intimated there was a better way to do it. Davison was worried that in this uncertain frame of mind the Queen would thrust the blame for carrying out the execution on him, as she had done with Lord Treasurer Winchester in the Norfolk case twenty-five years earlier. He turned to Hatton for advice; they went together to Burghley, who proposed consulting the whole Council, which was duly gathered in the Treasurer's chamber. After discussion they resolved unanimously to go ahead with the execution without further consulting the Queen.

Elizabeth called Davison for yet another interview, to tell him of a dream she had had which caused her to pause. She affirmed her resolve to go through with the matter, but complained again that there might have been a better way than this, which threw the whole burden on her. When Davison reminded her that she was the sovereign magistrate to whom the sword was entrusted by God, she retorted that there were others wiser than he. When on the following day Poulet's letter of rejection arrived, she grew very angry, denounced the weakness of 'these precisians', complained of the danger she stood in, and declared it a shame that the deed was not yet done. She wanted another letter to Poulet with direct instructions to act, but Davison urged that existing documents sufficed. The audience ended inconclusively.

In the mean time the Council had acted. Beale, the clerk of the Council, had been sent to carry out the instructions, his mission disguised as routine county business. He accomplished his mission with dispatch. The execution took place at Fotheringay on 8 February.

When the news was brought to Elizabeth, her unmeasured anger shook the frame of the court world. The whole council was roundly denounced for the concealment of their actions while the Queen hysterically disavowed having ordered the execution, declaring it was something she had never intended. Her wrath was directed specifically at Burghley and Davison. The latter was promptly sent to the Tower. The former was denied access to her presence; indeed, she refused even to receive his letters. Elizabeth, her irrational fury unabated, now proposed nothing less than hanging for Davison, a proceeding which Lord Chief Justice Anderson led her to believe was within her prerogative.[25] Only the most urgent advice from her councillors restrained her from this course. Burghley was finally received at court in March but only to be publicly abused by his mistress. A hearing was held under royal orders by the Lord Chancellor, the two Chief Justices, and the Archbishop of Canterbury at which Burghley was called upon to justify his action. He remained *persona non grata*; the unfortunate Davison was summoned for trial in Star Chamber where his late colleagues, thankful to find a scapegoat, condemned him to a £10,000 fine and imprisonment.[26]

Slowly the royal temper cooled, although even in early June she was saying harsh things of Burghley. Finally, later that month, a royal visit to Theobalds marked the return of the Lord Treasurer to the Queen's confidence.[27] The storm had blown itself out without permanent damage — except to the unlucky Davison. He was freed from prison after some eighteen months but his career was ended. (He did, however, receive his salary to the end of his life.)

Elizabeth's bout of sheer irrationality had made life miserable for her Council, but from their point of view it was a small price to pay for the elimination of Mary Stuart. From the day of her arrival she had been, as Burghley predicted, an ever-threatening menace to the regime, a dangerous infection within the body politic. Her alliance with the exile party and the King of Spain had raised the temperature to a fever pitch which threatened the existence of the regime. Her disappearance was a heavy blow to the exiles. They no longer had a standard-bearer within England around whose cause they could rally the Catholic forces. All their plotting had centred on the objective of freeing Mary Stuart and placing her on Elizabeth's throne. Henceforth their cause depended for its success solely on foreign invasion. Philip, too, was now pushed ever more to the realization that if the English regime was to be undone it could only be by his own arms.

These events marked a division within English Roman Catholic ranks. Few of the rank-and-file country gentry who were the backbone of the community were disposed to revolt against their queen. Indeed, they asserted their resolute loyalty to Elizabeth even while refusing to obey her laws on religion. Unlike the exiles, they had abandoned the hope of a restored Catholic regime in England. What they sought was an accommodation which would allow them at least a ghetto status in the kingdom, in return for their obedience in temporal matters. These goals led to rifts within their community. The resident Catholics resented the role of the exiles. The secular clergy came to blows with the Jesuits. Out of these disputes emerged a proposal to the crown that, in exchange for a pledge of obedience in things temporal, they should be allowed freedom of worship. Rome frowned on this scheme and the royal government remained coolly sceptical.

Thwarted for the present, the Catholic community pinned their hopes on the possibilities of a new reign.

By Elizabeth's death it was certain that English Roman Catholicism would survive. Threatened with death by inanition, it had been succoured in time. Revived by the ministrations of the seminary priests, it soon developed a sturdy toughness which was proof against the rigours of persecution. The reservoir of devoted clery proved inexhaustible. It was not a question of survival but rather of the terms under which it would be possible. That was a problem unresolved in 1603.

From the Queen's point of view, the survival of a dissident Catholic community defeated her purpose – the consolidation of a society in which realm and church would be totally congruent. Yet she could congratulate herself on a lesser but vitally important success. The great bulk of Catholic Englishmen were as loyal subjects of the Queen as she could wish. They were ready to obey without hesitation whatever commands she gave in her secular capacity, including resistance to foreign invasion led by a Catholic prince with papal sanction. They were not prepared to stifle their consciences by obedience to the supreme governor, but they were equally determined not to blemish their honour by disloyalty to the sovereign God had set over them.

30

The Queen and her Constituencies

*E*lizabeth from the first day of her reign had to deal with the
accumulated tangle of problems which were the result of her
three predecessors' actions. The consequences of this burdensome legacy would require her constant attention and consume much
of her energies for decades to come. They would force the Queen's
hand, pushing her into decisions often painful, sometimes dangerous,
but always unavoidable. The telling of that story has formed much of
the substance of this book.

There were also other legacies, inheritances from a remoter —
sometimes very distant — past. Individual acts of her predecessors,
responding to particular needs, had by repetition hardened into custom and then imperceptibly into institutions. Such were the law courts
and the exchequer or — later in time — Parliament. They provided the
machinery which was essential to the functioning of the monarchy.
However, they could also be an obstacle to the fulfilment of the royal
will. Under the Tudors the sprawling system of law courts, laden with
the business of a ligitious age, performed a valuable service easing
frictions which might otherwise have escalated into public violence.
Under the Stuarts the monarchs, faced by judicial checks on their
will, were driven to heavy-handed intervention.

The management of Parliament, docile enough under the Queen's
father, became, as this chronicle has shown, a major preoccupation in
her reign. Parliament was, in fact, only the tip of the iceberg, visible
embodiment of a much larger entity, for it contained in its ranks the
representatives of the political nation, the men on whose active loyalty
the success or failure of a particular ruler rested. In the coronation rite,
in Elizabeth's formal assumption of the royal office, all the symbols —

crown, sceptre, orb, sword — as well as the symbolic acts of acclamation and homage, expressed the power to command and the obligation of obedience. To ensure that obedience should in fact follow command was the very essence of statecraft, an art which required of the sovereign not only acts of will but the more subtle skills of persuasion. A sixteenth-century English monarch had to woo the complex of constituencies which collectively formed the political nation no less than a twentieth-century prime minister. The conditions of politics were radically different, but the necessity to win the favour, the confidence, and the loyalty of the political nation was no less imperative.

What was the political nation in the sixteenth century? It was substantially larger than it had been a century earlier, when the king had largely to deal with a small elite of great nobles to whom in turn the landholding classes of the counties looked for leadership. In the reconstruction of a badly damaged monarchy by the Yorkists and then by the Tudors, the crown had come into much more direct contact with the county elites. The mediating role of the nobles had largely dwindled away. Certainly, under Henry VIII the crown had sought to recruit its servants from the widest possible catchment pool. Men whose ancestors had looked to promote their careers in the entourage of a Neville, a Stafford, or a Percy now looked directly to the court as the theatre of advancement, while their less ambitious — or better endowed — brethren at home turned to the crown to mediate those local rivalries which were the stuff of domestic political life. The Tudor crown, by seeking to recruit its servants from a much wider catchment pool sought to build a broad base of support among the landholding classes of the whole kingdom, expanding the political nation from a noble elite to a nationwide gentry constituency.

This development was signalled by the astronomical increase in the armigerous families as gentry sought the visible and royally bestowed mark of distinction, a coat of arms. This was accompanied by the expansion of the squirearchy; in 1500 probably no more than one village out of five possessed a resident landlord; a century later it was something like four out of five. Economic circumstances were favouring influences, as grain prices soared and landed incomes swelled while the dissolution of the monasteries transferred thousands of acres of land into the hands of lay landowners. The impressive increase in the size of the Commons house during the same era, in no small part propelled by demand from below, was another token of a growing national political awareness.

Interest in Parliament arose in large part because so much business which concerned the localities was now transacted there — such problems as enclosures, the relief of the poor, or the regulation of the labour market. There was also the unprecedented experience of the religious upheavals. Parliamentary participation in the successive phases of religious alterations, along with the teachings of the reformers, begot the phenomenon of a nationwide public opinion. Men came to Parliament who held strong convictions about the right ordering of the nation's religious life and were prepared to press them on the floor of the Commons house. There was for the first time an ideological component to their debates. These same gentry through the sale of monastic properties had acquired much ecclesiastical patronage, which gave them power to appoint a significant segment of the parochial clergy.

These were the men on whom the crown depended for the governance of the realm. From their ranks would come the justices of the peace, those jacks of all trades — magistrates, police superintendents, road engineers, intelligence agents, poor-law supervisors — on whose shoulders rested the whole responsibility for public order throughout the kingdom. Many of them would be called on to serve as deputy lieutenants, controlling the county militias in peace time, conscripting and outfitting men in time of war. After 1585 it was they who raised the armies which fought on the Continent and in Ireland. Both as JPs and as deputy lieutenants they had local tax-raising powers. When Parliament levied a national subsidy, it was members of this group who would assess and collect the tax. When the crown went cap in hand asking for contributions to a privy seal loan, they would be at once assessors and collectors. They were likely to be called on to serve on myriad local commissions for special judicial or administrative purposes. Each year one of their number in each county would serve as sheriff. For none of these services were they paid.

Their active loyalty was the foundation on which the monarchy rested. When rebellion erupted, as in 1536, 1549, or later in 1569, they were the first line of defence. When the northern gentry collaborated with the rebels in 1536, the government faced a threat to its very existence; it was the unshaken loyalty of their fellows in other parts of the kingdom which saved Henry's regime. When the local elites reacted firmly to suppress disorder, as in the Midland counties in 1549, the situation was rapidly brought under control. Where they failed, in Norfolk and Devon, the royal government had to call on the militias of the neighbouring areas to defeat the rebellion in the field. Most spectacular of all instances was the spontaneous rising on behalf of Mary in 1553. Obviously, without the loyalty of these classes, the crown would be paralysed. Recalcitrant individuals could be cited before the Privy Council, but if they refused, as Northumberland did in 1569 – or Norfolk might have done in the same year – the crown had no ready instrument of coercion. In such instances it was the loyalty of the gentry which saved the situation.

A new ruler succeeded to the throne invested with the mystique of a divinely sanctioned right, which not all the water in the rough rude sea could wash away. Elizabeth's predecessors had for several generations done much to enhance the external majesty of the crown by an elaboration of court ceremonial which glorified the throne and its occupant. This intangible aura which surrounded the anointed monarch counted for much; but it was not sufficient in itself, as Shake-speare's Richard II painfully learned, to assure mastery. Like his Henry V, the incumbent on the throne had to embody in his own person the qualities ascribed to the office. Above all he must be visibly his own master; a puppet king or one under the sway of one or more of his own subjects was by definition no longer a true monarch. Elizabeth's immediate ancestors, Edward IV, Henry VII, and Henry VIII, had more than measured up to the requirements of the kingly office, filling it with self-assured authority. Could Elizabeth emulate them?

For a woman the demands made on the occupant of the throne were supremely difficult to meet, since the characteristic qualities which a monarch was expected to display were very largely masculine. How was Elizabeth to surmount this formidable barrier to effective ruler-ship? The acclaim which resounded in the London streets during her coronation procession was real enough, but it was compounded in one part of sheer relief that the succession had been untroubled and in another by a vague hope of better times to come which the mere fact of a new reign engendered. Elizabeth was shrewdly aware that the aura of her divinity was diminished by her sex and by the doubts which filled the minds of her counsellors after their unhappy experi-ence with her predecessor. It is hardly likely that the letters of advice which were showered on the new Queen would have been delivered to a male occupant of the throne. She was surrounded by men all too ready to ply her with counsel, hopeful of winning her ear and bending her to their will – or even winning her hand.

The first of the constituencies which made up the political nation she had to face was the Council. At once the smallest and the most important, it was one whose members she could choose. At her Council board would sit the men who would be her intimate associates, her advisers, and her principal servants. As the executors of her will, they were the dynamo which set the rest of the governmental machinery in motion. They could be her most valuable asset or alternatively a dangerous liability. Properly managed, they could provide vigorous direction to her government, informative advice, and wise counsel. They could be the sounding-board through which she could hear the voice of the larger political community of the counties. Weakly led, they could relapse into squabbling discord as ministers fought to win and monopolize the sovereign's ear, even to become a Wolsey or a Cromwell. The possibility of attaining such a place seemed all the more plausible when the throne was occupied by a woman who would look to them for guidance. Certainly, under Mary such rivalries had flared out of control. No sole minister had emerged, but the Council's utility as a serviceable instrument of the royal will had been diminished.

Mary had been unlucky since, on her accession, she was compelled to accept the services of a body of men who only a few days earlier had proclaimed Lady Jane Grey, a circumstance which chilled all future relations. Elizabeth inherited no such liability. She was free to retain or reject the incumbent members of the Council. While dismissing Mary's own personal servants and the committed Catholics in the old Council, the new Queen retained the services of a clutch of experienced courtiers who had served impartially all the religious regimes of the past decades. She balanced them with a group of men who were at once personal adherents and experienced civil servants. It was a combination which promised the reassurance of continuity along with an infusion of new blood.

The choice of councillors made, Elizabeth faced the next and more difficult task of establishing her unquestioned authority over its members. In the very first days of the new reign, contemporaries were aware of a formidable personality, entirely different from that of her sister. The elder among them soon drew comparisons with her father. However, mere assertion of her majesty was not enough; it had to be concretely manifest in the handling of the challenges which events forced upon her.

The first test came in the Scottish crisis, and revealed how uncertain was her touch when faced with painful and dangerous choices. She drew back nervously and, like a skittish mare, had to be coaxed, nudged, and manœuvred into action by the strong-minded Cecil. It was Secretary Cecil who called the tune. Elizabeth's resentments at having been manœuvred surfaced in the coldness which she displayed towards Cecil in the ensuing months. Her refusal to follow up the Scottish success by permanent patronage of the Moray regime, combined with the prospect of a Dudley marriage, led him to talk of retirement. Elizabeth was in a fair way to lose the confidence and the services of her ablest Councillor, whose doubts were shared by most of his colleagues.

Her handling of this crisis of confidence displayed her as a deft manager. Cecil's *amour propre* was soothed by the lucrative wards office and by the implied assurance of her continuing confidence in him. In the following months the Dudley match was put aside, but the favourite was given the handsome endowments which enabled him to launch his political career. Yet there was a price to pay. Both men had to bow to the royal will, Dudley to forget his marital ambitions, Cecil to accept as a colleague a man whom he thoroughly distrusted. For the Queen this was an act which subtly but unmistakably asserted her freedom of action. She continued to value Cecil's services and to respect his judgment, but by forcing him to share her confidence with a rival she removed the imputation that she was solely dependent on his advice and that her judgment was always swayed by his. By deliberately creating a rift within her Council, she had made herself an umpire to whose judgment the contenders would always have to bow.

It was a risky strategy; it assumed first that the rivals would submit, however reluctantly, to working in harness, and secondly, that if either kicked at the traces she could quickly bring him to heel. It displayed a superb self-confidence, since it assumed Leicester's willingness to exchange his place of privilege for the level field of political warfare. The test came when that lord, tempted by the wiles of the Scottish Queen, strayed from the path. Elizabeth's daring was triumphantly vindicated. At the very breath of her displeasure, he and his fellow delinquents melted into abject submission. Her control of the political arena would not be questioned again until the very last years of the reign.

The strategy by which Councillors were kept in constant competition was one which the Queen applied to the whole board. She took their advice individually, not collectively.[1] In the aftermath of the Darnley marriage, and again at the time of the Anjou match, each Councillor was required to submit his own individual written opinion. This made it difficult for the Council to unite as a body *vis-à-vis* their mistress, and it placed each individual Councillor in competition with his peers. As the years passed the Queen and her Councillors settled into a pattern of relationship at once stable and unstable. On the one hand, Councillors had to live with the basic rhythms of the royal personality — Elizabeth's basic indisposition to act until forced by events, and the distracting vacillations which then ensued. As a close observer wrote, she was 'by art and nature together so blended, it was difficult to find her right humour at any time. Her wisest men and best counsellors were oft sore troubled to know her will in matters of state.'[2] Much of this indecision was genuine, but it was also a convenient ploy for asserting her mastery of the scene; no Councillor or combination of Councillors could be assured that her consent, once given, would not be retracted. Above all it ensured that the monarch was indeed sovereign, raised above the swirling individual and factional rivalries of the courtiers, handing down decisions as she willed them without fear or favour.

The obverse of the Queen's indecision was the marked tendency to make snap decisions when her anger was aroused. This disposition became even more marked when war came. The faithlessness of Henry IV or the obstinacy of the States General would lead to arbitrary commands to withdraw her forces. Permission for Drake to sail would be retracted even while he waited for a favouring wind. To her vacillation the Councillors responded by a steady drum-beat of persuasive argument and to her anger by discreet braking manœuvres until her temper cooled. The success of such strategies revealed that beneath the surface of obstinate rigidity there was an underlying flexibility — and probably insecurity. So long as the Queen was not chivvied or pressured too obviously, she was willing to listen to counsel and to be persuaded. Such episodes are rarely fully documented. One instance when the curtain is lifted came in the Queen's dealings with Norris in Brittany. Wrestling with the uncertainties of the Breton venture, she resolved to withdraw altogether. The Council, urgent to keep the English forces there, urged their case. The Queen continued of the same mind, 'and yet, she saieth, she yieldeth unto your tarrying because she findeth us that be of her council to be of that mind'.[3] Again in 1596 she had yielded against her judgment to the Cadiz voyage, as her angry recriminations after the event showed.

The record is full of Councillors' laments about the Queen's capriciousness, either in delaying decisions or reversing them once made. These frustrations were not the only factors which contributed to the tensions of royal service. Elizabeth's encouragement of frankness and forthrightness in the giving of advice invited freedom of speech on their part and a relationship of mutual confidence.[4] The Queen's playful habit of giving nicknames to her councillors — Leicester her eyes, Walsingham her Moor, Hatton her sheep, or Burghley her spirit — suggests an atmosphere in which the overpowering egotism of the sovereign was tempered by a certain familiarity. The going was never easy. When displeased, the Queen had no hesitation in presuming on her royal privilege by searing explosions of the royal temper. Over and above the outbursts of royal temper, barbed with sardonic comment, all the principal Councillors, at one time or another, suffered banishment from the royal presence — Bacon over the Hales pamphlet on the succession, Walsingham and Leicester during the Anjou marriage crisis, and even Burghley, after the execution of Mary Stuart.

Yet underlying all the tempests which constantly agitated the surface of court life, was a rock-based stability. However rough her tongue or harsh her treatment of her servants, Elizabeth gave to them an enduring loyalty which was as dependable as her high temper or restless indecision were predictable. Her confidence, once given, was not withdrawn, however sharp-tongued her rebukes. With the obvious exception of Norfolk and Essex, almost all the royal Councillors remained at the council board until death carried them away. There was the all-important assurance that, however harsh her disapproval, it did not lead to the shipwreck of one's career. Here, as in other matters, Elizabeth's adherence to her motto, *semper eadem*, won for her worthwhile rewards — unquestioning obedience and heartfelt loyalty. This was the persona, in which the spontaneous outbursts of a high-tempered woman blended with the artifices of a calculating politician, with which the Queen's intimates had to live.

The existence of such stability at the top level of politics had consequences lower down the scale. Lesser men, in pursuit of their varying goals, promotion in the royal service or advantage over a local rival, needed landmarks to guide them through the intricate geography of the court. If these were constantly shifting or if a minister suddenly vanished, as Wolsey or Cromwell in the Queen's father's time, the ensuing confusion was likely to endanger the stability of the great and of the little political universes. Confidence in the effective functioning of the whole order was shaken when the lines of communication between the centre and the periphery were broken. The willingness to bear the weight of taxation even in peace, and to assume the burdens imposed by nearly two decades of war, owed much to the general sense of security which the Queen's enduring loyalty to her Councillors engendered.

The Council was, of course, the constituency closest to the sovereign, the innermost of a series of concentric circles of political communities orbiting around the crown. The Council itself overlapped two other such bodies, the peerage and Parliament, and its members were themselves also part of the extended, nationwide political communities, the county aristocracies. The peers were, next to the Council, those of her subjects with whom the Queen had most personal contact. Besides those who sat on the Council, other peers served as occupants of the great provincial offices such as the two regional presidencies. Sussex served in Ireland and the north, Huntingdon and Pembroke in the north and in Wales. Many nobles were familiar figures of the court world, but in the counties their influence had diminished.

The consistent policy of the royal house since 1485 had been to depress the status and power of the greatest magnates. In Henry's reign the proud Duke of Buckingham had been struck down remorselessly in 1521 and the dukedom suppressed. The third Duke of Norfolk had escaped with his head only because of Henry's opportune death. The Percys of Northumberland had been stripped of their lands. Mary had to some extent reversed this policy; she restored both the Howards and the Percys. Elizabeth kept the greater nobles at a distance. Norfolk was admitted to the Council at the same time as his bitter enemy, Dudley (November 1562). Although he played a role in promoting the Austrian match, his counsel clearly did not win a significant place in the royal estimation. His involvement with Mary Stuart forfeited what credit he had; his further commitment to the Ridolfi plot forced the Queen, reluctantly, to accede to his execution. The ducal title was extinguished; his son had to content himself with his maternal inheritance, the Arundel earldom. This earl's dabbling in Catholic intrigue brought him to the Tower, where he was to die. The Percys fared no better. The seventh Earl, cold-shouldered at court and excluded from office in his native region, stumbled into rebellion along with his fellow peer, Westmorland. Northumberland went to the block, Westmorland into exile, the last of his line. Northumberland's heir and successor, the eighth Earl, displayed the same fatal propensity as Arundel and met the same unhappy end. By the close of the reign three of the greatest noble houses had fallen into disgrace, unable to find a new role in the changed atmosphere of the Tudor monarchy.

With the peerage at large Elizabeth's relations were more comfortable. She was a natural snob, and held the dignity of the noble order high in her regard. Consequently — unlike her father, who rewarded service with noble title — she stinted her grants of hereditary honour to a bare mimimum, and the size of the peerage remained constant at some fifty odd families. Elizabeth had initially given a generous proportion of Council seats to peers, but over time, as death removed them, the proportions were somewhat diminished. Numbering nine out of twenty at the opening of the reign, they counted five out of thirteen at its close and of these five two (Buckhurst and Hunsdon) were creations of the Queen, while they and Nottingham were all kinsmen of their royal mistress. Virtually all the working noble members were essentially court-based. Of the great regional magnates who did sit, the Stanleys or the Talbots were sleepers, while Arundel and Norfolk ended in disgrace, the first in retirement, the second on the block. Considerations of merit bulked as large in noble appointments to the Council as they did in those of commoners.

At the opening of Elizabeth's reign there were a few restorations in rank of families which had fallen into disgrace under Edward or Mary — Dudley (Warwick), Parr (Northampton), and Seymour (Hertford). Faithful service was rewarded by a barony for Cecil and by promotions of the two lord admirals, Clinton and Howard of Effingham, to an earl's dignity. The sea service of Lord Thomas Howard earned him a barony. Personal favouritism won Dudley his earldom of Leicester. Two of Elizabeth's Boleyn kin, Hunsdon and Buckhurst, were elevated to noble rank. Other than that, Elizabeth's creations and promotions were politically unimportant and very few in number. On balance, the total peerage was no larger in 1603 than in 1558. The lesser dignity of knighthood was also awarded with a sparing hand. With a strong sense of the dignity of the noble order, the Queen was determined to maintain its prestige by limiting its numbers and by making no promotions which could not be sustained by the necessary wealth.

Both peers and Councillors sat in another body, another constituency, to which the Queen would have to give more attention than her predecessors. In forty-five years she would summon ten Parliaments, considerably less frequently than was the case in the decades from 1529 to 1559. However, the experience of those thirty years had wrought measurable change in the relations, particularly those of the lower house, with the sovereign. Under her father the break with Rome had led to far more frequent sessions than in the past; more important, it had made Parliament a participant in a revolution of state. The subsequent continuing alterations in religion had compounded their involvement. Most of the religious statutes pressed by the Henrician, Edwardian, or Marian regimes had passed with relative ease. Only when property rights came into question, as in the case of the monastic lands under Mary, did the Commons balk. When Elizabeth presented her religious programme in 1559, it was not the lower but the upper house which nearly wrecked her plans.

It was in her succeeding Parliaments that she was faced with a novel restlessness in the lower house, of a kind her predecessors had not known for some generations. The Commons became an arena in which a series of initiatives were launched; differing in kind, they were all designed to force the Queen to actions which she adamantly opposed. They fell under two general headings: the first, alterations to the 1559 settlement of religion; the second, requests that Elizabeth either marry or settle the succession to the crown. In later decades this issue was reshaped when the fate of Mary Stuart came to focus Commons attention. However, it would falsify the picture to suggest that these questions consumed the bulk of Parliament's attention. Much of its business concerned the implementation of social or economic regulation, or improvements in legal procedure. Priority was given to measures devised by the crown's ministers, facilitated by the sitting Privy Councillors and the royally nominated Speaker. The rest of the session was filled with private legislation, initiated by Members on behalf of their constituents, which included bodies such as the boroughs or the chartered companies as well as individuals.

What was novel in this reign was the appearance of a new kind of lobby – to use a modern term. The most vocal of these was the body of evangelically minded clergy, the advanced Protestants, who used their friends and patrons in the house to advance their cause. Less visible, but more potent, were interest groups within the official establishment. More than once members of the Council, in cooperation with peers and Commons members, frustrated by royal intransigence, sought to use Parliament to wear down the Queen's resistance to measures they favoured. These tactics were used both in the succession issue and in the attack on the Scottish queen. Yet the Commons were no mere puppets manipulated by the Councillors. Sharing the latter's concerns, they responded readily to Councillors' initiatives.

Of the two great questions of state which agitated Parliament during the reign, the first to appear was the royal marriage and the succession. The first term in this pairing necessarily faded out with the passing years, while the latter assumed concrete form in the claims of Mary Queen of Scots. The second question of national import – religion – emerged in 1566, and in successive Parliaments down to the last decade of the century. The advocates of religious change were by no means monolithic, but represented a whole spectrum of differing strains of opinion. In some cases they included bishops or Councillors; at the other extreme were those arch-radicals who would have done away with both the liturgy and the episcopal office. Against these varying pressures the Queen was resolute in fending off alterations of any kind, as we have seen (Chapter 25), although her tactics changed from issue to issue.

Out of her effort to silence the religious radicals there rose another, constitutional issue of great consequence, the Commons' liberty of speech. In these encounters between crown and Commons, Parliament was being imperceptibly transformed from its traditional function of presenting and remedying grievances, soothing frictions, and easing maladjustments in the social order, or amending obsolete legal process, into a forum in which the political classes were airing their views on large issues of state and, on their own, advancing schemes of action. These novel aspirations of the Commons aroused royal anger. The Queen objected to the substance of most of the proposals; she resented even more the intrusion into her prerogative, those great questions of state which were solely the monarch's concern. These changes pushed Elizabeth into a novel and difficult role. Far more than her predecessors, she had to intervene directly in the houses' business, either by instructions to the Speaker (or Lord Keeper) or in person. In most legislation the Speaker, primed by the Councillors, controlled the machinery of the committees and thereby the flow of public business. Only rarely was the Queen called upon to use her power of veto. In the changing atmosphere of this reign, these familiar techniques no longer sufficed.

To the major issues in dispute the Queen responded in different ways. We have seen how, on the marriage question, Elizabeth skilfully deflected the urgency of the houses by courteous but cloudily phrased half-promises, and by a series of pseudo-courtships, until the issue wore itself out with time. On the succession she resorted to persuasive argument, by pointing up the risks of a reversionary interest and the difficulties of uniting in choice of a nominee. Here again, time made the issue moot. The other great parliamentary question which drew the Queen into direct confrontation with the lower house, continuing reform of the national religion, could not be so easily dealt with, nor would it die out with time. In these cases the Queen had to deal with initiatives which trespassed on that sacred soil of her prerogative on which no subject's foot could tread. Her vision of Parliament's proper role in legislation was set out in a speech by Lord Keeper Bacon in 1571, which distinguished between matters of state and matters of commonwealth. On the latter the Commons were free to take the initiative; on the former they could act only at the royal pleasure: 'they should do well to meddle with no matters of state but such as should be proponed unto them'.[5] Religion fell under the former heading. The Queen would reiterate tirelessly the constitutional doctrine that matters of religion lay within her prerogative, not to be touched by the houses.

It was precisely upon this issue, the bounds between the untrammelled prerogative of the crown and the subjects' right to make heard their grievances and, through their representatives, to give counsel, that Queen and Commons clashed. The first of a long series of sparring matches between the two came in 1566, when a bill confirming the Thirty-Nine Articles of Religion, brought forward from the floor of the house, arrived in the Lords.[6] Elizabeth sent 'special commandment' to the Lord Keeper to halt it, not on the grounds of its contents but because it affected the royal prerogative. The Commons had to bow to her will, but they had their revenge – by refusing to pass a government measure to renew expiring statutes.

At the closing session of this Parliament the Queen herself came down to speak. In carefully tailored language she addressed the issue of the house's liberties, i.e. her interference in legislative process. Defending although not spelling out the legitimacy of her action, she told them they were 'sore seduced'. Fortunately they had 'met with a gentle Prince, else your needless scruple might perchance have bred your cause blame'. She laid the blame on those 'that broached the vessel not well fined, and began these attempts, not foreseeing well the end'. Others, 'deluded by pleasing persuasions of common good' or simply yielding to friends' persuasions, had been misled into supporting the bill. She ended: 'Let this my discipline stand you in stead of sorer strokes, never to tempt too far a prince's patience.'[7] The speech was a nice example of royal rhetoric. Condescending but gracious in tone, it took care to absolve the bulk of the Parliament men from blame, pinpointed the unwisdom of a few, and ended with a moderate but clearcut insistence that it was within the Queen's power to limit the parliamentary agenda. The case was argued as much on the superior wisdom of the sovereign as on larger constitutional grounds. On the main question the Queen had had her way, but the Commons had shown their claws could scratch when they were checked.

In 1571, after another struggle over the act for the Articles of Religion which Elizabeth reluctantly approved, the Lord Keeper was instructed to tell the houses, 'The prerogative toucheth her Majesty and her authority, which without her favour, ought not to be had in question.' As before, it was not the content of the bill which troubled her so much as the invasion of her rights.[8] 1572 saw a repeat performance: a measure to give clergy freedom to alter the liturgy at will was quashed when the Queen ordered the Speaker to hand over the bill to her. This time the house docilely obeyed.[9]

In 1576 a generally harmonious session was ruffled by the long speech delivered by Peter Wentworth, member for a Cornish borough, probably a protégé of Bedford. He now raised very explicitly the question of parliamentary freedom of speech. The issue had first come up in 1566 during the debates on the succession. The Queen had forbidden further discussion of the matter. In a petition drawn up by Cecil, the house had then defended as an ancient custom 'its "leeful" sufferance and dutiful liberty to treat and devise of matters honourable for your Majesty and profitable for your realm'. The Queen covered a diplomatic retreat with the polite fiction that there had been no general resolution of the house to press the suit, merely the speeches of a few individuals, and therefore she had no occasion to issue a prohibition.[10] The issue had risen in a different form in 1571 when Strickland, the member for Scarborough, introduced a bill for reforming the prayer book, which got a first reading. However, before proceeding further the Commons cautiously resolved to petition the Queen for permission to deal in the matter. The Queen's response was to summon Strickland before the Council and sequester him from the house.[11] This in turn led to protests from the floor of the house, silenced only when the sequestered member reappeared. Once again, a confrontation on the subject of parliamentary free speech had been blunted by discretion on both sides.

It was this theme on which Wentworth discoursed in 1576.[12] He pulled no punches in insisting on the house's right to bring forward all matters of public concern. He utterly denied the royal right to interfere in such discussions, and insisted on the need for forthright criticism of the Queen when her faults deserved it. He was halted in mid-passage by the Speaker and committed to the Tower by a shocked house. Although members might well feel some sympathy for the theme of their liberties, Wentworth's extravagances were too much for their digestion. His stay in the Tower lasted only a month, after which the Queen graciously freed him, forgiving and forgetting his offence.[13] Her mildness may well reflect the general feeling that Wentworth's performance was too eccentric to merit severe punishment.

These scenes were repeated in the Parliaments of the 1580s when the Puritan campaign against both the prayer book and episcopacy reached its climax (see Chapter 25). The Queen had now entrusted the execution of her policy to the capable hands of Archbishop Whitgift. The attack on him in the 1584–5 Parliament brought the Queen to his defence with an uncompromising statement of her position. Once again she reiterated her views. Parliament was not to 'meddle with matters of the Church, neither in reformation of religion or of discipline'. The Queen is 'Supreme Governor of this Church, next under God', with 'full power and authority both . . . by law of the crown as by law positive, by statute, to reform any disorders in the same'.[14]

In the 1586–7 Parliament the most radical of the Puritan bills – a proposal to abolish both liturgy and episcopacy – was quashed before it got a hearing. In the ensuing skirmishing between sovereign and Parliament, the indefatigable Peter Wentworth put a series of boldly phrased questions to his colleagues. Was not this house a place 'for any member . . . freely and without controlment of any person or danger of law, by bill or speech to utter any . . . griefs . . . touching the service of God, the safety of the Prince and this noble Realm?' And again, 'Whether it be not . . . against the law that the Prince or Privy Council should send for any Member . . . and check, blame, or punish them for any speech used in this place, except it be for traitorous words?' And finally, 'Whether it be not against the . . . liberties of this house to receive messages either of commanding or prohibiting, and whether the messenger be not to be reputed as an enemy to God, the Prince and State?'[15] For his pains he was again dispatched to the Tower, where he remained at least until the session was over.

Wentworth's zeal for the liberty of the house was not to be quenched. The religious issue faded away in the 1590s Parliaments, but Wentworth with characteristic insensitivity brought the free-speech question forward in a new guise by reviving the question of the succession. In 1587 he had drafted a tract urging the Queen to summon Parliament in order that the succession should be settled. His own actions denied him the opportunity to press it in the 1587 session. He now prepared a new campaign for 1593. A more cautious man might have hesitated after hearing the Queen's orders, conveyed by the Lord Keeper, 'Her Majesty commandeth me to tell you that to say yea or no to bills . . . with some short declaration of his reason therein, and therein to have a free voice — which is the very true liberty of the House.' It was not 'to speak there of all causes as him listeth and to frame a form of religion or a state of government, as to their idle brains shall seem meetest'.[16] Undeterred, Wentworth drew up a draft bill, a petition — and a thanksgiving for the Queen's gracious acceptance! In private meetings he solicited the cooperation of fellow members; word of this got about and Wentworth entered the Tower, this time not to leave it alive. (He died in 1597.) He had been punished for actions outside the house, and this time there was no echo from the floor to take up his cause. Only an innocent like Wentworth would have dreamed of tying the free-speech issue to a topic about which it was dangerous even to whisper.

Four years later the Parliament of 1597 met in a different atmosphere. Its preoccupations were domestic, and much of its time was spent in legislation on enclosures and poor relief; but there was also a new note of discontent in the attack on patents of monopolies, the royal grants of privilege to individuals which gave them exclusive control of the production or sale of commodities — or licence to dispense with penalties laid down by statute. Such grants were plainly within the crown's power. Criticism of their issuance directly touched the royal prerogative. On this occasion Parliament's complaints were diverted by royal promises to refer the cases to the courts.[17]

When the next Parliament, the last of the reign, met in 1601, the Queen's response to the petition for parliamentary privilege was somewhat softened; she simply urged that they should not waste time 'in idle and vain matters' or contentious speech. She did not anticipate the storm of protest over monopolies. This time the Councillors in the Commons had to listen to a barrage of angry outbursts from aggrieved members which they could not halt. Cecil found it impossible to silence the protest; the angry house pushed aside discussion of the subsidy act, giving priority to redress of grievances.[18] It was the Queen who resolved the impasse, by tactful retreat; she ordered a proclamation revoking a long list of monopolies. The house was appropriately grateful, but not quite at ease until the proclamation was actually in print. The Queen followed up this move with a stroke of political genius. She received some seventy or eighty Commons members in audience at Whitehall where the famous golden speech, the most famous of her orations, reduced her hearers to tears.[19] A masterpiece of rhetoric, it proved to be a valedictory message to the realm, reiterating the central themes of her government, the primacy of her people's welfare, her sense of responsibility to a higher power, her defence of her subjects from 'peril, dishonour, tyranny and oppression'. She continued, 'And though you have had and may have many princes more mighty and wise sitting in this seat, yet you never had nor shall have any that will be more careful and loving.'

Posterity has rightly applauded the Queen's political skill in this graceful withdrawal. It is interesting, however, to contrast this retreat before the assault on her prerogative rights with her unyielding defence of the supreme governorship. There, of course, the matter at issue was one of substance as well as procedure. The proposed changes were in themselves repugnant to the Queen; action by Parliament an invasion of her prerogative. This time there was less at stake. The monopolies had been granted largely as a means for relieving pressure on the crown by its exigent suitors. The ordinary sources of patronage were exhausted and yet the press of greedy claimants for royal favour grew ever more numerous. A Council letter of 1600 admitted 'that in our remembrance the court did never swarm with so many suitors'.[20] However, when the resentment of those who were excluded from the royal bounty outweighed the gratitude of the recipients it was easy for the Queen to shift the onus onto the shoulders of the unlucky monopolists, while displaying herself as the dispenser of justice and the protector of her people against the abuses of the monopolists. It was a shrewd move, but one which left untouched the power of prerogative, since it was not the power to grant which was touched but only the abuses of the grantees. It was left to her successor to face the larger issue when Parliament once again questioned the royal right to control the house's proceedings.

What is to be made of this long-drawn-out duel between the Queen and her Parliaments? It is tempting to read these events as a foretaste of the next two reigns. One must be cautious in drawing such connections; but before exploring that problem it is necessary to analyse the Elizabethan conflict. For the Queen the picture was black and white. The content of the proposed bills was unacceptable to her; more important still, she saw herself defending her prerogative against an indefensible attack. Hence there was no ground for discussion or compromise. The Commons' perspective was a more complex one.

On the one hand, whenever the Queen commanded them to drop a particular measure, they obediently gave way. Yet, in the face of her repeated command that they abstain altogether from any dealings in ecclesiastical causes, they persistently listened to and advanced proposals for reform of the church. How can one reconcile this apparent contradiction?

The force behind this persistent drive for further reformation came from a body of devout zealots, inside and outside the house, whose belief in their tenets was absolute since they believed them to rest on scriptural authority. These men had no hesitation in pressing such self-evident truths on their sovereign. If she did not listen, it was because of evil counsellors around her, the bishops and, ultimately, Whitgift in particular. Their consciences supported them in continuing to press unquestionable truths on a Queen ill-advised. Among the body of the house they found a generally sympathetic audience for measures of further reform. It is unlikely that a majority of the lower house would ever have voted the abolition of the prayer book or of episcopacy, but left to its own devices, free from royal control, it would probably have agreed to a moderate programme of changes from the 1559 settlement. Such sentiments were entertained by a wide spectrum, ranging from Lord Burghley and other Councillors, like Mildmay and Knollys, to the wild men who would have swept the ecclesiastical stage clear and started anew on the evangelical model. In practice this meant that moderate measures which more firmly imprinted on the English church its Protestant nature were likely to receive favourable consideration.

How did these 'fellow-travellers', who lacked the rock-like convictions of the evangelicals, justify such flouting of royal commands? In most cases they simply evaded the issue, but the bolder spirits among them defended their actions by raising the constitutional issue of parliamentary free speech. In the mouth of a Wentworth this was transformed into an even bolder doctrine which, by asserting the absolute freedom of the house to set its own agenda without royal or conciliar interference, pointed to an assertion of parliamentary independence. Most of his colleagues balked at pressing so sweeping a claim, but were ready in specific cases to petition for the release of fellow Members. Their intellectual confusion is a good index to the transitional position into which, crabwise, they were edging. Habitual deference and the habits of tradition had enough force to restrain them from flouting a direct command from the palace to shelve a particular bill, but they were ready to ignore the more general command to abstain from considering ecclesiastical legislation. The notion that they were indeed entitled to deal with matters of religion had taken root, but it was not yet deeply enough established to nerve them to a direct confrontation.

Plainly the Queen was on the defensive, although not against a considered attack on her prerogative. What she faced was a determined and articulate party of enthusiasts determined to advance their vision of the godly commonwealth. In their eagerness to achieve their goals, they were blind to such merely temporal considerations as the royal prerogative. Their motto was 'seek ye first the kingdom of God'. It was a dialogue of the deaf. The Queen, fortified in the citadel of her royalty, held unyielding to her course, unheeding of the advice even of her own trusted Councillors. For once, in a matter where the Queen's will was matched with a clearly conceived goal, she acted with as much decisiveness as her father. The church of England would bear the imprint of her stubborn determination for generations to come. Ecclesiastical uniformity was the goal nearest her heart; of all her acts its consequences would endure the longest.

There was, of course, a second bone of contention between sovereign and Parliament, one more likely to concern those more worldly-minded Parliamentarians who, while distressed at the Queen's religious conservatism, were more disturbed by her frequent prohibitions on free speech and, worse still, the confinement of men who spoke too boldly. Up to the 1590s the houses reacted consistently in protesting against such measures, and in reiterating what they conceived to be their ancient rights. They failed to move the Queen; in the 1593 Parliament no less than seven members were sequestered by the Queen.[21] However, the issue was by no means dead, as the *Apology* of 1604 was to demonstrate. The authors of that declaration enunciated a full-blown doctrine of parliamentary autonomy which would have warmed the heart of Peter Wentworth. In it they insisted that the prohibitions of the Queen's time were of a temporary nature, a concession to her sex and age.[22]

More successful than her predecessor, King Canute, Elizabeth had stayed the tides of parliamentary pressure, but it was a holding operation, not a victory. Her reluctance to act on such vital matters as the succession or, later, the fate of Mary Stuart had driven her own most loyal Councillors, even Burghley, to circumvent her by mobilizing Parliament, to act in what normally were 'matters of state' outside their cognizance. These were not merely manipulative operations in which the parliamentary members were docile instruments in the

Councillors' hands. The latter were exploiting shared convictions. Thus the unintentional consequence of these operations was to promote the growth of a new parliamentary self-perception. Commons members, stimulated by invigorating and novel experience, were coming to think of their house as a national forum, where they had the right to bring forward and to discuss what they conceived to be matters of national import. Elizabeth could check this momentum but not destroy it.

Fears about the succession were measurably eased by the execution of the Queen of Scots and gradually extinguished as the probability of James's accession hardened into certainty. Nevertheless, there were potent residues left behind by the parliamentary agitation of the reign. They were a powerful — although not exclusive — cause of the virulent anti-Catholicism which marked English life for generations to come. Beyond that the political classes of England had acquired a new vision. Their horizons were broadening out from the traditional limits of private and local concerns into larger interests of a national nature. At the same time there was emerging a sense that the house was a forum in which they were free to set their agenda, free from royal or conciliar restriction; further, they were free on the floor of the house to speak their minds, subject only to the discipline of their own body. This was an unresolved conflict, which Elizabeth bequeathed to her successors.

In dealing with council or Parliament Elizabeth was engaging in straightforwardly political activities, devising strategies to manipulate or to constrain opponents, to advance or to halt given measures. But there was a larger constituency which had to be wooed, the whole body of landholding aristocracy, the lesser nobility, and the gentry, large and small, on whose shoulders rested the whole task of government at grass-roots level. A representation of them would, of course, sit in Parliament, but the Queen needed the committed loyalty of a whole class. To win their support required an entirely different technique from that of political manipulation. What was required was the projection of an image of royalty which would elicit a personal devotion to Elizabeth herself.

In the management of the political establishment at Westminster the Queen had to play the role of a king, to bend men to her will and enforce their obedience to her commands, to outwit and outmanoeuvre them, to display the devious skills of Machiavelli's prince and the forthright wilfulness of Shakespeare's Henry V. To the greater community away from the court, in the counties, she projected another and wholly different image. In a conversation with her godson, the wit Sir John Harington, she told him that 'her state did require her to command, what she knew her people would willingly do from their own love to her'. He added: 'she surely did play her tables well to gain obedience thus without constraint.'[23] Another Harrington, the seventeenth-century political thinker, wrote percipiently of the 'perpetual love-tricks that passed between her and her people into a kind of romance'.[24]

It was here, in dealing with her largest constituency, that the Queen displayed her feminine visage. No longer the formidable, sharp-tongued, domineering virago who bullied her ministers, she was the embodiment of the female virtues, a lover of peace, the maternal guardian of her people's welfare, the beneficent goddess showering them with the blessings of a golden age of untroubled prosperity and enduring peace. In another, slightly different version she was the restorer of true religion, a modern Judith or Deborah, the liberator of her nation from alien and ungodly oppression. These were the themes of parliamentary oration or of royal proclamation; they were also played out in real life by the Queen herself. The stages on which the royal performer acted were highly public. The most obvious was the court itself. In her many residences, the river palaces of Hampton Court, Richmond, or Greenwich, the suburban splendours of Whitehall or St James's, or the more modest setting of a country house like Oatlands in Surrey, she moved in an atmosphere of decorous magnificence which was as much public as private.

The court was a microcosm of the aristocratic world. Its core was in the ladies and gentlemen of the chamber, the royal attendants whose personal services to the sovereign were of an honourable kind, as against those of the 'below-stairs' staff, who carried out the more menial tasks of the royal establishment. They were recruited from every part of the realm; families in every county had sons or daughters, nephews or nieces, cousins, aunts, and uncles who served as gentlemen pensioners, soldiers of the guard, or gentlemen and ladies of the privy chamber. Entrée to the public rooms of the court was easy for any person of appropriate dress and bearing; an introduction could easily be secured through family or neighbourly connections.

The experience of the young Welshman, Edward Herbert (later Lord Herbert of Cherbury), attending court for the first time in the last years of the reign, was characteristic.[25] Each Sunday the Queen walked in state to the chapel, along a route lined with kneeling courtiers. Herbert joined the waiting throng. 'As soon as she saw me,

375

she stopped and swearing her usual oath, "God's death!", demanded, "Who is this?" ' Sir James Croft, a Privy Councillor and Herbert's neighbour in the Welsh borders, told her who he was, and that he had married the daughter of Sir William Herbert of St Julians. To this the Queen observed, 'It is a pity he married so young.' The elite world to which young Herbert belonged was a small one, with many links of marriage and kinship. The scattered estates of a single family, the result of marriage or inheritance, often stretched across more than one county. Among the greater gentry there was forming a network of connections which reached out beyond a single region. The court was the natural gathering-place for this incipient national aristocracy, the Queen the focal point of their ambitions, either local or national. Here she could display herself to her best advantage, where, amidst the splendours of her royal state, she could show herself in majesty yet at the same time a smiling lady, at once gracious and witty, accessible to her well-born subjects, a presence both regal and winning. She could turn respect and awe for a distant sovereign into lively loyalty to a warm and vivid human being.

Elizabeth made of the court a public place where those of her subjects who travelled to the capital could see her in person. The movements of her peripatetic court from house to house in a wide circle around the capital, as well as her visits to London, to the civic corporation, the companies, or the Inns of Court, made her a familiar figure to much of the population of the capital and the adjoining counties of the Thames valley. For those who lived further off, the Queen took the initiative by going herself to visit them. This took the form of her famous progresses. With almost annual regularity Elizabeth set out on a visit to one or more counties in southern England. These summer progresses were a mixture of pleasure and business. They provided Elizabeth with a free holiday at her subjects' expense while yielding considerable political bonuses. Elizabeth revelled in the acclaim of her people as she moved through the countryside and the effusions of loyal sentiment which poured forth at every stop. For her personally they were perhaps a reassurance that she was in truth the beloved ruler of her subjects. It was also an admirable political device for stimulating a widespread personal devotion which transcended mere respect for the royal office.[26] Setting out from one or another of her usual residences in the Thames valley, she made her way slowly across the countryside, attended by her ladies of honour and an entourage large enough to sustain the image of royalty and yet striking a note of holiday relaxation. In a typical year, 1561, she was on the road from 10 July to 22 September, visiting four counties – Essex, Suffolk, Hertfordshire, and Middlesex, staying in eighteen houses and three towns. A similar progress thirty years later (1593) took her through eight counties, moving up the Thames valley from Surrey and Middlesex, through Buckinghamshire and Berkshire, on to Wiltshire and Gloucestershire and finally to Oxford. Some thirty-five private hosts provided hospitality, as well as the University of Oxford.[27] In the course of the reign her progresses took her to a large part of the populous counties south of Trent which contained the majority of the kingdom's inhabitants.

The leisurely passage of her procession along the country roads was a rural counterpart to the procession across the city in 1559. Country folk gathered along the wayside to admire, to cheer, and to witness such an episode as occurred when a Huntingdonshire lawyer shouted to the royal coachman, 'stay thy cart, that I may speak to the Queen. Whereat Her Majesty laughed, as she had been tickled ... although very graciously, as her manner is, she gave him great thanks and her hand to kiss.'[28] She lavished fulsome praise on the oratorical efforts of local spokesmen, and was profuse in her gratitude for local hospitality. As she left Norwich she paused: 'I have laid upon my breast such good will, as I shall never forget Norwich ... and said, Farewell! Norwich, with the water standing in her eyes.'[29]

For her hosts these visits stimulated mixed feelings. The honour was great, there was sometimes the reward of a knighthood, but the costs were staggering.[30] Apart from providing for her entourage, the host had to provide suitable gifts, a jewel, a dress, or some other costly trifle. Coventry put £100 in the cup which it offered. Individuals might well expend a year's income on a visit of a few days' duration. In the three-day visit to the Earl of Hertford at Elvetham in 1591, 300 men were set to work enlarging the house, digging a pond containing three islands. At the greater houses there were elaborate entertainments, costumed pageants, recitations in Latin and English, in verse and prose, and music both vocal and instrumental.

All this activity meant that the Queen, far from being a remote, awesome figure, was for a substantial number of her subjects a living presence, an smiling, affable princess, moving easily yet majestically among them. Elizabeth's assiduous cultivation of her popularity paid direct dividends in the wide personal popularity she came to enjoy. From about 1570 the custom quite spontaneously sprang up of local celebrations of her accession day, 17 November. There were, in Camden's words 'thanksgivings, sermons in churches, multiplied prayers, joyful ringing of bells, running at tilt and festival mirth'.[31]

These manifestations of the Queen's popularity she owed largely to her own efforts. These were independently augmented by the uncovenanted benefits which flowed from the cultural transformation of the English world during the course of her lifetime. She was witness to the springtime of an English literary high culture, of an outpouring of prose and poetry, unprecedented in volume and unrivalled in quality. In the Renaissance world the royal court provided inspiration, patronage, and audience for the aspiring writer. In the English case there were, even more excitingly, the special opportunities offered by a queen regnant. The celebration of her merits and her virtues gave the writer a subject and occasions for endless exploitation. The resulting repertory was vast, ranging from the simplest doggerel of the ballad broadsides to the sophisticated intricacies of the *Faerie Queene*. The rapid expansion of the printed word gave wide circulation to those effusions. They constituted a public-relations campaign — cost-free — which any modern public-relations specialist might envy.

From the Queen's point of view this was a windfall of great value. Without any effort of her own, she became the subject of an ever-growing genre of celebratory poetry and prose. She appeared in many guises — the lady of chivalry, surrounded by her loyal knights, a goddess — Diana, Astraea, Cynthia — adored by her devotees, or a heroine from the Old Testament, Deborah or Judith. The proliferation of these varying images gave the Queen great delight, gratifying as they were to her inordinate love of flattery. They also added measurably to her political capital. The royal image — the royal myth — which she inherited was, of course, that of divine-right kingship. Elizabeth made the most of this, but she had to work hard at it, for the qualities usually assigned to the sovereign were masculine. These literary personae generated by her admirers were a valuable addition to her stock in trade since they offered a series of images peculiarly feminine. The most famous of them was incorporated into the structure of court ritual — the annual accession-day jousts. Here the Queen held court as a lady of chivalric romance while her knights, arrayed in symbolic attire, wearing appropriate devices, fought for her favour.

Elizabeth had another literary role. She was not only the subject on whom countless versifiers bestowed their best effort but also the audience — or at least part of the audience — whom the new race of playwrights sought to please. The Queen delighted in the spectacles which at least since her father's time had provided entertainment in the winter months, when the court was largely at Whitehall. The most characteristic of these were the masques, a combination of dance and pageant. From the first years of the reign they were supplemented by the presentation of plays. Increasing in number from two or three a season early in the reign to six to ten later on, with eleven in 1601, they were a standard feature of court life in the festive season from Christmas to the beginning of Lent.[32]

Thus the court took its place along with the lawyers in the Inns of Court and the London companies as sponsors and audiences of the playwrights, such patrons ensuring by their prestige the acceptance of the new art form as part of the social and cultural fabric. That patronage was extended in another form when the players' companies were sponsored by the major courtiers and by the Queen herself. Early in the reign the plays were largely performed by boys from St Paul's, Eton, and Westminster schools or the royal chapels. With the building of the public theatres the companies of adult professionals came to the fore. These companies each bore the name of a noble patron — Leicester, Warwick, Oxford, the Lord Admiral, and others. The most famous were the Queen's Men. The company of twelve men was founded in 1583, the players being given the status of grooms of the Chamber. In the 1580s they gave no fewer than twenty-one performances at court besides, of course, their tours through the country, where royal patronage gave them an edge over their competitors.[33]

The importance of the court's role in the development of English drama in its brilliant springtime needs no restatement. The patronage of the Queen and her courtiers gave dignity and legitimacy to an art fundamentally popular in origin, and assured it a place in the burgeoning of English high culture.

Elizabeth would have been gratified by posterity's judgment in bestowing her name on the cultural achievement which blossomed in the latter years of her reign. She could claim only modest credit for it. She seems to have had no interest in the conflicting currents which agitated the literary world as the new vernacular forms sought to come to terms with the classical canons of humanist letters. Her tastes, so far as we can discover them, seem to have been as eclectic as those of her subjects, whose new country houses cheerfully blended a happy mixture of traditional English style with ornamental flourishes borrowed from the Renaissance architecture of France and Italy. In the pageants at Kenilworth or Elvetham, woodwoads and fairies jostled with the gods and goddesses of Greece and Rome. However, in the greatest of these spectacles, the accession-day tournaments, there was a clear preference for the traditional modes of medieval romance, the lady surrounded by her devoted knights, striving to win her favour. Yet if she played no conscious role in patronizing the new cultural forms, Elizabeth's obvious enjoyment of plays, instanced by the frequency of their presentation and her willingness to lend her countenance — and the modest wages of twelve men — to a players' company, was of inestimable advantage to playwrights and actors whose activities were regarded with deep disapproval in many quarters.

Elizabeth had made of her court, whether stationary or peripatetic, a brilliant theatre in which she, as the leading actress, was constantly on stage. A natural-born actress, she played out a role, written by herself but embellished by the creations of her admirers. The performance was continuous and lasted to the end of her life. Yet she never tired, for hers was a labour of love as much as of duty. The never-ceasing applause fed her insatiable appetite for admiration, and probably helped to fulfil the emotional needs of a lonely and isolated human being. Moreover, her success in evoking this immense surge of popular adoration realized the most difficult goal she set herself at her accession. In spite of her disabling gender she had won a ringing recognition of her royal status. No one could deny that she had 'the stomach of a king, aye, and of a king of England', that she was as fully a monarch as any of her male predecessors and, unlike most of them, not only feared but loved. For her it was a gratifying personal triumph; it was also a public achievement of first consequence to her kingdom. At a moment in history when England faced the threat of civil division as bloody and destructive as that which wasted her neighbours, France, Scotland, or the Low Countries, Elizabeth's projection of herself as a beneficent, peace-loving protectress of her people, willing to put aside all personal gratifications to devote herself to their welfare, proved a sovereign elixir to cure these threatening ills. She was able to attract her subjects into a common loyalty to her person and office which overrode the divisions of religion and united the country against an external foe and against subversive conspiracy. Of the four neighbours — England, Scotland, France, and the Low Countries — which were profoundly touched by the Protestant Reformation, it was only Elizabeth's kingdom which escaped the ravages of internecine violence. A lion's share of the credit for that great good fortune must be given to the English Queen.

31

An Economical Queen

The urgent problems which demanded the Queen's immediate attention at her accession – the unfinished war, the Scottish revolt, the religious question – were largely the creation of her three predecessors. Underlying them was another issue, endemic to all regimes in all times, but exacerbated in this instance by recent circumstance. This was the matter of finance.[1] The Tudors had inherited a fiscal system devised by their medieval forebears. It rested on a simple principle. The crown's recurrent income, from its lands, from customs duties, and from traditional fees, was reckoned sufficient to pay for 'ordinary' expenses. These were essentially the maintenance of the royal household plus such costs as judges' or diplomats' salaries – the normal running costs of a peacetime establishment. 'Extra-ordinary' expenses, invariably expenditures for war, would be provided for by one-shot grants of taxes voted by Parliament. The yield of the parliamentary tax (now known as the subsidy) had been substantially increased by Cardinal Wolsey's reassessment of the taxable wealth of the realm in the 1520s.

However, existing resources were far too small to meet the demands of Henry's great wars in France and Scotland. To finance the royal extravaganza of the 1540s, that King had sold off much of the newly acquired monastic lands (worth as much as the existing royal estate), had debased the currency, had borrowed abroad, and had bullied Parliament into cancelling the repayment of loans from his subjects. The continuance of the Scottish war under Edward had added to an already burdensome debt. Mary's efforts to reduce it were thwarted by the French war. Elizabeth inherited an accumulated debt and a nearly empty treasury.

The short-term solution to the fiscal problem was the grant of a parliamentary subsidy in 1559, but Elizabeth took a long-term view of financial matters. Control of finance became one of the central pillars of her whole system of government. On no other issues, except the church, did she exhibit so carefully articulated and firm a policy. Its principles were straightforward and simple, and would have won the hearty approval of Mr Micawber. Outgoings were not to exceed income. Better still, whenever possible, surpluses were to be squirrelled away as contingent funds against future urgencies. A tidy balance of cash in hand was for Elizabeth the be-all and end-all of royal financial practice.

The principles were simple; putting them into practice far less so. The old distinction between ordinary and extraordinary expenditures had begun to blur under Henry. In 1534 he had obtained a subsidy unrelated to present, past, or future war. Out of 'mere love and obedience' and gratitude for his 'wise and political governance, regiment and rule of this realm' for a quarter of a century, Parliament voted him a subsidy. There was some vague reference to the costs of previous wars against Scotland and the expense of coastal and border forts. A similarly phrased act was passed again in 1540.[2] Subtly the rhetoric of the subsidy acts was shifting to the new idea that the subjects were indebted to the monarch for the benefits derived from his quotidian care for their welfare. With the wars of the 1540s, however, the justificatory rhetoric returned to the ancient themes left over from the Hundred Years War, the recovery of the King's ancient lands and the defence of his honour. The tone changed radically under Edward and Mary, when the statutory prologue was couched in highly defensive terms, ascribing the need for money to the mistakes of Protector Somerset or simply to 'the great debts wherewith the imperial crown of this realm is charged'.[3]

The goal of Elizabeth and her ministers was first to wipe out the debt and then establish a pay-as-you-go policy for the future. Given the inherited debt and the troubled circumstances of the 1560s, this could be achieved only if each successive Parliament provided a single subsidy to supplement recurrent income. What began as a response to extraordinary occasions became, with time, an accepted convention. By the second decade of the reign it was taken for granted that such a tax was to be levied at every session. However, this was not accomplished without a transformation of the crown's own policy. The Queen's fiscal objectives were linked to new principles of royal governance which repudiated past practice, above all the actions of Elizabeth's father.

The Lord Keeper's speech at the opening of the 1559 Parliament spelled out those principles. The Queen, he said, would not for the satisfaction of 'her own will and fantasy' do anything 'to bring any servitude or bondage to her people nor allow any private affection to advance the cause or quarrels with any foreign prince or potentate'. He deplored the consequences of past such wars — 'the marvellous decays and wastes of the revenues of the crown, the inestimable consumption of the treasure, levied both of the crown and the subject'. The result was the 'incredible sum of money owing at this present and in honour due to be paid and the biting interest that is to be answered for forbearance of this debt'. However, he continued, the consequences of those wars were still with crown and subjects. He then retailed the heavy expenses for fortifications and ships which defence against continuing outside threats demanded. Drawing a mercantile analogy, he likened the payment of taxes to the costs of merchants' insurance, a prudent caution against contingent disaster. He went on to reassure his hearers that their money would be spent for public needs:

> This is not a matter of will, no matter of displeasure, no private cause which in times past have been sufficient for princes' pretences (the more pity) but a matter for the universal weal of this realm, the defence of our country, the preservation of every man, his home and family particularly.[4]

The contrast with the language of Henry's time was interesting. Both father and daughter were urging that the taxpayer contribute to the 'ordinary' costs of government as well as to the 'extraordinary' outlays for war. The justification differed in highly important ways. In the subsidy statute of 1545, the taxpayers expressed their gratitude to their protector with crouching humility, comparing themselves to 'the small fishes of the sea [who] in the most tempestuous and strong weather do lie quietly under the rocks and bankside untouched by the scourges of the water'. They begged him to accept their gift 'as it pleased the great king Alexander to receive thankfully a cup of water of a poor man by the highway side'. The implied relationship was one of humiliating dependence on one side and overweening power on the other. Compare this with the reasoned argument of Lord Keeper Bacon, offering a bargain — the exchange of the Queen's services as a protector for their tax money. Taxes are paid not as a humble offering to an earthly god but as recompense for services rendered.

A second, related theme which would be recited again and again was the Queen's determination not to spend upon her own pleasures. 'It hath been used in times past, that prince's pleasures and delights have been followed in matter of charge, as things of necessity. And now, because, God be praised, the relieving of the realms necessity is become the princes pleasure and delight, a noble conversion.' These were the words of the Lord Keeper in the 1571 Parliament. He went on to enumerate the gorgeous buildings, the glittering triumphs, the delectable pastime and shows on which money was wasted in times past. Now, in the twelve happy years of Elizabeth's reign, there had been no expenditures except 'for the weal and profit of the realm'.[5] These were large boasts, but not empty ones. It was true that expenditures had not fallen during this decade. The expedition to Scotland, a rising in Ulster, the Newhaven adventure, the rising in the north, and renewed intervention across the Scottish border had been costly. Yet in each case there was a strong argument that the action had served national interests; none had been pursued for the mere sake of glory. Moreover, they had preserved the peace. In 1566 Sir Ralph Sadler boasted that while all her neighbours 'have been and yet be in arms, in hostility and great garboil, only we rest here in peace, thanks be to God therefor and the good government of the Queen's Majesty'.[6] In 1571 Bacon could celebrate 'the inestimable benefit of peace during the whole time of ten whole years together and more . . . is not peace the mark and end that all good governments direct their actions unto?'

By the second decade of the reign Elizabeth had won parliamentary acceptance of the regular grant of one subsidy at every meeting of Parliament. (1572 was an exception, since the subsidy granted in the previous year was still being collected.) In the twenty-five peacetime years between 1559 and 1585 there were thirteen in which the taxpayer had to dig into his pocket, a burden which would have seemed intolerable to the early Tudor generations. The understandings which lay behind this practice have been laid out – an abstemious royal economy in domestic expenditure and a strictly defensive foreign policy. The old distinction of 'ordinary' and 'extraordinary' expenses had been blurred, so that the latter now included the prevention as well as the waging of war. In effect, the Commons had agreed to pay for the running costs of foreign policy.

This change had not been brought about through a mere exercise of enlightened reason; it was a hard-earned lesson brought about by a transformation in the nature of England's relations with other powers. The lingering habits of an age when war had been largely the rivalries of the Percys and Nevilles writ large, a dynastic contest for the advancement of a ruling family, were now replaced by the grim struggles of an age of confessional conflict which transcended national boundaries, where the stakes were those of survival. In this combat England was dangerously vulnerable.

By the early 1570s favouring circumstances plus careful fiscal management enabled Elizabeth to realize her goal. She was at last debt-free. The foreign creditors at Antwerp had been paid off; so had the domestic lenders. The government had won golden opinions among the English gentry by its handling of privy seal loans. These borrowings were in effect involuntary loans which the crown extracted from individual landowners. In the 1540s two such loans had been transformed into taxes by Parliament, bullied by the imperious King. Mary's loan of 1557 had not been repaid. In marked contrast, two such loans made in 1562 and 1569 had been promptly repaid within two years.[7] The restoration of a sound currency, debauched by successive debasements, had already begun under Mary; it was carried through to completion by her successor. The successful effort to pay off the debt was matched by a programme of severe economy in routine expenditures. Household costs were brought down well below those of Edward's reign, even though prices were increasing. Pensions fell from £30,000 a year to £23,000 in Burghley's first years in office. Naval costs were kept low by fitting out as few ships as possible. Rather than building new ships, old ones were remodelled. Not only was there no new building of royal residences, but maintenance costs were lowered from over £6,000 a year to a level between £3,000 and £4,000.[8]

The success of Elizabeth's fiscal policy owed much to the direction of her Lord Treasurer, the Marquis of Winchester. Holder of the office since 1550 and an administrative reformer of talent, he had initiated reform in Mary's reign. In particular he had issued a new schedule of customs rates, an updating of the assessed values of commodities which reflected the price inflation of the previous decades. This made for substantial increases in royal income. Under him the various treasuries spawned by the confiscation of church property had been united under the treasurer's control, with a consequent reduction in personnel costs and an improvement in efficiency. When his place was taken by Cecil, newly ennobled as Baron Burghley, the same rigorous economy was pursued with equal vigour.

In the 1570s the annual burden on the taxpayer decreased, an annual average of £33,000 compared with £56,000 in the previous decade. With the disappearance of the debt and the beginnings of a surplus in the treasury, Burghley might have hoped for a tax holiday. He was not to be so fortunate. In 1576 the Chancellor of the Exchequer, Sir Walter Mildmay, rose to make his customary request for a subsidy.[9] He began by celebrating the Queen's achievements, the restoration of religion, the expulsion of the French from Scotland, and now the liquidation of the crown's debts. Nevertheless, the skies were far from clear. 'The tail of these storms which are so bitter and boisterous in other countries may reach us also before they be ended.' The danger was made greater because of 'the hatred that is borne us by the adversary of our religion'. It was Parliament's business 'to consider aforehand the dangers that may come by the malice of enemies and to provide in time how to resist them'. The Queen must be 'sufficiently furnished of treasure . . . to answer anything that shall be attempted against her and us'.

While insisting that the Queen was not required to account for her expenditures to them, 'yet for your satisfactions I will let you understand such things as are very true'. Mildmay then listed the occasions of expenditure since their last meeting. This served to prove that 'her Majesty's very ordinary charges, which she cannot but sustain, are far greater by dearth of prices and other occasions, than in any other prince's days'. She must, as a regular charge, meet the costs of the navy, the ordnance, the armoury, the garrison of Berwick, and the standing garrison in Ireland. The last part of the Chancellor's speech reaffirmed what was now the prevailing convention, but the earlier section broke new ground. What he was asking of Parliament was to provide funds not to pay for unavoidable past expenditure but to provide for contingent future expenditure. The appeal for Parliament's aid rested explicitly on a common interest of the Queen and her people, the threat posed by their religious enemies.

In the next Parliament, in 1581, Mildmay repeated his performance. This time he was more direct in naming the Queen's enemy and his intentions. The Pope's 'implacable malice' and that of his confederates sprang from his view of the Queen and her state as the 'great obstacle which standeth between him and the over-flowing of the world again with Popery'.[10] His efforts to overthrow the Queen's regime were retailed, from the northern rebellion and the bull of 1570 to the recent incursions into Ireland. But he was not alone in his actions. He had underhanded confederates. Whence came the Irish invasion? Who provided the ships and men? His hearers knew well enough that it was Spain to which he referred. Mildmay pursued his argument to the same conclusion as in 1576. Elizabeth's enemies would 'procure the sparks of the flames that have been so terrible in other countries, to fly over into England and kindle as great a fire here'. The moral of the lesson was plain – more money, to give the Queen the means she needed to defend her people against these raging enemies.

The rhetoric of justification and the argument behind it was shifting. The Queen was praised again for 'having made us to live in peace for twenty two years', but she was now donning the mantle of a Judith or Deborah, to defend her people against an enemy of the gospel faith. The case for the subsidy was now more and more built on the defence of the realm against an enemy who threatened 'this noble realm, our native country, renowned of the world, which our enemies daily gape to overrun'. It struck a new note of national patriotism in place of the older appeal to chivalric loyalty to one's sovereign lord. It was Queen and country who were menaced, a national rather than a dynastic cause. It also ensured that the patriotic temperature was raised so that, if war came, the nation would be prepared not only financially but morally.

This tactic, of sounding a patriotic call while at the same time opening to the Commons the government's views of its international relations, paid off very well indeed. The Queen could rejoice in the accumulation of ever larger surpluses in her treasury, some £300,000 by 1584.[11] A lightening of the demands on her resources, improved income, and the subsidies had made it possible. For the Queen it was a moment of peculiar satisfaction. The popularity she had courted and the abstemious economy she had practised had now paid off handsomely. However, she would not have long to gloat over the accumulated treasures in the Tower, for in 1585 she was forced into war.

The nest-egg of the surplus plus the payments on the 1584 grant tided the government over for a time, but the standing costs in the Low Countries, the Armada, and now the subsidies to France brought the ministers cap in hand to Parliament in 1589, asking for the unprecedented grant of a double subsidy. In the wake of the previous year's events it was not hard to convince Parliament to agree. The houses, however, insisted on a proviso that this grant constituted no precedent. In 1593, with a war widened to the French theatre and with little prospect of an end visible, the ministers somewhat apprehensively sought yet another increase, a third subsidy. The committee's initial report in the lower house did not go beyond another double subsidy, even after the Lord Keeper painted a bleak picture of a new armada, conspiracy in Scotland, and the Spanish landing in Brittany. It took the intervention of the upper house, and of Lord Burghley particularly, to bring the Commons round. He offered figures to convince them; the Queen had received £280,000 from the 1589 subsidies; she had spent £1,030,000 in the intervening years. Even after this urging, there was more debate and a notable speech from Francis Bacon warning that the realm would be impoverished. The crown's spokesmen relied less on patriotic rhetoric and more on the force of brute fact.

In the two remaining Parliaments of the reign, circumstances favoured the government when it asked for money: in 1597 the Lopez plot against the Queen's life and in 1601 the Spanish landing in Ireland. In the latter case Cecil was also able to dangle the carrot of possible peace in the wake of the Spanish overtures in 1600. The houses were induced to raise the total levy to four subsidies. In all these grants the houses echoed the 1589 insistence that these increases beyond the single subsidy should not be a precedent.

The Queen herself was not directly involved in the management of these subsidy measures, but the general direction of war finance reflected her continuing determination to continue in wartime the same careful husbanding of her resources as in the pre-war years. Typical of her resolve not to change course was the handling of the two wartime privy seal loans. The first, levied in 1588, was repaid in 1592; the second, of 1592, repaid in 1595. In the end Elizabeth would come closer to paying for the war while fighting it than any government since her time. A very approximate estimate of war costs paid out of the treasury from 1585 to 1603 would be £4,500,000. Of this something over £2,000,000 was paid for by taxation; another £500,000 was raised by selling crown lands. On Elizabeth's death the debt stood at some £364,000 (with £60,000 in hand). The remaining payments due on the subsidy of 1601 would in theory have covered this shortfall. In fact much of it remained unpaid under her successor. (These figures do not take account of the local taxes levied for coat and conduct money and other mobilization expenses, all of which were locally levied. In sum they may well have equalled the money paid out through the royal exchequer.)

At every stage of the war Elizabeth's fiscal concerns took precedence over strategic goals. The great naval expeditions were all financed as far as possible by joint-stock ventures. On paper at least, the cost of both the Dutch and the French expeditions was financed by loans to be repaid after the war. The campaign of 1591 in the Seine valley was motivated in no small part by the expectation of holding the customs farm of Rouen as gage for the repayment of the French debt. In each of the overseas expeditions the Queen had high hopes of substantial booty; her disappointment was made known in the strongest terms.

Elizabeth was determined to apply the same fiscal principles in war as in peace. The great desideratum was to avoid at any cost the accumulation of debt. The contrast with the Continental monarchies could not be more striking. There, fiscal considerations were invariably subordinated to the needs of the state, above all of war. Ministers of finance were driven to every possible expedient in order to raise more funds — new taxes, increases in old ones, long- as well as short-term borrowing, the sale of offices, and if necessary a suspension of payments. The English Queen adhered strictly to ancient practice; the sole novelty, the doubling, trebling, and quadrupling of the subsidies, was introduced with the reasoned assent of Parliament, while the sovereign contributed her own sacrifice of assets.

Behind the Queen's obsession with a rigid economy stood a fundamental conception about the bounds of royal power. There was an underlying fear of taxpayer resistance. The old conception that parliamentary taxation was limited to wartime needs had been breached, but the notion that there was a limit to taxpayers' liability, that their willingness to pay was inelastic, remained rooted in the royal as in the popular consciousness. It had been manifest in the carefully argued strategy of persuasion, particularly in the Parliaments of 1576 and 1581. Continental monarchs may have had similar doubts about their subjects' taxpaying capacity, but they dealt with it by head-on challenge and by ruthless innovation.

The notion that Englishmen were peculiarly tax-resistant was not confined to the Queen. Bacon, in his 1593 speech, asserted, 'And in histories it is to be observed that of all nations the English are not to be subject, base, or taxable.'[12] That reluctance to pay was manifest in the steady decline in the yield of a single subsidy. This tax was, of course, locally collected and effectively self-assessed. Between 1564 and 1585 the yield of a single subsidy (levied at the same rate) fell from £150,000 to £100,000. At the end of the reign it brought no more than £67,000. Exhortations from the Council had no effect. The taxpayers were voting with their feet.

Yet, even if there was objective truth in the recalcitrance of the taxpayer, the Queen's parsimony had deep personal roots. They were compounded of a housewifely prudence, anxiety to pay the bills promptly and maintain a cash balance at the bankers, genuine revulsion against the wasteful male violence of war, and, lastly, her passionate desire to remain the adored ruler, guarantor of peace and the provider of prosperity. The coming of war threatened that image and, as the weary years passed, dimmed it. Yet Elizabeth did not opt to exchange the image of peace for that of war, to assume, as Essex and Ralegh would have had her do, the breastplate and armour of a warrior goddess. To the end she clung, *semper eadem*, to Astraea's role.

Part VII

The End of a Reign
1590–1603

32

The Earl of Essex

In the weeks when the Armada was battling its way through the northern seas, Elizabeth, even as she rejoiced in the Spaniards' repulse, suffered a grievous personal blow in the death of the Earl of Leicester, a sudden and seemingly unanticipated event which took place on 4 September. That event brought to an end the most important personal relationship of her life. It had begun in a love affair which had almost ripened into marriage, only to fade slowly but not unhappily into a lifelong companionship, durable and flexible enough to accommodate (just) Leicester's marriage with Lettice Knollys. Little remains to reveal Elizabeth's feelings on the occasion other than a brief notation, 'his last letter'. How strong the tie was had been revealed in the last weeks of the Earl's life, when Elizabeth proposed to make him Lieutenant-General of the realm during the invasion crisis.

It was a parting with larger resonances than the merely personal. Leicester, only three years older than the Queen, was the first of her generation to die, a sharp reminder of her own mortality. His death proved to be but the first in a long list, as one familiar face after another vanished from the court scene. Warwick, Leicester's brother, followed him in 1590. The invaluable Sir Walter Mildmay, Chancellor of the Exchequer and parliamentary spokesman, had gone in 1589. The most politically eminent was Secretary Walsingham, who survived Leicester by some eighteen months, dying in April 1590. He was followed by another royal intimate whose demise was both politically and personally consequential – Lord Chancellor Hatton in 1591. The death of three of the four confidants who had formed the Queen's inner council for some two decades necessarily shifted the balance of power within the Privy Council. Burghley alone remained, in solitary and unchallenged eminence. A court observer wrote in autumn 1591, 'old Saturnus is a melancholy and wayward planet but yet predominant here and if you have thus to do it must be done that way and whatsoever hope you have of any other believe it not'. The writer added that Sir Edward Norris had offended the Treasurer 'for nourishing and depending upon other besides His Lordship which will hardly be put up'.[1]

These circumstances powerfully affected war strategy. There was no longer an activist voice in the Council, prepared to push for an offensive strategy. This shift coincided with the failure of the English counter-stroke at Lisbon, a disaster which in any case left the Queen cold towards any further expeditions against the Spanish homeland or its colonies in America. The change in personnel as well as events converged, leading to a policy which was reactive, responding to the clamorous demands of the new King of France for all possible assistance or the equally insistent pleas of the Dutch, now that Count Maurice was mounting offensive campaigns.

However, domestic politics and, ultimately, war policy were dramatically deflected by the unanticipated entrance of a new actor on the political stage, as Elizabeth turned her eyes on a new favourite, stepson to the departed Robin — Robert Devereux, second Earl of Essex, barely twenty years old in 1588. His father had been promoted to an earldom by the Queen when he set out to found an English settlement in Ireland, a task in which he perished. The son, left an orphan at the age of nine, passed under the successive tutelage of Burghley, of his uncle, Sir William Knollys, and of the Lord President Huntingdon. He spent three years at Cambridge and about 1584 became a regular attendant at court. In 1585 he accompanied Leicester to the Low Countries, was made General of the Horse, and participated in the famous action at Zutphen, which won him his knighthood. When Leicester succeeded as Lord Steward in 1587, the Queen replaced him as her Master of the Horse by Essex. By the time of Leicester's death the young Earl was well established as favourite *en titre*.

His attractions were quite different from those which had won his stepfather royal favour. He was deeply touched by the high culture which was coming into full flower in the last years of the sixteenth century, and powerfully influenced by the model of Sir Philip Sidney, whose widow he married. He strove to embody the combination of humanist culture and chivalric idealism which had been personified in Sidney. That idealism was uneasily blended with a somewhat crasser ambition for conventional military fame, in which his own achievement as a great captain was to forward the twin causes of English national greatness and the Protestant faith. Add to this the immature psyche of a child of fortune who had won the glittering prizes too early and too easily and one had a recipe for strain, tension, and ultimately personal instability.

Early on it became evident that the new favourite was a very different style of player from his predecessors, Leicester and Hatton. They had accepted the rules set by the royal umpire, the first and greatest of which was unquestioning submission to the royal will. Neither of them dared openly cross a royal command. Leicester did not hesitate to resort to intrigue, both in the Norfolk marriage plot and at the time of the Anjou match, but faced by royal displeasure, he obeyed. He swallowed his disappointment in 1577 when the Queen reversed her decision to aid the States and accepted, however ruefully, her command that he marry Mary Stuart. Hatton was even more the Queen's humble servant, content to be the executor of her will. Essex, from the beginning of his career, refused to read the lines of his assigned part. As early as 1587 there was an episode in which the Queen commanded his sister, Penelope, to be confined to her chamber. The Earl turned on the Queen, reproaching her as a mere tool of Walter Ralegh (then his rival in her affections), and departed from the court, declaring he would sail to Flanders to join the siege of Sluys. A royal order halted him at Sandwich.[2]

More serious were his actions in 1589, when the Portugal expedition was preparing. Desperate to serve in the voyage, where he hoped to win both reputation and fortune, he flew in the face of an absolute royal command against his participation. Escaping from court, he preceded the fleet's departure from Plymouth and joined it off the Spanish coast. He continued in the voyage through the vain attempt at Lisbon, and had some satisfaction in striking his pike against the city's gates before finally bowing to the royal order for his return. In both these episodes Elizabeth, after a volcanic display of anger, received the truant back into grace. Even his secret marriage with Frances Walsingham, Sidney's widow, failed to shake his favour with the Queen for more than a moment. (His erstwhile rival, Ralegh, paid for his match by years of exile from court.)

Essex, restless and impatient, was always chafing against the very conditions of his status as favourite. The Queen, in return for her favour, expected a due return, in assiduous attendance on her person and in an appropriate posture of submission, expressed in both rhetoric and ritual, for which the model was drawn from the tradition of knightly romance. On the lips of Dudley and Hatton, contemporaries of the Queen, the language of knightly homage, the conventional praise of feminine beauty, tripped forth lightly, but when the devotee was a young man of twenty and the lady had rounded fifty, the fiction was harder to sustain. It was a role which Essex played uneasily and erratically.

The myth of a court romance comprehended more than the mere pairing of the lady and the suitor. Each favourite, like the heroes of a fairy tale, had, through the magic of their personal chemistry, been given the great and glittering prize of royal favour. Neither Leicester nor Hatton was so bemused by his good fortune not to perceive that, like other fairy gold, it had special characteristics. It was not automatically available; it could be withheld. Cautiously, warily, playing by the rules, they husbanded their treasure. Essex, recklessly self-confident, displayed no such prudence. He was exigent in his demands, insistent on their fulfilment and free in his displeasure when they were denied. He readily pushed aside the fiction of the supplicant, substituting that of the creditor, demanding his rightful due. Elizabeth flared angrily at his presumption, but invariably the royal displeasure cooled and the royal countenance again smiled benignly on the erring favourite. Behind the veil of courtly convention there was in fact a doting mother and a hopelessly spoiled child, whose tantrums and sulks were indulgently borne.

The appearance of the new favourite soon became a matter of more than mere court consequence. His appointment as Master of the Horse in 1587 made him a major household officer with constant access to the Queen — the same office Elizabeth had granted Leicester in the first days of the reign. Essex's interests were directed, however, not towards the court nor towards the conventional ambitions of the courtier — office, annuities, leases, the building materials for a family fortune — but to the great wars, to martial adventure overseas. When he returned from his madcap escapade in Portugal, he begged unsuccessfully for the command of the forces sent to Normandy to assist Henry IV in autumn 1589. The post went instead to Lord Willoughby, lately English commander in the Low Countries. In 1591 a new opportunity offered itself when the Queen agreed to send two expeditions to France. The first, destined for Brittany, went under the charge of the veteran soldier, Sir John Norris. The second command, that of the forces sent to join the French King at Rouen, gave promise of greater glory. Essex went down on his knees to beg for this post and enlisted the support of the French court. The dignity of the post demanded a noble appointee; Willoughby, the only other candidate, was in poor health. The Queen finally yielded to Essex's urging. The twenty-three-year-old Earl was placed at the head of an army of some 4,000 men. His previous military experience was limited to service as a gentleman volunteer under Leicester and in the Portugal voyage.

The Queen tried to hold him on a tight leash, restrained by a web of counsellors whose advice he was to take at every step. She herself kept close tabs on his actions as best she could, from London. There followed a fierce clash of wills as Essex strove to break his bonds, riding off on a dangerous journey to meet Henry IV and making his own troop dispositions. The Queen recalled him home and theatened to withdraw her whole force. Essex's anguish was such that he burst his buttons, rolling on his bed in a fit of sheer frustration. In the end the contest of wills ended with a relative advantage to the Earl. The Queen relaxed the strings, granted the dispatch of replacements, and allowed the expedition to continue. Essex did not, of course, win the martial successes he had hoped for. The siege fizzled out, and even before it ended he returned home, leaving a depleted force under Sir Roger Williams. However, blame for failure was diverted from his shoulders to those of the French. Essex's visit to Henry IV had made him as a confidant and close ally of the French King, confirming his reputation as a personage of international consequence. His experience in leading an army had established his position as the sole English nobleman with military credentials. (Willoughby's ill health had driven him into retirement.) Essex now became the patron of the martial careerists, the new officer class spawned by the war. These captains, seeking appointment or promotion in the Dutch, French, or — later — the Irish campaigns looked to him for their advancements.

Essex, upon his return from Normandy, turned over a new leaf. Putting aside, at least for a time, his ambitions for a military career, he pressed for admission to the centre of power, a seat on the Privy Council. His position as a major household officer, his recent role as a general, and above all his favour with the Queen, made the promotion a natural step. It was, however, a quantum leap in his career. The Queen, in making the appointment, was elevating him from the private status of favourite to the public one of a councillor of state, launching him on the political stage as she had launched Robert Dudley in the 1560s. It was a great gain in status and in consequence, but it also entailed costs. As favourite he had had a privileged and indulged position in which he could usually count on having his way, but as a Councillor he was one among equals. He had now to descend into the arena of play and to compete with his fellow Councillors for the Queen's ear. He would have to endure the give-and-take of a contest in which he would lose as often as he won. This was a lesson which Essex found hard to learn; he would never fully master it.

The rise of Essex in royal favour, his successive appointments, and above all his advancement to the Council table profoundly altered the world of high politics. The Elizabethan political system was a curious amalgam in which the cool calculations of *raison d'état* prevailing in relations with other princes or the management of the war were alloyed by the purely personal preferences of the ruler. The attractions of a young man in his twenties to an ageing woman, approaching her sixtieth birthday, pulled askew the whole network of personal relationships within which the conduct of English government had transpired for two decades past.

There was in this affair a re-enactment of events which had first taken place thirty years earlier. Then, as now, Elizabeth had startled the actors in the political drama by adding a new and unknown character to the plot, whose close relations with the Queen aroused their jealousy while his conduct led them to distrust his intentions and fear his ambitions. They had seen in Leicester an adventurer whose ambition to marry the Queen threatened the stability of the whole system. Those fears were gradually dissipated when it became clear she would not marry him nor give him a monopoly of her attention. Her favours would be distributed equitably. Leicester, on his side, showed a grasp of political reality, settling for a second-best prize. Nevertheless, there existed a deep fault-line in the political world, between the Lord Treasurer and the restless promoter of the evangelical cause at home and abroad. How deep and how lasting Burghley's suspicions were is revealed in the pages of Camden's annals.

The resemblance between the political scene of the 1590s and that of the 1560s was thrown into high relief by yet another duplication of earlier events. If Essex was in considerable measure a reincarnation of Leicester, he too faced a rival in yet another Cecil — in Robert, Burghley's second and favourite son. This young man, almost the same age as Essex, the son of that formidable lady, Mildred Cook, had inherited his father's talents and his disposition. Educated at Cambridge, initiated into public affairs as a member of the mission at Bourbourg in 1588, he was now ready to follow in his father's footsteps. Walsingham's death in 1590 vacated the key office of Secretary. Initially Burghley took over the duties he had laid down in 1571 when he was promoted to Treasurer, but the pressures of age and of his other responsibilities were too heavy for his shoulders. Various names were bandied about as possible appointees, but in the end, while the office itself remained unfilled, Robert Cecil entered the Privy Council (August 1591) with the implicit understanding that he would carry out the Secretary's duties under paternal supervision.

For the Cecils, father and son, this was the first step towards a greater goal. Burghley, by now seventy, had realized the ambitions of his own career — office, power, rank, wealth; now he entertained the hope that his son might be his political heir, stepping into his father's shoes as Councillor and minister. There was more yet. In the nature of things the Queen's reign was approaching its end; whoever stood at the centre of power on her death would have powerful leverage with her successor. Thus there were two prizes to be won, the first in the immediate present, the second in the contingent future. This hopeful prospect was now shadowed by the presence of the new favourite.

The Queen was quite aware that she was recreating the scenario of her early years, but entirely confident that, as she had held Leicester firmly in rein and kept him and Burghley harnessed together in her service, so she would manage the new team of the younger generation. The appointment reflected also a larger pattern of royal behaviour. Elizabeth was having great difficulty in accepting the mortality of her own generation. The disappearance of their familiar faces from the Council table and court shook her sense of security, and stirred her deep antipathy to any change in her inner circle. The compromise which she chose was to appoint her contemporaries' sons to fill their empty chairs. Hence William succeeded Francis Knollys; the second Lord Hunsdon the first; Buckhurst and Lord Admiral Howard took their fathers' places on the Council. As the Archbishop of York percipiently wrote, 'the race of nobles the Queen found at her accession has passed away'. Whatever the deficiencies of the new generation, he warned the Queen, 'he who watches the wind shall not sow and he who considers the clouds shall not reap'.[3]

The Cecils might look with dismay on the promotion of Essex but there was little they could do about it. Too shrewd to provoke his enmity, they cultivated civil relations. The hunchbacked Robert Cecil could not hope to rival the favourite's grace of presence. His best card was an assiduous attention to the duties of the secretarial office. It was a post which brought him into daily contact with the Queen and offered the opportunity to win her confidence in his administrative skill and the soundness of his judgment. A vignette from the pen of a hostile observer shows him in February 1594: 'Sir Robert goeth and cometh very often between London and the court so that he come out with his hands full of papers and head full of matter so occupied passeth through the presence like a blind man not looking upon any.'[4]

Essex now set about diligently learning his new trade as a Privy Councillor. His outward demeanour altered appropriately: 'His Lordship is become a new man, clean forsaking all his former youthful tricks, carrying himself with honourable gravity and singularly liked of, both in Parliament and at Council-table, for his speeches and judgment.'[5] The Earl was aware that he must carve out a role as a reponsible statesman if he were to obtain credit with his fellows at the Council board and with the Queen. To this end he recruited the services of a corps of able young assistants. Notable among them were the Bacon brothers. Francis, a rising lawyer with unfulfilled political ambitions, enjoyed the full confidence of his patron, to whom he acted as political adviser and general mentor in the mysteries of court politics. His brother, Anthony, newly returned from a long stay in France, where he had been one of Walsingham's intelligencers and established useful connections with the Protestant leadership, now took on a spider-like role as the centre of a web of agents, strategically placed on the Continent to gather intelligence. This intelligence service enabled Essex to provide a flow of information to the Queen's government at a time when the organization built up by Walsingham was in disarray.

His foreign correspondence was by no means limited to the reports of his intelligencers. He had regular contact with the French, both with the King, who looked on Essex as his advocate at the English court, and with the French Protestant magnates. His patronage of the fugitive Spanish secretary, Perez, whom he brought to England, gave him an additional link to Paris on the latter's return there.

A second link with a foreign sovereign which Essex forged had quite another significance. By the mid-1590s the earl had established a steady, albeit covert correspondence with James of Scotland, and was viewed by that monarch as the principal promoter and supporter of Stuart interests at the English court. Essex's cultivation of the Scottish King reflected Englishmen's consciousness of an inevitable event of which none dared speak. Elizabeth was now entering the last decade of the allotted biblical span. Her resolute refusal to countenance a 'rising sun' in her lifetime made the succession a taboo subject, yet one which was the anxious concern of all politically conscious Englishmen. Almost certainly the next sovereign would be James. The shrewder (and bolder) politicians with acute awareness of the situation were taking cautious steps. They had to tread warily, playing their cards in the current game while putting down a stake in another yet to be played.

Here Essex stole a march on his rivals. The Cecils as executive officers had to carry out royal policy, which involved in this case underhanded conspiracy with Scottish malcontents, a product of Elizabeth's distrust of James's ability to check Spanish intrigue with his nobles. The Cecils had also to bear the blame for the Queen's stinginess in the pension which she doled out to James. Had Elizabeth died in the middle 1590s the Cecils' prospects would have been very bleak. On Burghley's death it was said in Edinburgh that 'nothing but their greatest unfriend is gone'.[6]

Besides his intelligence-gathering activities, Essex essayed another role in Council. As the only Councillor with military experience he became a kind of unofficial minister of war. It was to him that the English commanders abroad, such as Vere or the governors of the cautionary towns in the Low Countries, reported and looked for direction. The lesser officers regarded him as the patron of their interests.

Essex also struck out in another direction, seeking to exploit his capital as a royal favourite by playing the role of a patronage broker. In 1593 the Attorney-General's post had fallen vacant by the promotion of Sir Thomas Egerton to the Keepership. It would, of course, be filled by a lawyer. Essex put forward his protégé and confidant, Francis Bacon, as his candidate. With characteristic impetuosity he importuned the Queen on every possible occasion. Rebuffs only made him even more persistent. His unavailing efforts led to unsolicited advice from his rival, Robert Cecil. While they were riding together in a coach the latter advised the Earl that he was wasting his time in pushing Bacon for the Attorney-Generalship. He should instead put him forward for an office of 'easier digestion' with the Queen, that of Solicitor-General. Essex's indignant reply was.

> Digest me no digestions for the attorneyship for Francis is what I must have and in that I will spend all my power, might and authority and amity [*sic*] and with tooth and nail procure the same for him against whensoever and whosoever gets this office out of my hands for any other; before he hath it shall cost him the coming by.[7]

The episode was a fair specimen of Essex's deficiencies as a courtier. He failed to understand the Queen's deep-lying resentment at any effort to force her will. Nor did he perceive that such appointments turned on the royal judgment of the candidates' competence, not on the persuasions of his friends. The post went to another lawyer, Sir Edward Coke, promoted from the Solicitorship. Essex did now push Bacon for the new vacancy, but with like ill success. Again, his advocacy was counterproductive. He had to accept defeat in a cause in which he had invested too much of his stock of influence.

Although this episode might seem to be a round in the Essex–Cecil rivalry, it is probable that the Cecils simply saw that Coke would be the royal choice in any case. Their advice to Essex was meant in good faith as a common-sense observation. It was not their fault that Essex chose to trip over his own feet. The Earl had a chance to recoup his political fortunes in the Lopez affair. Lopez, a Jewish Portuguese exile, was a physician who had risen to number the Queen among his clients. When he was accused of complicity in a Spanish plot to poison Elizabeth, Cecil expressed his doubts as to the veracity of the charge, while Essex's vehement assertion of the doctor's guilt won a royal rebuke. However, the Earl pressed the case and, as head of the investigating commission, proved Lopez's guilt and brought him to the block. Essex could now pose as the faithful and assiduous defender of his sovereign's threatened life, persistent in rooting out her enemies.[8]

In these years relations between the Earl and the Cecils, despite their occasional clashes, were civil and even friendly. Essex's disappointment at losing the Brest command won a sympathetic response from Robert Cecil. As it fell out, English success in that affair turned ultimately to Essex's advantage. The Queen now liquidated all her French commitments, confident that Henry could stand on his own feet. This freed English resources at a moment when intelligence of a new armada in preparation, said to be greater than the 1588 fleet, spread alarm in the English court. When the Queen, always especially sensitive to the threat of invasion, was persuaded to give her consent to a major offensive against Spain, Essex's hopes for a major command rose. The first of the three voyages which ensued was commanded by the veteran sea-dogs, Hawkins and Drake, but Essex had a hand in the enterprise. The soldiery in the expedition were commanded by the Earl's kinsman and protégé, Baskerville, and seven of the fourteen captains were members of his following.[9]

The second expedition, in 1596, offered Essex the longed-for opportunity for an achievement on the grand scale. The Queen had now agreed to an attack on the Spanish homeland. Her instructions were that her forces should do as much damage as possible to Spanish invasion preparations. That accomplished, and if conditions were favourable, they might assault a Spanish port, provide it was weakly defended. Finally, if the American plate fleet or East Indian merchantmen were heralded, they should seek to capture them. Command of the expedition was vested jointly in Essex and Lord Admiral Howard. They were supported by a council of senior officers, including Ralegh and Lord Thomas Howard.[10] Except for the Lord Admiral this was a corps of young men, of whom only Lord Thomas had actual naval experience. Although the command was a shared one, it was the Earl whose will was decisive in the first phase of the voyage.

His plan, revealed to the Queen and the Council only after he had set out, reached well beyond the goals set by the royal instructions. Confident that God had a great work for him to do, he saw his mission not as a mere harrying of Spanish naval preparations but as an effort to secure the key to victory by establishing an English base on Spanish soil. In his excited imagination it would lead to the triumphant realization of his ambitions, securing not only his fame but also his place as the architect of an achievement which would raise Elizabeth to heights of power unparalleled by her predecessors. The capture of Cadiz realized the first phase of his hopes, but the refusal of his colleagues to support his scheme for holding the city destroyed any prospect of their fruition. Essex's final effort, a proposal to send a squadron in pursuit of the plate fleet, was also vetoed by his colleagues.

In Essex's reception by the Queen on his return home there appeared the first signs of a rift between the monarch and the favourite. Instead of royal congratulations for a famous victory he was met with the Queen's sour complaint that, as she had anticipated, the expedition had been more of 'an action of honour and victory against the enemy and particular spoil to the army than any profitable to ourself'.[11] Essex's attempt to publish his own account of the voyage was suppressed at royal command. After a few weeks the royal ill temper subsided, while the news that the plate fleet had arrived home shortly after the English departure vindicated Essex's judgment and threw the blame on his colleagues' shoulders for the failure to capture it. Elizabeth's sardonic comment on Cadiz pointed up the deep gulf between her values and Essex's. 'Actions of honour' were to her mere masculine bravado, wasteful of men and money. Her pragmatic measure of success was straightforwardly material, the destruction of Spanish warships and — above all — the capture of Spanish silver. For her the glory of Cadiz was cancelled out by the failure to achieve either of these goals.

Moreover, there was a new vexation for the earl. During his absence Robert Cecil had received his long-coveted appointment as principal Secretary. This emphatic assertion of the Queen's confidence gave Cecil a new standing of his own, no longer a mere coadjutor to Burghley, but an officer of state, who could stand up as the Earl's peer among the royal Councillors. This he did in a confrontation in Council when Cecil secured the appointment of his dependant, Sir George Carew, as Commissioner for Prizes over Essex's strong objections. Allegations of corruption in the handling of booty floated about, as well as unpleasant innuendoes about the Earl's personal life.[12] The underlying rivalry between the favourite and the Secretary, inherent in their relationship since the early 1590s, now began to surface. It was heated up in the autumn when they became competitors for an important piece of patronage. Lord Cobham, Warden of the Cinque Ports, was dying. Cecil was backing his brother-in-law, the Cobham heir, for the post. Essex was promoting Robert Sidney, younger brother to the Earl's great friend, Philip. He was, as usual, intemperately insistent in his sponsorship.

Beneath these overt clashes there was a deeper and more dangerous current of suspicion and hostility. However much the Queen belittled the achievements of the past summer, they had aroused a very different response from her subjects. For them Essex was indeed 'England's glory and the wide world's wonder'. That wide acclaim was in the eyes of the Queen and the court a matter for grave concern. 'Popularity' was in sixteenth-century ears a word of sinister import, with undertones of intended sedition, even of treason. The Queen's subjects owed their loyalty solely to the sovereign. She could not tolerate that a subject should set himself up as a contestant for their affections. There could be no more be two suns in the political sky than in the heavens themselves.

Essex now commanded the loyalty of the new officer corps spawned by the war. Beyond that was his magnetic attraction for the younger generation of aristocrats, noble and gentle, who longed to seek the bubble reputation at the cannon's mouth. In the capital he was the darling of the London citizenry. Popular perception accorded him a dominating place in Council. Robert Sidney could write that 'the managing of all matters of war both by land and sea are almost in His lordship's hands'. How far popular perception went is expressed in a letter from an English clergyman in Zeeland: 'All men's eyes are upon you now at home and abroad . . . You are now expected to be as the steersman or master of the ship for counsel if God call my Lord Treasurer.'[13] To a leader of wide-ranging ambitions for himself and for the realm, the temptation to mobilize these constituencies against those ministers whose influence with the Queen thwarted his goals might be too powerful to resist. The Councillors had surely taken note of Essex's attempt to hold onto his army after returning, on the pretence of attacking Spanish-held Calais. It had not succeeded, but it was a straw in the wind. If the councillors had doubts about the reliability of their colleague, they were not assuaged by his conduct in the ensuing months.[14]

In the weeks following his return, Essex's characteristic moodiness became more marked as he alternated between elation and melancholy. The quarrel with the Cecils was made up, but the ill will remained. One of Essex's servants boasted that he 'had made the old fox crouch and whine'.[15] For a time the urgencies of the threatened Spanish fleet kept him busy, but when that crisis was past, he sank more and more into lethargy and depression, closeting himself in his chamber, refusing to attend upon the Queen. From melancholy he sank to self-pity, declining further into a persecution complex. In a surviving letter, to Lady Bacon, defending himself against reports of adultery, he goes on bitterly, 'I live in a place where I am hourly conspired against and practised upon. What they cannot make probable to the Queen that they give out to the world. They have almost all the house to serve for instruments.'[16]

In the late winter Essex talked of a long withdrawal from court by journeying to his Welsh estates. Anthony Bacon wrote that his master's health was worsened 'with just cause of undeserved discontents of mind'.[17] In March there was a duel of wills with the Queen.

> Full fourteen days His Lordship kept in; Her Majesty, as I heard, is resolved to break him of his will and to pull down his great heart, who found it a thing impossible and says he holds it from his mother's side, but all is well again and no doubt he will grow a mighty man in our state.[18]

The forecast was premature; before the same month was out there was more talk of a Welsh journey.

This fit of sulks, of sullen bad temper and paranoid suspicion was fed by a complex of causes. There was, of course, the bitter disappointment at the outcome of the 1596 expedition. More crushing still was the discovery that the Queen put little or no value on the triumph of his arms. His supreme offer of service – to raise his Queen to an imperial glory — was coldly put aside. Added to this was the overt hostility to him which surfaced within the Council. These were experiences which a more hardened politician, such as Leicester, might have shrugged off as part of the game. The delicate skin of the favourite, unused to disappointment or frustration, had not toughened sufficiently to bear these afflictions. Taken together, they had worked on him so as to expose an underlying instability. Spoiled child that he was, he had resorted to the characteristic ploy of sulky and spiteful withdrawal; he had sunk from fitful moodiness into a deepening depression in which his hold on reality was increasingly tenuous.

The events of the preceding summer no doubt fed the behaviour of the Earl, but they were entangled with a new development which took place in the winter months, about which we have only sketchy information. Another sea voyage had been in the planning stages since December, in response to reports of a second invasion fleet preparing in the Spanish ports. Essex had been consulted as to his views on the action; a joint command with the Lord Admiral was envisaged, for which a draft commission exists. However, rumours in the court had it that Essex would not be involved in the expedition, and Henry IV wrote jeeringly that 'S. M. ne laisseroit jamais son cousin d'Essex d'esloigner de son costillon' (Her Majesty would not allow her cousin of Essex away from her petticoats).[19] Essex may well have rejected another joint command with the man who had crossed his plans at Cadiz. Whatever the facts, the command was to play a major role in the dénouement which finally eventuated.

The English Achilles was finally induced to leave his tent through the ministrations of an old rival. Cecil had made overtures to the Earl, but they were rebuffed. It was Ralegh whose mediating efforts were successful in bringing about a general *entente*. It took the form of a three-sided treaty among Essex, Cecil, and Ralegh. The Earl was to have sole command of the naval expedition; Ralegh's fee for his mediatorial services was restoration to the court and to his post of Captain of the Guard. Cecil was to be rewarded with the Chancellorship of the Duchy. To this pact the Queen gave her warm approval. She commended Cecil for having made the first overture. When Essex balked because Elizabeth would not give Sidney the Wardenship of the Cinque Ports, he was soothed with a sweetener, appointment as Master of the Ordnance. The treaty settled the issue of the command and patched up the rift within the Council. At the same time, relations between the Queen and the favourite returned to smooth sailing. Just how strained they had been we cannot know; Essex seems to have been the temporary victor. In any case it was clear that Essex was to be treated as the prodigal son: in the joy of his return, past offence would be forgiven. Cecil had to accommodate himself to circumstances, even as his father had done when Elizabeth promoted Leicester thirty years earlier.

The court buzzed with the news of the *entente*. Not all took it at face value. Sir William Knollys, the Earl's uncle, wrote:

> If we live not in a cunning world, I should assure myself that Mr. Secretary were wholly yours, as seeming to rejoice at everything that may succeed well with you, and to be grieved at the contrary, and doth, as I hear, all good offices he may for you to the Queen. I pray God it may have a good foundation; and then is he very worthy to be embraced. I will hope the best, yet will I observe him as narrowly as I can.

Bacon's wry comment on the Earl's behaviour since the previous summer carried an implicit warning:

> My Lord, when I first came to you I took you for a physician who desired to cure the diseases of the state. But now I doubt you will be like to those physicians who can be content to keep their patients long, because they would always be in request.[20]

In any case the new amity between the rivals held good through the summer of 1597. When the attempt on Ferrol was foiled by bad weather, Cecil wrote hopefully of the Earl's chances of intercepting the plate fleet, adding soothingly, 'but if you bring home yourself we will not chide you'. Later he praised one of Essex's letters to the Queen, written 'more like angels than men, so much wisdom, so much caution, so much humility and providence; nay, so much good husbandry as I will keep it for a monument to your virtues'.[21] Essex limped home in October, empty-handed, battered by the same storm which scattered Philip's last armada.

Almost immediately there was a replay of the previous year's melodrama. This time the Earl, without having presented himself at court, retired to his house at Wanstead in Essex, pleading sickness. The Queen made her displeasure known, claiming his services as a Councillor but offering an olive branch if he would return. Both Hunsdon and Burghley vainly urged Essex to respond to the Queen's offer. The Lord Treasurer wrote, 'My good lord, overcome her with yielding without disparagement of your honour, and plead your own cause with your presence, whereto I will be as serviceable as any friend you have here.'[22] Another, anonymous correspondent warned him of the danger of absence: 'The greatest subject that is or ever was greatest in the prince's favour in his absence is not missed, and small discontinuance makes things that were as if they were not and breaks togetherness which gives way to wrath.'[23] Essex, he wrote, had '100,000 true hearts who wished his true contentment and the fall of them that love thee not'. Like Bacon, he insisted that Essex must shed the warrior's image for that of the courtier. The Earl remained at Wanstead, deaf to these pleas.

This time Essex's disappointment at the failure of the voyage was compounded by the Queen's criticism that he could have done more. Nor was he cheered by the news of Cecil's advancement to the Duchy office and, worse still, the young Cobham's appointment as Lord Warden. What drove him to a titanic explosion of anger was a new insult to his honour. Elizabeth had promoted Lord Admiral Howard to the Earldom of Nottingham. In the patent of promotion she cited him as the commander primarily responsible for the victory at Cadiz. Essex, incandescent with wounded pride, demanded a commission of inquiry; and even when the Queen yielded by amending the patent, he protested the change was made rather to pacify him than to admit the facts of the case. In a further concession to mollify his injured *amour propre*, the Queen appointed Essex Earl Marshal, an office of state which gave him precedence over the Admiral. Once again, for the last time as it proved, Essex bowed the Queen to his will. Restored to a calmer state, he would in the next few months surprise everyone by an astonishing *volte-face*, in which he would display himself as a self-sacrificing and public-spirited Councillor.

These two successive episodes in 1596 and 1597 bore witness to the power of Essex's attractions and his hold on the royal affections. He had exhibited all the worst traits of a spoiled child, self-pity, sulking withdrawal, peevish complaints, and, in the Nottingham affair, a fit of tantrums. His behaviour had angered the Queen, but in the end she had retreated before the gust of his fury and quieted his aggrieved pride with the grant of the Marshalcy. Twice the grave Councillor of state had relapsed into the petted court favourite and drawn on his seemingly bottomless fund of credit with the Queen.

After such a display his behaviour in the following spring of 1598 was all the more astonishing. France was drawing to a peace settlement with Spain. As that event became more and more a probablility, Elizabeth determined to send no less an envoy than her principal Secretary to France to sound out the King's intentions. Robert Cecil was by now the mainstay of her government; his father in rapidly failing health, was sinking to his grave. It is a testimony to Essex's position that he was seen as the only weighty Councillor who could stand in for Cecil in the latter's absence. In this hour of need both men put aside personal antipathies and rallied to their mistress's service. A kind of truce was drawn up. Essex was given a favoured bargain in the market for two valuable dyes, cochineal and indigo, worth (it was rumoured) £7,000.[24] In return, the Earl promised to assume Cecil's duties and protect his interests during the Secretary's absence. For the two months that Cecil was abroad, Essex diligently filled his shoes, carrying out the tasks of the Secretary's office, winning the approval of the dying father and the thanks of the son. It was a moment of unparalleled harmony. The soberly responsible conduct of the Earl in these spring months, coming after the childish exhibition of the past winter, gives a poignant tone to the history of this unhappy man, so badly miscast by historical circumstance. For an interval he had been able to achieve self-control, to halt the disintegation of his personality and display himself a mature servant of the crown.

The interlude was sadly brief. Cecil brought back the news of a peace concluded between Spain and France and a French-mediated overture from the Spanish for talks with Elizabeth's government. This development naturally led to prolonged discussion in Council as to the English response. Essex argued tenaciously against responding to the Spanish offer. He saw it as a plot to separate the English from their Netherlands ally. The argument grew warm and drew down Burghley's rebuke to the man of blood.[25] It was about this time that Essex told Lord Grey that he could not be friend to him and to Cecil; he must choose between the two; there could be no neutrality. What was becoming painfully apparent to Essex was that the beginning of peace talks, however tentative, saw the end of all his dearest hopes and ambitions for martial achievement. There would be no more grand expeditions against the ports or fleets of the Spanish King while the talks lasted. Moreover, he knew that the crisis in Ireland was now so acute that it was monopolizing all the resources of the realm. Essex, a man in his early thirties, faced the dreary prospect of rusting away in the tedium of a court life.

It was in fact the Irish question rather than the peace negotiations which led to a fateful scene in the Council, some time in July. The choice of a new deputy was urgent; the office had been vacant since Lord Burgh died in October 1597. Violence and disorder were growing daily as the country veered towards open insurrection. After the successive disasters of the past years the Irish deputyship seemed infected with a virus which was fatal to the career of any incumbent. Prospective nominees turned pale at the prospect of appointment. The Queen's preference was for Sir William Knollys, Essex's uncle and his faithful supporter in Council. The question became a factional one when the Earl pressed for the appointment of Sir George Carew, a Cecilian protégé. It was a nakedly political ploy, aimed at tactical advantage within the court and utterly disregardful of Irish needs. Knollys's career would be protected; an opponent would be removed from the court (and from the ordnance office, where he was Essex's deputy), while the blame for further disaster in Ireland would fall on the Cecilians.

When the Queen refused to listen to this proposal, the Earl lost his temper and insulted the sovereign by turning his back on her. She boxed his ears and told him to be gone and hanged. Essex, quite out of control, grasped his sword. The Admiral interposed himself. The Earl, swearing he would not endure such indignity even from Henry VIII, flung off in a rage and left for Wanstead.[26] How much the court at large knew of this scene we cannot be sure, but all were aware of the Earl's absence. For some three months the Earl absented himself from court and Council, but in the end it was he, not the Queen, who yielded. The crushing English defeat at the Yellow Ford in Ulster provided an excuse for his sullen return ('Duty was strong enough to rouse me out of my deadest melancholy'), but he refused to apologize for his absence from Council and reproached the Queen for listening to his enemies.[27]

There had been a serious effort to bring the Earl to reason. Both Knollys and Lord Keeper Egerton urged an apology, but Essex refused. 'I can neither yield myself to be guilty or this imputation laid upon me to be just.' He acknowledged his duty to the Queen but insisted she had treated him badly. 'What, cannot princes err? Cannot subjects receive wrong? I have received wrong and feel it.'[28] These words were reported to the Queen. However, some kind of submission was made; Essex returned to the Council. In the interval of Essex's absence Burghley had died, and the Secretary was uncontested first minister. Relations between him and the Earl were outwardly civil, but court opinion doubted their sincerity.

It was no longer the issue of the peace talks which now preoccupied the Council but, as in July, the Irish problem, now measurably worsened by a major military disaster to English arms. At last Elizabeth was forced to commit her government to a full-scale campaign aimed at crushing all Irish resistance. A great army was to be sent;

who was to command it? In what followed there was for Essex a tragic irony.

His pursuit of military fame had been crowned with a dangerous success. In reputation he was incontestably England's premier captain. Now, in this moment of national need, he was the only conceivable candidate for the Irish command. Duty to his Queen and his own reputation both inexorably drove him to accept the post. 'The Queen had irrevocably decreed it; the Council do passionately urge it; and I am tied by my own reputation to use no tergiversation.'[29] He accepted it with the greatest reluctance. This was a command which offered little hope of repeating the swift success of Cadiz. There would be no decisive blow, no ringing victory, but a long, slogging struggle in which experienced and skilful enemies would have the advantage. They would have to be winkled out of their fastnesses, step by weary step. There was little glory to be won and a fair prospect of humiliating failure. However, there was no alternative but to take up the heavy load.

It was not only the intrinsic difficulties of the campaign which quenched the Earl's old buoyant self-confidence, but the profound alteration in his relations with the Queen. The fatal scene in July snapped the bond which had held Elizabeth in thrall to him for a decade. Her refusal to appoint Carew to the Irish post was not a matter of first importance in itself, but it came at a moment when the Earl, deeply depressed by the move towards peace, so blighting to his own prospects, felt his power to influence policy fast waning. Given this mood, he saw the royal rejection of his nominee as yet more evidence that the Queen was turning to his enemies. The pent-up grievances of the past years exploded, but his anger was now directed not only toward his enemies in the court but towards the Queen herself. He could no longer brook being thwarted by this ageing woman who, obstinately refusing to listen to him, had frustrated his every effort to lead her and her realm along the path so clearly marked to glory and empire.

It was a fatal misstep. Elizabeth, however warm her favour to the Earl, would not tolerate this insult to her person nor the humiliation of a rebuke by a subject. Essex, having broken the taboo which shielded the royal person, compounded the offence by refusing to acknowledge he was in the wrong. Even worse, he questioned the validity of royal judgment. Denying any ambition for popularity or for his own glory, he went on to reproach the Queen: 'Princes were apt to find magna fama more dangerous than mala fama.' He sought either 'to be valued above them that are of no value or to forget the world and be forgotten by it'.[30] There was in these complaints an extraordinary strain of self-pity, yet without question the Queen's demeanour towards him was utterly changed. She now displayed a cold reserve; his complaints were brusquely dismissed and he was told to get on with his job. He was reminded that he commanded a far larger army than any of his predecessors at Dublin. Nothing was being spared that he might require to accomplish his task.

If Essex set off for Ireland gloomily presaging defeat, he left behind him a fearful Council, apprehensive as to what use he might make of the great army he now controlled. Like the Earl himself, they were caught in a trap from which they could not escape. It was imperative that the rebellion be crushed before Spanish forces appeared in the island. There was no other commander to whom they could turn, yet, knowing his animosity towards many of them, and aware of his popularity with the populace at large, they were terrified that he might divert the army, or part of it, to coerce the court. All may have dreaded this outcome, but some, according to the historian Camden, were, with Machiavellian deviousness, deliberately pressing his appointment in the expectation that he would fail and thus destroy himself.[31]

Nor were their fears unjustified. Before his departure Essex had sought out the medieval precedents relevant to the Earl Marshal's office. According to some sources he consulted, the Marshal (and the Constable, an office to which Essex had pretensions by right of birth) held a watching brief against abuse of the royal office by the incumbent, and were even entitled to arrest a erring monarch. While the Earl was in Dublin, he proposed to his stepfather, Sir Christopher Blount, and his intimate friend, the Earl of Southampton, that he take part of the army and return to Wales. With a base there he could march on the court. His counsellors were urgent in dissuading him from such a course. At the most, if he would go, he should take only enough men for his own protection. The Earl yielded to this advice and did nothing.[32]

At home there was a large-scale mobilization, officially occasioned by a threatened Spanish fleet, but some observers thought the real purpose was 'to show some that are absent that others can be followed as well as they and military service directed as if they were present'. (Cecil too could summon military support if the need arose.)[33] Camden asserts that the Queen said 'he [Essex] had something else in his mind than to do his prince service in Ireland', and the historian adds, 'I know not on what jealousy and suspicion'.[34]

In the end Essex fulfilled his own doom-laden prophecies and gratified the hopes of his enemies. He went to Ireland with precise instructions as to campaign strategy. His assigned objective was the destruction of Tyrone; to that end he was to carry out a pincer operation, trapping the Irish leader between his own army coming up from Dublin, another force landed at Lough Foyle on the northern Ulster coast, and a third assault from Connaught. Squeezed in the triple arms of the English embrace, Tyrone would be crushed.

Essex, instead of a prompt march northwards, undertook, on local advice, an expedition southwards into Munster, postponing Ulster to a later date. The Lough Foyle enterprise fell through for lack of ships (whether Essex or the home government were responsible is not clear). The Queen, disgusted with Essex's failure to confront the main enemy, angrily ordered him to delay no longer in assailing Tyrone. There was by now in Essex's letters from Ireland a rising hysteria, occasioned by his conviction that enemies at home were stabbing him in the back. He was unsparing in his reproaches against the Queen.

> But why do I talk of victory or success? Is it not known that from England I have received nothing but discomforts and soul's wounds? Is it not spoken in the army that Your Majesty's favour is diverted from me and that already you do bode ill both to me and to it?

Her response and that of the Privy Council were contemptuously dismissive of his allegations.[35]

Prodded by Elizabeth, Essex finally marched north, not, however, to engage Tyrone, but to parley with him. The Earls met, unattended, in a long conference, the outcome of which was a six-week truce, renewable to the following spring. Essex immediately left Ireland and sped with all haste to the court, bursting into the Queen's presence unannounced, with the mire of the journey still on him. Momentarily she smiled on him, but by that evening she gave orders to confine him to his chamber.

What followed seems in historical retrospect to have been preordained, but it did not appear so to contemporaries. In view of past experience, when the sinner had been absolved and restored to grace so many times, it seemed unimaginable that the well of favour had indeed dried up. After months of detention, Essex's case was heard by an *ad hoc* body, the Council augmented by a clutch of peers and four judges. Condemned on a variety of charges, ranging from incompetence to disobedience, he was suspended from most of his offices, genteelly confined for a time, and then dismissed into country exile,

Map 4: The Earl of Essex in Ireland

forbidden the court. The Earl wavered between humble submission to the royal will and continuing resentment at what he saw as unjust treatment. There were a few half-hearted royal concessions, but the acid test of Elizabeth's intentions came when Essex applied for the renewal of the sweet wines customs farm, a major source of his income and the main support of his credit with lenders. Elizabeth's harshly phrased refusal, 'an unruly horse must be abated of his provender, that he may be the easilier and better managed', spelled financial catastrophe; it also affirmed in a publicly humiliating way his utter and final disgrace.[36]

The blow loosened even more what hold the Earl still had on rationality. Convinced that his implacable enemies sought not only his disgrace but his life, he attempted a coup. In February 1601, gathering his supporters in his London residence, he proposed to storm the court, to remove the evil counsellors who were poisoning the Queen's mind against him and to force her to hear his cause. This feckless venture failed before it even got under way, and Essex speedily trod the path from prison, to trial, to the headsman's block.

For the Queen the whole sequence of events, from the stormy scene of July 1598 to the final act at the Tower in February 1601, acted out the most grievous episode in her life. She had bestowed her favour and affection on the young Earl, showered him with gifts and raised him to a high place in Council. She had expected in return his attendance on her person, the pleasure of his company, and the incense of his flattering devotion. She had been willing to put up with the moods, sulks, and occasional tantrums of this wayward man, and to yield to his importunate insistence on having his own way.

Elizabeth had also been willing to give him the coveted commands of the 1596–7 voyages, although she had been far from satisfied with the results, reproaching him for his itch for mere vainglory, leaving undone the real tasks of the expeditions. His neurotic behaviour in the autumns of 1596 and 1597 further strained the relationship, yet in the end all was forgiven and he was gratified with the Earl Marshal's office. His utter loss of self-control in July 1598 must have been the most painful experience of Elizabeth's adult life. The man who broke the taboo of royal inviolability was the pampered darling to whom so much had been given – and forgiven. His conduct had shattered the carefully nurtured fiction of the courtly romance, the devoted knight who displayed his lady's colours in the lists of accession day. For the first time in her life, Elizabeth had miscalculated her power to dominate another human being and to force him into the mould shaped by her own overwhelming ego. A personal tragedy for Elizabeth, it had very nearly been a political catastrophe for the realm. Only Essex's failure of nerve and bad judgment had averted an overt attack on the regime.

Essex's self-destructive act had cleared the stage for his rival. The Earl's exile from court left Robert Cecil without a peer within the Council. Neither of the senior Councillors, Buckhurst (now Lord Treasurer) nor Nottingham, were men of driving ambition; the rest of the Councillors were mere bureaucrats or courtiers. Cecil had won the game, more through his rival's ineptitude than by actively campaigning against the Earl. He may well have insinuated his fears of Essex's popularity in the Queen's ears, but the strength of his position lay in his indispensability to the Queen. He had taken Burghley's place as her man of business in domestic and foreign affairs and in the management of the Irish war. He was more truly sole minister of the crown than anyone since Thomas Cromwell. Cecil carried these burdens with ease, collaborating with Mountjoy in the successful conclusion of the Ulster war and keeping the peace negotiations (just barely) alive. At the same time he was already forging links with the prince who he knew would soon be his master.

33

The Queen and Ireland

A theme consistently reiterated in this book has been how many of the problems which circumstances thrust on the Queen's unwilling shoulders were a legacy from her predecessors. Some, like the question of religion or relations with Scotland, were, at the moment of accession, too urgent and too grave for delay. Ireland, initially less exigent in its demands, would reveal its unfolding complexities and their sheer intractability year by year, down to the last days of the reign.[1]

The nature of Irish problems was shaped by ancient circumstances and by a modern decision to alter them. The English conquest, begun four centuries earlier, had long since lost impetus. Ireland, where the English king bore the ambiguous title of lord, remained largely outside English domination. Dublin and the small area around it, the Pale, were English in culture and institutions, but in most of Leinster and Munster there was only a thin veneer of anglicization. The descendants of the Anglo-Norman Earls of Desmond, Ormond, and Kildare held sway over a society in which English influence only slightly diluted the older culture, while in most of the rest of the island the ancient Gaelic society remained untouched by the alien conqueror.

In the late fifteenth and early sixteenth centuries Ireland had lain on the periphery of English political consciousness. The English crown had been content to follow a policy of *laissez-faire* in the governance of its lordship of Ireland. The office of lord deputy had been entrusted to successive Earls of Kildare. Under the leadership of these great Old English[2] magnates, the government of Ireland at every level had been entirely in the hands of an Irish-born elite, and a rough equilibrium had existed between the two separate communities,

English and Gaelic. This era came to an end in the 1520s and 1530s with the gradual reassertion of effective royal control. After the crushing of a Kildare revolt in 1534, the English crown set about a deliberate expansion of royal authority throughout the whole island. Various factors lay behind this shift — Thomas Cromwell's efforts to extinguish all peripheral autonomy, fear of foreign intervention in the island, and, of course, the implementation of the Reformation. The new policy soon acquired a momentum of its own, although movement was slow and spasmodic. The change in title in 1541 — from Lord to King of Ireland — symbolized the coming of a new order.

The realization of this royal goal required two large-scale and fundamental changes in the Irish world. First, the feudal autonomy of the great earldoms, where royal authority barely penetrated, would have to be abolished. They would have to go the way of the marcher lords of the Welsh and Scottish borders. This meant establishing the ordinary machinery of English government, the law courts and the shire with its attendant officers. Secondly, there had to be a metamorphosis of Gaelic society. The native Irish had to suffer a disruption of their whole way of life. They were required to abandon the world of clanship, with all its interlocked ties of personal dependence and superiority, of property rights, and of military obligation; in short, the whole social order was to be demolished. The Gaels would have to learn a new language, wear a new style of clothing, even cut their hair in a different fashion and — with the coming of Protestantism — change their religion. Their chiefs were to become respectable nobles or country gentry, their clansmen tenant farmers. Irishmen must transform themselves into Englishmen.

These were the tasks the English governors set themselves; the goal was clear, but what strategies were to be employed to realize it? And — the corollary question — what means were available to turn these paper goals into solid social and political fact? The second question was easier to answer than the first. The government at Dublin had a bare trickle of income, hardly enough to cover its running expenses, and no more than a few hundred armed men to back up its commands. Whatever resources were needed for the task must come from England. This was a governing condition which narrowly constrained every action of the English governors.

The larger question, that of strategy, evoked a spectrum of proposed responses. All agreed that the body politic was diseased. How was it to be treated? One school of diagnosticians, largely Old English Palesmen, took the optimistic view that a steady application of mild therapy would suffice. This meant the gradual extension of the English legal and administrative institutions which already existed in the Pale. Tribal units would be replaced by counties and a concerted effort made to persuade the Gaelic elite to abandon the ambiguities of Irish customary law for the certainties of a royally granted land title, a change of far more than mere legal consequence since it would effectively destroy their chieftaincies, transforming them into mere landlords and their clansmen into tenants. The latter's personal dependence on the chief would end; they would now owe him only rent. Their loyalty and obedience would be owed solely to the crown and its officers. The proponents of this strategy based their hopes on the intrinsic appeal of what was to them a demonstrably superior social system, bestowing the blessings of order and civil peace.

This moderate course of treatment was attacked as inadequate to the malady, particularly by the growing colony of emigrant English officials whose numbers were increasing rapidly from the 1550s on. There were divergences of opinion in their ranks. Some called for radical surgery; they were convinced that peaceful transformation of the old order was impossible. It could only be dealt with by force; a work of demolition must precede reconstruction. Others regarded coercion as an instrument to be held in reserve if milder measures failed. An interesting variant was a scheme for colonization, for establishing immigrant English communities in Ireland which would act as models of 'civility' for the Irish to imitate. Some few envisaged a wholesale displacement of population, such as future colonists would undertake in North America. More commonly, the intention was to substitute for the existing elite a new class of English landlords, retaining the present cultivators as tenants. The necessary corollary of such a policy was an influx of new English settlers.

Elements of all these alternatives were visible in English conduct from the 1540s onwards. During that decade, Deputy St Leger pursued a policy of persuasion, but in 1547 he was replaced by a succession of deputies who over the next decade alternated between the carrot and the stick. In Leix and Offaly a first attempt at colonization was carried out; two fortified centres were surrounded by a settlement of English soldier-farmers who would be a nucleus of English 'civility' as well as a forceful manifestation of royal power in the whole area. During these years a substantial army was employed, kept busy in suppressing the revolts which the plantation policy provoked. All this was a heavy drain on the English treasury, where Ireland was becoming a permanent budget item. Consequently, when funds ran short,

the Dublin government pulled back its horns and took a more conciliatory line. Persuasion and coercion alternated with the flow of money
from England.

The shift to a more aggressive line of action in Ireland coincided
with the arrival of a new cast of characters on the Dublin stage,
immigrants from England, led by a high-placed English nobleman.
When Thomas Radcliffe, Earl of Sussex, was appointed Deputy in
1556, he brought in his train a clientage of relatives and friends who
would play a major role in Irish affairs for the next several decades;
many would settle in the island. This invasion heralded the recognition that Ireland was a land of opportunity for Englishmen who,
for reasons of birth or circumstance, were denied advancement
at home. They proved to be only the first contingent of a large
and ever-growing migration, the first beginnings of the English
ascendancy.

Moreover, this was a movement closely connected with the court.
Sussex, its first noble patron, soon became the voluble leader of the
anti-Dudley faction at court. The favourite, in responding to the challenge, assailed his rival's career in Ireland and himself set up as a
patron of the immigrants. His dependants – or Sussex's – would fill
the Deputyship for most of the years down to the end of the 1580s.
The consequence, of greatest importance to Irish affairs, was the
emergence of a new and potent interest group, the New English.
Hustling, greedy, ruthless, they sought to found their family fortunes
as a new ruling elite, in the process displacing the Old English elite
even as they set out to destroy the Gaelic chieftains.

This was the situation which Elizabeth faced at her accession. The
momentum for expanding English rule set in motion by her predecessors could not be halted; royal authority, once asserted, had to
be sustained by further measures. However, there was no urgency
requiring immediate action. Recent experience was not a helpful guide
for the future. The carrot-and-stick policy pursued in the preceding
decades had proved both costly and inconclusive. So matters could be
allowed to drift, shaped by events rather than by policy.

The two adjectives – costly and inconclusive – might well sum up
the history of the English regime in Ireland for much of Elizabeth's
reign. Some £1,300,000 laid out in Ireland between 1534 and 1572[3]
gave little to show in terms of diminished violence or increased civil
order. As far as the Queen's own role in this ill success goes, much
has to be ascribed to the force of circumstance. Events in Ireland
reached her through a kind of sound barrier, muted by distance and

the lapse of time. Perverse winds or howling gales might delay ship crossings for weeks at a time. Among her chief officers of state the Irish Deputy was the one most rarely in face-to-face contact. Information reached her through his letters, but was also filtered through many sources, members of the Dublin council, and interested parties in her own court and Council; but her Irish subjects were hard put to get a hearing at the court. The Gaels had virtually no one to speak for them, although Tyrone did for a time look to Leicester as a protector. The Old English were a little better off, since they had a spokesman with some clout in the Earl of Ormond, the Queen's distant kinsman and the one Irish nobleman at home in the court. Hence decisions about Irish affairs more often served the purposes of English politicians than the interests of the Queen's Irish subjects, English- or Gaelic-speaking. In general, Ireland, its people, and their problems got a hearing from the Queen only when events there forced themselves by their sheer urgency upon her reluctant attention.

There was also a lack of urgency which differentiated the Irish theatre from other areas of royal concern. The isolation of the island from the mainstream of European politics meant that, until the latter years of the reign, events there had little resonance outside the Queen's dominions. Ireland, unlike Scotland, did not trigger off threatening responses from the Continental monarchs which in turn compelled a reaction. Consequently, when the prospect of large outlays to deal with Irish unrest reared its ugly head, it became more sensible to come to a face-saving compromise with an offending chieftain and to postpone a showdown to a later time.

Elizabeth's indifference to Ireland and its affairs left a vacuum which was filled, at least in part, by the initiatives of her Deputies at Dublin. The Queen could turn her attention elsewhere, but the Irish government, on the other hand, was charged with the day-to-day running of sketchy and inadequate administrative machinery in the counties under English control, while pushing ahead with the herculean task of expanding its control in the other provinces. These imposed immediate problems which could not be shirked. Here the Queen's limitations as a ruler were acutely felt. Her pragmatic short-term vision could not be brought to focus on longer-term needs. Her preoccupation with immediate problems and her obsession with cutting costs made it impossible to attract her interest to long-range planning. Consequently, while her Deputies were left with considerable freedom in devising ways to meet needs to which the Queen was in principle willing to accede, her support was easily diverted when the question of expense loomed, or when rivals at court or the Old English party in Dublin dissuaded her from action.

The Deputies who governed the island from the late 1550s down to the late 1580s were men of large views who strove to deal with the long-term structural problems which had to be resolved if Ireland was to be reduced to obedience. The first of them, Sussex, already in office at Elizabeth's accession, was continued and indeed promoted to Lord Lieutenant, but his larger programmes of action were sidetracked by the immediate pressures of a turbulent and ambitious Gaelic prince, Shane O'Neill, the great lord of Ulster. Sussex's fruitless and costly campaigns gave ammunition to his court rival, Leicester, and lost him the royal confidence. When Sussex returned discomfited in 1564 he was followed at Dublin by another English politician, but one of lesser political stature. Sir Henry Sidney was brother-in-law to both Sussex and Leicester. He had come to Ireland under the wing of the former lord, but now judged it politic to shift his allegiance to the favourite. Sidney had spent considerable time in Ireland before his appointment as Lord President of Wales. He now returned with a programme for governing the dominion entrusted to him.

The most significant of Sidney's schemes was his plan to establish regional governments, presidencies modelled on the Council in the Welsh Marches and the Council of the North. A president, with a council of local notables, would exercise justice and give a backbone to the fledgling county governments being set up in the Gaelic areas. This would provide a framework within which the process of anglicization could be advanced. The president would have a small force at his command, but the essence of the strategy was to establish a consensual transformation to a new order.

After a hopeful start things began to go wrong. The Queen declined to confirm Sidney's nominee for the Munster presidency because of protests by the Old English, and then refused funds for a replacement. Unluckily, Sidney's actions had been sufficient to rouse an open revolt under a cadet of the Desmond house which involved much of the province. Similar risings took place in the Connaught presidency and in eastern Leinster.[4] Sidney's energies were siphoned off in the suppression of these disturbances. The presidencies, intended to be vehicles of civil rule, became largely martial in character. In Ulster Sidney was compelled to fight another campaign against the irrepressible Shane O'Neill. The latter's lands were ravaged although it was defeat in battle by the rival chieftain, O'Donnell, and his death at the hands of Scots mercenaries which eliminated him from the scene.

His fortunate death relieved the regime of a dangerous enemy, but a prospective settlement of Ulster in the wake of O'Neill's defeat was abandoned as soon as the scale of costs became visible. The O'Neill regime was reconstituted under a new chieftain.

When Sidney returned to England he was replaced as Deputy at Dublin by a protégé of Sussex. Sir William Fitzwilliam, also brother-in-law to Sidney, had been an Irish office-holder since 1556. Once again, the key Irish appointment was determined by the twists and turns of English politics, a symbol of the Queen's fundamental indifference to Irish affairs, where she allowed the initiative in appointment to remain in the hands of the court factions. Fitzwilliam was sent over with the usual royal instructions for strict economy. Dismayed by the heavy cost and lack of success in the introduction of the presidencies, the Queen now listened to proposals for experiments in which the cost could be shifted to private shoulders — colonization.

A beginning had been made in a scheme to establish an Ulster settlement in the wake of O'Neill's death. The backers had included a cluster of Leicester protégés, a contingent of West Country gentry, and some London merchant interests. The scheme fell through, significantly, when the Queen refused to pay for a garrison to protect the projected colony.[5] Another scheme, for a Munster settlement,[6] similarly failed to win royal financial support, but the agitation for these enterprises did lead to the formation of a Privy Council committee on Ireland. That in turn opened the way for an actual settlement, Sir Thomas Smith's colony in the Ards in County Down.[7] Smith was second Secretary of State and a Privy Councillor. He solved the problem of finance by raising private capital through a joint stock subscription (to which Cecil was a subscriber). Although several hundred participants went out to Ulster under Smith's son and, after his death, under Smith's brother, the project, faced by bitter local hostility, came to nothing.

A more ambitious scheme was launched by Walter Devereux, Earl of Essex, with a measure of royal backing; the Queen granted him a loan, secured by a mortgage on his estates. This venture was no more successful than Smith's and had to be bailed out by the crown, to the tune of some £80,000 spent on soldiers' pay.[8] The effect of these ill-starred attempts at colonization was to convince the backers that military conquest must precede colonization. That necessarily meant royal expenditure; only 'a prince's power and purse' could accomplish it. Yet Elizabeth remained as adamant as ever in her refusal to provide money for Irish purposes. Nevertheless, these experiments had hardened Gaelic opinion into a growing conviction that nothing less than confiscation of their lands and their own expulsion was aimed at.

The mounting costs of Irish government laid Fitzwilliam open to attack by the Leicester interest. He was recalled and Sidney returned as Deputy in 1575; but in order to win royal consent to his appointment, Sir Henry had to outbid competitors. The parsimonious monarch was won by his promise to make Ireland self-sufficient in three years, providing his pump was primed with a £40,000 subsidy and an army of 1,100 men.[9] Financial self-sufficiency would be accomplished by a new permanent, fixed land tax, the composition, to replace the old arbitrary levy, the cess. With much difficulty compositions were established in Munster and Connaught, but in the Pale organized protest by a delegation of lawyers persuaded the Queen to spare Leinster. Her confidence in Sidney waned as his expenditures soared beyond his estimates, and in March 1578 he was recalled for the last time.

For twenty years Elizabeth had given her half-hearted support to schemes for structural change in Irish government whose advocates promised both a settled peace and a long-term reduction of costs. In practice, the resistance which these schemes called forth made for repeated emergency demands on the royal purse. These the Queen had usually met, however grudgingly, but she adamantly refused proposals which would have forced her to long-term financial commitments, such as permanent garrisons or provincial bureaucracies. The result was mutual disillusionment. The Queen pointed to a country racked by endemic disorder and ever-mounting costs. The discontented Deputies, on their side, remained convinced that, had money been forthcoming, their policies would have succeeded. The Old English were increasingly disgruntled as they saw themselves shoved aside by the newcomers. The Old Irish viewed the intentions of the English government with ever-increasing distrust.

In the immediate wake of Sidney's departure a more moderate policy was pursued; concessions were made to local opinion. However, just at this moment, in 1579, the peace was shattered by the landing of a papally backed expedition led by a Desmond cadet, James Fitzmaurice. He was soon killed; a second, and larger, papal force which arrived in 1580 was trapped and massacred. The effort to raise a religious revolt failed, but in the volatile condition of Munster affairs the expedition served to trigger off a general rising of the discontented, both Old English and Gaelic, who resented the new extension of English power. The Earl of Desmond, exasperated by what he regarded as persecution, was drawn into rebellion and was followed, in a separate rising, by another Old English magnate, Lord Baltinglass, in Leinster. The long-drawn-out campaign of repression in Munster was graphically described by Spenser. In his words, Deputy Lord Grey was 'a bloody man who regarded not the life of Her Majesty's subjects no more than dogs, but had wasted and consumed all so now she had almost nothing left but to reign in their ashes'.[10] At the same time Grey had initiated a virtual reign of terror in the Pale which had aroused bitter opposition among the Old English. These events went far towards alienating the Old English interest, placing them in polar opposition to the New English immigrants. The growing influence of the latter in turn encouraged a policy of coercion.

By the 1580s, the obstacle which the great feudal lordships offered to English rule had been eliminated by the destruction of Desmond and the taming of Ormond. In Connaught, at the cost of considerable violence, but with the cooperation of the local earls, Clanricard and Thomond, English rule had been successfully rooted. With the skeleton of effective government in place in Leinster and Connaught and Munster's opposition broken, the completion of the English conquest in these provinces might have seemed within sight. The colonization of the forfeited Desmond lands was to be the next step forward in the process. The great unresolved problem was still Ulster, which, still untamed, remained outside effective English authority.

During these episodes the Queen, moved by Old English appeals, had more than once cast a critical eye on the abrasive conduct of her officers,[11] and after the suppression of the Desmond revolt had issued a general pardon (which was generally thwarted by the bloodthirsty Grey). A conciliatory move was the appointment of an Old English nobleman, Ormond, to replace Grey in command in Munster, where he mopped up the last remnants of resistance. Elizabeth was shrewd enough to discount the partisanship of the New English leaders, but, apart from these occasional gestures, she let affairs in Ireland take their bloody course.

Something of a new start was made when the Queen appointed Sir John Perrot as Deputy in 1584. A royal favourite and a protégé of Leicester, Perrot had had extensive experience in the island as president of Munster. He had won a reputation as a ruthless but fair-minded administrator. He now proposed to treat Irish- and English-born with equal impartiality. The Queen 'should govern Ireland equally, balancing her subjects according to their due desserts without respect of nation as having interest in God from them all alike'. He was soon at loggerheads with the New English officials at Dublin, while his influence with the Old English was not sufficient to pass his legislative programme through the Irish Parliament, where the Old English could still mount an effective opposition.[12]

Perrot's departure in 1588, to become a Privy Councillor, came at a highly unfortunate and potentially dangerous juncture of Irish affairs. The Old English community was drawing apart in sullen discontent, loyal still to the crown but in aggrieved retreat before the aggression of the New English. That party in turn, arrogant and greedily ambitious, painted their rivals as the enemies of religion and secretly disloyal to the Queen, whatever protestations they might make. At the same time a new uncertainty was rising in the one great surviving Gaelic lordship, Ulster, where the young Hugh O'Neill was pushing aside the old chieftain, Sir Turlough Luineach O'Neill, to assert his leadership in the province. Politically sophisticated, ardently ambitious, the young O'Neill was regarded by the English with a mixture of respect and apprehension. So far his behaviour had been highly correct, and the Queen had granted his desire by recognizing him as rightful holder of the family Earldom of Tyrone. Perrot and his successor, Fitzwilliam, had been instructed to keep on good terms with him.

Perrot's regime coincided with another, external event which would prove crucial for the course of Irish affairs – the coming of war with Spain in 1585. Ireland necessarily fell to the lowest priority on the English government's agenda. It was imperative that Irish waters be kept unruffled and that expenditure be pared to the bone. Yet, on the other hand, the war also gave the Queen new cause for worry about her wayward western realm. General fear of foreign intervention had stirred uneasily in the consciousness of English rulers since Henry VIII's time. They became sharply focused now, when it seemed all too probable Spain might imitate the English example by intervening in Ireland as its foe had done in the Low Countries. The choice of Sir William Fitzwilliam for a return engagement as Deputy proved an unfortunate one. His service in Ireland dated back to Sussex's time, and he had already served a term as Deputy between 1571 and 1575. In his earlier term he had the patronage of Sussex behind him, but that Earl was now dead, and the appointment of this sixty-year-old was a kind of *pis aller*, when other potential talent was required for the war.

It is hard to avoid the impression that during these early war years Ireland fell victim to increasing neglect by the Queen and her Councillors as their attention was diverted elsewhere. That neglect was doubly unfortunate because Fitzwilliam, early in his term, fell out with the New English party and then, by a fatally miscalculated act, aroused the deepest fears of the Old Irish community. More and more the regime at Dublin was rent by bitter internecine quarrels which divided its counsels at a time when the Earl of Tyrone, suspicious and fearful, was lurching towards direct collision with the English rulers.

Fitzwilliam's first quarrel was with Sir Richard Bingham, Governor of Connaught. That high-handed commander, in crushing revolt in northern Connaught, fell out with the Deputy, who rebuked the severity of Bingham's measures against the local Irish, appealing to Elizabeth's recommendation for a 'temperate course of government'.[13] Bingham appealed to his patron at court, Walsingham, from whom Fitzwilliam received a thorough dressing-down; the quarrel was only checked by the Queen when renewed trouble in the west forced their cooperation, but the antagonism remained to surface again. Another episode in the running warfare between moderates and hardliners, it was testimony to the chaos of English government in the island, in which inferior officers found it all too easy to go over their nominal chief's head to a patron at court.

The dispute with Bingham was an internal affair within the establishment, but the issue — what course to take with the Gaelic aristocracy — was a larger one. It arose in a different form in an episode in the borderlands of Ulster, County Monaghan.[14] When the local chieftain, Sir Hugh Ross MacMahon, died, dispute arose as to his rightful successor; the Deputy initially gave judgment for a certain Hugh Roe MacMahon. However, within a few months Fitzwilliam turned on the new chieftain, charging him first with cattle-raiding and then with treason. The case was referred to London and the Queen ordered MacMahon 'should be deprived of his lands, but not prosecuted'. Later the Privy Council authorized a trial. The Deputy set off for Monaghan with his unsuspecting prisoner, held a surprise trial, condemned and hanged him. MacMahon's lands were divided among a number of claimants, all holding directly from the crown. This effectually destroyed the chieftaincy and the clan's very existence. Similar action had followed Bingham's suppression of the O'Rourke rebellion in the west, but there it was punishment for active resistance. Here, so Irish opinion believed, the charges were trumped up, with MacMahon the victim of English treachery and the Deputy's greed.

The other Irish chieftains saw the operation as a trial run for a procedure which could destroy their whole order. A popular curse against an enemy was 'God send him the MacMahon lordship'.[15] English officials would in fact cite the Monaghan case as a prototype for future action.[16] Tyrone, to whom the late MacMahon had been a client, was deeply disturbed, and would cite this case as prime evidence of English perfidy. Russell, Fitzwilliam's successor, would write that this affair was 'the very seed of all our troubles'. Fitzwilliam had destroyed his standing among the Old Irish; worse still, he had roused the deepest suspicions about the intentions of the English governors.

The English determination to destroy the whole clan system by eliminating the chieftains and transforming the lesser men into tenants of the crown, portended by Bingham's actions in the west as well as the Monaghan affair, pushed the Gaelic lords more and more towards open defiance of the government. These developments came just at the moment when the greatest of the Gaelic leaders, Tyrone, was manœuvring himself into a position of maximum strength in Ulster. Master of the O'Neill inheritance, as the power of the old chieftain, Sir Turlough, declined, he reached out to form an alliance with the rival regional lord, O'Donnell of Tyrconnel, who now became his son-in-law. Tyrone, knowledgeable in English political ways, had no desire to break with the government, but, patronless since the death of Leicester, he was anxious to secure the strongest possible bargaining position *vis-à-vis* the English. He was determined to exclude from Ulster any effective official presence which would lessen his hold over his clientage.

During the next two years Tyrone walked a tightrope between the Dublin authorities and his Gaelic allies. He had powerful enemies at Dublin, who blackened his reputation at court and wanted to proceed against him as a traitor; but the Queen, her resources strained by war in France and the Low Countries, refused to allow the use of force against him. Temporary truces were patched up, although by this time Tyrone's distrust was so great that he refused to deal with the Deputy. He had now joined the other Gaelic leaders in an approach to Spain, although he was careful to let the government know these contacts. More important still, he was systematically training his soldiers in professional tactics, proposing to field an army which could face the English in open combat.

This dangerous game was encouraged by the feebleness of the English. Fission within the Irish council, intrigues against the Deputy, and the Queen's determination, burdened as she was, not to spend money in Ireland, encouraged the Earl to a more and more inflexible position and to larger and larger demands in his bargaining with Dublin. Elizabeth was receiving contradictory advice from the divergent factions in the Irish council; some held on to the hopes of an accommodation with Tyrone; others argued that only force would bring him to submission; the Queen, although insistent that he acknowledge his delinquency, clung to the hope of an accommodation. However, knowledge of Spanish contacts, as well as reports of a new armada assembling in Spain, alarmed her enough to augment the Irish garrison with experienced soldiers. When the capitulation of the Spanish fort at Brest ended her French involvement, she ordered part of the force to proceed directly to Ireland under their veteran commander, Sir John Norris, who was now given military command in the island.

This measure was stultified by the quarrel which soon sprang up between Norris and the new Deputy. Sir William Russell had taken over from Fitzwilliam in 1594. The latter had been begging for recall; his health was declining and he was quarrelling with his council. He had in addition lost the trust of Tyrone. A commentator summed up Fitzwilliam as a man whose 'experience made him able to know but his years did disable him to execute what he knew and to do what was requisite for so stirring a state'.[17] Russell had fought in Ireland under Grey and then served in the Low Countries under Leicester. Unemployed since his patron's death, he came to Ireland without major administrative experience or close acquaintance with the island's affairs. He seems to have had no reliable patron at court. On his arrival he faced a rapidly deteriorating situation. There was open warfare with Tyrone, who in February 1595 seized the English fort on the Blackwater on the Ulster borders; in May Enniskillen castle fell to the Irish; and in the same month they badly mauled in open-field fighting an English relief force at Clontibret.

In the face of open defiance, English policy faltered at every level. Russell and Norris quarrelled, each blaming the other and giving contradictory advice to London. The Queen, preparing the Cadiz expedition, wanted peace in Ireland at almost any cost. She insisted on a gesture from Tyrone; 'his proud heart' must come down 'to stand absolutely to Her Majesty's mercy', but 'mercy would not be denied him'.[18] In practical terms she was prepared to withdraw her garrisons from Armagh and Tyrconnel and tacitly to allow freedom of conscience for Catholics.[19] After wearisome negotiations Tyrone deigned to accept the royal pardon in July 1596. He was in fact now negotiating with the Spanish, a fact known to London. The Queen remained unmoved in her demands for a settlement. Robert Cecil rebuked Russell for having predicted that war would ensue in Ireland; Norris and the Irish Secretary, Fenton, were praised for their peace-making efforts. The Queen was still willing to believe in Tyrone's innocence if he would submit. Bingham, the obdurate hardliner in Connaught, was disgraced; his successor was given no additional soldiers and told to make his government self-supporting. In 1597 both Russell and Norris were recalled. The Queen summed up the Deputy's administration: 'as is too apparent to the whole world there never any realm was worse governed by all our ministers from the highest to the lowest'.[20] The Queen's vehement determination to keep the peace in Ireland at any price was, of course, conditioned by the demands made by the Cadiz expedition, and by the dearth which three years of failed harvest had produced in both islands. But it made her unable to face the unpalatable fact that Ireland was poised on the brink of a general insurrection.

The appointment of a successor to Russell reflected the fact that Ireland still stood low in the Queen's regard. Indeed, by now the Irish appointment was seen as the graveyard of careers, and potential appointees shrank away in dismay. The new Deputy, Lord Burgh, was a soldier who had served as governor of Brill, one of the cautionary towns in the Low Countries, but he had no experience of large command and no previous connection with Ireland. He had large ambitions, but inadequate resources quickly clipped his wings, and he had to resume the defensive posture which left much of Ulster and Connaught largely in rebel control. His career was cut short by death a bare six months after his arrival. Even now, with Tyrone in arms and unrest spreading outside Ulster, the Queen backed away from any firm policy in Ireland. French peace moves made the future uncertain, while the dearth continued to cripple the mobilization of an army. No new Deputy was appointed; a temporary commission composed of Archbishop Loftus and Chief Justice Gardiner held office for nearly two years. Ordered to reopen negotiations with Tyrone, they found he was raising his terms higher than ever. 'It is the alteration of the government and the State that he aimeth at,' declared the Dublin council.[21]

Slowly, however, the Queen and her ministers began to face the need for a large-scale, all-out effort. Preparations were put in hand to land a force on the north coast of Ulster at Lough Foyle to assault Tyrone's back door, but before it sailed there was news of an overwhelming defeat suffered by English arms. A relief force sent to the isolated English fort on the Blackwater was ambushed and wiped out at the battle of the Yellow Ford in August 1598. In its wake open rebellion flared in Leinster and Munster. This calamity finally jolted the Queen into decisive action. Fortunately, the Peace of Vervins opened the way for negotiations with Spain, while the Dutch had agreed to bear the main financial burden in the Low Countries. An army of 16,000 foot and 1,300 horse was to be mobilized — 'a royal army, paid, furnished in other sort than any king of this land hath done before'.[22] No expense was to be spared.

The awkward question was the choice of a commander. He needed to be of great reputation and high rank — England's premier soldier. Essex was, of course, the obvious choice. The problems which surrounded that choice have been discussed elsewhere (see Chapter 32). They cast a shadow over the expedition from its very inception. Essex assumed the post with the utmost reluctance, convinced that his enemies had the Queen's ear and bewailing his loss of her confidence. Doubtful of success, he prophesied failure before he set out. Nothing went right; the three-pronged strategy — an assault on Armagh by the Deputy, a landing at Lough Foyle on the north coast, and an attack on Tyrconnel from northern Connaught — went entirely astray. The army of the western commander, Sir Conyers Clifford, was overwhelmed and he was killed. No ships could be found for Lough Foyle. Essex himself, commanded by the Queen to attack Tyrone, instead parleyed with him and patched up yet another truce. Returning home, he was rebuffed by the Queen, stripped of his office, and his political career ended.

Who was to succeed him in Ireland? The need was more desperate than ever. The Queen's eye fell this time on another young soldier, to whom she had warmed earlier in his career. The charms of Charles Blunt, Lord Mountjoy, an impoverished baron of ancient descent, had once awakened Essex's jealousy although they had later become fast friends. An eager soldier, Mountjoy had served in the Low Countries, captained a ship in 1588 and campaigned with Norris in Brittany. In 1597 he commanded the land forces on the islands voyage. This time Elizabeth's choice proved as felicitous as the former appointment had proved disastrous. Mountjoy had many advantages. Not only was the Queen his steady supporter, but Robert Cecil threw all his considerable energies into giving the new Deputy everything he needed. A capable lieutenant, Sir George Carew, was appointed to the key post of Munster. Finally the three-pronged strategy, so often proposed in the past, was fully implemented. Mountjoy set about a systematic strangulation of Tyrone. The former was temporarily diverted by the arrival of Spanish forces in Munster in September 1601. Too little and too late, they landed in the wrong place. The Irish army which Tyrone had led south to Kinsale was no match for the Deputy's soldiers; the Irish unwisely sought a decision in the open field. Their defeat was quick and complete; the surrender of the helpless Spaniards soon followed.

Mountjoy was in a sense the last of Elizabeth's favourites. She had singled him out for the Irish appointment, indeed, would have preferred him to Essex. The long, slow campaign against Tyrone, far and away the greatest military effort of the reign, was hugely expensive and painfully protracted. Yet, except for an occasional flurry of bad temper, the Queen patiently accepted the drain on her treasury. When Mountjoy came under fire for the slow progress of the campaign, she wrote to him in her own hand, addressing him as 'Mistress kitchen-maid', assuring him that no one with such responsibilities could avoid mistakes, 'but I never heard of any had fewer'.[23] It was such a letter as hardly any other of the servants, least of all her captains, had ever received. It took Mountjoy three years from the time of his appointment to accomplish his task. With theatrical appropriateness, Tyrone's surrender came only a few days after Elizabeth's death (an event still unknown in Ireland).

With Tyrone's capitulation Elizabeth finished the task set by her father eighty years earlier, the completion of the English conquest of Ireland, the fulfilment after 400 years of the work Strongbow began. It was the greatest of Tudor enterprises and (apart from the Reformation) the most long-lasting in its consequences. It was achieved in agony and pain through the misery and deaths of countless of the Queen's subjects. It was altogether unheroic, the accomplishment of men who were not seeking the glories of imperial conquest or martial fame but struggling against a foe they despised, in a slogging campaign of attrition. It evoked on both sides a venomous outpouring of hatred which would permanently poison relations between the two islands. It bequeathed to the Queen's successors a problem of granite-like intractability.

What are we to say of the Queen's role? She was, in a constitutional or legal sense, clearly responsible. The government of Ireland was conducted in her name and the English governors acted under her instruction. Yet Elizabeth's participation in the government of her second kingdom obviously differed widely from her governance of England. In the larger kingdom she had considered views on the major problems of government – the church, the Catholics, relations with Scotland, France, or Spain. Foreign affairs in particular received her daily attention and close supervision. For better or worse, it was her will which shaped the course of public business.

Ireland remained peripheral in her concerns for a variety of reasons. Geographic distance was among them, as were the reluctance to spend money and the greater urgency of other problems. More fundamental, however, was the ambiguity of English attitudes towards Ireland and its people. There had been since the 1530s a continuing intention to bring the whole island under royal control, but the accomplishment of that goal was slackly pursued. Only at moments had it hardened into more determined purpose, but these efforts had been short-lived because that purpose was not matched by accepted strategy. Irishmen were to be transformed into Englishmen, but on how this was to be achieved there was little agreement among the English rulers.

To these problems Elizabeth contributed nothing. So far as possible she avoided them, invariably resorting to the cheapest remedy which would buy a short-term solution. Her near-sightedness was not entirely a liability in the swift ebb and flow of ever-changing international relations; but in Ireland it was only sustained, consistent, long-term policy which could hope to ameliorate the intrinsically painful process of cultural displacement which was posed by English aims. For this Elizabeth was wholly unfitted. She was not unresponsive to the plight at least of her Old English subjects, and from time to time attempted to check the brutality of her governors, but these impulses were short-lived. When men of larger vision, such as Sidney or Perrot, pressed for programmatic strategies aimed at structural adaptation, she was incapable of balancing short-term costs against long-term advantage. The final conquest of Ireland was at the best bound to be a long agony. It might have been eased in some measure had the English sovereign been a ruler of vision.

34

The Queen and Her Successor

During the first dozen years of her reign, Elizabeth's subjects were remorseless in pressing her either to marry or, failing that, to establish the succession. As to the first, the Queen successfully eluded all efforts to push her into matrimony. On the second she displayed a steely determination not to have a 'rising sun', a reversionary interest. She skilfully played on the disarray among her petitioners as to who the rightful heir was; the issue remained unsettled.

The marriage of the most plausible candidate for the succession, Mary Stuart, and the birth of James made it increasingly difficult to ignore the Scottish claim. However, Mary's own actions from 1567 onwards effectually stalemated the succession issue in English politics. Mary's reputation in English eyes was badly damaged. The succession issue took on a new character. Councillors and Parliament alike turned from a search for a successor to frantic effort to destroy the principal candidate, but the Queen's stubborn refusal to cooperate blocked their path. All they could do was to pray for the Queen's good health and hope that Providence would once again intervene on their favour. The issue would not become a live one for well over a decade after revelations of the Ridolfi plot.

English politicians, preoccupied with the captive Mary, paid little attention to her son, the boy King, during the first decades of his reign, focusing their attention on the men who ruled Scotland in his name for the first twenty years of his life. Mary's flight had been followed by the short-lived regency of the Earl of Moray, assassinated in January 1570. In the confusion which followed, Elizabeth allowed her lieutenant in the north, Sussex, to scourge the Scottish borderlands in pursuit of the English rebels lurking there and their hosts, but she refused to allow him to intervene on behalf of the pro-English party in the contest for a new regent. Fortunately for her, the ultimate victor in that contest was the Earl of Morton, who during the years of his tenure looked steadily southward for support against the Marian opposition. To those Councillors who would have made him an English pensioner, explicitly dependent on English aid, the Queen turned a deaf ear. She refused to spend her money to buy the doubtful loyalty of a Scottish magnate whom circumstances would in any case force him to turn to her as a suppliant in an emergency. During these years James was ignored, except when the Queen intervened to protect his reversionary interests in the act of 1571 against his mother.

Morton's fall from power in 1579 caught the English unprepared. They could only look on with disapproval when the Sieur d'Aubigny, the King's cousin, newly arrived from France, under Guisean auspices, quickly won first place in the young monarch's confidence. However, he was soon overturned by a noble conspiracy, the Raid of Ruthven, in which the King was kidnapped. This in turn was followed by a second coup which placed power in the hands of an adventurer, Captain James Stewart (created Earl of Arran). His opponents fled to England whence, with the Queen's encouragement, they were allowed to launch a successful return, ousting Stewart with ease in the autumn of 1585. The Queen's policy in these years of James's minority was simple and cynical: the Scots were to be left to their own devices. Only when their internal divisions threatened English interests was she prepared to intervene. Her preferred tactic was support for armed conspiracy against the anti-English regime. Her attitude towards Scottish politicians was not very different from that of her later successors towards troublesome tribal neighbours on the fringes of empire.

It was after the fall of Stewart that James, now almost twenty, emerged as a major actor on the Scottish political stage. It was also a moment when relations with Scotland became a crucial concern of the English crown. An English expeditionary force was crossing the North Sea to fulfil the commitments of the Treaty of Nonsuch. With a Spanish war looming, Elizabeth necessarily had to guard her back door. She sent an experienced negotiator, Thomas Randolph, to offer James an alliance. The Treaty of Berwick, an offensive and defensive league, was signed in July 1586. James seized the opportunity to bargain for some recognition of his rights to the English succession. What he obtained was an annual pension of £4,000, plus a guarded personal promise by the Queen not to prejudice his claims so long as

he behaved himself, i. e. kept to the path she set for him. The ink
was not long dry before the treaty was put to a searching test by the
trial and condemnation of the King's mother. James's position was a
particularly painful one, since in cold fact her removal from the scene
would work to his advantage. Her intrigues with the Catholic powers
threatened to endanger the Stuart claim altogether. The Act of Association, passed by Parliament in 1584, excluded from the throne anyone
conspiring against Elizabeth's life 'and their issues being any wise
assenting or privy to the same'.[1] Mary's death would ease his path
towards the coveted English throne. To accede without protest to
her execution would damage his own reputation grievously, perhaps
dangerously, while outright defiance, even the use of force, would run
the risk of a crushing defeat at English hands and the forfeiture of
support within England. James played for time by sending repeated
embassies to plead for his mother's life. When it became certain she
would die, he hedged as best he could; in two ambiguous statements
of protest, he left unstated an actual threat of retaliation, saying just
enough to square his honour and his interest.[2]

James made ritual protests after his mother's execution took place,
and normal diplomatic relations were not re-established until late
spring 1588. The English were then moved to woo his favour both
by the approach of the Armada and by concern over the Scottish
Catholics' attempts to unsettle the Edinburgh regime. During the
campaign the Queen sent another emissary to James, who, over-
stepping his instructions, offered the King a dukedom, a £5,000 pension, and English financial support for a personal guard. James did
indeed make preparations against the Spanish, but there was no need
to put them into effect. In the aftermath Elizabeth promptly repudiated her agent's promises, although she sent £3,000 to Edinburgh as
a sweetener.[3]

James had been manœuvring to gain some kind of quid pro quo
for his acquiescence in Mary's death. He got a very emphatic response
from the Queen. She would not be blackmailed. If he thought he
could pressure her by hinting that he might turn elsewhere,
he would be most unwise. She told him plainly that 'honourable and
secure' demands would be readily granted,

> but if any shall be required that my present estate shall not permit as sure
> for me, then abuse not your judgment with so contrarious thoughts, for
> never shall dread of any man's behaviour cause me to do aught that may
> 'esbrandil' the seat that so well is settled.[4]

Elizabeth's letter is a pointer to the differing views of their relationship which each sovereign entertained. The Queen was determined to treat James as a foreign monarch whose territories were breeding grounds for conspiracy against her throne. She had little confidence in his ability or his will to restrain these conspirators. She would use all the weapons in her well-stocked armoury, diplomatic, conspiratorial, financial, to bend him to her will. Neither the King's personal dignity nor his sovereign rights were much respected. That he was a probable successor was a consideration to be pointedly ignored. The furthest she would go was to promise not to prejudice his claims — if he conformed his actions to her direction.

James on his side set himself two separate goals. The most immediate was the assertion of his own authority as King over the unruly nobles of Scotland who had, for decades past, been free of royal restraint on their actions. His resources were, by comparison with those of the English monarchy, woefully scant. Nevertheless he was to prove himself a shrewd practitioner of his royal craft; by skilful manœuvre, by patiently playing one party against another, he won a degree of mastery over his realm which few, if any, of his predecessors had enjoyed. Scottish domestic politics were his preoccupation in the short term, but his eyes were always fixed on the day when Elizabeth would no longer be alive. It was the succession to the English throne which was the ruling ambition of his life. He would never cease in his efforts to secure recognition of his rights from Elizabeth, using whatever leverage he could devise, whether by bargaining with the Queen or by fishing for support outside Britain by intrigue at Paris, Madrid, or even Rome. Yet he knew that he would always have to dance to the tune which Elizabeth called.

The tortuous tactics by which he slowly advanced his own power within the realm did not always square with the demands of his southern neighbour. In the years following the Armada's defeat, relations between the two kingdoms were first ruffled in 1589, when a correspondence between Philip II and a clique of Scottish Catholic nobles was uncovered. The Queen became frantic in her insistence that they be punished. James's position was unenviable. He dare not fall out with the Queen, but his power to suppress the Catholic nobles was severely limited. His response was to vacillate: he imprisoned the guilty, only to release them. James discounted the serious intentions of his feckless nobles, and his low-key response was in fact far closer to the realities of Scottish politics than Elizabeth's over-excited reaction. It enabled him to pacify the Queen without too great a sacrifice of his own dignity.[5]

The next round in Anglo-Scottish relations was fraught by the antics of the Earl of Bothwell. This rogue male of the Scottish nobility, constant only in the inconstancy of his ephemeral alliances with other nobles, Protestant or Catholic, became a thorn in the King's flesh, and for several years Bothwell's escapades, during which he threatened the King with force, kept the Scottish political world in tumult. Elizabeth did not scruple to use Bothwell's services when she thought it would serve her purposes. The Catholic ogre raised its head again in late 1592 with the discovery of blank letters signed by four Scottish Catholic leaders, to be filled out as assurance of their cooperation with a Spanish invasion fleet.[6] This was the opening sentence in a long and stormy chapter in Anglo-Scottish relations. James, pressed to act against the signers of the blanks, again stalled, this time as much from force of circumstance as from policy. Scottish politics were in an even more bewildering state of flux than usual. A coalition of interests usually mutually hostile enabled the mischief-making Bothwell, who had been discreetly patronized by Elizabeth, to seize the court momentarily and extract a pardon (August 1593).[7] He bid for English assistance, offering to act as a counterweight to the Catholic party. Elizabeth unscrupulously bargained with both Bothwell and the Catholic lords.[8] An attempt by James to resolve the tension by a parliamentary act which pardoned the Catholic earls, on condition they submitted formally to the established Protestant faith, failed,[9] and he was unable to bring them to heel.

Elizabeth now turned to clandestine encouragement to Bothwell as a means to force James's hand (although at the same time putting out feelers to the Earl's great enemy, Chancellor Maitland). Bothwell was at this point in alliance with the leaders of the Kirk, who of course opposed the Catholic party. However, he failed to play his part.[10] When James made ready to move against the Catholic lords, Elizabeth grudgingly gave funds to support his preparations. Slowly and with great difficulty he mastered the situation; both the Catholic earls and Bothwell were forced into exile, and by March 1595 the affair of the blanks was over.[11]

During these years Elizabeth had been relentless in pushing James to do her will by suppressing the Catholic party. The King, beset by the Catholic lords and by the buccaneer Bothwell, lacked the power to act against both. Elizabeth repeatedly refused to give him the few thousand pounds he needed, preferring to use the familiar ploy of intrigue with the Scottish factions, which cost nothing. Negotiations were regularly punctuated by hectoring letters from the Queen, contemptuously reproachful of James's conduct, full of sententious advice and self-congratulation. James must have smarted under this treatment, but with his short-term need for money in order to master his own realm and his long-term hopes of the succession he could only endure it. Yet for all her bullying of James and her ruthless pursuit of English interests at his expense, Elizabeth did nothing which dimmed his hopes for the future. The pension, which was an implicit acknowledgment of his position as heir apparent, was paid with reasonable regularity.

These events did, however, affect James's relations with the leading English Councillors. At the end of the 1580s they had begun to take notice of the King. Leicester, Walsingham, and Burghley had all thrown out lines of communication.[12] After the deaths of the first two, there had been contacts with Essex. Burghley, as the Queen's chief minister, had been involved in the Bothwell intrigues, and James believed he had favoured them. Burghley too, as Lord Treasurer, was a necessary agent in the payment of James's pension and likely to be blamed when, for politic reasons, the Queen delayed remittance. Relations with Essex warmed accordingly, and from 1594 on that lord became the patron of James's causes at the English court. The Queen's absolute ban on the succession question made any such moves risky. Characteristically, it was Essex who was boldest in pushing them.[13] James's power to construct effective leverage against Elizabeth within the island was limited; the advantages all lay with the Queen, but abroad he might hope to be more successful in building up pressure points, or at least in securing friends who might be useful if a crisis arose. At least once James seriously considered the pros and cons of support for a Spanish invasion of England via Scotland. The King, though tempted, on a careful weighing of the probabilities decided the risks were too great, and that after all there was a good prospect of obtaining his goal peacefully.[14]

However, James had no hesitation in thrusting himself forward on the Continent by diplomatic ploys, partly to assert his present dignity and importance, partly to win friends who might be useful if the succession were contested. He made overtures for a treaty with France in 1590, but the English government saw that he was rebuffed. When the tripartite treaty of 1596 among France, England, and the States General was signed he was deliberately snubbed. Advances to the States General were similarly rejected, at English instance. Elizabeth took care that James should have no alliances outside the island with-out her consent, and deliberately thwarted every effort the Scottish King made to play some role in mainstream European politics. With the Catholic powers he had, of course, no formal links, but informal contacts existed, most of which were known to the well-informed English authorities.

James, for the most part, bore the ordeal of waiting patiently, but once in a while his anxieties boiled over, as in a speech to the Scottish Parliament in 1597 when he complained of his treatment by Elizabeth. This elicited a forthright warning from Burghley, reminding the King of Parliament's power to alter the succession. If by unjust allegations he offended the Queen or her Parliament, ' – it may bring with it harder consequences than were to be wished'.[15]

James's impatience carried him further away still when he listened to the siren voice of the Earl of Essex. While in Ireland in 1599 the latter had approached the King, asking support if he took a force back to England to coerce the court. Later, when after his return from Ireland Essex fell into disgrace, Mountjoy, about to leave for his new post, made similar proposals on the Earl's behalf. By the time James's reply came, Mountjoy had changed his mind, believing Essex no longer in mortal danger. To these overtures James had made ambigu-ously encouraging replies, but without any commitment. At the end of 1600 Essex, now driven almost mad by being thrust into the political wilderness, wrote seeking the King's countenance in the actions he was about to undertake against his enemies. He asked the King to send an ambassador, empowered to assist the Earl in his enterprise. James's ambassadors arrived only after the death of the Earl, bearing cautiously flexible instructions to sound out the situation.[16]

Elizabeth, of course, came to know much of this through the exam-ination of Essex's confederates after the rising of February 1601. She made no representations to James, nor did his name appear in any of the publicity at the trial or in official pamphlets. She allowed herself only one faint hint, in a letter of 1602: 'though many exceed me in many things, yet I dare profess that I can keep taciturnity for myself and my friends. My head may fail but my tongue shall never, as I will not say but yourself though not to me witness.'[17]

In all her dealings with James, Elizabeth's attitude had been con-stant. She had kept her eyes firmly fixed on the present. Any attempt by James to introduce future issues was quickly checked: 'He hasteth well that wisely can abide', and she added: 'Remember as well with whom you deal, as what you would obtain.'[18] Their relations had been those of two independent sovereigns; any suggestion of another relationship had been ignored. Elizabeth had pursued her self-interest relentlessly, exacting obedience to her demands. James had struggled with some success to assert his dignity, although on all major questions he had, of course, to yield, since his consuming ambition to inherit the English throne made him her prisoner. The Queen's awareness of this led her to treat him with a hectoring superiority, subjecting him to withering criticism for his failures while giving gratuitous instruction in the art of kingship in a tone suggesting that the pupil was an inept and stumbling learner.

Whatever the case, Elizabeth certainly assumed that James would succeed her. She accepted this fact, not because she esteemed him but because Providence – or circumstance – had made him the only plausible successor. Elizabeth might thank Providence not only for this blessing to her subjects but also for the benefits it shed on her. Here was a successor of impeccable credentials of birth and ancestry, an orthodox Protestant and a ruler acceptable to her people. Better still for her, he was a foreigner, by necessity absent from her court where an heir might have been the centre of a dangerous reversionary interest. In addition, the weakness of the Scottish monarchy made him financially and politically dependent upon the Queen. Circumstance thus left the way open to an untroubled succession by an heir too remote to be troublesome to the Queen.

What Elizabeth thought of her cousin we cannot know. She herself, conscious of her seniority among European monarchs and of her mastery of statecraft, looked down with impatient contempt on the bumbling efforts of such apprentice kings as James or Henry IV. However, the French King proved to be at least her match and often bested her. James, dependent on her favour and too weak at home to defy her, could be bullied mercilessly. Yet, however much she insisted on his toeing the line in all matters which touched her interests, so long as he bent to her will, she carefully refrained from any act which might disparage his claims to follow her on the English throne. Indeed, she did more. She was fully aware of virtually all his flirtations with Continental powers, even the proposeed cooperation with an invasion of the island and, above all, of his dealings with Essex. All these she chose to bury in oblivion. A Queen usually ready to flare into anger at any slight on her dignity or threat to her interests calmly overlooked an intrigue between her putative heir and her most dangerous subject. On this occasion at least, Elizabeth had risen above her own egotism to a longer vision of her kingdom's interests.

Epilogue

The final years of the reign were shadowed both by private and public events. The death of Essex had not only been a personal tragedy for Elizabeth; it had opened a rift between her and many of her subjects. Among them his fame still shone untarnished, and the Earl was seen as a victim, done to death by the malice of his enemies, pre-eminently Robert Cecil. In their view it was the hunchbacked secretary, his hatred for his brilliant rival masked in false civility, who had whispered in the ear of the Queen and poisoned her mind against the Earl. Circumstances lent some plausibility to their belief, for Cecil now stood in uncontested eminence in the royal confidence. The pluralism of counsel which had been characteristic in past decades had disappeared. The senior Councillors, Elizabeth's two cousins, Nottingham and Buckhurst (both born in 1536), were men of her generation, content with their honours and willing to follow the lead of the Secretary. The only younger courtier who might have challenged Cecil was Ralegh, but he was outside the Council. A character cut from very different cloth, his ambitions, like those of Essex, looked to other and less traditional goals than those of the ordinary courtier.

It was perhaps a sign of the Queen's slackening grasp that she was content to rely on a single Councillor who monopolized her confidence in a way no one had done since the earliest days of the reign, when the elder Cecil had enjoyed such a position. Certainly the Secretary's unique position added to the discontent not only of Essex's former adherents but of all those who felt excluded from access to the sovereign by Cecil's privileged place. It added to the restlessness of those who impatiently looked to the coming of a new reign.

In public matters the Queen was content to leave the burden of care in the Secretary's hands. The war had dwindled away to a mere murmur. The siege of Ostend, where an isolated garrison barely held the town against Spanish pressure, momentarily required attention, but the retention of the port was more a matter of honour than of high strategy. Ireland could be left to the capable and trusted Mountjoy, sustained by the steady support of Cecil. The Spanish landing at Kinsale, so long dreaded, was quickly turned into a resounding English victory over both the invader and their Irish allies. The moribund negotiations with Brussels had lost whatever urgency they had. In all these things the Queen's life was easier than it had been for decades past. She was no longer pressed for painful and costly decisions where all choices seemed equally repugnant. The constraints which had borne upon her since the first days of her reign were loosened as never before.

The routine of the court continued in its usual patterns. In 1601, besides numerous local visits, there was a month-long progress in late summer through Berkshire, Hertfordshire, and Surrey; and in the following year, a shorter perambulation in late July and early August in Middlesex and Buckinghamshire. The usual round of court entertainments was mounted; the last play was performed after the final remove to Richmond, in early March 1603.[1]

Nevertheless, there was a changed atmosphere in the court. Councillors and courtiers continued in their accustomed service to the Queen, but their eyes were turning more and more to the north, to the court at Edinburgh. Cecil had very promptly after Essex's death mended his fences and opened a regular correspondence with Holyrood house through an intermediary, Lord Henry Howard. James, making a realistic assessment of the English situation, saw the Secretary as his best guide to the labyrinth of Westminster. Others were throwing out lines to James as well – Ralegh, Lord Cobham, and Northumberland among them. For lesser men it was a time of deep anxiety. The fears and worries which Peter Wentworth had voiced a decade earlier were enhanced with time. The Spanish claim, put forward in Parsons's book,[2] aroused vague fears of intervention or of a local uprising; official silence on the subject of the succession served to heighten the tension.

The end when it came, on 24 March 1603, was mercifully swift. The Queen sank into a melancholy silence, refused food, and declined to go to bed until she actually collapsed. She lingered a few more days before death quietly came. Her Councillors had time to make preparations and to proclaim the new King without incident. Fears of disturbance faded swiftly as James VI set out from Edinburgh to become James I.

If the Queen in her final years ever paused to cast up her accounts, how would she have summed up her experience?[3] In her personal life Elizabeth had denied herself the pleasures and pains of marriage, but she had retained the lifetime companionship of two men to whom she was most strongly drawn, Leicester and Hatton. With their deaths, she turned to a third, Essex, whose magnetic attraction seemed to hold her in a spell. For a decade she gratified herself in indulging the tantrums of her unruly favourite, only to have him turn on her. They parted in the utmost bitterness, unforgiving coldness on her side, consuming self-pity on his. Cast out into the darkness of political exile, he had committed the ultimate folly of rebellion and paid the inevitable penalty. This last, troubled episode in her emotional life had ended in utter shipwreck, grievously wounding her personally and for a time threatening to shake her throne.

In the larger realm of her public life Elizabeth had more occasion for self-congratulation. Triumphantly disproving the doubts men had entertained about a woman's rule, she had imposed her will on her people as effectively as her father ever did. He had ruled by fear; she had won her people's loving devotion, and achieved a degree of personal popularity unequalled by her predecessors or successors.

Given her power to command obedience, how far had she been able to carry through the long-term objectives she set herself? More grandly, how far had she mastered the events which crowded on her, decade by troubled decade? Elizabeth had set her sights on two goals. The first was the establishment of the regime laid down in the 1559 settlement of religion. Her purposes were clearcut, her programme carefully tailored to achieve her ends, and she had fought stubbornly, against stiff resistance, to accomplish them. When she died, she had the satisfaction of seeing the church established by law also established in social fact.

The other goal she set before her was to keep her realm at peace, free from the bloody conflicts which ravaged her Continental neighbours. Here, unlike the ecclesiastical sphere, matters were much less in her own hands. After a somewhat shaky start, when policy was shaped more by the skills of William Cecil than by the Queen, she moved to assert control of her crucial relations with the two great Continental monarchies. In the decade of the 1570s she was successful, by discreetly supporting French and Dutch malcontents, in helping to keep the Valois princes and Philip II too preoccupied at home to interfere effectively in English affairs. But from the late 1570s events began to gain the upper hand. After the collapse of Spanish power opened the possibility of an autonomous Netherlands, Elizabeth, still seeking to avoid direct involvement, devised the grand strategy of the Anjou match. Very much an enterprise of her own making, it collapsed under its own weight; in the aftermath of its failure she could no longer contain the drift towards the war which came in 1585.

From that point on events more and more eluded her control, as the initiative passed to Philip, to Henry IV, and to the leaders of the new Dutch state. In these years the Queen's deficiencies as a ruler were more apparent, above all her reluctance to make decisions or to give her commanders leeway to act on the spot. Although she and Henry IV shared large political goals, at the level of actual cooperation the disjunction of their immediate interests prevented effective joint action. Henry's triumph over his enemies was his own doing. The Queen benefited from it but could claim little credit for the outcome. In Holland she could claim a larger role: the infusion of English men and money was a substantial, perhaps essential, contribution to the States' ultimate success, but the military initiatives were theirs, the English valuable auxiliaries. In this case there was mutual benefit to both sides, although credit for victory had to go largely to the Dutch leadership.

On the seas the stunning success of 1588, brought about by the skill and enterprise of her seamen, the ineptitude of Spanish strategy, and the winds and waves of the Atlantic, had not been followed (except fleetingly at Cadiz) by subsequent achievement. None of the naval enterprises to which the Queen gave her reluctant consent realized its stated goals, but two of them triggered off ill-considered responses by Philip which finally laid the ghost of another armada. Yet in the end, in spite of a history of ill-managed or ill-fated expeditions, the Queen found herself among the winners. It was not a triumphalist peace, but it was one which realized the goals for which the war had been fought — the re-establishment of a balance of power on the Continent which would hold in check the expansionist ambitions of either Spain or France and a Netherlandish state strong enough to maintain its independence from either of the two great monarchies.

As Spanish power on the Continent receded, the Queen was forced at last to turn her attention to her long-neglected second kingdom. The heavy bill for that neglect now fell due, and forced the Queen into the most costly enterprise she was to launch. In its outcome it

446

was both the greatest success and the greatest failure of her reign. The rebellion was crushed; conquest was complete; but the cost was permanent alienation of both the Gaels and the Old English. It was a poisoned legacy which she left her successors.

Elizabeth went to her grave, not in a blaze of glory, but with a lasting fame. She left behind her a nation which at home had been spared the horrors of those internecine wars that devastated her neighbours for a generation. Abroad, the threat of foreign intervention which had haunted Englishmen for half a century was at an end. This had not been achieved without great cost; the war years had strained English resources to the limit as her subjects groaned under nearly twenty years of unrelieved taxation. The popularity of her earlier years waned as the war dragged on without any sign of ending. The disgrace of the universally popular Essex, the hero of Cadiz, aroused bitter resentment in many quarters.

However, with the speedy conclusion of peace in 1604 and the cessation of warfare in Ireland, these shadows on the royal reputation faded away. As her reign receded into history, it was the successes which lingered in the collective memory. The end of a long era of foreign menace and the decades of peace which followed in the seventeenth century were ascribed to Elizabeth's leadership, the weary years of unsuccessful campaigns forgotten. It was not the vacillating ruler whose indecision hamstrung her commanders' best efforts, and whose frugality starved them of necessary resources, who went down to posterity. It was Gloriana, the beneficent and gracious queen of the annual progresses, the heroic leader of her people speaking to her soldiers at Tilbury.

Abbreviations

APC	*Acts of the Privy Council of England*, ed. J. R. Dasent, 32 vols. (London, 1890–1907)
Baschet	PRO, Baschet Transcripts
BL	British Library
Camden, *Annals*	William Camden, *Annals of Queen Elizabeth* (London, 1675)
Cotton	BL Cotton MSS
CPR	*Calendar of Patent Rolls:* Edward VI, 5 vols. (London, 1924–9); Elizabeth, 9 vols. (London, 1939–86)
CSPD	*Calendar of State Papers, Domestic*, 12 vols. (London, 1856–72)
CSPF	*Calendar of State Papers, Foreign* (Elizabeth), 23 vols. (London, 1863–1950)
CSPI	*Calendar of State Papers, Irish*, 11 vols. (London, 1860–1912)
CSP Rome	*Calendar of State Papers, Rome*, 2 vols. (London, 1916–26)
CSP Span	*Calendar of State Papers, Spanish*, 13 vols. (London, 1861–1954)
CSPSc	*Calendar of State Papers, Scottish*, 13 vols. (Edinburgh, 1898–1969)
CSPSp	*Calendar of State Papers, Spanish*, Elizabeth, 4 vols. (London, 1892–99)
CSPV	*Calendar of State Papers, Venetian*, 9 vols. (London, 1864–98)
DNB	*Dictionary of National Biography*
EHR	*English Historical Review*
Fénélon	B. de S. de la Mothe-Fénélon, *Correspondance diplomatique*, ed. A. Teulet, 7 vols. (London and Paris, 1838–40)

Harleian	BL Harleian MSS
Haynes	*Collection of State Papers . . . Left by William Cecil, Lord Burghley*, ed. Samuel Haynes (London, 1740)
HMC Hatfield	Historical Manuscripts Commission, *Calendar of the Manuscripts of the Marquis of Salisbury at Hatfield House*, 24 vols. (London, 1883–1976)
Journal Commons	*Journal of the House of Commons*, 17 vols. (London, 1803)
Journal Lords	*Journal of the House of Lords*, 19 vols. (London, 1767)
KL	Kervyn de Lettenhove and L. Gilliodts-Van Severen, *Relations politiques des Pays-Bas et de l'Angleterre, sous le règne de Philippe II*, 2 vols. (Brussels, 1882–1900)
L&A	*Lists and Analysis of State Papers Foreign*, 5 vols. (London, 1964–89)
L&P	*Letters and Papers, Foreign and Domestic, Henry VIII*, 11 vols. (London, 1862–1910)
Lansdowne	BL Lansdowne MSS
Murdin	*Collection of State Papers . . . Left by William Cecil, Lord Burghley*, ed. William Murdin (London, 1759)
PRO	Public Record Office
SP	PRO, State Papers
SR	*Statutes of the Realm*, 11 vols. (London, 1810–28)
ST	*A Complete Collection of State Trials and Proceedings for High Treason*, ed. William Cobbett *et al.*, 42 vols. (London, 1816–98)
TRHS	*Transactions of the Royal Historical Society*

Notes

Chapter 1

1. *L&P* VI, 1111, p. 464; Edward Hall, *The Lives of the Kings*, ed. Charles Whibley, 2 vols. (London, 1904), II, 242–4; Richard Grafton, *A Chronicle at large and meere History of the Affayres of England* (London, 1569), 1219–21.

2. *L&P* VI, 1486, p. 599; VII, 38, p. 17; 372, p. 154; 1171, pp. 456–7; VIII, 438–40, pp. 172–3; IX, 568, p. 189.

3. Ibid. VII, 1257, p. 484; VIII, 174, p. 58; 189, pp. 69–70; 339, p. 134; 342–3, pp. 137–8; 793, pp. 297–8; X, 410, p. 166.

4. Ibid. 141, p. 51.

5. Ibid. XI, 203, p. 90.

6. Ibid. 312, p. 130.

7. Ibid. 860, pp. 345–6.

8. Ibid. XII, pt. 1, 815–16, p. 361; see also 1315, p. 596.

9. Ibid. 911, pp. 318–20.

10. Ibid. XIII, pt. 1, 255, p. 89; 273, p. 93; XVI, 885, p. 432; 1090, pp. 519–20; XVII, 143, pp. 65–6; 200, pp. 90–1; XX, pt. 1, 91, p. 40; pt. 2, 639, p. 295; 890, p. 433.

11. *SR* III, 955–6 (35 Henry VIII, c. 1).

12. James K. McConica, *English Humanists and Reformation Politics* (Oxford, 1965), 215–17.

13. *The English Works of Roger Ascham* (London, 1761), 242, 350–6; *CSPV* 1534–54, p. 539; Camden, *Annals*, 6.

14. McConica, *English Humanists*, 231.

15. *L&P* XIX (2), 794, p. 466; McConica, *English Humanists*, 231.

16. Hastings Robinson (ed.), *Original Letters Relative to the English Reformation, 1531–58* (Cambridge, 1846), I, 76.

17. *L&P* XXI (2), 502, p. 258; 571, p. 294.

18. Louis Wiesener, *La Jeunesse d'Elizabeth d'Angleterre, 1533–58* (Paris, 1878), trans. C. M. Yonge, 2 vols. (London, 1879), I, 130; *APC* II, 251–2.

19. Haynes, 95–7, 99–101; *CSPD*, I, Edward VI, vi, 6, 19, 20, 21, 22; P. F. Tytler, *England under the Reigns of Edward VI and Mary*, 2 vols. (London, 1839), I, 70.

20. Haynes, 89–90.

21. Ibid. 70–1, 89–90.

22. John Aylmer, *An Harborowe for*

Faithfull and Trewe Subiectes (Strasburg, 1559), p. N.

23. *CPR* III, 415; in 1551 Elizabeth surrendered the grant of the previous year; a new patent was issued including most of the same properties, with an annual value of £3,064; for Hatfield see ibid. 238–42; for the household accounts see *Camden Miscellany* II, (London, 1853).

24. John Strype, *Ecclesiastical Memorials*, 3 vols. (Oxford, 1820–40), III, 26; *The Chronicle of Queen Jane*, ed. J. G. Nichols (London, 1850), 13, 14, 27.

Chapter 2

1. *CSPSpan* XI, 418; see also 292.
2. Ibid. 393–5.
3. Ibid. 188, 196, 220, 240, 252.
4. Ibid. 418, 440, 443–4.
5. Ibid. 169, 228, 263, 291, 400–1.
6. Ibid. 328, 254–5, 393–5.
7. Ibid. 393–4, 440, 454, 472.
8. Yonge, *Youth of Elizabeth*, 263; *CSPSp* XII, 40–1.
9. Ibid. 16.
10. E. H. Harbison, *Rival Ambassadors at the Court of Queen Mary* (London, 1940), 109–16; D. H. Loades, *Two Tudor Conspiracies* (Cambridge, 1965), 15–21.
11. *CSPSpan* XII, 51, 53–7, 77, 139–40.
12. Ibid. 8–9, 55–7, 125; Tytler, *Edward VI*, 426–7; *CSPD* I, Edward VI, iii, 21, 21-I.
13. HMC, *Second Report* (London, 1874), app. 154; *Chronicle of Queen Jane*, 68–70, 72–4. Wyatt may have made a confession under torture; see Loades, *Conspiracies*, 92 n.
14. John Foxe, *Acts and Monuments*, 8 vols. (London, 1837–41), VIII, 607; Thomas Heywood, *England's Elizabeth: her Life and Troubles*, (London, 1632), 89.

15. *CSPSpan* XII, 150–3, 166–7.
16. *CSPD* I (Mary), iv, 2.
17. Foxe, *Monuments* VIII, 610; Heywood, *England's Elizabeth*, 112–14.
18. *CSPSpan* XII, 151–3, 197–206; Loades, *Conspiracies*, 93–4. Gardiner claimed to have lost an intercepted dispatch which would have been very damaging.
19. Loades, *Conspiracies*, 96; *CSPSpan* XII, 218–19, 233–40, 261.
20. For Bedingfield correspondence see *Archaeological Society of Norfolk and Suffolk*, 4 (1855), 149–54.
21. Ibid. 158–9.
22. Ibid. 175–9.
23. Ibid. 176, 180–3.
24. Ibid. 182–3.
25. Ibid. 192–3, 196, 203.
26. Ibid. 204–9.
27. Ibid. 210–11.
28. Ibid. 221–2.
29. Ibid. 225–6.
30. *CSPV*, p. 61; Noailles's unpublished letter in the Archives du Ministère des Affaires Étrangères en Angleterre, 1553–6 (Paris), I, II, 287; *CSPSpan* XII, 310, 312.
31. Foxe, *Monuments* VIII, 621–2; *CSPV* VI, p. 148.
32. *CSPSpan* XIII, 251–2.
33. Ibid. XII, 51.
34. Loades, *Conspiracies*, 144, 176–217; *CSPSp* XIII, 147; *CSPV* VI, 31, 384.
35. *CSPD* I (Philip and Mary), viii, 52, 54; *CSPV* VI, 475, 479–80; VII, 836; *The Machyn Diary*, ed. J. G. Nichols (London, 1848), 4.
36. *CSPSpan* XIII, 150–3, 104, 285, 293, 359, 380–1.
37. Ibid. 387, 390, 400.
38. Ibid. 437–8.
39. KL I, 279–82; see also the dispatch from the Flemish envoy, D'Assonleville, 272–86.
40. See J. E. Neale, *Essays in*

Elizabethan History (London, 1958), 48–9, quoting HMC Hatfield IV, 189.

Chapter 3

1. For an account of Tudor governmental institutions, see Penry Williams, *The Tudor Regime* (Oxford, 1979).
2. R. B. Wernham, *England Before the Armada* (London, 1966), ch. 12.
3. E. A. Wrigley and R. S. Schofield, *The Population History of England 1541–1871* (Cambridge, Mass., 1981), 183 and tables 6.8, 6.10; app. 3, table A3.1.
4. For general acounts of economic history in this era, see Joyce Youings, *Sixteenth Century England* (London, 1984) or C. G. A. Clay, *Economic Expansion and Social Change: England 1500–1700*, 2 vols. (Cambridge, 1984).
5. G. R. Elton, *The Tudor Revolution in Government* (Cambridge, 1969), 316–69.
6. For the early career of Cecil see Conyers Read, *Mr Secretary Cecil and Queen Elizabeth* (London, 1955), chs. 2–5.

Chapter 4

1. See the introduction by J. E. Neale to *The Queenes Maiesties Passage through the Citie of London to Westminster the Day before her Coronacion*, ed. James M. Osborn (New Haven, Conn., 1960).
2. Norman L. Jones, *Faith by Statute* (London, 1982), 46, quoting G. L. Ross 'Il Schifanoya's Account of the Coronation of Queen Elizabeth', *EHR* (1908), 533–4; *CSPV* VIII, 24–5.
3. *CSPD* I (Eliz.), i, 9.
4. Amos Miller, *Sir Henry Killigrew* (Leicester, 1963), 37–44; Wernham, *Before the Armada*, ch. 28.
5. *CSPF* I, 137–9.

6. Ibid. 53–5; *CSPSp* I (Eliz.), 355; Jones, *Faith by Statute*, 53, n. 103.

Chapter 5

1. Jones, *Faith by Statue*, 8, quoting John Hayward, *Annals of the first Four Years of the Reign of Queen Elizabeth* (London, 1840), 4.
2. Jones, *Faith by Statute*, 36; see *APC* VII, 36.
3. Jones, *Faith by Statute*, 38; *APC* VII, 31.
4. *CSPSp* I, 17; HMC, *Seventh Report* (London, 1879), app. 614; Jones, *Faith by Statute*, 44.
5. Ibid. 46.
6. *CSPV* VII, 22–3.
7. Simonds D'Ewes, *The Journals of the Parliaments . . . of Queen Elizabeth* (London, 1693; repr. Wilmington, Del., 1974) 12.
8. Jones, *Faith by Statute*, 61; C. G. Bayne, 'The First House of Commons of Queen Elizabeth', *EHR* (1908), 643–82.
9. Jones, *Faith by Statute*, 63–5.
10. Ibid. 66–7.
11. David Loades, *The Reign of Mary Tudor* (London, 1979), 168–70, 325–6.
12. Ibid. 168–9.
13. Jones, *Faith by Statute*, 72–81.
14. *Journal Commons* I, 54.
15. J. E. Neale, 'The Elizabethan Acts of Supremacy and Uniformity,' *EHR* (1950), 304–32.
16. *CSPV* VII, 52.
17. Jones, *Faith by Statute*, 103 for names of peers; *CSPSp* I, 38.
18. Paul L. Hughes and James F. Larkin, *Tudor Royal Proclamations*, 2 vols. (New Haven, Conn., 1969), II, 109.
19. *Journal Commons* I, 58; *Journal Lords* I, 565; House of Lords Record Office, Memorandum 33 (1965), 1.
20. SP12/3/51, fo. 52; Raphael Holinshed, *Chronicles of England*,

Scotland and Ireland (London, 1577), 1801.

21. *APC* VII, 78; Holinshed, *Chronicles* (London, 1577), 1800; *CSPV* VII, 65.

22. Jones, *Faith by Statute*, 128–9; SP12/3/173.

23. *The Correspondence of Matthew Parker*, ed. John Bruce (Cambridge, 1857), 66; *Zurich Letters*, 2 vols. (London, 1842–5), I, 33.

24. E. Jeffrey Davies, 'An unpublished Manuscript of the Lords Journal for April and May 1559', *EHR* (1913), 538.

25. Ibid. 531–42.

26. Jones, *Faith by Statute*, 152; John Foxe, *Acts and Monuments*, 8 vols. (London, 1837–41), VIII, 691.

27. Corpus Christi College Cambridge MS 121, fos. 141–2.

28. Wallace T. MacCaffrey, *The Shaping of the Elizabethan Regime* (Princeton, NJ, 1968), 51–3.

Chapter 6

1. *CSPF* I, 518; *The State Papers and Letters of Sir Ralph Sadler*, ed. A. Clifford, 2 vols. (Edinburgh, 1809), I, 375; BL Lansdowne IV, fo. 9; Cotton Caligula B x 84.

2. Conyers Read, *Mr Secretary Cecil and Queen Elizabeth* (London, 1955), 142; *CSPF* I, 365.

3. Ibid. 519–23; Cotton Caligula B x 78–84; SP12/6/34.

4. *CSPF* II, 71, 72, 112.

5. Ibid. 186 n.; Lansdowne C II, fo. 1.

6. For the Imperial missions see Victor von Klarwill, *Queen Elizabeth and Some Foreigners* (London, 1928), 1–171.

7. *CSPSc* I, 367–9; HMC Hatfield I, 221.

8. Patrick Forbes, *A Full View of the Public Transactions in the Reign of*

Queen Elizabeth, 2 vols. (London, 1740), I, 454–7.

9. *CSPF* II, 104.

10. Haynes, 342–3; HMC Hatfield, I, 244.

11. Read, *Cecil*, 166–7.

12. *CSPF* III, 262.

13. Read, *Cecil*, 199.

Chapter 7

1. J. E. Neale, *Elizabeth I and her Parliaments, 1559–81* (London, 1953), 47–50; *CSPV* VII, 28; Camden, *Annals*, 25–6; Simonds D'Ewes, *The Journals of the Parliaments... of Queen Elizabeth* (London, 1693; repr. Wilmington, Del., 1974), 46.

2. *CSPSp* I, 12 n., 53–4, 102, 112, 114, 169, 174, 177.

3. Ibid. 22–3, 35.

4. SP12/13/21 (I).

5. *CSPSp* I, 58.

6. Dudley MSS, Longleat House, I, 21, 54, 161; *CSPSp* I, 106, 109; SP12/11/14; 13/12, 14.

7. *CSPSp* I, 95, 96, 98, 107.

8. Conyers Read, *Mr. Secretary Cecil and Queen Elizabeth* (London, 1955), 199, quoting BL Stow, fo. 180b and SP70/17; see also Winchester's letter, Haynes, 361.

9. *CSPF* III, 376–7.

10. *CSPSp* I, 176, 178.

11. Ibid. 178, 180–3.

12. BL Add. MS 35830, 74; *CSPF* IV, 23; *CSPSp*, I, 187–9.

13. KL, I 553; SP12/16/55, 66–8; 18/7, 8; *CSPF* IV, 104.

14. *CSPSp* I, 224–5.

15. *CPR* 1560–3, 181–91, 244, 361, 533–43.

16. For a discussion of Elizabethan court politics see Simon Adams, 'Eliza Enthroned? The Court and Its Politics', in C. Haigh (ed.), *The Reign of Elizabeth* (London, 1984); 'Faction, Clientage and Party: English Politics,

1558–1603', *History Today* 32 (Dec. 1982), 33–9.

17. *CSPF* IV, 608, 609.

18. Ibid. v, 262.

19. *CSPSp* I, 219, 226.

20. *CSPF* IV, 404; v, 36, 80, 129.

21. Ibid. v, 21, 22, 36.

22. Ibid. 268–9, 306–7.

23. Ibid. IV 609–10.

24. *Camden Miscellany* VI (London, 1871), 14–17; *CSPF* v, 575–7; P. Collinson (ed.), *Letters of T. Wood* (London, *Bulletin of Institute of Historical Research*, 1960, Supplement 5), p. ix; SP12/19/36.

25. Dudley MSS, Longleat House, I; *Wood Letters*, pp. xxi–xxiii.

26. *CSPF* VI, 110.

27. On Throckmorton, Cecil, and Smith, see Thomas Wright, *Queen Elizabeth and Her Times*, 2 vols. (London, 1838), I, 208.

28. *CSPF* VI, 480–1.

29. *CSPSp* I (Eliz.), 263; Patrick Forbes, *A Full View of the Public Transactions in the Reign of Queen Elizabeth*, 2 vols. (London, 1740), II, 188; *CPR* II, 534–43.

Chapter 8

1. *CSPSp* I, 262–4.

2. *CSPF* IV, 277; *Miscellaneous State Papers of. . . Earl of Hardwicke*, 2 vols. (London, 1778), I, 187; SP12/21/39, 55.

3. PRO SP12/28/20; *SCPSp* I, 321.

4. Ibid. 135; *CSPF* v, 12–17, 23–4; VI, 223–4, 415, 463; SP12/23/6.

5. *CSPF* IV, 163, 204, 248–9; *SCPSc* I, 542–3.

6. Ibid. 8, 22; *CSPSp* I, 308–15; Maurice Lee, *James Stuart, Earl of Moray* (New York, 1953), 114–15; Forbes, *Full View*, II, 2.

7. *CSPSc* II, 8, 19, 20, 22; *CSPSp* I, 338.

8. *CSPSc* II, 32.

9. Ibid. 44.

10. *Memoirs of Sir James Melville of Halhill*, ed. A. F. Steuart (London, 1929), 88–9, 92, 98; Camden, *Annals*, 75.

11. *CSPSc* II, 124; *CSPF* VII, 247; Lansdowne C II, fo. 66.

12. *CSPF* VI, 415; Lee, *Moray*, 123–255; *CSPSc* II, 60, 68, 75, 76–8.

13. Ibid. 141–7; A. Teulet, *Relations politiques de la France et de l'Espagne avec l'Écosse*, 5 vols. (Paris, 1862), II, 195–6; Baschet 5/2/1565.

14. *CSPSc* II, 150; *CSPF* VI, 384–7; Cotton Caligula B x, fos. 299–308, 350–3, 354–9; Lansdowne C II, fo. 112.

15. Ibid. fos. 13, 18, 20; BL Cotton Vespasian C VII 10/13/62; *CSPSp* I, 259, 297; *CSPF* v, 423; Wright, *Elizabeth*, I, 129; *CPR* IV, 63–4.

16. *Camden Miscellany* IX (London, 1895).

17. *CPR* III, 259.

18. Lansdowne C II, fo. 121; *CSPF* VII, 458, 478, 481.

19. BL Cotton Caligula B x, fos. 350–3; Teulet, *Relations politiques* II, 235.

20. *Memoirs of Sir James Melville of Halhill*, ed. A. F. Steuart (London, 1920), 131.

21. Lansdowne C II, fos. 89, 93, 102, 103; HMC Hatfield I, 290–1, not printed until 1713.

22. *CSPF* VII, 190.

23. BL Add. MS 33593, printed in *State Papers and Letters of Sir Ralph Sadler*, ed. A. Clifford, 2 vols. (Edinburgh, 1809), II, 557–61.

24. J. E. Neale, *Elizabeth I and Her Parliaments, 1559–81* (London, 1953), 101; *Journal Commons* I, 62–3.

25. Neale, *Parliaments 1559–81*, 107–9.

26. BL Add. MS 32379, fos. 17–20.

27. Neale, *Parliaments, 1559–81*, 113, citing *CSPSp* I, 317; SP12/28/20.

28. Neale, *Parliaments, 1559–81*, 126–8, citing Cotton Titus F I, f. 77

ff.; Harleian 5176, fo. 97; Lansdowne xciv, fo. 30.

29. HMC Hatfield i, 283, 285; *CSPF* vi, 558; Wright, *Queen Elizabeth*, i, 207–8.

30. PRO, Baschet 16/2 17/2, 10/5, 20/5 6/6, 18/6/1565; Teulet, *Relations politiques*, ii, 217; Lansdowne C ii, fo. 114; *CSPSp*, i, 443.

31. Ibid. 365; Baschet 7/3/65; Lansdowne C ii, fos. 110, 121.

32. Ibid.; *CSPSp* i, 377.

33. Haynes, 444.

34. Camden, *Annals*, 79.

35. Lansdowne C ii, f. 121.

36. Camden, *Annals*, 79; SP12/36/ 66; Murdin, 760; *CSPSp* i, 445–6, 511, 554; Conyers Read, *Mr Secretary Cecil and Queen Elizabeth* (London, 1955), 332–3, quoting SP63/18/19.

37. *CSPSp* i, 382, 438, 517–18, 544, 575–6; SP12/39/31.

38. SP12/40/91.

39. Neale, *Parliaments, 1559–81*, 130.

40. Murdin, 762; Neale, *Parliaments, 1559–81*, 132–3.

41. National Library of Scotland, Murray MSS, LaForêt to Charles IX, 21 Oct. 1566; I am indebted to Professor J. E. Neale for a copy of this dispatch.

42. *CSPSp*, i, 589–90.

43. Murray MSS, LaForêt to Charles IX, 21 Oct. 1566.

44. Ibid. 27 Oct. 1566; *CSPSp* i, 591–2; Murdin, 762.

45. Neale, *Parliaments, 1559–81*, 146–50; Cambridge University Library, MS Gg iii, 34, fos. 208 ff.

46. SP12/41/20, 21, 22.

47. SP12/41/30/31; 27/45 (misplaced under 1563).

48. Lansdowne 1236, fo. 42.

49. *CSPSp*, ii, 382, 438, 517–18, 544, 575–6, 636–7; SP12/39/31; *CSPF* viii, 257.

50. Ibid. 360, 361.

51. SP12/44/42, 46, 53; Cotton Titus B ii 328; for Norfolk's letter see HMC, *Calendar of the Manuscripts of the Marquis of Bath at Longleat*, 5 vols. (London, 1904–80), ii, 17–19; *CSPF* viii, 377–8, 382; Wright, *Queen Elizabeth* i, 265.

Chapter 9

1. Cotton Caligula B x 472; *CSPSc* ii, 310.

2. Ibid. i, 450, 474, 483, 485, 497– 9, 507–8, 516–17, 523; *CSPSc* ii, 198, 210, 272, 278, 294, 457, 627–8.

3. SP12/43/36, 39.

4. *CSPF* viii, 232, 252; *CSPSc* ii, 336, 340, 342.

5. Ibid. 378–9, 385–6, 389; *Cabala Sive Scrinia Sacra* (London, 1691), 130; *CSPF* viii, 383.

6. *CSPSc* ii, 407–9.

7. Ibid. 410–13; *CSPF* viii, 469, 473; Cotton Caligula B ix, 290; Thomas Wright, *Queen Elizabeth and Her Times*, 2 Vols. (London, 1838), i, 272; Cuthbert Sharpe, *Memorials of the Rebellion of 1569* (London, 1840), 340–1.

8. *CSPSc* ii, 418–19.

9. Ibid. 463–4, 469.

10. Ibid. 424–7, 431–5, 459–60; Camden, *Annals*, 110; A. Teulet, *Relations politiques de la France et de l'Espagne avec l'Écosse*, 5 vols. (Paris, 1862), ii, 369–70; *CSPSp* ii, 35–6.

11. *CSPSc* ii, 418–19, 438–40.

12. Ibid. 462–3, 470–1, 509, 510.

13. Ibid. 520, 523, 527, 528, 529, 532–5, 552, 581, 583, 590; E. Lodge, *Illustrations of British History . . .*, 3 vols. (London, 1838), i, 458–64; HMC Hatfield i, 369.

14. Ibid. 365–6; Haynes, 487–8.

15. *CSPSc* ii, 583–4, 590.

16. Ibid. 589–92.

Chapter 10

1. *CSPD* Addenda 1566–79, 402; *CSPSp* II, 96; Sharpe, *Memorials*, 189–90, 192, 194.
2. Haynes, 548, 581, 586.
3. *Memoirs of Sir James Melville of Halhill*, ed. A. F. Steuart (London, 1920), 88–9, 114–19; *CSPF* VII, 247.
4. For a life of Norfolk see Neville Williams, *Thomas Howard, Fourth Duke of Norfolk* (London, 1964).
5. Murdin, 45 (misplaced and misdated under 1571), 51 ff.; *CSPSc* II, 693–4; *ST*, I, 975–8, 979–82, 988; Fénélon I, 17–18; Haynes, 574–5; W. Robertson, *The History of Scotland* (London, 1759), II, app. 58–61.
6. J. H. Pollen, *The English Catholics in the Reign of Queen Elizabeth* (London, 1920), 131; *CSPSp* II, 163; Fénélon I, 158; Murdin, 42; *CSP Rome* I, 302–5.
7. Haynes, 542.
8. *CSPSc* II, 693–4; IV, 33–4; Robertson, *Scotland* II, app. 58–62; *ST* I, 979–82; Murdin, 52–4; Haynes, 574–5, 542.
9. *CSPSc* II, 642 ff.; Fénélon II, 6–7.
10. *CSPSc* II, 642–8, 664–5, 673; Robertson, *Scotland*, II, app. 58–61.
11. Haynes, 549–50; *CSPD* Add. 1566–79, 236, 402 ff.; Sharpe, *Memorials*, 193.
12. *CSPSp* II, 167, 189, 209, 210; Fénélon II, 126–7; KL v, 438.
13. Camden, *Annals*, 122; SP12/85/20.
14. HMC Hatfield I, 409; Cotton Titus B II, 336; Lansdowne C II, fo. 143.
15. *CSPSp* II, 111; Fénélon I, 233, 258 ff.
16. Ibid. 69–70; Ridolfi was pressing the Pope to back this scheme (*CSP Rome* I, 302).
17. Fénélon I, 204, 233, 258–62.
18. Ibid. 235–6; KL v, 307, n. 1.
19. Fénélon I, 217–23, 322; KL v, 333 ff., 360.
20. HMC Hatfield I, 409; Cotton Titus B II, 336; Lansdowne C II, f. 143.
21. *CSPSp* II, 167; Fénélon II, 51–4; Williams, *Norfolk*, 117–18.
22. Camden, *Annals*, 129–30; *CSPSc* IV, 36; *ST* I, 989, 994–5; Fénélon II, 236; HMC Hatfield I, 541; Murdin, 23, 44, 50, 126.
23. Camden, *Annals*, 131; Haynes, 528–9; Fénélon II, 247–8, 272; KL V, 451, 456, 458–9 for de Spes's account.
24. See Williams, *Norfolk*, ch. 5.
25. Haynes, 531–2.
26. Ibid. 533–4.
27. *Cabala*, 156–7.
28. Haynes, 571–2; Camden, *Annals*, 145; Fénélon II, 379.
29. *Cabala*, 156–7; *CSPD* Add. 1566–79, 83–4; *CSPSc* II, 684.
30. Fénélon II, 19–28.

Chapter 11

1. *CSPD* Add. 1566–79, 407; Sharpe, *Memorials*, 204.
2. SP12/67/59; *CSPD* Add. 1566–79, 274, 403; Murdin, 30; *CSPSc* II, 487; *CSPSp* II, 167; R. Reid, 'The Rebellion of the Earls, 1569', *TRHS* n.s., 20 (1906), 171–203; Sharpe, *Memorials*, 192, 193; Fénélon I, 325, 398.
3. *CSPSp* II, 196, 199, 208; *CSPD* Add. 1566–79, 404–5, 413; Haynes, 595–6; Murdin, 217, 226–7; SP/12/67/59; Cotton Caligula C I, 514; Sharpe, *Memorials*, 100–195; KL *V*, 479.
4. *CSPD* Add. 1566–79, 85, 88, 89, 93, 95; Cotton Caligula C I, 472; Haynes, 550.
5. SP12/59/20; 12/60/18; *CSPD* Add. 1566–79, 89, 407; Sharpe, *Memorials*, 204.
6. Reid, 'Rebellion', 197; *CSPD*, Add. 1566–79, 11; Sharpe, *Memorials*,

39–42, 184; Haynes, 564; Harleian 6990, 89.

7. *CSPSc* III, 84; *CSPD* Add. 1566–79, 193, 241–2.

8. Ibid. 86, 89, 144, 119–20, 123–4, 187–8, 235; *CSPSc* II, 674; SP12/67/59; Haynes, 553; Cotton Caligula B IX, 375, 382, 398; HMC Hatfield I, 465; Lodge, *Illustrations*, I, 500–3.

9. *CSPSp* II, 214, 218; Fénélon II, 379, 385–6; Murdin, 38, 39; Williams, *Norfolk*, 73–81.

10. *Cabala*, 159.

11. *CSPSc* III, 87–8, 171–2, 182–3, 187–9, 196–8, 204–5.

12. Fénélon III, 144 ff.; *CSPSc* III, 137–9, 182–4.

13. Ibid. 103, 358; Cotton Caligula B IX, 395; Fénélon III, 95.

14. Fénélon III, 100, 125; Cotton Julius F XI, 22–41; Caligula C II, 551–64.

15. Fénélon III, 95, 123, 139, 162, 189.

16. Ibid. 188.

17. SP12/63/16; *Cabala*, 167.

18. *CSPSc* III, 358–9.

19. Haynes, 608–14; *CSPSc* III, 358, 363–4; Fénélon III, 308, 328–9.

20. *CSPSc* III, 498, 501.

21. Fénélon IV, 14, 51.

22. E. Lavisse, *Histoire de France*, 9 vols. (Paris 1911), I, 114–15; III, 461; VIII, IV, 11, 41, 59; Dudley Digges, *The Compleat Ambassador* (London, 1655), 62–3.

Chapter 12

1. Murdin, 26, 27, 37, 42, 76, 81, 82, 135; *CSPSc* III, 385–6; [Philip, 2nd Earl of Hardwicke,] *Miscellaneous State Papers from 1501 to 1726*, 2 vols. (London, 1778), I, 190–4; Cotton Caligula C II, 70, 72, 73 and Caligula B IX, 315; Fénélon II, 301–2, *CSP Rome* I, 330–2.

2. SP12/85/11; Murdin, 26, 37, 42, 65; HMC Hatfield I, 555.

3. Murdin, 24, 56; Camden, *Annals*, 154, 162–3; Cotton Caligula C II, 518.

4. *CSP Rome* I, 393–400.

5. Murdin, 100, 113; *CSPSp* II, 323, 349–50.

6. *CSPSp* II, 274, 288; Fénélon III, 401, 422–3, 458; SP/12/74/41.

7. *ST* I, 991.

8. *CSPD* Add. 1566–79, 391; *CSPF* IX, 571; Murdin, 212; *CSPSc* IV, 85, 113; Digges, *Compleat Ambassador*, 199; Camden, *Annals*, 177; Fénélon IV, 410–11.

9. J. E. Neale, *Elizabeth I and Her Parliaments, 1559–81* (London, 1953), 225–6.

10. Ibid. 232.

11. Digges, *Ambassador*, 198, 199; Fénélon IV, 411, 412.

12. Neale, *Parliaments 1559–81*, 244–5.

13. Ibid. 249–50.

14. Ibid. 252–7.

15. Ibid. 260.

16. Ibid. 268–74.

17. Ibid. 281–3.

18. Ibid. 309–10.

Chapter 13

1. *CSPF* VIII, 394.

2. Haynes, 587.

3. *CSPF* VIII, 573; IX, 20–1, 107; SP/12/46/38

4. Fénélon I, 217–23; *CSPF* IX, 32, 39.

5. Fénélon III, 188.

6. KL III, 1–9, 14–17; see also *CSPF* IV, 641 n.

7. G. D. Ramsay, *The City of London in International Politics at the Accession of Elizabeth Tudor* (Manchester, 1975), 96.

8. Cecil to Sidney, *CSPF* VIII, 547.

9. For this whole episode see Ramsay, *City of London*, ch. 1.

10. Ibid. 202–3.

11. G. D. Ramsay, *The Queen's*

Merchants and the Revolt of the Netherlands (Manchester, 1986), 49; see KL IV, 434–8, 438–40; *CSPSp* II 566, 577, 583, 598–9, 610–13.

12. Ibid. 683; 1, 8–9.
13. Ibid. 26–8.
14. Ibid. 52–4, 54–9.
15. Ibid. 54–9, 60, 62–3.
16. Ibid. 10.
17. Ibid. 13.
18. Ibid. 83–5.
19. SP12/48/50, 60, 62.
20. *CSPF* VIII, 585–6.
21. *CSPSp* II, 102–4.
22. Ibid. 90.
23. KL V, 253–62; *CSPSp* II, 102–4.
24. Ibid. 97.
25. Ibid.
26. Fénélon I, 69–72.
27. *CSPSp* II, 85–8.
28. *CSPF* VIII, 588; Fénélon I, 97.
29. Haynes, 583–4.
30. For this paragraph see Ramsay, *The Queen's Merchants*, ch. 6.
31. Ibid. 158.
32. *CSPF* IX, 384–5.
33. Ibid. 419–20.
34. Fénélon III, 300.
35. Ibid. 357–8.
36. *CSPF* IX, 383–4, 391.
37. Ibid. 483, 538–9.
38. M. Dewar, *Sir Thomas Smith* (London, 1964), 129–31; Harleian 253, fos. 143–52.
39. *CSPSp* II, 381.
40. Haynes, 579.
41. Eric S. Brooks, *Sir Christopher Hatton* (London, 1946), 30.
42. Ibid. 111, quoting J. Bond, *History of Corfe Castle*. (London, 1883).
43. P. W. Hasler (ed.), *The House of Commons, 1558–1603*, 3 vols. (London, 1981). 276.
44. Brooks, *Hatton*, 197, 333–4.

Chapter 14
1. Camden, *Annals*, 152.
2. *APC* VIII 44, 46–7, 49, KL VI,

183–5; G. D. Ramsay, *The Queen's Merchants and the Revolt of the Netherlands* (Manchester, 1986), 174–5.
3. KL VI, 370–3, 393–6, 414–18; Dudley Digges, *The Compleat Ambassador* (London, 1655), 189, 203.
4. KL VI, 420–1, 425–7; Digges, *Compleat Ambassador*, 212; Kervyn de Lettenhove, *Les Huguenots et les Gueux... 1560–85*, 6 vols. (Bruges, 1883–5), III, 47–8; *CSPF* X, 123.
5. KL VI, 488–9.
6. Fénélon IV, 355–7; *CSPF* X, 10, 36.
7. Digges, *Compleat Ambassador*, 250, 251.
8. Ibid. 258.
9. Fénélon V, 120–31; Digges, *Compleat Ambassador*, 246–50, 253, 258.
10. Fénélon V, 194–6, 218–19, 228–9.
11. Ibid 306–7, 314–15, 326; *CSPF* X, 429; Fénélon VI, 67, 71–2, 74–5.
12. Digges, *Compleat Ambassador*, 336.
13. *CSPF* X, 319, 322; Fénélon V, 324, 350–2; Lettenhove, *Huguenots* III, 232–5.
14. Fénélon V, 417; *CSPF* X, 418.
15. For the whole episode see SP78/1/144–48v and *CSPF* X, 484, 485, 486–7, 491, 507.
16. Ibid. 560–4, 584; Fénélon VI, 228–35, 242, 290–1, 340; Lettenhove, *Huguenots* III, chs. 6, 7.
17. *CSPF* XI, 39–40, 49, 115; Fénélon VI, 357–8, 395, 421, 425–6.
18. Ibid. 484–91, 498–506; *CSPF* XI, 123–4, 125, 140–2, 155, 177.
19. Ibid. 190–2, 239–40, 241–2, 251, 297, 302–4, 323, 325–9; Baschet, 23 Mar., 8 Apr. 1576; Lettenhove, *Huguenots* III, 638.
20. For the Maisonfleur intrigue see ibid. 107–35; HMC Hatfield II, 27–35, 36; *CSPF* X, 200, 220, 234,

255–6; Digges, *Compleat Ambassador*, 311–14.

21. KL VI, 420–1, 425–7; Digges, *Compleat Ambassador*, 212; *CSPF* X, 123.

22. Digges, *Compleat Ambassador*, 299; KL VI, 568–70.

23. Paul L. Hughes and James F Larkin, *Tudor Royal Proclamations*, 2 vols. (New Haven, Conn., 1969), II, 371.

24. KL VI, 736–7, 744, 745, 750, 780, 785, 789, 803; *CSPSp* II, 469; *CSPF* X, 348.

25. Ibid. 365, 394–5, 398.

26. Murdin, 274; HMC Hatfield II, 295–6; Camden, *Annals*, 208.

27. KL VI, 685, 724, 732, 733, 760.

28. Ibid. VII, 318–20, 328; 476, 491; VIII, 17–31; *CSPF* XI, 28, 75–6, 84–5, 156; *CSPSp* II, 510; BL Add. MS 48084, fos 32–54; G. P. Gachard, *Correspondance de Philippe II sur les affaires des Pays-Bas*, 3 vols. (Brussels, 1858), III, 259.

29. *CSPF* X, 480–1; KL VII, 93, 104, 168, 174, 196, 201, 205–8, 215–16, 222. See also Julian Corbett, *Drake and the Tudor Navy*, 2 vols. (London, 1898), I, 203–6.

30. KL VIII, 109–11, 118–20, 121–3, 188–94, 198–215; *CSPF* XI, 243.

Chapter 15

1. Ibid. 431, 437, 438; KL IX, 23–4.

2. Ibid. 82–3, 96–7, 102–3, 139; Cotton Titus B VII, fo. 273; Galba C, V, fo. 363; *CSPF* XI, 456, 480–1.

3. Ibid. 583, 600; KL IX, 356–62; Cotton Galba C V, fo. 133.

4. Ibid. 452–3; Harleian 285, fo. 36; *CSPF* XII, 54–5.

5. KL IX, 294; Cotton Galba VI, pt. i. fo. 45.

6. KL IX, 487–91.

7. Ibid. 540–5, 549–50; *CSPF*, XII, 201–4, 207.

8. KL X, 14–16; *CSPF* XII, 203–4, 260–2.

9. KL IX, 556–8; *CSPF* XII, 221–2, 266–8, 271–2.

10. *CSPF* XII, 271–3, 320–3.

11. KL X, 103–6; Cotton Galba C VI, pt. i, fos. 73, 74; *CSPF* XII, 247–8, 292–3, 329–30, 364–9, 382–3.

12. KL X, 109–11, 119–20.

13. Ibid. 122–3.

14. Ibid. 125–9, 152–4; Cotton Galba C VI, pt. i, fo. 59; *CSPF* XII, 204.

15. KL X, 172, 215–17, 219–21.

16. Ibid. 263; Cotton Galba C VI, pt. i, fo. 14.

17. KL X, 249–52, 260; *CSPF* XII, 479–80, 482–3, 497.

18. KL X, 274–6; Cotton Galba C VI, pt. i, fo. 12; *CSPF* XII, 490–1.

19. *CSPF* XII, 497–8.

20. KL X, 281; *CSPF* XII, 497.

21. KL X, 311–13; Harleian 1582, fo. 128.

22. Cotton Galba C VI, pt. ii, fos. 73, 75; *CSPF* XII, 529–30, 556–8.

23. *CSPF* XII, 531, 556; KL X, 281–2.

24. Ibid. 335–6, 391–2.

25. *CSPF* XII, 690–2; Cotton Titus B II, fo. 493; Galba C VI, pt. ii, fos. 10, 33; Vespasian F XII, fo. 135; *CSPF* XIII, 105.

26. KL X, 626–8; Cotton Galba C VI, pt. ii, fo. 101; *CSPF* XII, 58, 72–4, 81–2, 101–2.

27. KL X, 733–6; 678–82, 698–701, 708–10, 722–3, 724–7, 731–2; Cotton Galba C VI, pt. ii, fos. 33, 59, 109, 127, 128, 132.

28. KL X, 743–5, 764–5; Cotton Galba C VI, pt. ii, fos. 40, 42; *CSPF* XIII, 158.

29. *CSPF* XIII, 357–8, 407–8.

Chapter 16

1. KL IV, 48–60; *CSPF* XII, 320–3, 324–7.

2. Ibid. 597, 650–1; XIII, 4, 11–13, 14, 18, 42; Baschet 31/3/27 (4 July 1578).

3. L. Van den Essen, *Alexandre Farnese . . . (1549–92)*, 5 vols. (Brussels, 1933–7), II, 88.

4. *CSPF* XIII, 437–8.

5. Ibid. 120–2.

6. Baschet 15/1/79, 22/2/79, 8/3/79, 29/4/79.

7. Ibid. 25/3/79; HMC Hatfield II, 291–3.

8. Baschet 14/6/79, 18/6/79.

9. Ibid. 6/7/79; HMC Hatfield II, 293; *CSPSp* III, 688–94.

10. Hatfield II, 238, 239, 245, 249–53; Murdin, 319–21.

11. HMC Hatfield II, 244–5.

12. E. Lodge, *Illustrations of British History . . .* , 3 vols. (London, 1838), II, 148–50; Harris Nicolas, *Memoirs of the Life and Times of Sir Christopher Hatton* (London, 1847), 81–9; *CSPF* XIII, 161–3.

13. Ibid. 120–1.

14. Hatfield MS 148, fos. 23–38, quoted in Mitchell Leimon, 'Sir Francis Walsingham and the Anjou Marriage Plan, 1574–81' (Ph.D. dissertation, University of Cambridge, 1989), 119–20.

15. Paul L. Hughes and James F. Larkin, *Tudor Royal Proclamations*, 2 vols. (New Haven, Conn., 1969), II, 445–9.

16. Camden, *Annals*, 270.

17. *CSPSp* II, 693.

18. Camden, *Annals*, 232; HMC Hatfield II, 277–80.

19. Baschet 29/10/79.

20. John Stubbs, *The Discourse of a Gaping Gulf* (London, 1579), ed. Lloyd E. Berry (Charlottesville, Va., 1968), 44–5.

21. *Complete Works of Sir Philip Sidney*, ed. A. Feuilleret, 3 vols. (Cambridge, 1923), III, 51–60.

22. Stubbs, *Discourse*, 34, 36.

23. Ibid. 92.

24. Murdin, 322–33.

25. Harleian 6265, fos. 104–10.

26. Murdin, 336–7.

27. Ibid.; HMC Hatfield II, 267–74.

28. *CSPSp* II, 704–6; *CSPF* XIV, 95, 97, 108–9; HMC Hatfield II, 273, 275–6, 293, 298.

29. *CSPF* XIV, 267–9, 343–9.

30. Ibid. 231–2, 424–8, 510.

31. Baschet 10/2/81; *CSPF* XIV, 535–6; XV, 105–6, 131–2.

32. Baschet 2-9-28/4/81; *CSPF* XIV, 172–3.

33. Ibid. XV, 209–13, 234–5, 255–63.

34. Dudley Digges, *The Compleat Ambassador* (London, 1655), 352–4; *CSPF* XV, 271–9.

35. Digges, *Compleat Ambassador*, 377–8, 387–8, 408.

36. *CSPF* XV, 206–9, 299–300, 304, 305, 313, 331; HMC Hatfield II, 424; Digges, *Compleat Ambassador*, 367–8, 397–8.

37. *CSPF* XV, 190, 194, 341–2; HMC Hatfield II, 449–51; Camden, *Annals*, 267–8; *CSPSp* III, 226. Anjou had planned a visit in June, only to be thwarted by contrary winds.

38. Ibid. 227–9; Camden, *Annals*, 268.

39. *CSPF* XV, 368–9, 388–9.

40. Ibid. 409, 449–51, 484, 489–90, 500.

41. Ibid. XVII, 19–22, 405–6; XVIII, 197; HMC Hatfield III, 10–11.

42. BL Add. MS 48094, fos. 2–56 *passim*, esp. fo. 19.

43. Digges, *Compleat Ambassador*, 353, 354; see also 377–8 for other instances in which this theme is repeated.

44. BL Add. MS 48084, fos. 6–8.

45. *CSPF* XVIII, 461, 553–5, 584, 625, 628–9, 635, 653–5.

46. Ibid. XIX, 149–51, 176–81.

47. Ibid. 273–6, 295–8, 315–21.
48. Ibid. 326, 515–16, 557–9, 609, 618, 630–1, 655, 668–9.

Chapter 17

1. *Documents Concerning English Voyages to the Spanish Main 1569–80*, ed. I. A. Wright, Hakluyt Society 2nd series, 71 (London, 1932), p. xlvii.
2. Camden, *Annals*, 255; Julian Corbett, *Drake and the Tudor Navy*, 2 vols. (London, 1898), I, 336.
3. *CSPSp* III, 59, 60, 65, 78, 83; Corbett, *Drake* I, 344; HMC Hatfield II, 515.
4. *CSPSp* III, 128–9, 132–6, 140–2, 185–90.
5. Ibid. 185–90, 324–6, 362–4, 406–8.
6. Ibid. II, 626–7, 645–8.
7. HMC Hatfield III, 67–9.
8. Camden, *Annals*, 319–20.
9. *CSPF* XIX, 37–8, 55, 61–2, 101, 103–6, 119–20.
10. Ibid. 84–5, 239–41, 333–4, 352.
11. Ibid. 423–4.
12. Conyers Read, *Lord Burghley and Queen Elizabeth* (London, 1960), 314–21.
13. J. S. Corbett (ed.), *Papers Relating to the Navy During the Spanish War, 1558–87*, Navy Record Society 2 (London, 1898), ix.
14. Conyers Read, *Mr. Secretary Walsingham and the Policy of Queen Elizabeth*, 3 Vols. (Cambridge, Mass., 1925), III, 103.
15. Ibid. 108.
16. Ibid. 110, quoting J. L. Motley, *The Rise of the Dutch Republic*, 3 vols. (London, 1903–4), I, 330 ff.
17. *CSPF* XX, 67.
18. Ibid. 8, 172; SP12/181/1; 182/24, 32; T. Rymer, *Foedera* etc., 20 vols. (London, 1704–32), XV, 799; John Bruce (ed.), *Correspondence of Robert Dudley, Earl of Leicester, 1585–1586*,

Camden Society 27 (London, 1844), 4, 5, 8.
19. *CSPF* XX, 129; Foedera XV, 590; Bruce, *Dudley*, 5, 166; BL Add. MS 48084, fo. 134v.
20. *CSPF* XVIII, 10, 34.
21. Bruce, *Dudley*, 20, 57–63; *CSPF* XX, 6, 140–1, 175, 192.
22. Ibid. 322–4; Bruce, *Dudley*, 105–6.
23. Ibid. 95, 103, 117–21, 165–7, 168–71, 188–90, 193–9, 204–5; *CSPF* XX, 371–2, 446, 450–2, 500, 510–11.
24. For the whole episode see J. E. Neale, *Elizabeth I and Her Parliaments, 1584–1601* (London, 1957), 166–7. The sources are in Simonds D'Ewes, *The Journals of the Parliaments . . . of Queen Elizabeth* (London, 1693; repr Wilmington, Del., 1974), 408–10 and Harleian 7188, fos. 89–103; 6845, fos. 30–42.
25. BL Add. MS 22563, fo. 23; *CSPF* XXI (ii), 45, 56–9, 78–80; for a short history of these negotiations up to Aug. 1586 see ibid. XIX (ii), 143–4.
26. Ibid. XXI (i), 304; (ii), 16–17, 320–1, 343–5, 428–9, 435–7; Cotton Galba C XI, 114–18.
27. Bruce, *Dudley*, 214–19, 290, 379, 393, 395; *CSPF* XX, 525, 677–9; XXI (ii), 163.
28. Ibid. 94, 163–4, 168–9, 174–5, 187–8, 189.
29. Harleian 287, fo. 22; *CSPF* XXI (iii), 20–1, 69–70; HMC Hatfield III, 265; SP15/30/24.

Chapter 18

1. Camden, *Annals*, 402–3.
2. For the Armada see Garret Mattingly, *The Defeat of the Spanish Armada* (London, 1959); Colin Martin and Geoffrey Parker, *The Spanish Armada* (London, 1988).
3. J. Williamson, *Hawkins of Plymouth* (London, 1969), 256–91.
4. *CSPD* II, ccvi, 41.

5. Ibid. I, cviii, 41–3.
6. Ibid. 72.
7. Ibid. II, ccix, 40.
8. Ibid. 89.
9. Ibid. ccviii, 30, 31; latter has reference to possible cessation of arms.
10. Ibid. ccxi, 47, 48, 50.
11. Ibid. ccxii, 18.
12. J. K. Laughton (ed.), *State Papers Relating to the Defeat of the Armada*, 2 vols. (London, Navy Record Society, 1894), I, 6.
13. *CSPD* II, ccxii, 80.
14. Ibid. ccviii, 46.
15. Camden, *Annals*, 404.
16. *CSPD* II, ccxiii, 38.
17. Ibid. 46.
18. John Stow, *Chronicle* (London, 1598), 415.
19. Ibid. 417.
20. John Strype, *Annals of the Reformation*, 4 vols. (Oxford, 1820–40), IV, 149–56.
21. Camden, *Annals*, 419.
22. *CSPD* II, ccxv, 65.
23. Anthony Wingfield, 'A true discourse (as is thought) by Colonel Antonie Wingfield employed in the voyage to Spain and Portugal, 1589', printed in Richard Hakluyt, *The Principal Navigations, Voyages, Traffiques of Discoveries of the English Nation*, 10 vols. (London and New York, 1929), 306–54.
24. *CSPD* II, ccxxii, 89; E. M. Tenison, *Elizabethan England*, 13 vols. (Leamington Spa, 1933–60), VIII, 18–22.
25. *CSPD* II, ccxvii, 79; ccxxiii, 76; Tenison, *Elizabethan England*, VIII, 61–3.
26. Wingfield, 'Voyage', 312–17; *CSPD* II 27; Sir Walter Ralegh, *Works*, 8 vols. (London, 1829), VIII, 480; R. B. Wernham, *After the Armada* (Oxford, 1984), 127.
27. *CSPD* II, ccxxiv, 50, 53; ccxxvi, 4; ccxxviii, 32, 35; *CSPV* VIII, 431; *The Naval Tracts of Sir William Monson*, ed. M. Oppenheim, 5 vols., Navy Record Society (London, 1902–14), I, 197–200; E. Lodge, *Illustrations of British History . . .* , 3 vols. (London, 1838), II, 379–82; SP12/238/45; 225/42.
28. *Monson* I, 177.
29. Kenneth R. Andrews, *Elizabethan Privateering* (Cambridge, 1964), 124–5, 128.

Chapter 19
1. *CSPF* XXI (4), 186, 200; XXIII, 260–3, 275.
2. *CSPD* I, xxiii, 349; Lansdowne 104, 26/57–9.
3. *CSPD* II, ccxxvi, 13, 14, 18, 19.
4. *CSPF* XXI (1), 186–200; *L&A* I, 471, 483; II, 455.
5. Ibid. I, 714; Lawrence Stone, *An Elizabethan: Sir Horatio Palavicino* (London, 1956), 149–62.
6. Howell Lloyd, *The Rouen Campaign, 1590–92* (Oxford, 1973), 140–7: *L&A* II, 725–8; *APC* XVII, 419.
7. SP78/22/143, 163.
8. SP78/22/134.
9. SP84/41/52; 78/23/161–2.
10. SP78/23/161; Lloyd, *Rouen*, 60; *L&A* II, 529.
11. See L. Grégoire, *La ligue en Bretagne* (Paris and Nantes, 1856).
12. *L&A* III, 453, 457, 464.
13. Ibid. 320–3.
14. Ibid. II, 511, 513.
15. SP78/24/49, 53.
16. *L&A* II, 566.
17. Ibid. 514.
18. *A Compilation . . . Evidence . . . to Illustrate the Life and Character of Thomas Egerton, Lord Ellesmere* (Paris, 1812), 317, 331, 332, 349–51; HMC, *Manuscripts of the Earl of Ancaster at Grimsthorpe* (London, 1907), 307; Walter Devereux, *Lives and Letters of the Devereux, Earls of Essex, 1540–1646*, 2 vols. (London, 1853), I, 213–14;

Tenison, *Elizabethan England*, VIII, 306.

19. *L&A* III, 550–1, 552.

20. *L&A* III, 664.

21. Ibid. 91–2, 659.

22. Ibid. 385, 398, 403–13; *The Correspondence of Sir Henry Unton*, ed. J. Stevenson (London, 1847), 413–16, 433–4, 436–7.

23. SP78/30/165, 172, 179, 197, 210, 213, 222, 260, 262, 287.

24. SP78/32/193.

25. SP78/28/121, 133, 154, 180; *Unton*, 457–8.

26. SP78/29/29, 31, 34, 35, 51, 52, 59, 68, 72, 78, 132.

27. SP78/30/161, 170, 189–90, 237; *The Edmondes Papers*, ed. C. G. Butler (London, 1913), 54.

28. SP78/31/222–3.

29. SP78/32/234, 287, 366, 370–1; 78/33/5, 7.

30. SP78/33/298, 301, 309, 317, 319, 331, 356, 369, 379.

31. Murdin, 664–5, 666–7.

32. SP78/35/31, 50, 57; *Edmondes*, 207–11, 219–22.

33. SP78/36/32–5, 52–55, 113, 119–28; *Edmondes*, 270–1, 280.

34. SP78/37/25, 50.

35. SP/78/37/202, 209, 226.

36. SP78/38/199, 237–8; 39/3, 21, 58, 62.

Chapter 20

1. For Dutch affairs see Geoffrey Parker, *The Dutch Revolt* (London, 1977) and Jan den Tex, *Oldenbarnevelt*, 2 vols. (Cambridge, 1973).

2. SP84/44/286.

3. *CSPF* XXIII, 199–200, 278, 284, 352; *L&A* I, 89–90, 268, 273, 283, 290; den Tex, *Oldenbarnevelt* I, 182.

4. *L&A* II, 226.

5. SP84/297, 318, 326, 337; 45/2–6, 9–10, 27, 39.

6. SP84/45/130, 132–3, 134–5, 138, 148–9, 158, 162–3, 179, 189, 215.

7. SP84/45/244–6, 275, 299–302, 361–2.

8. SP84/47/11–12, 13, 15, 57.

9. SP84/48/23–4, 55–6, 88–9, 91, 104–5.

10. SP84/48/230–2, 247, 251, 255, 272, 281–2; 49/30, 224.

11. For the details of this negotiation see W. T. MacCaffrey, *Elizabeth I: War and Politics, 1588–1603* (Princeton, NJ, 1992), 273–8.

Chapter 21

1. *The Last Voyage of Drake and Hawkins*, ed. K. R. Andrews, Hakluyt Society, 2nd series, 142 (London, 1972), 36–40, 48–50, 86; HMC Hatfield V, 495–6; *The Naval Tracts of Sir William Monson*, ed. M. Oppenheim, 5 vols., Navy Record Society (London, 1902–14), II, 29; E. M. Tenison, *Elizabethan England*, 13 vols. (Leamington Spa, 1933–60), X, 558.

2. *CSPD* IV, ccliii, 30, 31, 70, 76; HMC Hatfield V, 285, 290, 307.

3. Ibid. 319; *CSPD* IV, Eliz., ccliii, 79, 87.

4. *Letters and Memorials of State*, ed. A. Collins, 2 vols. (London, 1746), I, p. ii, 343–4.

5. HMC Hatfield VI, 188–9; Thomas Birch, *Memoirs of the Reign of Queen Elizabeth*, 2 vols. (London, 1754), II, 8.

6. Cotton Otho E IX, fo. 343; *APC* XXVII, 84–9.

7. *CSPD* IV, Eliz., cclix, 12, printed in Walter Devereux, *Lives and Letters of the Devereux, Earls of Essex, 1540–1646*, 2 vols. (London, 1853), I, 349–56.

8. Ibid. 350.

9. *APC* XXVI, 84–9.

10. Cotton Otho E ix, fos. 363–4, 368–71.

11. Ibid. fos. 363–4, 368–70.

12. HMC Hatfield VII, 109–11; *Monson* II, 15.

13. Birch, *Memoirs* II, 343; *Letters and Memorials of State . . .* , collected by Sir Henry Sidney, ed. A. Collins, 2 vols. (London, 1746), II, 52–3; *CSPD* IV, Eliz., cclxii, 19, 13 April unnumbered, 120, 124, 20 April unnumbered, 140, 145, 150; cclxiii, 50, 74, 99, 102; cclxiv, 3, 5, 19; Hatfield VIII, 48–9; *Monson* II, 38–40.

14. *An Apologie for the Earl of Essex* (London, 1603), B3v.

15. HMC Hatfield VII, 211–12, 236–7, 291; *CSPD* IV, Eliz., cclxiv, 11, 21, 50; cclxvi, 69, unnumbered p. 481; Samuel Purchas, *Hakluyt Posthumus or Purchas his Pilgrim* (London, 1625; repr. Glasgow, 1905–7, 20 vols.), xx 25–6; *Apologie*, Biv.

16. HMC Hatfield VII, 346–9; *Apologie*, Biv.

Chapter 22

1. SP78/40/223, 236, 238, 254; *The Edmondes Papers*, ed. C. G. Butler (London, 1913), 296–302, 304–11.

2. SP78/41/48–54, 59–68, 120, 149.

3. SP78/41/236–8, 239–41, 246–8, 251, 253, 255, 256b.

4. SP78/44/13.

5. HMC Hatfield VIII, 118–27, 154.

6. SP84/56/157–61.

7. den Tex, *Oldenbarnevelt* I, 275–7; SP84/57/36–7, 68, 76, 260–1.

8. SP78/42/9, 124, 171–6.

9. SP78/43/25–31; also Lansdowne 103:87/248–51, 252–6; Harleian 6998, fos. 76–9, 163–9; Lansdowne 103:87:8/31–2 and 160; 89–91; John Strype, *Annals of the Reformation*, 4 vols. (Oxford, 1820–40), IV, 51–64; Camden, *Annals*, 546–7; E. Lodge, *Illustrations of British History . . .* , 3 vols. (London, 1838), II, 512–14.

10. Camden, *Annals*, 555.

11. *Actes des États Généraux de 1600*, ed. M. L. Gachard (Brussels, 1849), introd. pp., xxff.; P. Laffleur de Kermaingant, *L'Ambassade de France en Angleterre sous Henri IV: Mission de Jean de Thumery, Sieur de Boissise*, 2 vols. (1598–1603; repr. Paris, 1886), II, 16–18, 29–31, 40–2.

12. Ralph Winwood, *Memorials of State . . . Queen Elizabeth and King James I*, ed. E. Sawyers, 3 vols. (London, 1725), I, 139–40, 156–7; Baschet 31/8/31, Feb.–Mar. 1600; SP78/43/41; *Actes des États Généraux*, xxvi; *Mission de Boissise*, 98–9.

13. PRO 31/3/31, 31 Mar. 1600; *Actes des États Généraux*, xxix; Winwood, *Memorials* I, 139–57, 171–5; SP77/6/142, 146, 148.

14. Winwood, *Memorials* I, 171.

15. SP78/44/113–17; Harleian 1858, fos. 11–28; Camden, *Annals*, 586–7.

16. Winwood, *Memorials*, I, 216–18.

17. SP77/6/184, 185; Winwood, *Memorials*, I, 219–20.

18. Ibid. 222–4.

19. Ibid. 224; Helen G. Stafford, *James VI of Scotland and the Throne of England* (New York, 1940), 278.

20. John J. Silke, *Kinsale* (Liverpool, 1970), 31, 74; Winwood, *Memorials* I, 231.

Chapter 23

1. Norman L. Jones, *Faith by Statute* (London, 1982), 47–9.

2. *Documents Illustrative of English Church History*, ed. H. Gee and W. J. Hardy (London, 1896), 417–42.

3. Henry Gee, *The Elizabethan Clergy and the Settlement of Religion, 1558–1564* (Oxford, 1898), chs. 12–14; Henry N. Birt, *The Elizabethan Religious Settlement* (London, 1907), chs. 4, 5.

4. W. P. Haugaard, *Elizabeth and the English Reformation* (Cambridge, 1968), 315, citing *CSP Rome* I, 97; C. G. Bayne, *Anglo-Roman Relations, 1558–65* (Oxford, 1913), 290–1.

5. Haugaard, *Elizabeth*, 295–302.

Chapter 24

1. Ibid. 57–61, 121–3, 170–2.

2. *Parker Correspondence, 1535–75*, ed. J. Bruce and T. T. Perrowne (Oxford, 1853), 223–7; John Strype, *Life and Acts of . . . Matthew Parker*, 3 vols. (Oxford, 1822), 301–2.

3. *Parker Correspondence*, 227–30, 233–5, 236–8; Gee and Hardy, *Documents*, 467–75.

4. *Parker Correspondence*, 262–4, 271–2.

5. Ibid. 267–9, 269–70, 280.

6. *Zurich Letters*, ed. H. Robinson, 2 vols. (Oxford, 1842–5), II, 58–9, 168–70, 175–81.

7. *Parker Correspondence*, 237–8, 243, 245.

Chapter 25

1. SP12/41/36; *Parker Correspondence*, 290–4; J. E. Neale, *Elizabeth I and Her Parliaments, 1559–81* (London, 1953), 159–81, 166–70.

2. *Sermons of Edwin Sandys, Archbishop of York*, ed. J. Ayre (Cambridge, 1842), 42–3; Cotton Tiberius F, fos. 123–5.

3. *Puritan Manifestoes*, ed. W. H. Frere and R. E. Douglas (London, 1954), pp. xvii–xx; proclamation against Admonition in Paul L. Hughes and James F. Larkin, *Tudor Royal Proclamations*, 2 vols. (New Haven, Conn., 1969), 375–6.

4. *Puritan Manifestoes*, 9, 21, 16.

5. P. Collinson, *The Elizabethan Puritan Movement* (Berkeley, Calif., 1967) 112–13.

6. Ibid. 145.

7. *Parker Correspondence*, 410.

8. *Puritan Manifestoes*, pp. xxxii, xxiii, quoting Lansdowne 17, xvii, 43.

9. Collinson, *Puritan Movement*, 147.

Chapter 26

1. These paragraphs and the general treatment of Grindal are based on Patrick Collinson's biography, *Archbishop Grindal, 1519–83* (London, 1979).

2. Ibid. 174.

3. Ibid. 191–2, citing Cambridge University Library Fe.11.34, fos. 151–61; *Parker Correspondence*, 456–8; BL Add. MS 21565, fo. 16; Lambeth Palace Library MS 2003, fo. 27; *Norfolk Record Society* 43 (1974), 74–5, for Parkhurst letter-book.

4. Collinson, *Grindal*, 192–3, citing Lambeth PL 2003, 29.10; BL Add. MS 29546, fo. 56.

5. Lansdowne 23, 4 fo. 7.

6. *Grindal's Remains*, ed. W. Nicholson (Cambridge, 1843), 376–90.

7. John Strype, *Life and Acts . . . of Edmund Grindal*, vols. (Oxford, 1821), 574–6; Nicholson, *Remains*, 467.

8. SP12/113/17.

9. Gee and Hardy, *Documents*, 481–4; John Strype, *Life and Acts . . . of John Whitgift*, 3 vols. (London, 1822), I, 227–32.

10. Collinson, *Puritan Movement*, 249–53.

11. Strype, *Whitgift* I, 318–22; III, 81–7; I, 318–22.

12. SP12/172/1; BM Add. MSS 48039, fos. 40–50; 22473, fos. 18–20, 20–1.

13. Simonds D'Ewes, *The Journals of the Parliaments . . . of Queen Elizabeth* (London, 1693; repr. Wilmington, Del., 1974), 359–60.

14. J. E. Neale, *Elizabeth I and Her Parliaments, 1584–1601* (London,

1957), 73–5, quoting Harleian 6853, fos. 285–7.

15. Neale, *Parliaments 1581–1601*, 154–7; Simonds D'Ewes, *The Journals of the Parliaments . . . of Queen Elizabeth* (London, 1693; repr. Wilmington, Del., 1974), 410–11.

Chapter 27

1. J. E. Neale, *Elizabeth I and Her Parliaments, 1559–81* (London, 1953), 192; SP12/71/16.
2. Camden, *Annals*, 223–4.
3. Ibid. 145–7; A. O. Meyer, *England and the Catholic Church under Elizabeth* (1915; repr. London, 1967), 87. For recent scholarship on the Elizabethan Catholics, see C. Haigh, *The English Reformation Revised* (Cambridge, 1987); 'The Church of England, the Catholics and the People', in C. Haigh (ed.), *The Reign of Elizabeth I* (London, 1984), 195–220; John Bossy, *The English Catholic Community, 1570–1850* (London, 1975).
4. Paul L. Hughes and James F. Larkin, *Tudor Royal Proclamations*, 2 vols. (New Haven, Conn., 1969), II, 341–3.
5. *SR* I, 13 Eliz. c. 2.
6. Camden, *Annals*, 166–7, 224.
7. Meyer, *English Catholics*, 132, quoting *First and Second Diaries of the English College at Douai* ed T. F. Knox (London, 1878), 24ff.
8. *Harleian Miscellany*, 10 vols. (London, 1808–13), III, 565–8.
9. Meyer, *English Catholics*, 138–44.
10. Philip Hughes, *The Reformation in England*, 3 vols. (New York, 1951–4), III 342.
11. *SR* I, 27 Eliz. c. 2.
12. See *Folger Documents in Tudor and Stuart Civilization*, ed. Robert Kingdon (Ithaca, NY, 1965).
13. Ibid. 8.

14. Ibid. 37.
15. See *Folger Documents*.
16. Hughes, *Reformation* III, 293.
17. F. X. Walker, 'The Implementation of the Elizabethan Statutes against Recusancy, 1581–1603' Ph.D. thesis (University College London, 1961) 149–54, 158–9, 165, 189, 193–5, 200, 201, quoting SP12/185/64, 207–8.
18. Ibid. 149–54, 158–9, 165, 189, 193–5, 200.
19. Neale, *Parliaments, 1559–81*, 121, citing *Parker Correspondence, 1535–75*, ed. J. Bruce and T.T Perrowne (Oxford, 1853), 173–5.
20. Ibid. 191–2.
21. Ibid. 304, 349.
22. Ibid. 388–90.
23. Camden, *Annals*, 271.

Chapter 28

1. T. M. Veech, *Dr Nicholas Sanders and the English Reformation, 1530–81* (Louvain, 1935), 208–9, 212–15, 229–30, 260.
2. Alexandre Labanov, *Lettres, instructions et mémoires de Marie Stuart*, 7 vols. (Paris, 1844), VII, 24–30.
3. See P. O. DeTorne, *Don Juan d'Autriche et ses projets de conquête de l'Angleterre . . . 1568–78*, 2 vols. (Helsinki, 1912, 1928) for a full acount of Don John's career in these years.
4. Conyers Read, *Lord Burghley and Queen Elizabeth* (London, 1960), 357; *CSPF* XI, 75–7, 490, 516, 567.
5. KL IX, 404.
6. Read, *Burghley*, 238–40.
7. *CSPSp* II, 665–6; Murdin, 324; CSPIII, 162.
8. A. Teulet (ed.), *Relations politiques de la France et l'Espagne avec l'Écosse*, 5 vols. (Paris, 1862), V, 213–14; 'Letters and Memorials of William Allen', ed. T. F. Knox, in *Records of the English Catholics under the Penal Laws*, II (London, 1882), pp. xxxiv–xlii.

9. 'Allen Letters', pp. xlvi–vii; J. H. Pollen, 'Negotiations with Mary', in *Publications of the Scottish Historical Society* (Edinburgh, 1901), 412, 413; see also Meyer, *English Catholics*, 269–71, app. 490–1.

10. 'Allen Letters', pp. liii–lv, 416–19; Teulet, v, 369–79.

11. See Throckmorton's account in *Harleian Miscellany* III, 190–200, for full account of conspiracy.

12. See ibid. III, 192–3; SP12/173/4.

Chapter 29

1. Read, *Walsingham*, II, 399–405.

2. SP12/173/81, 82, 83; 176/23.

3. J. E. Neale, *Elizabeth I and her Parliaments, 1584–1601* (London, 1957), 17–18.

4. Ibid. 33–7, 50–3.

5. Conyers Read, *Mr Secretary Walsingham*, 3 vols. (Oxford, 1925), III, 5; *CSPSc* VIII, 102.

6. Read, *Walsingham* III, 1–3.

7. *CSPSc* VIII, 85–6, 389, 390.

8. J. H. Pollen, 'Mary Queen of Scots and the Babington Plot', *Scottish Historical Society*, 3rd series, 3 (1922), 51.

9. Ibid. pp. lxxxiv–vi, xc–xcii, 52–4, 56–7, 59–60.

10. Read, *Walsingham* III, 32; *The Letter Books of Sir Amyas Poulet*, ed. John Morris (London, 1874), 234–6.

11. Read, *Walsingham* III, 32–44; Pollen, 'Babington Plot,' 26–37.

12. *Poulet Letter Books*, 245, 246.

13. Ibid. 267–8.

14. *The Bardon Papers*, ed. Conyers Read (London, 1909), 44–7.

15. Ibid. 46–7; Pollen, 'Babington Plot', 63–6.

16. Read, *Burghley*, 351.

17. Neale, *Parliaments, 1584–1601*, 104; *CSPSc* VIII, 701.

18. Neale, *Parliaments 1584–1601*, 106.

19. Ibid. 116–21, citing Lansdowne 94, fos. 84–5; Raphael Holinshed, *Chronicles of England, Scotland and Ireland* (London, 1587), 1582–3.

20. Neale, *Parliaments 1584–1601*, 132, quoting SP12/195/22.

21. Ibid. 133.

22. Murdin, 576–7; *CSPSc* IX, 262–3, 296–7; *CSPF* XXI (ii), 274–5.

23. *Poulet Letter Books*, 359–62.

24. See N. H. Nicolas, *Life of William Davison* (London, 1823), app. A31–55, for an account of events at this juncture.

25. See Neale, *Parliaments, 1581–1601*, 141–2; Lansdowne 108/54; see also BL Add. MS 48027, fos. 609b, 402; *CSPF* XXI (i), 241.

26. Nicolas, *Davison*, app. F, 302–30.

27. SP12/202/1; *CSPD* II (ccii), 56.

Chapter 30

1. John Harington, *Nugae Antiquae*, ed. T. Park, 2 vols. (London, 1804), I, 358.

2. Ibid. 354.

3. SP78/32/103, 231.

4. Harington, *Nugae Antiquae* I, 358–9.

5. J. E. Neale, *Elizabeth and Her Parliaments, 1559–81* (London, 1953), 189; John Hooker, in *Transactions of the Devonshire Association* 11 (1879), 465; on Elizabethan Parliaments, besides J. E. Neale, *The Elizabethan House of Commons* (London, 1963) and his two volumes on the individual Parliaments cited above, see G. R. Elton, *The Parliament of England, 1559–81* (Cambridge, 1986).

6. Neale, *Parliaments, 1559–81*, 167, 169.

7. Ibid. 174–6.

8. Neale, *Parliaments 1559–81*, 238.

9. Ibid. 302.

10. Ibid. 152–7.

11. Ibid. 198, 200–3.

12. Ibid. 318–24, quoting Inner Temple Petyt MS 538/17, fos. 1–6.

13. Neale, *Parliaments, 1559–81*, 329–30.

14. J. E. Neale, *Elizabeth I and Her Parliaments, 1584–1601* (London, 1957), 74, quoting Harleian 6853, fos. 285–7.

15. Cotton Titus F 1, fos. 289–90; Lansdowne 105, fo. 182, printed in J. E. Neale, 'Peter Wentworth', *EHR* 39 (1924), 48.

16. Harleian 6265, fos. 113ff (printed in *EHR* 31 (1916), 128–37); Neale, *Parliaments, 1581–1601*, 249–50

17. Ibid. 352–3.

18. Ibid. 375–80, 384.

19. H. Townshend, *Historical Collections* (London, 1680), 263–6.

20. *APC* xxx, 354, 455.

21. Neale, *Parliaments 1584–1601*, 278.

22. *Constitutional Documents of the Reign of James I*, ed. J. R. Tanner (Cambridge, 1930), 222; see also G. R. Elton, *Studies in Tudor and Stuart Politics and Government*, 4 vols. (Cambridge, 1974–92), II, 174.

23. Harington, *Nugae Antiquae* (1804), 354–7.

24. *The Political Works of John Harrington*, ed. J. G. A. Pocock (Cambridge, 1977), 198.

25. *The Life of Edward, first Lord Herbert of Cherbury written by himself* (1770), ed. V. M. Shuttleworth (London, 1976), 36–7.

26. For the progresses see John Nichols, *The Progresses and Public Processions of Queen Elizabeth*, 3 vols. (London, 1823).

27. E. K. Chambers, *The Elizabethan Stage*, 4 vols. (Oxford, 1923), IV, 79, 107.

28. J. E. Neale, *Queen Elizabeth* (London, 1934), 207.

29. Nichols, *Progresses* I, 166.

30. F. Peck, *Desiderata Curiosa*, 2 vols. (London, 1779), I, 25, which reports that Burghley spent some £2,000–3,000 on twelve separate entertainments.

31. Camden, *Annals*, 152.

32. Chambers, *Elizabethan Stage*, IV, 77–115.

33. Ibid. II 4, 5, 104; IV, 100–4.

Chapter 31

1. For Elizabethan finance see F. C. Dietz, *English Public Finance, 1485–1641*, 2 vols. (London, 1964).

2. *SR* III, 516–24, 812–24; 26 Henry VIII, c. 19; 32 Henry VIII, c. 50. See G. R. Elton, *Studies in Tudor and Stuart Politics and Government*, 4 vols. (Cambridge, 1974–92), III, 216–33; G. L. Harriss, 'Thomas Cromwell's New Principle', *EHR* 93 (1978), 721–38; J. D. Alsop, 'Theory and Practice,' *EHR* 97 (1982), 14–26.

3. Dietz, *Finance*, 199, quoting SP/12/28/52, *SR* IV (1), 176; 7 Edward VI, c. 12.

4. Simonds D'Ewes, *The Journals of the Parliaments . . . of Queen Elizabeth* (London, 1693; repr. Wilmington, Del., 1974), 14; T. F. Hartley, *Proceedings in the Parliaments of Elizabeth I, 1558–81* (Leicester, 1981), 38.

5. D'Ewes, *Journals*, 139.

6. *State Papers and Letters of Sir Ralph Sadler*, ed. A. Clifford, 2 vols. (Edinburgh, 1809), II, 548–52.

7. Dietz, *Finance* II, 17, 25–6.

8. Ibid. 35–7.

9. D'Ewes, *Journals*, 244–6; Hartley, *Proceedings*, 440–4.

10. D'Ewes, *Journals*, 285–6; Hartley, *Proceedings*, 502–8.

11. Dietz, *Finance*, 48 gives £298,954; R. B. Outhwaite, 'Studies

in Elizabethan Government and Finance' (Ph.D. dissertation, University of Nottingham, 1964), 21 gives £324,000.

12. D'Ewes, *Journals*, 493.

Chapter 32

1. *Letters and Memorials of State* . . . , Collected by Sir Henry Sidney, ed. A. Collins, 2 vols. (London, 1746), I, 231, [331]-332.

2. Walter B. Devereux, *Lives and Letters of the Devereux, Earls of Essex*, 2 vols. (London, 1853), I, 186–9; *Memoirs of Robert Cary*, ed. F. H. Mares (Oxford, 1972), 11–12.

3. *CSPD* IV, cclxii, 64.

4. T. Birch, *Memoirs of the Reign of Queen Elizabeth*, 2 vols. (London, 1754), I, 155.

5. Devereux, *Lives* I, 282–3.

6. H. G. Stafford, *James VI of Scotland and the Throne of England* (New York, 1940), 201.

7. Birch, *Memoirs* I, 152–3.

8. *CSPD* III, ccxlvii, 69, 70, 73, 82, 84, 93, 100, 102, 103; ccxlviii, 7, 12, 15, 16, 20 (I), 22; unnumbered, 14 March, p. 462.

9. K. R. Andrews, *The Last Voyage of Drake and Hawkins*, Hakluyt Society 2 ser.; 142 (Cambridge, 1972).

10. Cotton Otho E ix, fo. 343; *APC* XXVII, 84–9.

11. Cotton Otho E ix, fos. 363–4.

12. Birch, *Memoirs* II, 131, 140–2.

13. HMC Hatfield VII, 156; VI, 478.

14. Birch, *Memoirs* II, 77–8, 93–4, 98–9, 100–1; *The Naval Tracts of Sir William Monson*, ed. M. Oppenheim, 5 vols. (London, Navy Record Society, 1902–14), II, 12.

15. Birch, *Memoirs* II, 159–60.

16. Ibid. 218–20.

17. *Sidney Letters* II, 16–17; Birch, *Memoirs* II, 281–2.

18. *Sidney Letters* II, 19–20; Birch, *Memoirs* II, 284–5.

19. Ibid. 289–90, 385.

20. Ibid. 50–1, 345.

21. *CSPD* IV, cclxiv, 5, 10, 19, 49, 61; E. M. Tenison, *Elizabethan England*, 13 vols. (Leamington Spa, 1933–60), X, 26–8.

22. HMC Hatfield VII, 479–80; *CSPD* IV, cclv, 7, 6, 14, 23.

23. Ibid. cclxv, 10.

24. *Sidney Letters* II, 83–4.

25. Camden, *Annals*, 555.

26. Ibid. 555–6.

27. HMC Hatfield VIII, 281, 318.

28. Ibid. 281, 333; Camden, *Annals*, 555–6; *CSPD* V, cclxviii, 56, 71, 75, 111; cclxx, 28; Birch, *Memoirs* II, 389, 390–1.

29. HMC Hatfield IX, 4, 9–11.

30. Ibid. 4, 9–11.

31. Camden, *Annals*, 567–9.

32. *Correspondence of James VI of Scotland with Sir Robert Cecil and others in England*, ed. J. Bruce, Camden Society 78 (London, 1861), 107–8; HMC Hatfield XI, 72–3.

33. For the invasion scare, see *CSPD* V, cclxxii, 1–68; for the popular belief see ibid., 68 (Chamberlain to Carlton), and John Stow, *Annales of England* (London, 1605), 1309–10.

34. Camden, *Annals*, 572.

35. Devereux, *Lives* II, 36–41; Birch, *Memoirs* II, 415; Fynes Moryson, *An History of Ireland from the Year 1599 to 1603*, 2 vols. (Dublin, 1735), 80–5. For further expressions of this kind see *CSPI* VIII, 76–7, 95–6.

36. Camden, *Annals*, 603.

Chapter 33

1. For sixteenth-century Ireland see Richard Bagwell, *Ireland under the Tudors*, 3 vols. (London, 1885–90); S. G. Ellis, *Tudor Ireland* (London, 1985); N. P. Canny, *The Elizabethan Conquest of Ireland, 1565–76* (Hassocks, Sussex, 1976); Brendan Bradshaw, *The Irish Constitutional Revolution of the*

Sixteenth Century (Cambridge, 1979).

2. The term 'Old English' denotes the descendants of the Anglo-Norman invaders of the twelfth century.

3. Canny, *Conquest*, 32, quoting SP63/1/72, 73.

4. Ibid. 142.

5. Ibid. 69–76.

6. Ibid. 77–81.

7. Ibid. 85–8.

8. Ibid. 81; Ellis, *Tudor Ireland*, 268.

9. Ibid. 269.

10. Bagwell, *Ireland and the Tudors*, III, 97–9, quoting Edmund Spenser.

11. Ellis, *Tudor Ireland*, 280.

12. ECS [Sir Edward Cecil, Viscount Wimbledon], *The Government of Ireland . . . under Sir John Perrot* (London, 1626), 49–50.

13. *CSPI* IV, 142–4, 167, 204–5, 208–9, 216–17; Bagwell, *Ireland under the Tudors* III, 212–17.

14. For this affair see *CSPI*, IV, 142–77 *passim*, 464–5; also Peader Macduinnshleibhe, 'The Legal Murder of Aodh Ruadh McMahon, 1590', *Clogher Record* (1915), 39–52.

15. SP63/169/3; *Chronicle of Ireland by Sir James Perrot*, ed. H. Wood (Dublin, 1933), 68; *Itinerary written by Fynes Moryson*, 4 vols. (Glasgow, 1907–8), pt. 2, 10; Fynes Moryson, *An History of Ireland from the Year 1599 to 1603*, 2 vols. (Dublin, 1735), I, 24–6.

16. Hiram Morgan, 'The End of Gaelic Ulster: A Thematic Interpretation of Events between 1534 and 1600', *Irish Historical Review* 26/101 (Mayo, 1988), 8–32.

17. Perrot, *Chronicle*, 57.

18. *CSPI* V, 364.

19. *Calendar of Carew Manuscripts*, 6 vols. (London, 1867–73) IV, 167.

20. *CSPI* VI, 266.

21. *CSPI* VII, 182.

22. *Carew Manuscripts* III, 293.

23. Ibid. 481–2.

Chapter 34

1. *SR* IV, pt. I.

2. See *King James' Secret*, ed. Robert S. Rait and A. I. Cameron (London, 1927) for a full account; *Letters and Papers relating to the Master of Grey*, ed. Thomas Thompson (Edinburgh, 1835), 107–17; *SCPSc* IX, 164–5.

3. Helen G. Stafford, *James VI of Scotland and the Throne of England* (New York, 1940), 24–5.

4. HMC Hatfield XIII, 384, quoted in Stafford, *James VI*, 25.

5. Ibid. 41–8.

6. Ibid. 76; *CSPSc* X, 829–33.

7. Stafford, *James VI*, 90–1.

8. Ibid. 92–7.

9. Ibid. 98–9.

10. Ibid. 102–8.

11. Ibid. 110–15.

12. Ibid. 19–21.

13. *CSPSc* X, 799–800; Stafford, *James VI*, 117–18.

14. HMC Hatfield IV, 214–16.

15. Stafford, *James VI*, 192, quoting *SCPSc* XIII (1), 148.

16. Ibid. 216, quoting BL Add. MS 31022, fos. 107–8, printed in Stafford, *James VI*, 221–4; T. Birch, *Memoirs of the Reign of Queen Elizabeth*, 2 vols. (London, 1754), II, 510, 511–13; *Correspondence of King James VI of Scotland with Sir Robert Cecil and Others*, ed. John Bruce (London, 1861), 89–90.

17. Stafford, *James VI*, 218; *CSPSc* XIII (2), 1013–14.

18. Stafford, *James VI*, 193; *CSPSc* XIII (1), 195–6.

Epilogue

1. E. K. Chambers, *The Elizabethan Stage*, 4 vols. (Oxford, 1923), IV, 113–16.

2. In 1594 Robert Parsons had written, under the pseudonym Doleman, a book asserting the right of the Infanta of Spain to the English succession.

3. For a general consideration of Elizabeth see C. Haigh. *Elizabeth I* (Harlow, 1988).

Index

'Admonitions' to Parliament, 312–13
Advertisements, 305–7
Aerschot, Duke of, 189, 192
Albert, Archduke of Austria, 264, 287
Alençon/Anjou, François Hercules,
    Duke of, 178, 179, 180–1, 195, 200,
    208–9, 216
Alva, Duke of, 106, 118, 136–7, 156
Amiens, 264
Allen, William, Cardinal, 329, 332–3,
    341
Anderson, Sir John, 352
Andreas, Cardinal of Austria, 289
Anjou, Duke of, see Alençon; Henry III,
    King of France
Anne Boleyn, Queen of England
Antonio, Pretender of Portugal, 207,
    219, 246
Antwerp, 155–6, 191, 216–17
Armada campaign, 238–9; map 240
Articles of Religion, 311, 316
Arundel, Charles, 207
Arundel, Earl of, see Fitzalan
Ascham, Roger, 6
Ashley, Kate, 9–10, 26
Ashridge, Bucks., 11, 15, 24, 25
Austria, Don John of, 136, 189, 191,
    192, 193, 196, 339–40

Babington, Anthony, 346–8
Bacon, Anthony, 400
Bacon, Francis, 400–1, 407
Bacon, Sir Nicholas, Lord Keeper, 40,
    51, 67, 93, 109, 141, 170, 310

Ballard, John, 346
Beale, Robert, 290, 352
Bedford, Earl of, see Russell, Francis
Bedingfield, Sir Henry, 20–3
Bertie, Peregrine, Baron Willoughby,
    251, 257, 268
Bingham, Sir Richard, 427
Blavet, 253
Blois, Treaty of, 165
Blount, Charles, Baron, Mountjoy,
    431–2, 440
Blount, Sir Christopher, 412
Bodley, Sir Thomas, 267, 271
Bond of Association, 344, 350
Bothwell, see Hepburn, James; Stewart,
    Francis
Breda, 269
Brill, rising at, 1572, 177
Brest, 261
Bristol, Treaty of, 162, 185
Brittany, 254–5, 259–60; map 252
Bromley, Sir Thomas, Lord Keeper,
    170, 205, 348
Brooke, William, Baron Cobham,
    137–8, 195–6
Browne, Anthony, Viscount Montague,
    130
Butler, Thomas, Earl of Ormond, 421,
    425

Cadiz, 277–8
Calais, 263, 277
Cambrai, 263
Campion, Edmund, 330

Carew, Sir George, 404, 410, 431

Carew, Sir Peter, 16, 17, 24

Carlos, Infante of Spain, 84

Carrillo, Councillor, 290

Cartwright, Thomas, 313, 315

Cary, George, 2nd Baron Hunsdon, 290, 399, 407

Cary, Henry, 1st Baron Hunsdon, 42, 129–30, 170, 205, 209, 239, 399

Casimir, Duke John, 189, 193

Casket letters, 108

Cateau-Cambrésis, Treaty of, 46–7, 62, 147

Catherine de Medici, Queen of France, 150, 164, 181, 198

Cave, Sir Ambrose, 40

Cecil, Sir Robert, Secretary, entrance into politics and appointment to Privy Council, 398–9; appointed Secretary, 404; mission to Henry IV, 283–5, 409; meets with Flemish envoy, 290; and Boulogne negotiations, 291–2; and Essex over Bacon candidacy, 401; challenges Essex, 404; entente with Essex, 406–7, 408–9; dominance in Privy Council, 416; supports Mountjoy in Ireland, 431

Cecil, Sir William, Baron Burghley, Secretary and Lord Treasurer, appointed as Secretary, 39; his Scottish policy, 1559–60, 63–4, 67, 359–60; mission to Edinburgh, 65; threatens resignation, 68; Master of Wards, 73; presses Austrian match, 91; rivalry with Leicester, 91–2; supports Austrian match, 99; views on Mary after her flight, 106–7; urges hearing Moray, 109; on menace of Mary in England, 114; plot to overthrow him, 118–21; opposes treaty with Mary, 133; and the Spanish treasure, 159; state paper of 1569, 166–7; attitude towards Leicester and relations with Queen, 1679; appointed Lord Treasurer, 169; attitude towards Alençon match (1572), 179; opposes intervention in Low Countries, 190, 193; advice on Anjou match, 200, 201–2, views on

war strategy, 244–5; gravely ill, 1598, 283; supports peace effort, 1598, 288; writes *Execution of Justice*, 331; and execution of Mary, 350–3; Queen's treatment of him and Leicester, 360; dominance in Council 1591, 394; relations with James VI, 439; urges Essex to conciliation with Queen, 407

Champernoun, Sir Arthur, 149

Charles, Archduke of Austria, 64, 71, 91, 99

Charles IX, King of France, 84, 91, 132, 164, 179

Chatillon, house of, 77, 150, 163

Clifford, Sir Conyers, 431

Clifford, George, Earl of Cumberland, 248

Clinton, Edward Fiennes de, Baron Clinton, Earl of Lincoln, Lord Admiral, 40, 67, 99, 108–9, 129, 205

Clontibret, battle of, 429

Cobham, *see* Brooke

Cobham, Sir Henry, 185

Coeverden, 270

Coligny, Gaspard de, Admiral of France, 152, 177, 178

Commons, House of, composition, 1559, 52–3; and settlement of 1559, 48–59; and Mary Stuart (1571), 140–2 (1586), 348–9; petition to Queen to marry (1559), 71, (1563), 89–90; motion for settling succession, 94–6, 344–5; bill to abolish *Book of Common Prayer*, 325; relations with Queen, 364–8; free speech issue, 368–71, 373

Condé, Henry, Prince of, 178, 181

Condé, Louis, Prince of, 77

Connaught, 424, 425

Convocation, 1563, 303–4

Cooper, Thomas, Bishop of Lincoln, 319

Corunna, 247, 278

Courtenay, Edward, Earl of Devon, 14, 16, 24

Cox, Richard, Bishop of Ely, 50–1, 203

Croft, Sir James, 16, 18, 24, 72, 228

Cumberland, Earl of, *see* Clifford

Dacre, Leonard, 114, 129
d'Assonleville, Councillor, 156, 161
Davison, William, Secretary, 216, 223, 351–3
Defence of English Catholics, 332–3
Derby, Earl of, *see* Stanley
Desmond, Earl of, *see* Fitzgerald
Devereux, Robert, Earl of Essex, accompanies Leicester to Low Countries, 225; patron of hawks, 245; joins Lisbon voyage, 247; appointed to Rouen command, 257–8, 262–3; sponsors 1595 voyage, 275; joint commander 1596 and plans for expedition, 277–8; reception by Queen on return, 278–9; chosen to head 1597 fleet, 279–80; stands in for Cecil 1598, 283–4; opposes peace 1598, 288; rise to favour, 394; relations with Queen, 395–6; commands in Normandy, 396–7; Privy Councillor, 397–8, 400–1; and Bacon appointment, 401–2; Lopez affair, 402; Cadiz, 401–3; quarrels with Cecils, 404; his popularity, 404–5; Islands voyage, 406–7; appointed Earl Marshal, 408; insults Queen, 409–10; appointed to Irish command, 411; proposes to take army to England, 412; leaves Ireland, 413; revolt, 415; relations with James VI, 439
Devereux, Walter, 1st Earl of Essex, 423
Dieppe, 255
Dombes, Prince of, 254
Donington, Berks., 24
Douay, 329
Douglas, James, 4th Earl of Morton, 341, 435
Douglas, Lady Margaret, Countess of Lennox, 15, 70, 73, 83
Drake, Sir Francis, 219–20, 224, 237, 246, 247, 275-6
Dudley, Ambrose, Earl of Warwick, 41, 76, 78, 129, 170, 393
Dudley, John, Duke of Northumberland, 41, 42, 45
Dudley, Robert, Earl of Leicester, appointed Master of Horse, 45, 69;

prospective husband for Queen, 71–2; grants of land, 76; promotes Newhaven venture, 77–8; Privy Councillor, 80; proposed as husband for Mary Stuart, 83–6; presses French match, 95; rebuked by Queen, 95; opposes Austrian match, 99; supports hearing Moray, 108; supports Norfolk match, 115–17; attacks Cecil in Council, 120; forgiven for Norfolk plot, 123; presses for treaty with Mary, 132–3; his role after Norfolk match, 167–8, 173; leads interventionists, 190; disappointed at Queen's refusal to send troops 1577, 194; forbidden Privy Council at time of Anjou match, 205; accompanies Anjou to Flushing, 209; backs Drake voyage, 219; chosen to command Dutch expedition, 1585, 224–5; Governor-General, 216–17; warns Grindal of disorderly preaching, 319; Queen's treatment of, 360; Elizabeth and his death, 393; Irish patronage, 410; and James VI, 439
Dyer, Sir Edward, 173

Edmondes, Thomas, 289, 290
Edward VI, King of England, 4, 5, 8
Egerton, Sir Thomas, Lord Keeper, 291, 410
Elizabeth, Queen of England, birth and childhood, 1–4; education, 5–8; Seymour affair, 9–11; relations with Queen Mary, 13; arrested and sent to Tower, 1–18; imprisoned at Woodstock, 19–22; freed, 23; accedes to throne, 33; chooses Council, 38–42, 359; coronation procession, 43–4; religious position, 49–51; her reactions to Scottish crisis, 1559–60, 64–5, 359–60; her response to petition for marriage, 1563, 90–1; answers Parliament on succession issue, 95–6; reactions to Mary Stuart's dethronement, 104–5; instructions on hearing of Mary's case, 107–8; permits Moray to submit casket letters, 108; retrospect on reign to

Elizabeth, Queen of England – *cont.*
1569, 110–13; summons Norfolk to
explain match with Mary, 121–2;
vetoes bill against Mary 1571, 142;
policy towards France after
Bartholomew, 181–3; attempts
mediation in Low Countries 1574,
185; promises men and money to
States General, then backs Casimir,
192–4; indicates interest in Anjou
match, 196, 198; refuses to commit
herself to French alliance 1581, 208;
agrees to Treaty of Nonsuch, 223–4;
negotiates with Parma, 228; speech at
Tilbury, 239–40; presses Norman
campaign, 256; withdraws from
France, 261–2; evades alliance with
France, 263–4; authorizes Picard
campaign, 264; interferes with
Maurice's campaigns, 270; presses for
repayment of Dutch debt, 272–3;
critical of Cadiz commanders, 278–9;
renegotiates Treaty of Nonsuch, 286;
opens negotiations with Spain, 287–9;
her conception of religious policy,
298–300; her attitudes towards
religious reformers in Parliament,
310–11; supports Whitgift against
Commons, 325; Queen's views on
toleration of Catholics, 327, 335;
checks measures against Mary Stuart
1584, 345; authorizes trial of Mary,
348; and execution of Mary, 350–3;
relations with Privy Council, 361–2;
with peerage, 363–4; with Parliament,
364–71, on marriage and succession,
366, religion, 367, 371–3, freedom of
speech, 367–70, monopolies, 370–1;
her court, 375–6; her progresses,
376–7; and literary culture, 378–9;
fiscal policy, 382–3; her frugality,
384–5; taxation policy, 386–8; Privy
Seal loans, 388; relations with Essex,
395–6; insulted by Essex, 409–10;
refuses to forgive him, 415–16;
attitude towards James VI, 441
Emden, 156
Essex, Earl of, *see* Devereux
Execution of Justice in England, 331–2

Farnese, Alexander, Prince (later Duke)
of Parma, 197, 206, 209, 228, 25?
Faro, 278
Fenelon, *see* Mothe-Fenelon
Feria, Count of, 27
Ferrol, 280
Fitzalan, Henry, Earl of Arundel, 40, 42,
87, 109, 116, 119, 120, 122, 123, 169,
199
Fitzgerald, Gerald, Earl of Desmond,
42
Fitzmaurice, James, 339, 340, 424
Fitzwilliam, Sir William, 423, 424,
426–7
Francis II, King of France, 62, 83
Freke, Edmund, Bishop of Rochester,
319
Frobisher, Sir Martin, 248, 261, 276

Gilpin, George, 271
'Gaping Gulf', 202–5
Gardiner, Stephen, Bishop of
Winchester, 15, 17, 18, 23, 24
Gertruydenburg, 268
Gifford, Gilbert, 346
Gregory XIII, Pope, 340, 341
Greville, Fulke, 173
Grey, Arthur, Baron Grey, 425
Grey, Lady Catherine, 70, 83
Grindal, Edmund, Bishop of London,
Archbishop of York, Canterbury,
305–6, 316–17, 319–21
Grindal, William, 6
Groningen, 271–2
Guise, house of, 76, 150, 216, 221,
341–2

Hales, John, 94
Hastings, Henry, Earl of Huntingdon,
71, 73, 83, 122, 199, 306, 308
Hatton, Sir Christopher, 1702, 205, 219,
226, 244, 314, 345, 349, 393
Hamburg, 161
Hatfield, Herts., 11, 25
Hawkins, Sir John, 219, 236–7, 248,
275–6, 314
Henry VIII, King of England, 4, 34, 36,
44–5
Henry II, King of France, 46, 62

Henry III, King of France (formerly Duke of Anjou), 163, 179, 180, 250

Henry IV, King of France and Navarre (Bourbon), 179, 180, 216, 250–1, 254, 258, 260, 285, 406

Hepburn, James, Earl of Bothwell, 103–4

Herbert, Henry, 2nd Earl of Pembroke, 199, 202

Herbert, John, 284, 290

Herbert, William, 1st Earl of Pembroke, 40, 67, 95, 99, 108–9, 116–17, 120, 122, 123, 169

Hertford, Earl of, *see* Seymour

High Commission, 312

Horsey, Edward, 191

Howard, Charles, 2nd Lord Howard of Effingham, Earl of Nottingham, Lord Admiral, 209, 237, 238, 278, 290, 299, 408, 416

Howard, Lord Henry, 103

Howard, Lord Thomas, Baron Howard de Walden, 277, 280, 403

Howard, Thomas, 4th Duke of Norfolk, 72, 80, 87, 92, 94–5, 99, 107, 115–16, 119, 120, 121–3, 136, 138–9

Howard, William 1st Lord Howard of Effingham, 17, 40, 67, 99, 108, 169

Hunsdon, Baron, *see* Cary

Huntingdon, Earl of, *see* Hastings

Injunctions of 1559, 300–1

Ireland, 409–16, 417–33 *passim*; map 414

James VI, King of Scotland, 89, 133, 345; accession to power, 434–5; goals, 437–8; and Essex, 440

Joinville, Treaty of, 216

Katherine Parr, Queen of England, 5–9

Kildare, earls of, 417

Killigrew, Sir Henry, 46, 258

Knollys, Sir Francis, 40, 41, 42, 99, 105–6, 226, 308, 312, 319, 325, 399

Knollys, Sir William, 299, 407, 410

Leicester, Earl of, *see* Dudley, Robert

Leighton, Sir Thomas, 258

Leinster, 425

Leslie, John, Bishop of Ross, 117, 122, 123, 136, 158

Leix and Offaly, 419

Lisbon, 247

Lords, House of, composition, 53–4; rejects uniformity bill, 55; passes it, 57; petition to Queen to marry 1563, 90

Lopez, Roderigo, 402

Lough Foyle, 413, 431

Louis of Nassau, 158, 183, 184

Louvain, 339

MacMahon, Hugh Roe, 427

Madre di Dios, 249

Maisonfleur, 182

Maitland, Sir William of Lethington, 84, 86, 117–18

Man, John, 155

Mary I, Queen of England, 4–5, 12, 14, 19, 23, 27, 359

Mary, Queen of Scotland, born, 35; widowed and returns to Scotland, 83–4; offered Leicester's hand, 84–5; marries Darnley, 87; murder of Rizzio, 88; turns against Darnley and marries Bothwell, 103; abdictes, 104; escapes to England, 105; hearings on Moray's charges, repudiated by Mary, moved to Tutbury, 109; proposed Norfolk mariage, 115–18; agrees to Ridolfi plot, 136; and Throckmorton plot, 221; turns to Philip for support, 338; and Babington plot, 347–8; trial, 348; execution, 352

Mason, Sir John, 40, 46, 67

Matthias, Archduke of Austria, 189, 192, 193

Maurice of Nassau, 228, 266, 267, 270, 291

Mayne, Cuthbert, 330

Melville, Sir James, 115

Mendoza, Don Bernardino de, 218–19, 220–1, 341–2, 346

Mercoeur, Duke of, 253, 254

Mildmay, Sir Walter, 104, 133, 205, 226, 314, 319, 325, 345, 349, 386, 389

Monaghan, 427

Montmorency, house of, 150, 178, 180–1
Moray, Earl of, *see* Stuart, Lord James
Morton, Earl of, *see* Douglas
Mothe-Fénélon, de la, Bertrand de Salignac, 118, 119, 120, 138, 164, 178
Munster, 424, 425

Neville, Charles, Earl of Westmorland, 118, 126–8, 129
Neville, Sir Henry, 290
Newhaven (Le Havre), 79
Nonsuch, Treaty of, 217
Norfolk, Duke of, *see* Howard, Thomas
Norris, Sir John, 224, 229, 230, 245, 246, 254–5, 259–61, 361, 429
Northampton, Marquis of, *see* Parr, William
Northumberland, Duke of, *see* Dudley, John
Northumberland, Earl of, *see* Percy, Thomas
Nottingham, Earl of, *see* Howard, Charles

O'Donnell, Hugh, of Tryconnel, 428
Oldenbarnvelt, Jan von, 229, 266, 267, 268, 284–6
O'Neill, Hugh, Earl of Tyrone, 413, 428, 429–30, 432
O'Neill, Shane, 422
Ormond, Earl of, *see* Butler, Thomas

Pacification of Ghent, 191
Paget, Charles, 346
Paget, William, Baron Paget, 42
Palavicino, Sir Horatio, 253
Parker, Matthew, Archbishop of Canterbury, 304–5, 316
Parkhurst, John, Bishop of Norwich, 318–19
Parma, Duke of, *see* Farnese
Parr, William, Marquess of Northampton, 40, 41, 95, 99, 120
Parry, Sir Thomas, 9–10, 20, 28, 39, 40, 42, 73
Parry plot, 344
Parsons, Robert, 341

Paulet, William, Marquess of Winchester, Lord Treasurer, 40, 67, 93, 169, 385
Pembroke, Earl of, *see* Herbert
Penal legislation (1571), 328; (1572), (1585), 330, 335
Percy, Thomas, Earl of Northumberland, 105, 114, 119, 120, 126–8, 129
Perez, Antonio, 400
Perrot, Sir John, 425–6
Petre, Sir William, 40, 67
Philip II, King of Spain, 14, 71, 103, 137, 206, 216
Philip III, King of Spain, 289
Piedmont, Emmanuel Philibert, Prince of, 19, 26
Pius V, Pope, 328, 330, 332, 335
Poulet, Sir Amyas, 345, 348, 350
Privy Council, 38–42, 360–1
Prophesyings, 317–19
Puerto Rico, 276

Quadra, Alvaro de, Bishop, 72–4, 154, 302

Radcliffe, Thomas, Earl of Sussex, 92, 99, 107, 108, 118, 127, 130, 132, 170, 201, 205, 420, 422
Ralegh, Sir Walter, 173, 277, 278, 280, 403, 406
Randolph, Thomas, 84, 435
Recusants, 334
Renard, Simon, 15, 19, 25
Requesens, Luis de, 186, 188
Richardot, Jean, 290
Ridolfi, Roberto, 116, 119, 120, 122, 123, 136, 137
Rizzio, David, 88
Robsart, Amy (Dudley), 72
Rogers, Sir Edward, 40, 41, 99
Rouen, 79, 255, 258–9
Russell, Francis, Earl of Bedford, 40, 41, 86, 88, 19?
Russell, Sir William, 429

Sackville, Sir Richard, 40, 42
Sackville, Thomas, Baron Buckhurst, 42, 163, 229, 290, 291, 416

Sadler, Sir Ralph, 89, 107, 108, 205
St Lo, Sir William, 17
Sampson, Thomas, 306
Sanders, Nicholas, 339, 340
Sandys, Edwin, Bishop of London, Archbishop of York, 310, 314, 399
Seymour, Edward, Duke of Somerset, Lord Protector, 45
Seymour, Edward, Earl of Hertford, 83
Seymour, Thomas, Lord Seymour of Sudeley, 8–10
Shelton, Sir John, 5
Shrewsbury, Earl of, *see* Talbot
Sidney, Sir Henry, 41, 78, 170, 422–3, 424
Sidney, Lady Mary, 72, 73
Sidney, Sir Philip, 173, 202–3
Sidney, Robert, 404
Silva, Guzmán de, Don Diego, 92, 93, 154, 158, 162
Simier, Jean, 199
Smith, Sir John, 191
Smith, Ottywell, 256
Smith, Sir Thomas, 79, 164, 169, 319, 423
Somerset, Duke of, *see* Seymour
Spes, Guerau de, 118, 119, 126, 127, 137, 159–60, 161, 162, 163
Stanley, Edward, Earl of Derby, 40, 118, 120
Stanley, Sir William, 229
States General, 191, 192–3, 195, 216, 267–8
Steenwyck, 270
Stewart, Francis, Earl of Bothwell, 438
Stewart, James, Earl of Arran, 435
Strickland, William, 311
Stuart, Esmé, Sieur d'Aubigny, 207, 341, 435
Stuart, Henry, Lord Darnley, 83, 86–7, 103
Stuart, Lord James, Earl of Moray, Regent of Scotland, 65, 84, 88, 106, 108, 116, 132
Stuart, Matthew, Earl of Lennox, 86, 133
Stubbs, John, 202–5
Stukely, Thomas, 339, 340

Supremacy, statute of, 56–7, 299
Sussex, Earl of, *see* Radcliffe
Sweveghem, councillor, 191

Talbot, Francis, 5th Earl of Shrewsbury, 40
Talbot, George, 6th Earl of Shrewsbury, 109, 120, 170, 199, 345
Terceira, 280
Throckmorton, Sir Nicholas, 41, 49, 73, 77, 79, 86–7, 92, 105, 115, 116, 121, 123–4
Throckmorton conspiracy, 221, 341
Trent, Council of, 74, 302
Troyes, Treaty of, 80
Turenne, Henry de la Tour d'Auvergne, 253
Tyrone, Earl of, *see* O'Neill
Tyrwhitt, Sir Robert, 10

Uniformity, statute of, 56–7, 299
Unton, Sir Henry, 257, 263

Vere, Edward de, Earl of Oxford, 172–3
Vere, Sir Francis, 269, 271, 280
Verney, Francis, 26
Verreykens, Louis, 290, 292
Vigo, 247
Vitelli, Chiapin, 61

Waldegrave, Sir Edward, 74
Walsingham, Sir Francis, Privy Councillor and Secretary, 169–70; mission to Low Countries, 195–6; forbidden Council at time of Anjou match, 205; mission to Paris 1581, 207–9; backs Drake voyuage, 210; backs Bodley against Dutch, 267; warns Grindal of disorderly preaching, 319; detects Throckmorton plot, 342; and Babington plot, 346–8; prepares Mary's condemnation, 350; dies, 393; Irish patronage, 427; relations with James VI, 439.
Warwick, Earl of, *see* Dudley, Ambrose
Wentworth, Peter, 325
Whitgift, John, Archbishop of Canterbury, 41, 323–4

Wilbraham, Thomas, 141–2

Wilkes, Sir Thomas, 229, 230, 258, 284

William, Prince of Orange, 151, 158, 183, 184, 189, 206, 215

Williams, Sir Roger, 245, 253, 255–6, 259

Willoughby, Baron, *see* Bertie

Wilson, Sir Thomas, 170, 195, 205

Winchester, Marquess of, *see* Paulet

Wingfield, Anthony, 245

Wotton, Sir Nicholas, 40, 67

Wriothsley, Henry, 2nd Earl of Southampton, 130

Wriothsley, Henry, 3rd Earl of Southampton, 412

Wyatt, Sir Thomas, 15, 17, 24

Ziericksee, 186, 191